*'A good hotel is where the guest comes first'*

Hilary Rubinstein, founding editor
(1926–2012)

The Newt in Somerset, Bruton

# CONTENTS

# goodhotelguide.com

Our website has many handy features to help you get
the most out of your Guide.

- **Explore offers and discounts**
- **View special collections**
- **Read the latest news**
- **Search for a hotel near you**
- **Search for a hotel near a particular destination**
- **Submit a review**
- **Join the Good Hotel Guide Readers' Club**
- **Order a copy of the printed Guide**

DESKTOP

TABLET

SMARTPHONE

Make it even easier to get on the Good Hotel Guide website while
you're on the go: add an icon to the home screen of your iPhone or iPad
for one-touch smartphone access. Go to **goodhotelguide.com** on your
mobile browser. Tap on the rectangle with an arrow pointing upwards,
at the bottom of the screen. Then tap on the + sign
('Add to Home Screen') that pops up.

# INTRODUCTION

As the country went into lockdown and hotels closed their doors, it was a tough call whether to go ahead with this year's Guide. We have no regrets that we decided to publish. The decision was made on behalf of our many thousands of loyal readers and our carefully selected properties, which are chosen on merit alone. But the result is that this edition, our 44th, has been produced in challenging circumstances. We have not done as many inspections as we would have liked; reports from readers about their visits have understandably dried up. Fortunately, we have reserves of knowledge and capital built up over more than four decades, which is why we have been able to continue to publish a Guide proud of its reputation for independence.

This year's edition, with more than 750 hotels, inns, B&Bs and guesthouses, has been edited by two distinguished travel journalists, Jane Knight, former travel editor of The Times, and Kate Quill, formerly her deputy. We have benefited from their experience and detailed knowledge of the hospitality industry. Together with Niki Davies and Astella Saw who edited the Shortlist, they have brought their collective skills and keen eyes to discovering new properties such as a Michelin-starred pub in Co. Clare and a restaurant-with-rooms just outside Stratford-upon-Avon that offers fantastic value as well as serving good food.

The Guide's range of entries is deliberately eclectic, with Editor's Choice selections in 20 categories that range from romantic and dog-friendly to pubs-with-rooms and places to stay offering great value. Our top-ten awards, the Césars, include a 400-year-old farmhouse reached by a horse-drawn cart on a remote car-free island and a stylish seaside Cornish hotel loved by millennials for its cool environmentalism.

As they reopened, our selected hotels faced many challenges, not least the safety measures they needed to take to reassure guests. The situation is fast-moving, which is why readers should contact properties to find out about current conditions. Despite the problems, I am confident about the future. Our selected properties are not just the pick of the best, they have hospitality built into their very fabric. This country is a superb holiday destination, and with international travel disrupted there has never been a better time to discover what is on offer. There are more than 50,000 hotels and B&Bs in the UK and Ireland. We have space for only a fraction, which is why we refine our selections year on year. The ultimate judges of which properties get an entry are you, our readers. So please keep writing to us.

Adam Raphael
July 2020

# HOW TO USE THE GOOD HOTEL GUIDE

## MAIN ENTRY

The 412 main entries, which are given a full page each, are those we believe to be the best of their type in Great Britain and Ireland.

Colour bands identify each country; London has its own section.

An index at the back lists hotels by county; another lists them by hotel name.

Hotels appear alphabetically under the name of the town or village.

The maps at the back of the book are divided into grids, with a small house indicating a main entry, and a triangle a Shortlist entry.

If a hotel has received one of our César awards either this year or in the last ten years, that is indicated here. If a hotel is making its first appearance, is returning after an absence or has been upgraded from the Shortlist, this is indicated by a 'new' emblem.

This hotel has agreed to give Guide readers a 25% discount off its normal bed-and-breakfast rate for one night only, subject to availability. Terms and conditions apply.

We try to indicate whether a hotel is wheelchair-accessible or is unsuitable for the disabled. It's always worth calling the hotel to check the details of this.

The panel provides useful information, such as contact details, number of bedrooms and facilities.

We name readers who have endorsed a hotel; we do not name inspectors, readers who ask to remain anonymous, or those who have written a critical report.

We give the range of room, bed-and-breakfast and/or dinner-bed-and-breakfast prices. The price for dinner is for a set meal, or the average cost of three courses from an à la carte menu.

If the Shortlist (see opposite) also has one or more entries for this village or town, a cross-reference to the Shortlist appears here.

---

**Sample entry panel:**

384　SCOTLAND　　goodhotelguide.com

PITLOCHRY Perth and Kinross　　MAP 5:D2

KNOCKENDARROCH HOTEL
♥ Previous César winner

Pitlochry's renowned Festival Theatre was born in 1951 in the grounds of this Victorian mansion, run today as a welcoming hotel by Struan and Louise Lothian. Bedrooms are traditionally furnished, with Scottish art, perhaps a wall of statement wallpaper, floral and plaid accents, a balcony or dual-aspect windows, views of woodland and mountains. Suites have a coffee machine, a drinks cooler, smart TV. We hear praise for a 'polite European receptionist' and 'prompt service'. Barely had a Guide trusty sunk into a leather armchair by a roaring log fire than 'canapés of smoked haddock mousse and haggis were brought'. A cabinet is stocked with more than 50 malt whiskies. A lounge menu offers light lunches, while in the dining room Nick Imrie's nightly-changing menus include such dishes as assiette of seafood, braised feather blade of Highland beef, and a creative veggie option. At breakfast there are free-range eggs, Perthshire sausages, smoked haddock. Summer packages include a pre-theatre dinner and transport across the river to catch, as it might be, Private Lives or The Pasadena Roof Orchestra. (Robert Gower, and others)

**25% DISCOUNT VOUCHERS**

Higher Oakfield
Pitlochry PH16 5HT

T: 01796 473473
E: bookings@knockendarroch.co.uk
W: knockendarroch.co.uk

BEDROOMS: 14, 2 on ground floor.
OPEN: Feb–early Dec.
FACILITIES: 2 lounges, restaurant, in-room TV (Freeview), 2-acre wooded garden, bicycle storage, car park (electric charging points), unsuitable for disabled.
BACKGROUND MUSIC: in restaurant in evening.
LOCATION: central.
CHILDREN: not under 10.
DOGS: not allowed.
CREDIT CARDS: Amex, MC, Visa.
PRICES: per room B&B £175–£345, D,B&B £225–£395. Set dinner £49. 1-night bookings sometimes refused Sat.

**SEE ALSO SHORTLIST**

# HOW TO USE THE GOOD HOTEL GUIDE

## SHORTLIST ENTRY

The Shortlist complements our main section by including interesting new entrants and a selection of places in areas in which we have limited choices. It also includes some hotels that have previously been in the Guide but have not had sufficient feedback this year.

Shortlist hotels are included in both indexes at the back of the book, where (S) indicates that it is a Shortlist entry.

This hotel is making its first appearance in the Shortlist or is returning after an absence.

Many readers tell us they find background music irritating. We say whether music is played and where you might encounter it.

We list the principal credit cards accepted by the hotel (with MC standing for Mastercard).

This hotel has agreed to give Guide readers a 25% discount off its normal bed-and-breakfast rate for one night only, subject to availability. Terms and conditions apply.

We give the range of room, bed-and-breakfast and/or dinner-bed-and-breakfast prices. The price for dinner is for a set meal, or the average cost of three courses from an à la carte menu.

# CÉSARS 2021

We give our César awards to the ten best hotels of the year. Named after César Ritz, the most celebrated of hoteliers, these are the Oscars of hotel-keeping.

## 🏆 NEWCOMER OF THE YEAR
### Baraset Barn, Alveston

Fantastic food, amazing value and a side serving of culture in nearby Stratford-upon-Avon are the hallmarks of this restaurant-with-rooms. The barn is as atmospheric as they come, with a flagstone floor and an impossibly high vaulted ceiling. (Page 78)

## 🏆 COUNTRY HOUSE HOTEL OF THE YEAR
### The Grasmere Hotel, Grasmere

Walks from the doorstep, views of Helm Crag, and fires to gather round for pre-dinner drinks make the Winsland family's Victorian country house hotel a clear winner. As is the food, with imaginative menus, homemade bread, and kippers for breakfast. (Page 192)

## 🏆 SEASIDE HOTEL OF THE YEAR
### The Scarlet, Mawgan Porth

Readers' complimentary reports on this adults-only hotel flood our inbox. The seaside setting, spa and smiling service, alongside an effective environmental policy, win repeated praise. Over the past year we haven't had a single negative comment. (Page 236)

## 🏆 ISLAND HOTEL OF THE YEAR
### La Sablonnerie, Little Sark

Reached by horse-drawn carriage over a scenic isthmus, Elizabeth Perrée's 400-year-old farmhouse on car-free Sark is as charming as its owner. There are cliffs and coves to explore before returning to tuck into local lobster and scallops. (Page 445)

## 🏆 ROMANTIC HOTEL OF THE YEAR
### Lewtrenchard Manor, Lewdown

With stucco ceilings, antique-filled rooms and ornate fireplaces, the Murray family's manor house is clearly made to be shared with someone special. After dinner à deux in the wood-panelled dining room, you can retire to a sleigh bed or four-poster. (Page 222)

### ❦ B&B OF THE YEAR
**Swan House, Hastings**
Historic mixes with hip in this half-timbered house with
inglenook fireplace that has been given a stylish makeover.
Brendan McDonagh gets as much praise for his warm
welcome and breakfasts as his partner, Lionel Copley, does
for his interior design. (Page 203)

### ❦ INN OF THE YEAR
**The Angel Inn, Hetton**
Local ales are served as well as Michelin-starred food at
this Dales pub with beams and luxury rooms. Chef/patron
Michael Wignall uses local food but global inspiration to
create such dishes as Yorkshire duck with soy, black bean
and miso. (Page 205)

### ❦ GREEN HOTEL OF THE YEAR
**Coes Faen, Barmouth**
Proof positive that sustainability can be stylish, Sara and
Richard Parry-Jones's hotel has the wow factor as soon as
the door opens to a glass staircase built into the hillside.
There is biomass heating, and roofs have sheep's wool
insulation. (Page 411)

### ❦ IRISH HOTEL OF THE YEAR
**Roundwood House, Mountrath**
There's a library in the double-height stables and a
delicious dinner is served with a serenade from chef Paddy
Flynn, who runs this 18th-century country house with
his wife, Hannah. The Georgian interiors have a relaxed,
homely atmosphere. (Page 473)

### ❦ SCOTTISH RESTAURANT-WITH-ROOMS OF THE YEAR
**The Peat Inn, Peat Inn**
Our inspectors were bowled over by the food created by
Michelin-starred chef/patron Geoffrey Smeddle in his old
coaching inn with modern interior. Dishes might include
pastrami of sea trout, loin of deer. (Page 382)

# REPORT OF THE YEAR COMPETITION

Readers' contributions are the lifeblood of the Good Hotel Guide. Everyone who writes to us is a potential winner of the Report of the Year Competition. Each year we single out the writers of the most helpful reports. These correspondents win a copy of the Guide and an invitation to our annual launch party in the autumn.

*This year's winners are:*

**Carol Bulloch**, of Grantown-on-Spey
**John and Gillian Charnley**, of Bromley
**Jill Cox**, of Powick
**Peter Foster**, of Lanark
**Lara Good**, of London
**Susan Grossman**, of London
**Tony Hall**, of Slinfold
**Edward Mirzoeff**, of London
**Kevin and Victoria Seymour**, of Seaford
**Felicity Taylor**, of Oxford

# JOIN THE GOOD HOTEL GUIDE READERS' CLUB

**Send us a review of your favourite hotel.**
As a member of the club, you will be entitled to:
- A pre-publication discount offer
- Personal advice on hotels
- Advice if you are in dispute with a hotel
- Monthly emailed Guide newsletter

The writers of the ten best reviews will each win a free copy of the Guide and an invitation to our launch party. And the winner of our monthly web competition will win a free night, dinner and breakfast for two at one of the Guide's top hotels.

*Send your review via*
our website: goodhotelguide.com
or email: editor@goodhotelguide.com
or fax: 020 7602 4182
or write to:
Good Hotel Guide
50 Addison Avenue
London W11 4QP
England

# EDITOR'S CHOICE

From glamorous spa hotels to great value B&Bs and
dog-friendly pubs with treats behind the bar, here are
some of the places that have caught our eye this year.
Turn to the full entry for the bigger picture.

Eckington Manor, Eckington

### BLACKADDIE HOUSE
SANQUHAR

Don't fill up on the shortbread in the rooms of this Scottish manse, especially if you're having the eight-course tasting menu. Ian McAndrew creates interesting dishes such as roast-onion ice cream as well as classic aged Scotch beef. (Page 392)

### UNIVERSITY ARMS
CAMBRIDGE

The restaurant may resemble a traditional college buttery but Tristan Welch's modern fare couldn't be further from canteen fodder. Alongside Norfolk fruits de mer and truffle risotto, he does, though, do a very special bolognese. (Page 141)

### THE OLLEROD
BEAMINSTER

Fish goes straight from the boats to Chris Staines's door, where he uses it on menus strong in local produce but with worldwide influences. So there's smoked eel in sweet soy, duck with wasabi mash and a 15-leaf salad from the garden. (Page 97)

### BELMOND LE MANOIR AUX QUAT'SAISONS
GREAT MILTON

French chef Raymond Blanc has held two Michelin stars in this quintessential English hotel for more than three decades – and you can see why with each bite of the tasting menu. Cookery school courses reveal some of his kitchen secrets. (Page 194)

### BALLYMALOE HOUSE
SHANAGARRY

You know they take their food seriously when you hear that chef Dervilla O'Flynn doesn't compose her menus until the afternoon, when fresh fish is delivered. Fruit and vegetables are from the walled garden, meat from their organic farm. (Page 479)

### ECKINGTON MANOR
ECKINGTON

Food can't get much more farm-to-fork than on this Avon Valley estate, which rears Aberdeen Angus cattle and Gloucester Old Spot pigs. Produce from the orchard and the vegetable and herb gardens is used in both the restaurant and the cookery school. (Page 176)

### THE PIG IN THE FOREST
BROCKENHURST

A decade after opening, Robin Hutson's first Pig hotel is as obsessive as ever about locally sourced food, used to create outstanding, original and unpretentious dishes. Alongside plenty of piggy bits are options for vegetarians. (Page 131)

### THE PIPE AND GLASS INN
SOUTH DALTON

You can order something as simple as a sarnie with a pint at James and Kate Mackenzie's historic inn. But in the bar and the restaurant, you'll also find Michelin-starred cuisine such as rabbit with black pudding and white-bean crumble. (Page 299)

### KYLESKU HOTEL
KYLESKU

It's a long drive to this remote spot, but it's worth it for lochside views and fish so fresh it practically swims to the door. Tommy Barney can turn his hand to local langoustine or lamb. And you can get a picnic to take seal spotting. (Page 379)

### HARBOURMASTER HOTEL
ABERAERON

The quayside position here means you can expect plenty of locally landed fish and seafood on the menu. Other local specialities from Welsh lamb to laver bread also feature among Ludo Dieumegard's unpretentious but flavourful dishes. (Page 406)

## PRESTONFIELD
### EDINBURGH
The opulent Owner's Suite is entered via a turret stairway, and has a four-poster draped in crimson damask and a book-lined bathroom with a chariot bath big enough for two. The candlit restaurant will put you in the mood for a proposal. (Page 361)

## LIME WOOD
### LYNDHURST
Snuggle up in perfect privacy for the weekend in a pretty Pavilion room at this chic New Forest getaway. With a vast bed, open fire, lounge, terrace, fully stocked pantry, and roll-top bath in a bay window, there'll be no reason to leave. (Page 231)

## STRATTONS
### SWAFFHAM
You won't have to remortgage to enjoy a romantic weekend at this 19th-century villa filled with art, antiques and eccentricities. The Red Room suite has a Jacobean four-poster, scarlet velvet everywhere, an open fire and courtyard garden. (Page 308)

## LANGAR HALL
### LANGAR
Head off to a place loved by the queen of romance herself, Barbara Cartland. Many rooms feature fully draped four-posters, delicate flower prints and antique furniture. Or you can book the chalet overlooking the croquet lawn. (Page 217)

## GREGANS CASTLE HOTEL
### BALLYVAUGHAN
This manor house in the wild karst landscapes of the Burren, on Ireland's west coast, has quiet rooms (no TV) overlooking the bay or mountains; some have private gardens. Candles are lit as dusk falls, and the restaurant serves gourmet food. (Page 456)

## PORTOBELLO HOTEL
### LONDON
Follow in the footsteps of celebrity couples who have stayed at this citadel of Notting Hill bohemia. It's as decadent as ever, with flamboyant canopied beds, exotic fabrics and an honesty bar whenever a toast to everlasting love calls. (Page 68)

## BARNSLEY HOUSE
### BARNSLEY
A dreamy country garden designed by Rosemary Verey, chic contemporary rooms, including a Secret Garden Suite with hot tub, four-poster and complimentary champagne, all add up to a blissful Cotswolds retreat. (Page 88)

## LYMPSTONE MANOR
### EXMOUTH
Sumptuously decorated five-star rooms, panoramic views of the Exe estuary, sleek marble bathrooms with roll-top baths, and Michael Caines's Michelin-starred food can't fail to inspire an amorous mood at this Relais & Châteaux hotel. (Page 184)

## THE THREE CHIMNEYS AND THE HOUSE OVER-BY
### DUNVEGAN
This crofter's cottage on a ruggedly beautiful spot by Loch Dunvegan is a highly regarded restaurant-with-rooms, now in the capable hands of luxury hotelier Gordon Campbell Gray. Next door are sea-view rooms with rain showers and gardens. (Page 359)

## JEAKE'S HOUSE
### RYE
Ideal for lovers on a budget, this creaky 17th-century house in a cobbled street has cosy, individually styled rooms with beams, four-posters, toile de Jouy wallpapers, a rather theatrical bar and an open fire in the parlour. (Page 281)

Barnsley House, Barnsley

## THE NARE
### VERYAN-IN-ROSELAND
Not only does this family-friendly hotel have beautifully landscaped gardens leading to a secluded bay, but it also has two boats for outings on the ocean. You can explore the creeks and rivers of the Cornish coast by yacht or motor launch. (Page 327)

## GWESTY CYMRU
### ABERYSTWYTH
Room 6 is the one to book for a bath with a sea view at this hotel overlooking the Victorian promenade and Cardigan Bay. If you visit in winter, take a seat on the lawn and watch the starlings return to roost under the pier at sunset. (Page 410)

## THE SHIP INN
### ELIE
With its own cricket team and a pitch on the beach a stone's throw away, this Scottish pub looking out across the Firth of Forth is pretty unique. Games are tide dependent but the bay views from nautical rooms should bowl you over all the time. (Page 364)

## THE WHITE HOUSE
### HERM
Where better than an island for an idyllic seaside stay? Car-free Herm may be small, but it has sandy beaches in spades. Everything is an easy stroll from the delightfully old-fashioned harbourside hotel, with dazzling views. (Page 444)

## RATHMULLAN HOUSE
### RATHMULLAN
It may be on the Wild Atlantic Way but this family-run hotel also has a three-kilometre beach on the shores of Lough Swilly at the bottom of its garden. There are lough views from some of the rooms, and the restaurant features local seafood. (Page 477)

## ARTIST RESIDENCE BRIGHTON
### BRIGHTON
For somewhere that encapsulates the spirit of bohemian Brighton, look no further than this mural-bedaubed hotel, with views to pebbles and pier. There's a fun atmosphere, with cocktails and ping-pong as well as sea views and street art. (Page 122)

## SOAR MILL COVE HOTEL
### SALCOMBE
You get the very best of the British seaside at Keith Makepeace's family-friendly hotel. A trail leads to the uncrowded beach, bedrooms have sea views, the menu is rich in seafood and there is easy access to the South West Coast Path. (Page 288)

## THE PIG ON THE BEACH
### STUDLAND
Robin Hutson's litter of Pig hotels is known for its foodie credentials, but in this one the specials on the menu come with a sea view. A path leads down to Studland Bay and the hotel's beach hut; spa cabins look on to the waves. (Page 306)

## SCARISTA HOUSE
### SCARISTA
The sea may be a tad frosty from the three-mile stretch of sand in front of this Isle of Harris hotel, but it's gloriously remote and crowd free. Try your hand at sea sports on the island, including surfing, kayaking and sailing. (Page 393)

## ST AIDAN HOTEL & BISTRO
### SEAHOUSES
The day starts with breakfast in sight of golden beaches and Bamburgh Castle. Then you can take a boat trip to see puffins on the Farne Islands, hike along the coast, and use the binoculars in the rooms to scan harbour and horizon. (Page 290)

The Nare, Veryan-in-Roseland

Seaham Hall, Seaham

## MULLION COVE HOTEL
MULLION COVE

Forget whale music: at this cliff-top spa hotel, the lapping sea provides the relaxation soundtrack. With an outdoor pool and hot tub, seaweed treatments and a wall of windows to show off the view, it makes the most of the seaside setting. (Page 241)

## CHEWTON GLEN
NEW MILTON

If you feel a twinge after using the hotel's golf course, you can book a massage using golf balls. There is something for everyone, with dance classes and kids' treatments. There's also an ozone-treated pool, hydrotherapy pool and hot tub. (Page 244)

## THE DEVONSHIRE ARMS
BOLTON ABBEY

There's no need to venture into the Yorkshire Dales to get muddy when you can do so in the rasul temple, with different muds to treat the face, body and hair. The spa, in an ancient, adjacent barn, features a pool beneath a high beamed ceiling. (Page 111)

## ILSINGTON COUNTRY HOUSE
ILSINGTON

Wine isn't just for dinner at this Dartmoor hotel: spa treatments use vinotherapy, based on the antioxidant qualities of grapes. You can enjoy a premier cru facial or a crushed cabernet body treatment and toast the healthy side of wine. (Page 212)

## SUMMER LODGE
EVERSHOT

Other spas embrace the darkness, but Summer Lodge is true to its name, with its pool and gym in an impressive light-filled conservatory. There are mindfulness classes, and both reiki and reflexology as well as Elemis treatments. (Page 182)

## SEAHAM HALL
SEAHAM

A destination spa with a boutique hotel attached, Seaham has at its heart a toasty 20-metre hydrotherapy pool. Designed according to feng shui principles, the spa comes with outdoor hot tubs, a variety of sauna and steam cabins and a modern gym. (Page 289)

## LAKE COUNTRY HOUSE HOTEL & SPA
LLANGAMMARCH WELLS

Indulge in champagne and truffles – as a facial, rather than at dinner, although you do get a complimentary glass of bubbles too, putting the treat into this Temple Spa treatment. There is a hot tub overlooking the lake as well as a pool. (Page 429)

## THE ROYAL CRESCENT HOTEL & SPA
BATH

What could be better for the soul than swimming in the pool as shards of light penetrate the church-style windows of this boutique spa? A door opens on to a walled garden for more relaxation after an Elemental Herbology treatment. (Page 95)

## WHATLEY MANOR
EASTON GREY

For extra effect, you can book a treatment in the Natura Bissé Bubble Suite, where filtered air is 99.95 per cent pure. As well as an impressive inside/outside hydrotherapy pool, the spa has heated recliners in the tepidarium and thermal suite. (Page 175)

## HARTWELL HOUSE
AYLESBURY

The terracotta walls, arches and statues lend a Roman vibe to this spa set in the garden orangery. And after your pick from a range of Aromatherapy Associates therapies, you should feel like a Roman god or goddess. (Page 83)

## BARLEY BREE
### MUTHILL
It's the perfect pairing: French cuisine using the finest Scottish seafood and game (you might even find haggis and onion tartlet on the menu). Chef/patron Fabrice Bouteloup also has the perfect partner in his wife, Alison, a wine expert. (Page 380)

## THE WHITEBROOK
### WHITEBROOK
Michelin-starred chef Chris Harrod forages for plants and herbs in the Wye valley to create his original dishes. They might include suckling pig with lamb's sorrel, pigeon with wild chervil or pumpkin with three-cornered garlic. (Page 442)

## THE NEPTUNE
### OLD HUNSTANTON
A stone's throw from Hunstanton beach on the north Norfolk coast, Kevin Mangeolles's Michelin-starred restaurant is big on seafood dishes such as lobster tortellini and monkfish with Brancaster mussels. There are four immaculate rooms. (Page 252)

## LA FLEUR DE LYS
### SHAFTESBURY
A passion for provenance means Marc Preston and David Griffin-Shepherd's food wins high praise from readers. You can feast on dishes such as tart of local scallops and prawns on smoked salmon, and pan-fried saddle of Dorset lamb. (Page 292)

## THE COTTAGE IN THE WOOD
### BRAITHWAITE
The forest on the doorstep, the Lake District fells and west coast harbours all supply Michelin-starred Ben Wilkinson with ingredients for menus that might include Eden Valley pork with black truffle or salt-baked beetroot with sheep's curd. (Page 119)

## THE CROSS AT KINGUSSIE
### KINGUSSIE
After working up an appetite in the surrounding Cairngorms national park, guests at this former Victorian mill can do justice to David Skiggs's tasting menu which showcases Highlands produce, such as wild venison. (Page 377)

## RESTAURANT JAMES SOMMERIN
### PENARTH
Outside, views are of the Severn Estuary, while inside, guests can watch Michelin-starred James Sommerin prepare locally sourced dishes from lobster to lamb. Tables can order bespoke tasting menus, with many dishes delivered by the chefs. (Page 436)

## MORSTON HALL
### HOLT
Guests sit down at 8 pm for the seven-course tasting menu cooked by Michelin-starred Galton Blackiston. The hall is two miles from the north Norfolk coast so you can expect perhaps King's Lynn brown shrimps or wild sea bass on the menu. (Page 207)

## LAKE ISLE
### UPPINGHAM
Readers who have been visiting the Burtons' restaurant for years tell us they have never had less than a perfect dinner. The irresistibly inventive menus feature dishes such as guineafowl with sherried lentils and black pudding crumb. (Page 324)

## THE SEAFOOD RESTAURANT
### PADSTOW
They specialise in simple seafood dishes with classic flavours at Rick Stein's Padstow flagship, with a seafood bar in the middle. Whether it's cod and chips or Indonesian seafood curry, you can be sure the fish is super fresh. (Page 258)

Morston Hall, Holt

Widbrook Grange, Bradford-on-Avon

## THE ROSE & CROWN
### ROMALDKIRK

In addition to a 'Dog Hall of Fame' on the website, where you can send in a photo of your satisfied mutt lounging in the bar, this village inn makes a fuss of guest pooches with beds and Welly-bix treats. There is also a drying area and there are no extra charges. (Page 279)

## EDDRACHILLES HOTEL
### SCOURIE

A £10 fee entitles four-legged guests to the BowWOW service – personalised pampering that includes bedding, towels, washing facilities (with warm water, mind), mats and cushions. They are allowed in one part of the restaurant, where a 'three-bark' rule applies. (Page 394)

## THE CASTLE HOTEL
### BISHOP'S CASTLE

A dog welcome box (mat, bowl, towel, lead, treats, poo bags), cooked sausage at breakfast, great local walks on the doorstep and no supplementary charge make this a perennial favourite with Guide hounds. (Page 107)

## THE MASTER BUILDER'S
### BEAULIEU

As if staying on Lord Montagu's Beaulieu Estate were not enough of a treat for Bonzo, he also has his own bed, bowls, treats and a delicious Doggy Room Service menu. And he can join you for dinner in the Yachtsman's Bar. (Page 98)

## TALLAND BAY HOTEL
### TALLAND-BY-LOOE

A Cornish beach on the doorstep, a blanket, bowl, feeding mat and doggy treat, sausage breakfast and chicken dinner – what more could your beloved best friend wish for? They can also join you for a meal in the conservatory. (Page 309)

## THE GROVE OF NARBERTH
### NARBERTH

Six dog-friendly rooms, with French doors leading on to the garden or a terrace, plus towels, blanket, treats and a doggy dining menu, means pets should enjoy their stay here just as much as you do. There is a charge of £20 per night. (Page 432)

## THE ROSE & CROWN
### SNETTISHAM

This gregarious pub has always welcomed dogs in all areas except the dining room. Now two refurbished garden-access rooms, with a special welcome pack for mutts, have been designed to appeal particularly to pet owners and families. (Page 296)

## WIDBROOK GRANGE
### BRADFORD-ON-AVON

Snoopy not only has a comfy bed and treats here but can also enjoy a doggy afternoon tea, with a tennis ball to take home, wet food, organic dog biscuits and puppichino. Or splash out with a bottle of Pawsecco, a healthy drink for pets. (Page 117)

## THE GURNARD'S HEAD
### ZENNOR

There are no fees for pets at this Cornish pub-with-rooms that welcomes dogs as much as their owners. It has restaurant tables where Fido can sit with you, and rooms with doggy biscuits, blanket, bowls and towels. (Page 343)

## ENNISCOE HOUSE
### CASTLEHILL

Dogs are allowed in all the public rooms except the restaurant at this grand, family-owned Georgian house. Book a 'Dog Lovers' package, which includes a treat box and your pet's photo on the hotel's Facebook page. Fame for Fido at last. (Page 457)

Headlam Hall, Darlington

## THE NEWT IN SOMERSET
### BRUTON
As well as grand Georgian architecture, refined interiors, and a spa at The Newt, you will find a treetop walk, wild swimming pool, ice-cream parlour, and even an interactive gardening museum. And don't forget the cyder bar. (Page 132)

## THE GROVE OF NARBERTH
### NARBERTH
This beautifully restored Jacobean mansion oozes laid-back luxury, from four-posters to candlelit dining. Add to that views of the Preseli hills, extensive grounds, and one of Pembrokeshire's prettiest market towns just down the road. (Page 432)

## CORSE LAWN HOUSE
### CORSE LAWN
As the decades have rolled by, this handsome Queen Anne-style house beside a pond quacking with ducks has resisted fads and fashions without compromising on quality. Returning guests love its peach-coloured rooms, loose-leaf tea and G&Ts on the terrace. (Page 155)

## HEADLAM HALL
### DARLINGTON
The warm welcome and informal atmosphere at Headlam are much praised by readers. That's not to say that certain traditions aren't observed, but alongside afternoon tea, fine dining and period features, there is a spa and modern touches. (Page 162)

## THE TORRIDON
### TORRIDON
A long drive along a single track leads to this Victorian hunting lodge in a spectacular location overlooking Loch Torridon. Kayak, hike and star-gaze; dine on the best Highland produce. Bedrooms have mesmerising views. (Page 402)

## CURRAREVAGH HOUSE
### OUGHTERARD
The past is a foreign country at this beautiful 180-acre estate beside Lough Corrib; it has been in the same family since 1890. Step back into another era: no door keys, no TV, and a gong to summon you for a delicious four-course dinner. (Page 476)

## PENDRAGON COUNTRY HOUSE
### CAMELFORD
Replete with references to local Arthurian legend, this vicarage between Pentire Point and Bodmin Moor is renowned for excellent food and attention to detail. Prefer a light-tog duvet to goose down, or perhaps fine wool blankets? Not a problem. (Page 142)

## KINLOCH LODGE
### SLEAT
Marcello Tully's destination restaurant is reason enough to visit this heirloom-filled former hunting lodge owned by Lord and Lady Macdonald. The setting is pretty special, too, with spectacular views of Loch Na Dal from some of the rooms. (Page 395)

## THE HOUSE AT TEMPLE SOWERBY
### PENRITH
Dine on fine food in a circular conservatory overlooking a walled garden at this Georgian house in the Eden valley. Bedrooms are homely and traditional, but with crucial spoiling extras, such as spa baths and hydrotherapy showers. (Page 261)

## GRAVETYE MANOR
### EAST GRINSTEAD
Jeremy and Elizabeth Hosking's Elizabethan manor enjoys the perfect setting, with beautiful gardens amid 1,000 acres of woodland. Inside, it's just as good, with slick service, antique-filled rooms and Michelin-starred dining. (Page 171)

## AUSTWICK HALL
### AUSTWICK
This restored Italianate garden, set into a hillside, is a delight throughout the year: in winter, admire the drifts of snowdrops in the woodland; in spring, displays of daffodils and bluebells. Art lovers will enjoy the sculpture trail. (Page 81)

## HILTON PARK
### CLONES
The 600-acre grounds of this glorious 18th-century mansion form one of Ireland's four accredited wildlife estates, where red squirrels still happily scamper. It has three lakes, a 19th-century parterre, a rose garden and woodlands. (Page 461)

## HOTEL ENDSLEIGH
### MILTON ABBOT
Humphry Repton's swan song (his last commission, in 1814), these gardens are as dreamily picturesque as Olga Polizzi's hotel. Overlooking the Tamar are a formal garden, dell with bridges, arboretum, cottage orné and herbaceous border. (Page 239)

## LONGUEVILLE MANOR
### ST SAVIOUR
A walk through this 18-acre estate, landscaped by a Victorian clergyman, offers the pleasures of a lake, kitchen garden and woods that are home to red squirrels and woodpeckers. Beyond, country lanes take you into idyllic Jersey scenery. (Page 449)

## CONGHAM HALL
### KING'S LYNN
Love herbs? Congham Hall is right up your patch. With 400 varieties, these beautifully laid-out herb gardens are a popular attraction in their own right. A stroll in the early morning or at dusk is a sensual delight for the eye and nose. (Page 213)

## GRAVETYE MANOR
### EAST GRINSTEAD
These historic gardens were designed by William Robinson, the Irish pioneer of the wild garden, in 1885. His spirit lives on in the romantic flower garden, pergola, kitchen garden, orchard and woodland garden. (Page 171)

## BODYSGALLEN HALL AND SPA
### LLANDUDNO
The formal gardens here are as aristocratic as the 17th-century house. Wander through the restored parterre and the walled and rose gardens, and admire the lily ponds and follies, before exploring the 200-acre estate. (Page 428)

## GREYWALLS
### GULLANE
These six-acre gardens are attributed to Gertrude Jekyll and one can sense her hand in the elegant Edwardian design, with its promenades, radiating pathways, rooms and vistas, and perfectly placed spots for sun, shade and privacy. (Page 371)

## STOBERRY HOUSE
### WELLS
Frances and Tim Meeres Young have created a lushly landscaped garden that makes the most of views of Wells Cathedral and Glastonbury Tor. Wildlife ponds, vivid planting, sculptures and night illumination make it a pleasure at all hours. (Page 330)

## THE NEWT IN SOMERSET
### BRUTON
These 800-acre gardens, comprising cultivated and landscaped areas, deer park, wild flower meadows and woodland, are no pleasing add-on to Hadspen House, but the star of the show. A dedicated museum tells the 'Story of Gardening'. (Page 132)

Gravetye Manor, East Grinstead

Gara Rock, East Portlemouth

## GARA ROCK
### EAST PORTLEMOUTH
You can swim in the pool and see the sun dip into the ocean, or watch boats as you wallow in the hot tub at this clifftop hotel above a beautiful beach. Most of the rooms, suites and cottages have a sea view, plus a balcony or garden. (Page 173)

## THE COOKIE JAR
### ALNWICK
Ramparts can be seen from the terraced garden, with full views of Alnwick Castle from some bedrooms. The interiors in this former convent provide a striking contrast, with blue walls, patterned carpets, and stained glass in the Chapel room. (Page 77)

## LINDETH FELL
### BOWNESS-ON-WINDERMERE
The beautifully kept gardens already create the perfect picture at this Edwardian house. Add the glorious views of Windermere and surrounding fells and you won't want to look away. Lake-view rooms Windermere and Grasmere are the best. (Page 116)

## LLWYNDU FARMHOUSE
### BARMOUTH
There is even a sea view through the window of a walk-in wardrobe at Peter and Paula Thompson's Tudor farmhouse. There's no need to linger among the coat hangers; Cardigan Bay and the Llyn peninsula can be seen from other rooms. (Page 412)

## DUNKERY BEACON COUNTRY HOUSE
### WOOTTON COURTENAY
The highest point of Exmoor, after which the hotel is named, can be seen from the veranda and from one of the bedrooms. This former Edwardian hunting lodge makes a great base for exploring the moorlands – and for night-sky viewing. (Page 339)

## ROSLEAGUE MANOR
### LETTERFRACK
Beautiful gardens run down to scenic Ballinakill Bay, with the mountains of Connemara beyond, at Mark Foyle's creeper-clad manor. Rooms at the front of the house command the best watery vistas, but garden views are lovely, too. (Page 468)

## MAISON TALBOOTH
### DEDHAM
It is Constable country on the Essex–Suffolk border and you could be gazing at your own landscape from this quirky boutique hotel. One room, Shelley, has a double aspect, looking out to the gardens, the pool and across Dedham Vale. (Page 167)

## HAMBLETON HALL
### HAMBLETON
A Michelin-starred meal in sight of Rutland Water makes a feast for the eyes as well as the stomach. The same stunning panorama can be seen from some bedrooms and from the flower-filled terrace and pretty ornamental gardens. (Page 198)

## COLL HOTEL
### ARINAGOUR
The epic seascape showcasing Mull, Staffa and the Treshnish Isles is visible from most of the rooms at Coll's only hotel and pub. It's also on show from the waterside gardens and restaurant, where you can enjoy the freshest seafood. (Page 347)

## TRESANTON
### ST MAWES
Olga Polizzi's seaside hotel cascades down the hillside above the sea. Each of its bedrooms looks on to the water, and from the restaurant terrace and beach club you can gaze over the water to St Anthony's Lighthouse. (Page 286)

## DAISYBANK COTTAGE
### BROCKENHURST
Ciaran and Cheryl Maher will welcome you like old friends to this Arts and Crafts house in the New Forest, whose pretty, immaculate rooms have espresso machines and chocolates. There is home-made granola and American pancakes for breakfast. (Page 130)

## OLD WHYLY
### EAST HOATHLY
Handily situated for Glyndebourne, Sarah Burgoyne's Georgian farmhouse is homely and comforting, with a lovingly tended garden ablaze with seasonal blooms. There is also an outdoor pool. She's a trained cook, so breakfasts are tip-top. (Page 172)

## THE OLD MANOR HOUSE
### HALFORD
This lovely 16th-century house overlooking the Stour seems too good to be true. It has antique-filled interiors, comfy, oak-beamed bedrooms, a drawing room with an open fire and, outside, a tennis court and the option to fish in the river. (Page 196)

## LOW MILL GUEST HOUSE
### BAINBRIDGE
The past comes alive at this converted 18th-century watermill in Wensleydale hill country: the old waterwheel is a highlight of the rustic, playful interior, with its stone walls and jazzy fabrics. In the morning, wake up to home-baked bread. (Page 86)

## NUMBER THIRTY EIGHT CLIFTON
### BRISTOL
A great deal of care has gone into making this B&B look so stylish, from the unusual vintage furniture, contemporary art and Zoffany wallpapers to the special features in the rooms, such as four-posters and copper baths. (Page 125)

## THE COACH HOUSE
### BRECON
Kayt and Hugh Cooper usher you in to their 19th-century former coaching inn with tea and bara brith. Spacious rooms are soothing, in shades of sage green and cream. Walkers will appreciate the big breakfasts and option of a packed lunch. (Page 414)

## 2 BLACKBURNE TERRACE
### LIVERPOOL
A discerning eye characterises Sarah and Glenn Whitter's Georgian town house, with its carefully curated collection of furniture, books and paintings. Sleep in richly coloured rooms; at breakfast the table is laid with silver and crystal. (Page 223)

## THE DULAIG
### GRANTOWN-ON-SPEY
On the edge of the Cairngorms, this Edwardian house was designed by the chap behind London's Waldorf Hotel; inside, a sense of timeless comfort prevails in its Arts and Crafts furniture, home-baked treats, and superb breakfasts. (Page 369)

## CHAPEL HOUSE
### PENZANCE
This Georgian house with crisp white interiors overlooks the harbour. Bedrooms with just a dash of colour – cerulean, sunburnt orange – all have sea views. They serve a fine breakfast and you can join a communal dinner at weekends. (Page 265)

## MILLGATE HOUSE
### RICHMOND
Lovers of fine Georgian interiors, antiques and the chime of many clocks will adore this Regency house with an award-winning garden, which is run by two passionate collectors. Some of the elegant bedrooms have views of the garden and river. (Page 277)

Old Whyly, East Hoathly

Mornington House, Multyfarnham

## EES WYKE COUNTRY HOUSE
### NEAR SAWREY
Beatrix Potter holidayed here, and no wonder. This country hotel overlooks Esthwaite Water, and most rooms enjoy views across the lake to the fells of the Old Man of Coniston, the Langdale Pikes and Grizedale Forest. B&B doubles start at £99. (Page 242)

## THE BECKFORD ARMS
### TISBURY
There's plenty to like about this Wiltshire pub-with-rooms: down-to-earth food (Ploughman's, Beckford beef burger), local ales, and sophisticated rooms with oak floors and fine Welsh blankets. Better still, B&B doubles start at £95. (Page 317)

## MORNINGTON HOUSE
### MULTYFARNHAM
Enjoy the pleasures of a grand, family-owned Irish country manor house – enormous, high-ceilinged rooms, Victorian wallpapers, antiques, slouchy sofas, flower-filled gardens – but without the eye-watering bill. B&B doubles cost from €160. (Page 474)

## NEWBEGIN HOUSE
### BEVERLEY
Walter and Nuala Sweeney will welcome you like trusted regulars to their atmospheric Georgian house, with its shuttered sash windows, fine antique furniture, family heirlooms, books, paintings and walled garden. Doubles, with fresh milk and biscuits, cost £90–£100. (Page 102)

## GRASSHOPPERS
### GLASGOW
The perfect city-centre bolt-hole – it's right next to the station – with bright, design-conscious bedrooms. Big breakfasts include a full Scottish. There is a bar and the option of a simple meal in the evening. B&B doubles are £90–£148. (Page 366)

## BRITANNIA HOUSE
### LYMINGTON
Tobias Feilke is your genial host at this double-fronted Victorian house overlooking a marina. Rooms are lavishly decorated with swags, drapes and plump sofas, and Tobias cooks up a mean breakfast in the morning. B&B doubles are £99–£149. (Page 230)

## TREREIFE
### PENZANCE
This Cornish Queen Anne house delights Guide regulars. Charming, higgledy-piggledy interiors, with lots of antiques, are complemented by bedrooms with views of the parkland and gardens, and hearty breakfasts. B&B doubles are £100–£160. (Page 266)

## RIVERWOOD
### PITLOCHRY
This Arts and Crafts-style house with sleek, modern interiors (shoes off when you enter), is set in secluded gardens beside the River Tay. Rooms are spacious and well-equipped; four have patios or terraces. B&B doubles are £120–£155. (Page 385)

## CNAPAN
### NEWPORT
The Coopers settle you into their B&B with tea and Welsh cakes, before showing you to a bright and immaculate bedroom. Munch on kippers or Glamorgan sausages at breakfast, and read in the sunny garden. Doubles start at £85. (Page 433)

## YALBURY COTTAGE
### LOWER BOCKHAMPTON
Deep in Thomas Hardy country, this charming former shepherd's cottage has cosy bedrooms with bucolic views, a garden with comfortable seating, and an excellent restaurant working wonders with West Country produce. B&B doubles are £99–£125. (Page 228)

The Felin Fach Griffin, Felin Fach

## THE BONNIE BADGER
### GULLANE

Tom and Michaela Kitchin's classy gastropub has a nature-to-plate philosophy (and serves everything from ham, egg and chips to Orkney scallops), while the coolly luxurious bedrooms reflect the soft colours of the East Lothian countryside. (Page 370)

## THE LAMB INN
### BURFORD

Set in former weavers' cottages, with a beamed and flagstoned interior and a jumble of antiques and armchairs, this is a classic old English pub, but with a smart dining room, and 17 rather swish rooms attached, some of them with four-posters. (Page 136)

## THE STAR INN AT HAROME
### HAROME

This exceptional pub in a thatched village cottage is worth a long detour. Andrew Pern serves Michelin-starred food, the bar was built by a master craftsman, and the bedrooms across the road are charmingly eccentric and very comfortable. (Page 200)

## THE CAT INN
### WEST HOATHLY

From its tile-hung facade to Harvey the resident spaniel snoozing in front of the fire, this is a quintessential Sussex village pub. The kitchen is passionate about local sourcing, and the bedrooms have Vispring beds and posh toiletries. (Page 331)

## PENTONBRIDGE INN
### PENTON

This stylish former coaching inn with views across Cumbria is run with a five-star touch. Chris Archer serves local food, much of it grown in the kitchen garden. Contemporary bedrooms have fresh flowers and wet-room showers. (Page 264)

## THE SUN INN
### DEDHAM

The Sun continues to shine with its winning blend of modern pub food, beamed interiors and a jolly atmosphere. Bedrooms are graceful, with solid oak beds, and an indulgent fry-up at breakfast will set you up for a day in Constable country. (Page 168)

## THE PEAR TREE INN
### WHITLEY

A gorgeous 17th-century pub, lovingly restored by Jackie Cosens and Adrian Jenkins, has got everything right, from chic-farmhouse interiors to delicious seasonal food – so local that meat can be traced right back to the individual animal. (Page 333)

## THE FELIN FACH GRIFFIN
### FELIN FACH

Not far from the book-lovers' paradise of Hay-on-Wye is this laid-back dining pub with famously comfortable beds in its retro rooms. Menus are brief, to maintain the chef's fierce commitment to the fresh, seasonal and locally sourced. (Page 422)

## THE ROYAL OAK
### TETBURY

Plant eaters will be happy at this funky inn, with a jukebox inside, an Airstream trailer outside, and rustic chic bedrooms. Chef Stergios Pikos specialises in excellent vegan and vegetarian dishes, alongside traditional pub favourites. (Page 315)

## THE TALBOT INN
### MELLS

This relaxed 15th-century coaching inn offers food of a consistently high standard, whether it's a simple Ploughman's or a dry-aged Stoke Marsh Farm sirloin steak. Bedrooms have Egyptian cotton sheets, Welsh blankets and cosy armchairs. (Page 238)

### BALLYVOLANE HOUSE
CASTLELYONS

It's a home rather than a hotel, say owners Jenny and Justin Green, and a very family-friendly one at that. You can expect trampolines and a tree house, animals to feed, eggs to collect, bikes to ride and games galore. There are glamping tents in summer. (Page 458)

### BEDRUTHAN HOTEL AND SPA
MAWGAN PORTH

This sister hotel to the nearby adults-only Scarlet goes all out for families, with dawn-to-dusk activities. Take them surfing on the beach or enjoy a family spa session. You'll find all the clobber you need for young children, too. (Page 235)

### AUGILL CASTLE
KIRKBY STEPHEN

If staying in a Victorian folly of a castle isn't enough of a treat for the kids, there's a games room, cinema and tennis court at Augill. It's antique-filled but relaxed, with some seriously romantic bedrooms for the grown-ups. (Page 215)

### THE COLONSAY
COLONSAY

It feels like a family holiday from yesteryear at this easy-going island hotel, reached by ferry. There are beaches to comb, seals to spot and bikes to hire. Families and locals mingle in the bar and the restaurant has children's menus. (Page 356)

### MOONFLEET MANOR
FLEET

Take a hotel on Chesil Beach with fossils and smugglers' tales galore, add a huge indoor play area with traversing wall and soft play area, a spa with indoor pools, plus an Ofsted crèche, and you've got the recipe for a happy family holiday. (Page 187)

### PORTH TOCYN HOTEL
ABERSOCH

It's no surprise that parents who visited this coastal hotel as children return with their own families: it has everything from high chairs and cots to a games room and outdoor pool. It's gloriously relaxed, with different dining options. (Page 409)

### TREFEDDIAN HOTEL
ABERDOVEY

A favourite for multi-generational families, and five minutes from the beach, Trefeddian has oodles of space for all ages. After time in the pool or in the indoor or outdoor play area, there's early supper or kids' menus at family meals. (Page 407)

### WOOLLEY GRANGE
BRADFORD-ON-AVON

An unstuffy atmosphere reigns in this Jacobean manor with crèche, where little ones can go egg collecting or pond-dipping while adults enjoy the spa. Kids can tuck into high tea before being tucked up, and there's fine dining for grown-ups. (Page 118)

### CHEWTON GLEN
NEW MILTON

Be prepared to be nagged to return here once the youngsters have experienced the fairytale children's club, indoor and outdoor pools, cooking classes, golf and tennis. And if you book a treehouse suite, they may never agree to leave. (Page 244)

### CALCOT & SPA
TETBURY

It's not just about the kids at this play-and-stay option, which has set splash times in the pool, so adults get some quiet time. On hand is everything from a crèche to a cinema, plus more baby gear than some people have at home. (Page 313)

Bedruthan Hotel and Spa, Mawgan Porth

The White Horse, Brancaster Staithe

## FOREST SIDE
GRASMERE
Just ten minutes on foot from
this is an idyllic spot for walkers o
abilities, from ramblers to serious hik
Luxury rooms and a Michelin-starred
restaurant will do wonders for aching feet
and hungry tummies on your return.
(Page 191)

## MOOR OF RANNOCH –
## RESTAURANT & ROOMS
RANNOCH STATION
There's no TV, radio, Wi-Fi or mobile
signal here – just miles of moorland
sometimes described as Britain's last
great wilderness. By turns desolate and
uplifting, it has been lauded by writers
from William Wordsworth to Robert
Macfarlane. (Page 390)

## THE ROCK INN
NEWTON ABBOT
There is no shortage of beautiful walks
from the front door of this cosy inn through
Dartmoor's huge spaces, and staff will
provide plenty of detailed information on
them. South Devon and the Coast Path are
a short drive away. (Page 248)

## THE WHITE HORSE
BRANCASTER STAITHE
Walk to the end of the garden of this
family-run hotel, and you'll find the
Norfolk Coast Path, with its miles of beach,
marshland, bridleways, quiet country lanes,
abundant birdlife and enormous skies.
(Page 121)

## PEN-Y-DYFFRYN
OSWESTRY
Walking holidays are a speciality here,
thanks to the hotel's blessed situation
amid the hills and footpaths of the Welsh
Borders. You can do 30-minute strolls to
full-day treks. Offa's Dyke long-distance
trail is less than a mile away. (Page 254)

su
with y

## THE PEAC
ROWSLEY
The Peak District na
doorstep here, and staff
a wide range of walks. Try t
round-trip to Chatsworth House
the River Derwent, stopping for a pi
at the Red Lion in Bakewell en route.
(Page 280)

## AEL Y BRYN
EGLWYSWRW
Pembrokeshire's dramatic coastal paths
and the Preseli hills are waiting to be
discovered on foot from this friendly,
adults-only B&B. On your return there is a
drying room for muddy clothes, and pre-
arranged evening meals. (Page 421)

## BLUE HAYES
ST IVES
The gardens at this glamorous, sun-soaked
hotel on Porthminster Point lead on to the
South West Coast Path – ideal for walks
that will conveniently take you past many
foodie and cultural points of interest, such
as Tate St Ives. (Page 282)

## LORUM OLD RECTORY
BAGENALSTOWN
The Blackstairs mountains and South
Leinster Way are a short stroll from
this country house, as is the Barrow
Navigation Towpath. Curracloe beach,
where the D-Day scenes of Saving Private
Ryan were filmed, is an hour's drive away.
(Page 452)

Grasmere,
fall
rs.

## THE BELL AT SKENFRITH
### SKENFRITH
Six circular walks, taking in glorious
Monmouthshire countryside, start
from the Bell's front door; staff provide
illustrated guides charting the route,
history and wildlife of each one. In
...mer, you can order a picnic to take
... (Page 439)

...OCK AT ROWSLEY

...ional park is on your
...ill recommend
...e eight-mile
...along

...o you
...ms and
...with its
...eals a
...g is for

...USE

...e lantern
...here are
... Downs, too,
... stay in the
...n the tower,
... ladder.

You can seek sanct...
Sutheran's imaginatively convert...
19th-century chapel with its arched
windows, wood flooring and double-height
living room. Even the original carved
pulpit and the harmonium are still present.
(Page 291)

**TALLAND BAY HOTEL**
TALLAND-BY-LOOE
Whether you're sitting on a zebra-print
sofa looking at the 3D Mickey Mouse on
the wall or perched on a wooden bench
with giant budgies in the garden with its
fairy statues, you'll find this coastal hotel
'curiouser and curiouser'. (Page 309)

**NO.15 GREAT PULTENEY**
BATH
The Georgian facade may be traditional
but there's a world of eccentricity within:
the spa is in a former coal cellar, room
keys are kept in a doll's house, and The
Dispensary restaurant holds the contents of
an antique chemist's shop. (Page 93)

... bar and the
...s 18th-century
...ining room, with
its original beam... ...he bedrooms have
access to the millstream, where swans
glide in sight of the enormous chimney.
(Page 321)

**THE QUAY HOUSE**
CLIFDEN
Don't be surprised to find a Buddha statue
rubbing shoulders with a Cupid in the
Foyles' harbourside B&B, packed with
curios, including clocks – broken and
working – a collection of bovine horns and
family photos a-plenty. (Page 459)

**THE CEILIDH PLACE**
ULLAPOOL
The Urquhart family's hotel has only 13
rooms, but it also has a bookshop, coffee
shop and events space as well as the more
traditional bar and restaurant. There's
even a bunkhouse across the car park for
those travelling on a budget. (Page 403)

The Old Railway Station, Petworth

The Traddock, Austwick

## THE ZETTER
### LONDON
A 1,500-foot borehole supplies water to flush the loos and cool the rooms; if you open a window, the air conditioning will cut out. Made from eco-friendly material, the hotel recycles all glass and paper and has bikes for hire and a Green Team. (Page 71)

## Y GOEDEN EIRIN
### DOLYDD
Alongside a warm Welsh welcome from Eluned Rowlands, guests at this B&B receive recycling instructions in bedrooms that are big on local slate and timber. There are solar panels and dimmer switches; and electric cars can be charged onsite. (Page 420)

## CAEMORGAN MANSION
### CARDIGAN
When Beverley and David Harrison-Wood renovated their 19th-century B&B, they added heating and hot water from a biomass boiler. Solar panels and LED lighting help cut down on electricity, and food is locally sourced where possible. (Page 416)

## THE OLD RECTORY
### BOSCASTLE
Sally and Chris Searle live the real Good Life here. They grow fruit and veg, collect eggs and cure bacon. Waste goes to the wormery and old carpets become weed suppressants. They have solar panels and an electric car, too. (Page 114)

## THE PIERHOUSE
### PORT APPIN
Towels aren't tumble-dried at The Pierhouse: a pulley system is employed instead. Using everything from eco-friendly cleaning products to a septic tank for waste, this Lochside hotel has been awarded a gold award for Green tourism. (Page 387)

## PENDRAGON COUNTRY HOUSE
### CAMELFORD
Even the website of this Cornish hotel is hosted by a carbon neutral server. Families can benefit from a free washable nappy service, those who drive in electric cars can recharge, and there are solar panels and a biomass boiler. (Page 142)

## THYME
### SOUTHROP
Most of the food you eat at this country estate is farmed on site. What's more, heating comes from a ground source heat pump and wood pellet boiler. Even the bin liners are paper and the hotel is looking to introduce wooden key cards. (Page 302)

## WHATLEY MANOR
### EASTON GREY
You can tuck into Michelin-starred meals with a clear conscience at this eco-friendly hotel, which uses a company to turn food waste into fuel. Though with Niall Keating cooking, we doubt there will be much left on your plate. (Page 175)

## THE TRADDOCK
### AUSTWICK
The gorgeous Yorkshire Dales setting of this creeper-clad hotel has inspired the Reynolds family to do everything they can to minimise its impact on the environment. That includes recycling, energy saving, woodland restoration and organic food. (Page 82)

## ARGYLL HOTEL
### IONA
It may be in the Hebrides, but this hotel still aims to dry as much laundry as possible on the lines, after washing it with biodegradable products. Their goal is to protect the pristine island by cutting food miles and upgrading insulation. (Page 374)

Star Castle, St Mary's

## LLANTHONY PRIORY HOTEL
### LLANTHONY
The ruins of a medieval Augustinian abbey are the backdrop to this hotel, in the former prior's lodging. There's still a certain monastic simplicity to the rooms, four of which are in the tower, with no en-suites, TV or Wi-Fi. (Page 430)

## KNOCKINAAM LODGE
### PORTPATRICK
You can stay in the room where Churchill slept (and soak in the enamelled-concrete bath he used) when he and Eisenhower planned the D-Day landings from this secluded Victorian hunting lodge. Churchillian levels of luxury abound. (Page 388)

## CASTLE LESLIE
### GLASLOUGH
The Leslie family can apparently trace its origins to Attila the Hun, though its Irish estate is much more recent, dating back to the 17th century. The current Victorian pile is home to such oddities as the first plumbed bath in Ireland. (Page 464)

## PLAS DINAS COUNTRY HOUSE
### CAERNARFON
For fans of the TV series The Crown: Princess Margaret regularly stayed at this former home of the Armstrong-Jones family when she was married to Lord Snowdon. Royal memorabilia is on show; the Princess Margaret suite has a four-poster. (Page 415)

## ASKHAM HALL
### PENRITH
Charles Lowther's ancestral pile comes with a medieval pele tower and a 17th-century topiary garden. Prince Philip stayed in the Admiral's Room on his visits to the hall over 30 years during the Lowther Show carriage-driving event. (Page 260)

## CLIVEDEN HOUSE
### TAPLOW
You name them, they've stayed at this Thameside Italianate summer palace. Former guests include most British monarchs since George I, plus personalities such as Charlie Chaplin. Not to mention a certain Christine Keeler and John Profumo. (Page 310)

## HARTWELL HOUSE
### AYLESBURY
The exiled French king Louis XVIII set up his impoverished court at Hartwell for five years after 1809, farming livestock on its roofs. He signed his accession to the throne in the library. The mansion is now run by the National Trust. (Page 83)

## THE ASSEMBLY HOUSE
### NORWICH
Madame Tussaud exhibited her waxworks in this Georgian building, Franz Liszt gave a concert in the music room, and the local gentry danced beneath the chandeliers in the magnificent Great Hall to celebrate Nelson's victory at Trafalgar. (Page 250)

## THE LYGON ARMS
### BROADWAY
There's history from both sides of the English Civil War to be found among the beams and inglenooks. Charles I stayed in 1649; his coat of arms can be seen over a fireplace in his room. And Oliver Cromwell slept here before battle in 1651. (Page 128)

## STAR CASTLE
### ST MARY'S
The bar is in the dungeon and the beamed dining room in the former officers' mess of this Elizabethan fortress, built in star formation to defend the Isles of Scilly. Some rooms are in the original ramparts, so may have an unusual shape. (Page 284)

## GILPIN HOTEL AND LAKE HOUSE
### WINDERMERE
The Lake House, which you can hire exclusively with 100 acres of grounds, has six suites, lakeside views, lounge, outdoor hot tubs, sauna and indoor pool. After your vows, there is Michelin-starred dining in the Conservatory or marquee. (Page 336)

## THE INN AT WHITEWELL
### WHITEWELL
Couples can marry in the orangery of this mullion-windowed 18th-century inn overlooking the Forest of Bowland, or in a charming church, built in 1821, which is in the grounds. In addition to 23 rooms, there is a private cottage. (Page 332)

## LLANGOED HALL
### LLYSWEN
Welsh country house hospitality awaits spouses-to-be at this impressive hall in the Wye valley. Exchange vows with a view of the Black mountains, dine on locally sourced cuisine, and wander arm-in-arm through wild flowers in the grounds. (Page 431)

## BURGH ISLAND HOTEL
### BIGBURY-ON-SEA
Have the island and this retro-glamorous Art Deco hotel, which has hosted luminaries from Winston Churchill to Noël Coward, entirely to yourself as the tide draws in. With 25 rooms, it can host 50 guests for exclusive use. (Page 103)

## THE HORN OF PLENTY
### TAVISTOCK
Fine weather permitting, couples can tie the knot outdoors with a magnificent view across the Tamar valley from this four-star, creeper-clad Georgian country house. Large suites in the main house or coach houses have balconies and terraces. (Page 311)

## MARLFIELD HOUSE
### GOREY
Fairy-tale weddings are a mainstay of this luxurious Relais & Châteaux hotel, set in 36 acres of glorious gardens. Say 'I do' in the Print Room, elegant Turner-style Conservatory or garden; spend your wedding night in a lavish State Room. (Page 465)

## LORDS OF THE MANOR
### UPPER SLAUGHTER
This romantic Cotswold manor house set in eight acres of gardens prides itself on offering bespoke extravagant ceremonies for up to 150 people, as well as discreet, intimate affairs with just a handful of guests. (Page 323)

## NEW HOUSE FARM
### LORTON
The wedding photos here will win you bragging rights for the rest of your days. Couples have a mesmerising backdrop of dramatic fells, brooks and gardens at this Lake District farmhouse. Marry in a rustic hayloft with exposed stone walls. (Page 227)

## JUDGES
### YARM
Wedding nerves will be calmed by a warm Yorkshire welcome at this clubby hotel in a Victorian country mansion. Marry in the lovely garden gazebo with acres of gardens and woods as the backdrop, and dine on excellent food. (Page 340)

## GLENAPP CASTLE
### BALLANTRAE
Church of Scotland ceremonies can be held in a Victorian chapel on this splendid Ayrshire estate, or in the turreted castle hotel. In the evening, watch the sun set over Ailsa Craig and the Mull of Kintyre, and retire to a sea-view suite. (Page 350)

Burgh Island Hotel, Bigbury-on-Sea

## TEMPLE HOUSE
BALLYMOTE

Monster pike of up to 46 pounds lurk in the 200-acre Temple House Lake – the one on the hall's mantelpiece weighs a measly 32 pounds. This is a great place for coarse fishing, including perch and bream, with four boats to take on the water. (Page 455)

## THE PEACOCK AT ROWSLEY
ROWSLEY

Only guests at Lord and Lady Manners's hotel can fish for trout in low season on the 15 miles of banks along four rivers running through the Haddon Estate. One is the Derbyshire Wye, known for its population of wild rainbow trout. (Page 280)

## NEWPORT HOUSE
NEWPORT

The fishing rights to eight miles of the Newport river are held by this Georgian mansion overlooking the estuary. It is one of the few Irish fisheries where spring salmon can be fished from a boat. Your catch can be frozen or smoked. (Page 475)

## THE DEVONSHIRE ARMS
BOLTON ABBEY

Running through the Duke and Duchess of Devonshire's Bolton Abbey Estate is the River Wharf. You can fly fish for trout and grayling along a 4½-mile stretch surrounded by the scenic Yorkshire Dales. (Page 111)

## FORSS HOUSE
THURSO

A 42-pound salmon was landed in 1954 at the bottom of this Highland retreat's garden, looped around by the River Forss. We can't guarantee anything similar but occasional rods are available to rent, with permits available on other rivers. (Page 401)

## HOTEL ENDSLEIGH
MILTON ABBOT

A ghillie will give you tips on the best way to cast and catch salmon on eight miles of the Tamar at Olga Polizzi's country hotel, built as a fishing lodge for Georgiana, Duchess of Bedford. Tackle and tuition are available. (Page 239)

## LAKE COUNTRY HOUSE HOTEL & SPA
LLANGAMMARCH WELLS

It's a short walk from Jean-Pierre Mifsud's former fishing lodge to the well-stocked trout lake. More experienced anglers can try their luck for trout and grayling on seven miles of the River Irfon, which runs through the hotel grounds. (Page 429)

## SHIELDAIG LODGE
GAIRLOCH

You can join a local fisherman for creel fishing on a sea loch and the lodge's chefs will cook a seafood platter with your spoils. Shieldaig also has loch and river fishing on its 26,000-acre Highland estate, with ghillies and tuition. (Page 365)

## THE INN AT WHITEWELL
WHITEWELL

On the banks of the Hodder in the Forest of Bowland, this rural inn has residents-only rights to fishing on seven miles of riverbanks. There are 14 pools and interesting runs, along with the services of a ghillie should you need them. (Page 332)

## GLIFFAES
CRICKHOWELL

Bedrooms look on to the River Usk, where guests can fish for trout and salmon on one of the hotel's three beats along a mile of left-bank fishing, with more beats upriver. If you land a trout, the kitchen can cook it for your breakfast. (Page 417)

Forss House, Thurso

Trefeddian Hotel, Aberdovey

## BUDOCK VEAN
MAWNAN SMITH

The golf bar has views over the fairway, Sky Sports is tuned to the golf channel, and the nine-hole course has one of the longest par-fives in the country. Better still, green fees at the Barlow family's resort hotel are included. (Page 237)

## ROMNEY BAY HOUSE
NEW ROMNEY

On one side of this 1920s mansion built by Clough Williams-Ellis lies the English Channel, while on the other is Littlestone golf course. It's a scenic, isolated spot, whether you're playing on the Championship Links or The Warren. (Page 245)

## TREFEDDIAN HOTEL
ABERDOVEY

The nine-hole putting course at this family-friendly, dog-friendly hotel on the coast is just a warm-up for the real thing: Trefeddian overlooks Aberdovey's 18-hole championship golf course. Coaching and caddies are available if needed. (Page 407)

## HILTON PARK
CLONES

There's a double bonus for guests staying at the sprawling Madden family estate, home to Clones golf course: not only are greens fees complimentary, but the rolling woodland course features 20 holes, after an extra two were added in 2005. (Page 461)

## GREYWALLS
GULLANE

The only thing separating this Lutyens-designed house from Muirfield golf course is a ha-ha. Some rooms have links views, and you can drink or dine overlooking the green of the 18th hole. It is possible to tee off on 22 golf courses within ten miles. (Page 371)

## PARK HOUSE, HOTEL & SPA
BEPTON

If you like to mix your golf with other activities, Seamus O'Brien's South Downs leisure hotel may be the place. As well as a putting lawn and six-hole 18-tee golf course, there are two pools and a spa, plus tennis, croquet and bowls. (Page 101)

## THE ATLANTIC HOTEL
ST BRELADE

There are ocean views from every hole at Jersey's La Moye golf course, plus a few rocky outcrops on the fairway. At the adjacent Atlantic Hotel, rooms without sea views overlook the fairways. The food is well above par. (Page 446)

## BOATH HOUSE
AULDEARN

Two championship golf courses are in Nairn, while Castle Stuart, home of the Scottish open, is nearby, and Royal Dornoch is one of 30 golf courses within an hour's drive. But first you need to tear yourself away from the exquisite hotel grounds. (Page 349)

## BEECHWOOD HOTEL
NORTH WALSHAM

Guests at Emma and Hugh Asher's country house hotel can enjoy special deals at Mundesley and Royal Cromer golf clubs. In the evening, there's a different clubby atmosphere back at Beechwood, with a rolling programme of evening events. (Page 249)

## BALLYMALOE HOUSE
SHANAGARRY

For a bit of fun or practice, there is a five-hole course in front of this hotel, with golf balls and clubs available at reception. For something more serious, there are courses at nearby Castlemartyr, Fota Island and Harbour Point. (Page 479)

Each of these hotels has a tennis court (T)
and/or a swimming pool (S)

Chewton Glen, New Milton

## ENGLAND
**Hartwell House,**
  Aylesbury (T,S)
**Royal Crescent Hotel & Spa,**
  Bath (S)
**Park House, Hotel & Spa,**
  Bepton (T,S)
**Burgh Island Hotel,**
  Bigbury-on-Sea (T,S)
**The Blakeney Hotel,**
  Blakeney (S)
**The Devonshire Arms,**
  Bolton Abbey (S)
**Widbrook Grange,**
  Bradford-on-Avon (S)
**Woolley Grange,**
  Bradford-on-Avon (S)
**The Lygon Arms,**
  Broadway (S)
**The Newt in Somerset,**
  Bruton (S)
**Hell Bay Hotel,**
  Bryher (S)
**Brockencote Hall,**
  Chaddesley Corbett (T)
**Tor Cottage,**
  Chillaton (S)
**Corse Lawn House,**
  Corse Lawn (T,S)

**North House,**
  Cowes (S)
**The Rectory Hotel,**
  Crudwell (S)
**Headlam Hall,**
  Darlington (T)
**Dart Marina,**
  Dartmouth (S)
**Maison Talbooth,**
  Dedham (T,S)
**Old Whyly,**
  East Hoathly (T,S)
**Gara Rock,**
  East Portlemouth (S)
**Whatley Manor,**
  Easton Grey (S)
**Summer Lodge,**
  Evershot (T,S)
**Moonfleet Manor,**
  Fleet (S)
**Fowey Hall,**
  Fowey (S)
**The Old Manor House,**
  Halford (T)
**Hambleton Hall,**
  Hambleton (T,S)
**The Pheasant,**
  Harome (S)

**Ilsington Country House,**
Ilsington (S)
**Congham Hall,**
King's Lynn (S)
**Augill Castle,**
Kirkby Stephen (T)
**Mallory Court,**
Leamington Spa (S)
**Lime Wood,**
Lyndhurst (S)
**Bedruthan Hotel and Spa,**
Mawgan Porth (T,S)
**The Scarlet,**
Mawgan Porth (S)
**Budock Vean,**
Mawnan Smith (T,S)
**Mullion Cove Hotel,**
Mullion Cove (S)
**Chewton Glen,**
New Milton (T,S)
**Askham Hall,**
Penrith (S)
**Star Castle,**
St Mary's (T,S)
**Soar Mill Cove Hotel,**
Salcombe (T,S)
**Seaham Hall,**
Seaham (S)
**Thyme,**
Southrop (S)
**Plumber Manor,**
Sturminster Newton (T)
**Cliveden House,**
Taplow (T,S)
**Calcot & Spa,**
Tetbury (T,S)
**The Royal Hotel,**
Ventnor (S)
**The Nare,**
Veryan-in-Roseland (T,S)
**Gilpin Hotel and Lake House,**
Windermere (S)
**Middlethorpe Hall & Spa,**
York (S)

## SCOTLAND
**Glenapp Castle,**
Ballantrae (T)
**Shieldaig Lodge,**
Gairloch (T)

**Glengarry Castle Hotel,**
Invergarry (T)
**Douneside House,**
Tarland (T,S)

## WALES
**Trefeddian Hotel,**
Aberdovey (T,S)
**Porth Tocyn Hotel,**
Abersoch (T,S)
**Gliffaes,**
Crickhowell (T)
**Bodysgallen Hall & Spa,**
Llandudno (T,S)
**Lake Country House Hotel & Spa,**
Llangammarch Wells (T,S)

## CHANNEL ISLANDS
**The White House,**
Herm (T,S)
**The Atlantic Hotel,**
St Brelade (T,S)
**Greenhills Country House Hotel,**
St Peter (S)
**Longueville Manor,**
St Saviour (T,S)

## IRELAND
**Ballyvolane House,**
Castlelyons (T)
**Killiane Castle Country House and Farm,**
Drinagh (T)
**Marlfield House,**
Gorey (T)
**Rosleague Manor,**
Letterfrack (T)
**Currarevagh House,**
Oughterard (T)
**Rathmullan House,**
Rathmullan (S)
**Coopershill,**
Riverstown (T)
**Ballymaloe House,**
Shanagarry (T,S)

Each of these hotels has at least one bedroom equipped for a visitor in a wheelchair. You should telephone to discuss individual requirements.

Coes Faen, Barmouth

## LONDON
The Beaumont
The Goring
The Zetter
The Zetter Townhouse Clerkenwell
The Zetter Townhouse Marylebone

## ENGLAND
The Wentworth,
  Aldeburgh
The Cookie Jar,
  Alnwick
Baraset Barn,
  Alveston
Hartwell House,
  Aylesbury
Red Lion Inn,
  Babcary
Barnsley House,
  Barnsley
The Cavendish,
  Baslow
No.15 Great Pulteney,
  Bath
Park House, Hotel & Spa,
  Bepton
The Blakeney Hotel,
  Blakeney
The Lord Crewe Arms,
  Blanchland
The Devonshire Arms,
  Bolton Abbey

Leathes Head Hotel,
  Borrowdale
The Millstream,
  Bosham
Lindeth Fell,
  Bowness-on-Windermere
Widbrook Grange,
  Bradford-on-Avon
Woolley Grange,
  Bradford-on-Avon
The White Horse,
  Brancaster Staithe
The Lygon Arms,
  Broadway
The Pig in the Forest,
  Brockenhurst
The Newt in Somerset,
  Bruton
University Arms,
  Cambridge
Pendragon Country House,
  Camelford
Blackmore Farm,
  Cannington
The Pig at Bridge Place,
  Canterbury
Brockencote Hall,
  Chaddesley Corbett
Captain's Club Hotel,
  Christchurch
Beech House & Olive Branch,
  Clipsham

The Bay Hotel,
Coverack

Hipping Hall,
Cowan Bridge

Clow Beck House,
Croft-on-Tees

Headlam Hall,
Darlington

Dart Marina,
Dartmouth

The Red Lion Freehouse,
East Chisenbury

Whatley Manor,
Easton Grey

The Duncombe Arms,
Ellastone

The Ellerby Country Inn,
Ellerby

Summer Lodge,
Evershot

Lympstone Manor,
Exmouth

The Carpenters Arms,
Felixkirk

Fowey Hall,
Fowey

The Pig at Combe,
Gittisham

Forest Side,
Grasmere

Belmond Le Manoir aux Quat'Saisons,
Great Milton

The Pheasant,
Harome

Castle House,
Hereford

Congham Hall,
King's Lynn

Augill Castle,
Kirkby Stephen

Mallory Court,
Leamington Spa

Lewtrenchard Manor,
Lewdown

Lime Wood,
Lyndhurst

The Talbot,
Malton

Bedruthan Hotel and Spa,
Mawgan Porth

The Scarlet,
Mawgan Porth

Budock Vean,
Mawnan Smith

Hotel Endsleigh,
Milton Abbot

Chewton Glen,
New Milton

Jesmond Dene House,
Newcastle upon Tyne

The Assembly House,
Norwich

Hart's Hotel,
Nottingham

Old Bank,
Oxford

Old Parsonage,
Oxford

Tebay Services Hotel,
Penrith

The Yorke Arms,
Ramsgill-in-Nidderdale

The Black Swan,
Ravenstonedale

The Coach House
at Middleton Lodge,
Richmond

Boskerris Hotel,
St Ives

Idle Rocks,
St Mawes

Seaham Hall,
Seaham

St Cuthbert's House,
Seahouses

La Fleur de Lys,
Shaftesbury

Brocco on the Park,
Sheffield

The Rose & Crown,
Snettisham

Glazebrook House,
South Brent

The Pipe and Glass Inn,
South Dalton

Thyme,
Southrop

The Harcourt Arms,
Stanton Harcourt

Plumber Manor,
Sturminster Newton

Cliveden House,
Taplow

The Horn of Plenty,
Tavistock

The Hare and Hounds,
  Tetbury
The Royal Oak,
  Tetbury
The Gunton Arms,
  Thorpe Market
Titchwell Manor,
  Titchwell
Tuddenham Mill,
  Tuddenham
The Royal Hotel,
  Ventnor
The Nare,
  Veryan-in-Roseland
The Pear Tree Inn,
  Whitley
Gilpin Hotel and Lake House,
  Windermere
Middlethorpe Hall & Spa,
  York

## SCOTLAND
Loch Melfort Hotel,
  Arduaine
Boath House,
  Auldearn
Glenapp Castle,
  Ballantrae
Monachyle Mhor,
  Balquhidder
Coul House,
  Contin
The Three Chimneys
and The House Over-By,
  Dunvegan
Prestonfield,
  Edinburgh
Kylesku Hotel,
  Kylesku
The Peat Inn,
  Peat Inn
The Green Park,
  Pitlochry
Viewfield House,
  Portree
Blackaddie House,
  Sanquhar
Kinloch Lodge,
  Sleat
The Inn at Loch Tummel,
  Strathtummel
Douneside House,
  Tarland

Forss House,
  Thurso
The Torridon,
  Torridon

## WALES
Harbourmaster Hotel,
  Aberaeron
Trefeddian Hotel,
  Aberdovey
Coes Faen,
  Barmouth
Gliffaes,
  Crickhowell
Penbontbren,
  Glynarthen
Tyddyn Llan,
  Llandrillo
Bodysgallen Hall & Spa,
  Llandudno
Lake Country House Hotel & Spa,
  Llangammarch Wells
The Grove of Narberth,
  Narberth
Restaurant James Sommerin,
  Penarth
Twr y Felin Hotel,
  St Davids

## CHANNEL ISLANDS
Greenhills Country House Hotel,
  St Peter

## IRELAND
The Mustard Seed at Echo Lodge,
  Ballingarry
Stella Maris,
  Ballycastle
Gregans Castle Hotel,
  Ballyvaughan
The Quay House,
  Clifden
The Wilder Townhouse,
  Dublin
Castle Leslie,
  Glaslough
Rayanne House,
  Holywood
No. 1 Pery Square,
  Limerick
Viewmount House,
  Longford

# LONDON

London Eye

# LONDON

MAP 2:D4

## ARTIST RESIDENCE LONDON

♔ Previous César winner

Amid the historic streets and squares of Pimlico, a 19th-century pub has been reinvented as a hip hotel, with café and cocktail bar. This Artist Residence was a third venture for Justin and Charlotte Salisbury – see also Artist Residence in Brighton, South Leigh and Penzance (Shortlist entry), with a changing display of curated artwork throughout. A new general manager, Leutrim Grbavci, has been appointed, but the funky style and the modus operandi remain the same, with local residents encouraged to drop by for a drink or a bite at any time, in the café, in the club room or on the terrace. The ten bedrooms have a mix of contemporary, vintage and distressed furnishings, a Roberts radio, mini-fridge and espresso machine. The Art Deco-style Club Suite has a super-king-size handmade bed, a velvet sofa and battered leather club chairs, a large bathroom with a roll-top bath and walk-in shower. The Loft, under the eaves, has a French-style 1930s bath and bare brick walls. Breakfast, charged extra, includes fresh pastries, pancakes, smashed avocado, the full English or vegan; at other times, you can order small plates, burgers, fish and chips and cauliflower risotto – or a champagne cream tea.

52 Cambridge Street
Pimlico
London SW1V 4QQ

**T:** 020 3019 8610
**E:** london@artistresidence.co.uk
**W:** artistresidence.co.uk/london

**BEDROOMS:** 10. 2 suites.
**OPEN:** all year.
**FACILITIES:** cocktail bar, restaurant, club room lounge, games/private dining/meetings room, small 'hidden' garden, in-room TV (Freeview), unsuitable for disabled.
**BACKGROUND MUSIC:** in public areas.
**LOCATION:** Pimlico, underground Pimlico.
**CHILDREN:** all ages welcomed, cot available for larger rooms, no extra beds for children sharing.
**DOGS:** only allowed in the restaurant.
**CREDIT CARDS:** Amex, MC, Visa.
**PRICES:** per room £255–£595. Cooked breakfast from £6, full English £12, vegan £10, à la carte £40. 1-night bookings sometimes refused weekends.

**SEE ALSO SHORTLIST**

# LONDON

MAP 2:D4

## THE BEAUMONT     **NEW**

'It has an air of luxury and style,' says a trusted reviewer, of this 'quiet and peaceful' hotel on a garden square in Mayfair. The handsome Art Deco building, adorned with a giant Antony Gormley sculpture (the interior of which is now a guest room), was converted into a hotel in 2014, though 'its sense of gravitas makes you think it's been here for ever'. The interior has a glamorous '1920s vibe', with 'suited and booted staff' and glossy dark wood finishes. 'Impeccable' bedrooms combine period detailing with contemporary mosaic-and-marble bathrooms that bring them up to date. 'Charming small touches' include illustrated postcards and writing paper. All meals are taken in the New York speakeasy-style Colony Grill where 'the sommelier in particular is a delight' and gives excellent recommendations. Our reviewer chose a 'fantastic roast hake with beetroot and chard'; at breakfast they ordered eggs that were wonderfully cooked. 'Staff couldn't have been nicer' and 'we had an unquestionably beautiful time'. (BF)

Mayfair
London W1K 6TF

**T:** 020 7499 1001
**E:** reservations@thebeaumont.com
**W:** thebeaumont.com

**BEDROOMS:** 73. Some rooms suitable for disabled.
**OPEN:** all year.
**FACILITIES:** bar, restaurant, private dining room, spa, electric shuttle limousine; in-room smart TV (free movies), public rooms wheelchair accessible, adapted toilet.
**BACKGROUND MUSIC:** yes.
**LOCATION:** Mayfair, mews parking, underground Bond Street, valet parking.
**CHILDREN:** all ages welcomed.
**DOGS:** by arrangement.
**CREDIT CARDS:** Amex, MC, Visa.
**PRICES:** per room £470–£4,500 (with continental breakfast). Cooked breakfast £23.75, à la carte £53.

**SEE ALSO SHORTLIST**

# LONDON

MAP 2:D4

## DURRANTS

There is an Edwardian, clubby feel about this hotel, occupying four Georgian town houses, and celebrating a centenary in the care of the Miller family. 'It is a slightly eccentric enterprise,' writes a trusted reader. However, 'they are unfailingly welcoming, with old-fashioned courtesies such as bags swept up in a moment from the taxi'. Bedrooms, from singles to suites, have classic furnishings, a bath or shower room with L'Occitane toiletries. 'Those at the rear are cosy rather than grand.' Some have been refurbished this year, and even the shortcomings endear. 'Usually my bathroom sink is blocked or slow on my arrival, but it is swiftly cleared.' The 'staff are plentiful', and 'service has markedly improved'. A coal fire burns in the George bar, while in the panelled Grill Room the menu offers chargrilled steaks, shepherd's pie, maybe pumpkin and spinach risotto, Sunday roasts from the trolley. 'Breakfast is very grand, with pots of this and that crowding the table, and specially cooked calorific dishes balanced by astringent pressed juices.' (Keith Salway, RW)

26–32 George Street
Marylebone
London W1H 5BJ

T: 020 7935 8131
E: enquiries@durrantshotel.co.uk
W: www.durrantshotel.co.uk

BEDROOMS: 92. 7 on ground floor.
OPEN: all year, restaurant closed 25 Dec evening.
FACILITIES: lifts, bar, restaurant, lounge, meeting/events rooms, in-room TV (Freeview), use of nearby fitness club, public areas wheelchair accessible, no adapted toilet.
BACKGROUND MUSIC: none.
LOCATION: off Oxford Street, underground Bond Street, Baker Street.
CHILDREN: all ages welcomed.
DOGS: allowed in George bar only.
CREDIT CARDS: Amex, MC, Visa.
PRICES: per room B&B single from £190, double £221–£401. Fixed-price menu £20–£33 (Sun £28–£33), à la carte £55.

SEE ALSO SHORTLIST

# LONDON

## 11 CADOGAN GARDENS     NEW

London's only Relais & Châteaux hotel sprawls
over four red brick Victorian town houses built
by Lord Chelsea, its sleeping quarters reached by
a warren of staircases and hallways and serviced
by a 'very old-fashioned lift'. Until recently a
private members' club, it is now part of the Iconic
Luxury Hotels group (see also Cliveden House,
Taplow; Chewton Glen, New Milton; and Lygon
Arms, Broadway). Apart from the Union flag,
'from the outside, you wouldn't know it was a
hotel', says a Guide inspector. Individually styled
bedrooms, 'many with extraordinary furnishings',
range from singles to the splendid Sloane Suite,
with canopied four-poster and floor-to-ceiling
windows overlooking leafy Cadogan Gardens.
Silk wallpapers and Arabescato marble bathrooms
give a luxurious touch. You can read in the library,
relax in the drawing room, drink cocktails in
the atmospheric bar, and eat from an all-day
menu in Hans' Bar and Grill. Meals feature
kippers or a full English at breakfast, and later,
spatchcocked baby chicken, grass-fed steak or
'excellent chickpea and coriander burger and tuna
tartare'. The 'super-friendly, very polite' staff are
'a highlight'.

11 Cadogan Gardens
Chelsea
London SW3 2RJ

T: 020 7730 7000
E: reception@11cadogangardens.com
W: 11cadogangardens.com

**BEDROOMS:** 56 (incl. 25 suites).
**OPEN:** all year.
**FACILITIES:** small lift, drawing room,
library, cocktail bar, Hans' Bar and
Grill (wine room, conservatory),
private dining/meetings/events
rooms, in-room TV (Freeview), gym,
decked terrace, grill and public rooms
wheelchair accessible. adapted toilet
by grill.
**BACKGROUND MUSIC:** everywhere
except the library.
**LOCATION:** Chelsea, underground
Sloane Square.
**CHILDREN:** all ages welcomed (cots,
extra bed in suite free for under-17s,
£72 for over-16s, babysitting available).
**DOGS:** only assistance dogs.
**CREDIT CARDS:** Amex, MC, Visa.
**PRICES:** per room B&B single from
£250, double £310–£1,250. À la carte
£40, market menu £28–£35.

**SEE ALSO SHORTLIST**

# LONDON

## THE GORING

A long-time favourite of its royal neighbours, this Belgravia grand dame is 'charmingly old-school', with red-liveried footmen, Michelin-starred restaurant, and one of the largest private gardens in London. The now 'very expensive' hotel was founded in 1910 by Otto Goring. His great-grandson Jeremy – aided by long-serving managing director David Morgan-Hewitt – runs things today. The public areas are 'immaculate'; the busy cocktail bar and lounge lead off a chequered-floor lobby. Down the hall is The Dining Room, where a mix of classic and more contemporary dishes includes the late Queen Mother's favourite, Eggs Drumkilbo, and a signature fillet of beef Wellington. Siren is Nathan Outlaw's seafood restaurant, overlooking the garden; it serves simple dishes made with the freshest Cornish produce. The grandest bedroom is the Royal Suite, which comes with a dedicated footman and life-size portrait of Queen Victoria, but less grand rooms are all fit for a minor royal, with their silk-lined walls, bespoke furniture and Asprey toiletries. Breakfast brings a choice of continental or hot dishes, served in The Dining Room. (AB)

15 Beeston Place
Grosvenor Gardens
London SW1W 0JW

T: 020 7396 9000
E: reception@thegoring.com
W: thegoring.com

**BEDROOMS:** 69. 2 suitable for disabled.
**OPEN:** all year.
**FACILITIES:** lifts, lounge, bar, restaurant, private dining rooms, gym, in-room TV (Sky), civil wedding licence, business centre, fitness room, veranda, 1-acre garden (croquet), public rooms wheelchair accessible, adapted toilet.
**BACKGROUND MUSIC:** none.
**LOCATION:** Belgravia, mews parking, underground Victoria.
**CHILDREN:** all ages welcomed.
**DOGS:** only assistance dogs allowed.
**CREDIT CARDS:** Amex, MC, Visa.
**PRICES:** B&B single from £455, double from £485, D,B&B double from £525. À la carte (3 courses) from £67, pre-theatre dinner (2 courses) £32, Siren restaurant from £65.

**SEE ALSO SHORTLIST**

# LONDON

MAP 2:D4

## THE GRAZING GOAT

You can graze throughout the day at this dining-pub-with-rooms in an area of trendy independent shops dubbed Portman Village, two minutes from the homogenous stores of Oxford Street. Despite the central location, its rooms are a good size with rustic-chic styling and blond wood fittings reminiscent of a country house hotel. A room at the top might be a climb (there is no lift) but traffic noise is no more than a distant hum. Cafetière coffee is a welcome bonus. Downstairs, the vibe is youthful and laid-back, the service friendly. Imaginative breakfast choices in the café/bar include chilli cornbread with smashed avocado, spinach omelette and smoked ham hock. The full English comes with Cumberland sausage and black pudding. In the first-floor dining room you can browse fixed-price, limited-choice menus, or eat à la carte dishes such as haddock and chips, roast Lyons Hill Farm pheasant, choucroute and port jus, or salt-baked celeriac with barley, crispy shallots and Madeira sauce. There are tables on a pavement patio too. (See also its sister pub in Pimlico, The Orange.)

6 New Quebec Street
Marble Arch
London W1H 7RQ

T: 020 7724 7243
E: reservations@thegrazinggoat.co.uk
W: thegrazinggoat.co.uk

BEDROOMS: 8.
OPEN: all year.
FACILITIES: bar, dining room, patio, in-room TV.
BACKGROUND MUSIC: all day in bar.
LOCATION: central, underground Marble Arch.
CHILDREN: all ages welcomed (cot or child's bed available).
DOGS: allowed in public rooms, not in bedrooms.
CREDIT CARDS: Amex, MC, Visa.
PRICES: per room £219–£269. Breakfast mains from £8, full English £12.50, à la carte £35, set menus £27–£46.

**SEE ALSO SHORTLIST**

# LONDON

MAP 2:D4

## HAZLITT'S

A slice of literary history in lively Soho, this
former home of English essayist William Hazlitt
creaks with authenticity. Now a boutique B&B,
it is much more luxurious than it was when the
impoverished Hazlitt lived here. Made from three
adjoining town houses with a fourth behind,
it's owned by Peter McKay and Douglas Blain,
founding members of a charity that protects
historic buildings. Bedrooms are opulent, their
ornate carved beds dressed with rich fabrics
and plush cushions; some have gilded cherubs.
Spacious bathrooms have restored period fixtures
and fittings, and might feature a classical statue
or a lavatory concealed in a Jacobean-style love
seat. It's full of surprises: the Duke of Monmouth
duplex suite has a 'courtyard garden' with a
sliding glass roof; a wall panel in the Teresa
Cornelys junior suite springs open to reveal a
dressing table. In the panelled library you will
find a real fire, squashy sofas, an honesty bar and
plenty to read. An optional breakfast is served on
a tray in your room. (The Rookery, London, is a
sister – see entry.)

6 Frith Street
Soho
London W1D 3JA

T: 020 7434 1771
E: reservations@hazlitts.co.uk
w: hazlittshotel.com

BEDROOMS: 30. 2 on ground floor.
OPEN: all year.
FACILITIES: lift, library, private
lounge/meeting room, in-room TV
(Freeview), public rooms wheelchair
accessible, adapted toilet.
BACKGROUND MUSIC: none.
LOCATION: centre of Soho,
underground Tottenham Court Road,
Leicester Square.
CHILDREN: all ages welcomed.
DOGS: not allowed.
CREDIT CARDS: Amex, MC, Visa.
PRICES: room only single from £193,
double £232–£484. Breakfast £12,
limited room-service menu £25.

**SEE ALSO SHORTLIST**

# LONDON

## THE ORANGE

A pocket-handkerchief-sized park with London plane trees and a statue of the young Mozart lies just across the road from this stuccoed Victorian pub in Pimlico, now a buzzy bar, café and restaurant with four guest bedrooms. A sister to The Grazing Goat, Marble Arch (see entry), it has the same stripped-back style that they term 'countryside-chic', with bare floors, high ceilings, a real fire, vintage advertising posters, pot plants and unadorned tables and chairs. The bedrooms, at the top, are classed 'standard' and 'superior', but all are of a decent size. A corner room has three sash windows overlooking the main road. In the restaurant, you will find such dishes as haddock with kohlrabi and mussel, clam and caper sauce. Imaginative vegan options might include Jerusalem artichoke, wild mushroom and celeriac hotpot. Breakfast, charged separately, brings freshly squeezed orange juice, brioche French toast with caramelised banana and maple syrup, free-range eggs with creamed spinach, and Cumberland sausage.

37 Pimlico Road
Pimlico
London SW1W 8NE

T: 020 7881 9844
E: reservations@theorange.co.uk
W: theorange.co.uk

BEDROOMS: 4.
OPEN: all year.
FACILITIES: restaurant, 2 bars, private dining room, in-room TV, ground-floor pub/dining area wheelchair accessible, adapted toilet.
BACKGROUND MUSIC: in public areas.
LOCATION: Pimlico, underground Sloane Square.
CHILDREN: all ages welcomed.
DOGS: allowed in bedrooms by prior agreement, public rooms, except first-floor dining room.
CREDIT CARDS: Amex, MC, Visa.
PRICES: per room £214–£249. Breakfast cooked dishes from £8, full English £12.50, à la carte £38, fixed-price menus £27–£46.

**SEE ALSO SHORTLIST**

# LONDON

## PORTOBELLO HOTEL

There is still bags of bohemian spirit in this legendary rock and roll hotel converted from two neoclassical mansions, thanks to its eclectic collection of rooms containing many pieces from nearby Portobello market. They range from the traditional cosy attic rooms to more generous suites, one with a circular bed, another with a four-poster from Hampton Court Palace. They might be Moroccan themed, or have a mural on the wall, but all come with rich colours, vintage and antique furniture, lots of details such as piles of books and quirky ornaments everywhere. Smaller rooms are shower-only, while the biggest have a Victorian bath, sometimes behind a curtain. Breakfast, in the charming sitting room or your room, is a simple continental with cooked items, such as scrambled eggs and smoked salmon, or the full English, for an extra charge. In the evening, help yourself to a drink from the honesty bar in the drawing room and pair it with a sandwich, sharing board or perhaps a risotto from the short menu (which can be enjoyed in your room). Or check out the discounts at hand-picked neighbourhood eateries.

22 Stanley Gardens
Notting Hill
London W11 2NG

T: 020 7727 2777
E: stay@portobellohotel.com
W: portobellohotel.com

BEDROOMS: 21.
OPEN: all year.
FACILITIES: lift, sitting room/breakfast room with honesty bar, in-room TV (Freeview), unsuitable for disabled.
BACKGROUND MUSIC: 'chill-out' in sitting room.
LOCATION: Notting Hill, underground Notting Hill Gate.
CHILDREN: all ages welcomed.
DOGS: allowed in 1 room, not in breakfast room.
CREDIT CARDS: Amex, MC, Visa.
PRICES: per room B&B single £190–£200, double £220–£460. Cooked breakfast £6–£10, light snacks £8–£12. 1-night bookings sometimes refused Sat, public holidays.

**SEE ALSO SHORTLIST**

# LONDON

## THE ROOKERY

Powder your wig and imagine you're arriving
by sedan chair at this singular hotel, occupying
a Georgian terrace and presented as a piece of
living history. Some 30 years ago, self-styled 'old
gits' Peter McKay and Douglas Blain bought the
properties, close to Smithfield Market, and created
a glorified B&B. They also own Hazlitt's, London
(see entry), and behind their apparent whimsy lies
a deep impulse to preserve the old and beautiful.
A fire burns in a clubby conservatory lounge,
with well-stocked honesty bar and leafy patio.
Bedrooms are replete with heavy silk curtains or
shutters, impressive antiques, oil paintings and
quaint vintage bathroom fittings, along with
such modern comforts as air conditioning and a
minibar. A ground-floor suite named after the
founder of the nearby Charterhouse (because
numbers are impersonal) has a carved four-poster
and panelled sitting room. You can order dishes
from a room-service menu, breakfast on delicious
pastries and freshly squeezed orange juice, and
dine in great restaurants in this trendy area,
a den of thieves in Dickens's day, nicknamed
'The Rookery'.

12 Peter's Lane
Cowcross Street
London EC1M 6DS

**T:** 020 7336 0931
**E:** reservations@rookery.co.uk
**W:** rookeryhotel.com

**BEDROOMS:** 33. 1 on ground floor.
**OPEN:** all year.
**FACILITIES:** conservatory lounge,
meeting rooms, in-room TV (Sky),
small patio garden, unsuitable for
disabled.
**BACKGROUND MUSIC:** none.
**LOCATION:** Clerkenwell, underground
Farringdon, Barbican.
**CHILDREN:** all ages welcomed (under-
13s, sharing with parents, stay free in
some rooms).
**DOGS:** not allowed.
**CREDIT CARDS:** Amex, MC, Visa.
**PRICES:** per room £274–£374. Breakfast
from about £12, à la carte (from
limited room-service menu) £28.

**SEE ALSO SHORTLIST**

# LONDON
MAP 2:D4

## SAN DOMENICO HOUSE

On a quiet street moments from the King's Road,
two red brick Victorian mansions, built in what
Pevsner describes as the 'semi-Dutch, semi-
Queen Anne style', conceal a veritable palazzo.
This was formerly the renowned Sloane Hotel,
created by interior designer Sue Rogers, who
furnished it with auction finds, all for sale. Today
it is owned by the Melpignano family (see Guide
website, Masseria San Domenico in Savelletri di
Fasano, Italy), and you could not put a price on
the antiques, china, cherubs, rare 18th-century
English and Italian paintings and untold metres
of designer fabric that fill the interiors. The
bedrooms are individually themed, some with a
balcony. Junior suites have a 25-foot-tall draped
bedhead, toile de Jouy fabrics and a marble
bathroom; gallery suites have a seating area and
steps down to a bedroom with bespoke four-poster
like a silk-draped palanquin. All rooms have air
conditioning, Molton Brown toiletries and room
service. There is a drawing room, a breakfast
room and scenic roof terrace, Outwardly similar,
inwardly another world, 11 Cadogan Gardens (see
entry) is just around the corner.

29–31 Draycott Place
Chelsea
London SW3 2SH

T: 020 7581 5757
E: info@sandomenicohouse.com
W: sandomenicohouse.com

BEDROOMS: 19.
OPEN: all year.
FACILITIES: lift, lounge, breakfast room,
roof terrace, in-room TV (Freeview),
unsuitable for disabled.
BACKGROUND MUSIC: in lounge and
breakfast room.
LOCATION: Chelsea, underground
Sloane Square.
CHILDREN: all ages welcomed
(children's menu).
DOGS: not allowed.
CREDIT CARDS: Amex, MC, Visa.
PRICES: per room B&B £259–£349
(includes continental breakfast).

**SEE ALSO SHORTLIST**

# LONDON

## THE ZETTER

Housed in a converted Victorian warehouse, this design-conscious boutique hotel is a perfect fit for east London's creative hub. A modern chandelier and funky tree mural in the lobby set the tone; a roomy bar and restaurant continue the theme with a mid-century design aesthetic. The new chef here is Rasheed Shahin, who focuses on simple, well-balanced dishes that allow seasonal British produce to shine – maybe escabèche of Orkney scallop and mussel, followed by a rib-eye steak from the Cooked over Coal menu. Vintage-modern bedrooms and suites vary in size, from bijou Guest to spacious refurbished Rooftop Deluxe Studios, the latter with a large decked terrace with roll-top bath and cityscape views. Decor is inspired by the building's industrial heritage, perhaps a steel-and-marble coffee table or a geometric-patterned feature wall. All are supplied with Penguin paperbacks, magazines, hot-water bottles in a woolly jacket, pink mood lighting and an honesty refreshment tray. In the bathrooms are REN toiletries and drench showers. Complimentary bicycle use is available for guests of a daring disposition.

86–88 Clerkenwell Road
London EC1M 5RJ

T: 020 7324 4444
E: info@thezetter.com
W: thezetter.com

BEDROOMS: 59. 2 suitable for disabled.
OPEN: all year.
FACILITIES: 2 lifts, atrium, bar/restaurant, terrace (alfresco dining), in-room TV (Freeview, some with smart TV), in-room spa treatments, reduced rates at local gym, bicycles to borrow, NCP 5 mins' walk, public areas wheelchair accessible, adapted toilet.
BACKGROUND MUSIC: in bar/restaurant.
LOCATION: Clerkenwell, NCP garage 5 mins' walk, underground Farringdon.
CHILDREN: all ages welcomed.
DOGS: only guide dogs allowed.
CREDIT CARDS: Amex, MC, Visa.
PRICES: per room £125–£394. Breakfast buffet £15.50, full English £16, à la carte £45.

**SEE ALSO SHORTLIST**

# LONDON

## THE ZETTER TOWNHOUSE CLERKENWELL

♥ Previous César winner

'We've been raving about it to everyone!' enthuses a recent guest of this zany boutique hotel on Clerkenwell's St John's Square. This was the first of Mark Sainsbury and Michael Benyan's 'themed' town house hotels. Here, rich colours and textures evoke the home of a much-travelled great-aunt. The lounge is a hotchpotch of gilt-framed paintings, taxidermy and velvet upholstery; the deep red cocktail bar a cosy cocoon of Persian rugs and fringed lampshades. Bedrooms and suites are no less eccentric: one has a four-poster bed festooned with Union flag bunting, another a wardrobe painted in broad stripes. Contemporary creature comforts include drench showers, REN toiletries and an honesty tray of snacks and drinks. Breakfast – continental or cooked – and a sumptuous afternoon tea are served in the lounge. Cocktails, both classic and wacky, are accompanied by a menu of small plates, such as lobster brioche rolls, charcuterie and warm madeleines with bergamot curd. 'We'd go back in a heartbeat,' says our captivated reviewer. (See also The Zetter, previous entry, and The Zetter Townhouse Marylebone, next entry.)

49–50 St John's Square
Clerkenwell
London EC1V 4JJ

T: 020 7324 4567
E: reservations@thezetter.com
W: thezettertownhouse.com

BEDROOMS: 13. 1 suitable for disabled.
OPEN: all year.
FACILITIES: cocktail lounge, private dining room, games room, in-room TV (Freeview), civil wedding licence, cocktail lounges wheelchair accessible.
BACKGROUND MUSIC: in cocktail lounge.
LOCATION: Clerkenwell, underground Farringdon.
CHILDREN: all ages welcomed.
DOGS: assistance dogs only.
CREDIT CARDS: Amex, MC, Visa.
PRICES: per room B&B £222–£550. Cooked breakfast £16, à la carte £30.

**SEE ALSO SHORTLIST**

# LONDON

MAP 2:D4

## THE ZETTER TOWNHOUSE MARYLEBONE

Mark Sainsbury and Michael Benyan's second Zetter town house hotel is every bit as eccentric as the first, the design conceit here being that it was once the home of 'wicked Uncle Seymour' (the inspiration for Seymour being Edward Lear, former incumbent and real-life eccentric). It was the imaginary Seymour who crammed these candlelit public spaces with Victoriana, books, clocks, Persian rugs and mismatched vintage furniture. He, too, who filled the bedrooms and suites with tasselled lamps, oriental artwork and antiques, adding a four-poster bed here, a writing desk there. One top-floor apartment – named after Lear – has a roof terrace and alfresco bath. Spoiling comforts include hot-water bottles in a hand-knitted jacket, powerful rain showers, tea- and coffee-making facilities and sweet-smelling toiletries. There's no formal restaurant, but a hefty afternoon tea, small plates and sharing boards, and Aunt Wilhelmina's 'Drop of Sherry' trifle are available in Seymour's Parlour, which serves a mean cocktail, too. (See also the two previous entries, The Zetter Townhouse Clerkenwell and The Zetter).

28–30 Seymour Street
Marylebone
London W1H 7JB

**T:** 020 7324 4544
**E:** reservations@thezetter.com
**W:** thezettertownhouse.com/
  marylebone

**BEDROOMS:** 24. 2 suitable for disabled.
**OPEN:** all year.
**FACILITIES:** lift, cocktail lounge/restaurant, in-room TV (Freeview).
**BACKGROUND MUSIC:** all day in cocktail lounge.
**LOCATION:** central, underground Marble Arch.
**CHILDREN:** all ages welcomed.
**DOGS:** only guide dogs allowed.
**CREDIT CARDS:** Amex, MC, Visa.
**PRICES:** per room B&B £222–£631 (includes £16 continental buffet, which can be traded for equivalent cooked option, including a full English). À la carte £35.

**SEE ALSO SHORTLIST**

# ENGLAND

Land's End, Cornwall

# ALDEBURGH Suffolk

## THE WENTWORTH

Nothing much alters from year to year at Michael
Pritt's Victorian hotel, just across from a shingle
beach washed by the North Sea. And that is the
way his loyal guests like it. 'Our annual visit to our
favourite hotel,' writes one reader. 'It is great to be
welcomed by the same staff.' The ethos is proudly
traditional. 'It may seem "old-fashioned" but that
is an advantage, as really nothing needs changing.'
Public rooms are 'attractive and comfortable',
with acres of carpet and soft furnishings. Another
reader 'tried hard, but couldn't find any fault
except a poor hairdryer'. A third, however, felt
her large sea-view double, with a 'very compact'
bathroom, was 'drab' and did not live up to
its picture on the website. In the restaurant,
Tim Keeble's seasonal fare was enjoyed by our
devotees. 'The food was really good this year,
with plenty of choice for non-meat-eaters like
us. Delicious fish, too.' (Maybe grilled lemon sole
and chervil butter, or caramelised onion and Brie
tart.) 'Michael Pritt is always so friendly. We just
hope he will continue.' (Simon Rodway, Edward
Gosnell, and others)

### 25% DISCOUNT VOUCHERS

Wentworth Road
Aldeburgh IP15 5BD

T: 01728 452312
E: stay@wentworth-aldeburgh.co.uk
W: wentworth-aldeburgh.com

BEDROOMS: 35. 7 in Darfield House
opposite, 5 on ground floor, 1 suitable
for disabled.
OPEN: all year except possibly 2 weeks
in Jan.
FACILITIES: 2 lounges, bar, restaurant,
private dining room, conference room,
in-room TV (Freeview), 2 terrace
gardens, courtyard garden, public
rooms wheelchair accessible, adapted
toilet.
BACKGROUND MUSIC: none.
LOCATION: seafront, 5 mins' walk from
centre.
CHILDREN: all ages welcomed.
DOGS: allowed in bedrooms (£5 per
dog per night) and public rooms, not
in restaurant.
CREDIT CARDS: Amex, MC, Visa.
PRICES: per room B&B £113–£330,
D,B&B £135–£370. Set dinner
£25–£31. 1-night bookings refused Sat.

# ALNWICK Northumberland

MAP 4:A4

## THE COOKIE JAR

**NEW**

It may be a former convent, but there's nothing remotely ascetic about this well-upholstered hotel in a 'sympathetic conversion' a stone's throw from Alnwick Castle. Behind the doors of a sober Georgian terrace, Debbie Cook has rejected conformity in favour of striking blue-grey interiors bursting with dizzy ikat-inspired fabrics. Well-padded chairs and sofas abound, along with swirly patterned rugs and shelves of books and ornaments. Bedrooms have a complimentary cookie jar (obviously), king- or super-king-size Hypnos bed, Amazon Echo; bathrooms offer drench shower and Penhaligon toiletries. The Chapel suite, with castle views, has stained-glass windows, and a roll-top copper bath behind a screen (which might have raised a few blushes among the Sisters of Mercy). It's all set up for shooting parties, with a gunroom, and kennels for the dogs. In the bistro, John Blackmore offers appetising modern British dishes with an imaginative flourish – smoked salmon arancini, or slow-cooked lamb shank with curried aubergine and cauliflower, while breakfast brings grilled Craster kippers and basket of home-made bakery. (Peter Anderson)

12 Bailiffgate
Alnwick NE66 1LU

T: 01665 510465
E: hello@cookiejaralnwick.com
W: cookiejaralnwick.com

BEDROOMS: 11. 1 suitable for disabled.
OPEN: all year, bistro open till 4 Tues–Sat, Fri/Sat evenings.
FACILITIES: lounge, bistro, drying room, secure gunroom, in-room TV (Freeview), lift, terrace with fire pit (alfresco dining), garden.
BACKGROUND MUSIC: in public spaces.
LOCATION: near town centre.
CHILDREN: all ages welcomed.
DOGS: in some bedrooms, not in public areas, 5 kennels for gun dogs.
CREDIT CARDS: MC, Visa.
PRICES: per room £165–£360. Set 3-course dinner £42.50.

# ALVESTON Warwickshire                           MAP 3:D6

## ❦BARASET BARN    [NEW]

César award: newcomer of the year

'Foodie heaven, with the bonus of nearby culture
in Stratford-upon-Avon', this restaurant added
rooms in 2019 and is new to the Guide after an
insider was bowled over by its 'amazing value and
fantastic meals'. The first hotel for Warwickshire
gastro group Lovely Pubs it 'hopefully will be
followed by more'. The barn makes a 'spectacular,
atmospheric setting' for the modern British
food, with flagstones, high-beamed ceiling and
modern fittings; there is also an outside deck.
'My scallops with sticky pomegranate and sesame
pork belly zinged with flavour.' Barbecue ribs
come with 'unusual but delicious' watermelon,
chilli, ginger and coriander; ice-cream sundaes are
'piled high with goodies'. There are gluten-free
and vegetarian menus. The 'pleasant, spacious
rooms with neutral palette and splashes of colour'
are in a modern 'barn' across a stylish courtyard.
All have floor-to-ceiling windows looking on
to a meadow; those at the top have a balcony,
those at the bottom a terrace. Bathrooms have an
'impressively powerful' shower. 'We cycled on the
hotel bikes to Shakespeare's birthplace – too close
to work off the calories.' (JK)

### 25% DISCOUNT VOUCHERS

Pimlico Lane
Alveston
Stratford-upon-Avon CV37 7RJ

T: 01789 295510
E: barasetbarn@lovelypubs.co.uk
W: barasetbarn.co.uk

BEDROOMS: 16. In separate annexe,
1 suitable for disabled.
OPEN: all year, hotel closed Sun nights.
FACILITIES: restaurant with private
mezzanine, conservatory, bar lobby,
in-room TV (Freeview), courtyard
garden, patio area, hotel bicycles,
public area and restaurant wheelchair
accessible, adapted toilet.
BACKGROUND MUSIC: in public rooms at
meal times.
LOCATION: rural, 2 miles NE of
Stratford-upon-Avon.
CHILDREN: all ages welcomed.
DOGS: allowed in garden and
conservatory, not bedrooms.
CREDIT CARDS: Amex, MC, Visa.
PRICES: per room B&B £99–£180. À la
carte £40.

# AMPLEFORTH Yorkshire

MAP 4:D4

## SHALLOWDALE HOUSE

The welcome couldn't be warmer for guests of Phillip Gill and Anton van der Horst at their 1960s house in a beautifully tended hillside garden, on the edge of the North York Moors national park. Readers mention the hosts' 'great kindness', with the 'whole place centred on guests' comfort', making it a 'real pleasure' to stay. They return year after year. On cold days a fire blazes in the sitting room, where tea and home-baked scones are served every afternoon. Interiors have a tasteful mix of contemporary and traditional furniture, books and artwork. Large windows afford lovely views to the Howardian hills. The bedrooms have Penhaligon toiletries and little treats such as a bowl of chocolates. With notice, Anton cooks an 'imaginative and delicious' dinner of local, seasonal produce, served at 7.30 pm at tables laid with crisp white linen. Perhaps asparagus, duck breasts in Marsala, a pear and blueberry tart, with 'an excellent choice of house wines'. A cooked breakfast with freshly squeezed orange juice sets you up for a visit to Rievaulx Abbey or Castle Howard. Then again you might just want to gaze at the vista. (MH, and others)

West End
Ampleforth YO62 4DY

T: 01439 788325
E: stay@shallowdalehouse.co.uk
W: shallowdalehouse.co.uk

BEDROOMS: 3.
OPEN: all year except Christmas/New Year, closed 'occasionally at other times'.
FACILITIES: drawing room, dining room, sitting room/library, in-room TV (Freeview), 2½-acre gardens, unsuitable for disabled.
BACKGROUND MUSIC: none.
LOCATION: edge of village.
CHILDREN: not under 12.
DOGS: not allowed.
CREDIT CARDS: MC, Visa.
PRICES: per room B&B single £130–£145, double £150–£175. Set dinner £49.50 (min. 48 hours' notice). 1-night bookings occasionally refused weekends.

# AUGHTON Lancashire                                MAP 4:E2

## MOOR HALL RESTAURANT WITH ROOMS   `NEW`

Millions have been poured into the restoration of a Tudor manor house on a lake, today a restaurant-with-rooms and theatre for the skills of co-proprietor/chef Mark Birchall. Within 19 months of opening, it had two Michelin stars, matching the success of L'Enclume in Cumbria where Mr Birchall was Simon Rogan's head chef. Here is Lancashire on a plate. In the restaurant you can watch the brigade working with produce from the kitchen garden and glasshouse, preparing such dishes as black pudding with pickled gooseberry; Aynhoe Park fallow deer, kale and elderberry; and garden apples with birch sap and apple marigold. A more casual meal in The Barn might bring Herdwick lamb saddle, caramelised turnips, new-season garlic and pot-roast shoulder. Individually styled bedrooms (two at ground level in The Gatehouse) blend rustic charm and oak beams with modern comforts. All have a lake view, coffee machine, mini-fridge, maybe an emperor bed, a slipper bath and walk-in shower. Breakfast, served tasting-menu style, brings yogurt, fruit and pastries, charcuterie made in-house, then a traditional full English.

Prescot Road
Aughton L39 6RT

T: 01695 572511
E: enquiry@moorhall.com
W: moorhall.com

BEDROOMS: 7. 2 on ground floor in Gatehouse.
OPEN: hotel open all year except 1–21 Jan, 2–17 Aug, 23–26 Dec, restaurant closed Mon/Tues (contact hotel for Dec/New Year opening).
FACILITIES: bar, lounge, 2 restaurants, in-room TV (Freeview), 5-acre grounds, ground floor public areas wheelchair accessible, lift to one restaurant, adapted toilet.
BACKGROUND MUSIC: in public areas.
LOCATION: on B5197, 2½ miles SW of Ormskirk.
CHILDREN: well-behaved children of all ages welcomed.
DOGS: not allowed.
CREDIT CARDS: Amex, MC, Visa.
PRICES: per room B&B £220–£450. Moor Hall 4-course lunch £70, 8-course dinner £155, à la carte (Barn) £56 (plus 12.5% discretionary service charge).

# AUSTWICK Yorkshire

MAP 4:D3

## AUSTWICK HALL

From the grand entrance hall with its flamboyant staircase to the antique-furnished bedrooms and Italianate garden, this country house B&B adds an exotic touch to a Yorkshire Dales village. Owners Eric Culley and Michael Pearson – who 'carried our case to our room' – welcome guests with tea in the fire-warmed hall, one of several public rooms in the 16th-century manor house, with its curios, paintings and vast fireplaces. The stairs lead to 'large and generously furnished' bedrooms with rugs on shining floorboards, 'extravagantly thick curtains' and fine furniture that might include a writing desk, or a rococo or four-poster bed. Bathrooms are palatial, with roll-top bath, and most have a separate shower and views. The gardens are 'a delightful place to sit and read'. 'Very good breakfasts' include home-made granola, eggs from their own hens, and local bacon. Michael advises on local places 'for a hearty Yorkshire supper' including The Traddock (see next entry), which impressed readers. On the edge of Austwick village, the house is 'blissfully quiet' – 'only birdsong' – and well placed for walks. (TL, and others)

Townhead Lane
Austwick LA2 8BS

T: 01524 251794
E: info@austwickhall.co.uk
W: austwickhall.co.uk

BEDROOMS: 4.
OPEN: all year except 24–26 Dec.
FACILITIES: hall, drawing room, dining room, in-room TV (Freeview), 14-acre gardens, hot tub, unsuitable for disabled.
BACKGROUND MUSIC: none.
LOCATION: edge of village.
CHILDREN: 16 and upwards welcomed.
DOGS: not allowed.
CREDIT CARDS: MC, Visa.
PRICES: per room B&B single £110–£140, double £125–£155. 1-night bookings refused bank holiday weekends.

# AUSTWICK Yorkshire

## THE TRADDOCK

♘ Previous César winner

The high number of returning guests speaks volumes about the warm welcome, quiet luxury and generous comforts of this country house hotel, set amid glorious Dales walking country. 'We're always happy there,' reports one reader. 'A small hotel with brilliant staff,' says another regular. The creeper-covered Georgian and Victorian house, run for many years by the Reynolds family, has a refined yet homely atmosphere (dogs are welcomed), its public rooms filled with antiques, plump sofas and rich wallpapers. In the sitting rooms and garden, someone is always on hand to bring tea or drinks: 'staff are excellent, friendly and efficient'. Bedrooms are country house style with boldly coloured or papered walls, a sprinkling of antiques; 'comfy beds and nice towels'. Most have a bath as well as a shower; all spoil with fruit and home-made biscuits. The 'imaginative' modern English menu is praised: 'The food is so good here.' Main courses might include cod with morels and wild garlic, or poussin with ceps and asparagus, while the extensive breakfast choice includes poached haddock and a full Yorkshire. (Franz Kuhlmann, PA)

Graystomber Lane
Austwick LA2 8BY

T: 01524 251224
E: info@thetraddock.co.uk
W: thetraddock.co.uk

BEDROOMS: 14. 1 on ground floor.
OPEN: all year.
FACILITIES: 3 lounges, bar, 2 dining rooms, function facilities, in-room TV (Freeview), 1½-acre grounds (sun deck), ground-floor restaurant wheelchair accessible.
BACKGROUND MUSIC: in public areas except 1 lounge.
LOCATION: 4 miles NW of Settle.
CHILDREN: all ages welcomed.
DOGS: allowed in bedrooms and on lead in public rooms, not in dining rooms, but owners may eat in bar area with their dogs (£5 per dog per night).
CREDIT CARDS: MC, Visa.
PRICES: per room B&B double £99–£230. À la carte 2-courses £31, 3-courses £40. 1-night bookings refused Sat.

# AYLESBURY Buckinghamshire

MAP 2:C3

## HARTWELL HOUSE

Visitors this year were 'very happy with everything' at this former stately home set in landscaped gardens and parkland on the edge of the Chilterns. The Grade I listed, part Jacobean, part Georgian building, filled with original antiques and paintings, was restored by Historic House Hotels, and given to the National Trust in 2008. Grand but 'relaxing' public rooms, with damask-covered walls and ornate stuccoed ceilings, are perfect for 'tea and cakes' on arrival. The 'sumptuous' bedrooms and suites are mostly in the main house. The first-floor 'Royal Suites' (the exiled King Louis XVIII of France lived here from 1809 to 1814) have a spacious bathroom, a sitting room and south-facing views. 'Royal' rooms are equally plush; some have a four-poster bed. 'Classic rooms' have a sofa, writing desk and king-size bed, but one older reader was 'unable to use the over-bath shower'. Dinner in the formal but unstuffy dining room might be crab and courgette cannelloni followed by pan-roasted fillet of cod, cooked to perfection by chef Daniel Richardson and his team. 'An awesome place to stay.' (Geoffrey Bignell, and others)

Oxford Road
Stone
Aylesbury HP17 8NR

T: 01296 747444
E: info@hartwell-house.com
W: hartwell-house.com

BEDROOMS: 48. 16 in stable block, some on ground floor, 1 (main house) suitable for disabled.
OPEN: all year, closed for lunch Mon/Tues.
FACILITIES: great hall, morning room, drawing room, library, 2 dining rooms, function facilities, in-room TV (Sky, Freeview), civil wedding licence, spa (swimming pool), 94 acres of gardens and parkland, tennis, public rooms wheelchair accessible, adapted toilet.
BACKGROUND MUSIC: none.
LOCATION: 2 miles W of Aylesbury.
CHILDREN: not under 6.
DOGS: allowed in some annexe bedrooms with access to grounds.
CREDIT CARDS: Amex, MC, Visa.
PRICES: per room B&B single £210–£250, double £220–£780. À la carte £47–£53, Bill of Fare menu £55–£67.

# BABBACOMBE Devon

MAP 1:D5

## CARY ARMS & SPA

Queen Victoria thought of Italy as she viewed the 'red cliffs and rocks and wooded hills' that surround pebbly Babbacombe Bay, and for la dolce vita look no further than this spa hotel. Sitting beneath Babbacombe Downs and the Coast Path, it is spread across several levels at the water's edge; there's even a bell to ring if you spot dolphins while dining outside. Coastal-chic bedrooms which bring to mind a New England inn are designed to take advantage of the lovely situation, most with a balcony or terrace. Two ground-floor doubles are dog-friendly, with access to the terraced gardens, while above, suites have a log-burner. Duplex beach huts have hand-made furniture, modern artwork, and wall-to-wall glass doors that fold back on to a sun deck, affording views across Lyme Bay to Portland Bill. In the cosy pub, decorated with nautical artefacts, seasonally inspired dishes run from a crab sandwich or a pint of prawns to Lyme Bay lobster and Devon beef, with a separate menu for vegans and vegetarians. The resident pianist plays on Saturday night, while a guitarist will sing to you over your Sunday roast.

Beach Road
Babbacombe TQ1 3LX

T: 01803 327110
E: enquiries@caryarms.co.uk
W: caryarms.co.uk

BEDROOMS: 18. 6 beach huts, 2 beach suites. Plus 4 self-catering cottages.
OPEN: all year.
FACILITIES: saloon, bar/restaurant, in-room TV (Freeview), civil wedding licence, spa (hydrotherapy pool, mini-gym, steam room), garden unsuitable for disabled.
BACKGROUND MUSIC: all day in inn, saloon and bar.
LOCATION: by beach, 2¼ miles N of Torquay harbour.
CHILDREN: all ages welcomed.
DOGS: allowed in some bedrooms, part of restaurant.
CREDIT CARDS: Amex, MC, Visa.
PRICES: per room B&B double £269–£399, beach huts £389, family suites £399–£459, spa use £15. À la carte £40 (vegetarian/vegan £28). 1-night bookings often refused weekends.

# BABCARY Somerset

MAP 1:C6

## THE RED LION

With regional ales and ciders on tap, the charismatic Red Lion is as much a local watering hole as it is a contemporary pub-with-rooms, where owners Clare and Charlie Garrard ensure that in the cosy bar, with its ancient flagstone floors, exposed beams and open fires, both villagers and residents feel at home. Boutique-style bedrooms are in a converted barn next to the pub. One reviewer found his Superior Double on the first floor 'exceptionally spacious'. Decorated in neutral tones, all the rooms have tea- and coffee-making facilities, luxury toiletries and fine Egyptian cotton bedlinen. Dinner can be taken in the bar or the slightly more formal restaurant, with its flagstoned floor, rugs and Windsor chairs; in summer, enjoy a wood-fired pizza outside. There's good choice for vegetarians, including Turkish shakshuka and asparagus, pea and feta risotto, as well as plenty to keep carnivores happy. Another guest found the service 'friendly though a little haphazard'. Breakfast brings a full English made from local free-range ingredients plus Dorset Cereals muesli and bread from West Camel.

Babcary TA11 7ED

T: 01458 223230
E: info@redlionbabcary.co.uk
W: redlionbabcary.co.uk

BEDROOMS: 6. All in converted barn, 1, on ground floor, suitable for disabled.
OPEN: all year.
FACILITIES: bar, snug, restaurant, private dining room, seasonal outdoor pizza bar, meeting/function facilities, in-room TV (BT), garden (with play area), bar wheelchair accessible.
BACKGROUND MUSIC: in bar area.
LOCATION: 5 miles E of Somerton.
CHILDREN: all ages welcomed.
DOGS: allowed in bar only.
CREDIT CARDS: Amex, MC, Visa.
PRICES: per room B&B single £95–£115, double £115–£135. À la carte £29.

# BAINBRIDGE Yorkshire

MAP 4:C3

## LOW MILL GUEST HOUSE

Spending a night on a riverbank, in an 18th-century watermill, with Wensleydale's gentle hills all around: what could be more restorative for the soul? This 'wonderful guest house' has been renovated by Neil and Jane McNair with flair and imagination. Public rooms of 'stone walls and huge beams' are furnished eclectically with retro sofas, colourful rugs, artefacts and a toasty range fire in the lounge, home to the grinding stone. Bedrooms are equally spacious and quirky, with a 'copper bath big enough for two' and mill machinery in the Workshop, vintage furniture in others. All have views: 'Our room overlooked the river and garden to hills beyond.' The McNairs' 'attention to detail is second to none', with home-made fudge and cake, fresh milk and Temple Spa toiletries. 'They could not do enough to help us with advice on walks and booking pubs for dinners,' writes a visitor who stayed for nine nights. There are no evening meals, but breakfasts are 'comprehensive', including home-made bread and granola, omelettes and the full works (with veggie option). 'Staying here is a unique experience, not to be missed.' (Tessa Stuart, and others)

Bainbridge
Leyburn DL8 3EF

T: 01969 650553
E: lowmillguesthouse@gmail.com
w: lowmillguesthouse.co.uk

BEDROOMS: 3.
OPEN: all year except Christmas–27 Dec.
FACILITIES: lounge, dining room, small library, in-room TV (Freeview), ¼-acre riverside garden with seating, secure bicycle storage, unsuitable for disabled.
BACKGROUND MUSIC: none.
LOCATION: 5 miles E of Hawes.
CHILDREN: not under 15.
DOGS: allowed in bedrooms, not in dining room, on lead in other public areas.
CREDIT CARDS: MC, Visa.
PRICES: per room B&B single £90–£170, double £110–£190. 1-night bookings refused some Sats, bank holidays.

**SEE ALSO SHORTLIST**

# BARLOW Derbyshire

MAP 4:E4

## THE PEACOCK AT BARLOW  `NEW`

A traditional pub in a Peak District village, the former Old Pump now struts its stuff as the Peacock dining pub-with-rooms and onsite brewery. A long-time friend of the Guide was so impressed with his visit that it has been given a full entry this year. 'A large car park leads to the first-floor entrance, with an imposing sculpture.' Bedrooms are 'tastefully designed and furnished, complete with robes, safe and minibar', not to mention air conditioning, a coffee machine, smart TV, a Porcelanosa bathroom and White Company toiletries. Four rooms are in an adjoining converted barn. Each is named after a variety of hop. Fuggles has a wall of Timorous Beasties 'Thistle' wallpaper and a valley view. Boadicea has a dressing area, a freestanding bath and walk-in shower. The vibe is free and easy (dogs and children welcome – grab a table and eat when you like). A menu of hearty pub grub includes handmade pies, curries, Chatsworth lamb and Derbyshire beef. 'I enjoyed promptly served vegan pumpkin and sage ravioli and succulent grilled salmon.' Breakfast brings local sausages, farm eggs, smashed avocado and smoked salmon. (Robert Gower)

Barlow
Chesterfield S18 7TD

T: 01142 890340
E: cheers@thepeacockatbarlow.co.uk
W: thepeacockatbarlow.co.uk

BEDROOMS: 8. 4 in barn conversion. 2 on lower floor with step-free access, 2-bedroom self-catering cottage.
OPEN: all year.
FACILITIES: orangery dining area, tap room (open fire and lounge area), brewery with tasting/function room, in-room TV (Freeview), terraces (outdoor seating), large car park, car charging points, wheelchair accessible.
BACKGROUND MUSIC: in all public areas including upper terrace, not brewery.
LOCATION: on outskirts of village, 10 miles S of Sheffield.
CHILDREN: all ages welcomed.
DOGS: in cottage bedroom and all pub areas.
CREDIT CARDS: MC, Visa.
PRICES: per room B&B double £89–£249. À la carte £30.

# BARNSLEY Gloucestershire                    MAP 3:E6

## BARNSLEY HOUSE

The late Rosemary Verey, doyenne of the
20th-century English country garden, created
the flourishing grounds at this 17th-century
Cotswold stone mansion, her home from the
late 1950s. Now it is a hotel, part of the Calcot
Collection (see also The Painswick, Painswick;
Calcot & Spa, Tetbury; and The Lord Crewe
Arms, Blanchland). Bedrooms, with restful if
unremarkable decor, range from snug, 'elegant'
doubles to four with a garden view, comfy seating,
perhaps a modern four-poster and side-by-side
roll-top baths. The Secret Garden suite has an
outdoor hot tub; the Rosemary Verey suite has a
conservatory and private courtyard with grotto.
Some duplex rooms are in a purpose-built block.
All rooms have an espresso machine, snacks,
stylish bathroom fittings and REN toiletries. In
the Potager restaurant, produce from the prolific
kitchen garden and local suppliers appears on
Mediterranean-inspired menus, in such dishes as
Barnsley House Crown Prince squash risotto with
candied pumpkin seeds, and Gloucester lamb and
baba ganoush with minted couscous. You can eat
more cheaply at The Village Pub (same management),
from a list of pub classics. Reports, please.

Barnsley
Cirencester GL7 5EE

T: 01285 740000
E: info@barnsleyhouse.com
w: barnsleyhouse.com

BEDROOMS: 18. 7 in stableyard, 4 in
courtyard, 1 in cottage, 1 suitable for
disabled.
OPEN: all year.
FACILITIES: 2 lounges, bar, restaurant,
cinema, meeting room, in-room TV
(Sky, Freeview), civil wedding licence,
11-acre garden (spa, hydrotherapy
pool), restaurant and lounge
wheelchair accessible.
BACKGROUND MUSIC: in lounge and
restaurant.
LOCATION: 5 miles NE of Cirencester.
CHILDREN: not under 14.
DOGS: allowed in stableyard rooms, not
grounds or public areas.
CREDIT CARDS: Amex, MC, Visa.
PRICES: per room B&B single
£262–£632, double £280–£789, family
£320. À la carte £45 (pub £35). 1-night
bookings sometimes refused.

**SEE ALSO SHORTLIST**

## BARWICK Somerset

MAP 1:C6

### LITTLE BARWICK HOUSE

'Amid gentle Somerset countryside', a Georgian country house is home to Emma and Tim Ford's 'utterly charming' restaurant-with-rooms. 'It offers peace, comfort and sublime food,' writes a regular returnee. The long and sloping garden, sheltered by fine, mature trees, is a pleasant place for drinks or a complimentary tea on arrival, another reader avers. Spacious country-house-style bedrooms have home-made shortbread, cafetière coffee, fresh milk, Duck Island toiletries and, should you wish, sheets and blankets. Each is liked, especially one with direct garden access, apart from one with an in-room basin and 'tiny, cramped' shower room. Any gripes, however, are soon forgotten at lunch or dinner in the 'bright and spacious dining room', over plates of Tim's 'sublime food'. 'Intense flavours were brought out in two fine main courses, veal sweetbreads and saddle of roe deer.' The wine list is 'substantial and well chosen'. 'The welcome and service are warm, efficient and knowledgeable.' Breakfast brings 'perfectly cooked scrambled eggs'. (Carolyn Hicks, Edward Mirzoeff, SR)

**25% DISCOUNT VOUCHERS**

Rexes Hollow Lane
Barwick
Yeovil BA22 9TD

T: 01935 423902
E: info@littlebarwick.co.uk
W: littlebarwickhouse.co.uk

BEDROOMS: 7. 1 for week-long let.
OPEN: all year except 25 Dec, New Year, 3 weeks in Jan, every Sun, Mon, lunchtime Tues.
FACILITIES: 2 lounges, restaurant, conservatory, in-room TV (Freeview), 3½-acre garden (terrace, paddock), restaurant wheelchair accessible.
BACKGROUND MUSIC: none.
LOCATION: ¾ mile outside Yeovil.
CHILDREN: not under 5.
DOGS: allowed in some bedrooms, sitting rooms (£20 a night), only assistance dogs in restaurant.
CREDIT CARDS: MC, Visa.
PRICES: per room B&B single occupancy from £95, double £154, D,B&B with afternoon tea, per person £135. Set 3-course dinner £57.95. 1-night bookings sometimes refused at weekends.

# BASLOW Derbyshire

MAP 3:A6

## THE CAVENDISH

The slightly austere facade of the Duke and Duchess of Devonshire's hotel on the Chatsworth Estate belies the country house comforts within. 'We so appreciated the deep pile and warmth on a snowy day,' write trusted readers. 'Our rooms were wonderfully cosy, with fabulous views.' All bedrooms have a minibar with fresh milk, 'scrumptious Chatsworth biscuits' and luxury toiletries. Many have a four-poster, while works of art from the owners' collection are displayed throughout. The staff are 'watchful without being intrusive, so that wishes were guessed at and granted'. Tea by 'a roaring fire' elicited a niggle ('my delicious macaroons were just a bit too cold') – the exception that proves the rule of all-round excellence. In the Gallery restaurant, Adam Harper uses Chatsworth farm and estate produce in his fixed-price menus for carnivores and vegetarians. 'The food was beautifully prepared and imaginatively presented.' You can eat more simply in the Garden Room. An 'outstanding breakfast' is served at the table, 'no hopping up and down to a buffet'. (Abigail Kirby-Harris, Jill and Mike Bennett, and others)

**25% DISCOUNT VOUCHERS**

Church Lane
Baslow DE45 1SP

T: 01246 582311
E: reception@cavendishbaslow.co.uk
W: cavendish-hotel.net

BEDROOMS: 28. 2 on ground floor, 4 in converted coach house, 2 suitable for disabled.
OPEN: all year.
FACILITIES: lounge/bar, 2 restaurants, 2 private dining rooms, function facilities, in-room TV (Freeview), civil wedding licence, ½-acre grounds, public rooms wheelchair accessible.
BACKGROUND MUSIC: none.
LOCATION: on edge of village.
CHILDREN: all ages welcomed.
DOGS: guide dogs allowed in 2 bedrooms.
CREDIT CARDS: Amex, MC, Visa.
PRICES: per room B&B single £160–£350, double £180–£450. Tasting menu £85, set menus £58, Garden Room à la carte £32 (pus 5% for distribution to staff). 1-night bookings sometimes refused at weekends.

## BASLOW Derbyshire

MAP 3:A6

### FISCHER'S AT BASLOW HALL

The style is 17th century and the interiors Jacobean, but Max and Susan Fischer's manor house in 'stunningly beautiful' grounds on the edge of a Peak District village was built in 1907. House bedrooms (refurbished since last year) are individually styled. Haddon, overlooking an arboretum, has a new bathroom. Rutland has a sitting room with a 'very comfortable sofa', 'a bathroom with a really deep bath', 'a comfortable bed with effective reading lights', a view of the 'impressive vegetable garden'. More contemporary-style annexe rooms have their own walled garden. All have a coffee machine and organic toiletries. Max Fischer and James Payne create ten-course tasting menus for omnivores and vegans. The three-course menu might include pan-braised halibut with fennel, orange and langoustine bisque or sirloin of Baslow beef. 'Dinner was everything others have written effusively about.' The staff are 'charming and helpful'. A new sound system is likely to divide opinion. Breakfast includes 'freshly squeezed juice, wonderful granola, perfect kippers, and honey from hives to go with fresh croissants'. (Andrew Warren, and others)

Calver Road
Baslow DE45 1RR

T: 01246 583259
E: reservations@fischers-baslowhall.co.uk
W: fischers-baslowhall.co.uk

BEDROOMS: 11. 5 in Garden House, 4 on ground floor.
OPEN: all year except 25/26 Dec, restaurant closed Mon.
FACILITIES: lounge/bar, main dining room, drawing room, wine room, function facilities, in-room TV (Freeview), civil wedding licence, 5-acre grounds, restaurant and lounge wheelchair accessible.
BACKGROUND MUSIC: in bar/lounge and dining rooms.
LOCATION: edge of village, 5 miles NE of Bakewell.
CHILDREN: all ages welcomed, no under-8s in restaurant.
DOGS: not allowed.
CREDIT CARDS: Amex, MC, Visa.
PRICES: per room B&B single £185–£265, double £260–£339, D,B&B £366–£496. Set menu £78.50, tasting menu £90.

# BATH Somerset

## APSLEY HOUSE

Said to have been built by the Duke of Wellington for one of his mistresses, this late Georgian house turned B&B has elegant proportions, a grand piano, and the city of Bath at its feet. It does share its name, at least, with his magnificent Hyde Park residence, No. 1 London, and the bedrooms are all named in the Iron Duke's honour. For instance, Wellington, allegedly where he stayed, has a hand-carved king-size bed, a minibar fridge, a slipper bath and walk-in shower. Ground-floor Wellesley has a four-poster and a French armoire. Copenhagen (Wellington's horse) is located not, as you might hope, in the stables, but in a semi-basement, and can be paired with Mornington, which has a silk-draped four-poster and French doors to the garden. Breakfast, served in a south-facing drawing room at tables laid with crisp linen, brings porridge, granola, eggs Benedict, scrambled eggs with smoked salmon, or a full English. Helpful managers Miroslav Mikula and Katarzyna Kowalczyk live in, and are ready to advise on where to eat in the city, a half-hour walk or a short drive down the hill.

141 Newbridge Hill
Bath BA1 3PT

T: 01225 336966
E: info@apsley-house.co.uk
W: apsley-house.co.uk

BEDROOMS: 12. 1 on ground floor, plus 1 self-catering 2-bedroom apartment in coach house.
OPEN: all year except 24–26 Dec.
FACILITIES: bar/drawing room, dining room, in-room TV (Freeview), ¼-acre garden, parking, unsuitable for disabled.
BACKGROUND MUSIC: Classic FM in drawing and dining rooms.
LOCATION: 1¼ miles W of city centre.
CHILDREN: all ages welcomed.
DOGS: only guide dogs allowed.
CREDIT CARDS: MC, Visa.
PRICES: per room B&B double £148.50–£240. 1-night bookings refused Sat in peak season.

**SEE ALSO SHORTLIST**

## BATH Somerset

MAP 2:D1

### NO.15 GREAT PULTENEY

The Georgian facade of this Grade I listed building on long, wide, very grand Great Pulteney looks like something Jane Austen would recognise. Inside, though, lies not just a luxury hotel with a spa in a former coal cellar but an intriguing curiosities gallery. You get a taste of what's to come at reception, where room keys are kept in a large doll's house. There is something everywhere to catch the eye, from a lost-earring chandelier to collections of beaded evening bags. New owners (family-run Guest Holdings) have made one change that pleased a reader. 'Dogs are now permitted in most bedrooms, and in Bar 15 – this has an all-day menu.' Even the least expensive cosy doubles have bespoke artwork, a coffee machine, a larder of complimentary soft drinks and snacks, and 100 Acres toiletries. In a neo-Gothic coach house annexe, junior suites have a freestanding double bath and a rain shower. The entire contents of an antique chemist's shop furnishes The Dispensary, where dinner brings such dishes as cod with caviar fish cream, wild mushroom and red dulse. 'Good value and very well located.' (Chris and Erika Savory)

15 Great Pulteney Street
Bath BA2 4BR

**T:** 01225 807015
**E:** reception@no15greatpulteney.
  co.uk
**W:** no15greatpulteney.co.uk

**BEDROOMS:** 40. 8 in coach house, 1 suitable for disabled.
**OPEN:** all year, restaurant open daily for breakfast, dinner, Sun brunch.
**FACILITIES:** lift, lounge, bar, restaurant, private dining room, in-room TV (Sky), spa (treatments, hot tub, sauna), small garden terrace, parking permits, public rooms wheelchair accessible, adapted toilet.
**BACKGROUND MUSIC:** all day in lounge, bar and restaurant.
**LOCATION:** central.
**CHILDREN:** all ages welcomed.
**DOGS:** allowed in bedrooms except top floor, bar, not in restaurant.
**CREDIT CARDS:** Amex, MC, Visa.
**PRICES:** per room B&B £189–£383. À la carte £35. 1-night bookings sometimes refused at weekends.

**SEE ALSO SHORTLIST**

# BATH Somerset

## THE QUEENSBERRY

Near the city centre but surprisingly quiet, this stylishly quirky hotel with a Michelin-starred restaurant occupies a quartet of Georgian town houses, each backed by a garden. They were built for the 8th Marquess of Queensberry, whose passion for boxing can be traced throughout. Owners Laurence and Helen Beere are hands-on alongside manager Joss Roussanne, all overseeing the final stages of a four-year refurbishment. Bedrooms offer a smart home-from-home feel. Georgian features – marble fireplaces, high ceilings, sash windows – are complemented by designer wallpapers and colourful furnishings; toiletries are by The White Company. After a drink in the Old Q bar – perhaps a G&T made with 6 O'Clock Gin from Bristol – dinner guests proceed downstairs to the Olive Tree where chef Chris Cleghorn produces such culinary delights as longhorn-beef tartar with Exmoor caviar and Woolley Park Farm duck with beetroot, sea beet and kumquat. In the bar hangs a spoof of the Queensberry Rules. Top of the list: 'Manners, decorum and kindness to be shown at all times.' It's a rule that the 'attentive and friendly' staff take seriously.

**25% DISCOUNT VOUCHERS**

4–7 Russel Street
Bath BA1 2QF

T: 01225 447928
E: reservations@thequeensberry.co.uk
W: thequeensberry.co.uk

BEDROOMS: 29. Some on ground floor.
OPEN: all year, restaurant closed Mon, midday Tues–Thurs.
FACILITIES: lift, residents' drawing room, bar, 2 sitting rooms, restaurant, meeting room, in-room TV (Freeview), 4 linked courtyard gardens, unsuitable for disabled.
BACKGROUND MUSIC: in restaurant and bar.
LOCATION: near Assembly Rooms.
CHILDREN: all ages welcomed.
DOGS: assistance dogs only.
CREDIT CARDS: Amex, MC, Visa.
PRICES: per room B&B £125–£475. Tasting menus £70–£90, à la carte £60. 1-night bookings sometimes refused weekends.

**SEE ALSO SHORTLIST**

# BATH Somerset

MAP 2:D1

## THE ROYAL CRESCENT HOTEL & SPA

Behind the golden-stone facade of two mansions, at the centre of Bath's magnificent Georgian crescent, lies a luxurious hotel with an oasis garden, spa and 12-metre pool. 'What a pleasant hotel this is,' writes one reader, who was particularly impressed by the 'staff who engage, not in a subservient way'. Uniquely styled bedrooms range from the 'deluxe', with a queen-size bed and contemporary styling, through 'heritage', overlooking the garden or the Royal Crescent lawn, to 'master' rooms in the main mansion or coach houses, each with a separate living area. There are also family master rooms, such as Jane Austen, with a conservatory. An all-day menu is served in the Montagu bar (perhaps a croque-monsieur or fish and chips), while in the Dower House restaurant head chef David Campbell's menus include such dishes as roasted Cornish halibut, Falmouth mussels, spring onions and curry oil. Breakfast brings Agen prunes in Earl Grey tea, Viennoiserie, Manx kipper and more, including something for vegetarians. There is valet parking, a car charging point, and you can order a picnic before setting off to explore this beautiful city.

16 Royal Crescent
Bath BA1 2LS

T: 01225 823333
E: info@royalcrescent.co.uk
W: royalcrescent.co.uk

BEDROOMS: 45. 10 in Dower House, 14 in annexes, 8 on ground floor.
OPEN: all year.
FACILITIES: lift, bar, lounge, library, restaurant, function facilities, in-room TV (Sky, Freeview), civil wedding licence, 1-acre garden, spa (12-metre pool), public rooms wheelchair accessible.
BACKGROUND MUSIC: in library and restaurant.
LOCATION: ½ mile from High Street.
CHILDREN: all ages welcomed, not under 13 in spa.
DOGS: allowed in some bedrooms, public rooms, not in restaurant or bar.
CREDIT CARDS: Amex, MC, Visa.
PRICES: per room B&B double £330–£1,080. À la carte £72, tasting menu £82. Min. 2-night stay Sat.

**SEE ALSO SHORTLIST**

# BAUGHURST Hampshire

MAP 2:D2

## THE WELLINGTON ARMS

An emphasis on organic home-grown products, together with spacious beamed bedrooms and a 'friendly welcome, including for our dog', characterise this dining-pub-with-rooms. It is a labour of love for the owners, Simon Page and chef Jason King. Outside, Jacob sheep graze in a field; fruit, vegetables and herbs are grown in the kitchen garden. Milk and home-baked bread are organic; fish arrives daily from Brixham. The bedrooms, three in outbuildings, have pale Farrow & Ball paint finishes, oak furniture and a heated slate floor or sisal carpet. They also have everything you need for a good cup of tea including home-baked biscuits and fine china, the teapot snug in a mohair cosy knitted by Simon's mum. A suite above the pub has a sitting room furnished with antiques. At dinner, there is little to tempt vegans, but carnivores get their teeth into chargrilled steak, home-reared lamb or roe deer pot pie. Breakfast brings new-laid eggs, avocado, Uig Lodge smoked salmon and French toast with crispy bacon. It's not a big place, but in summer drinkers spill out into the garden for drinks on the lawn. 'It exceeded our high expectations.'

Baughurst Road
Baughurst RG26 5LP

T: 0118 982 0110
E: hello@thewellingtonarms.com
W: thewellingtonarms.com

BEDROOMS: 4. 3 in converted outbuildings.
OPEN: all year except 1–21 Jan, restaurant closed Sun night, Mon.
FACILITIES: bar, restaurant, in-room TV (Freeview), 2-acre garden, parking, dining room wheelchair accessible.
BACKGROUND MUSIC: in bar and restaurant.
LOCATION: equidistant between Reading, Basingstoke and Newbury.
CHILDREN: all ages welcomed.
DOGS: allowed in 2 bedrooms (£10 per night), public areas.
CREDIT CARDS: MC, Visa.
PRICES: per room B&B £125–£220. À la carte £37.

## BEAMINSTER Dorset

MAP 1:C6

### THE OLLEROD

An ancient, honey-stone priest's house turned hotel in a pretty market town has been given a chic make-over as a restaurant-with-rooms. The owners, Silvana Bandini and Chris Staines, have impressive credentials – she in hotel management, he in Michelin-starred kitchens – but there is nothing swanky about The Ollerod (Dorset dialect for 'cowslip'). It hosts a book club, supper clubs and art exhibitions. It is child-friendly, and locals are encouraged to drop in for drinks in the bar, or in the snug with its roaring fire. In the restaurant or walled garden, the seasonally driven menus of local and home-grown produce include small plates and choices for children and vegans. Typical dishes include roast haunch of venison with smoked chocolate sauce; spiced roasted cauliflower, cauliflower quinoa, tea-soaked sultanas, hummus and aubergine compote. The bedrooms (four in the old coach house) are stylish, with dramatic patterned wallpaper, an espresso machine and organic toiletries. Some have a king-size four-poster. A garden-view room is obviously best, but street-facing rooms are well insulated against traffic noise.

3 Prout Bridge
Beaminster DT8 3AY

T: 01308 862200
E: enquiries@theollerod.co.uk
W: theollerod.co.uk

BEDROOMS: 13. 4 in coach house, 4 on ground floor.
OPEN: all year.
FACILITIES: lounge, bar, sun room, conservatory, restaurant, in-room TV (Freeview), treatment room, civil wedding licence, walled garden, covered terrace.
BACKGROUND MUSIC: in public rooms.
LOCATION: 100 yards from centre.
CHILDREN: all ages welcomed.
DOGS: allowed in 2 bedrooms, bar and terrace, not in restaurant.
CREDIT CARDS: Amex, MC, Visa.
PRICES: per room B&B £145–£275.
À la carte £40.

# BEAULIEU Hampshire

MAP 2:E2

## THE MASTER BUILDER'S

Views of the Beaulieu river can be enjoyed from this former 18th-century shipbuilder's house, which has a 'lovely setting down quiet lanes' in a New Forest hamlet of Georgian cottages. The flags of Nelson's conquests adorn reception (a reminder of the warships built here for Trafalgar), while the crew in the bar sport Breton stripes. You can eat from the bar menu – perhaps a venison or falafel burger – or dine more stylishly in the restaurant, from a short, appealing menu of such dishes as Brixham cod with mussels, chickpeas and venison chorizo. In summer there are garden barbecues. Bedrooms in the main house have original features, antiques and artwork, perhaps a four-poster or an old sea chest. In the newer Henry Adams wing, named after the original resident master shipwright, shipshape bedrooms have contemporary blue-and-white decor. Several rooms are so dog-friendly, Fido can even order from a room-service menu, while humans breakfast on smoked haddock, free-range eggs and New Forest mushrooms. 'The maritime museum in the village is worth a visit (get a discount from reception),' a reader advises.

Buckler's Hard
Beaulieu SO42 7XB

T: 01590 616253
E: enquiries@themasterbuilders.co.uk
W: themasterbuilders.co.uk

BEDROOMS: 26. 18 in newer Henry Adams wing.
OPEN: all year.
FACILITIES: lounge, bar, restaurant, terrace with river views, in-room TV (Freeview), civil wedding licence, ½-acre garden, bar and restaurant wheelchair accessible, no adapted toilet.
BACKGROUND MUSIC: in bar and restaurant.
LOCATION: 6 miles NE of Lymington.
CHILDREN: all ages welcomed.
DOGS: allowed in some bedrooms, lounge, the Yachtsman's bar, not in restaurant.
CREDIT CARDS: Amex, MC, Visa.
PRICES: per room B&B £155–£225, D,B&B £220–£275. À la carte £40 (restaurant), £30 (bar).

# BEAULIEU Hampshire

MAP 2:E2

## MONTAGU ARMS

Perfectly placed to explore the New Forest, this Victorian Arts and Crafts inn, on the Beaulieu river near Lord Montagu's home, is a mix of cosy bolt-hole, luxury hotel and fine-dining restaurant, with a pub in a 1920s wing. Beyond the stone dogs that guard the door you find 'great ambience': beams, panelling and open fires. There is a wide choice of bedrooms, each different, with a mix of antique and contemporary styling. All have a king- or super-king-size bed and White Company toiletries; many have a four-poster. Duplex Hayloft suites, in a converted Georgian barn, have a private terrace overlooking the Gertrude Jekyll-inspired gardens. In the Terrace restaurant, Matthew Whitfield's ambitious à la carte and tasting menus, including one for vegans, feature locally sourced and home-grown ingredients in such dishes as chalk-stream trout with pine nuts and Hampshire watercress. You can eat less expensively in Monty's Inn, with imaginative fare such as garden herb sausage roll, potato and garden artichoke rösti, fish pie or a burger with Laverstoke mozzarella. The staff are 'helpful and attentive'.

Palace Lane
Beaulieu SO42 7ZL

T: 01590 612324
E: reservations@montaguarmshotel.co.uk
W: montaguarmshotel.co.uk

BEDROOMS: 24. 2 in Hayloft suites.
OPEN: all year. Terrace restaurant closed Mon all day, Tues lunch.
FACILITIES: lounge, conservatory, library/bar/brasserie, restaurant, in-room TV (Freeview), civil wedding licence, 3-acre garden, public rooms wheelchair accessible, adapted toilet.
BACKGROUND MUSIC: Classic FM all day in reception.
LOCATION: village centre.
CHILDREN: all ages welcomed, no under-12s in Terrace restaurant at dinner, but welcome in Monty's.
DOGS: assistance dogs allowed.
CREDIT CARDS: Amex, MC, Visa.
PRICES: per room B&B £219–£449. Tasting menu £75–£90, à la carte £60 (Terrace restaurant), £28 (Monty's Inn). 1-night bookings sometimes refused Fri/Sat, peak season.

# BEESANDS Devon

MAP 1:E4

## THE CRICKET INN

Fish and chips within sound of the waves, local crab and lobster, and the day's catch cooked over charcoal are among the attractions at this expanded pub in a small village overlooking Start Bay. The position is 'absolutely beautiful', between countryside and sea, and if the approach is slightly hairy, via 'narrow lanes with some steep hills and sharp bends', it is 'worth it once you get there'. Inside it has a nautical feel slightly at odds with cricket theming. First opened in 1867, it was taken over 20 years ago by the Heaths, who added a dining space with rooms above. Rachel Heath runs the inn with son Scott, who previously worked as the chef but is now the owner, assisted by Jamie Smith in the kitchen. Blue-and-white bedrooms, three sleeping a family, have a New England lightness, a shower room, nothing fancy, though Botham and Trueman each have a modern king-size four-poster. 'We stayed in Oval, with a seat in the large bay window, and very much liked the style of decoration.' In the dining room there are children's portions, steaks and burgers. Seafood Sundays are popular, so book ahead, don't just bowl up.

Beesands
Kingsbridge TQ7 2EN

T: 01548 580215
E: enquiries@thecricketinn.com
W: thecricketinn.com

BEDROOMS: 7. 4 in extension.
OPEN: closed Christmas Day (no rooms Christmas Eve).
FACILITIES: bar, restaurant (alfresco dining), private dining facilities, free (intermittent) Wi-Fi, in-room TV (Freeview), parking, restaurant and bar wheelchair accessible, adapted toilet.
BACKGROUND MUSIC: all day.
LOCATION: in village, on South West Coast Path.
CHILDREN: all ages welcomed, children's menu, family rooms.
DOGS: allowed in bar only.
CREDIT CARDS: MC, Visa.
PRICES: per room B&B (double and family rooms) £110–£150, D,B&B (double) £150–£190 (up to £50 per couple for dinner). À la carte £30. Min. 2-night stay preferred at weekends in high season.

# BEPTON Sussex

MAP 2:E3

## PARK HOUSE, HOTEL & SPA

Now a luxury spa hotel in a 'magnificent' setting, this country house was a family home when it first opened its doors to the Cowdray Park set back in 1949. Two generations on, owner Seamus O'Brien has transformed it into a leisure resort, with a six-hole golf course, tennis courts, croquet and bowls. It is a welcoming place where the staff effortlessly 'make you feel you are at home'. 'Housekeeping is assiduous.' 'Bedding preferences were discussed when we booked.' Traditional bedrooms in the main house have views over the South Downs national park, perhaps a separate sitting area, toile de Jouy wallpaper, and a patio or balcony. All come with hand-made biscuits and Voya toiletries. There are further rooms with more facilities in cottages in the grounds. An all-day menu is on offer in the bar, its walls crowded with photos of family and the polo fraternity. In the dining room, Callum Keir's 'competent if not memorable' menus change only seasonally and include such dishes as Sussex rib-eye steak and red Thai chickpea hotpot. Breakfast brings free-range eggs, kippers and oak-smoked salmon. (Andrew Wardrop, BR)

Bepton Road
Bepton
Midhurst GU29 0JB

T: 01730 819000
E: reservations@parkhousehotel.com
W: parkhousehotel.com

BEDROOMS: 21. 5 on ground floor, 1 suitable for disabled, 9 in cottages in grounds.
OPEN: all year, except 24–26 Dec.
FACILITIES: drawing room, bar, dining room, conservatory, function rooms, in-room TV (Sky), civil wedding licence, 10-acre grounds, spa, heated indoor and outdoor swimming pools, tennis, public rooms and spa wheelchair accessible.
BACKGROUND MUSIC: in restaurants.
LOCATION: village centre.
CHILDREN: all ages welcomed.
DOGS: allowed in some bedrooms with garden access, not public rooms.
CREDIT CARDS: Amex, MC, Visa.
PRICES: per room B&B £150–£320, D,B&B £230–£340. Set dinner £45. Min. 2-night stay Fri/Sat.

# BEVERLEY Yorkshire

## NEWBEGIN HOUSE

In a 'wonderful' walled garden, yet just minutes from the centre of Beverley, this classic Georgian town house is brimful of family treasures accumulated by owners Walter and Nuala Sweeney, who 'treat their guests as friends'. It has a 'superb' yet 'comfortably furnished' interior of shuttered sash windows, polished-wood floors, chandeliers, marble fireplaces, antiques, books, artwork and family photos. The 'first-class welcome' includes a large pot of tea in the sitting room and, later, a 'personal tour of the lovely garden' if you wish. Bedrooms, which 'feel like guest rooms in a friend's rather grand house', have family heirlooms, big solid beds, comfy armchairs and crammed bookcases. One overlooks the garden, another, 'ridiculously large', has two double beds and a sweep of sash windows. 'Excellent amenities' include sherry, fresh milk, flowers and teas and coffees. The 'wide choice for breakfast' includes omelettes, poached eggs with prosciutto and cheese, as well as a traditional Yorkshire. Readers enthuse: 'A memorable stay', 'Walter and Nuala were perfect hosts.' (Mark Mulrooney, and others)

10 Newbegin
Beverley HU17 8EG

T: 01482 888880
E: wsweeney@wsweeney.karoo.co.uk
W: newbeginhousebbbeverley.co.uk

BEDROOMS: 3.
OPEN: all year except when owners take a holiday.
FACILITIES: sitting room, dining room, small conference facilities, in-room TV (Freeview), ¾-acre walled garden, unsuitable for disabled.
BACKGROUND MUSIC: none.
LOCATION: central.
CHILDREN: all ages welcomed.
DOGS: not allowed.
CREDIT CARDS: none accepted.
PRICES: per room B&B single £60, double £90–£100. 1-night bookings sometimes refused during the Early Music Festival.

# BIGBURY-ON-SEA Devon

MAP 1:D4

## BURGH ISLAND HOTEL

♔ Previous César winner

This decadent Art Deco grande dame, set on its own tidal island, 'harks back to a more glamorous age', and a recent refurbishment has been given the thumbs up by faithful regulars. After a glass of champagne, a trusted reviewer was shown to 'Jane Marple', a cosy double room on the first floor 'with views over the lawn and the Mermaid pool beyond'. It was compact, with both an in-room bath tub and basin. Larger doubles and suites are more spacious, some with a vast bathroom, and have sweeping views of the bay. All rooms are 'age-appropriately furnished', and well equipped without being 'boutiquified', though the lighting may be 'too dim to read by'. Evenings begin in the 1930s-style Palm Court Lounge, perhaps with a Burgh Bramble mixed by long-standing barman Gary, followed by a black-tie dinner of 'imaginative and perfectly executed' dishes in the Grand Ballroom. Sometimes there is dancing. Breakfast brings a buffet of breads, pastries and cereals or hot dishes cooked to order, including 'kedgeree, porridge and full English'. Service is 'friendly and efficient at all times'. 'I loved every minute.'

Burgh Island
Bigbury-on-Sea TQ7 4BG

T: 01548 810514
E: reception@burghisland.com
W: burghisland.com

BEDROOMS: 25. 1 suite in Beach House in grounds, apartment above Pilchard Inn.
OPEN: all year, except Jan.
FACILITIES: lift, bar, 2 restaurants, ballroom, sun lounge, billiard room, private dining room, spa, civil wedding licence, 17-acre grounds, sea bathing pool, tennis court.
BACKGROUND MUSIC: period in public rooms.
LOCATION: off Bigbury beach. Private garages on mainland.
CHILDREN: not under 5, no under-13s at dinner.
DOGS: allowed in Beach House, Artist's Studio, and Pilchard Inn.
CREDIT CARDS: Amex, MC, Visa.
PRICES: per room B&B £345–£815, singles from £295. À la carte £75. 1-night bookings refused weekends, some bank holidays.

# BIGBURY-ON-SEA Devon

MAP 1:D4

## THE HENLEY

'The views are stunning' from Martyn Scarterfield and Petra Lampe's Edwardian holiday cottage-turned-B&B, which gazes over the Avon estuary to Burgh Island. As well as a 'gorgeous' outlook from the dining room and the decked sun terrace, guest bedrooms are all sea facing. They are traditionally furnished and homely, with 'thoughtful touches' including sherry and biscuits. Throughout, the atmosphere is 'relaxing and informal', with a wood-burning stove in the lounge. Dogs are welcomed. After a full Devon breakfast with Aune Valley bacon and sausages, kippers, eggs Benedict or scrambled eggs with smoked salmon, you might play a round at Bigbury Golf Club, take the steps down to the beach, or walk the South West Coast Path. Then hitch a ride on the sea tractor across the sands to the island for lunch at the 700-year-old Pilchard Inn. Give three days' notice if you want to dine in. Martyn's home cooking could give London chefs a run for their money, says one regular visitor. A typical meal might be pea soup with asparagus and pea girasole, pan-fried John Dory, and Rote Gruetze, a red berry pudding.

Folly Hill
Bigbury-on-Sea TQ7 4AR

T: 01548 810240
E: info@thehenleyhotel.co.uk
W: thehenleyhotel.co.uk

BEDROOMS: 4.
OPEN: Mar–end Oct, restaurant closed Sun eve.
FACILITIES: 2 lounges, dining room, reception, in-room TV (Freeview), small terraced garden (steps to beach, golf, sailing, fishing), Coast Path nearby, unsuitable for disabled.
BACKGROUND MUSIC: jazz/classical in the evenings in lounge, dining room.
LOCATION: 5 miles S of Modbury.
CHILDREN: not under 12.
DOGS: allowed in bedrooms (not on bed), lounges, not in dining room (£7 per dog per night).
CREDIT CARDS: MC, Visa.
PRICES: per room B&B single £106, double £145–£175, D,B&B (2-night min.) single £134, double £200–£233. Set dinner £36. 1-night bookings sometimes refused weekends.

# BIGGIN-BY-HARTINGTON Derbyshire    MAP 3:B6

## BIGGIN HALL

With a 'spectacular location' in a small village high in the White Peak landscape, James Moffett's Grade II* listed manor house with its stone floors, oak beams and mullioned windows also offers 'excellent value for money'. Beer and Prosecco are offered on arrival, though you might prefer to order tea by the fire in the sitting room, with its massive stone fireplace and oak panelling. The complimentary drinks are just part of the service: 'We were very pleasantly surprised to be presented with a packed lunch', perfect to eat while exploring the Peak District national park. Walkers with dogs can stay in the annexe. Comfortable bedrooms done in traditional style range from two single rooms, which share a bathroom, to the Master Suite, which has a four-poster bed. Regular visitors, on their 25th stay, had only praise for 'our favourite hotel'. However, another reader disliked the music at dinner. Although not fancy, the locally sourced food hits the spot, with such dishes as chargrilled High Peak fillet steak, and a separate vegetarian menu. (Michael and Patricia Blanchard, Jonathan Rose, and others)

**25% DISCOUNT VOUCHERS**

Biggin-by-Hartington
Buxton SK17 0DH

T: 01298 84451
E: enquiries@bigginhall.co.uk
W: bigginhall.co.uk

BEDROOMS: 21. 13 in annexes, some on ground floor.
OPEN: all year, restaurant closed Mon lunch.
FACILITIES: sitting room, library, dining room, meeting room, in-room TV (Freeview), civil wedding licence, 8-acre grounds, restaurant, toilet wheelchair accessible.
BACKGROUND MUSIC: in restaurant.
LOCATION: 8 miles N of Ashbourne.
CHILDREN: not under 12.
DOGS: allowed in annexe bedrooms, not main house, no charge unless for damage.
CREDIT CARDS: MC, Visa.
PRICES: per room B&B single from £80, double £120–£160. À la carte £32, Indulgence menu Fri and Sat (for whole table) £70 per person, incl. wine. 1-night bookings sometimes refused weekends.

# BILDESTON Suffolk

MAP 2:C5

## THE BILDESTON CROWN

In a thriving village of gaily painted and ancient black-and-white houses, this hotel is set in a 15th-century merchant's house-turned-coaching inn. Run by Hayley and Chris Lee, manager and chef, it was awarded 'a firm tick' this year by a trusted reader. 'Full endorsement, excellent food.' The staff are 'smiley, friendly and welcoming', Guide insiders concur. 'Gaily checked-carpeted corridors' lead to 'characterful and colourful' bedrooms, one with an antique four-poster. All have personal touches: portraits, landscapes, a wall of Jane Clayton's 'Hot Dogs' wallpaper, a double-ended bateau bath and walk-in shower. Fires burn in public rooms while, in 'several large dining areas', menus include produce supplied by the Crown's farmer owner, James Buckle. Dishes range from a simple sausage roll to sea bream with bouillabaisse sauce. Singled out for praise this year are the 'very freshly cooked duck liver', chicken curry, and truffle risotto. Surprisingly, the breakfast room was cold, but 'an ample cooked breakfast' comes with 'delicious potatoes' and 'a jug of fresh orange juice'. (Robert Gower, and others)

104 High Street
Bildeston IP7 7EB

T: 01449 740510
E: reception@thebildestoncrown.co.uk
W: thebildestoncrown.com

BEDROOMS: 12.
OPEN: all year, no accommodation 24–26 Dec, New Year's Day.
FACILITIES: 2 bars, restaurant, 2 private dining areas, lift, in-room TV (Freeview), courtyard, 3 small patios, parking, mobile phone reception variable, restaurant and bar wheelchair accessible, adapted toilet.
BACKGROUND MUSIC: in public areas.
LOCATION: village centre, 10 mins' drive from Lavenham.
CHILDREN: all ages welcomed.
DOGS: allowed in some rooms and in bar, not in restaurant.
CREDIT CARDS: Amex, MC, Visa.
PRICES: per room B&B single £70–£180, double £95–£180. À la carte £40.

# BISHOP'S CASTLE Shropshire

MAP 3:C4

## THE CASTLE HOTEL

Walkers and those with four-legged friends are among the happy customers of the 'ultimate dog-friendly hotel' built on the ruins of a hilltop Norman castle with views to the south Shropshire hills. A sister to Pen-y-Dyffryn, Oswestry (see entry), it is run by Henry Hunter and is 'superb'. 'The building was quirky with its uneven floors, but the decor was lovely.' 'We revelled in the historic surroundings and warm welcome.' Bedrooms mix original features with contemporary furnishings; a master double has an in-room, claw-footed bath. One reader, though, points out that bedside lights are 'too dim'. The self-catering Elephant Gate House is not a nod to former landlord Clive of India but to its stint as a refuge for homeless circus elephants in the war. Dogs stay for free and can join their owners if they eat in one of three bars, or on a vine-covered terrace. In the panelled dining room Steve Bruce's daily menus run the gamut of pub classics and fancier fare, with vegan options. A 'magnificent' breakfast features kippers, and the full Shropshire – plus sausages for Fido. (Brian Robinson, Tracey Brydges, Ian Nuttall, and others)

Market Square
Bishop's Castle SY9 5BN

T: 01588 638403
E: stay@thecastlehotelbishopscastle.co.uk
W: thecastlehotelbishopscastle.co.uk

BEDROOMS: 14. 2 suites in converted town house opposite.
OPEN: all year except first week Jan.
FACILITIES: 3 bar areas, dining room, in-room TV (Freeview), in-room spa treatments, patio, terrace, garden, parking, bars and restaurant wheelchair accessible, adapted toilet.
BACKGROUND MUSIC: in bar areas.
LOCATION: in small market town centre.
CHILDREN: all ages welcomed.
DOGS: allowed in bedrooms, bar, at owner's side at meal times in dog-friendly areas, not in restaurant. Welcome box, no charge.
CREDIT CARDS: MC, Visa.
PRICES: per room B&B single £100–£115, double £125–£170. À la carte £30. 1-night bookings sometimes refused Sat.

# BLAKENEY Norfolk

MAP 2:A5

## THE BLAKENEY HOTEL

♀ Previous César winner

On the quayside overlooking the estuary and salt marshes, in the luminous landscape of north Norfolk, Emma Stannard's 'lovely, comfortable', child-friendly hotel gets another thumbs-up from a trusted reader. Bedrooms are smart and contemporary, with views of the water or south-facing gardens. Some have a balcony, maybe a four-poster; others open on to a patio and are ideal for guests with a dog. Interconnecting rooms suit a family; cots and extra beds can be supplied. Menus at lunch and dinner include locally farmed beef and lamb, local crab, Norfolk cheeses, sandwiches and platters (perhaps a Blakeney seafood plate). As well as two lounges, a bar, a billiard and games room, a mini-gym, steam and sauna room, there is 'an excellent pool' overlooking a sun terrace. Breakfast brings plenty of choice, though our reader was single-minded. 'I had kippers for breakfast every morning, from the nearby Cley smokehouse – perfection.' Birdwatchers are in their watery element in this part of the world, and a boat trip to Blakeney Point with its grey seals is certainly worth making. (David Sefton, SW)

The Quay
Blakeney
Holt NR25 7NE

T: 01263 740797
E: enquiries@blakeneyhotel.co.uk
W: blakeneyhotel.co.uk

BEDROOMS: 64. 16 in Granary annexe opposite, some on ground floor, 1 suitable for disabled.
OPEN: all year.
FACILITIES: lift, lounges, bar, restaurant, in-room TV (Freeview), function facilities, heated indoor pool, steam room, mini-gym, games room, terrace, ¼-acre walled garden, public rooms wheelchair accessible, adapted toilet.
BACKGROUND MUSIC: none.
LOCATION: on the quay.
CHILDREN: all ages welcomed.
DOGS: allowed in some bedrooms, not in public rooms.
CREDIT CARDS: Amex, MC, Visa.
PRICES: per person B&B £130–£215, D,B&B (2-night min.) £142–£227. À la carte £36, fixed-price dinner £34. 1-night bookings sometimes refused weekends, bank holidays.

# BLANCHLAND Northumberland

MAP 4:B3

## THE LORD CREWE ARMS

♀ Previous César winner

Blending 12th-century stone origins with 21st-century country-inn comforts, plus robust food, this handsome hotel attracts walkers and weekenders. In a 'charming stone-built village by a river', the former abbot's lodgings oozes atmosphere with its flagged floors, mullioned windows, a barrel-vaulted bar and dining areas that vary from cosy and fire-warmed to chic. (It's part of the Calcot Collection; see Barnsley House, the Painswick, and Calcot & Spa.) Food is modern British and might include home-made pâté on sourdough, followed by hogget rump with creamy polenta or chalk-stream trout with chickpea fritters. One reader commented on small portions but others spoke of 'punchy flavours' and 'unpretentious' dishes. Although only four of the 21 bedrooms are in the main inn (the rest are across the square, or round the corner in former miners' cottages), all share the same 'light and airy, modern country look'. There are 'splendid bathrooms' and 'nice touches' of books, fudge, hot-water bottles. Some rooms have a window seat, others a log-burning stove. There is no excuse not to explore: there are walking routes, and wellies to borrow. (HP)

The Square
Blanchland DH8 9SP

T: 01434 675469
E: enquiries@
lordcrewearmsblanchland.co.uk
W: lordcrewearmsblanchland.co.uk

BEDROOMS: 21. 7 in adjacent miners' cottages, 10 in The Angel across road, some on ground floor, 1 suitable for disabled.
OPEN: all year.
FACILITIES: reception hall, lounge, restaurant, bar, Gatehouse events space, in-room TV (Freeview), civil wedding licence, beer garden, 1 dining area wheelchair accessible with ramp.
BACKGROUND MUSIC: in dining room and bar.
LOCATION: in Blanchland village on the B6306, 9 miles S of Hexham.
CHILDREN: all ages welcomed.
DOGS: well-behaved dogs allowed in bedrooms, public rooms, not in dining room.
CREDIT CARDS: Amex, MC, Visa.
PRICES: per room B&B £149–£274.
À la carte £34.

# BLEDINGTON Gloucestershire

MAP 3:D6

## THE KING'S HEAD INN

'The staff were friendly and helpful, the setting on the village green was delightful – what a wonderful place to stay,' says a trusted reviewer of this Cotswolds inn-with-rooms. Locals have been propping up the bar here since the 16th century, and owners Archie and Nicola Orr-Ewing have maintained the pub's authentic heritage feel – oak settles, flagstone floors, ancient support beams – while adding all the luxury accoutrements of contemporary hospitality. 'Very comfortable' rooms are in the main building or the nearby courtyard where our reviewer had 'a large upstairs room with a good bathroom', and their friends a downstairs room which was 'quite a lot smaller with less natural light'. Bathrooms all have handmade toiletries from Nicola's own Bantam Bodycare range. After a drink, perhaps in the courtyard garden, guests can enjoy a hearty dinner in the elegant dining room, the bar, or out on the terrace. 'Local produce, large portions and plenty of choice' are the order of the day, with a regular burger night featuring Bledington beef. At breakfast our reviewer found a 'good buffet table and excellent cooked dishes'. (Sara Price)

The Green
Bledington OX7 6XQ

T: 01608 658365
E: info@kingsheadinn.net
W: thekingsheadinn.net

BEDROOMS: 12. 6 in courtyard annexe, some on ground floor.
OPEN: all year except 25/26 Dec.
FACILITIES: bar, restaurant, snug, courtyard, in-room TV (Freeview), children's play area.
BACKGROUND MUSIC: most of the day, in bar.
LOCATION: on village green.
CHILDREN: all ages welcomed.
DOGS: allowed in bar and certain bedrooms by arrangement, not in restaurant.
CREDIT CARDS: MC, Visa.
PRICES: per room B&B single £80–£105, double £110–£140, D,B&B double £170–£200. À la carte £35. 1-night bookings refused Sat.

# BOLTON ABBEY Yorkshire

MAP 4:D3

## THE DEVONSHIRE ARMS

The Duke and Duchess of Devonshire's luxury hotel has come a long way since starting life as a 17th-century inn. On the 30,000-acre Bolton Abbey estate in the Yorkshire Dales, it features decor overseen by the Duchess which blends contemporary style and comfort with 'quality period furnishings'. Walls are hung with works from the Chatsworth Devonshire Collection, and some pricier rooms, in the 18th-century wing, have a four-poster. Even the cheapest 'classics', overlooking the Italian box garden, have a coffee machine, minibar and fresh milk. An atmospheric spa can be found in an adjacent barn. Our inspector took a drink in the cocktail bar, its walls 'festooned with canine silhouettes' (courtesy of Osborne & Little). In the restaurant, Peter Howarth's tasting menu might be 'almost curt in its brevity' (including St Austell Bay mussels, sardine purée, Barolo and, for vegetarians, confit fennel, smoked ricotta, dill, apple, quinoa), but dishes are long on flavour and high in quality. The wine list comes 'in an enormous folder'. You can eat more cheaply in the modern brasserie. (See also The Cavendish, Baslow.)

Bolton Abbey Estate
Bolton Abbey
Skipton BD23 6AJ

T: 01756 718100
E: reception@thedevonshirearms.
  co.uk
W: thedevonshirearms.co.uk

BEDROOMS: 40. Some on ground floor suitable for disabled.
OPEN: all year, restaurant closed Mon eve, brasserie open all week.
FACILITIES: 4 lounges, brasserie, restaurant, private dining rooms, in-room TV, civil wedding licence, spa (indoor pool, spa bath), gardens, helicopter pads, public areas wheelchair accessible, adapted toilet.
BACKGROUND MUSIC: in public areas.
LOCATION: 6 miles E of Skipton.
CHILDREN: all ages welcomed.
DOGS: allowed in most bedrooms, public areas, not spa or dining areas.
CREDIT CARDS: Amex, MC, Visa.
PRICES: per room B&B single £149–£359, double £169–£379, D,B&B £309–£519. Set menu £75, tasting menu £85 (restaurant), à la carte £35 (brasserie).

# BORROWDALE Cumbria

MAP 4: inset C2

## HAZEL BANK

♀ Previous César winner

Occupying a prime spot in what is arguably the Lake District's most picturesque valley, Hazel Bank has 'stunning mountain views', walks from the doorstep, and the chance of spotting a red squirrel. Sitting above Rothswaite village in Borrowdale, the Victorian house – fictional home for 'Rogue Herries' in Hugh Walpole's novels – is a classic country house on an intimate scale. Owners Gary and Donna MacRae are 'friendly and attentive hosts', ensuring 'a cheerful, warm atmosphere' and 'a luxury welcome', with sherry, home-made biscuits and fine chocolates in bedrooms. The latter are elegant, with pretty wallpapers, comfortable armchairs, valley views and a top-notch bathroom, including under-floor heating and L'Occitane toiletries. And then there's the food. Donna and MasterChef finalist Darren Cornish cook 'outstanding' evening meals that might include teriyaki mackerel with roasted watermelon followed by seared Cumbrian beef with smoked potato. There is a 'comprehensive, sophisticated wine list'. Served by the MacRaes in the garden-view dining room, 'all diners felt themselves to be suitably spoilt'. (Carolyn Speirs, DD-L)

**25% DISCOUNT VOUCHERS**

Borrowdale
Keswick CA12 5XB

T: 01768 777248
E: info@hazelbankhotel.co.uk
W: hazelbankhotel.co.uk

BEDROOMS: 7. 1 on ground floor with walk-in shower.
OPEN: all year except 14 Dec–23 Jan.
FACILITIES: lounge, dining room, drying room, in-room TV (Freeview), 4-acre grounds (croquet, woodland walks).
BACKGROUND MUSIC: Classic FM at breakfast.
LOCATION: 6 miles S of Keswick on B5289 to Borrowdale.
CHILDREN: not under 16.
DOGS: not allowed.
CREDIT CARDS: MC, Visa.
PRICES: per room B&B double £160–£210. Set dinner £45. Min. 2-night bookings except by special arrangement.

# BORROWDALE Cumbria

## LEATHES HEAD HOTEL

In a 'wonderful location', with uninterrupted valley and fell views, this Edwardian country house is an elegant retreat for outdoors lovers who appreciate their creature comforts. There's a log-burner in the lounge, glorious views from the conservatory dining room, and a terrace for afternoon tea; a great spot for admiring the three-acre garden with its birds and wildlife. 'We often saw red squirrels prancing on the wall opposite.' Bedrooms are lightly traditional, with pale colours, soft carpets and a contemporary bathroom. There is much praise for chef Noel Breaks's 'excellent' cooking, focusing on locally grown, reared and foraged produce, although readers point out that dinner is a short-choice menu that changes only seasonally. Lamb from nearby Yew Tree Farm was 'tender and full of flavour'. There is home-made bread at the nicely presented breakfast which will set you up for a day's exploring; many walks are from the doorstep. 'A really nice, relaxed atmosphere about the hotel; staff were delightful, attentive without overdoing it.' (John Barnes, Sara Price)

Borrowdale
Keswick CA12 5UY

T: 01768 777247
E: reservations@leatheshead.co.uk
w: leatheshead.co.uk

BEDROOMS: 11. Some on ground floor, 1 suitable for disabled.
OPEN: all year except Christmas and Jan (but open New Year).
FACILITIES: lounge, bar, conservatory restaurant, in-room TV (Freeview), civil wedding licence, drying room, terrace, 3-acre grounds, public rooms wheelchair accessible.
BACKGROUND MUSIC: in public rooms.
LOCATION: 4½ miles S of Keswick.
CHILDREN: not under 15.
DOGS: not allowed.
CREDIT CARDS: Amex, MC, Visa.
PRICES: per room B&B £150–£240, D,B&B £190–£300. Set 4-course dinner £42.95. 1-night bookings refused Sat, May–Sept.

# BOSCASTLE Cornwall                    MAP 1:C3

## THE OLD RECTORY

The old rector was none other than the great-grandfather of Sally Searle, who, with husband Chris, welcomes guests to their loved and lived-in Victorian home. Here, too, in 1870 Thomas Hardy met his first wife, Emma Gifford. The Searles are energetic hosts, maintaining the walled garden, keeping ducks, hens, bees, rare breed pigs and Jacob sheep. They grow fruit and vegetables, make sausages, cure bacon, and collect eggs and honey. House bedrooms are furnished with antiques. All have 'comfort and charm'. The Stables has a rustic feel, the Rector's Room has a whirlpool bath with shower over it. 'We had Emma's Room, overlooking the super garden; it was really spacious, with extra blankets, a full tray with teapot, a glorious modern wet room' and original 'thunderbox' loo, 'fully working, of course'. At breakfast there is Cornish bacon and hog's pudding, home-grown tomatoes, locally smoked fish, Cornish rarebit and much more. At night they will drive you to a local restaurant of your choice. 'It felt almost like staying with a friend.'

St Juliot
Boscastle PL35 0BT

T: 01840 250225
E: sally@stjuliot.com
W: stjuliot.com

BEDROOMS: 4. 1 in Stables (connected to house via conservatory and with separate entrance).
OPEN: normally Feb–end Oct, 'but please check', limited evening meals by arrangement.
FACILITIES: sitting room, breakfast room, conservatory, in-room TV (Freeview), 3-acre garden (croquet lawn, 'lookout', walled kitchen garden), electric charging point, unsuitable for disabled.
BACKGROUND MUSIC: none.
LOCATION: 2 miles NE of Boscastle.
CHILDREN: not under 12.
DOGS: up to 2 allowed, only in stable room (£10 per dog/stay).
CREDIT CARDS: Amex, MC, Visa.
PRICES: per room B&B single £72–£108, double £95–£120. 1-night bookings only accepted if a late vacancy or quiet period.

# BOSHAM Sussex

MAP 2:E3

## THE MILLSTREAM

In an 'adorable' South Coast village, and just a short walk from Bosham Quay, this family-run hotel stands set back from the road, in pretty gardens bisected by a stream. The building centres on a conversion of three workmen's cottages, with a modern extension. We hear a smattering of applause this year from readers praising the 'very helpful, pleasant' staff, the 'super-high standard', and even the 'softest water and softest towels'. Some bedrooms are traditionally styled, others more contemporary. Across the stream are two suites with private patio in a separate thatched cottage. Extras include a coffee machine and mini-fridge with fresh milk, paraben-free toiletries and 24-hour room service. You can eat such dishes as bream fillet with shellfish bisque and crab beignet in the elegant dining room, or more cheaply in the modern brasserie, with striped chairs and bare-wood floor (tempura cod and chips, lamb tagine, vegan options). Breakfast brings free-range eggs, local sausages, smoked haddock and waffles with maple syrup. 'Gorgeous food well presented, and comfortable without pretension.' (IM, and others)

Bosham Lane
Bosham
Chichester PO18 8HL

T: 01243 573234
E: info@millstream-hotel.co.uk
W: millstreamhotel.com

BEDROOMS: 35. 2 in cottage, 7 on ground floor, 2 suitable for disabled.
OPEN: all year.
FACILITIES: lounge, bar, restaurant, brasserie, conference room, in-room TV (Freeview), civil wedding licence, front lawn (alfresco dining), residents' garden (stream, gazebo), public areas wheelchair accessible.
BACKGROUND MUSIC: all day in bar, lounge and restaurants.
LOCATION: 4 miles W of Chichester.
CHILDREN: all ages welcomed.
DOGS: not allowed.
CREDIT CARDS: MC, Visa.
PRICES: per room B&B single £86–£212, double £122–£245, D,B&B £180–£310. À la carte (restaurant) £43, (brasserie) £27. 1-night bookings sometimes refused Sat.

# BOWNESS-ON-WINDERMERE Cumbria    MAP 4: inset C2

## LINDETH FELL

With glorious views of Windermere and seven
acres of spectacular grounds, this guest house feels
more like a country house hotel, complete with
wood panelling and ornate ceilings. Yet while 'the
style is gracious', it is 'never hushed and formal' in
the Edwardian house which Diana Kennedy and
her daughters have transformed into a relaxed
and welcoming haven. A scattering of family
books and photographs can be found among the
large sofas and plump window seats. These make
the perfect place for the cream tea offered on
arrival, which features 'Diana's legendary scones'.
Bedrooms are more contemporary: there are bold
wallpapers, smart armchairs and pale carpets.
'Lots of thoughtful extras' include sherry, iced
water, digital radio, robes and coffee machines.
Throughout the day, soup, sandwiches and cake
are available, all deliciously home made. You can
enjoy them on the terrace if it's sunny, or in the
dining room, where the picture windows overlook
the lovely gardens. Handsome supper platters
can be pre-ordered, as can a popular Sunday
lunch, 'cooked with such flair by Jo Kennedy'.
(Ralph Wilson, HP)

---

### 25% DISCOUNT VOUCHERS

Lyth Valley Road
Bowness-on-Windermere LA23 3JP

T: 015394 43286
E: kennedy@lindethfell.co.uk
W: lindethfell.co.uk

BEDROOMS: 14. 1, on ground floor,
suitable for disabled.
OPEN: all year except 24–26 Dec,
3 Jan–11 Feb, open New Year.
FACILITIES: 2 lounges, bar, entrance
hall with seating, dining room, in-
room TV (Freeview), 7-acre grounds
(terrace, gardens, lawn games),
complimentary access to local gym,
spa, pool 10 mins' drive away.
BACKGROUND MUSIC: classical in dining
room, bar.
LOCATION: 1 mile S of Bowness.
CHILDREN: all ages welcomed.
DOGS: only assistance dogs allowed.
CREDIT CARDS: MC, Visa.
PRICES: per room B&B single £69–£120,
double £139–£290. Pre-ordered
Sunday lunch £24.50, evening platters
£14.50. 1-night bookings sometimes
refused.

# BRADFORD-ON-AVON Wiltshire

MAP 2:D1

## WIDBROOK GRANGE

'Staying here was an experience,' wrote Guide inspectors of Nick Dent's Georgian farmhouse hotel, which is so dog-friendly it even hosts doggie birthday parties, and where creative reuse has been raised to an art form. A scrap-metal horse crops the grass. A sheep sports a spark-plug fleece. Within, even a bicycle has been upcycled as a washstand. The decor is 'genuinely rustic, with wooden boxes piled up to form shelving … lots of interesting visual stimuli'. Yet there is nothing Steptoe here. House and annexe bedrooms have modern comforts, maybe an in-room roll-top bath, an emperor bed, 'crisp bedlinens', Bramley toiletries. There is a gin bar off 'a clubby sitting room', while in the restaurant gin features along with home-grown produce in many of Sandor Szucs's dishes. For instance, ham-wrapped monkfish with a saffron gin sauce, or pear and mango cake, blackberry mousse, mulberry gin sorbet. A kids' menu is mercifully free of mother's ruin. Meanwhile, four-legged friends can tuck into sausages at breakfast, have afternoon tea, or hold a party, with optional bow ties and neckerchiefs along with a menu of cookies and cakes.

Trowbridge Road
Bradford-on-Avon BA15 1UH

T: 01225 864750
E: stay@widbrookgrange.com
W: widbrookgrange.com

BEDROOMS: 19. 15 in outbuildings, 1 suitable for disabled.
OPEN: all year.
FACILITIES: gin bar, snug, restaurant, conservatory, in-room TV (Freeview), civil wedding licence, function facilities, 11-acre grounds, 11-metre indoor heated swimming pool, gym, giant chess, parking, public rooms wheelchair accessible, no adapted toilet.
BACKGROUND MUSIC: soft, all day in public rooms.
LOCATION: 2 miles S of Bradford-on-Avon.
CHILDREN: all ages welcomed.
DOGS: allowed in certain bedrooms (£15 per dog per night), public rooms, not restaurant.
CREDIT CARDS: Amex, MC, Visa.
PRICES: per room B&B double £155–£215, D,B&B £225–£285. À la carte £40, tasting menu £59.

**SEE ALSO SHORTLIST**

# BRADFORD-ON-AVON Wiltshire                    MAP 2:D1

## WOOLLEY GRANGE

Fun time, mucking-in time and adult 'me time' are all part of the deal at this rambling Jacobean manor turned child-friendly and dog-friendly hotel, with extensive grounds. It was the first venture for Nigel Chapman's popular Luxury Family Hotels (see also Fowey Hall, Fowey, and Moonfleet Manor, Fleet), and while the business has been sold, we are promised that it will be pleasure as usual. The house is 'beautiful but quirkily unstuffy', with unusual touches: a fairground carousel bear here, a sphinx there. Lounges have blazing fires, baggy sofas – and toy boxes. Family and interconnecting bedrooms, baby video monitoring, babysitting, an Ofsted crèche, games room, swimming pools and a spa make for complete relaxation. The children won't be bored, with nature trails, fruit to pick, eggs to collect and even soap-making and pond-dipping. They can enjoy high tea or family meals in the orangery, with candlelit fine dining using a wealth of home-grown produce for adults. A trusted reader this year enjoyed a birthday celebration: 'The staff were fantastic, helpful at every stage; the food was delicious.' (Fiona Miller)

Woolley Green
Bradford-on-Avon BA15 1TX

T: 01225 864705
E: info@woolleygrangehotel.co.uk
W: woolleygrangehotel.co.uk

BEDROOMS: 25. 11 in annexes, 2 on ground floor, 1 suitable for disabled.
OPEN: all year.
FACILITIES: 2 lounges, 2 restaurants, cinema, 2 private dining rooms, in-room TV (Freeview), crèche, spa, heated indoor and outdoor swimming pools, civil wedding licence, 14-acre grounds, wheelchair accessible.
BACKGROUND MUSIC: in restaurants.
LOCATION: 1 mile NE of Bradford-on-Avon, 8½ miles SE of Bath.
CHILDREN: all ages welcomed.
DOGS: allowed in bedrooms, public rooms, not restaurants.
CREDIT CARDS: Amex, MC, Visa.
PRICES: per room B&B double £179–£319, family £219–£469. Fixed-price dinner £37.50, à la carte £40. 1-night bookings sometimes refused weekends.

SEE ALSO SHORTLIST

# BRAITHWAITE Cumbria

MAP 4: inset C2

## THE COTTAGE IN THE WOOD

Now with a Michelin star, this restaurant-with-rooms has confirmed its status as one of the Lake District's top foodie places – and is set in an enviably tranquil location. Liam and Kath Berney's 17th-century cottage, its surroundings teeming with wildlife, is tucked into woodland on Whinlatter Pass with views to Skiddaw. After a day's walking and canapés in the 'comfortable lounge', it's time to move into the candlelit restaurant for Ben Wilkinson's 'awesome dinners'. These make creative use of local produce: salt-baked beetroot with sheep's curd and horseradish, perhaps, or Eden Valley pork with shallot and black truffle. 'The iced cream cheese with strawberries was delicious,' one reader relates. Afterwards, you can retire to boutique-style bedrooms with shimmery wallpapers and pale-wood furnishings as well as fresh milk and home-made shortbread. Bigger rooms with the best fell views are 'light and airy, and very comfortable' but one had a 'tiny' bathroom. Breakfasts feature 'perfect eggs' although one reader bewails the 'lack of fresh orange juice' at this 'unique, special place'. (Sara Price, and others)

**25% DISCOUNT VOUCHERS**

Magic Hill
Whinlatter Forest
Braithwaite CA12 5TW

T: 01768 778409
E: relax@thecottageinthewood.co.uk
W: thecottageinthewood.co.uk

BEDROOMS: 9. 1 in the garden with separate entrance.
OPEN: all year except 25/26 Dec, 2nd and 3rd week Jan, closed Sun, Mon.
FACILITIES: lounge, restaurant, in-room TV (Freeview), drying room, secure bicycle storage, terraced garden, 2 acres of woodland, restaurant and public areas wheelchair accessible, adapted toilet.
BACKGROUND MUSIC: none.
LOCATION: 5 miles NW of Keswick.
CHILDREN: not under 10.
DOGS: not allowed.
CREDIT CARDS: MC, Visa.
PRICES: per room D,B&B double £230–£320. Set dinner £55, tasting menu £75. 1-night bookings refused weekends.

# BRAMPTON Cumbria

MAP 4:B3

## FARLAM HALL

**NEW**

Despite a change of ownership, this quintessential country house hotel in a peaceful Cumbrian village is still in safe hands, report readers. After 44 years in the Quinion family, the Relais & Châteaux member is now owned by Joseph Walter and Kathy Mares, previous guests of 20 years' standing, who ensure that the creeper-covered Victorian house maintains 'its sense of tradition'. Furnishings are in keeping with the period of the house – patterned and striped wallpapers, substantial sofas, fires in the sitting rooms – but with a light touch. Evening meals are 'a proper dining experience with canapés and petits fours' and might include Cumbrian venison tartare followed by shin of beef, as well as 'a proper cheese course' and a wine list with 'a good selection by the glass'. Large bedrooms are firmly traditional with big-patterned wallpapers, pelmeted curtains, armchairs and sofas, and a mix of reproduction and antique furniture. All rooms have garden views; most have a bath as well as a shower. 'Clearly a hotel with loyal guests,' concludes a reader who met one who returns every year 'despite the long drive from London'. (John Barnes)

**25% DISCOUNT VOUCHERS**

Hallbankgate
Brampton CA8 2NG

T: 01697 746234
E: farlam@farlamhall.co.uk
W: farlamhall.co.uk

BEDROOMS: 12. 2 on ground floor, 1 in stables 3 mins' walk from house.
OPEN: all year except 24–28 Dec (restaurant open Christmas Eve), 5–23 Jan.
FACILITIES: 2 lounges, restaurant, in-room TV (Freeview), civil wedding licence, 6-acre grounds, public rooms wheelchair accessible.
BACKGROUND MUSIC: in public areas, including restaurant.
LOCATION: on A689, 2½ miles SE of Brampton.
CHILDREN: all ages welcomed.
DOGS: allowed in bedrooms (not unattended), public rooms, but not in restaurant.
CREDIT CARDS: Amex, MC, Visa.
PRICES: per room B&B single £108–£155, double £210–£270, D,B&B single £165–£195, double £310–£370, À la carte £38, tasting menu £65.

# BRANCASTER STAITHE Norfolk

MAP 2:A5

## THE WHITE HORSE

♥ Previous César winner

You can dine in the conservatory or alfresco at the Nye family's hotel, and gaze across tidal salt marshes to the sea that supplied what is on your plate. The panoramic views, which take in Scolt Head Island, are even better appreciated now, after refurbishment of the conservatory, restaurant, dining area and bar, with the addition of larger paned windows. The bedrooms are also influenced by the landscape: all have a coastal palette of aquamarine, teal, lavender and sand, while eight garden rooms in an annexe have a sedum roof to blend into the surroundings. 'Lovely rooms,' writes a repeat visitor. 'Nice hotel, brilliant location.' Fran Hartshorne's menus are naturally strong on fish and shellfish. Expect such dishes as Staithe Smokehouse haddock, pan-fried hake with mussels and curried chowder, wild mushroom risotto. Our reader sent back his skate, which he found over-seasoned, but says 'food is generally very good' and 'they dealt with it well'. A breakfast of smoked salmon, kippers, roast ham, or a full English will set you up to walk the Norfolk Coast Path, which passes the foot of the garden. (Peter Anderson, and others)

Main Road
Brancaster Staithe PE31 8BY

T: 01485 210262
E: reception@whitehorsebrancaster.co.uk
W: whitehorsebrancaster.co.uk

BEDROOMS: 15. 8 on ground floor in annexe, 1 suitable for disabled.
OPEN: all year.
FACILITIES: open-plan bar, lounge areas, conservatory restaurant, dining room, in-room TV (Freeview), ½-acre garden (terrace, covered sunken garden), in-room therapies, public rooms wheelchair accessible, adapted toilet.
BACKGROUND MUSIC: 'subtle' in restaurant.
LOCATION: centre of village.
CHILDREN: all ages welcomed, children's menu, high chair.
DOGS: allowed in garden rooms (£10 per night), bar.
CREDIT CARDS: Amex, MC, Visa.
PRICES: per room B&B £120–£240. À la carte £33.

# BRIGHTON Sussex                                    MAP 2:E4

## ARTIST RESIDENCE BRIGHTON

Right-on Brighton rocks to a bohemian rhythm, encapsulated by Charlotte and Justin Salisbury's mural-bedaubed hotel on a Regency square with view to the eerie remains of the West Pier. The quirky style for four further hotels was set here in 2008, when Justin invited artists to decorate his parents' B&B in exchange for free board. You might go for a small sea-view room with work by street artists and upcycled furniture, or trade up to a master room with a balcony, a bespoke super-king-size four-poster, and a copper roll-top bath for two. In either, you'll have a Roberts radio, a minibar, an espresso machine and organic Bramley toiletries. One reader's room had the 'perfect view down to the i360', another a 'small but well-equipped bathroom'. There is informal dining from lunch through to dinner in The Set restaurant, from a menu of such dishes as bream bisque with fennel, and venison with pear and shallots, while drinks are served in The Fix bar. Breakfast brings 'tasty cooked dishes', including a full vegan with sourdough from Flint Owl Bakery in Lewes, home-smoked salmon with kimchi hollandaise. (D and JB, and others)

34 Regency Square
Brighton BN1 2FJ

T: 01273 324302
E: brighton@artistresidence.co.uk
W: artistresidence.co.uk

BEDROOMS: 24.
OPEN: all year, restaurant closed 25/26 Dec.
FACILITIES: lift, lounge, cocktail bar, private bar (events), restaurant, ping-pong/meeting room, in-room TV (Freeview), unsuitable for disabled.
BACKGROUND MUSIC: in public areas.
LOCATION: town centre.
CHILDREN: all ages welcomed (under-16s not unsupervised in bedrooms).
DOGS: allowed in some bedrooms (£15 per dog per night).
CREDIT CARDS: Amex, MC, Visa.
PRICES: per room double £89–£275. Cooked breakfast from £7.50, full English £12, vegetarian/vegan £11, fixed-price menu (Mon–Sat) £34–£38, à la carte £32. 1-night bookings refused weekends.

**SEE ALSO SHORTLIST**

# BRIGHTON Sussex

MAP 2:E4

## DRAKES

'A really memorable experience without stuffiness or formality,' write our trusted reviewers of this stylish boutique hotel on Brighton's Marine Parade. After a warm welcome, they were shown to a 'light and airy' sea-facing room on the first floor with three floor-to-ceiling bay windows giving it the feel of an observation deck – a telescope is helpfully provided. Traffic noise from the busy road outside was 'not too intrusive and we slept soundly'. All rooms are beautifully furnished with handcrafted beds and designer fabrics, some with a bathtub in the bay window, and generously stocked with luxury items, including cafetière with freshly ground coffee, complimentary slippers, waffle dressing gowns and White Company toiletries. In the elegant restaurant, chef Andy Vitez serves 'truly delicious' dishes, including the 'most tender beef' one reader had ever eaten, though 'only one dish (out of five) on the menu changed over our three-night stay'. The true strength of Drakes lies in its 'friendly, enthusiastic and helpful' staff. 'Whatever we requested, they delivered.' (Andy and Sylvia Aitken)

**25% DISCOUNT VOUCHERS**

43–44 Marine Parade
Brighton BN2 1PE

T: 01273 696934
E: info@drakesofbrighton.com
W: drakesofbrighton.com

BEDROOMS: 20.
OPEN: all year.
FACILITIES: lounge/bar, restaurant, meeting/private dining room, in-room TV (Sky), civil wedding licence, off-road parking, unsuitable for disabled.
BACKGROUND MUSIC: in bar and restaurant.
LOCATION: ½ mile from centre, on seafront.
CHILDREN: all ages welcomed.
DOGS: only assistance dogs allowed.
CREDIT CARDS: Amex, MC, Visa.
PRICES: room only £120–£360, DB&B £190–£430. Breakfast £7.50–£15, 5-course tasting menu £65, table d'hôte menu £40–£50. Min. 2-night stay Sat, but check availability.

**SEE ALSO SHORTLIST**

# BRISTOL

MAP 1:B6

## BROOKS GUESTHOUSE

A stroll from the harbour and Old Vic, Carla and
Andrew Brooks's imaginative conversion of a
1950s office block impressed our inspectors this
year. 'It has a touch of pizzazz, with improbable
silver caravans gleaming on its roof,' providing
novel accommodation, and 'fun for a family'. A
courtyard garden is planted with 'hedge shrubs
and lavender'. A double room (some are king-
size) was 'neat, well lit and tastefully decorated
with classily understated' Cole & Son floral
wallpaper. There was some criticism of poor
luggage space and absent-minded housekeeping,
and a small shower room was 'just about
adequate' and could have done with better
lighting. Still, the open-plan lounge/breakfast
room had 'rugs on polished floors, chairs and
sofas grouped around old travelling trunks'. A
'well-executed, freshly cooked' breakfast included
'vegan options and a range of less usual dishes,
organic jams and compotes, and daily specials
chalked on a blackboard'. Overall, it is terrific
value and perfect for younger guests. 'We'd be
happy to recommend it.'

Exchange Avenue
St Nicholas Market
Bristol BS1 1UB

T: 0117 930 0066
E: info@brooksguesthousebristol.com
W: brooksguesthousebristol.com

BEDROOMS: 27. 4 in Airstream-style
caravans on roof.
OPEN: all year except 24–26 Dec.
FACILITIES: lift, lounge/breakfast room,
honesty bar, in-room TV (Freeview),
courtyard and rooftop garden,
unsuitable for disabled.
BACKGROUND MUSIC: in lounge and
breakfast area.
LOCATION: central, next to St Nicholas
Market.
CHILDREN: all ages welcomed.
DOGS: only assistance dogs.
CREDIT CARDS: Amex, MC, Visa.
PRICES: per room B&B single £80–£150,
double £89–£112, triple £89–£130,
caravans £99–£148. Min. 2-night
stay Sat.

# BRISTOL

MAP 1:B6

## NUMBER THIRTY EIGHT CLIFTON

♕ Previous César winner

Everything was shipshape and Bristol fashionable at Adam Dorrien-Smith's 'handsome, double-fronted' Georgian merchant's house turned boutique B&B when our inspector visited. 'At one of the highest points of the city, it overlooks the wide sweep of the downs on one side, rooftops and distant hills on the other.' Bedrooms and suites are 'deeply comfortable', styled with 'unfussy good taste' and some with wood panelling. A large loft suite with 'a spectacular outlook' had a bath and walk-in shower. The smallest rooms have just a shower, but all have a super-king-size bed, a minibar fridge and 100 Acres bath products. A rear terrace with outdoor seating is 'reached via rather precipitous stairs'. You can order a cocktail in the lounge until 8 pm, when the 'friendly and efficient' staff stand down. They can also recommend great restaurants. At breakfast there is a buffet with fresh pastries, 'delicious compote and granola'. A cooked breakfast, charged extra and 'well worth it', includes free-range eggs and smashed avocado on sourdough with bacon. 'Try to nab a table with a view', and request a parking permit when you book.

38 Upper Belgrave Road
Clifton
Bristol BS8 2XN

T: 0117 946 6905
E: info@number38clifton.com
W: number38clifton.com

BEDROOMS: 12.
OPEN: all year.
FACILITIES: lounge, breakfast room, meeting space, in-room TV (Freeview), terrace, limited number of parking permits on request, unsuitable for disabled.
BACKGROUND MUSIC: in public areas 8 am–8 pm.
LOCATION: 2½ miles from city centre.
CHILDREN: not under 12.
DOGS: not allowed.
CREDIT CARDS: Amex, MC, Visa.
PRICES: per room B&B single £115–£240, double £130–£255, cooked breakfast £5 surcharge.

# BRISTOL

## OLD CHURCH FARM  **NEW**

You know it's going to be grand when you hear that this 16th-century manor, 'an attractive and characterful house', was formerly a hospitality venue for Rolls-Royce. Today, under owners Christopher Trim and Kathryn Warner, it has become 'five-star hotel meets the very best of British B&Bs'. In the grounds there is a conference centre, a skittle alley, the tower of ruined St Helen's church, rose gardens, a fishpond with fountain, croquet lawn and walled kitchen garden. Our inspectors' bedroom was 'spacious', and 'handsomely furnished', with some antiques and a king-size bed with Hypnos mattress, although lighting was 'slightly too dim for comfortable reading'. Music is provided courtesy of Alexa devices. Public rooms have a wealth of original features, including 'remarkable plaster ceilings'. One depicts a pelican, a Christian symbol of self-sacrifice, but there is no need to tighten your belt as you sit down at the same table with fellow guests for a breakfast or dinner cooked by Cordon Bleu-trained Kathryn, in which local, seasonal and home-grown ingredients shine. (Emma Hooper, and others)

Church Road
Rudgeway
Bristol BS35 3SQ

T: 01454 418212
E: stay@old-church-farm.co.uk
W: old-church-farm.co.uk

BEDROOMS: 7.
OPEN: all year.
FACILITIES: snug, drawing room, breakfast room, dining room, in-room TV (Freeview), conference facilities, civil wedding licence, croquet, table tennis, terrace, 8-acre gardens, only conference centre wheelchair accessible, adapted toilet.
BACKGROUND MUSIC: classical or guests' own choice, in drawing room, dining room.
LOCATION: 12 miles N of Bristol, on the edge of a south Gloucestershire village.
CHILDREN: not under 12.
DOGS: not allowed.
CREDIT CARDS: Amex, MC, Visa.
PRICES: room only, single £130–£240, double £150–£240. Breakfast £15, set dinner £32.50. 1-night bookings refused weekends May–Sept.

# BROADWAY Worcestershire

MAP 3:D6

## THE BROADWAY HOTEL

Golden stone abuts Tudor black-and-white at this historic hotel, which has a large terrace for alfresco dining overlooking a picture-postcard village green. The first of the Cotswold Inns and Hotels group, it was not part of Fuller's takeover, and is still owned by Michael and Pamela Horton. Our inspectors found it very professionally run under manager Richard Tebay. A horsey theme runs throughout, referencing the proximity of Cheltenham Racecourse. Bedrooms – some in the 15th-century part of the building – have original features, modern fabrics, some antiques, maybe a wall of GranDeco Library wallpaper behind a four-poster. All rooms have Molton Brown toiletries and an espresso machine. Dining options are flexible, from a club sandwich in the galleried Jockey bar, or a grilled Barnsley chop from the all-day garden menu, to such dishes as pan-roast hake loin with shellfish bouillabaisse from chef Eric Worger's menu in Tattersall's Brasserie. Breakfast brings freshly squeezed orange juice, smoked haddock and a full English with hash brown and black pudding. The hotel makes a good base for a tour of the Cotswolds.

The Green
Broadway WR12 7AA

T: 01386 852401
E: reception@broadway-hotel.co.uk
W: broadway-hotel.co.uk

BEDROOMS: 19. 1 on ground floor.
2 self-catering cottages nearby.
OPEN: all year.
FACILITIES: sitting room, bar, brasserie, in-room TV (Freeview), courtyard, garden (residents-only terrace), car park (electric charging point), unsuitable for disabled.
BACKGROUND MUSIC: ambient in public areas.
LOCATION: village centre, 'best to request a parking space before you arrive, especially in summer'.
CHILDREN: all ages welcomed (children's menu).
DOGS: well-behaved dogs allowed in some bedrooms and in public areas, not in restaurant.
CREDIT CARDS: Amex, MC, Visa.
PRICES: per room B&B £150–£290, D,B&B £223–£363. À la carte £39.

**SEE ALSO SHORTLIST**

# BROADWAY Worcestershire                    MAP 3:D6

## THE LYGON ARMS

An impressive list of famous guests, including
both Charles I and Oliver Cromwell, have
stayed at this rambling Tudor coaching inn
with beams and inglenooks, panelled walls and
leaded windows. Edward VII motored down
in 1905. Evelyn Waugh visited, and no doubt
revisited. It was in the doldrums when Iconic
Luxury Hotels (see also Chewton Glen, New
Milton, and Cliveden House, Taplow) came to
the rescue in 2017. Today it offers a wide choice
of accommodation, from doubles furnished
with antiques and paintings to four-poster
suites. Modern, airy courtyard suites open
on to landscaped terraced gardens. Despite
refurbishment and redesign of the 'wonderful
building', adding a spa and a 13-metre indoor
pool, a reader noted a chipped bath, and reported
that 'the air con sounded like Concorde'. The
ambience is family-friendly. You can take tea by
the fire or alfresco, order panini and pizzette in
the wine bar, or dine on such classics as fish and
chips or beef Wellington in the Grill, its walls
crammed with historic portraits. 'Our meal was
fine. Italian friends were astonished by the natural
beauty of the surroundings and loved the place.'
(Jonathan Rose, and others)

High Street
Broadway WR12 7DU

T: 01386 852255
E: reservations@lygonarmshotel.
co.uk
W: lygonarmshotel.co.uk

BEDROOMS: 86. 26 on ground floor,
some in cottages, some courtyard
suites, 2 suitable for disabled.
OPEN: all year.
FACILITIES: 7 lounge areas, wine bar/
restaurant, bar/grill, cocktail bar,
in-room TV (Freeview), civil wedding
licence, 3-acre garden, indoor pool,
spa, public areas (not spa) wheelchair
accessible, adapted toilet.
BACKGROUND MUSIC: in lounges.
LOCATION: village centre.
CHILDREN: all ages welcomed.
DOGS: in some bedrooms, all lounges
(£25 per dog per night).
CREDIT CARDS: Amex, MC, Visa.
PRICES: per room B&B £195–£465.
À la carte £40. 1-night bookings
sometimes refused Sat, always at
Christmas/New Year.

**SEE ALSO SHORTLIST**

# BROADWAY Worcestershire

MAP 3:D6

## RUSSELL'S

Tables are set for some seriously good dining at Andrew and Gaynor Riley's restaurant-with-rooms, occupying the former showroom of Sir Gordon Russell, wartime pioneer of utility furniture, in a picture-postcard Cotswold village. In the years since our inspector found Russell's tip-top in every respect, we have heard no dissenting word. Immaculate bedrooms have a smart natural-stone bathroom with luxury toiletries. A spacious suite has exposed stone and timbers, a spa bath and walk-through shower, with no hint of make-do-and-mend. Nor will you need ration books at lunch and dinner, when Jorge Santos uses local produce, Cotswold meats and game in such dishes as pan-fried guineafowl breast in Parma ham with pistachio-crumb confit leg, pickled beluga and tarragon jus. Items on the veggie menu might include Vale of Evesham asparagus or wild mushroom and spinach pithivier. But, for days when only fish and chips will do, Russell's also has a first-rate chippy nearby, serving the usual fried fish, plus a catch of the day, prawn cocktail and lemon and herb squid. 'Delicious fishcakes' were 'efficiently served'. Reports, please.

**25% DISCOUNT VOUCHERS**

20 High Street
Broadway WR12 7DT

T: 01386 853555
E: info@russellsofbroadway.co.uk
W: russellsofbroadway.co.uk

BEDROOMS: 7. 3 in adjoining building, 2 on ground floor.
OPEN: all year, restaurant closed Sun evening and bank holiday Mon.
FACILITIES: residents' lounge, bar, restaurant, private dining room, in-room TV (Freeview), patio (heating, meal service), restaurant and bar wheelchair accessible.
BACKGROUND MUSIC: in restaurant.
LOCATION: village centre.
CHILDREN: all ages welcomed, under-2s stay free.
DOGS: allowed in certain bedrooms, some areas of restaurant.
CREDIT CARDS: MC, Visa.
PRICES: per room B&B £140–£300. Set dinner (Mon–Fri) £25–£29, à la carte £55, vegan £32. 1-night bookings refused weekends.

**SEE ALSO SHORTLIST**

# BROCKENHURST Hampshire                    MAP 2:E2

## DAISYBANK COTTAGE    NEW

Deep in the New Forest, Ciaran and Cheryl
Maher have created a smart B&B in an Arts and
Crafts, Charles Rennie Mackintosh-inspired
house. It gains a full entry this year on the
strength of glowing reports. 'Ciaran and Cheryl
are the best hosts, so friendly and kind,' writes one
reader. 'They enjoy spoiling their guests, and love
to share their local knowledge.' The bedrooms
are 'amazing, with special added touches'.
All have an espresso machine, a mini-fridge,
handmade chocolates and luxury bath products.
The Marryat Suite, opening on to the garden,
has a copy of Captain Marryat's classic, The
Children of the New Forest. In the Gardener's
Cottage, redesigned by an award-winning local
architect, the Dandelion Suite has under-floor
heating, a volcanic-limestone bath, a separate rain
shower and a private patio. The breakfast, too, is
'amazing', another reader writes. You are asked
to order the night before from a menu of farm
produce, home-made granola, American pancakes
with maple syrup, free-range eggs, gluten-free and
vegan options. 'Our only advice is to stay longer.'

### 25% DISCOUNT VOUCHERS

Sway Road
Brockenhurst SO42 7SG

T: 01590 622086
E: info@bedandbreakfast-newforest.
  co.uk
W: bedandbreakfast-newforest.co.uk

BEDROOMS: 8. 2 in Gardener's Cottage,
all on ground floor, plus 1-bed
shepherd's hut available Apr–Sept,
some suitable for disabled but not
fully adapted.
OPEN: all year, except 1 week over
Christmas.
FACILITIES: 2 sitting rooms, breakfast
room, in-room TV (Freeview), ½-acre
garden, parking.
BACKGROUND MUSIC: none.
LOCATION: ¾ mile S of Brockenhurst
village.
CHILDREN: over-7s welcomed.
DOGS: not allowed.
CREDIT CARDS: MC, Visa.
PRICES: per room B&B single £95–£155,
double £110–£165. 2-night min. stay
preferred weekends.

# BROCKENHURST Hampshire

MAP 2:E2

## THE PIG IN THE FOREST

This year marks the tenth anniversary of the opening of Robin Hutson's mother Pig, in a New Forest hunting lodge, and it seems 'on better form than ever', writes a trusted reader after an annual visit. With food sourced from its bountiful kitchen gardens and within a 25-mile radius, this first Pig saw the creation of the smallholding's signature rustic-chic style (for other Pigs, see index). Judy Hutson designed the interiors for an imaginary Great-Aunt Maud, an easy-going old bird and a bit of a tippler, to judge by the wide choice of libations in the bar. Choose a bedroom in the main house or the grounds – perhaps a forest hut with floor-to-ceiling windows and private terrace, or a cabin with four-poster, in-room bath and monsoon shower. Wherever you stay, service is 'excellent': 'What's most striking is the flexibility and initiative of the many young staff.' The food is 'truly outstanding and original without being pretentious', say Guide insiders. As well as dishes such as Salisbury veal with hazelnuts and pickled shallots, there are plenty of options for vegetarians. (Anna Brewer, and others)

Beaulieu Road
Brockenhurst SO42 7QL

T: 01590 622354
E: info@thepighotel.com
W: thepighotel.com

BEDROOMS: 32. 10 in stable block (100 yds), some on ground floor, 2 lodges and a cabin in the garden, 1 courtyard room suitable for disabled.
OPEN: all year.
FACILITIES: lounge, library, bar, restaurant, in-room TV (Freeview), civil wedding licence, treatment rooms, kitchen garden, 6-acre grounds, public rooms wheelchair accessible, adapted toilet.
BACKGROUND MUSIC: in public areas.
LOCATION: 1 mile E of Brockenhurst village.
CHILDREN: all ages welcomed.
DOGS: guide dogs only.
CREDIT CARDS: Amex, MC, Visa.
PRICES: per room £185–£499. Breakfast £12–£16, à la carte £35. 1-night bookings refused at weekends, Christmas, New Year.

# BRUTON Somerset

## THE NEWT IN SOMERSET    `NEW`

Palladian Hadspen House, home to the Hobhouse
family from 1785, and to gardener Penelope
Hobhouse until 1979, is now a luxurious
country house hotel. It stands on an estate with
orchards, gardens and deer park, cyder press
and bar. The name refers not to the famously
bibulous amphibians, but to the protected great
crested newts discovered on site. Interiors
have been designed by Karen Roos, wife of
South African billionaire owner Koos Bekker,
whose Babylonstoren Cape farm estate is world
renowned. House bedrooms have antique
furniture, original Georgian features, a smart
bathroom and well-stocked larder. Rooms in
converted outbuildings are styled with a sense
of fun. Stable rooms take rustic-chic to a new
level, with heritage stalls, a wood-burning stove
and a roll-top copper bath. In the Botanical
Rooms, ingredients from the estate appear on
menus composed by chef Ben Abercrombie and
depending on what was picked in the morning.
There is plant-based fare in the Garden Café, and
a walled garden with 267 apple varieties, a farm
shop, bakery, cheese room, and much more.

Bruton
Castle Cary BA7 7NG

T: 01963 577777
E: reservations@thenewtinsomerset.
   com
W: thenewtinsomerset.com

BEDROOMS: 23. 10 in converted
outbuildings. 1 suitable for disabled.
OPEN: all year.
FACILITIES: restaurant, bar, lounge,
drawing room, library, lift, in-room
TV (Sky), spa (hydrotherapy pools,
swimming pool), 300-acre estate
(parkland, woods, orchards, café,
cyder bar, farm shop), restaurant and
bar wheelchair accessible, adapted
toilet.
BACKGROUND MUSIC: in public rooms.
LOCATION: on the A359 between Castle
Cary and Bruton.
CHILDREN: all ages welcomed, allocated
times for children's swimming and
dining in restaurant, babysitting by
arrangement.
DOGS: not allowed.
CREDIT CARDS: Amex, MC, Visa.
PRICES: per room B&B £275–£450,
D,B&B £365–£540.

**SEE ALSO SHORTLIST**

# BRYHER Isles of Scilly

MAP 1: inset C1

## HELL BAY HOTEL

♋ Previous César winner

New England meets Newquay at the UK's most westerly hotel, a stylish coastal retreat 30 miles from the Cornish mainland, on the smallest of the inhabited Isles of Scilly. Once a pub (before that a farmhouse), overlooking a quiet cove on the island's rugged Atlantic coast, it's part of Robert Dorrien-Smith's Tresco Estate. The public rooms and bedrooms provide the perfect backdrop for the family's collection of Cornish art. Most of the clapboard suites, some with a patio or balcony, have sea views. The Emperor Suite has a private decked area with sun loungers and a white picket fence. All rooms are 'beautifully decorated', and have an upmarket beach house aesthetic, the Caribbean blue of the external woodwork reflected in the bright and breezy furnishings. Equally upmarket is Richard Kearsley's cooking which makes the most of fresh island produce, including Bryher lobster and Tresco beef. Or head down to the Crab Shack housed in an old net loft for Bryher crab, mussels and scallops, served with chips and salad and followed by Eton mess.

Bryher TR23 0PR

T: 01720 422947
E: contactus@hellbay.co.uk
W: hellbay.co.uk

BEDROOMS: 25 suites. In 5 buildings, some on ground floor.
OPEN: 12 Mar–22 Oct.
FACILITIES: lounge, games room, bar, 2 dining rooms, in-room TV (Freeview), gym, treatment shed, yoga studio, grounds (heated swimming pool, playground), public rooms wheelchair accessible, adapted toilet (island reached by ferry).
BACKGROUND MUSIC: in the bar.
LOCATION: W side of island, boat from St Mary's (reached by boat/plane from mainland).
CHILDREN: all ages welcomed.
DOGS: allowed (charge) in bedrooms, bar, not in restaurant.
CREDIT CARDS: Amex, MC, Visa.
PRICES: per person B&B £95–£320, D,B&B double £145–£360. Set dinner £50. Min. 2-night weekend bookings.

# BUCKLAND MARSH Oxfordshire                    MAP 2:C2

## THE TROUT AT  **NEW**
## TADPOLE BRIDGE

You can mess about in boats with a fishing rod,
sip a pint of bitter in the sunshine or enjoy classic
gastropub fare at this cheerful pub-with-rooms
beside the Thames, with moorings that are free
to guests. Guide inspectors were enchanted by
the former 18th-century toll house's 'wonderful
setting by a narrow stone bridge', a large garden
running down to the riverside, and 'a welcome
that could not have been bettered' from manager
Tom Brady. Above the flagstoned and beamed bar
are three bedrooms. Another three are set around
a courtyard garden, each named after a fishing
fly. All are decorated in an individual rural style:
a large wooden or brass bed, vintage furniture,
and bathrooms with rain shower and eco-friendly
toiletries. Some have river views; others a record
player. Downstairs, the busy kitchen serves pub
favourites – beer-battered cod with triple-cooked
chips, burgers and steaks, and locally caught oak-
smoked trout. Breakfast brings cereals, pastries,
and a full range of cooked dishes 'all served
exactly as requested'. Small wonder the Trout is
reeling us in.

Buckland Road
Buckland Marsh SN7 8RF

T: 01367 870382
E: info@troutinn.co.uk
W: troutinn.co.uk

BEDROOMS: 6. 3 in courtyard garden.
OPEN: all year.
FACILITIES: bar, dining area, breakfast
area, private dining room, in-room
TV (Freeview), civil wedding
licence, 2-acre garden (pagoda, river,
moorings), public areas wheelchair
accessible, adapted toilet.
BACKGROUND MUSIC: in all public areas.
LOCATION: off the A420, 15 miles SW
of Oxford.
CHILDREN: all ages welcomed.
DOGS: allowed in 4 bedrooms (£15 per
dog per night), and public areas.
CREDIT CARDS: MC, Visa.
PRICES: per room B&B double
£120–£300. À la carte £33. 1-night
bookings refused Sat.

# BUDE Cornwall

MAP 1:C3

## THE BEACH

You can drink a cocktail on the sun terrace at Susie and Will Daniel's stay-and-play youthful, family-friendly hotel, and see when surf's up on Summerleaze Beach below. The Victorian hotel has been made over in New England style, with natural wood furniture, Lloyd Loom chairs and relaxing 'Fabbo and Ball' greys and whites. The bedrooms range from rear-facing super-king-size doubles or twins to sea-facing deluxe doubles, four with a private terrace. Superior rooms have a Juliet balcony. All rooms have a smart modern bathroom. There are now two suites, one sleeping four, with lounge and terrace, the other sleeping six, with a lounge and kitchen/diner. A reader who found the meals 'too big' need not fear. In the bar and restaurant, and alfresco, award-winning chef Jamie Coleman's menus comprise small, large and sharing plates, with a list for vegetarians and vegans. Typical dishes include lamb scrumpet with whipped goat curd, sea buckthorn and heritage carrots, scampi and fries with Bloody Mary ketchup, and chickpea and butternut squash burger. When the tide is out, Summerleaze's sea-bathing pool is revealed.

---

### 25% DISCOUNT VOUCHERS

Summerleaze Crescent
Bude EX23 8HJ

T: 01288 389800
E: enquiries@thebeachatbude.co.uk
W: thebeachatbude.co.uk

BEDROOMS: 18. 1 on ground floor, 2 family suites.
OPEN: all year except a few days over Christmas.
FACILITIES: lift, bar, lounge area, restaurant, in-room TV (Freeview), terrace, ground floor wheelchair accessible, adapted toilet.
BACKGROUND MUSIC: all day in public areas.
LOCATION: above Summerleaze beach.
CHILDREN: all ages welcomed, children's menu.
DOGS: allowed in 1 dog-friendly suite only, not in public areas except the terrace.
CREDIT CARDS: Amex, MC, Visa.
PRICES: per room B&B single £105–£235, double £125–£255, suite £295–£355. À la carte £30.

# BURFORD Oxfordshire

MAP 3:D6

## THE LAMB INN

The very model of an olde worlde inn, with its
flagstones, beams, blazing fires and jumbled
interiors, The Lamb sits on the edge of a picture-
perfect Cotswolds wool town, in the aptly named
Sheep Street. Cobbled together from ancient
weavers' cottages, it became a coaching inn in the
1700s, and is now owned by Fuller's. Individually
designed bedrooms have a mix of antique
furniture and contemporary styling, an espresso
machine, home-made flapjacks, and Molton
Brown toiletries. Allium suite, with views over the
walled garden and the grounds of Burford Priory,
has a plasma-screen TV over a roll-top bath in a
large bathroom. Shepherd, with antique four-
poster, is 'very comfortable', reports a reader, who
liked the 'friendly, helpful staff and the relaxing
atmosphere'. In the restaurant, you can eat dishes
such as roast pork belly with celeriac and potato
rösti and Toulouse sausage, or in the popular bar
or lounges, where 'delicious fare' includes beer-
battered haddock, fishcakes or sausage and mash.
Breakfast brings freshly squeezed juices, grilled
kippers with lemon, Wiltshire cured ham and
free-range eggs. (David Ganz)

Sheep Street
Burford OX18 4LR

T: 01993 823155
E: info@lambinn-burford.co.uk
W: cotswold-inns-hotels.co.uk/lamb

BEDROOMS: 17. 1 with private garden,
1 on ground floor.
OPEN: all year.
FACILITIES: 3 lounges, bar, restaurant,
in-room TV (Freeview), courtyard,
½-acre walled garden.
BACKGROUND MUSIC: subtle in all public
areas.
LOCATION: 500 yds from High Street.
CHILDREN: all ages welcomed.
DOGS: allowed by prior arrangement in
some bedrooms, bar, lounges, garden,
not in restaurant (£20 per night for
one, £10 for each additional dog).
CREDIT CARDS: Amex, MC, Visa.
PRICES: per room B&B single
£130–£210, double £160–£670, D,B&B
(double) £230–£740. À la carte £40.

SEE ALSO SHORTLIST

# BURTON BRADSTOCK Dorset

MAP 1:D6

## THE SEASIDE BOARDING HOUSE

Order a crab sandwich on the terrace, gaze out over Lyme Bay from this white-painted hotel above Chesil Beach, and you can half imagine you're in Edward Hopper's Cape Cod. The ironically named 'boarding house' is the creation of Mary-Lou Sturridge and Tony Mackintosh, formerly of London's Groucho Club, and it has a cool, laid-back ambience with 'efficient but relaxed staff'. The sea-facing bar and the restaurant, with its row of French windows, are light and airy, with bare floorboards and nautically themed art, while the library is positively snug. 'Bright, light, seasidey rooms' have touches of Edwardian style, a claw-footed bath or walk-in shower, cleverly chosen books and a Roberts radio. Each has at least an oblique sea view. Executive chef Alastair Little and head chef James Raybould devise seasonal menus, big on seafood – fish soup, mussels and chips, a half lobster – with maybe bavette steak or roast chicken. 'An excellent tasty meal.' A regular says there wasn't 'much choice at dinner this time' but adds she still wants 'to move down there for the summer'. (JB, and others)

Cliff Road
Burton Bradstock DT6 4RB

T: 01308 897205
E: info@theseasideboardinghouse.com
W: theseasideboardinghouse.com

BEDROOMS: 9.
OPEN: all year.
FACILITIES: cocktail bar, restaurant, library, function facilities, in-room TV on request, civil wedding licence, terrace, lawn, restaurant and bar wheelchair accessible.
BACKGROUND MUSIC: classical music in bar.
LOCATION: ½ mile from village centre, 3½ miles SE of Bridport.
CHILDREN: all ages welcomed.
DOGS: allowed in some bedrooms, bar, library and on terrace, not in restaurant.
CREDIT CARDS: Amex, MC, Visa.
PRICES: per room B&B single £200–£260, double £220–£280. À la carte £40. 1-night bookings refused Sat.

# BUXTON Derbyshire

MAP 4:E3

## THE ROSELEIGH

Swans glide on the lake in gardens laid out by
Joseph Paxton of Crystal Palace fame in front
of this bay-fronted Victorian home, close to the
opera house. Trusted readers who are repeat
visitors report again this year how much they love
both house and hospitality at Gerard and Maggi
Heelan's B&B. 'It's very attractive and richly –
and colourfully – decorated, in keeping with the
traditional style of the building and the area, with
lots of carpeting and soft furnishings.' Everywhere
there are leather armchairs, heavy drapes,
period furniture. However, another reader who
declared that the spa town of Buxton 'is a national
treasure' could only summon up an 'okay' for The
Roseleigh. No doubt a front-facing, dual-aspect
room would have been preferred to the ground-
floor, side-facing room that he found 'dark'.
The Heelans, former tour guides, are a mine of
local information, handy for exploring the Peak
District. At breakfast there are free-range eggs,
local jams and honey, a summer pudding made
with muesli, pear purée, yoghurt and fresh fruit.
(Stephen and Pauline Glover, and others)

19 Broad Walk
Buxton SK17 6JR

T: 01298 24904
E: enquiries@roseleighhotel.co.uk
W: roseleighhotel.co.uk

BEDROOMS: 13. 1 on ground floor,
1 single with private bathroom (not
en suite).
OPEN: 15 Jan–12 Dec.
FACILITIES: lounge (computer for
guests' use), breakfast room, in-room
TV (Freeview), parking, unsuitable
for disabled.
BACKGROUND MUSIC: classical/baroque
in breakfast room.
LOCATION: central.
CHILDREN: not under 6.
DOGS: not allowed.
CREDIT CARDS: MC, Visa.
PRICES: per room B&B single £55–£61,
double £90–£120. 1-night bookings
usually refused weekends, bank
holidays (call to check).

# CAMBER Sussex

MAP 2:E5

## THE GALLIVANT

A trusted reviewer had a 'great stay' in 2020 at this 'very welcoming' restaurant-with-rooms, a skimming stone's throw from the dunes of Camber Sands. Owner Harry Cragoe transformed the run-down motel into the epitome of Californian beach-chic just over a decade ago. Bright and breezy bedrooms, all on the ground floor, have direct or easy access to the garden. Baby Hampton rooms have light oak flooring, window seat and compact marble bathroom. New Garden rooms are more dramatic, with colourful detailing and wooden decking. Our reviewer's Luxury Garden room 'was well thought out, with sliding bathroom wall, and French windows looking on to a small garden'. New head chef is Jamie Guy, who cooks with locally sourced ingredients. A whole fish to share is a speciality: our reviewer's plaice was 'superb'. Other local delights might include Dungeness crab, Romney salt marsh lamb or braised Hastings cuttlefish. Breakfast brings everything to set you up for a day on the beach: home-made granola and fruit, a full English or perhaps avocado on toasted sourdough made in Rye. 'We are very happy here.' (Richard Bright, DH)

New Lydd Road
Camber TN31 7RB

T: 01797 225057
E: enquiries@thegallivant.co.uk
W: thegallivant.co.uk

BEDROOMS: 20. All on ground floor, 12 with direct access to garden.
OPEN: all year.
FACILITIES: bar, sitting room, reading room, restaurant, private dining room, in-room TV (Freeview), civil wedding licence, function facilities, spa treatment room, terrace, car park, 1-acre garden, restaurant and bar wheelchair accessible.
BACKGROUND MUSIC: in bar and restaurant.
LOCATION: 3¾ miles SE of Rye.
CHILDREN: up to 18 months and over-10s welcome, but not allowed in restaurant after 8 pm.
DOGS: allowed in some bedrooms, bar, terrace.
CREDIT CARDS: MC, Visa.
PRICES: per room B&B £145–£349, D,B&B £215–£419. À la carte £38.

# CAMBRIDGE Cambridgeshire

MAP 2:B4

## DUKE HOUSE

In a quiet neighbourhood of Victorian terraced houses on the edge of Christ's Pieces, this boutique B&B is well placed for those wishing to see the city. Previous owners include a notable computer scientist, and the current Duke of Gloucester, to whom the house owes not just its name but some of its architectural features, including the staircase. The 'very helpful' owners, Liz and Rob Cameron, extended the association by naming each bedroom after a different dukedom. The first-floor Gloucester (HRH's former room) is decorated in fresh tones of cream and white, and has the original fireplace. Cambridge, on the second floor, has a separate sitting room and its own balcony; York is smaller, but has a large bathroom with tub and shower. Guests can relax with a drink in the pretty sitting room, with pale lilac-blue walls, seagrass matting and open fireplace, before dining at a local eatery (there's a good choice within walking distance). Breakfast brings free-range eggs, tomatoes, mushrooms and fruit, with Clarks of Ware sausages and bacon and salmon from the acclaimed River Farm Smokery in Bottisham. Reports, please.

1 Victoria Street
Cambridge CB1 1JP

T: 01223 314773
E: info@dukehousecambridge.co.uk
W: dukehousecambridge.co.uk

BEDROOMS: 5. 1 in adjacent cottage, plus self-catering apartment.
OPEN: all year except over Christmas period.
FACILITIES: sitting room, breakfast room with courtyard, balcony, in-room TV (Freeview), limited parking (by arrangement), unsuitable for disabled.
BACKGROUND MUSIC: during breakfast.
LOCATION: city centre.
CHILDREN: babies and over-10s welcomed.
DOGS: not allowed.
CREDIT CARDS: MC, Visa.
PRICES: per room B&B single £125–£160, double £140–£195. 1-night bookings refused weekends.

**SEE ALSO SHORTLIST**

# CAMBRIDGE Cambridgeshire

MAP 2:B4

## UNIVERSITY ARMS

You can't miss the nods to the university at this 'fantastic city hotel with stylish decor and superb food' on Parker's Piece green: Cambridge blue walls; corridor carpets striped like the student tie; and suites named after famous graduates, from Virginia Woolf to Stephen Hawking. 'It's tasteful, not tacky,' says a Guide insider. Although the hotel has 192 rooms, it still has an 'individual feel', retaining period features such as copper-topped turrets and fireplaces but with modern touches. Bedrooms, with striped fabric headboards and velvet chairs, have old-fashioned reading lamps and blackout curtains. Bathrooms have traditional-style tiles over under-floor heating. In 'buzzy' Parker's Tavern, you can sip a Cambridge cocktail in the atmospheric bar before sampling Tristan Welch's amazing modern fare – the spaghetti bolognese 'melts in the mouth'; the truffle risotto is 'a treat'. 'The setting is as deliciously relaxed as the food', done out like a college buttery, with wooden tables, leather banquettes and library-style lights. 'There is even complimentary bicycle use so you can see Cambridge as the students do.' (JK)

Regent Street
Cambridge CB2 1AD

T: 01223 606066
E: enquiries@universityarms.com
W: universityarms.com

BEDROOMS: 192. 10 suitable for disabled.
OPEN: all year.
FACILITIES: library, bar/bistro, ballroom, meeting rooms, fitness centre, in-room TV, civil wedding licence, bicycles, limited guest parking, public areas wheelchair accessible, adapted toilet.
BACKGROUND MUSIC: in bar and restaurant.
LOCATION: city centre.
CHILDREN: all ages welcomed, children's menu, interconnecting rooms.
DOGS: only assistance dogs allowed.
CREDIT CARDS: Amex, MC, Visa.
PRICES: per room B&B £183–£499. À la carte £43.

**SEE ALSO SHORTLIST**

# CAMELFORD Cornwall                                    MAP 1:C3

## PENDRAGON COUNTRY HOUSE

Legendary hosts Sharon and Nigel Reed provide 'thoughtful touches, too many to mention' at their former Victorian vicarage, themed in celebration of local hero King Arthur. A suit of armour guards the hall. Fires blaze in the drawing rooms with leather sofas and generously stocked honesty bar. Bedrooms are named after Arthurian knights. And so to Bedivere, with a cherry-wood four-poster. Or to dual-aspect Lamorak, with four-poster and 'such beautiful views' of Bodmin Moor. Kay has a four-poster built for one, ground-floor Pelleas a wet room. All have complimentary sherry, a choice of bedding, under-floor bathroom heating and handmade herbal toiletries. Guests gather for drinks before a 'beautifully presented' dinner of 'exceptional standard'. 'Nigel cooked a different meal each evening, and Sharon made desserts.' A typical dish: rolled blade of beef slow-roasted in red wine, sage-infused roast potatoes, seasonal roots, butter-wilted kale. 'Breakfast is delicious, with locally sourced and home-grown ingredients' – free-range eggs, hog pudding and Cornish kipper. (Sally Crowley, Phillip Jesson, Tanya Gist, and others)

**25% DISCOUNT VOUCHERS**

Old Vicarage Hill
Davidstow
Camelford PL32 9XR

T: 01840 261131
E: enquiries@
   pendragoncountryhouse.com
W: pendragoncountryhouse.com

BEDROOMS: 7. 1 on ground floor suitable for disabled.
OPEN: all year except Christmas, restaurant closed Sun eve.
FACILITIES: sitting room, lounge with honesty bar, dining room, games room (pool table), in-room TV (Freeview), 1¾-acre grounds, electric charging point in car park.
BACKGROUND MUSIC: none.
LOCATION: 3½ miles NE of Camelford.
CHILDREN: all ages welcomed.
DOGS: allowed in ground-floor bedroom (£5 charge), lounge but not restaurant, except guide dogs.
CREDIT CARDS: Amex, MC, Visa.
PRICES: per room B&B single £65–£75, double £110–£150, D,B&B single £90–£100, double £145–£208. Set menu £31.50–£35.

## CANNINGTON Somerset

MAP 1:B5

### BLACKMORE FARM

Gazing upon the Quantock hills, Ann and Ian Dyer's 15th-century, red sandstone manor house B&B on the family farm is redolent of history. Beyond a wisteria-festooned porch, the interiors have beams, stone floors and arches, yawning fireplaces, venerable antiques and artefacts, even a chapel. 'Having breakfast in the great hall at a table that could seat about 20 was a bit like being in the 16th century,' writes a reader. Two of the three main-house bedrooms have a four-poster. Rustic suites in converted farm buildings are set up for guests who want more space and independence, with sitting and dining areas. Those in the Wagon House have a fridge, microwave and toaster. The Cider Press, sleeping four, has a fully equipped kitchen, patio and small garden. There is also a shepherd's hut in a secluded garden. A full English brings free-range eggs from the farm hens and award-winning sausages. An on-site farm shop can provide you with the makings of a picnic before you walk the River Parrett Trail; a cream tea in the café awaits your return. (Clive Ringrose)

**25% DISCOUNT VOUCHERS**

Blackmore Lane
Cannington TA5 2NE

T: 01278 653442
E: dyerfarm@aol.com
W: blackmorefarm.co.uk

BEDROOMS: 14. 10 in annexes, with 6 on ground floor, 1 in shepherd's hut in grounds, 1 suitable for disabled.
OPEN: all year.
FACILITIES: lounge/TV room, Great Hall/breakfast room, in-room TV (Freeview), 1-acre garden (stream, coarse fishing), children's play area, farm shop/café, lounge and dining room wheelchair accessible.
BACKGROUND MUSIC: none.
LOCATION: 3 miles W of Bridgwater.
CHILDREN: all ages welcomed.
DOGS: allowed in some bedrooms by prior arrangement, not in public rooms.
CREDIT CARDS: Amex, MC, Visa.
PRICES: per room B&B single £90–£100, double £120–£140. Shepherd's hut £75 per person. 1-night bookings refused bank holiday weekends.

# CANTERBURY Kent                              MAP 2:D5

## THE PIG AT BRIDGE PLACE

'Possibly the best of the litter', the sixth in Robin
Hutson's Pig smallholding occupies a Grade
I listed mansion, built in 1701, almost within
the sound of Canterbury bells. 'Everything is
deliciously quirky,' a Guide insider reports, from
posters in the loos recalling the house's days as a
rock venue, to the bar 'done out in deep burgundy,
including the ornate ceiling'. The 'beautiful decor'
is the work of Judy Hutson, with 'shabby-chic
bedrooms, some with beams, one with gold-
scalloped cornicing and mezzanine bathroom'.
They range from 'extremely small' (albeit one
large enough for an 'impressive oak four-poster'),
through hop pickers' huts, to the two-storey
'Barn'. As with all the Pigs, the kitchen garden
is the engine of the hotel, supplying produce
straight to the kitchen. You can go hog wild in the
greenhouse restaurant with 'open kitchen serving
Pigalicious food', home grown or locally sourced.
'I still dream of the chorizo wood-fired flatbreads
served outside from the garden oven.' There is a
'wonderful breakfast choice (of note are the carrot
and beetroot juices, eggs from their own hens,
gluten-free fig and walnut bars)'. (JK, MAS)

Bourne Park Road
Bridge
Canterbury CT4 5BH

T: 0345 225 9494
E: info@thepighotel.com
W: thepighotel.com

BEDROOMS: 29. 7 in main house,
12 in coach house, 4 on ground floor,
2 suitable for disabled, 2 family-
friendly lodges, converted barn, and
7 hop pickers' huts.
OPEN: all year.
FACILITIES: restaurant, bar/lounge,
snugs, study, 2 treatment rooms,
gardens, terrace, wheelchair access to
the garden, with gravel tracks around
the property.
BACKGROUND MUSIC: in public areas.
LOCATION: on edge of village, 3 miles
S of Canterbury.
CHILDREN: all ages welcomed.
DOGS: not allowed.
CREDIT CARDS: Amex, MC, Visa.
PRICES: per room £139–£469. Breakfast
buffet £12, cooked £16, à la carte £42.
2-night bookings only at weekends.

# CARTMEL Cumbria

## AYNSOME MANOR

In wooded grounds in a valley looking over farmland to pretty Cartmel village, this 400-year-old manor house, long owned and run by the Varley family, offers reassuringly traditional comforts. Readers (many of whom return year after year) call it 'an oasis of peace and tranquillity in beautiful countryside'. In its lounges are comfortable, deep sofas, china ornaments and brass fenders around open fires. 'An ideal venue to relax over coffee and talk with other guests – no background music here!' The windows frame pleasing views. 'Good-sized bedrooms' are furnished in simple country house style with patterned wallpapers and modern oak furniture; second-floor rooms have beams and a sloping ceiling. In the panelled Georgian dining room, daily-changing menus offer 'excellent' and sophisticated British dishes such as guineafowl and leek terrine, and oven-baked cod with prawn and shallot butter; the choice of two-to-five courses is appreciated by readers. Breakfast includes locally smoked haddock with poached egg as well as the full Cumbrian. Staff 'combine efficiency with first-class service in a friendly and unobtrusive manner'.

**25% DISCOUNT VOUCHERS**

Aynsome Lane
Cartmel
Grange-over-Sands LA11 6HH

T: 01539 536653
E: aynsomemanor@btconnect.com
W: aynsomemanorhotel.co.uk

BEDROOMS: 12. 2 in cottage across courtyard.
OPEN: all year except 23–27 Dec, 2–28 Jan, lunch served Sun only.
FACILITIES: 2 lounges, bar, dining room, in-room TV (Freeview), ½-acre garden, unsuitable for disabled.
BACKGROUND MUSIC: none.
LOCATION: ¾ mile N of village.
CHILDREN: all ages welcomed, no under-5s in dining room in evening.
DOGS: in bedrooms only and must not be unattended (£7 per night).
CREDIT CARDS: Amex, MC, Visa.
PRICES: per room B&B £80–£140 (£165 on race weekends). Set dinner £24–£39. 1-night bookings occasionally refused weekends.

# CHADDESLEY CORBETT Worcestershire

MAP 3:C5

## BROCKENCOTE HALL

A long winding drive leads past a lake to this Victorian mansion, remodelled in the 1940s in the style of a Loire château, with parkland, fountain and 17th-century dovecote. 'We were impressed with the service, ambience and accommodation,' writes a reader this year. Part of the Eden Hotel Collection (see also Mallory Court, Leamington Spa), it has a country house feel with its impressive hallway and fireplace, though 'the bar looked as if it could have been shipped in from the Premier Inn'. The hotel now welcomes dogs, who can stay in some of the 21 rooms. These are 'spacious, with a comfy bed, more easy chairs than guests to fill them', and have a modern bathroom. There are 'nice touches such as cafetière coffee, fresh fruit, savoury nibbles and home-made biscuits'. At dinner – 'fantastic, beautifully presented and delicious' – Tim Jenkins caters to all tastes, with such dishes as crispy chestnut polenta, Jerusalem artichoke, sprouts and elderberries, or braised ox cheek, Roscoff onions, salsify and port jus. 'Breakfast has a good choice. I was especially cheered to be able to enjoy some Bury black pudding.' (Jill Cox, and others)

Chaddesley Corbett DY10 4PY

T: 01562 777876
E: info@brockencotehall.com
W: brockencotehall.com

BEDROOMS: 21. Some on ground floor, 1 suitable for disabled.
OPEN: all year.
FACILITIES: lift, hall, lounge, conservatory, bar, library, restaurant, function facilities, in-room TV (Freeview), civil wedding licence, 72-acre grounds (fishing, croquet, tennis), public rooms wheelchair accessible, adapted toilet.
BACKGROUND MUSIC: all day in public areas.
LOCATION: 3 miles SE of Kidderminster.
CHILDREN: all ages welcomed.
DOGS: allowed in some rooms, garden and bar.
CREDIT CARDS: Amex, MC, Visa.
PRICES: per room B&B single from £105, double £115–£365, extra bed for child up to age 12, £25. Market menu £39–£50, seasonal menu £45–£60, tasting menu (whole table) £75.

# CHESTER Cheshire

MAP 3:A4

## EDGAR HOUSE

On the Roman city walls, overlooking the River Dee, this handsome boutique hotel is 'very well run' by owners Michael Stephen and Tim Mills. Their 'great attention to detail' is revealed in both the service – guests are welcomed with a glass of fizz and greeted by name – and the striking design, which includes artwork loaned by Castle Fine Art in Chester. Four of the bedrooms overlook the river, two have a balcony. All have bespoke furniture, comfy sofa and super-king-size bed. Bathrooms offer Molton Brown toiletries and rain showers; some have a freestanding bath. In the restaurant Twenty2, new chef Rafal Kweik focuses on seasonal produce in both the regularly changing à la carte menu and flagship tasting menus. Readers enjoyed the duck and blackberry Bakewell and ballotine and Kiev of guineafowl. A 'proper' afternoon tea was 'delicious'. Breakfast dishes included 'wonderful' Rumbledethumps (crushed potato and greens topped with avocado, crispy bacon and poached egg). There is a riverside garden to enjoy when the sun shines, and a cosy garden lounge with an open fire for when it does not. (Frances Thomas)

22 City Walls
Chester CH1 1SB

T: 01244 347007
E: hello@edgarhouse.co.uk
W: edgarhouse.co.uk

BEDROOMS: 7.
OPEN: all year, restaurant from noon Fri, Sat, lunch only first Sun of month.
FACILITIES: garden lounge, mini-cinema, restaurant, in-room smart TV, sun terrace, riverside garden (alfresco meals), free allocated parking, restaurant wheelchair accessible, adapted toilet.
BACKGROUND MUSIC: Classic FM in lounge, music in restaurant 'appropriate to relaxing setting'.
LOCATION: central, on the river.
CHILDREN: not under 14.
DOGS: not allowed in hotel, but welcome in garden and when dining outside.
CREDIT CARDS: MC, Visa.
PRICES: per room B&B single £164–£284, double £179–£299, D,B&B double £280–£359. À la carte £35, tasting menu £69.

**SEE ALSO SHORTLIST**

## CHETTLE Dorset                                    MAP 2:E1

### CASTLEMAN

Change is afoot at this former dower house, which opened as a hotel in 1996 under Barbara Garnsworthy, in an estate village of thatched limestone cottages amid the rolling chalk downs of Cranborne Chase. She has now handed over to Niki and Jez Barfoot, who own The Tickled Pig in Wimborne Minster and share the cherished values of the Castleman, where staff are 'efficient, helpful and friendly and the food is excellent'. An 18th-century staircase sweeps up to bedrooms graded simply 'standard' and 'large', one with a four-poster. They have had a revamp, but not at a cost to the eccentricity that is so much a part of the charm. All are supplied with Bramley toiletries in refillable dispensers. Enlarged over the centuries, the building has two 19th-century drawing rooms, one with a Jacobean fireplace and ornate carved woodwork, the other with Regency plasterwork. In the kitchen, Richard Morris and Jez Barfoot cook a seasonal menu of such locally sourced rustic dishes as venison stew braised in sixpenny ale with juniper, or veggie hotpot with garden greens. It is early days, but we are optimistic.

Chettle
Blandford Forum DT11 8DB

T: 01258 830096
E: enquiry@castlemanhotel.co.uk
W: castlemanhotel.co.uk

BEDROOMS: 8. 1 family room.
OPEN: all year, except 25/26 Dec, 31 Dec/1 Jan, lunch on Sun only.
FACILITIES: 2 drawing rooms, bar, restaurant, in-room TV (Freeview), 2-acre grounds (stables for visiting horses), riding, fishing, shooting, cycling nearby, public rooms wheelchair accessible.
BACKGROUND MUSIC: none 'except for the occasional piano-playing chef'.
LOCATION: village, 1 mile off A354 Salisbury–Blandford.
CHILDREN: all ages welcomed.
DOGS: allowed in 1 bedroom (£20 a night), not in public areas.
CREDIT CARDS: MC, Visa.
PRICES: per room B&B single £90, double £115–£130, D,B&B (Sun–Thurs) double £145–£165. À la carte £35, supper Mon–Wed from £20.

# CHILLATON Devon

MAP 1:D3

## TOR COTTAGE

In its own secluded wooded valley, this B&B
is ideal for guests who want to come and go as
they please. Only one room is in owner Maureen
Rowlatt's cottage, but it is in a private wing
with a sitting room. Four rooms are in garden
annexes, three of them equipped for self-catering,
with a microwave, grill and full-size fridge, and
outdoor seating. They each have a log-burner and
a king-size bed. Laughing Waters is a secluded
bedsit, in its own garden and woodland, designed
in New England style, with maple furniture, a
patchwork quilt, a fridge, cutlery and crockery,
veranda, a decked barbecue area and steps down
to a stream. Breakfast, in the conservatory or on a
flower-decked terrace, is the only meal provided,
and brings a buffet and a choice of kedgeree, a
full English or a vegetarian grill. In summer, the
heated pool is available to guests; there is also
a river for fishing. If you want to eat out, you
might drive the six miles to The Horn of Plenty
in Gulworthy (see entry under Tavistock), or
into Tavistock proper, with its choice of pubs,
restaurants and cafés. Dartmoor and the Tamar
valley are on the doorstep.

Chillaton
Lifton PL16 0JE

T: 01822 860248
E: info@torcottage.co.uk
W: torcottage.co.uk

BEDROOMS: 5. 4 in garden annexes.
OPEN: Feb–mid-Dec.
FACILITIES: sitting room, large
conservatory, free Wi-Fi in reception
and public areas, in-room TV
(Freeview), 28-acre grounds (2-acre
garden, heated outdoor swimming
pool, 12 by 6 metres, May–Sept) with
pool house, river (fishing ½ mile).
BACKGROUND MUSIC: none.
LOCATION: ½ mile S of Chillaton,
6½ miles N of Tavistock.
CHILDREN: not under 15.
DOGS: only guide dogs allowed.
CREDIT CARDS: MC, Visa.
PRICES: per room B&B single £98,
double £150. Platters £32 for 2.
Normally min. 2-night stay, 'but check
availability'.

# CHRISTCHURCH Dorset

MAP 2:E2

## CAPTAIN'S CLUB HOTEL

With the shiny promise of a cruise ship, Robert Wilson and Tim Lloyd's spa hotel by the River Stour is as family- and dog-friendly as you please. Room choices range from a 'spacious' double to a 'fabulous' three-bedroom suite with lounge and kitchen, while 24-hour room service, a coffee machine and aromatherapy toiletries are standard. Visitors awake to a river view through floor-to-ceiling windows, and relax into the free-and-easy vibe. 'I visited with my 93-year-old mum,' a reader writes. 'The beds were very comfortable, with two chairs by the window, and everything was spotless.' The day begins with breakfast in the lounge (maybe Loch Fyne smoked salmon or eggs Benedict with Dorset ham). You can graze on Quay bar nibbles, order lunch or afternoon tea from an all-day menu in the lounge or alfresco, and dine in the restaurant on such dishes as fillet steak, moules marinière or Sri Lankan monkfish curry. There are menus for vegetarians and children, and babysitting by arrangement. 'Service was very friendly and helpful and the food was delicious.' 'We'd recommend this hotel to anyone.' (Jill Cox, IM)

Wick Ferry
Christchurch BH23 1HU

T: 01202 475111
E: enquiries@captainsclubhotel.com
W: captainsclubhotel.com

BEDROOMS: 29. 2 suitable for disabled.
OPEN: all year.
FACILITIES: lifts, open-plan bar/lounge/restaurant, function facilities, in-room TV (Sky, Freeview), civil wedding licence, riverside terrace, spa (hydrotherapy pool, treatments, sauna), moorings for guests, public rooms wheelchair accessible.
BACKGROUND MUSIC: in public areas, live jazz every other Sun lunchtime.
LOCATION: on the river.
CHILDREN: all ages welcomed.
DOGS: allowed in suites, on terrace, areas of bar/lounge (£20 per dog).
CREDIT CARDS: MC, Visa.
PRICES: per room B&B doubles £159–£299, suites (3–6 guests) £219–£699. À la carte £40. 1-night bookings normally refused Sat.

# CLEARWELL Gloucestershire

MAP 3:D4

## TUDOR FARMHOUSE

♥ Previous César winner

'A hit! Just our kind of hotel,' say trusted reviewers of this 'small but luxurious' retreat set in 'ravishing countryside' in the Forest of Dean. Owners Hari and Colin Fell have given the 13th-century farmhouse and clutch of farm buildings a boutique feel, so that rooms with beams and exposed stonework are equipped with 'everything of the highest quality'. Bedrooms vary in size (the smallest 'is not big but is well furnished'); all have a coffee machine and Bramley toiletries. Families might opt for the cottage suite – 'perfect for us upstairs and the little ones on the ground floor', with direct access to the 'lovely' garden. New chef Joe Williams joined last autumn but 'style and quality' of the seasonal dishes, made from local ingredients where possible, remain unchanged. The tasting menu is 'quite superb', and includes such delights as duck liver parfait with red onion marmalade, and pork belly with pickled pear and parsnip purée. Breakfast is 'utterly delicious', in particular the scrambled eggs. 'The chef has changed but the house style and quality haven't.' 'Superb in every way.' (Peter Anderson, Andrew Kleissner, T and SR)

High Street
Clearwell GL16 8JS

T: 01594 833046
E: info@tudorfarmhousehotel.co.uk
W: tudorfarmhousehotel.co.uk

BEDROOMS: 20. 8 on ground floor, 4 in farmhouse, 9 in barn, 7 in cider house.
OPEN: all year.
FACILITIES: lounge, bar, 2 dining rooms, in-room TV (Freeview), 14-acre grounds (garden, ancient grassland), restaurant and lounge wheelchair accessible, adapted toilet.
BACKGROUND MUSIC: in restaurant and lounge at lunch and dinner.
LOCATION: 7 miles SE of Monmouth.
CHILDREN: all ages welcomed.
DOGS: allowed in 3 bedrooms, grounds, not in public rooms.
CREDIT CARDS: Amex, MC, Visa.
PRICES: per room B&B £129–£299. Tasting menu £60, à la carte £49. Min. 2-night stay at weekends, some bank holidays.

# CLEE STANTON Shropshire

MAP 3:C5

## TIMBERSTONE

Five miles from the foodie town of Ludlow, two
300-year-old cottages have been brought together
as a B&B known for producing its own delicious
meals. Owners Tracey Baylis and Alex Read have
created a rural haven, with beautiful long views to
the Clee hills. 'The countryside is gorgeous, living
up to the poetry of AE Housman and the music
of George Butterworth.' A party of six adults, an
11-year-old boy and their pooch report a perfect
stay. 'We all enjoyed ourselves very much and felt
very much at home.' Bedrooms have rustic charm,
a king-size bed, shortbread and paraben-free
Faith in Nature toiletries. Oak room has exposed
beams and an extra double sofa bed. Slate will
sleep a family of five. In the garden, a cabin retreat
has a small kitchen and French doors that open
on to decking, a fire pit and a private hot tub. At
some time in the afternoon, says another reader,
Tracey, who earlier worked with a Michelin-
starred chef, asks who will be staying in for a
communal dinner and discusses what she might
cook. 'We enjoyed all our breakfasts and evening
meals. The damson mess was a real treat.' (Jean
and Denis Jukes, DB)

Lackstone Lane
Clee Stanton SY8 3EL

T: 01584 823519
E: timberstone1@hotmail.com
W: timberstoneludlow.co.uk

BEDROOMS: 5. 1 in garden cabin.
OPEN: all year except Christmas and
New Year.
FACILITIES: lounge/dining room,
conservatory, in-room TV (Freeview),
½-acre garden.
BACKGROUND MUSIC: none.
LOCATION: 5 miles NE of Ludlow.
CHILDREN: all ages welcomed
(babysitting, travel cots).
DOGS: allowed by arrangement (£10
per night), not in dining room.
CREDIT CARDS: MC, Visa.
PRICES: per room B&B single £90–£140,
double £120–£175. Set menus £25–£30.
Min. 2-night booking in cabin retreat.

# CLEY-NEXT-THE-SEA Norfolk      MAP 2:A5

## CLEY WINDMILL

Rising above the reed beds and River Glaven in a pretty village no longer 'next the sea', Julian and Carolyn Godlee's 19th-century windmill offers characterful accommodation. Bedrooms (some huge) are within the brick tower and converted outbuildings. A door from the circular, beamed Stone Room leads to a wraparound viewing platform. New this year, the Old Cart Shed has an oak four-poster, a heated flagstone floor with oriental rugs, a Shaker kitchenette and glass doors to the harbour. The walled garden has been redesigned, and David Mears has taken over as chef. On most nights a three-course dinner with amuse-bouche is served in the circular dining room – maybe chicken liver parfait, herb-crusted hake, then chocolate tart. 'They check that you are happy with the menu, and will make adjustments, but there is no choice as such,' advises a Guide inspector. On 'off' nights you may order a hamper. At breakfast there is fish from a local smokehouse, or a full English cooked to order. 'Staff are pleasant and happy to chat. The atmosphere is relaxed and informal, yet everything runs smoothly.'

The Quay
Cley-next-the-Sea NR25 7RP

T: 01263 740209
E: info@cleywindmill.co.uk
W: cleywindmill.co.uk

BEDROOMS: 10. 1 in Boat House, 1 in Long House, 1 in Cart Shed.
OPEN: all year, self-catering only over Christmas/New Year, dinner most evenings.
FACILITIES: bar/lounge, dining room, in-room TV (Freeview), civil wedding licence, ¼-acre garden.
BACKGROUND MUSIC: in dining room, soft classical and jazz.
LOCATION: in northerly village next to River Glaven, less than a mile from the sea.
CHILDREN: all ages welcomed.
DOGS: allowed in 1 room.
CREDIT CARDS: MC, Visa.
PRICES: per room B&B double £159–£295. Set menu £34.50, hampers £65–£95. Min. 2-night stay weekends.

# CLIPSHAM Rutland

MAP 2:A3

## BEECH HOUSE & OLIVE BRANCH

꩜ Previous César winner

Just a couple of miles from the A1, down a tree-lined road, is a great combination of gastropub and luxury B&B. 'Such a good place to stay when we're travelling north.' The mellow stone village pub was rescued from closure by Ben Jones and Sean Hope (ex-Hambleton Hall, see entry) in 1999. Contemporary-rustic in style with stripped-wood floors and mismatched chairs, it serves modern British cooking which focuses on local produce, although one regular writes that dinners are 'veering a bit towards the pretentious'. Dishes might include lamb with burnt shallot and crispy potatoes, or roast pollack with curried pearl barley. Smitten? Take a class in the cookery school, or buy produce from the pub shop. Bedrooms, across the road in the buttermilk-coloured Georgian Beech House, don't stint on luxuries: hand-made mattresses, antiques, proper coffee, fresh milk. Aubergine, with 'Art Deco fittings', has the appearance of 'a mini-Claridge's'. Biscuit has a double-ended bath and garden views. 'Excellent' breakfasts include 'superb kedgeree'. Staff are 'consistently cheerful', 'even recommending a cheaper wine'. (Mary Milne-Day, and others)

Main Street
Clipsham LE15 7SH

T: 01780 410355
E: info@theolivebranchpub.com
W: theolivebranchpub.com

BEDROOMS: 6. 2 on ground floor, family room (also suitable for disabled) in annexe.
OPEN: all year except 25 and 31 Dec, 1 Jan, pub on Sun nights, all day Mon and Tues.
FACILITIES: pub, dining room, breakfast room, in-room TV (Freeview, Netflix), small terrace, garden, public rooms wheelchair accessible, adapted toilet.
BACKGROUND MUSIC: classical/jazz in pub.
LOCATION: in village 7 miles NW of Stamford.
CHILDREN: all ages welcomed (children's menu).
DOGS: allowed in ground-floor bedrooms and bar.
CREDIT CARDS: MC, Visa.
PRICES: per room B&B £125–£215, D,B&B £175–£290. Set dinner (5 courses) £45, à la carte (3 courses) £40.

# CORSE LAWN Gloucestershire

## CORSE LAWN HOUSE

Pink without and peachy within, this Queen Anne-style mansion, in a rural hamlet with views to the Malvern hills, has been owned by the Hine family since 1978. Run today by Baba Hine, with a team of long-serving staff, it inspires loyalty among Guide readers. 'It is just lovely,' writes one who has known it for 18 years and has seen little change. Public rooms done in shades of apricot and pastel orange have 'wonderfully quirky furniture' and paintings by Baba's great-grandmother. 'Don't expect "boutique"', but if you want a 'comfortable, traditional, not overly formal hotel', with pool and tennis court, here it is. 'The welcome is warm', bedrooms are spacious: 'You can dance about in them without hitting the furniture.' Some have a four-poster or canopy bed, perhaps a balcony; all have leaf tea, a cafetière, fruit, home-made biscuits and a fridge with fresh milk. New chef Chris Exley's sustainably sourced cooking is served in the bistro, the restaurant or alfresco. A typical dish might be charred lamb fillet, confit shoulder and salsa verde. 'It never ceases to delight.' (Joanna Gibbon and Paul Lindsell, and others)

### 25% DISCOUNT VOUCHERS

Corse Lawn GL19 4LZ

T: 01452 780771
E: enquiries@corselawn.com
W: corselawn.com

BEDROOMS: 18. 5 on ground floor.
OPEN: all year.
FACILITIES: 2 drawing rooms, snug bar, restaurant, bistro, private dining/meeting rooms, in-room TV (Sky, BT, Freeview), civil wedding licence, 12-acre grounds (croquet, tennis, indoor heated swimming pool), unsuitable for disabled.
BACKGROUND MUSIC: none.
LOCATION: 5 miles SW of Tewkesbury on B4211.
CHILDREN: all ages welcomed.
DOGS: allowed in bedrooms, on lead in public rooms, not in eating areas.
CREDIT CARDS: Amex, MC, Visa.
PRICES: per room B&B single £75–£85, double £130–£150, D,B&B £175–£195. Fixed-price dinner (restaurant) £35.50, (bistro) £21.50–£25.50, à la carte £37.50.

## COVERACK Cornwall

MAP 1:E2

### THE BAY HOTEL

**NEW**

Tiered gardens step down to the sands at this dog-friendly hotel, in an unspoilt fishing village on the Lizard peninsula, with the South West Coast Path passing through. 'Small and superbly maintained', it is promoted from the Shortlist this year following a change of ownership and a glowing report from a trusted reader. The coast-facing bedrooms, varying in size, have a seaside palette of sand, sky and surf, and a shower room with power shower. Some have a seating area in a bay window, while the best suites have French doors to a private patio, and a large bathroom with bath and walk-in shower. 'My lovely top-floor room had a generous, quite luxurious bathroom with, refreshingly, natural light and space.' Drinks can be taken in the bar or on the sun terrace. In the small restaurant, chef Sam Jones creates 'beautifully presented' dishes of ethically sourced seasonal Cornish produce. 'A sea bass and asparagus main course was cooked and flavoured really well.' In the morning there are 'tasty breakfasts where they even get the toast right'. In sum, 'real care and pride are put into every detail'. (Mike Craddock)

North Corner
Coverack
Helston TR12 6TF

T: 01326 280464
E: enquiries@thebayhotel.co.uk
W: thebayhotel.co.uk

BEDROOMS: 14. 1, on ground floor, suitable for disabled.
OPEN: 1 Mar–27 Dec.
FACILITIES: lounge, bar/restaurant, conservatory, in-room TV (Freeview), 2 tiered gardens, large sun terrace, parking.
BACKGROUND MUSIC: quiet classical music or blues in bar and restaurant.
LOCATION: village centre, 9 miles SE of Helston.
CHILDREN: all ages welcomed ('we are not suitable for babies or very young children').
DOGS: allowed in bedrooms and on lead in grounds, not in public rooms.
CREDIT CARDS: MC, Visa.
PRICES: per room B&B single £150–£281, double £187–£351. À la carte £35. 1-night bookings sometimes refused.

# COWAN BRIDGE Lancashire

MAP 4: inset D2

## HIPPING HALL

Between the Yorkshire Dales and the Lake District – and just ten minutes from the M6 – Hipping Hall is a surprising foodie find with understated but luxurious bedrooms, a relaxed atmosphere and restful views. A sprawl of buildings – from the medieval dining room and 17th-century main hall to converted cottages and stables – set among gardens, it feels like a mini-country estate. Bedrooms are quietly sophisticated, ranging from cosy cottage rooms with bold wallpapers to soft-coloured main-house rooms. The Scandi-style affairs in the converted stables are 'splendid, with a nice, large bathroom, pleasant sitting room, space outside and an outlook of fine countryside'. The main event is the 'exceptional' dinner, served in the atmospheric medieval hall with beams and grand fireplace. Chef Oli Martin's food is about 'purity, simplicity and freshness', a 12-course fortnightly-changing tasting menu whose quirky starkness belies the intricate preparations: eggy bread and caviar; cod with truffle; for pudding, apple, Douglas fir and honey. Service is 'first class from really friendly staff'. (See also sister property Forest Side, Grasmere.)

Cowan Bridge
Kirkby Lonsdale LA6 2JJ

T: 01524 271187
E: info@hippinghall.com
W: hippinghall.com

BEDROOMS: 15. 3 in cottage, 5 in stables, 1 suitable for disabled.
OPEN: all year, restaurant closed Mon, Tues.
FACILITIES: lounge, orangery, bar, restaurant, 'chef's kitchen', civil wedding licence, in-room TV (Freeview), 12-acre grounds, orangery, restaurant and lounge wheelchair accessible.
BACKGROUND MUSIC: in lounge, restaurant.
LOCATION: 2 miles SE of Kirkby Lonsdale, on A65.
CHILDREN: all ages welcomed, no under-12s in restaurant in evening.
DOGS: allowed in stable bedrooms (max. 2), orangery.
CREDIT CARDS: Amex, MC, Visa.
PRICES: per room B&B £199–£329, D,B&B £299–£459. Dinner tasting menu £80.

# COWES Isle of Wight

MAP 2:E2

## NORTH HOUSE

♀ Previous César winner

'Anyone visiting the Isle of Wight should spend at least one night here,' say fans of this Grade II listed town house in Cowes old town. Renovated by 'approachable' owners, Lewis Green and Luke Staples, the 'relaxed and unstuffy' hotel offers 'exceptionally fine service'. Stylish rooms (Lewis and Luke run an interiors shop, too), some with sea views, are categorised as Spacious, Comfortable and Cosy; all are 'very well appointed', with 'comfortable' bed, in-room pantry, bath robes and REN toiletries. 'Even the smallest' have space for 'a couple of tub chairs'; some bathrooms have a freestanding bath and walk-in shower. The 'tastefully decorated' restaurant provides an 'excellent choice' of 'well-cooked' dishes such as twice-baked Gallybagger cheese soufflé with an apple and walnut salad and Breton fish stew with sea bass, crevettes, scallops, mussels and langoustine. Breakfast has fresh juices, pastries, cereals, fruit, boiled eggs, smoked salmon, cheeses and charcuterie, and a cooked breakfast at the weekend. A 'totally unexpected delight' with 'everything pleasing to the eye'. (Chris and Erika Savory, and others)

Sun Hill
Cowes PO31 7HY

T: 01983 209453
E: reception@northhousecowes.co.uk
W: northhousecowes.co.uk

BEDROOMS: 14.
OPEN: all year, restaurant closed Mon, Tues (except bank hols).
FACILITIES: bar, library, restaurant, private dining room, in-room TV (Freeview), civil wedding licence, garden, outdoor heated swimming pool.
BACKGROUND MUSIC: in bar and restaurant.
LOCATION: in centre of Old Town.
CHILDREN: all ages welcomed.
DOGS: allowed in some bedrooms, bar, library, in restaurant by special request.
CREDIT CARDS: Amex, MC, Visa.
PRICES: per room B&B £110–£295. À la carte £36.

# CROFT-ON-TEES Yorkshire

MAP 4:C4

## CLOW BECK HOUSE

The personal welcome, horizon-stretching views, homely touches and feeling of space make this former farmhouse a relaxing place to stay. David and Heather Armstrong run their Yorkshire-stone home, which has been in David's family for more than 100 years, with a down-to-earth friendliness. There's nothing pretentious, with a neat, conservatively furnished lounge, a large, rustic dining room with slate floor, open beams and fire in a stone fireplace, and bedrooms in converted outbuildings. Rooms range from traditional, with the odd antique, elegant sofa and botanical prints, to more contemporary, with startling wall decorations such as blown-up photographs of Audrey Hepburn. All rooms have thoughtful extras, including hot-water bottles, hairspray, sweets and home-made biscuits. David cooks generous portions of homely farmhouse-style meals from a surprisingly extensive menu. You can dine while overlooking the beautiful gardens with box hedge knot garden, pond, terrace, hidden corners with seats; a miniature cricket team on a lawn, and plenty to entertain children. Reports, please.

Monk End Farm
Croft-on-Tees DL2 2SP

T: 01325 721075
E: reservations@clowbeckhouse.co.uk
W: clowbeckhouse.co.uk

BEDROOMS: 6 in garden buildings, some on ground floor, 1 suitable for disabled.
OPEN: all year except Christmas and New Year.
FACILITIES: lounge, restaurant, in-room TV (Freeview), small conference facilities, 2-acre grounds on 100-acre farm.
BACKGROUND MUSIC: classical, 'easy listening' in restaurant.
LOCATION: 3 miles SE of Darlington.
CHILDREN: all ages welcomed.
DOGS: not allowed.
CREDIT CARDS: Amex, MC, Visa.
PRICES: per room B&B single £90, double £140. À la carte £35.

# CROSTHWAITE Cumbria

MAP 4: inset C2

## THE PUNCH BOWL INN

In a quietly beautiful area of the Lake District –
the lovely Lyth valley – this smart village inn has
a deserved reputation for good food and cosseting
bedrooms. 'Always a favourite,' declares one
reader, 'with lots of atmosphere.' Locals come
to sip real ales at the bar, but the food is the star
attraction, whether eaten in the slate-floored and
beamed bar area with toasty log-burner, the more
formal dining room, or outside on the terrace
overlooking the neighbouring church. Dishes
from new head chef Alex Beard (formerly of
the three-Michelin-starred Waterside Inn, Bray)
might include prawn tempura with avocado and
wasabi dip, duck breast with blood orange brûlée
and the signature lemon tart with damson sorbet.
No two bedrooms are alike, though they share a
contemporary-country style of pale-wash colours,
thick carpets and vintage or solid-oak furniture.
Many have beams, low windows and valley views;
all have an 'inviting' bathroom with tongue-and-
groove panelling, roll-top bath and under-floor
heating. 'Efficient and cheerful' staff welcome
arriving guests with home-made scones and tea.
(S and KT)

Crosthwaite
Kendal LA8 8HR

T: 01539 568237
E: info@the-punchbowl.co.uk
W: the-punchbowl.co.uk

BEDROOMS: 9.
OPEN: all year.
FACILITIES: bar, bar dining area,
restaurant, in-room TV (Freeview),
civil wedding licence, 2 terraces, bar
and restaurant wheelchair accessible,
adapted toilet.
BACKGROUND MUSIC: in public areas.
LOCATION: 5 miles W of Kendal, via
A5074.
CHILDREN: all ages welcomed.
DOGS: allowed in bar only.
CREDIT CARDS: Amex, MC, Visa.
PRICES: per room B&B £125–£320.
À la carte £35. 1-night bookings
usually refused 25 Dec, 31 Dec.

# CRUDWELL Wiltshire

MAP 3:E5

## THE RECTORY HOTEL

'At the heart of a quintessentially Cotswold village', this Georgian rectory turned laid-back but stylish hotel proved 'enough to make a pair of Londoners consider giving up city life'. With sister dining pub The Potting Shed opposite, it is a first venture into hospitality for music industry executive Alex Payne, but the style bears the signature of Dan Brod and Charlie Luxton (see Beckford Arms, Tisbury). Bedrooms, painted in muted shades, with seagrass flooring, are classed 'Big' (with in-room roll-top bath), 'Medium' and 'Small' (not poky). A small room had hooks and hangers but no wardrobe. Nice touches include smart TV with a film library, a cafetière, home-made shortbread and Bramley bath products. Help yourself to milk from the fridge or a drink from the honesty bar on the landing. A cocktail bar opens on to a garden with a 13th-century dovecote and a pool. You can eat 'exquisite' meals with 'bread fresh from the oven' in the glasshouse or the pub, from inventive, unfussy modern menus with great vegan options. 'The perfect antidote to busy London life. Our favourite hotel in the UK.' (Lara Good, and others)

Crudwell
Malmesbury SN16 9EP

T: 01666 577194
E: info@therectoryhotel.com
W: therectoryhotel.com

BEDROOMS: 18. 3 in cottage in garden.
OPEN: all year.
FACILITIES: living room, drawing room, dining room, card room, bar, in-room TV (Freeview, film library), meeting facilities, civil wedding licence, 3-acre garden, heated outdoor swimming pool (10 by 15 metres, May–Oct), restaurant and bar wheelchair accessible, no adapted toilet.
BACKGROUND MUSIC: in public areas.
LOCATION: 4 miles N of Malmesbury.
CHILDREN: all ages welcomed.
DOGS: allowed in 3 bedrooms and public rooms, not in dining room.
CREDIT CARDS: Amex, MC, Visa.
PRICES: per room B&B £125–£300. À la carte £40. Min. 2-night bookings at weekends, usually.

# DARLINGTON Co. Durham                MAP 4:C4

## HEADLAM HALL          **NEW**

This country hotel ticks all the boxes – historic
building, beautiful gardens, smart bedrooms,
relaxed dining, spa and pool – while retaining a
homely feel. 'The warmth of the welcome by staff
continued to impress,' says one fan; 'a beautiful
hotel in glorious surroundings,' enthuses another.
Surrounded by the Robinson family's farmland,
the hall – dating from Jacobean times – is
impressive. Tartan carpets on flagged or polished-
wood floors, tweed-covered armchairs, and walls
with hunting prints and Victorian watercolours
create 'a comfortable yet informal atmosphere'.
There is space to relax, from the elegant drawing
room or cosy library bar to the spa and the terraces
overlooking the gardens. Bedrooms are 'modern
country house' in style, and range from the main
hall, with original features, to more contemporary
spa bedrooms, and rustic mews and coach house
rooms. The restaurant wins praise for its 'quality,
value and variety of menus'. Meals include steak
and ale pie, bistro dishes such as herb-crusted
hake, plus vegetarian choices. 'All in all a
delightful place to stay.' (Alwyn and Thelma Ellis,
Ralph Wilson, HP)

### 25% DISCOUNT VOUCHERS

Gainford
Darlington DL2 3HA

T: 01325 730238
E: reception@headlamhall.co.uk
W: headlamhall.co.uk

BEDROOMS: 38. 9 in coach house, 6 in
mews, 7 in spa, 2 suitable for disabled.
OPEN: all year except 24–27 Dec.
FACILITIES: lift, bar, restaurant, spa
brasserie, lounge, drawing room,
private dining rooms, in-room TV
(Freeview), civil wedding licence,
function facilities, 4-acre garden,
spa, tennis, 9-hole golf course, public
rooms wheelchair accessible, adapted
toilet.
BACKGROUND MUSIC: all day in bar,
restaurant.
LOCATION: 8 miles W of Darlington.
CHILDREN: all ages welcomed.
DOGS: allowed in bedrooms, public
rooms.
CREDIT CARDS: Amex, MC, Visa.
PRICES: per room B&B single
£115–£205, double £145–£235, D,B&B
double £216–£306. À la carte £35.

# DARTMOOR Devon

MAP 1:D4

## PRINCE HALL

Dramatic moorland views are part of the allure at this isolated Georgian mansion, where former guests are said to have included Sir Arthur Conan Doyle. Was he inspired here to write The Hound of the Baskervilles? Possibly. More certain, though, is the welcome today's hounds will get, with dog-washing facilities, treats, and the chance to accompany their owners in the bistro, where the same menu is served as in the restaurant. Two-legged guests also find Chris Daly's hotel a 'truly special' place, with 'warm, friendly young staff'. Bedrooms range from a single with courtyard views and a walk-in shower, to superior doubles such as Haytor, with a sleigh bed and 'lovely view across the moor'. All have fresh milk from a fridge on the landing, and botanical toiletries. Chris's son Luke cooks a seasonally changing menu, with veggie and gluten-free options, and was happy to provide more variety for readers staying a while. Expect such dishes as pea and shallot tortellini with Cornish blue cheese and pesto, or hake with caper sauce. 'Very delicious dinner and breakfast,' say Guide insiders. (SR) NOTE: As the Guide went to press, Prince Hall announced that it was changing to become an exclusive-use venue.

Princetown
Dartmoor PL20 6SA

T: 01822 890403
E: info@princehall.co.uk
W: princehall.co.uk

BEDROOMS: 9.
OPEN: all year, booking advised for restaurant.
FACILITIES: lobby, bar, lounge, dining room, free Wi-Fi in some rooms and bar/bistro, in-room TV (Freeview), civil wedding licence, terrace, 5-acre grounds, public rooms wheelchair accessible.
BACKGROUND MUSIC: none.
LOCATION: 3 miles E of Princetown.
CHILDREN: all ages welcomed, no children's menu, but smaller portions offered.
DOGS: 'very much' allowed (treats, facilities for food storage and dog-washing, pet-friendly garden and grounds), not in restaurant, but same menu available in bistro for owners with dogs.
CREDIT CARDS: MC, Visa.
PRICES: per room B&B single £95–£117, double £176–£220. À la carte £35.

# DARTMOUTH Devon

MAP 1:D4

## BAYARDS COVE INN

Behind its Tudor black-and-white facade, a
medieval merchant's house close to the water's
edge, and once carved up as shops and flats, is
today a welcoming bar, restaurant and hotel. 'The
atmosphere is lovely. You could happily spend all
day drinking coffee, eating cake and watching
the world go by.' The bedrooms have the feel of
a historic inn: 'The walls are uneven, as are the
floors, but it is cosy' with diamond-pane leaded
windows. Drake duplex suite has a double bed
under a cruck beam roof, bunks and a sofa bed.
Mountbatten has a king-size bed, a lounge area
with sofa bed, bare floorboards, a blend of original
features, period and contemporary furniture.
Extras include a cafetière, teapot, shortbread and
good toiletries. 'Our spacious double was perfect
for us and our dog.' All-day menus kick off with
a cooked breakfast and vegan smoothies. Later
come a locally sourced beef and bone-marrow
burger, the catch of the day with salsa verde,
Devon sirloin steak and veggie options. 'In winter
it is warming in every sense, and in summer its
prime position is perfect to enjoy the liveliness
of the town.'

27 Lower Street
Dartmouth TQ6 9AN

T: 01803 839278
E: info@bayardscoveinn.co.uk
W: bayardscoveinn.co.uk

BEDROOMS: 7. 2 family suites.
OPEN: all year.
FACILITIES: bar, restaurant, in-room
TV (Freeview), bicycle storage,
private parking nearby (reservation
required, £15 per day), public areas
wheelchair accessible, adapted toilet.
BACKGROUND MUSIC: in public areas.
LOCATION: in centre, close to
waterfront.
CHILDREN: all ages welcomed,
children's menu.
DOGS: allowed throughout (£12 per
dog per night).
CREDIT CARDS: Amex, MC, Visa.
PRICES: per person B&B double
£165–£225, family room £220–£275.
À la carte £35. Min. 2-night stay at
weekends.

**SEE ALSO SHORTLIST**

# DARTMOUTH Devon

MAP 1:D4

## DART MARINA

Devoted to leisure and pleasure, Richard
Seton's spa hotel overlooking the Dart estuary
is a perennial readers' favourite. It is 'faultless',
writes one this year. Winter or summer, says
another, 'everything ticks over to perfection'.
Rooms, designed to soak up the ever-changing
river view, are painted in muted pastels and
washed with watery light. Some have French
doors to a balcony; others, sliding glass doors
to decking with glass balustrade. Junior suites
have a dual-aspect lounge and a wet room with
drench shower. All rooms have air conditioning,
a coffee machine, fresh milk, and binoculars
for porpoise-spotting. The staff are 'fabulous',
under 'ever-present' manager Paul Downing. In
the restaurant, Peter Alcroft uses local produce,
freshly landed fish and shellfish for his unfussy
dishes – perhaps a risotto, fish pie or dry-aged
South Devon beef. There is a lounge menu and, in
season, Cloud Nine pop-up van-bar parks on the
waterfront to serve drinks and lunches – Exmouth
mussels, pulled pork and ciabatta – to eat alfresco
as you watch people messing about in boats. (Ian
Malone, Peter Anderson, and others)

Sandquay Road
Dartmouth TQ6 9PH

T: 01803 832580
E: reception@dartmarina.com
W: dartmarina.com

BEDROOMS: 49. 4 on ground floor,
1 suitable for disabled, plus
4 apartments.
OPEN: all year.
FACILITIES: lounge/bar, restaurant,
in-room TV (Freeview), lawn, terrace,
spa (heated indoor swimming pool,
8 by 4 metres, gym), lounge and
restaurant wheelchair accessible.
BACKGROUND MUSIC: in restaurant and
lounge/bar during the day.
LOCATION: on waterfront.
CHILDREN: all ages welcomed.
DOGS: allowed in some bedrooms and
lounge, not in restaurant.
CREDIT CARDS: MC, Visa.
PRICES: per room B&B single
£170–£368, double £190–£408, D,B&B
double £261–£480. À la carte £40.
1-night bookings usually refused
weekends at peak times.

**SEE ALSO SHORTLIST**

# DEDHAM Essex                                 MAP 2:C5

## DEDHAM HALL

There is 'nothing chichi' about Wendy and Jim
Sarton's 15th-century manor house, which stands
in 'pleasantly rural, overgrown tranquillity' in
gardens where rabbits skitter. Lounges have
a country, comfy, lived-in feel, with exposed
beams, open fires, squashy sofas. Bedrooms are
traditionally styled, with a 'comfortable bed,
high-quality linen'. One Guide insider noted a
hint of eccentricity, but enjoyed his stay. Another
was plied with tea and home-made brownies in
'a private parlour with a bright fire' on arrival.
If you come with children, he advises, this is the
ideal rural retreat. But the special appeal is to
artists, who can take residential courses here in the
heart of Constable country. At night Wendy cooks
a three-course dinner – typical dishes include
beef fillet with wild mushrooms and red wine,
pan-fried lemon sole, mushroom and cream-
cheese pancake. Vegans should consult before
booking. Service is 'prompt and courteous', wine
is affordable. In the morning, 'buttery scrambled
eggs and home-baked bread' are served on
'attractive vintage china'. It's a perfect prelude
to a visit to the Munnings Art Museum half
a mile away.

### 25% DISCOUNT VOUCHERS

Brook Street
Dedham
Colchester CO7 6AD

T: 01206 323027
E: sarton@dedhamhall.co.uk
W: dedhamhall.co.uk

BEDROOMS: 20. 16 in annexe around art
studio, some on ground floor suitable
for disabled.
OPEN: all year except Christmas–New
Year.
FACILITIES: 2 lounges, bar, dining
room, studio, in-room TV (terrestrial),
6-acre grounds (pond, gardens, fields),
lounge and dining room wheelchair
accessible.
BACKGROUND MUSIC: none.
LOCATION: end of village High Street
(set back from road).
CHILDREN: all ages welcomed.
DOGS: allowed in some bedrooms, not
in public rooms.
CREDIT CARDS: MC, Visa.
PRICES: per room B&B single £80,
double £130, D,B&B single £110,
double £190. À la carte/fixed-price
dinner, for residents only (or by prior
arrangement), £35.

## DEDHAM Essex

### MAISON TALBOOTH   `NEW`

In 1952, Gerald Milsom stopped at some Tudor tea rooms beside the River Stour and liked them so much he bought them. Thus began the Talbooth story, with a renowned restaurant and, later, this luxury hotel with fine views. Gerald died in 2005, but the business is still run by the Milsom family, who also own The Pier at Harwich, Harwich (see entry). A Guide insider praised the friendly ambience, 'eye-catching furniture', and 'staff who can't do enough for you'. Bedrooms, each named after a poet, have fresh milk and Aromatherapy Associates toiletries. Shakespeare has a sunken bath, Kipling a wet room, and Browning a roll-top bath and walk-in shower. 'Shelley has a sublime view over Dedham Vale that could be straight out of a Constable painting.' Best of all is 'the lovely pool house in its own walled garden, with an open fire in winter, honesty bar, lounge, and changing facilities'. The nearby road can get busy, but guests are driven by courtesy car to Le Talbooth for riverside dining on such dishes as Dedham Vale beef Rossini or ricotta and cèpe dumplings. Breakfast and lunch are served back at base in the Garden Room. (JK)

**25% DISCOUNT VOUCHERS**

Stratford Road
Dedham CO7 6HN

T: 01206 322367
E: maison@milsomhotels.com
W: milsomhotels.com/maison-talbooth/

BEDROOMS: 12. 5 on ground floor with walk-in shower.
OPEN: all year.
FACILITIES: lounge, Garden Room, courtesy car to restaurant 1 minute away, 5-acre grounds (tennis), outdoor heated pool (pool house, hot tub, honesty bar), in-room TV (Sky, Freeview), spa, civil wedding licence, parking ramp, some public areas wheelchair accessible, adapted toilet.
BACKGROUND MUSIC: none.
LOCATION: ½ mile W of Dedham village.
CHILDREN: all ages welcomed.
DOGS: allowed in bedrooms and lounge, on terrace and in lounge area of brasserie, but not in Talbooth restaurant.
CREDIT CARDS: Amex, MC, Visa.
PRICES: per room B&B £295–£375, D,B&B £400–£415. À la carte £65 (Talbooth), £37 (Milsoms).

# DEDHAM Essex

MAP 2:C5

## THE SUN INN

In the heart of Constable country, Piers Baker's 14th-century inn is 'what pubs were meant to look like', from the eye-catching sign outside to the beamed ceilings and wooden floors within. The panelled lounge, with 'old books on the window ledges', is home to a log-burning stove, sofas arranged around it. In the bar, a 'convivial local gathering spot', the walls are hung with original artwork, old photographs and advertising posters. The 'restful, gracefully homey rooms' are a mix of period and contemporary styling, with perhaps a brass, oak or half-tester bed. Two, above the dining room, are accessed from the 'small, paved beer garden' via a Tudor staircase – the twin had a bathroom separated 'by a partition that didn't reach the ceiling'. A Guide inspector noted with approval 'a powerful rain shower', ground coffee, Abahna toiletries, and the soothing chimes from St Mary's church. Chef Jack Levine cooks 'modern pubby food' such as rare breed meats, and hake with squid ink sauce; there is also a vegan menu. A locally sourced breakfast with fresh-baked bread sets you up for a tour of the famous landscape.

High Street
Dedham
Colchester CO7 6DF

T: 01206 323351
E: office@thesuninndedham.com
W: thesuninndedham.com

BEDROOMS: 7. 2 across the terrace, approached by Tudor staircase.
OPEN: all year except 25/26 Dec.
FACILITIES: lounge, bar, dining room, in-room TV (Freeview), 1-acre walled garden (covered terrace, children's play area, garden bar), unsuitable for disabled.
BACKGROUND MUSIC: all day in public areas.
LOCATION: village centre.
CHILDREN: all ages welcomed.
DOGS: in bar and Oak Room, in guest bedrooms by arrangement and subject to terms and conditions (not in dining room).
CREDIT CARDS: Amex, MC, Visa.
PRICES: per room B&B single £90–£135, double £150, D,B&B double £200. À la carte £36, weekly set menu £25.50.

# DUNSTER Somerset

MAP 1:B5

## THE LUTTRELL ARMS HOTEL

You can almost hear the clatter of hoofs and the trundling of wheels at Nigel and Anne Way's Tudor coaching inn in a medieval village on the Dartmoor borders, dominated by its hilltop castle. The bedrooms have a mix of vintage and contemporary furniture. The most spectacular has an antique four-poster and an ornate 17th-century overmantel, while some have a private courtyard and access to the garden. There is an atmospheric bar with carved oak windows that extend over two floors, best admired from the courtyard that they overlook. An all-day bar menu is also served in an eclectically furnished lounge with log-burner, grandfather clock and armchairs dressed in patchwork. On sunny days, you might eat in the garden, while in Psalter's restaurant (named after the Luttrell Psalter in the British Library) Barrie Tucker's ambitious menus include such dishes as smoked haddock and seafood chowder, and game-stuffed saddle of rabbit with white bean and chorizo cassoulet. At breakfast there is kedgeree, a full Somerset with free-range eggs and black pudding, and smashed avocado on toast. Reports, please.

32–36 High Street
Dunster TA24 6SG

T: 01643 821555
E: enquiry@luttrellarms.co.uk
W: luttrellarms.co.uk

BEDROOMS: 29. Some on ground floor, 1 with 'easy access'.
OPEN: all year.
FACILITIES: lounge, 2 bars, snug, restaurant, function rooms, in-room TV (Freeview), civil wedding licence, courtyard, garden (alfresco dining), lounge and restaurant wheelchair accessible, no adapted toilet.
BACKGROUND MUSIC: in restaurant.
LOCATION: village centre, 3½ miles SE of Minehead.
CHILDREN: all ages welcomed, some rooms not suitable for under-14s (call to check availability).
DOGS: allowed in most bedrooms, bar, not in restaurant.
CREDIT CARDS: Amex, MC, Visa.
PRICES: per room B&B single £97.50–£167.50, double £130–£185. À la carte £35. Min. 2-nights weekends.

# EAST CHISENBURY Wiltshire

MAP 2:D2

## THE RED LION FREEHOUSE

♀ Previous César winner

On the edge of Salisbury Plain not far from
Stonehenge, this thatched 19th-century beer house
is run as a friendly village local and Michelin-
starred pub-with-rooms by chef/proprietors Guy
and Brittany Manning. 'It has real character,'
readers write. 'We were welcomed by a friendly
barman who recognised us from a previous
visit.' The food is the star here, with carefully
sourced, home-grown and foraged ingredients
in such dishes as Salisbury Plain venison with
celeriac, cavallo nero, prunes and sauce poivrade;
and roast Cornish cod with gyoza and pak choi.
Pastry chef Brittany turns her hand to such
delights as Yorkshire 'rhubarb and custard' tart
with hazelnut crunch and Negroni sorbet. The
boutique bedrooms don't disappoint either. In a
modern bungalow opposite, they have full-height
glass doors on to decking beside the River Avon,
a king-size bed, minibar and smart, modern
bathroom. The largest has its own entrance, a
leather sofa bed for an extra guest, a roll-top bath
and rainfall shower. 'We chatted to a couple who
decided to stay on for a second night, they were so
impressed.' (Terence Bendixson, C and ES)

East Chisenbury
Pewsey SN9 6AQ

T: 01980 671124
E: troutbeck@redlionfreehouse.com
W: redlionfreehouse.com

BEDROOMS: 5. On ground floor,
1 suitable for disabled.
OPEN: all year except 25 Dec, kitchen
closed Sun evening, all day Mon/Tues.
FACILITIES: bar/restaurant, private
dining room, in-room TV (Freeview),
½-acre garden.
BACKGROUND MUSIC: in pub/restaurant.
LOCATION: in village, 6 miles S of
Pewsey.
CHILDREN: all ages welcomed, travel
cot from £15, extra bed for child £50.
DOGS: allowed in 1 bedroom by
arrangement (£10 a night).
CREDIT CARDS: Amex, MC, Visa.
PRICES: per room B&B £160–195
(£245 Sat and peak times), D,B&B
£195–£245 (Wed–Fri, non-peak
times). 3-course fixed-price menu
£24–£28, à la carte £60, pre-booked
7-course tasting menu £75.

# EAST GRINSTEAD Sussex

## GRAVETYE MANOR

♧ Previous César winner

Jeremy and Elizabeth Hosking's beloved and beautiful Elizabethan manor house stands in glorious gardens, amid 1,000 acres of woodland. 'It is absolutely exceptional,' runs a typical report of this Relais & Châteaux country house hotel. 'The professionalism of the staff, the high quality of the rooms, the extraordinary garden, the paintings and the delicious dinner.' Bedrooms have fine antiques, original features and views of those gardens, created by former resident William Robinson, which are Gravetye's great glory. Public rooms have blazing log fires, oak-panelled walls, portraits and fresh flowers. A smart-casual dress code in the glass-walled dining room reflects the hotel's relaxed, spoiling ethos. Michelin-starred chef George Blogg uses produce from the kitchen gardens and orchard in such dishes as tasting of Creedy Carver duck with young parsnip, honey and Gravetye lavender. 'The passion fruit soufflé was to die for,' writes one reader, and the service continues to win high praise. 'Gravetye is certainly expensive but it appears to have a very satisfied clientele.' (Bill Bennett, Jonathan Rose, F and IW, and others)

Vowels Lane
West Hoathly
East Grinstead RH19 4LJ

T: 01342 810567
E: info@gravetyemanor.co.uk
W: gravetyemanor.co.uk

BEDROOMS: 17.
OPEN: all year.
FACILITIES: 2 lounges, bar, restaurant, 2 private dining rooms, in-room TV (Sky), civil wedding licence, 1,000-acre grounds (woodland, ornamental and kitchen gardens, meadow, orchard, lake, croquet lawn, glasshouses), restaurant wheelchair accessible, adapted toilet.
BACKGROUND MUSIC: in bar.
LOCATION: 4 miles SW of East Grinstead.
CHILDREN: not under 7 in dining room.
DOGS: not allowed.
CREDIT CARDS: Amex, MC, Visa.
PRICES: per room B&B £295–£950. Set dinner £80, tasting menu £95 (plus discretionary service). 1-night bookings sometimes refused at weekends.

# EAST HOATHLY Sussex

## OLD WHYLY

'The house is beautiful, the garden is glorious,' writes a reader this year, after a return visit to Sarah Burgoyne's Georgian farmhouse, so handy for Glyndebourne. Interiors of this 'delightful' B&B are filled with antiques and paintings. Cheery fires burn on winter days. The bedrooms are spacious, pretty and traditional. One has a shower, another a bath en suite; two have a private bathroom. The gardens blaze with year-round colour, from the first spring bulbs through azalea time to autumn. Guests have full use of a hard tennis court in the orchard, and an outdoor pool with wisteria-draped pool house. They can take tea alfresco, and walk in an adjoining estate, spotting rare orchids. At night, Paris-trained Sarah cooks a three-course dinner, using local and home-grown produce for such dishes as curried squash soup, spring Southdown lamb and chocolate tart. Breakfast is 'as good as you'll find anywhere', with 'delicious home-made stewed fruit and jams', new-laid eggs from the ducks and hens, honey from the hives in bee heaven. A picnic is provided on request. 'Highly recommended.' (Catrin Treadwell, and others)

London Road
East Hoathly BN8 6EL

T: 01825 840216
E: stay@oldwhyly.co.uk
W: oldwhyly.co.uk

BEDROOMS: 4.
OPEN: all year.
FACILITIES: drawing room, dining room, in-room TV (Freeview), 4-acre garden, heated outdoor swimming pool (14 by 7 metres), tennis, unsuitable for disabled.
BACKGROUND MUSIC: none.
LOCATION: 1 mile N of village.
CHILDREN: all ages welcomed.
DOGS: allowed in drawing room, not in dining room or unattended in bedrooms.
CREDIT CARDS: none.
PRICES: per room B&B £99–£150, D,B&B £139–£190. Set dinner £40, hamper £42 per person. 1-night bookings may be refused at weekends in summer season.

# EAST PORTLEMOUTH Devon

MAP 1:E4

## GARA ROCK

'The perfect pit stop' on the Coast Path between Salcombe and Dartmouth, Gara Rock stands 'high on the cliff above a beautiful beach'. Driving there is quite an adventure, down country roads where your satnav might send you on a scenic detour. It's worth the trip, though, to find, as a Guide insider did, a 'stylish yet relaxed hotel with sublime sea views', built on the footprint of old coastguard cottages. Sea-facing bedrooms, in earth tones, have a balcony or terrace. Loft suites have a freestanding roll-top bath and an en suite rainfall shower. 'Enormous garden suites open on to the lawn and are perfect for dog owners and families.' A reader loved the setting, the beach, two pools and plush cinema, but 'maintenance needs a bit of an overview' with 'lots of lights not working at night'. The open-plan public space includes an all-day bistro, with sea views 'enhanced by the curved floor-to-ceiling windows'. Here, they serve 'unpretentious, tasty dishes such as excellent fish and chips and Salcombe crab', although 'limited menu choices' for children mean it is only 'fine for one night'. (JK, C and ES, and others)

East Portlemouth
Salcombe TQ8 8FA

T: 01548 845946
E: info@gararock.com
W: gararock.com

BEDROOMS: 30. Accessed externally, 1 suite separate from hotel.
OPEN: all year.
FACILITIES: restaurant, private dining area, lounge bar, spa, cinema room, terrace, indoor and outdoor pool, in-room TV, civil wedding licence, public rooms wheelchair accessible, adapted toilet on floor below, reached via lift.
BACKGROUND MUSIC: in public areas.
LOCATION: on cliff-top, 1 mile SE of East Portlemouth.
CHILDREN: all ages welcomed.
DOGS: allowed in some rooms, grounds, lounge bar and restaurant (£40 per dog).
CREDIT CARDS: Amex, MC, Visa.
PRICES: per room B&B £225–£1,100. À la carte £42, fixed-price menu £19.50–£24.50.

# EASTBOURNE Sussex

MAP 2:E4

## BELLE TOUT LIGHTHOUSE

The lantern room at this remote B&B between
the Seven Sisters chalk cliffs and Beachy Head
commands 360-degree views over the sea and the
South Downs. Built in 1832 and decommissioned
in 1902, the lighthouse has been welcoming guests
since 2010. The atmospheric Keeper's Loft, with
exposed brick, fireplace, small window and double
bed reached by a ladder, is the only bedroom in
the tower. The others – lighter and brighter – are
in the adjoining house. Here, the Captain's Cabin,
'although rather small, has all you would expect
from a well-fitted-out hotel room', write readers
this year, who were 'made very comfortable'. Ian
Noall, the manager and 'very informative host',
invites all guests for drinks between 5 and 6 pm
in the cosy lounge with fireplace, lots of comfy
seating and great views through plate-glass
windows. Some eat a picnic supper here, having
made a beeline for the Beehive deli in East Dean,
a short drive away, where The Tiger Inn also
provides 'a very good pub supper'. Then it's back
up to the lantern to play CDs and gaze at stars. In
all, 'a fascinating experience'. (Richard Bright)

Beachy Head Road
Eastbourne BN20 0AE

T: 01323 423185
E: info@belletout.co.uk
W: belletout.co.uk

BEDROOMS: 6. 5 in house, 1 in
lighthouse tower (bunk bed).
OPEN: all year except Christmas/New
Year.
FACILITIES: 2 lounges, breakfast room,
free Wi-Fi (in some rooms and some
public areas), in-room TV (Freeview),
terrace, garden, unsuitable for
disabled.
BACKGROUND MUSIC: none.
LOCATION: 3 miles W of Eastbourne,
2 miles S of East Dean village (pub,
deli).
CHILDREN: not under 15.
DOGS: not allowed.
CREDIT CARDS: MC, Visa.
PRICES: per room B&B £180–£240. Min.
2 nights, though 1-night bookings
may be accepted (check for availability
in the week before proposed stay).

**SEE ALSO SHORTLIST**

# EASTON GREY Wiltshire

MAP 3:E5

## WHATLEY MANOR

From the moment your car is valet-parked and luggage whisked to your room, you know this honeyed Cotswold manor house will deliver cosseting luxury – and star-spangled dining (Relais & Châteaux). Impressive public areas are 'decorated in the best possible taste', reports our inspector, with wood panelling, rugs on polished floors, paintings, and table lamps creating intimate spaces. Relax in the spa or the gardens, and prepare for dinner. In 2019, Niall Keating gained a second Michelin star for 'daring and innovative' cooking which, for The Dining Room's taster menu, might include chorizo risotto plus scallop and caviar or grilled Wagyu with kimchi. Less costly is Grey's Brasserie with dishes such as pork belly porchetta. There are vegan and vegetarian menus. Bedrooms are uncluttered but comfortable with all the right touches: good reading lights, fruit, robes, chocolates. Bathrooms, with under-floor heating and L'Occitane products, have 'candles for romantic bathing'. The 'very good' breakfast menu includes 'perfectly cooked poached eggs' while 'the head waiter greets each person by name'.

Easton Grey SN16 0RB

T: 01666 822888
E: reservations@whatleymanor.com
W: whatleymanor.com

BEDROOMS: 23. Some on ground floor, 1 suitable for disabled.
OPEN: all year. Dining Room restaurant open Thurs–Sun eve; Grey's Brasserie open all week.
FACILITIES: 3 lounges, 2 bars, brasserie, restaurant, cinema, gym, spa, in-room TV (Sky, Freeview), 12-acre garden, civil wedding licence, conference facilities, public areas and restaurants wheelchair accessible, adapted toilet.
BACKGROUND MUSIC: in public areas.
LOCATION: 6½ miles from Tetbury.
CHILDREN: over-11s welcomed.
DOGS: allowed in some bedrooms (£30 per night), garden, public areas except restaurant and bar.
CREDIT CARDS: Amex, MC, Visa.
PRICES: per room B&B £249–£699. Tasting menu (Dining Room) £130, à la carte (Brasserie) £50. 1-night bookings usually refused at weekends.

# ECKINGTON Worcestershire

## ECKINGTON MANOR

Judy Gardner's restaurant-with-rooms and
purpose-built cookery school sit amid a working
farm in the Avon valley. Bedrooms in the timber-
frame farmhouse and outbuildings have a Fired
Earth bathroom and White Company toiletries.
Pricier rooms have hand-painted silk wallpaper,
perhaps an in-room roll-top bath or a log-burning
stove. Some rooms, under a sloping ceiling, have
only a skylight window. From Wednesday to
Saturday there is afternoon tea in the Garden
bar, and lunch and dinner in the restaurant, as
well as Sunday lunch. New chef Greg Newman's
farm-to-fork menus showcase meat from the farm
and ingredients from local suppliers in such dishes
as roast rump of Eckington beef, caramelised
cauliflower, Berkswell cheese and smoked bone
marrow – for vegans, hay-baked celeriac, smoked
celeriac purée, toasted hazelnuts, wild mushrooms
and celeriac jus. Dinner is 'the highlight of this
hotel', the service 'first class'. Breakfast is cooked
to order, and picnic hampers are available. When
the restaurant is closed, a 20-minute drive to
Broadway suggests itself.

**25% DISCOUNT VOUCHERS**

Hammock Road
Eckington WR10 3BJ

T: 01386 751600
E: info@eckingtonmanor.co.uk
W: eckingtonmanor.co.uk

BEDROOMS: 17. All in courtyard
annexes, some on ground floor.
OPEN: all year except 25/26 Dec,
restaurant closed Sun evening, Mon,
Tues.
FACILITIES: lift, 2 sitting rooms (1 with
bar area), restaurant, function rooms,
in-room TV (Freeview), civil wedding
licence, cookery school, 260-acre
grounds (lawns, herb garden, orchard,
farm), public areas wheelchair
accessible, adapted toilet.
BACKGROUND MUSIC: in garden bar and
restaurant.
LOCATION: 4 miles SW of Pershore.
CHILDREN: not under 8.
DOGS: allowed in 1 bedroom, not in
public rooms.
CREDIT CARDS: MC, Visa.
PRICES: per room B&B £149–£365. Set
dinner £48, tasting menus £75.

# EGTON BRIDGE Yorkshire

## BROOM HOUSE
## AT EGTON BRIDGE

With its uninterrupted views of moors and farmland, this smart farmhouse B&B in an acre of garden feels remote, yet is only a ten-minute walk from the riverside village of Egton Bridge. The Victorian building has been stylishly modernised with slate floors, pale oak doors and soothing Farrow & Ball colours: 'modern, clean and well thought through'. Most bedrooms have 'a cottagey feel', done with 'a light touch', with pale-coloured furniture, muslin curtains and modern bathroom; two are more contemporary in style, while second-floor rooms are cosier, with beams, and have the best views. Go for walks on the moors from the doorstep – the coast-to-coast path is only half a mile away – and return to a fire in the sitting room on wintry days, or birdsong on the large, stone terrace in summer. Two village pubs are within walking distance. Although a 'short menu', breakfast, taken in the large, modern dining-room extension, has good local sourcing, 'very friendly service' and 'particularly good scrambled egg'. Throughout guests' stay, the feeling is 'relaxed and peaceful'. (HP, and others)

Broom House Lane
Egton Bridge YO21 1XD

T: 07423 636783
E: info@broom-house.co.uk
W: broom-house.co.uk

BEDROOMS: 7. 1 in cottage annexe.
OPEN: Apr–Oct 2020, limited availability Nov–Feb, fully reopen Mar 2021.
FACILITIES: lounge, breakfast room, in-room TV (Freeview), 1-acre garden.
BACKGROUND MUSIC: in breakfast room.
LOCATION: ½ mile W of village.
CHILDREN: only over-12s welcomed.
DOGS: not allowed.
CREDIT CARDS: MC, Visa.
PRICES: per room B&B £90–£140. Min. 2-night bookings for summer weekends.

# ELLASTONE Staffordshire

MAP 3:B6

## THE DUNCOMBE ARMS

Immortalised as 'The Donnithorne Arms' in George Eliot's Adam Bede, this Victorian pub was boarded up before Johnny and Laura Greenall stepped in to save it. Now, it makes both a handy and a comfortable base from which to explore the Peak District, or to visit Chatsworth or Alton Towers. Fires burn in cosy but contemporary Johnny's bar and in the split-level main dining room. Here, Jake Boyce wins acclaim for such locally sourced dishes as artichoke, truffle and cultured cream, roast plaice with tarragon and chicken and butter sauce, and guineafowl with oyster mushroom, leek and kohlrabi. Air-conditioned bedrooms at the back, in Walnut House, are decorated with artisan wallpaper and are hung with artwork for sale. Extras include a Roberts radio, home-baked biscuits, Bamford bath products, and an umbrella in case it is raining when you head to the bar. A reader's room had French doors on to a terrace, and a coffee machine and fresh milk in the lobby. Most rooms have a bath and walk-in shower; four have a shower only. Breakfast includes freshly squeezed OJ, 'a detox concoction', and home-baked sourdough toast.

**25% DISCOUNT VOUCHERS**

Ellastone
Ashbourne DE6 2GZ

T: 01335 324275
E: hello@duncombearms.co.uk
W: duncombearms.co.uk

BEDROOMS: 10. All in Walnut House annexe, with 2 family rooms, 1 suitable for disabled.
OPEN: all year.
FACILITIES: bar, 2 dining rooms plus private dining room, in-room smart TV, no mobile signal, garden (alfresco dining, fire pit), car park, electric charging points, bar and dining room wheelchair accessible, adapted toilet.
BACKGROUND MUSIC: quiet in bar and restaurant.
LOCATION: on B5032, 5 miles SW of Ashbourne.
CHILDREN: all ages welcomed.
DOGS: allowed in some bedrooms (£20 charge), bar (dog-friendly tables for dining).
CREDIT CARDS: MC, Visa.
PRICES: per room B&B £160–£190, D,B&B from £195. À la carte £40, market menu (Mon–Thurs) £18.50–£22.50.

# ELLERBY Yorkshire

## THE ELLERBY COUNTRY INN

**NEW**

'A really good find – an inn where residents come first.' In 2020, a long-time friend of the Guide discovered this family- and dog-friendly Yorkshire village hostelry. With a pretty garden, crisp bedrooms and good pub food, the sandstone inn, with its climbing roses and colourful planters, sits in a row of cottages in pin-neat Ellerby, a mile from the sweep of Runswick Bay. 'Immaculate housekeeping' makes the simple, quiet bedrooms – breezy colours, modern oak furniture – perfect for a good night's sleep after a day's walking. Some of the shower-only bathrooms can be a squeeze, but they are modern, and all rooms have fresh milk, robes and king- or super-king-size bed. The best share a balcony overlooking the garden. Dine alfresco if the weather allows; otherwise choose the bar or restaurant. 'Superior classic pub food' ranges from Whitby scampi and home-made pies to sea bass or steak, and there are good vegetarian options. Owners Mark and Georgie Alderson are 'keen to ensure you have everything you need'. A 'lovely place to stay – and eat'. (Lynn Wildgoose)

12–14 Ryeland Lane
Ellerby
Whitby TS13 5LP

T: 01947 840342
E: relax@ellerbyhotel.co.uk
W: ellerbyhotel.co.uk

BEDROOMS: 10. 4 on ground floor, 1 suitable for disabled.
OPEN: all year.
FACILITIES: bar, snug, restaurant, conservatory/lounge, garden, in-room TV (Sky), public rooms wheelchair accessible, adapted toilet.
BACKGROUND MUSIC: public areas.
LOCATION: in village, 8 miles W of Whitby.
CHILDREN: all ages welcomed.
DOGS: allowed in 3 bedrooms, garden and lounge/conservatory, not in bar or restaurant.
CREDIT CARDS: MC, Visa.
PRICES: per room B&B single £70–£120, double £100–£150. 3-course à la carte £27.

# ERMINGTON Devon

MAP 1:D4

## PLANTATION HOUSE

Between Dartmoor and the sea, in a village
remarkable for its crooked church spire, Richard
Hendey's former Georgian rectory is today 'a
really good hotel'. Readers on a return visit were
'greeted with a warm welcome back', and shown
to a 'clean, spacious, very comfortable' room 'with
a super-king-size bed', armchairs and coffee table.
Pleasing touches include home-made cake, fresh
fruit, a cafetière, flowers from the garden and
White Company toiletries. Some bathrooms have
a bath and separate shower. What impresses above
all is the commitment to seasonal, local produce,
with everything possible made on the premises,
from breads and pastries to truffles. Richard
Hendey and John Raines cook a nightly-changing
menu with a 'surprise appetiser' and at least four
choices at each course. A typical dish: fillet of
brill on a Maris Piper chive potato cake with lime
hollandaise, ginger courgettes and asparagus.
Breakfast (in bed, if you choose) is 'of a similar
high standard', with freshly squeezed orange
juice, freshly baked croissants, smoked haddock
and the full Devon. (Steve Hur)

**25% DISCOUNT VOUCHERS**

Totnes Road
Ermington
Plymouth PL21 9NS

T: 01548 831100
E: info@plantationhousehotel.co.uk
W: plantationhousehotel.co.uk

BEDROOMS: 8.
OPEN: all year, restaurant (dinner only)
closed some Sun evenings.
FACILITIES: lounge/bar, 2 dining rooms,
in-room TV (Freeview), in-room
massage, terrace, 1-acre garden,
restaurant, bar and lounge wheelchair
accessible, no adapted toilet.
BACKGROUND MUSIC: background jazz
(sometimes live) in public rooms,
classical 'when required or deemed
suitable'.
LOCATION: 10 miles E of Plymouth.
CHILDREN: all ages welcomed.
DOGS: allowed in 1 bedroom, not in
public rooms.
CREDIT CARDS: Amex, MC, Visa.
PRICES: per room B&B single £90–£195,
double £110–£230. Set dinner £40–£45
(items can be charged separately).
1-night bookings sometimes refused
on bank holiday weekends.

# EVERSHOT Dorset

MAP 1:C6

## THE ACORN INN

A literary past accompanies this former 16th-century coaching inn, which features as the Sow and Acorn in the novel Tess of the d'Urbervilles and in two of Thomas Hardy's short stories. Bedrooms make the most of the literary link with names inspired by Hardy's characters and fictional locations. Snug rooms are small but stylishly done; larger rooms might have a bay window overlooking the village, or perhaps an antique four-poster carved with acorns. The loft suite has a separate sitting room. A member of the Red Carnation group (see Summer Lodge, next entry), the inn has a cosy lounge with roaring fire, country bar and smart restaurant with elegant hamstone fireplace (more carved acorns). Here, chef Robert Ndungu offers hearty seasonal dishes with ingredients from local and sustainable sources. Perhaps rump of Dorset Horn lamb or crispy belly of Dorset pork followed by a cheeseboard of regional favourites, including Dorset Red and Glastonbury Twanger Cheddar. Breakfast is equally fortifying, with scrumptious cooked-to-order choices as well as a vegetarian and fish option, and bread from the village bakery. Reports, please.

28 Fore Street
Evershot DT2 0JW

T: 01935 83228
E: stay@acorn-inn.co.uk
W: acorn-inn.co.uk

BEDROOMS: 10.
OPEN: all year.
FACILITIES: 2 bars, restaurant, lounge, in-room TV (Sky, Freeview), skittle alley, beer garden, access to spa, gym at sister hotel opposite (£15 per day), bar and restaurant wheelchair accessible, toilet not adapted.
BACKGROUND MUSIC: in bar and restaurant.
LOCATION: in village, 10 miles S of Yeovil.
CHILDREN: all ages welcomed.
DOGS: allowed (£12 charge per dog per night, water bowls, towels, treats).
CREDIT CARDS: Amex, MC, Visa.
PRICES: per room B&B £105–£240, D,B&B £185–£330. À la carte £35. Min. 2-night stay at weekends during peak season.

## EVERSHOT Dorset                                   MAP 1:C6

### SUMMER LODGE

A Georgian dower house extended to designs
by Thomas Hardy, this luxury hotel and spa
(Relais & Châteaux) stands in landscaped grounds
adjoining a deer park. 'We are big fans of this
lovely hotel,' write regular visitors. 'Bedrooms
are all different; all beautifully and traditionally
furnished.' They have gentle touches of humour
– a print of Lowry's The Schoolyard, vintage
political caricatures. Even the smallest rooms have
fresh fruit and flowers, and REN toiletries. You
can take a cream tea in the beautiful drawing
room, the conservatory or whisky lounge. In the
restaurant, Steven Titman's locally sourced menus
range from pasta to such dishes as Lyme Bay
gurnard and king prawn with lobster risotto; for
vegans, chickpea and roasted red pepper chilli.
Under-12s can dine in the conservatory and it's
a short walk down the road to The Acorn Inn
(previous entry), also part of the Red Carnation
group. Special praise this year goes to joint general
manager Jack Mackenzie. 'When a guest was
taken ill after 10 pm, he insisted on driving him
and his wife to A&E, waited with them, and
returned them to the hotel.' (Ian Dewey)

9 Fore Street
Evershot DT2 0JR

T: 01935 482000
E: summerlodge@rchmail.com
W: summerlodgehotel.com

BEDROOMS: 24. 6 in coach house, 3 in
courtyard house, 5 in cottages, 1 on
ground floor suitable for disabled.
OPEN: all year.
FACILITIES: lounge, drawing room,
restaurant, conservatory, meeting
room, in-room TV (Sky), indoor
pool, spa, civil wedding licence,
4-acre grounds (tennis), public rooms
wheelchair accessible, adapted toilet.
BACKGROUND MUSIC: in bar/whisky
lounge.
LOCATION: 10 miles S of Yeovil.
CHILDREN: all ages welcomed.
DOGS: allowed in some bedrooms,
whisky lounge.
CREDIT CARDS: Amex, MC, Visa.
PRICES: per room B&B double
£235–£690. Fixed-price dinner
£58–£75, vegetarian £47–£60, à la carte
£38 (conservatory). 1-night bookings
sometimes refused.

# EXETER Devon

MAP 1:C5

## SOUTHERNHAY HOUSE

Ⓠ Previous César winner

A sense of old-world elegance where 'style is a central feature' can be found in this independent boutique hotel not far from the cathedral. Owners Deborah Clark and Tony Orchard have added a 20th-century sensibility to the Grade II listed town house, the original Georgian features complemented by soft Farrow & Ball colours, quirky antiques and designer furnishings. A Guide inspector found that 'exquisite' bedrooms had none of the 'charmingly dog-eared features often present in even the nicest of places'. All rooms have a comfortable seating area, and overlook the pocket garden or leafy Southernhay Gardens. Some larger rooms have an in-room roll-top bath tub. A new self-contained apartment has just been added. On the ground floor, a glamorous bar, with a new glass pavilion extension, is the place for cocktails and fine wines. The 'exceptional food' is 'an experience in its own right', with a changing menu of seasonal dishes, simply cooked, and served in the 'intimate' dining room. Breakfast brings a wide array of hot dishes cooked to order. 'I would go there purely for the hotel, irrespective of whether I wanted to visit the city.'

36 Southernhay East
Exeter EX1 1NX

T: 01392 439000
E: home@southernhayhouse.com
W: southernhayhouse.com

BEDROOMS: 12.
OPEN: all year.
FACILITIES: bar, restaurant, private dining, in-room TV (Freeview), small lawn, veranda, terrace, civil wedding licence, public rooms wheelchair accessible.
BACKGROUND MUSIC: in public areas.
LOCATION: central Exeter.
CHILDREN: children over 14 welcomed on an adult basis.
DOGS: only in the bar and terrace.
CREDIT CARDS: MC, Visa.
PRICES: per room B&B £141–£301. À la carte £35.

# EXMOUTH Devon

## LYMPSTONE MANOR

The chef/patron at this country house hotel on the Exe estuary is Michael Caines, whose eye for detail informs everything, from the hand-painted wallpaper to the Michelin-starred cuisine. References to the abundant local birdlife are ubiquitous, from the hanging birdcage seats in the lobby to the avian-inspired names of the luxurious bedrooms and suites, each with its own distinct plumage: Kingfisher has a vivid blue bedhead and fireplace tiles to match, Greenfinch its own private garden, Woodwarbler an outdoor fire pit and soak tub. All rooms have L'Occitane toiletries and a gin tray. In the public spaces, muted colours and clean lines reflect the beauty of the surroundings. Assistant manager Anca Paraschiv has been promoted to general manager, so there are unlikely to be any unsettling changes. Top of the pecking order, naturally, is Caines's modern European cuisine, with a tasting menu that wings its way from langoustine cannelloni to white chocolate candle, via galantine of quail, salted cod and Newlyn crab, partridge and loin of Powderham venison, each dish paired with wine from the hotel's extensive cellar.

Courtlands Lane
Exmouth EX8 3NZ

T: 01395 202040
E: welcome@lympstonemanor.co.uk
W: lympstonemanor.co.uk

BEDROOMS: 21. 5 on ground floor, 1 suitable for disabled.
OPEN: all year.
FACILITIES: 3 dining rooms, reception lounge, lounge, bar, 28-acre grounds (vineyard), in-room TV (Freeview), civil wedding licence, public areas wheelchair accessible, adapted toilet.
BACKGROUND MUSIC: all day in public rooms.
LOCATION: in centre, close to waterfront.
CHILDREN: all ages welcomed (no under-5s in restaurant).
DOGS: in 2 bedrooms.
CREDIT CARDS: Amex, MC, Visa.
PRICES: per room B&B £350–£1,147, D,B&B £630–£1,427. Tasting menus £150–£160, à la carte £140 (discretionary service charge of 12½% is added to food).

# FAVERSHAM Kent

MAP 2:D5

## READ'S

✿ Previous César winner

'We can see why you awarded it a César,' writes a trusted reader about this restaurant-with-rooms which has been run by David and Rona Pitchford for 45 years. The Georgian Macknade Manor makes 'a perfect hideaway for a special occasion or base for exploring the North Kent coast'. Our inspector found everything 'perfectly orchestrated'. 'The staff gave the impression that our well-being was their absolute priority.' Huge bedrooms are furnished with antiques. Dual-aspect Chestnut is 'especially lovely', Laurel has a four-poster and Cedar 'a nice sitting area, a spacious, well-equipped bathroom, sherry – if you like it!' Outside there was 'an honesty bar and tea and coffee facilities'. In the dining room, tables are well spaced, courses are well paced. At lunch and dinner, David's cooking is 'very special' but the menu 'seems not to change very often'. Stay more than five days and you could be round again to the slow-raised new Kentish lamb neck brioche, or Aylesbury duckling with blackberries and apple purée. Is that a hardship? At breakfast 'each ingredient seemed to have been carefully chosen'. (Ian Dewey, and others)

Macknade Manor
Canterbury Road
Faversham ME13 8XE

T: 01795 535344
E: enquiries@reads.com
W: reads.com

BEDROOMS: 6.
OPEN: all year except 4 days at Christmas, first 2 weeks Jan, 2 weeks Sept, restaurant closed Sun/Mon.
FACILITIES: sitting room/bar, 3 dining rooms, in-room TV (Freeview), civil wedding licence, 4-acre garden (terrace, outdoor dining), restaurant wheelchair accessible, toilet adapted.
BACKGROUND MUSIC: none.
LOCATION: ½ mile SE of Faversham.
CHILDREN: all ages welcomed.
DOGS: allowed in bedrooms only.
CREDIT CARDS: MC, Visa.
PRICES: per room B&B single £140–£195, double £180–£210, D,B&B single £185–£250, double £290–£320. Set lunch £32, dinner £65, tasting menu £65.

# FELIXKIRK Yorkshire

MAP 4:C4

## THE CARPENTERS ARMS

At this smart village inn, with views over the
Vale of York, visitors can chat with locals over
a pint of real ale, dine on classy pub food, and
sleep in spacious, chalet-style rooms. Close to the
North York Moors, it has 'a great location' and
'helpful staff'. From its whitewashed exterior,
bright with hanging baskets, to its rustic-chic
interiors, it's clear that thought has gone into
its design. The bar retains a pubby feel, with
rich-red walls, beams and open fire. Dine here or
in the restaurant, on food that is strong on local
sourcing, including the inn's own kitchen garden.
Menus mix pub classics – eg, pie of the day – with
more considered dishes, eg, slow-braised pork
belly with caramelised shallot, or roasted cod with
chorizo and clams. The two bedrooms in the main
building, in modern rustic style, are 'cosy rather
than spacious', while the eight chalet-style rooms,
arranged around a 'landscaped garden', are larger
and lighter, with space for a sofa. Glass doors
open to patios, and there is under-floor heating
in the modern bathrooms. Breakfasts, including
omelettes and smoked haddock, will set you up
for a day's walking.

Felixkirk
Thirsk YO7 2DP

T: 01845 537369
E: enquiries@
    thecarpentersarmsfelixkirk.com
W: thecarpentersarmsfelixkirk.com

BEDROOMS: 10. 8 in single-storey
garden annexe, 1 suitable for disabled.
OPEN: all year.
FACILITIES: bar/sitting area, restaurant,
private dining room, in-room TV
(Freeview), terrace (alfresco meals),
garden, public rooms on ground floor
wheelchair accessible, adapted toilet.
BACKGROUND MUSIC: at mealtimes in
bar and restaurant.
LOCATION: in village 3 miles NE of
Thirsk.
CHILDREN: all ages welcomed.
DOGS: welcomed in garden bedrooms,
bar and some dining areas.
CREDIT CARDS: Amex, MC, Visa.
PRICES: per room B&B £145–£185,
D,B&B £185–£225. À la carte £30–£35.

# FLEET Dorset

MAP 1:D6

## MOONFLEET MANOR

It's one long round of fun at this family-friendly hotel, centred on a Georgian manor house overlooking Chesil Beach and the Fleet Lagoon. Moonfleet is part of the Luxury Family Hotels group (see also Woolley Grange, Bradford-on-Avon, and Fowey Hall, next entry) which recently changed hands, but the formula remains the same, with a spa, an Ofsted crèche, swimming pool, cinema, trampoline, high teas and high jinks. A huge indoor play area houses everything from air hockey and table tennis to a traversing wall and indoor football pitch. It's not smart or swanky: the real luxury for adults is the chance to relax while the children have a whale of a time. A reader praises the 'warm, friendly, attentive staff', and the comfy lounges, 'particularly the one with huge squashy red sofas', but adds that the 'spacious and comfortable' bedroom was 'slightly drab, and smelt a little musty'. For dinner, Michael Culley sources local produce for such dishes as pan-fried sea bass or Jurassic Coast rib-eye. Breakfast has 'lots to choose from on the cereal/Danish pastry front, and really good fruit salad'. 'I felt so at home that I forgot we were due to check out.' (Diana Goodey, and others)

Fleet Road
Fleet DT3 4ED

T: 01305 786948
E: info@moonfleetmanorhotel.co.uk
W: moonfleetmanorhotel.co.uk

BEDROOMS: 36. 3 in coach house, 3 in villa, 3 ground floor.
OPEN: all year.
FACILITIES: 2 lounges, snug, restaurant, playroom, crèche, cinema, in-room TV (Freeview), civil wedding licence, indoor swimming pools, terrace, 5-acre garden, public areas wheelchair accessible, no adapted toilet.
BACKGROUND MUSIC: in restaurant.
LOCATION: 7 miles W of Weymouth.
CHILDREN: all ages welcomed, last entrance for children in dining room 7.30 pm.
DOGS: allowed in bedrooms, on lead in public rooms, not in restaurant (£15 a night).
CREDIT CARDS: Amex, MC, Visa.
PRICES: per room B&B £109–£549, D,B&B £179–£619. À la carte £38. 1- and 2-night bookings sometimes refused weekends.

# FOWEY Cornwall

MAP 1:D3

## FOWEY HALL

♛ Previous César winner

There are lots of good things to report about this family-friendly spa hotel this year. Bedrooms, bathrooms and public spaces have all been refurbished. The four-acre garden has had subtle landscaping. The library has hundreds of new books. The sleek new look updates rather than obliterates the legacy of the coastal manor's original owner, Sir Charles Hanson, MP for Bodmin and one-time Lord Mayor of London. Bedrooms in the main house have a soft grey wooden floor, vintage furniture and handmade oak bed. Those in the courtyard annexe have a more modern feel with designer furnishings and wallpapers. Children's rooms have bespoke bunk bed and desk. Head chef is Wesley Pratt, who works with the best local producers, from fishermen and dairy farmers to ice-cream makers, producing both casual and fine dining. Themed afternoon teas, such as a Beatrix Potter-inspired edible garden, are another speciality. Breakfasts are a hit with the whole family, with a bounteous buffet and hot dishes cooked to order. (See also Moonfleet Manor, Fleet, and Woolley Grange, Bradford-on-Avon.)

Hanson Drive
Fowey PL23 1ET

T: 01726 833866
E: info@foweyhallhotel.co.uk
W: foweyhallhotel.co.uk

BEDROOMS: 36. 8 in courtyard, some on ground floor, 1 suitable for disabled.
OPEN: all year.
FACILITIES: morning room, drawing room, library, restaurant, in-room TV (Freeview), crèche, billiard room, games rooms, civil wedding licence, spa, 12-metre indoor pool, 5-acre grounds, public rooms wheelchair accessible, adapted toilet.
BACKGROUND MUSIC: in bar, lounge, restaurant.
LOCATION: ½ mile from town centre.
CHILDREN: all ages welcomed.
DOGS: allowed in main house bedrooms (£15), in lounge, bar on lead, not in restaurant.
CREDIT CARDS: Amex, MC, Visa.
PRICES: per room B&B £139–£249. Set dinner £30–£38, à la carte £45. 1-night bookings refused some weekends.

**SEE ALSO SHORTLIST**

# GITTISHAM Devon

## THE PIG AT COMBE

The Empress of Blandings among Robin Hutson's Pig hotels (see index), this honey-stone Elizabethan manor house in the Otter valley is reached by a mile-long carriage drive. 'A beautiful house', with rococo plasterwork, mullioned windows, fireplaces and panelling, it has been filled by Judy Hutson with antiques, paintings, Paris trade-fair finds, Zoffany fabrics and signature rustic-chic pieces. Readers' 'comfy luxe' bedroom had a 'long, narrow bathroom with freestanding bath at the window, and a walk-in shower with an amazing drench head'. Many have an in-room roll-top bath. The Horsebox, in the old stable, has the original stall partitions. A Guide insider loved the 'drawing rooms, all with roaring fireplace, and magnificent hall turned into a striking bar' but a regular reader felt 'there was a faux air about the hotel'. However, 'the 25-mile menu shows impressive commitment to local sourcing, as does the beautiful kitchen garden'. Meals in 'the lovely dining room' feature local venison, Lyme Bay fish and home-grown produce by the bushel. 'Breakfast was terrific.' (Michael Gwinnell, David Birnie, SR)

Gittisham
Honiton EX14 3AD

T: 01404 540400
E: info@thepighotel.com
W: thepighotel.com

BEDROOMS: 30. 10 in stable yard, 5 in cottages (2 for family), 3 rooms suitable for disabled.
OPEN: all year.
FACILITIES: bar, 2 lounges, restaurant, Folly (communal dining), private dining rooms, in-room TV (Freeview), civil wedding licence, spa treatment rooms, 3,500-acre grounds, public rooms wheelchair accessible, adapted toilet.
BACKGROUND MUSIC: in public areas.
LOCATION: on outskirts of village.
CHILDREN: all ages welcomed.
DOGS: not allowed.
CREDIT CARDS: Amex, MC, Visa.
PRICES: per room £175–£389, family £309–£399. Continental breakfast £12, cooked £16, à la carte £35, set menus £22.50–£28.50. 1-night bookings sometimes refused.

# GRANTHAM Lincolnshire                    MAP 2:A3

## THE BROWNLOW ARMS

With her infectious laugh and ready endearments,
hostess Lorraine Willoughby is the life and soul
of this gastropub-with-rooms in a friendly rural
village, but there is much besides to like. 'We
had expected a distinctly rustic feel,' readers
write. 'In fact, the decor and furnishings are fresh
and very tasteful.' Armchairs are drawn up to
a log fire in the beamed bar, where table lamps
shed a cosy glow, and quiz nights are a popular
draw. Bedrooms are in every sense cosy, and
have antiques, good-quality fabrics and a drench
or power shower. 'Our room, in an adjoining
building, was attractively fitted out, with a very
comfortable bed – a matter to which Lorraine had
given careful attention.' There has been a change
of chef since last year, with Dean Carroll now
presiding. You can eat in the smart, blue-panelled
dining room or on the terrace, with views over the
countryside. A typical 'beautifully presented' dish
might be Burghley Estate lamb, shepherd's pie,
thyme carrot and redcurrant jus. 'The roast pork
was outstanding.' (Robert and Joan Grimley, RG)

Grantham Road
Hough-on-the-Hill
Grantham NG32 2AZ

T: 01400 250234
E: armsinn@yahoo.co.uk
W: thebrownlowarms.com

BEDROOMS: 5. 1 on ground floor in barn
conversion.
OPEN: all year except 25/26 Dec,
31 Dec/1 Jan, closed Sun evening,
Mon, Tues lunch.
FACILITIES: bar, 3 dining rooms, in-
room TV (Freeview), unsuitable for
disabled.
BACKGROUND MUSIC: in public areas.
LOCATION: rural, 2 miles E of town
centre.
CHILDREN: no under-8s in restaurant
in the evening.
DOGS: only guide dogs allowed.
CREDIT CARDS: MC, Visa.
PRICES: per room B&B single £90,
double £140. À la carte £40.

# GRASMERE Cumbria

MAP 4: inset C2

## FOREST SIDE

♙ Previous César winner

This Victorian Gothic mansion, one of Andrew Wildsmith's small, sophisticated group (see also Hipping Hall, Cowan Bridge), manages to be stylish yet relaxed. And, with its gourmet restaurant under a new head chef, it continues to turn out imaginative meals. One returning couple declared of their visit: 'It certainly won't be our last.' With glorious views towards Grasmere, a ten-minute walk away, Forest Side stands in large grounds; the walled potager produces much of the restaurant's needs. The light and airy oak-floored dining room is the star of the show, with Paul Leonard (ex-Isle of Eriska and Devonshire Arms) turning out dishes of startling combinations such as BBQ lobster, kohlrabi and pine or chocolate with buckthorn. There are vegetarian menus, and wines 'superbly chosen by the gifted sommelier'. Bedrooms, with garden views and home-made biscuits, have Zoffany fabrics, Herdwick wool carpets and beds by local company Harrison Spinks. 'Fantastic' bathrooms have Bramley natural plant-based products. Spot red squirrels during a cooked-to-order breakfast, before enjoying walks from the doorstep. (Lynn Middleton, and others)

Keswick Road
Grasmere LA22 9RN

T: 01539 435250
E: info@theforestside.com
W: theforestside.com

BEDROOMS: 20. 1 suitable for disabled.
OPEN: all year, restaurant closed Mon/Tues, and Wed lunch, hotel closed Mon/Tues Nov–Apr.
FACILITIES: lounge, bar, restaurant, function/private dining rooms, civil wedding licence, in-room TV (Freeview), terrace, 43-acre grounds with kitchen garden, public rooms wheelchair accessible, adapted toilet.
BACKGROUND MUSIC: in public areas.
LOCATION: outskirts of village.
CHILDREN: all ages welcomed, 8 and above only in dining room in evening.
DOGS: allowed in some bedrooms (max. 2 per room, £25 per dog, includes welcome pack).
CREDIT CARDS: Amex, MC, Visa.
PRICES: per room B&B £229–£369, D,B&B £329–£559. Tasting menus (6 courses) £80, (10 courses) £105.

**SEE ALSO SHORTLIST**

# GRASMERE Cumbria

## ♔ THE GRASMERE HOTEL

César award: country house hotel of the year

'I cannot recommend it highly enough,' concludes a visitor to this little hotel in postcard-pretty Grasmere. 'I do wish there were more family-owned and family-run hotels of this quality around.' The Winslands – Kevin, Nicki and two daughters – run their Victorian country house hotel with an assured hand, from the 'immaculately presented' bedrooms to the extensive dinner menu. There are views to Helm Crag, and a garden running down to the River Rothay. The 'very comfortable' lounges, with log fires, 'make a superb venue to enjoy canapés and drinks' before dinner. The latter puts a European spin on local dishes: Herdwick lamb with pea purée and tarragon pesto, perhaps, or sea bass with stir-fry and cashew nuts. 'How good to see kippers, haddock and salmon on the breakfast menu,' writes another reviewer, who also rhapsodises about the home-made bread. Bedrooms, all with views, are modern, with breezy colours, feature walls and simple furnishings. 'In all our travels around the UK, we cannot recall another hotel that offers food and service of this quality at such a bargain price.' (Ian Dewey, B and JH)

Broadgate
Grasmere LA22 9TA

T: 01539 435277
E: info@grasmerehotel.co.uk
W: grasmerehotel.co.uk

BEDROOMS: 11. Some on ground floor.
OPEN: all year except 31 Dec–31 Jan.
FACILITIES: two lounges, restaurant, in-room TV (Freeview), ½-acre garden, unsuitable for disabled.
BACKGROUND MUSIC: in lounge and restaurant during mealtimes.
LOCATION: in village.
CHILDREN: over-10s welcomed.
DOGS: allowed, by arrangement, in 1 ground-floor bedroom, not in public rooms.
CREDIT CARDS: MC, Visa.
PRICES: per room B&B single £71–£76, double £132–£168. Set 4-course dinner £37.50 (£30 for residents). 2-night min. stay normally required (check for 1-night availability), Sat and bank holiday Sun night reservations must include dinner.

SEE ALSO SHORTLIST

# GRASSINGTON Yorkshire

MAP 4:D3

## GRASSINGTON HOUSE

Overlooking the cobbled square in one of the most attractive Dales villages, this smart restaurant-with-rooms combines chic bedrooms and creative food with a warm Yorkshire welcome. It's hard to miss Sue and John Rudden's handsome Georgian house, whose terrace is a perfect spot for post-walk pints or a spoiling afternoon tea. Inside, it is anything but traditional: a bistro-style dining room has bold contemporary lighting and shimmery colours, while bedrooms are luxuriously modern. Expect oversized headboards, velvet cushions; in larger rooms, perhaps a gold-painted French-style bed, chandelier and roll-top bath. Smaller rooms are cosy 'but comfortable', with 'a very powerful shower' and a view of the village square. All rooms have bathrobes, home-made biscuits and Sedbergh Soap toiletries. John's creative food is as striking as the decor; dishes from this 'very inventive chef' might include Gloucester Old Spot pork belly with ham fritter and tarragon jus or duck breast with vanilla parsnip and rhubarb. Breakfast includes home-smoked salmon, and bacon and sausages from their own pigs. It is 'so good that the memory lingers all day'.

**25% DISCOUNT VOUCHERS**

5 The Square
Grassington
Skipton BD23 5AQ

T: 01756 752406
E: bookings@grassingtonhouse.co.uk
W: grassingtonhousehotel.co.uk

BEDROOMS: 9.
OPEN: all year except Christmas Day.
FACILITIES: lounge, bar, restaurant, in-room TV (terrestrial), civil wedding licence, function facilities, terrace, cookery classes, parking, public rooms wheelchair accessible.
BACKGROUND MUSIC: in public areas.
LOCATION: in village square, 16 mins' drive from Skipton.
CHILDREN: all ages welcomed.
DOGS: allowed in bar and terrace only.
CREDIT CARDS: MC, Visa.
PRICES: per room B&B single £117, double £135–£175, DB&B compulsory on Sat, single £160, double £235–£265. Tasting menu (Sun & Mon) £55 for two, market menu (lunch Mon–Sat, early dinner Tues–Thurs) £18–£20, à la carte £35.

# GREAT MILTON Oxfordshire                    MAP 2:C3

## BELMOND LE MANOIR AUX QUAT'SAISONS

**NEW**

It's not just in the two-Michelin-starred restaurant of Raymond Blanc's honey-stone Oxfordshire hotel (Relais & Châteaux) that you get great attention to detail: in the bedrooms, even the sugared almonds are colour coded according to the decor. The chef 'has let his creative soul spill from the kitchen to the bedrooms' to create what a Guide insider says is 'probably the best hotel I have stayed in'. Elegant bedrooms, some with private garden, draw inspiration from Blanc's past. A trip to China produced Lemongrass, with its bed on a raised dais and lime-green furnishings, and started Blanc growing the plant in the 'beautiful gardens', which include an orchard and organic kitchen garden supplying the restaurant. 'It's neither stuffy nor overbearing'; children are welcome guests. Staff are perfectly trained so they are 'there when needed, never intrusive'. As for the food, 'prepare to be blown away' with dishes such as chargrilled Scottish langoustine, and squab pigeon wrapped in salt crust. Even the breakfast table is a 'work of art': Blanc spent a year perfecting it. 'It's expensive, but for a special occasion, it's worth it.' (JK)

Church Road
Great Milton OX44 7PD

T: 01844 278881
E: lemanoir@belmond.com
W: belmond.com/lemanoir

BEDROOMS: 32. 22 in garden buildings, some on ground floor, 1 suitable for disabled.
OPEN: all year, restaurant closed for lunch Mon–Wed.
FACILITIES: 2 lounges, champagne bar, restaurant, private dining room, in-room TV (Sky, BT, Freeview), cookery school, civil wedding licence, 27-acre grounds (orchard, Japanese tea garden), public rooms wheelchair accessible, adapted toilet.
BACKGROUND MUSIC: in some public areas.
LOCATION: 8 miles SE of Oxford.
CHILDREN: all ages welcomed.
DOGS: allowed in some bedrooms and public rooms, kennels provided.
CREDIT CARDS: Amex, MC, Visa.
PRICES: per room B&B £570–£2,160. À la carte £180, 7-course set meal £194.

# GURNARD Isle of Wight

## THE LITTLE GLOSTER

So close to the Solent that it's practically afloat, Ben and Holly Cooke's restaurant-with-rooms has a cool Scandinavian vibe. 'It's absolutely wonderful,' writes a reader who celebrated her birthday here. The sea-view restaurant has bare floorboards, sails looped from the ceiling, and is 'beautifully decorated, with a nautical theme'. Holly manages the friendly waiting staff who 'couldn't do enough for us', while Ben uses local produce in menus with influences from his Danish granny. For instance, home-cured Hampshire trout gravadlax, day-boat hake with lobster velouté, roast pork loin with crackling and asier (a Danish pickle). 'The lobster, scallops and gurnard with hollandaise were very fresh, and simply but beautifully cooked, and to top it all, they brought me a cup cake with a candle.' Two of the immaculate, Scandi-chic bedrooms in an adjoining building can sleep a family, and all have an espresso machine. One has a balcony, another a sitting room and decked terrace. 'Binoculars are thoughtfully provided.' Breakfast, ordered the night before, is served until 11 am. (Maureen Knight, and others)
NOTE: As the Guide went to press, The Little Gloster announced that it was closing.

31 Marsh Road
Gurnard PO31 8JQ

T: 01983 298776
E: info@thelittlegloster.com
W: thelittlegloster.com

BEDROOMS: 3. All in adjoining building.
OPEN: see website for closures, restaurant opens Thurs pm–Sun pm Oct–1 June, Wed–Sun 6 pm (2 June–30 Sept), plus bank holidays and Sun pm on bank holiday weekends.
FACILITIES: restaurant, bar, in-room TV (Freeview), seaside garden, public rooms wheelchair accessible, adapted toilet.
BACKGROUND MUSIC: in dining room.
LOCATION: on the coast, a 5-min. drive W of Cowes.
CHILDREN: all ages welcomed, high chairs, cots, camp beds.
DOGS: allowed in restaurant (not bedrooms).
CREDIT CARDS: MC, Visa.
PRICES: per room B&B £130–£240. À la carte £35, fixed-price menu £19–£24 (not Sat or bank holidays). 1-night bookings sometimes refused.

# HALFORD Warwickshire

## THE OLD MANOR HOUSE

'B&Bs this good are rare,' write hoteliers who stayed at Jane and William Pusey's 16th-century manor house. Set in extensive gardens sloping down to the River Stour, it is just ten minutes' drive from Stratford-upon-Avon. Cordon Bleu-trained Jane runs the show, but William proved 'the perfect host' when Guide readers arrived in her absence. He showed them to a spacious, comfortable bedroom. 'The bathroom was larger than in most hotel bedrooms; it had a bath and walk-in power shower.' All the rooms have period charm, fresh milk on request, bathrobes and ila Spa toiletries. Rowley, reached by its own staircase, adjoins a single room that can be used for a friend or family member. You can take tea in the drawing room or on the terrace. 'Piles of books, knick-knacks, antiques, and the clock in the breakfast room playing music every four hours make it feel like staying at a friend's house.' Retriever Summer welcomes canine guests, by arrangement. Breakfast brings home-baked organic bread, organic yogurts and local bacon, before a day's fishing or a game of tennis. For dinner we suggest The Howard Arms at Ilmington (see entry). (Sue and John Jenkinson)

Queen Street
Halford
Shipston-on-Stour CV36 5BT

T: 01789 740264
E: oldmanorhalford@btinternet.com
W: oldmanor-halford.co.uk

BEDROOMS: 3.
OPEN: 28 Feb–14 Dec.
FACILITIES: hall, dining room, drawing room, in-room TV (Freeview), bicycle storage, 3½-acre grounds (tennis, fishing).
BACKGROUND MUSIC: none.
LOCATION: northern edge of village.
CHILDREN: aged 7 and over welcomed.
DOGS: allowed (confirm when booking, £15 per night), not in dining room.
CREDIT CARDS: MC, Visa.
PRICES: per room B&B single £90 Mon–Thurs (double occupancy rate weekends), double £115–£120. Phone to check for 1-night bookings.

# HALNAKER Sussex

## THE OLD STORE

It may have lost its old store, but a pretty village on Goodwood's doorstep has an excellent B&B instead. A wishing well stands before the 'gorgeous' red brick and stone facade, but you could not wish for hosts more 'accommodating' and 'thoughtful' than Patrick and Heather Birchenough. Bedrooms have contemporary decor, a shower room, and are supplied with fresh milk, biscuits and chocolates. Some have a view across countryside as far as the Isle of Wight. 'The beds were very comfortable, the en suite was modern and well-equipped,' write trusted readers. And while their bedroom looked on to a 'not particularly busy' road, triple glazing screened out any noise. A Guide insider writes of a 'powerful' shower with lashings of hot water. New arrivals may be greeted by 'a pleasant smell of baking' and the offer of tea and cake in the small sitting room. Breakfast, in a 'sun-filled', street-facing room, brings 'a nice buffet', Sussex apple juice, organic eggs, local sausages, home-made bread and American-style pancakes. A walk up to Halnaker Windmill, through a magical tunnel of trees, is a must. (Hugh Allan, and others)

Stane Street
Halnaker
Chichester PO18 0QL

T: 01243 531977
E: theoldstore4@aol.com
W: theoldstoreguesthouse.co.uk

BEDROOMS: 7. 1 on ground floor with step between bathroom and bedroom.
OPEN: Mar–mid-Dec.
FACILITIES: lounge, breakfast room, in-room TV (Freeview), ¼-acre garden with seating.
BACKGROUND MUSIC: none.
LOCATION: 4 miles NE of Chichester.
CHILDREN: all ages welcomed.
DOGS: not allowed.
CREDIT CARDS: MC, Visa.
PRICES: per room B&B single £63–£120, double £85–£125, family from £115 (higher for Goodwood 'Festival of Speed' and 'Revival' meetings). 1-night bookings refused weekends, sometimes other nights in high season.

# HAMBLETON Rutland

MAP 2:B3

## HAMBLETON HALL

♔ Previous César winner

From the landscaped gardens with 'a five-star view' over Rutland Water to the Michelin-starred dining, Tim and Stefa Hart's acclaimed hotel nails English country house excellence. 'Courtesy, helpfulness and a constant search for perfection remain the standards here,' sighs one regular. 'Baggage was in our room in a trice, followed by a nice tray of tea and biscuits.' The handsome Victorian mansion has a sweep of public rooms with panelled walls, deep sofas and open fires. Bedrooms are classic country house: rich fabrics and wallpapers, antiques, a roll-top bath, fresh flowers and home-made treats. In the Michelin-starred restaurant, Aaron Patterson creates meals 'magnificent in style and quality, brilliance and richness'. Menus might include poached fillet of halibut, mushroom tortellini, lemon verbena sauce, or startling combinations such as rabbit in a liquorice sauce. One quibble: residents find it is 'not always possible to find seating in the lounge' before dinner. With 'outstanding service', this Relais & Châteaux hotel inspires loyalty: 'When we go there it is like returning to old friends.' (Anthony Bradbury, CF, and others)

Hambleton
Oakham LE15 8TH

T: 01572 756991
E: hotel@hambletonhall.com
W: hambletonhall.com

BEDROOMS: 17. 2-bedroom suite in cottage.
OPEN: all year.
FACILITIES: lift, hall, drawing room/bar, restaurant, 2 private dining rooms, in-room TV (Sky), civil wedding licence, 17-acre grounds (tennis, swimming pool – heated May–Sept – croquet, vegetable garden), electric charging point, public rooms wheelchair accessible, no adapted toilet.
BACKGROUND MUSIC: none.
LOCATION: 3 miles SE of Oakham.
CHILDREN: all ages welcomed, no under-5s in restaurant.
DOGS: allowed in bedrooms (not unattended), hall.
CREDIT CARDS: Amex, MC, Visa.
PRICES: per room B&B single £210–£225, double £295–£775. Set dinner £78, tasting menu £98. 1-night bookings normally refused weekends (call to check).

# HAROME Yorkshire

MAP 4:D4

## THE PHEASANT

In an idyllic setting, overlooking the village pond, this hotel in a collection of stone buildings around a pretty courtyard maintains high standards for food, comfort and service. 'A first-class stay', with 'young, enthusiastic, hard-working staff who are proud of their hotel'. A former blacksmith's, shop and barns have been converted into a hotel that feels informal yet is deeply comfortable. Three lounges – rich wallpapers, tweedy armchairs, books, piano – are 'luxuriously appointed', one with 'a wood-burner creating a cosy environment'. Bedrooms have a modern country house look, with bold wallpapers, bright headboards and the occasional antique, and feature fresh milk and sloe gin. Some have a four-poster, others a big sofa; all have a rustic-chic bathroom with under-floor heating and Cowshed toiletries. Peter Neville's 'superb dinners' include sophisticated dishes such as beetroot-cured salmon, or salt-aged Yorkshire duck with charred little gem. There are good vegetarian and vegan options, too. Breakfast is 'outstanding in every respect', especially the 'perfectly prepared scrambled egg'. (P and AD, and others)

Mill Street
Harome YO62 5JG

T: 01439 771241
E: reservations@thepheasanthotel.
   com
W: thepheasanthotel.com

BEDROOMS: 16. 3 on ground floor, 4 in courtyard, 1 room in hotel suitable for disabled.
OPEN: all year.
FACILITIES: bar, lounge, conservatory, restaurant, in-room TV (Freeview), civil wedding licence, heated indoor swimming pool, terrace, ½-acre garden, public areas wheelchair accessible, no adapted toilet.
BACKGROUND MUSIC: in public areas.
LOCATION: village centre.
CHILDREN: all ages welcomed.
DOGS: allowed in 2 bedrooms, on terrace and in garden, not in public rooms.
CREDIT CARDS: MC, Visa.
PRICES: per room B&B single £95–£240, double £190–£290, D,B&B single £135–£280, double £270–£370. Tasting menu £55–£75, à la carte £46.

# HAROME Yorkshire

## THE STAR INN AT HAROME

♞Previous César winner

On the edge of the North Yorkshire moors, this postcard-perfect thatched village pub continues to delight with its Michelin-starred cooking and quirky bedrooms. 'Wow, what a wonderful place this is!' It's divided into two halves: guests dine in the low-beamed pub with its jolly bar, flagged floors and smart, but unstuffy dining rooms, and sleep across the road in farm buildings converted into characterful bedrooms. With beams and odd shapes, they're modern-rustic in style, with country-scene wallpapers, chunky furniture and eclectic objects – riding boots, a piano, even a snooker table. 'We were bowled over by the lovely rooms.' A hunting lodge-style lounge is the place to 'sit by the log stove with a whisky from the honesty bar'. But it's Andrew Pern's 'modern Yorkshire' cooking that is the main event. Championing local produce, he produces flavour-dense dishes of unusual combinations such as black treacle-glazed duck with lovage tortellini, or cod with Hispi cabbage carbonara. 'Exceptional. Wonderful-tasting dishes, well presented.' 'Sensational' breakfasts are served at a huge table. (Jonathan Rose, and others)

High Street
Harome
Helmsley YO62 5JE

T: 01439 770397
E: reservations@thestarinnatharome.
co.uk
W: thestaratharome.co.uk

BEDROOMS: 9. All in Cross House Lodge, opposite, 4 on ground floor.
OPEN: all year, restaurant closed Mon lunch, last orders Sun 6 pm.
FACILITIES: bar, restaurant, cocktail bar, private dining room, alfresco dining (all in main pub), lounge, breakfast/private dining room (in building with bedrooms), in-room TV (Freeview), civil wedding licence, terrace, 2-acre garden, restaurant wheelchair accessible.
BACKGROUND MUSIC: in lounge, dining room.
LOCATION: village centre.
CHILDREN: all ages welcomed.
DOGS: allowed in 3 bedrooms by arrangement, not in restaurant or pub.
CREDIT CARDS: MC, Visa.
PRICES: per room B&B £150–£270. Market menu £20–£25, à la carte £50–£60, tasting menu £85.

# HARWICH Essex

MAP 2:C5

## THE PIER AT HARWICH

Fishing boats and ferries, cruise liners and container ships form a constantly shifting waterscape in this port town, best enjoyed from the wrought iron balcony of the Milsom family's harbourside hotel. It occupies an Italianate Victorian building, with seven further bedrooms in the former Angel pub next door, including the Mayflower Suite, with a telescope in its massive five-sash bay window. Other bedrooms, with neutral decor and matching fabric headboard and furnishings, may have free soft drinks in a minibar and Aromatherapy Associates toiletries, but our inspector felt that, though well equipped, they 'lacked pizzazz'. The public rooms, by contrast, have a 'chic-industrial style'. Nordic-inspired small plates and sharing platters are served in the bar, with 'suave leather banquettes' and an impressive gin selection, as well as on the street terrace. In the first-floor restaurant, where general manager Stephen Robson is also now co-head chef with John Goff, there are oysters, mussels, burgers, fish and chips, menus for kids, vegans and vegetarians.

**25% DISCOUNT VOUCHERS**

The Pier
Harwich CO12 3HH

T: 01255 241212
E: pier@milsomhotels.com
W: milsomhotels.com

BEDROOMS: 14. 7 in annexe, 1 on ground floor suitable for disabled.
OPEN: all year.
FACILITIES: bar, lounge (in annexe), restaurant, private dining room, small lift, in-room TV (Sky, BT, Freeview), civil wedding licence, balcony, small front terrace; restaurant, bar wheelchair accessible.
BACKGROUND MUSIC: in the bar.
LOCATION: on quay, in old town.
CHILDREN: all ages welcomed.
DOGS: allowed in bedrooms, bar, lounge.
CREDIT CARDS: Amex, MC, Visa.
PRICES: per room B&B £145–£225. À la carte £40.

# HASTINGS Sussex

MAP 2:E5

## THE OLD RECTORY

Five minutes' walk from Hastings Contemporary, this Georgian rectory-turned-B&B provides a showcase for the works of artists from Hastings and St Leonard's. It is owned by designer Lionel Copley, who also co-owns Swan House, Hastings (next entry) with his partner, Brendan McDonagh. As you would expect, then, the public rooms are stylish, with rugs on sanded floorboards, pale paint finishes and bespoke wallpapers. Meanwhile, the bedrooms have a muted palette. Nice touches include home-made biscuits, fresh milk and Lionel's Made by the Sea toiletries. Street-facing Ebenezer has a deep grey wall hung with Wedgwood calendar plates. A private corridor leads to All Saints, overlooking the garden, with hand-printed Deborah Bowness floral wallpaper and hand-painted headboard, a bathroom with freestanding claw-footed bath and a wet room. Rob Hills cooks a locally sourced breakfast, with organic apple juice, free-range eggs, kippers and smoked haddock from Rock-a-Nore Fisheries, home-made sausages, bread and preserves. The walled garden is tended by Zeline Dupraz, who has worked at Great Dixter and Sissinghurst.

**25% DISCOUNT VOUCHERS**

Harold Road
Hastings TN35 5ND

T: 01424 422410
E: info@theoldrectoryhastings.co.uk
W: theoldrectoryhastings.co.uk

BEDROOMS: 8. One 2-bed suite.
OPEN: all year except 1 week Christmas, 2 weeks Jan, open for New Year.
FACILITIES: 2 lounges (honesty bar), breakfast room, treatment rooms, sauna, in-room TV (Freeview), civil wedding licence, 1-acre walled garden, unsuitable for disabled.
BACKGROUND MUSIC: in breakfast room and main lounge.
LOCATION: edge of Old Town (limited parking spaces, complimentary permits).
CHILDREN: not under 10.
DOGS: not allowed.
CREDIT CARDS: Amex, MC, Visa.
PRICES: per room B&B single £90–£115, double £110–£180. 1-night bookings refused weekends.

**SEE ALSO SHORTLIST**

# HASTINGS Sussex

MAP 2:E5

## ♛SWAN HOUSE

César award: B&B of the year

Brendan McDonagh is 'the most welcoming of hosts' at this half-timbered Tudor B&B on a quiet cul-de-sac in the trendy Old Town. It is 'a successful combination of stylish and homely, a warm, comfortable, well-cared-for historic house', writes a trusted reader. Visitors step inside to find a beamed lounge/breakfast room with an inglenook fireplace and a courtyard garden to the rear. 'An old staircase led to our luxury room overlooking a church,' another reader relates. 'Very comfortable bed with lovely, crisp linen, big, soft towels and dressing gowns.' There is one ground-floor room off the lounge. Brendan's partner, Lionel Copley (see previous entry, Old Rectory), has brought his designer's eye to the interiors, creating 'the most stylish of houses' without being flashy; bedrooms are all 'delightfully elegant and whimsical'. Breakfast, cooked by Brendan, brings real orange juice and 'an amazing selection of locally sourced produce. The smoked salmon and the kippers were particularly delicious.' Secure parking is a short walk away. (Diana Goodey, Dan Clarke, Eric Heller, Charley Holmes, and others)

**25% DISCOUNT VOUCHERS**

1 Hill Street
Hastings TN34 3HU

T: 01424 430014
E: info@swanhousehastings.co.uk
W: swanhousehastings.co.uk

BEDROOMS: 5. 1 on ground floor, 2 adjoining.
OPEN: all year except 24–26 Dec.
FACILITIES: lounge/breakfast room, in-room TV, patio garden, secure allocated parking 10 mins' walk away (permits supplied), unsuitable for disabled.
BACKGROUND MUSIC: background during breakfast.
LOCATION: in Old Town, near seafront.
CHILDREN: 5 and upwards in Renaissance Suite, by prior arrangement.
DOGS: not allowed.
CREDIT CARDS: Amex, MC, Visa.
PRICES: per room B&B single £99–£110, double £120–£150. 1-night bookings usually refused weekends but check, £10 supplement for Sat night only, if available.

**SEE ALSO SHORTLIST**

# HEREFORD Herefordshire    MAP 3:D4

## CASTLE HOUSE

'We thoroughly enjoyed the whole experience,' wrote trusted readers after a stay at the Watkins family's stucco-fronted, balconied hotel overlooking the moat of the long-gone castle. Staff are 'welcoming and ultra-efficient' and appear to be a cohesive 'long-standing team'. Bedrooms, in the main house and a Georgian town house, range from small singles to suites, and have antiques and artwork. Some have French doors to the garden and private terrace, a bath and separate shower. Generous extras include fresh milk in a mini-fridge, a decanter of sherry, fresh fruit and L'Occitane toiletries. A new garden restaurant opened in 2020, and in fine weather you can eat on the terrace. Chef Gabor Katona delights in devising menus with produce from the family's farm and kitchen garden. 'Interesting flavours and choices, plus beautiful presentation tempted us all to three courses.' There is a 'good wine list', too. An enticing breakfast menu includes local pear juice, free-range eggs, charred halloumi, or the full Hereford with free-range pork sausage, black pudding and potato and apple cake. (S and JJ, S and PG)

**25% DISCOUNT VOUCHERS**

Castle Street
Hereford HR1 2NW

T: 01432 356321
E: reception@castlehse.co.uk
W: castlehse.co.uk

BEDROOMS: 24. 8 in town house (a short walk away), some on ground floor, 1 suitable for disabled.
OPEN: all year.
FACILITIES: lift (in main house only), lounge, bar/bistro, restaurant, in-room TV (Freeview), civil wedding licence, terraced garden, ground floor wheelchair accessible.
BACKGROUND MUSIC: occasionally in restaurant, bistro and reception.
LOCATION: central.
CHILDREN: all ages welcomed.
DOGS: not allowed except in garden, on a lead.
CREDIT CARDS: Amex, MC, Visa.
PRICES: per room B&B single £140–£210, double £155–£260, D,B&B double £210–£325. Tasting menu £50, à la carte (restaurant) £40, (bistro) £30.

# HETTON Yorkshire

MAP 4:D3

## ⚜ THE ANGEL INN

César award: inn of the year

This landmark Dales pub, with sublime views, creeper-covered stonework and 15th-century beams, is flying high with a Michelin star. It is owned by chef Michael Wignall (ex Gidleigh Park) and his wife, Johanna, and is a place to enjoy local ales as well as a first-rate dining experience and a luxurious night's sleep. 'High standards of comfort and cuisine underpin the business, which is clearly customer-centred,' reports our inspector. Expect relaxed but smart interiors – wood-panelled bar, log fires, fuss-free decoration, and intimate dining spaces. The food, described as 'truly magnificent' by one reader, is locally sourced but globally inspired, such as Yorkshire salt-aged duck with pumpkin, soy, black bean and miso, or skrei cod with razor clam and barbecued celeriac. There are good vegetarian menus, too. Bedrooms are cottagey or rustic-chic; most are in the adjoining building or converted barns. Suites may include a roll-top bath or a private patio. All come with Dyson hairdryers and hand-made chocolates. 'I loved the warm atmosphere and the fabulous food. It is definitely one of my favourite hotels.' (Trevor Lockwood)

Hetton
Skipton BD23 6LT

T: 01756 730263
E: info@angelhetton.co.uk
W: angelhetton.co.uk

BEDROOMS: 13. 5 in barn conversion, 4 in cottage, 2 on ground floor suitable for disabled.
OPEN: all year except 25 Dec, 2–14 Jan, 24 Dec lunch and dinner only, 26 Dec and 1 Jan lunch only, rooms and restaurant closed Tues, Wed.
FACILITIES: bar, restaurant, private dining room, civil wedding licence, terrace, in-room TV (Freeview), some public areas wheelchair accessible.
BACKGROUND MUSIC: bar area.
LOCATION: village centre.
CHILDREN: all ages welcomed, children's menu.
DOGS: allowed in 2 bedrooms and bar.
CREDIT CARDS: Amex, MC, Visa.
PRICES: per room D,B&B only £265–£345. Tasting menu £80, à la carte £55 (vegetarian £40).

# HINTON ST GEORGE Somerset

MAP 1:C6

## THE LORD POULETT ARMS

In a thriving village amid rolling farmland this thatched dining-pub-with-rooms has been made over in the signature style of sister inns The Talbot, Mells, and The Beckford Arms, Tisbury (see entries). Our inspectors found the bar and restaurant, with central fireplace, 'splendidly atmospheric', furnished 'in keeping with the 17th-century building'. Bedrooms have a rustic, dressed-down chic, with seagrass flooring, Welsh blankets, comfy armchairs, Bramley toiletries; and hooks and hangers in place of furniture. One has an in-room claw-footed bath and separate shower room. A family room has bunk beds for children. Philip Verden's frequently changing menus range from such classics as cider-battered fish and chips and pie of the day to more adventurous dishes, with a vegan option. 'Roasted brill on a bed of peas and spinach was spectacularly tasty.' At breakfast there are home-baked pastries, home-made toasted granola, a full Somerset with pork and marmalade sausage and black pudding. The efficient waiting staff have 'charisma, charm, a sense of humour'. In summer, children can run in the garden; in winter, adults enjoy mulled wine by the roaring fires.

High Street
Hinton St George TA17 8SE

T: 01460 73149
E: reservations@lordpoulettarms.com
W: lordpoulettarms.com

BEDROOMS: 6. 4 with en suite, 2 with private bathroom, 1 for family.
OPEN: all year except 25 Dec.
FACILITIES: bar, restaurant, private dining room, in-room TV (Freeview), 1-acre grounds, unsuitable for disabled.
BACKGROUND MUSIC: throughout pub.
LOCATION: in village, 4 miles NW of Crewkerne.
CHILDREN: all ages welcomed.
DOGS: in 1 bedroom and all public areas.
CREDIT CARDS: MC, Visa.
PRICES: per room B&B single £75–£95, double £85–£120, family £160, D,B&B £145–£170. À la carte £35.

# HOLT Norfolk

MAP 2:A5

## MORSTON HALL

'Amazingly gorgeous.' 'Top of my list.' 'Superb food.' Readers lavish praise on Tracy and Galton Blickiston's restaurant-with-rooms on the north Norfolk coast. 'We had a delicious dinner,' reads the latest endorsement. 'The service is impeccable and the food very high quality.' House bedrooms in country house style are named after local stately homes. Blickling has a lovely bathroom with roll-top bath and walk-in shower. Beamed Mannington is tucked away under the eaves with a view of the herb garden, while a garden pavilion offers suites with a seating area, coal-effect fire and a terrace. A report tells of fresh milk and (hooray!) sheets and blankets. At breakfast there are freshly squeezed juices, home-baked croissants, locally smoked haddock, boudin noir, and free-range eggs. But whoever said that breakfast is the most important meal cannot have experienced Galton's Michelin-starred seven-course tasting menus in the light-filled conservatory. Typical offerings include butternut squash velouté with King's Lynn brown shrimps; spelt risotto with ewe's curd and peas; and wild sea bass with butter sauce. (JB, and others)

Morston
Holt NR25 7AA

**T:** 01263 741041
**E:** reception@morstonhall.com
**W:** morstonhall.com

**BEDROOMS:** 13. 6 on ground floor, 100 yds from house, in garden pavilion, 1, in main house, suitable for disabled.
**OPEN:** all year except 24–26 Dec, 1–29 Jan.
**FACILITIES:** reading lounge, sun lounge, conservatory, restaurant, in-room TV (Freeview), civil wedding licence, 3-acre garden (pond, croquet), restaurant wheelchair accessible, adapted toilet.
**BACKGROUND MUSIC:** none.
**LOCATION:** 2 miles W of Blakeney.
**CHILDREN:** all ages welcomed, children's portions.
**DOGS:** allowed in bedrooms, some public rooms, not in restaurant.
**CREDIT CARDS:** Amex, MC, Visa.
**PRICES:** per person D,B&B single occupancy £250–£310, double £185–£210. Set dinner £95.

**SEE ALSO SHORTLIST**

## HOPE Derbyshire

### UNDERLEIGH HOUSE

✿ Previous César winner

'We felt as if we had been invited to stay with friends,' says one reviewer of this welcoming B&B in the heart of Jane Eyre country. Indeed, the converted cottage and long barn were built for a scion of the real-life Eyre family in the 19th century. Today it's the home of Vivienne and Philip Taylor, who are the 'best hosts'. The three first-floor bedrooms have views across the valley to Win Hill or Lose Hill or towards Shatton Edge. Townhead Garden Suite, on the ground floor, offers direct access to the lovely garden as well as to a patio and rose garden where feeders and nest boxes attract local birdlife. All have a large modern bathroom, with walk-in shower or shower-bath, and White Company toiletries. Breakfast is a hearty feast of home-made and local produce, taken in the beamed dining hall in the 'wonderful company of the other guests'. There's plenty of interest nearby, including Haddon Hall, which has stood in for Rochester's Thornfield Hall in several screen adaptations of Jane Eyre. 'One of our favourite places to stay out of the many trips we have taken,' says one reviewer. (Denise Pierce)

Lose Hill Lane
off Edale Road
Hope S33 6AF

T: 01433 621372
E: underleigh.house@btconnect.com
W: underleighhouse.co.uk

BEDROOMS: 4. 3 suites with a private lounge.
OPEN: all year except mid-Dec to mid-Feb.
FACILITIES: lounge, breakfast room, in-room TV (Freeview), ¼-acre garden, unsuitable for disabled.
BACKGROUND MUSIC: none.
LOCATION: 1 mile N of Hope.
CHILDREN: not under 12.
DOGS: allowed in 1 suite by prior arrangement, not in public rooms.
CREDIT CARDS: Amex, MC, Visa.
PRICES: per room B&B single £80–£110, double £100–£130. 1-night bookings normally refused Fri/Sat, bank holidays.

# HUNSTANTON Norfolk

MAP 2:A5

## NO. 33

A stroll from the seafront, a bay-fronted house has been transformed into a B&B by Jeanne Whittome, with a strong emphasis on customer care. Tea and cake await new arrivals. The bedrooms have bespoke furniture, pale paint finishes, perhaps a wall of Zoffany 'Verdure' or 'Gondolier' wallpaper, a very Marie Antoinette white bombe chest. 'The bold contemporary design is not necessarily to everyone's taste,' one visitor commented, 'but it all seemed to work.' Extra touches include a cafetière and biscuits. Spacious Room 3 has a modern four-poster, a balcony with a distant sea view, a bath and drench shower. Room 5, on the ground floor, has a walk-in shower, a bath, and access to a small courtyard. There are bigger, pricier suites down the road at a sister enterprise in Thornham, above a deli and licensed café. Breakfast, in the dining room (or in bed), brings locally sourced juices, home-made granola, smoked salmon and cream cheese bagels, pastries and cooked dishes. A concierge service helps with restaurant bookings, bike hire, walking, sailing, birdwatching or what you will, and you can order a hamper for a picnic.

33 Northgate
Hunstanton PE36 6AP

T: 01485 524352
E: reception@33hunstanton.co.uk
W: 33hunstanton.co.uk

BEDROOMS: 5. 1 on ground floor.
OPEN: all year.
FACILITIES: small sitting room, breakfast room, in-room TV (Freeview), small garden.
BACKGROUND MUSIC: radio during breakfast.
LOCATION: town centre.
CHILDREN: well-behaved children welcomed, Z-bed for children under 14 (max. 1 per room), cots and high chairs available.
DOGS: allowed in bedrooms, max. 1 per room (£5 per night), not in dining room.
CREDIT CARDS: MC, Visa.
PRICES: per room B&B double (Hunstanton) £95–£190, suites (Thornham) £140–£205, single occupancy discount £10 a night, third person £30, infant £10.

# HUNTINGDON Cambridgeshire                    MAP 2:B4

## THE OLD BRIDGE

It's much easier to enjoy the 'exceptional wine list' and elegant interiors of this ivy-clad town house hotel, owned by a Master of Wine and an interior designer, now that Huntington's High Street has been pedestrianised, cutting down traffic noise. John Hoskins oversees the on-site wine shop, where 24 wines a day can be tasted; his wife, Julia, is the creator of the stylish bedrooms, with contemporary fabrics and some antique furniture. Room 6 has a four-poster and a huge bathroom with varnished wood floor, roll-top bath and walk-in shower. 'I was upgraded to a large double with all you could want,' a trusted reader relates. Another regular correspondent found the hotel 'too geared to businessmen'. Not so a third reader, who enjoyed 'very good food' and 'good communal areas with a buzz'. Pramod Jadhav has stepped up from senior sous-chef to run the kitchen, cooking such dishes as chargrilled cauliflower 'steak' with chunky chips, or real Aberdeen Angus rib-eye. 'The breakfast is very good – tasty kipper with mustard butter and lemon, and tremendous marmalade.' (David Sefton, and others)

1 High Street
Huntingdon PE29 3TQ

T: 01480 424300
E: jh@huntsbridge.co.uk
W: huntsbridge.com

BEDROOMS: 24. 2 on ground floor.
OPEN: all year.
FACILITIES: lounge, bar, restaurant, private dining room, wine shop, business centre, in-room TV (Freeview), civil wedding licence, 1-acre grounds (riverside patio for private events), parking, unsuitable for disabled.
BACKGROUND MUSIC: none.
LOCATION: 500 yds from town centre, station 10 mins' walk.
CHILDREN: all ages welcomed.
DOGS: allowed in 2 bedrooms, lounge and bar, not in restaurant.
CREDIT CARDS: MC, Visa.
PRICES: per room B&B (weekdays) single from £99, double from £148, D,B&B (weekends and bank holidays) single from £148, double from £229. À la carte £38.

# ILMINGTON Warwickshire

MAP 3:D6

## THE HOWARD ARMS

Overlooking the green in a Cotswolds village, and decked with hanging baskets, this pretty pub-with-rooms was in the doldrums before two local families took it on and spruced it up. The perfect pub essence is now distilled in a bar with beams, flagstones, exposed stone walls and battered leather armchairs drawn up to an inglenook. 'The welcome was lovely, staff were friendly, helpful and efficient, and made sure everyone was enjoying themself,' trusted readers wrote. Country-chic bedrooms are home to a mix of contemporary and antique furnishings. One has a half-tester bed. A couple have sloping ceilings that reduce usable space. All have percolator coffee, biscuits and Temple Spa toiletries. 'Very good food' is served in the bar, the mezzanine dining area and outside. Gareth Rufus's menus range from pub classics and Sunday roasts to such dishes as pan-fried bream with mussel beurre blanc sauce. Breakfast brings real orange juice, porridge with Cotswold honey, Wye valley smoked salmon, home-baked bread. Shakespeare's Stratford is eight miles away. Your dog is welcome in the bar but not the dining area. (S and JJ)

Lower Green
Ilmington
Stratford-upon-Avon CV36 4LT

T: 01608 682226
E: info@howardarms.com
W: howardarms.com

BEDROOMS: 8. 4 in extension, 1 on ground floor.
OPEN: all year.
FACILITIES: snug, bar, restaurant, in-room TV (Freeview), terrace, garden (alfresco dining), bar wheelchair accessible, toilet not adapted.
BACKGROUND MUSIC: all day in public areas.
LOCATION: 8 miles S of Stratford-upon-Avon, 6 miles NE of Chipping Campden.
CHILDREN: all ages welcomed, travel cots and Z-beds.
DOGS: allowed in bar and on patio only.
CREDIT CARDS: Amex, MC, Visa.
PRICES: per room B&B single £112–£130, double £120–£190. À la carte £32. 1-night bookings sometimes refused.

# ILSINGTON Devon

## ILSINGTON COUNTRY HOUSE

'We would certainly go again,' write trusted readers after a stay at the Hassell family's country house hotel and spa in wooded grounds, with Dartmoor on the doorstep. On arrival at reception – redesigned since last year – they were 'greeted by a charming lady', but no one offered to help with their luggage. Rooms are decorated in restful shades, with antique pieces and a sleigh bed. Most have a bath and overhead shower. Two deluxe rooms have a roll-top bath and walk-in shower. 'Our spacious superior room overlooked the terrace and the nicely kept front garden.' There were 'moreish' flapjacks on the tea tray. After a game of croquet, guests can take a cream tea on the lawn. In the dining room, chef Mike O'Donnell uses local, seasonal produce and day-boat fish in dishes such as seared beef fillet with an ox-cheek fritter, hake with slow-cooked octopus and squid-ink gnocchi. For veggies, there was risotto, all 'very flavoursome and nicely presented'. Pre-dinner drinks in the lounge were accompanied by 'a tasty canapé'. Breakfast brings 'very tasty' bread too, and eggs from happy hens. (Steve Hur)

---

**25% DISCOUNT VOUCHERS**

Ilsington
Newton Abbot TQ13 9RR

T: 01364 661452
E: hotel@ilsington.plus.com
W: ilsington.co.uk

BEDROOMS: 25. 6 on ground floor.
OPEN: all year except 3–14 Jan.
FACILITIES: lift, 2 lounges, bar, restaurant, bistro, conservatory, function facilities, spa, indoor pool, in-room TV (Freeview), 10-acre grounds, spa/public rooms wheelchair accessible, adapted toilet, ramps.
BACKGROUND MUSIC: in bar, restaurant during day, some areas of spa.
LOCATION: just W of village, 7 miles NW of Newton Abbot.
CHILDREN: all ages welcomed.
DOGS: allowed in some bedrooms, 1 lounge area, bar, conservatory, garden (on lead).
CREDIT CARDS: MC, Visa.
PRICES: per room B&B single £110, double £125–£220. Set dinner £33.50–£39.50, tasting menu (Fri, Sat) £58. 1-night bookings refused peak times.

# KING'S LYNN Norfolk

MAP 2:A4

## CONGHAM HALL

**NEW**

In summer, visitors buzz like contented bees around a garden of almost 400 herb varieties at Nicholas Dickinson's Georgian merchant's house-turned-hotel. Trusted readers were 'impressed from the moment we stepped into the beautifully decorated entrance hall and lounge area'. Main-house bedrooms are presented in classic style, with restful decor and an updated bathroom. There are more contemporary, dog-friendly rooms around the spa garden, with their own furnished patio, a freestanding bath and waterfall shower. All have a coffee machine, home-made cookies and fresh milk. 'Our garden room, across a small courtyard full of flowers and herbs, was beautifully decorated and spotless.' There is praise, too, for the service: 'All requests were responded to straight away, and the staff seemed genuinely pleased to help.' Other readers laud James O'Connor's cooking of dishes such as 'seared wood pigeon breast with creamed polenta, sea trout with sauce vierge, and thyme panna cotta with poached rhubarb and rhubarb sorbet – all delicious'. In the spa, treatments use herbs from the garden. (Andy and Sylvia Aitken, Carol Jackson)

Lynn Road
Grimston
King's Lynn PE32 1AH

T: 01485 600250
E: info@conghamhallhotel.co.uk
W: conghamhallhotel.co.uk

BEDROOMS: 26. 6 garden rooms, 1 suitable for disabled.
OPEN: all year.
FACILITIES: bar, sitting room, library, restaurant, in-room TV (Freeview), civil wedding licence, conference facilities, terrace, spa, 12-metre indoor swimming pool, 30-acre grounds, EV charging point, public areas wheelchair accessible, adapted toilet.
BACKGROUND MUSIC: in bar, restaurant.
LOCATION: 6 miles E of King's Lynn.
CHILDREN: all ages welcomed.
DOGS: allowed in some bedrooms, public rooms.
CREDIT CARDS: MC, Visa.
PRICES: per room D,B&B £240–£460, room only £175–£420 (Mon–Thurs, breakfast £8/£15, continental/cooked). À la carte £40. 1-night bookings sometimes refused Sat.

**SEE ALSO SHORTLIST**

# KIRKBY LONSDALE Cumbria

MAP 4: inset C2

## THE SUN INN

In an old market town, this dog-friendly historic inn by the river and church has quirky rooms, open fires and cheery staff. 'Warm welcome, amazing food. Can't recommend it enough!' The whitewashed building, with 17th-century origins, is 'deceptively big' and has been carefully updated to keep its 'traditional pub feel but with a modern touch'. The large bar with beams and stripped-wood floor has a wood-burning stove, Windsor chairs and light country colours, while the dining area has exposed-stone and claret-red walls. 'Food is modern British, 'imaginative and good' – expect beef tartare with pickled plum, salt-aged duck with smoked beetroot, or 'beautifully pink' lamb. Most bedrooms are 'on the compact side', but have original features such as window seats. Handmade furniture and jolly checks and tartans keep a country feel, while bathrooms are 'bright and reasonably spacious', with sweet-smelling soaps from local producer Bath House. Breakfast includes a 'generous' buffet, cooked dishes using local produce, and berry smoothies. 'We would happily stay there again.' (SP, HP, and others)

6 Market Street
Kirkby Lonsdale LA6 2AU

T: 01524 271965
E: admin@sun-inn.info
W: sun-inn.info

BEDROOMS: 11.
OPEN: all year, restaurant closed Mon lunch.
FACILITIES: bar, restaurant, in-room TV (Freeview), parking (permits supplied), bar and restaurant wheelchair accessible, adapted toilet.
BACKGROUND MUSIC: in bar.
LOCATION: town centre.
CHILDREN: all ages welcomed.
DOGS: allowed in bedrooms, public rooms (separate dog-friendly area in restaurant).
CREDIT CARDS: MC, Visa.
PRICES: per room B&B single £90–£130, double £95–£195, D,B&B £151–£259. À la carte £34. 1-night bookings usually refused Sat but ring to check.

# KIRKBY STEPHEN Cumbria

MAP 4:C3

## AUGILL CASTLE

♀ Previous César winner

With its towers and battlements, wood-panelled walls and ornate ceilings, this Victorian-folly castle set in acres of grounds still manages to be 'very relaxed; we never felt we had to be on our best behaviour'. 'Like staying in a friend's grand country estate,' adds an inspector, 'supremely enjoyable.' Owners Simon and Wendy Bennett are 'never intrusive, always attentive'. Plenty of activities are on offer: tennis, a private cinema and a games room. Bedrooms, spread between castle, stables, orangery and separate buildings, range from big to vast. Eccentrically furnished with antiques, sale-room finds and bold wallpapers, they might include a four-poster, roll-top bath or fireplace. 'Our room had an open fire which we were encouraged to light, an enormous bath, lashings of hot water!' New chef Justin Woods offers modern British menus of 'gorgeously cooked local food', such as braised beef cheek and roasted roots, and more-ish puddings, including damson Bakewell. 'Magnificent breakfasts', too, for which children can collect the eggs. 'A magical home from home.' (Heather Cole, and others)

---

**25% DISCOUNT VOUCHERS**

South Stainmore
Brough
Kirkby Stephen CA17 4DE

T: 01768 341937
E: enquiries@stayinacastle.com
W: stayinacastle.com

---

BEDROOMS: 17. 2 on ground floor, 9 in stables, orangery, coach house, 1 suitable for disabled.
OPEN: all year, dinner nightly (excl. Mon), children's suppers daily.
FACILITIES: hall, drawing room, library, sitting room, conservatory bar, dining room, cinema, in-room TV (Freeview), civil wedding licence, 20-acre grounds (landscaped garden, tennis), public rooms wheelchair accessible, adapted toilet.
BACKGROUND MUSIC: none.
LOCATION: 3 miles NE of Kirkby Stephen.
CHILDREN: all ages welcomed.
DOGS: allowed in 2 bedrooms, not public rooms.
CREDIT CARDS: Amex, MC, Visa.
PRICES: per room B&B £180–£280. À la carte £35. 1-night bookings often refused school holidays, Sat.

# LACOCK Wiltshire

MAP 2:D1

## SIGN OF THE ANGEL

You may feel a sense of déjà vu at Tom and Jack Nicholas's timber-frame coaching inn: it starred as the Babberton Arms in Harry Potter films, while the picturesque streetscape has stood in for Cranford in the BBC drama. In a National Trust village on the edge of the Cotswolds, the Angel today is a popular hotel and restaurant – but still keeps the past alive. 'It would be hard to find somewhere more olde worlde than this 15th-century coaching inn' with Tudor fireplace, 17th-century panelling, flagstone floors and exposed beams. On our last inspectors' visit everything was top-notch. Bedrooms, with 'cottagey decor', have original features, sometimes a 'beam to be wary of', antique pieces, creaky floorboards and modern plumbing. You can take a cream tea by a stream in the orchard garden, and dine in one of three areas. Former sous-chef Ashley Jackson now heads the kitchen, cooking steaks, venison and the like, and with a separate vegan menu. On our covert visit, there was no mobile phone signal, so no diners fixated on their screens, and breakfast proved 'excellent', with smoked haddock and perfect scrambled eggs.

6 Church Street
Lacock SN15 2LB

T: 01249 730230
E: info@signoftheangel.co.uk
W: signoftheangel.co.uk

BEDROOMS: 5.
OPEN: all year except New Year's Eve (phone to check festive dates).
FACILITIES: bar, 3 dining rooms, sitting room, private dining room, no mobile phone signal, cottage garden, restaurant and garden wheelchair accessible.
BACKGROUND MUSIC: in restaurant, radio option in sitting room.
LOCATION: in village, 4 miles S of Chippenham.
CHILDREN: all ages welcomed, cots and blow-up beds available.
DOGS: allowed in bedrooms (£15 charge for cleaning), public rooms.
CREDIT CARDS: Amex, MC, Visa.
PRICES: per room B&B single £85–£140, double £110–£155. À la carte £38, vegan £36, tasting menu £48 (for whole tables ordering in twos or fours).

# LANGAR Nottinghamshire

## LANGAR HALL

A linden avenue leads to this apricot-washed Georgian mansion in parkland, beside St Andrew's church in a Vale of Belvoir village, with a river running through. 'The surroundings are beautiful,' write trusted readers. In the same family since 1868, it was opened as a hotel in 1983 by the late, much-missed Imogen Skirving. Today, her granddaughter, Lila Arora, continues the welcoming tradition. Each bedroom has character, from The Nursery to Barbara Cartland's favourite, no longer pink but with Cole & Son silver birch wallpaper. Edwards has the original four-poster. Dog-friendly Barristers, beloved of a learned friend, is on the ground floor. Cottage-style Cricketers, in a separate wing, has a country cottage feel. It's not perfect ('our room was small and the window could not be shut') but it has many saving graces. Chef Gary Booth, in his 19th year here, devises menus around local ingredients. For instance, braised shoulder of Langar lamb, roast Belvoir partridge or wild mushroom risotto. Breakfast is served in a 'cheerful, sunny conservatory', cocktails in the bar, tea on the lawn. (J and JM)

Church Lane
Langar NG13 9HG

T: 01949 860559
E: info@langarhall.co.uk
W: langarhall.com

BEDROOMS: 13. 1 on ground floor, 3 in annexe, 1 in garden chalet, 1 pod.
OPEN: all year.
FACILITIES: study/sitting room, bar, garden room, main dining room, Indian room, in-room TV (Freeview), civil wedding licence, 30-acre grounds, restaurant wheelchair accessible.
BACKGROUND MUSIC: at lunch and dinner.
LOCATION: 12 miles SE of Nottingham.
CHILDREN: all ages welcomed.
DOGS: in some bedrooms, sitting room and bar, not in restaurant (£20 a night).
CREDIT CARDS: Amex, MC, Visa.
PRICES: per room B&B single £110–£180, double £130–£225, Agnews/Pod £110–£125. Fixed-price dinner £25–£32.50 (Sun, Mon), £42.50–£47.50 (Tues–Thurs), £54.50 (Fri, Sat).

# LASTINGHAM Yorkshire                          MAP 4:C4

## LASTINGHAM GRANGE

Where the road turns into a moorland track, this country hotel offers peace, seclusion and comfort far removed from the modern world. On the edge of the North York Moors, the former 17th-century farmhouse – all sash windows and wisteria – has been run by the Wood family for 60 years. Their style is firmly traditional (some might say a time warp) but they make guests feel 'very welcome and comfortable'. The lounge and dining room have views of the terrace and rose garden, real fires, newspapers, and home-made scones and tea for guests on arrival. Bedrooms, although a little 'dated', have all 'the creature comforts', including fresh milk, coffee machines and baths with showers. There's a drying room for recovering from a day's walking. Dinner is a five-course affair that might start with game ballotine and continue with local partridge with Pernod hollandaise. Generous portions can leave guests 'too full for pudding, but we chose raspberries in elderflower jelly – light and delicately flavoured'. The hotel charms: 'A nurturing place for people to escape from ordinary life.' (RB, and others)

**25% DISCOUNT VOUCHERS**

High Street
Lastingham YO62 6TH

T: 01751 417345
E: reservations@lastinghamgrange.com
W: lastinghamgrange.com

BEDROOMS: 11. Plus self-catering cottage in village.
OPEN: all year except 22 Nov–4 Mar.
FACILITIES: hall, lounge, dining room, in-room TV (Freeview), 10-acre grounds (terrace, garden, orchard, croquet, boules), restaurant wheelchair accessible.
BACKGROUND MUSIC: none.
LOCATION: 5 miles NE of Kirkbymoorside.
CHILDREN: all ages welcomed.
DOGS: allowed in bedrooms with prior consent, lounge, garden but not in dining room.
CREDIT CARDS: Amex, MC, Visa.
PRICES: per room B&B single £140–£144, double £198–£220, D,B&B double £275–£290. À la carte £42.

# LAVENHAM Suffolk

MAP 2:C5

## THE GREAT HOUSE

In one of England's most perfect medieval villages, this timber-framed house may show the world a handsome Georgian face but within, it is all beams and slanted ceilings. Run as a restaurant-with-rooms and long 'loved for its French ambience', it has lost none of its je ne sais quoi since it was bought by Dominique Tropeano, owner and saviour of Colchester Zoo. Each bedroom has its own style. Bastille, though short on storage, is 'lovely', with a separate seating area. 'The bed was very comfortable, with blanket and sheets as we'd asked,' reported our inspectors. Versailles has a Jacobean four-poster. Extras include a coffee machine, minibar, fresh fruit and sherry. There is no lounge, but a small bar, and a patio for alfresco dining. Chef Swann Auffray cooks inventive dishes such as lemon sole with sautéed mushrooms, porcini oil foam and Jerusalem artichoke purée; for vegans, carrots every which way, with cumin caviar and orange-scented quinoa. At breakfast there is a buffet with freshly squeezed orange juice, cheeses, charcuterie, home-baked croissants and Lavenham honey, with cooked dishes charged extra.

Market Place
Lavenham CO10 9QZ

T: 01787 247431
E: info@greathouse.co.uk
W: greathouse.co.uk

BEDROOMS: 5.
OPEN: open all year except Jan, restaurant closed Sun eve, all Mon, Tues lunch.
FACILITIES: restaurant, in-room TV (BT, Freeview), patio dining area, unsuitable for disabled.
BACKGROUND MUSIC: in restaurant.
LOCATION: town centre (free public car park).
CHILDREN: all ages welcomed (cot, high chair, children's portions).
DOGS: only assistance dogs allowed.
CREDIT CARDS: Amex, MC, Visa.
PRICES: per room B&B £129–£204 (continental buffet, cooked dishes £6 extra). Set dinner £37.50, tasting menu £58, à la carte £52. 1-night bookings sometimes refused Sat.

**SEE ALSO SHORTLIST**

# LEAMINGTON SPA Warwickshire

MAP 2:B2

## MALLORY COURT

This Lutyens-style Arts and Crafts manor house with wood panelling and leaded windows presides over landscaped grounds, with lawns, ponds, rose and herb gardens. 'They would look glorious in bloom,' mused a trusted reader. The enterprise is part of the Eden Hotel Collection (see also Brockencote Hall, Chaddesley Corbett), and is as indulgent to families as to laptop-tapping business folk. Main house bedrooms have lovely original features, but perhaps the best are the new rooms above the spa in the Orchard House. The style varies from traditional to contemporary and many rooms will sleep three or four, with views over the herb garden or countryside. All have ESPA products, a coffee machine and turn-down service. 'The room was wonderful at every level, perfect,' writes a reader this year. Food is good too (Relais & Châteaux), with a choice between brasserie classics and ambitious cooking in the atmospheric dining room, where produce from the kitchen garden appears on modern menus. 'Lunch in the little restaurant was excellent.' The breakfast cook passes the scrambled eggs test. (Carole Bloch, RG)

Harbury Lane
Bishop's Tachbrook
Leamington Spa CV33 9QB

T: 01926 330214
E: info@mallory.co.uk
W: mallory.co.uk

BEDROOMS: 43. 11 in Knight's Suite, 12 in Orchard House, 2 suitable for disabled.
OPEN: all year, restaurant for dinner, Thurs–Sat, Sun lunch; brasserie for lunch Wed–Sun, dinner nightly.
FACILITIES: 2 lounges, brasserie (Thurs jazz pm), restaurant, lift, in-room TV (Freeview), civil wedding licence, spa (indoor pool), 10-acre garden, public rooms wheelchair accessible.
BACKGROUND MUSIC: in public rooms.
LOCATION: Bishop's Tachbrook, 3 miles from Leamington Spa.
CHILDREN: all ages welcomed.
DOGS: in some bedrooms, gardens, not public rooms, charges apply.
CREDIT CARDS: Amex, MC, Visa.
PRICES: per room B&B single from £124, double £129–£401. À la carte £65, set menus £67.50.

# LETCOMBE REGIS Oxfordshire

## THE GREYHOUND INN

At the centre of a village at the foot of the Berkshire Downs, Martyn Reed and Catriona Galbraith's 18th-century pub-with-rooms brims with community spirit. There are quiz nights, pizza nights, special tasting nights, and on Bonfire Night, after fireworks on the recreation ground, it's all back for mulled cider and free nibbles at The Greyhound, from where the Riot Act was read for the last time in England one November 5 when the locals got out of hand. There are no riots today, just high spirits in the main bar, which has a 'jolly and noisy' atmosphere. Here, and in three more restful dining rooms, new chef Liam Whittle's locally sourced menus might include lamb rump with Roscoff onions, or sea bream with chive butter sauce. 'Charming location,' writes a trusted reader, who stopped in for coffee. 'We were given a tour of the rooms. They looked good.' Some are small, but two suites will sleep a family, and all are smart. Extras include home-baked biscuits, fresh milk and Bramley toiletries. At breakfast there are freshly baked pastries, smoked haddock, the full English or full vegetarian. (John Barnes)

**25% DISCOUNT VOUCHERS**

Main Street
Letcombe Regis
Wantage OX12 9JL

**T:** 01235 771969
**E:** info@thegreyhoundletcombe.co.uk
**W:** thegreyhoundletcombe.co.uk

**BEDROOMS:** 8.
**OPEN:** all year except 24/25 Dec, 1 week in Jan.
**FACILITIES:** bar with snug, 3 dining rooms (1 available for private dining/meetings), function room, in-room TV (Freeview), garden, bar/restaurant, garden wheelchair accessible, adapted toilet.
**BACKGROUND MUSIC:** occasionally in public rooms.
**LOCATION:** in village, 2 miles SW of Wantage.
**CHILDREN:** all ages welcomed.
**DOGS:** allowed in 2 bedrooms (£15 per night), bar, garden, not dining rooms.
**CREDIT CARDS:** MC, Visa.
**PRICES:** per room B&B single £80–£130, double £95–£145, family £145–£185, D,B&B double £155–£205. À la carte £35, 2-course Midweek Fix dinner (Wed) £15.

# LEWDOWN Devon

MAP 1:C3

## ⚘LEWTRENCHARD MANOR

César award: romantic hotel of the year
'A most beautiful building in lovely, peaceful grounds with a wooded walk down to the river,' say Guide insiders of the Murray family's splendid stone manor house. Although Jacobean in origin, it is largely the creation of the Revd Sabine Baring-Gould, an ebullient Victorian best known for penning 'Onward Christian Soldiers'. 'There is a beautiful gallery with two pianos', a library, Renaissance woodwork, a Jacobean ceiling and Rococo fireplace. Bedrooms – some with a sleigh bed or four-poster – are luxurious, with views of parkland laid out by Walter Sarel and a dovecote designed by Baring-Gould. 'Over all these years, nothing has diminished,' write readers who have been coming here for 20 years. Others say it is ideal for a romantic break. In the atmospheric, oak-panelled dining room, hung with gilt-framed portraits, chef Tom Browning's 'fresh and engaging' menus make extensive use of local and home-grown ingredients in such dishes as grilled brill fillet, Cornish pastis, mussels and dill. The bar menu offers simpler fare. A full Devon breakfast comes with freshly squeezed juice.
(Gage McKinney, C and AR)

Lewdown
Okehampton EX20 4PN

T: 01566 783222
E: info@lewtrenchard.co.uk
W: lewtrenchard.co.uk

BEDROOMS: 14. 1 in folly, 4 with separate entrance, 1 suitable for disabled.
OPEN: all year.
FACILITIES: lounge, bar, library, restaurant, function facilities, in-room TV (Freeview), civil wedding licence, 12-acre gardens, public rooms wheelchair accessible.
BACKGROUND MUSIC: none.
LOCATION: rural, 10 miles N of Tavistock.
CHILDREN: all ages welcomed, no under-8s in restaurant in evening.
DOGS: allowed in bedrooms (not unattended), in public rooms, not in restaurant.
CREDIT CARDS: Amex, MC, Visa.
PRICES: per room B&B single £115–£230, double £175–£280, D,B&B double £270–£370. Set dinner £49.50, tasting menus £74–£89. 1-night bookings sometimes refused Sat.

# LIVERPOOL Merseyside

MAP 4:E2

## 2 BLACKBURNE TERRACE

In the cultural district, this boutique B&B between the city's two cathedrals is ideally located for the Liverpool Philharmonic and Everyman and Unity theatres. A 'calm, relaxing place to stay', it has a few artistic flourishes of its own too. The handsome Georgian town house, set behind mature lime trees, provides the blank canvas for owners Sarah and Glenn Whitter's idiosyncratic creativity. Art books are neatly stacked on a tangerine ottoman, original paintings grace the walls. A private gallery is open to guests by appointment. Bedrooms are individually styled – Room 2 has sumptuous gold and yellow fabrics and paintings by Korean artist Eun Sook Choi; Room 1 an enormous sofa in cerulean blue velvet and a 19th-century mahogany compactum. All rooms have Egyptian cotton sheets, fresh flowers, Duffy's chocolate and a small bottle of local artisan gin. Breakfast – an opulent spread of hot and cold dishes – is served in the art-filled dining room, the polished purple table laid with silver cutlery and cut crystal. 'A real find in this wonderful city.'

2 Blackburne Terrace
Liverpool L8 7PJ

T: 0151 708 5474
E: info@2bbt.co.uk
W: 2blackburneterrace.com

BEDROOMS: 4.
OPEN: all year except 24 Dec–1 Jan.
FACILITIES: drawing room, dining room, in-room smart TV (Freeview), walled garden, unsuitable for disabled.
BACKGROUND MUSIC: classical at breakfast.
LOCATION: city centre.
CHILDREN: not under 11.
DOGS: not allowed.
CREDIT CARDS: MC, Visa.
PRICES: per room B&B £180–£300.

**SEE ALSO SHORTLIST**

# LODSWORTH Sussex

## THE HALFWAY BRIDGE

In the heart of the South Downs national park, this 18th-century inn is a well-judged mix of friendly local and restaurant-with-rooms. The A272 outside is now a busy road, but inside, it's still atmospheric, with beams and inglenook fireplace; when our inspectors last visited, drinkers nursed their Arundel ales as dogs snoozed by their feet. Proprietors Sam and Janet Bakose also own The Crab & Lobster, Sidlesham (see entry), and chef Clyde Hollett oversees both kitchens. On the short menu can be found both pub classics and more inventive dishes such as hake in bouillabaisse sauce – 'tasty and beautifully presented'. It's not a quick trip upstairs to bed though: bedrooms are in the inn's old stables, a 165-yard walk away and across a narrow country road. Our inspectors' room was huge, with beams and a high ceiling, and a picture window looking out over fields. Fresh milk and organic toiletries were welcome extras. The look was a bit generic, with wall-to-wall carpeting and flower prints, but it was comfy for all that, with good lighting to read by. Reports, please.

Lodsworth
Petworth GU28 9BP

T: 01798 861281
E: enquiries@halfwaybridge.co.uk
W: halfwaybridge.co.uk

BEDROOMS: 7. In converted barns, 165 yds from main building.
OPEN: all year.
FACILITIES: bar, restaurant, in-room TV (Freeview), bar terrace, small beer garden, unsuitable for disabled.
BACKGROUND MUSIC: 'quiet' in bar and restaurant.
LOCATION: 3 miles W of Petworth, on A272.
CHILDREN: all ages welcomed.
DOGS: allowed in bar area only.
CREDIT CARDS: Amex, MC, Visa.
PRICES: per room B&B single £95–£115, double £150–£230. Set lunch menu £26, à la carte £32. 1-night bookings refused Fri and Sat, when single occupancy is charged at full double rate.

# LONG SUTTON Somerset

MAP 1:C6

## THE DEVONSHIRE ARMS

A former hunting lodge in a village that was once part of the Devonshire estate, this inn has been given a smart make-over by hands-on owners Philip and Sheila Mepham. Whether you book the 'small but well-furnished' room experienced by one reader or the 'big comfortable one overlooking the village green' where another reader stayed, bedrooms are contemporary in style, painted in pale shades and uncluttered, with dark-wood furniture and seagrass flooring. Most rooms have a shower only but the modern four-poster bedroom has a bath and separate shower. Downstairs, locals drop in to drink Harry's cider, brewed in the village, in a bar with an open fire. In the wood-floored dining area, its deep blue walls hung with caricatures, 'the goat's cheese mousse was very good, the confit duck leg faultless'. There is alfresco dining in a garden planted with lavender and olive trees. Breakfast isn't quite as impressive; one reader was disappointed to find bottled orange juice. If you stay in winter, you can see the spectacle, at dawn and dusk, of murmurations of starlings flying over the Somerset Levels. (RC)

Long Sutton
Langport TA10 9LP

T: 01458 241271
E: info@thedevonshirearms.com
W: thedevonshirearms.com

BEDROOMS: 9. 2, on ground floor, in annexe behind main building.
OPEN: all year except 24–26 Dec.
FACILITIES: open-plan bar and restaurant, private dining room, in-room TV (Freeview), courtyard, garden (croquet lawn, vegetable garden), public areas wheelchair accessible, no adapted toilet.
BACKGROUND MUSIC: in bar.
LOCATION: by the village green.
CHILDREN: all ages welcomed (children's menus, free travel cot, Z-bed £20).
DOGS: allowed in bar only.
CREDIT CARDS: MC, Visa.
PRICES: per room B&B £120–£170 (single £90, Sun–Thurs, subject to availability). À la carte £30. 1-night bookings sometimes refused weekends.

# LONGHORSLEY Northumberland                    MAP 4:B3

## THISTLEYHAUGH FARM

A perfect example of a traditional farmhouse
B&B: huge and comfortable bedrooms, generous
hospitality, breakfasts to fuel the day, and the
restorative peace of the countryside. The Nelless
family's organic farm feels remote (down a
network of country lanes), yet is only two miles
from the main road. 'A wonderful and peaceful
location in rural Northumberland,' say fans. The
creeper-covered Georgian farmhouse, surrounded
by gardens and farmland, is picture-book-
perfect. Inside, Enid Nelless's passion for art and
antiques is clear: polished tables, collections of
silver and china, paintings and sketches fill the
rooms. Bedrooms are elegantly old-fashioned
– mahogany wardrobes, 'proper towel rails and
dressing tables', pretty lampshades and broderie
anglaise bedcovers. All rooms have fresh milk and
home-made biscuits; there are roll-top baths in the
bathrooms. Enid and her daughters-in-law, Zoe
and Janice, are praised for their 'endlessly helpful'
manner, whether suggesting walks or nearby
pubs, or drying muddy clothes. 'Lovely' breakfasts
include home-produced bacon, eggs and honey
from neighbours, and local Craster kippers. (HP)

**25% DISCOUNT VOUCHERS**

Longhorsley
Morpeth NE65 8RG

T: 01665 570629
E: thistleyhaugh@hotmail.com
W: thistleyhaugh.co.uk

BEDROOMS: 4.
OPEN: all year except 18 Dec–8 Jan.
FACILITIES: lounge, garden/breakfast
room, hall, in-room TV (Freeview),
¼-acre garden (summer house),
fishing, shooting, golf, riding nearby.
BACKGROUND MUSIC: none.
LOCATION: 10 miles N of Morpeth,
W of A697.
CHILDREN: all ages welcomed.
DOGS: not allowed (kennels nearby).
CREDIT CARDS: MC, Visa.
PRICES: per room B&B single £75–£90,
double £100. Snack supper £12.50.

# LORTON Cumbria

## NEW HOUSE FARM

In the scenic Vale of Lorton, in the peaceful
northwest corner of the Lake District
national park, Hazel Thompson's Grade
II listed farmhouse B&B stands against a
beautiful backdrop of fells. The landscape is a
photographer's dream, and weddings are hosted
in the rustic tea rooms in a converted cow byre, so
call ahead and check if you want a light lunch of
panini, Whitby scampi or a Cumberland sausage
bap, to eat inside or alfresco. Overnight guests are
welcomed with a cream tea, and have use of the
outdoor hot tub. Bedrooms, two in outbuildings,
are named after their views or former function.
They have period furnishings, original features
but contemporary art and a modern bathroom.
The ground-floor Old Dairy and Stable each have
an antique four-poster. The former has exposed
stone walls and a double-ended slipper bath.
Whiteside has a double air-jet bath. Swinside
(source of the house spring water) has a double
power shower with body jets. You might dine at
the pub in Lorton, two miles away, or drive six
miles to Wordsworth's birthplace, Cockermouth,
for a host of golden opportunities. Reports, please.

Lorton
Cockermouth CA13 9UU

T: 07841 159818
E: hazel@newhouse-farm.co.uk
W: newhouse-farm.com

BEDROOMS: 5. 1 in Stable, 1 in Old
Dairy.
OPEN: all year, tea room closed end
Oct–mid-Mar, every Sat, and some
Tues.
FACILITIES: entrance hall, 2 lounges,
dining room, civil wedding licence,
17-acre grounds (garden, hot tub,
streams, woods, field, lake and river,
safe bathing 2 miles), unsuitable for
disabled.
BACKGROUND MUSIC: none.
LOCATION: on B5289, 2 miles S of
Lorton.
CHILDREN: not under 6.
DOGS: 'clean and dry' dogs with own
bed allowed in bedrooms (£10 per
night), not in public rooms.
CREDIT CARDS: MC, Visa.
PRICES: per room B&B £140–£180.
1-night bookings usually refused
(check availability).

# LOWER BOCKHAMPTON Dorset          MAP 1:D6

## YALBURY COTTAGE

♔ Previous César winner

Lower Bockhampton is in Thomas Hardy country, and what could be more Hardyesque than this 'pretty cottage hotel' in the former home of a local shepherd? 'We have been there several times since Jamie and Ariane Jones bought it, and it remains a favourite,' say recent guests. Ariane is 'a warm and skilful front-of-house' manager while chef Jamie produces 'unfussy but attractively presented' dishes, such as Portland crab fritter and Lyme Bay scallop and beef brisket with Dorset black garlic crumb. A 'very good wine list offers at least three red and three white wines by the glass', and several 'special occasion' wines. Bedrooms, in the modern part of the building, are decorated in simple cottage style and have bucolic views over sheep-scattered fields or the hotel gardens. There's plenty of choice at breakfast – smoked haddock with poached egg and chive butter sauce, perhaps, or a grilled Bridport kipper. The winning combination of 'people, food and location make Yalbury Cottage outstanding', comments one regular reviewer. (David Birnie, Michael and Betty Hill)

**25% DISCOUNT VOUCHERS**

Lower Bockhampton
Dorchester DT2 8PZ

T: 01305 262382
E: enquiries@yalburycottage.com
W: yalburycottage.com

BEDROOMS: 8. 6 on ground floor.
OPEN: all year except 23 Dec–21 Jan.
FACILITIES: lounge, restaurant, in-room TV (Freeview), garden with outdoor seating.
BACKGROUND MUSIC: 'easy listening' in lounge in evening.
LOCATION: 2 miles E of Dorchester.
CHILDREN: all ages welcomed, no under-12s in restaurant after 8 pm.
DOGS: allowed in bedrooms, lounge, not in restaurant.
CREDIT CARDS: MC, Visa.
PRICES: per room B&B single £75–£85, double £99–£125, D,B&B single £105–£120, double £175–£195. À la carte £42.50.

# LUDLOW Shropshire

MAP 3:C4

## OLD DOWNTON LODGE

♀ Previous César winner

Hidden away down a 'long winding track', Pippa and Willem Vlok's restaurant-with-rooms has a secluded, 'away from it all' feel. This 'friendly and efficient' establishment is set in converted farm buildings, some medieval in origin, and arranged around a courtyard garden. Individually decorated bedrooms are 'lovely and comfortable', some have a modern four-poster bed; all have a state-of-the-art bathroom. The dining room, with exposed stone walls and timbered vaulted ceiling, is impressive. Food equally so, created from Shropshire's natural larder by new chef Nick Bennett. The market menu might include sea bass with octopus, piquillo and garlic, and plum panna cotta to finish. Bennett, who was a MasterChef Professionals finalist, also offers a six-course tasting menu. Arriving late, one trusted reviewer enjoyed a 'cheeseboard of Shropshire specialities' and an 'excellent' bottle of wine in the 'relaxing' lounge bar. Breakfast is also 'first class'. The hotel is minutes from foodie haven Ludlow, ideal for exploring the blue remembered hills of Shropshire. (Lindsay Hunt and John Fisher, I and FW, PC, and others)

**25% DISCOUNT VOUCHERS**

Downton on the Rock
Ludlow SY8 2HU

T: 01568 771826
E: bookings@olddowntonlodge.com
W: olddowntonlodge.com

BEDROOMS: 10. In buildings round courtyard.
OPEN: all year, except Christmas, afternoon tea Tues–Sat 3–5 pm, restaurant closed for lunch Mon–Wed and for dinner Sun, Mon.
FACILITIES: sitting room, dining room, 'museum' (function room), in-room TV (Freeview), civil wedding licence, 1-acre courtyard, 2 Tesla car charging points, unsuitable for disabled.
BACKGROUND MUSIC: soft classical in sitting and dining rooms.
LOCATION: 6 miles W of Ludlow.
CHILDREN: over-12s only.
DOGS: allowed in some bedrooms by prior arrangement, not in public rooms.
CREDIT CARDS: Amex, MC, Visa.
PRICES: per room B&B £165–£285, D,B&B £225–£325. Market menu (2–3 courses) £40–£50, tasting menu (6 courses) £65.

**SEE ALSO SHORTLIST**

# LYMINGTON Hampshire                              MAP 2:E2

## BRITANNIA HOUSE

Trusted readers this year 'greatly enjoyed' this 'small and quirky hotel' overlooking one of three marinas in a historic New Forest coastal town. Genial, 'larger-than-life' host Tobias Feilke has a winning, 'direct, friendly approach'. He is also no amateur: Rhineland-born Tobias trained at the prestigious Brenners Park-Hotel & Spa in Baden-Baden, then moved to Chewton Glen, New Milton (see entry) via a BSc in hotel management. He has brought something of the grand country house look to a former Victorian public house. When it comes to boutique-chic, Britannia waives the rules. The hallway is hung with a magnificent array of hats, and the interiors are a riot of swags and tassels. The Britannia Suite is positively imperial, done out in gold and black. On the ground floor, The Courtyard looks on to a small garden, while The Forest promises 'reminders of the New Forest national park'. A dual-aspect first-floor lounge has a marina view. 'Breakfast is communal, in the kitchen, and very friendly.' Tobias, at the Aga, cooks everything to order, and is a mine of 'information and recommendations'. (Geoffrey Bignell)

Station Street
Lymington SO41 3BA

T: 01590 672091
E: enquiries@britannia-house.com
W: britannia-house.com

BEDROOMS: 5. 2 on ground floor, one 2-storey apartment.
OPEN: all year except over 'the festive season'.
FACILITIES: lounge, kitchen/breakfast room, in-room TV (Freeview), courtyard garden, parking, unsuitable for disabled.
BACKGROUND MUSIC: none.
LOCATION: 2 mins' walk from High Street/quayside, close to station.
CHILDREN: not under 8.
DOGS: not allowed.
CREDIT CARDS: MC, Visa.
PRICES: per room B&B single £89–£139, double £99–£149. 1-night bookings refused weekends.

# LYNDHURST Hampshire

MAP 2:E2

## LIME WOOD

Designed for pure leisure and pleasure, this Georgian New Forest lodge is run as a glamorous yet relaxed country house hotel for today's savvy guest. 'It really does encapsulate laid-back luxury at its best,' says a Guide insider. Neutral-tone rooms are 'romantic, some tucked away up towers, with open fire and wood floor'. The simplest, under the eaves, have garden and forest views. There are two-storey suites, pavilions with a lounge and private terrace, and a cabin by the lake with outdoor bath. Public rooms are beautiful, but 'none as enticing as the light-filled Courtyard bar, with glass-ceiling', marble bar and leather chairs. Sunbathe on the herb-planted roof of the spa, order small plates from an all-day menu, or dine on modern Italian fare from Luke Holder and Angela Hartnett (maybe 'particularly good truffle ravioli', or crab risotto with orange and fennel). 'Staff are so well trained that when a spider crawled on me in the restaurant, the waiter leant over and calmly palmed it, then stood and chatted to me with it in his hand.' You can borrow boots to head into the forest, with trails from the door. (JK)

Beaulieu Road
Lyndhurst SO43 7FZ

T: 02380 287177
E: info@limewood.co.uk
W: limewoodhotel.co.uk

BEDROOMS: 33. 5 on ground floor, 2 suitable for disabled, 16 in pavilions and cottages in the grounds.
OPEN: all year.
FACILITIES: lifts, 2 bars, 3 lounges, 2 restaurants, private dining rooms, in-room TV (Freeview), civil wedding licence, spa (indoor pool), 14-acre gardens, cookery school, public rooms wheelchair accessible.
BACKGROUND MUSIC: all day in public areas.
LOCATION: in New Forest, 12 miles SW of Southampton.
CHILDREN: all ages welcomed, children's menus and swimming times.
DOGS: allowed in outside bedrooms (£30 charge), not in main house.
CREDIT CARDS: MC, Visa.
PRICES: per room £395–£2,500. Breakfast £22, à la carte £65. 1-night bookings refused most weekends.

# MALTON Yorkshire

## THE TALBOT

**NEW**

This former Georgian coaching inn in Yorkshire's 'food capital' has a winning combination of cool style, informal atmosphere and robust food. Part of the Naylor-Leyland family estate, the building's interiors mix bold colours, vintage finds and rustic-chic styling. 'High-quality soft furnishing and interesting art make the lounge restful,' reports a reader, while 'candlelit tables lent intimacy to the dining room'. Food is punchy and strongly local, and might include steak tartare with horseradish followed by smoked haddock and corn chowder. Be aware: 'a lack of portion control left us with no room for pudding'. Bedrooms, with scrubbed-wood furniture, vary from light, if plain, top-floor rooms with views to dark-hued affairs with four-poster. Some are perhaps too sparse with 'dim lighting' and 'no view', but a 'comfortable and spacious bed'. Home-made biscuits and fresh milk were appreciated, along with 100 Acres toiletries in bathrooms, which often have a roll-top bath. A large breakfast buffet, with 'freshly squeezed juice and molten poached egg', will set you up for exploring Malton's artisan producers. (Robert Gower)

Malton YO17 7AJ

T: 01653 639096
E: enquiries@talbotmalton.co.uk
W: talbotmalton.co.uk

BEDROOMS: 26. 1, on ground floor, suitable for disabled.
OPEN: all year.
FACILITIES: sitting room, bar, restaurant, private dining room, in-room TV (Freeview), civil wedding licence, 2 terraces, garden, most public areas wheelchair accessible, adapted toilet.
BACKGROUND MUSIC: in all public areas.
LOCATION: town centre.
CHILDREN: all ages welcomed.
DOGS: allowed in some bedrooms, all public areas except restaurant.
CREDIT CARDS: Amex, MC, Visa.
PRICES: per room B&B double £119–£410. À la carte £30.

# MARKET DRAYTON Shropshire     MAP 3:B5

## GOLDSTONE HALL

A vast, prolific kitchen garden is the perennial glory of John and Sue Cushing's red brick Georgian manor house in flower-filled acres amid gentle countryside. But there is much more to admire, not least 'very comfortable rooms and excellent food'. The bedrooms, one with an antique four-poster, have a classic feel but modern furnishings. Each has a deep bath and separate power shower, a fridge with fresh milk, and home-baked biscuits. Garden rooms have views of the walled garden, an old acacia tree, and rose beds. In the restaurant, Liam Philbin's menus sing of home-grown produce – fermented gooseberries with grilled mackerel; carrot and coriander rösti and fennel pollen yogurt with pigeon breast; pumpkin blackcurrant leaf ice cream, blueberry and violet Alaska. Breakfast in the orangery brings real orange juice, good muesli, great vegetarian options and fresh fruit from the gardens. The latter are open to the public from March to October under the Royal Horticultural Society Partner Garden scheme; several other gardens are in the area. (K and LB)

Goldstone
Market Drayton TF9 2NA

T: 01630 661202
E: enquiries@goldstonehall.com
W: goldstonehall.com

BEDROOMS: 12. 2 on ground floor.
OPEN: all year.
FACILITIES: bar, lounge, drawing room, dining room, orangery, in-room TV (Sky, Freeview), function facilities, civil wedding licence, 5 acres of grounds (walled garden, kitchen garden, Great Lawn), public rooms and garden wheelchair accessible, adapted toilets.
BACKGROUND MUSIC: in bar and dining room.
LOCATION: 5 miles S of Market Drayton.
CHILDREN: all ages welcomed.
DOGS: not allowed.
CREDIT CARDS: Amex, MC, Visa.
PRICES: per room B&B single £95–£115, double £150–£180, D,B&B single £138–£158, double £246–£276, child sharing with parents £11.50–£28. Set dinner £49.

## MARTINHOE Devon                    MAP 1:B4

### THE OLD RECTORY HOTEL

✿ Previous César winner

Standing high on verdant, hog-backed cliffs above
the Exmoor coast, Huw Rees and Sam Prosser's
rectory-turned-hotel is wonderfully remote. The
bedrooms, in the main house and coach house,
are a blend of contemporary and traditional style,
with a modern bathroom, Noble Isle toiletries
and spring water on tap. A new annexe duplex
suite this year offers two bedrooms, a lounge with
a log-burner, a bathroom and shower room. The
conservatory is a comfortable jumble of sofas
overlooking mature gardens with a stream and
waterfall. At afternoon tea, cakes freshly baked
by Huw are a dangerous temptation. Guests
gather for drinks and canapés before a dinner
of local and home-grown produce and day-boat
fish, cooked by Michael Caines alumnus Thomas
Frost: maybe Ilfracombe crab, a fillet of Devon
Red Ruby beef with chateaubriand sauce or a
vegetarian choice. At breakfast there is local apple
juice, eggs Florentine or the full Devon, with
Exmoor honey, jams and Marmite. 'Very good
as per your comments. Food is exceptional,'
writes a reader this year, short and to the point.
(Alan Renwick)

Berry's Ground Lane
Martinhoe EX31 4QT

T: 01598 763368
E: info@oldrectoryhotel.co.uk
W: oldrectoryhotel.co.uk

BEDROOMS: 12. 2 on ground floor, 3 in
coach house, 1 in cottage annexe.
OPEN: Mar–early Nov.
FACILITIES: 2 lounges, orangery, dining
room, in-room TV (Freeview), 3-acre
grounds, public rooms including
restaurant wheelchair accessible, toilet
not adapted.
BACKGROUND MUSIC: 'very quiet' in
dining room only.
LOCATION: 4 miles W of Lynton.
CHILDREN: not under 14.
DOGS: not allowed.
CREDIT CARDS: Amex, MC, Visa.
PRICES: per room B&B double £190–
£250, D,B&B £230–£290, for single
deduct £15 (B&B) or £45 (D,B&B).
À la carte £35, 1-night bookings
occasionally refused weekends.

# MAWGAN PORTH Cornwall

MAP 1:D2

## BEDRUTHAN HOTEL AND SPA

♦ Previous César winner

There are grandparents who today cherish childhood memories of holidays at this family-friendly hotel. Set into the cliff-top above the sandy beach, it has been owned by the same family since 1959. The interiors have been updated over the decades (out with purple carpet and orange bedspreads, in with Scandi-style), but the walls are still hung with work by Cornish artists, and floor-to-ceiling windows frame the same Atlantic views. The atmosphere is lively and inclusive, with activities for children from dawn until dark, while parents can relax in the spa. It can be rumbustious ('not for the faint-hearted', said a reader who visited on a bank holiday), but everything is well organised. Bedrooms come in various configurations, some with a balcony or terrace. You can dine in The Herring restaurant, on such dishes as hake fillet with curry sauce and pea shoots. ('Food is generally pretty good, and value for money.') There is simpler dining in the Wild Café, where breakfast brings daily specials such as eggs Benedict. If peace and quiet are what you seek, choose the adults-only sister hotel, The Scarlet (next entry). (SW)

Trenance
Mawgan Porth TR8 4BU

T: 01637 860860
E: stay@bedruthan.com
W: bedruthan.com

BEDROOMS: 101. 1 suitable for disabled, apartment suites in separate block.
OPEN: all year.
FACILITIES: lift, bar, restaurant, café, lounge, in-room TV (Freeview), spa (indoor pool), civil wedding licence, 5-acre grounds (3 heated pools, tennis), several areas wheelchair accessible.
BACKGROUND MUSIC: in restaurant, café and bar.
LOCATION: 4 miles NE of Newquay.
CHILDREN: all ages welcomed.
DOGS: allowed in some bedrooms (£12 per dog), some public areas.
CREDIT CARDS: MC, Visa.
PRICES: per room B&B single from £95, double £165–£335, D,B&B £217–£387. Set dinner £38 (Herring), à la carte £26 (Wild Café).

# MAWGAN PORTH Cornwall

MAP 1:D2

## ☼THE SCARLET

César award: seaside hotel of the year

While children let rip at sister hotel Bedruthan (previous entry), all is serene at the adults-only Scarlet, 'perfectly located overlooking the beach and ocean', with Ayurvedic-inspired spa and outdoor hot tubs. There are no negatives in the many reports readers send about this modern hotel, which has 'lovely art scattered everywhere, and a real sense of connection to nature, with the outdoor freshwater pool and landscaping'. Each bedroom has a private courtyard, garden terrace or balcony, with sea views. 'We had a "Just Right" room, with its own private patio leading to a path to the beach.' 'The staff are top class, young, friendly, knowledgeable; everything is done with grace and a smile.' In the Atlantic-view restaurant, Mike Francis's imaginative, locally sourced menus include such dishes as glazed native beef with crispy oyster, or curried aubergine with pickles and samosa. 'The food is wonderful, great choice, freshly cooked breakfasts with local produce.' 'If something wasn't on the menu that wasn't a problem – the kitchen would rustle up what you wanted.' (Andy Driscoll, Peter Francis, and many others)

Tredragon Road
Mawgan Porth TR8 4DQ

T: 01637 861800
E: stay@scarlethotel.co.uk
W: scarlethotel.co.uk

BEDROOMS: 37. 2 suitable for disabled.
OPEN: all year except 2–31 Jan, house parties Christmas (4 days) and New Year (3 days).
FACILITIES: lift, 2 lounges, bar, library, restaurant, in-room TV (Freeview), civil wedding licence, spa, terrace, meadow garden, public areas wheelchair accessible, adapted toilet.
BACKGROUND MUSIC: all day in bar and restaurant.
LOCATION: 4 miles NE of Newquay.
CHILDREN: not allowed.
DOGS: allowed in 5 selected bedrooms, some public areas.
CREDIT CARDS: MC, Visa.
PRICES: per room B&B single £200–£460, double £220–£480. Fixed-price dinner £49.95. 1-night bookings refused Fri/Sat.

# MAWNAN SMITH Cornwall

MAP 1:E2

## BUDOCK VEAN

'The setting could hardly be more enticing' at this spa hotel and golf resort on a 'magical' part of the Helford river. It stands in 'exotic gardens, with a large enclosed swimming pool and lovely rooms that overlook the course and the rich woodlands'. In an 18th-century manor house, the hotel has been owned by the Barlow family since 1987, and some guests have been coming here for almost as long. One reader notes a 'clubby feeling – guests all seemed to know each other'. In the past year, Signature bedrooms have been refurbished in more contemporary style; Standard and Superior rooms are scheduled for an update. 'We were upgraded to a Signature room. It was spotless, and had an excellent bathroom and a large shower.' There are tennis courts, an outdoor hot tub, a snooker table, kayaking, painting and bridge breaks. Dinner, with a separate vegetarian menu, is a dress-up affair, but it divides opinion somewhat. 'Food good (traditional),' reads one report. 'Perhaps the cooking could be a bit more ambitious,' ventures another. In all events, try for a window table and gaze out over the valley. (Mike Craddock, Josie Mayers, SL)

nr Helford Passage
Mawnan Smith
Falmouth TR11 5LG

T: 01326 252100
E: relax@budockvean.co.uk
W: budockvean.co.uk

BEDROOMS: 55. Plus 4 self-catering cottages, 1 suitable for disabled, with wheelchair access from rear of hotel.
OPEN: all year except 2–22 Jan.
FACILITIES: lift, 2 lounges, cocktail bar, conservatory, bar, restaurant, in-room TV (Freeview), civil wedding licence, 65-acre grounds, spa, sauna, indoor swimming pool, bar and lounges wheelchair accessible, adapted toilet.
BACKGROUND MUSIC: 'gentle' live piano or guitar at dinner.
LOCATION: 6 miles SW of Falmouth.
CHILDREN: all ages welcomed.
DOGS: allowed in most bedrooms, terrace, not in public rooms.
CREDIT CARDS: MC, Visa.
PRICES: per person B&B £74–£149, D,B&B £102–£177. Fixed-price dinner £28 (£47 for non-residents).

## MELLS Somerset

## THE TALBOT INN

♥ Previous César winner

Take a historic village inn, then reinvent it as a dining-pub-with-rooms, in shabby-chic style, for the modern era. It's a formula which Dan Brod, Charlie Luxton and Matt Greenlees have perfected with their trio of Bramley Bars (see also The Beckford Arms, Tisbury, and The Lord Poulett Arms, Hinton St George). The Talbot, a 15th-century coaching inn built around a cobbled courtyard, also features a beamed coach house where food is grilled on charcoal and wood, as in traditional inns. In addition, the restaurant is a 'sequence of homely rooms' where the food is 'of a very high standard'. It might include anything from a simple ploughman's or burger to dishes such as salted Atlantic cod, duck-fat pommes Anna, cauliflower purée and pickled cauliflower. Upstairs, the keenly priced bedrooms are more contemporary, with an emperor bed, vintage Welsh blankets, seagrass flooring, comfy chairs and handmade Bramley toiletries. Do visit the sitting room in the old tithe barn, which has a mural by local artists Fleur Kelly and Diana Byrne, depicting the magic of Mells through time (including the exploits of local man little Jack Horner).

Selwood Street
Mells
Frome BA11 3PN

T: 01373 812254
E: info@talbotinn.com
W: talbotinn.com

BEDROOMS: 8. 1 on ground floor.
OPEN: all year except 25 Dec.
FACILITIES: sitting room, bar, restaurant, coach house grill room, in-room smart TV (including Freeview), cobbled courtyard, small garden.
BACKGROUND MUSIC: in public areas.
LOCATION: in village.
CHILDREN: all ages welcomed.
DOGS: allowed in 1 bedroom (£10 one-off charge), and in all public areas.
CREDIT CARDS: MC, Visa.
PRICES: per room B&B £100–£160, family suite £200. À la carte £30. 1-night bookings refused weekends.

# MILTON ABBOT Devon

## HOTEL ENDSLEIGH

♨ Previous César winner

'It's hard to fathom just how many things the Endsleigh does right,' says one reader, of this Grade I listed hotel set in 200 acres of fairy-tale gardens in the Tamar valley. The house was built 200 years ago for the Duchess of Bedford, who fell in love with the 'unreal natural beauty' of the valley. Readers feel the same, praising the 'simply spectacular' parkland created by Humphry Repton. Two drawing rooms and a library for afternoon tea are stylish and comfortable. Bedrooms are testament to owner Olga Polizzi's fine eye for detail, mixing period features with modern comfort. Many have garden views; one has a chaise longue, another a bathroom fashioned from the original owner's private chapel. Toiletries are by Mitchell and Peach. A 'heavenly' dinner is cooked by chef Tom Ewings using seasonal ingredients sourced from local producers, and served in the wood-panelled dining room. Service is 'very personal', an extension of the 'harmonious relationship of the hotel, the grounds and all its animal life'. The 'awful' mobile phone reception is no bad thing, serving to preserve the hotel's unruffled atmosphere.

## 25% DISCOUNT VOUCHERS

Milton Abbot
Tavistock PL19 0PQ

T: 01822 870000
E: info@hotelendsleigh.com
W: hotelendsleigh.com

BEDROOMS: 19. 1 on ground floor, 3 in stables, 1 in lodge (1 mile from main house), 1 suite suitable for disabled.
OPEN: all year.
FACILITIES: drawing room, library, card room, bar, 2 dining rooms, in-room TV (Freeview), civil wedding licence, 108-acre estate (fishing, ghillie), public rooms wheelchair accessible, adapted toilet.
BACKGROUND MUSIC: none.
LOCATION: 7 miles NW of Tavistock.
CHILDREN: all ages welcomed.
DOGS: allowed in bedrooms, lounges, not in restaurant or library at tea time.
CREDIT CARDS: Amex, MC, Visa.
PRICES: per room B&B £211.50–£485, D,B&B £251.50–£590. Breakfast £20. À la carte £52.50. 1-night bookings refused Fri, Sat.

## MOUSEHOLE Cornwall

MAP 1:E1

## THE OLD COASTGUARD

♛ Previous César winner

'Perfection – time seems to slow down the moment you enter,' says one trusted reviewer of this contemporary take on a traditional coastal inn, which exudes a wonderfully relaxed and cheerful atmosphere. Recently refurbished bedrooms (the hotel suffered a fire in 2019) have a full or partial sea view; most have a balcony. Each is 'warmly decorated', with tongue-and-groove panelling and paintings by local artists. Homely touches include a Roberts radio and a 'proper tea tray with a cafetière'. In the restaurant, Jamie Porter's brasserie-style dishes are 'consistently delicious', while the staff are 'knowledgeable about the food and alcohol, and will do whatever they can to make your stay more enjoyable'. One reviewer so enjoyed the scallops with coral sauce that he ordered it three nights running. Breakfast brings a cooked Cornish, smoked salmon with scrambled eggs or home-made muesli. 'A true gem,' says a recent guest. 'We can't wait to return,' says another. See also entries for sister properties The Gurnard's Head, Zennor, and The Felin Fach Griffin, Felin Fach, Wales. (Kate Bailey, Vicky Lloyd, and others)

**25% DISCOUNT VOUCHERS**

The Parade
Mousehole
Penzance TR19 6PR

T: 01736 731222
E: bookings@oldcoastguardhotel.
co.uk
W: oldcoastguardhotel.co.uk

BEDROOMS: 14.
OPEN: all year except 24/25 Dec.
FACILITIES: bar, sun lounge, restaurant, sea-facing garden with path to beach, restaurant and bar wheelchair accessible.
BACKGROUND MUSIC: Radio 4 at breakfast, selected music at other mealtimes.
LOCATION: 2-min. walk from village, 3 miles S of Newlyn.
CHILDREN: all ages welcomed.
DOGS: allowed in bedrooms (treats, towels, dog bowls), not in dining room.
CREDIT CARDS: MC, Visa.
PRICES: per room B&B £150–£250, D,B&B £205–£305. Set dinner £19.50–£27, à la carte £29. 1-night bookings only rarely refused.

# MULLION COVE Cornwall
MAP 1:E2

## MULLION COVE HOTEL

This striking cliff-top hotel on the Cornish Coast Path is on 'excellent form' and as 'welcoming, friendly and helpful as ever', says a fan. Built by the Great Western Railway in 1898, and bought by the Grose family more than a decade ago, it has recently added a spa decked out in copper, silver and granite to evoke Cornwall's mining history. Many of the 'lovely' big, light-filled rooms have spectacular coastal views, and a 'very comfortable' Vispring bed to sink into. All are furnished in classic-meets-contemporary style, and painted in light-reflecting hues. Some suites have garden access. In the kitchen, new chef James Heath makes the most of local produce, from line-caught fish to meat, cheese and organic veg. One reader thought the 'food had improved' since his last visit. Dinner in the Atlantic View restaurant, after an aperitif in the Art Deco-style bar, might be steamed mussels followed by honey and soy-glazed duck breast, or a trio of Helford River oysters. The 'impressive' breakfast offers a choice of cold and hot dishes. 'Our visit was all too short,' lamented one reader. (Peter Govier, and others)

Cliff Road
Mullion Cove
Helston TR12 7EP

T: 01326 240328
E: enquiries@mullion-cove.co.uk
W: mullion-cove.co.uk

BEDROOMS: 30. Some on ground floor.
OPEN: all year.
FACILITIES: lift, 3 lounges, bar, restaurant, in-room TV (Freeview), 1-acre garden, 10-metre heated outdoor swimming pool, public areas wheelchair accessible, adapted toilet.
BACKGROUND MUSIC: at mealtimes and in bar.
LOCATION: on edge of village.
CHILDREN: all ages welcomed.
DOGS: allowed in some bedrooms, 1 lounge.
CREDIT CARDS: Amex, MC, Visa.
PRICES: per room B&B single £85–£320, double £99–£335, D,B&B double £170–£405. Set dinner £40, à la carte £33. 1-night bookings sometimes refused bank holiday Sat.

# NEAR SAWREY Cumbria

## EES WYKE COUNTRY HOUSE

More guest house than hotel, this Georgian country house overlooking Esthwaite Water has the feel of a comfortable family home, a bit lived-in – and what an outlook. There are spectacular views to the Langdale Pikes and Grizedale Forest (a scene painted by Beatrix Potter when she holidayed here). A stay here is 'quite an intimate experience; you can't help but get friendly with the staff and other guests'. Arriving visitors may be greeted by owner Richard Lee wearing his chef's hat, 'very friendly, despite being in the middle of preparing dinner'. He is a famously personable host, and 'in a three-day stay, Ees Wyke exerted its considerable charm'. The staff are 'approachable without being intrusive'. Bedrooms are traditionally styled, with a mix of antique and contemporary furniture, complimentary sherry and Penhaligon toiletries. A limited-choice, locally sourced three-course dinner might include Morecambe Bay shrimps, lamb, and that great Lakeland invention, sticky toffee pudding. 'Breakfasts were excellent, with a Loch Fyne kipper, smoked haddock and home-made croissants.' (L Roberts, Lesley Hattersley, Andrew Butterworth)

**25% DISCOUNT VOUCHERS**

Near Sawrey
Ambleside LA22 0JZ

T: 01539 436393
E: mail@eeswyke.co.uk
W: eeswyke.co.uk

BEDROOMS: 9. 1 on ground floor, 7 en suite, 2 with separate private bathroom.
OPEN: all year except Christmas.
FACILITIES: 2 lounges, restaurant, in-room TV (Freeview), veranda, ½-acre garden, unsuitable for disabled.
BACKGROUND MUSIC: none.
LOCATION: edge of village 2½ miles SE of Hawkshead on B5285.
CHILDREN: not under 12.
DOGS: not allowed.
CREDIT CARDS: MC, Visa.
PRICES: per room B&B single £85–£145, double £99–£195. Set dinner £38. 1-night bookings sometimes refused weekends, bank holidays.

# NETHER WESTCOTE Oxfordshire                    MAP 3:D6

## THE FEATHERED NEST

♔ Previous César winner

An 18th-century malthouse on a hilltop, with spectacular views across the Evenlode valley, is today a village hub, pub and foodie destination. The previous proprietors have now flown the nest, and Adam Taylor is cock-a-hoop to have fulfilled his ambition of running his own Cotswold restaurant. New head chef Matt Weedon gained a Michelin star first at Glenapp Castle, Ballantrae, Scotland, then at Lords of the Manor, Upper Slaughter (see entries). You can eat on the rear terrace, or in the restaurant, with its wall of valley-facing windows, where ambitious dishes might include halibut with langoustine ravioli, shellfish and vanilla bisque; venison with salt-baked parsnip and black pudding hash; or gnocchi, brassicas, wild mushrooms, truffle and pecorino. There are real ales and occasional live music in the cosy, beamed bar, where a short menu offers unusual snacks (Parmesan and truffle chips, or the day's bread with home-made butter and Marmite beef dripping). Smart, contemporary bedrooms have a coffee machine, home-made cookies, a decanter of port, and Bramley toiletries. The best has a roll-top bath and walk-in drench shower.

Nether Westcote
Chipping Norton OX7 6SD

T: 01993 833030
E: info@thefeatherednestinn.co.uk
W: thefeatherednestinn.co.uk

BEDROOMS: 4.
OPEN: closed Mon/Tues (except special trading days), open on Christmas Day 2020.
FACILITIES: 2 bars, small lounge, dining room, in-room TV (Freeview), civil wedding licence, 45-acre grounds, restaurant and bar wheelchair accessible, adapted toilet.
BACKGROUND MUSIC: in bar all day, occasionally live.
LOCATION: in hamlet, 5 miles S of Stow-on-the-Wold.
CHILDREN: all ages welcomed, children's menu.
DOGS: allowed in bar only.
CREDIT CARDS: Amex, MC, Visa.
PRICES: per room B&B £225–£295. 3-course dinner £58, 6-course tasting menu £65.

# NEW MILTON Hampshire

## CHEWTON GLEN

Readers are 'unable to fault anything at all' at this ivy-clad country house hotel on the edge of the New Forest, 'the ultimate luxurious and indulgent treat'. It is a 'lovely place to celebrate a special occasion or recharge the batteries', with plenty to occupy all ages, including cookery classes, tennis, golf and kids' club. It has 'one of the best' hotel spas one reader has ever experienced, with an indoor pool and hydrotherapy pool. The hotel's 130 acres of woodland, gardens and parkland, close to the coast, are 'idyllic and peaceful'. Staff are 'attentive in an understated and relaxed way'. Bedrooms, suites, some with hot tub, and tree-house suites are a blend of classic comfort and contemporary luxury, with 'everything we needed'. Food 'will not disappoint', with Executive Chef Luke Matthews creating 'exceptional' dishes from locally sourced ingredients. The mushroom risotto, Emmental soufflé, venison and sea bass were all 'heavenly' and the sommelier was 'amazingly knowledgeable'. 'We will certainly be going back.' (Mervin and Judith Knight, Alexandra Heaton, Paul Solomons, and many others)

Christchurch Road
New Milton BH25 6QS

T: 01425 275341
E: reservations@chewtonglen.com
W: chewtonglen.com

BEDROOMS: 72. 14 on ground floor, 14 tree-house suites in grounds, 1 suitable for disabled.
OPEN: all year.
FACILITIES: lounges, bar, 2 restaurants, function rooms, in-room TV (Sky), civil wedding licence, cookery school, spa, indoor pool, 130-acre grounds (heated pool, tennis, golf), public rooms (not spa) wheelchair accessible.
BACKGROUND MUSIC: 'subtle' in public areas.
LOCATION: on S edge of New Forest.
CHILDREN: all ages welcomed.
DOGS: allowed in tree-house suites, on terraces.
CREDIT CARDS: Amex, MC, Visa.
PRICES: per room B&B £370–£4950. À la carte £70. 1-night stays sometimes refused Sat.

# NEW ROMNEY Kent

MAP 2:E5

## ROMNEY BAY HOUSE

🏆 Previous César winner

With a superb sea view amid the elemental
landscape of Romney Marsh, haunt of both
writers and smugglers, this 1920s mansion was
built by Clough Williams-Ellis. There are just the
golf links on one side and the English Channel on
the other. Guests arriving on four wheels bump
down a rutted road but receive a warm welcome.
Hosts Lisa and Clinton Lovell 'could not be more
gracious'. Two bedrooms have a four-poster, and
all have binoculars ('On the French coast, the light
gleams, and is gone,' to quote Matthew Arnold).
'We had an excellent room, perfectly serviced.'
A cosy first-floor lounge is home to a log fire,
books and games. Four nights a week, classically
trained chef Clinton cooks a 'delicious' candlelit
dinner 'designed around what he has bought fresh
that day' (maybe locally landed cod or salt marsh
lamb). On other nights you can order a simple
supper. 'We enjoyed a wonderful cheese platter
with Merlot, looking out to sea as the sun went
down.' 'The conservatory is a very nice spot' for
a 'fabulous' breakfast. (Jill and Mike Bennett,
William and Hilary Rogers, and others)

**25% DISCOUNT VOUCHERS**

Coast Road
Littlestone
New Romney TN28 8QY

T: 01797 364747
E: enquiries@romneybayhousehotel.
   co.uk
W: romneybayhousehotel.co.uk

BEDROOMS: 10.
OPEN: all year except Christmas and
New Year, dining room open Tues/
Wed/Fri/Sat for dinner only.
FACILITIES: bar, sitting room, first-
floor lounge with sea views, dining
room, in-room TV (Freeview), small
function facilities, 1-acre garden,
unsuitable for disabled.
BACKGROUND MUSIC: none.
LOCATION: 1½ miles from New
Romney.
CHILDREN: 14 and upwards welcomed.
DOGS: only guide dogs allowed.
CREDIT CARDS: Amex, MC, Visa.
PRICES: per room B&B single £80–£95,
double £115–£160. Set dinner £49.
1-night advance bookings refused
weekends.

## NEWBIGGIN-ON-LUNE Cumbria

MAP 4:C3

### BROWNBER HALL

With its quirky hipster vibe, thoughtful touches and soul-stirring views of the Howgills, this Victorian country house has charmed many readers. 'We can't wait to return!' Outdoors-lovers Peter and Amanda Jaques-Walker fled the City in 2016 to transform the original B&B into the stylish yet laid-back haven of today. The 'well-appointed shabby-chic' look mixes modern, vintage and antique furnishings. Expect to find chandeliers and Ercol sofas, rustic wooden tables and Regency chairs, modern art and Victorian prints – and a '50s cocktail bar. 'The help-yourself bar gave the tone of how relaxing this place was.' Light and uncluttered bedrooms are similarly mismatched: cast iron bedsteads, Anglepoise bedside lights, stripy blanket throws. 'The views were of never-ending green landscapes', and the 'attention to detail was so good'. The evening's pizza menu, with sourdough bases by 'charming and attentive' Peter, 'was a stroke of genius'. (John Longcroft-Neal, CV, and others)

NOTE: As the Guide went to press, Brownber Hall announced that it was changing to become an exclusive-use venue for private rental for up to 15 guests.

Newbiggin-on-Lune
Kirkby Stephen CA17 4NX

T: 01539 623208
E: enquiries@brownberhall.co.uk
W: brownberhall.co.uk

BEDROOMS: 8.
OPEN: all year except Christmas and New Year, restaurant only Thurs–Sun evenings
FACILITIES: 2 lounges (log fire, honesty bar), dining room, in-room TV (Freeview), 1-acre garden, bicycle storage, unsuitable for disabled.
BACKGROUND MUSIC: all day in public rooms.
LOCATION: 6¼ miles SW of Kirkby Stephen – 'follow the hosts' clear directions, not satnav'.
CHILDREN: all ages welcomed.
DOGS: allowed in 2 bedrooms, public rooms.
CREDIT CARDS: MC, Visa.
PRICES: per room B&B single £75, double £100–£220. À la carte (3 courses) £25.

# NEWCASTLE UPON TYNE Tyne and Wear    MAP 4:B4

## JESMOND DENE HOUSE

♀ Previous César winner

You get the best of both worlds here: although it's in the city suburbs just a ten-minute drive from the centre, Jesmond Dene House, named after the lush wooded valley it overlooks, 'feels as if it's in the country'. The Arts and Crafts mansion, once home to Victorian industrialist Lord Armstrong's business partner, is all battlements, tall chimneys and mullioned windows. Interiors are 'impressive yet inviting', with plenty of original features, including two spacious wood-panelled rooms with 'grand fireplaces'. Bedrooms are 'contemporary and understatedly elegant' – velvet armchairs, muted colours, feature wallpapers – with 'welcoming touches such as pot plants, fresh milk and glossy magazines'. Terraces, window seats and grand windows feature in some. Chef Danny Parker has Michelin-star experience, offering dishes such as hake with curry and saffron sauce, accompanied by 'a very good wine list'. There's a simpler all-day bar menu, popular afternoon tea and 'extensive' breakfast choice, the last served in the light-filled conservatory overlooking the garden. Throughout the hotel, 'staff are consistently attentive'. (HP, and others)

Jesmond Dene Road
Newcastle upon Tyne NE2 2EY

T: 0191 212 3000
E: info@jesmonddenehouse.co.uk
W: jesmonddenehouse.co.uk

BEDROOMS: 40. 8 in adjacent New House, 2 suitable for disabled.
OPEN: all year.
FACILITIES: lift, lounge, cocktail bar, restaurant, conference/function facilities, terrace, in-room TV (Sky), civil wedding licence, parking, ¼-acre garden, public areas accessible by wheelchair, adapted toilet.
BACKGROUND MUSIC: in public areas and restaurant.
LOCATION: 2 miles from city centre.
CHILDREN: all ages welcomed.
DOGS: allowed on restaurant terrace only.
CREDIT CARDS: Amex, MC, Visa.
PRICES: per room B&B £119–£299. À la carte £45.

# NEWTON ABBOT Devon

MAP 1:D4

## THE ROCK INN

Built from granite quarried beneath massive Haytor, this whitewashed village inn is a perennially popular local and makes a good base for exploring Dartmoor. It dates from 1820, along with surrounding quarry workers' cottages and the now-disused granite tramway – and it is rock steady. Run by the Graves family since 1983, it is a firm favourite with a trusted reader, who has known it for almost as long. 'The atmosphere remains warm … the food is delicious, the service efficient, friendly and unobtrusive.' Cosy bedrooms, each named after a Grand National winner, have exposed beams, contemporary and antique furniture, views over the garden and countryside. Sheila's Cottage has a four-poster bed. Master Robert has a smart bathroom with roll-top bath and walk-in shower, and far-reaching moorland views from a balcony. You can eat in the bar with its oak furniture and log fires, or in any of the small dining rooms. Dishes include roast chicken breast, sweet potato fondant, braised red cabbage; Start Point hake, Exmouth mussels, butterbean, fennel and lemon; wild garlic risotto with goat's cheese and truffle oil. (Diana Goodey)

Haytor Vale
Newton Abbot TQ13 9XP

T: 01364 661305
E: info@rock-inn.co.uk
W: rock-inn.co.uk

BEDROOMS: 9.
OPEN: all year except 25/26 Dec.
FACILITIES: bar, restaurant, snug bar, conservatory, in-room TV (Freeview), ½-acre garden, bar and restaurant wheelchair accessible, no adapted toilet.
BACKGROUND MUSIC: in bar/restaurant.
LOCATION: 3 miles W of Bovey Tracey.
CHILDREN: all ages welcomed, no under-14s in main bar area, children's menu.
DOGS: allowed in some bedrooms, bar, 1 dining room.
CREDIT CARDS: MC, Visa.
PRICES: per room B&B £110–£170. À la carte £35, fixed-price £22.50–£28.50 (2–3 courses, selected dishes from main menu). Sat night bookings must include dinner. 1-night bookings sometimes refused.

# NORTH WALSHAM Norfolk

MAP 2:A6

## BEECHWOOD HOTEL

'A bright spot' in a north Norfolk market town, Emma and Hugh Asher's hotel is also something of a night spot, with a rolling programme of events: taster nights, comedy nights, murder mystery nights (a nod to Agatha Christie, who stayed often when this was a private house), and South African Nights (to celebrate Hugh's native land). 'Staff helpful, room comfortable, food good, gin menu tempting,' notes a reader. New this year are two garden rooms with hot tub and sauna. Some main-house rooms have French doors to the garden, perhaps a half-tester or a four-poster bed and a Victorian bathroom with walk-in shower and slipper bath. Expect to linger over drinks in the lounge or in the 'beautiful garden', before dining on Steven Norgate's locally sourced dishes (maybe lamb with baby leeks, goat curd and mint jelly, or a vegetarian option). And if our reader's serving of cheese was small (was it a Fawlty Towers night?), breakfast brought 'the best and hugest portion of scrambled eggs I have ever tasted'. Golfers' packages include special deals with Mundesley and Royal Cromer golf clubs. (Mariana Lamperty, SP)

### 25% DISCOUNT VOUCHERS

20 Cromer Road
North Walsham NR28 0HD

T: 01692 403231
E: info@beechwood-hotel.co.uk
W: beechwood-hotel.co.uk

BEDROOMS: 20. 4 on ground floor, 2 garden spa rooms with deck, hot tub and sauna.
OPEN: all year except 27/28 Dec.
FACILITIES: bar, 2 lounges, restaurant, in-room TV (Freeview), 100-metre landscaped garden (croquet).
BACKGROUND MUSIC: all day in public rooms.
LOCATION: near town centre.
CHILDREN: all ages welcomed.
DOGS: allowed in bedrooms, public rooms, not in restaurant.
CREDIT CARDS: Amex, MC, Visa.
PRICES: per room B&B single £70–£95, double £100–£195, D,B&B £175–£265 (murder mystery nights), £215–£305 (taster nights). À la carte £40 (vegetarian £23).

# NORWICH Norfolk

## THE ASSEMBLY HOUSE

People danced beneath the crystal chandeliers in the magnificent Great Hall of the 'House of Assemblies' to celebrate Nelson's Victory at Trafalgar in 1805, and they're dancing still. 'It isn't a hotel as such,' wrote a reader, who had 'an excellent lunch' here. Rather, it is a stunning events venue with rooms, café, restaurant and cookery school. You cross a courtyard garden to check in under gilded Corinthian columns in a soaring space flooded with natural light (the residents' lounge, sometimes hosting a party). In an adjacent, older building, bedrooms described as 'contemporary Georgian' were launched in 2016 by chef Richard Hughes and hotelier Iain Wilson, former owner of The Dial House, Reepham (see entry). They have a mix of antique and reproduction furniture, a coffee machine, Arran Aromatics toiletries, maybe a four-poster, a roll-top bath and drench shower, a lounge and patio. Locals drop in for a light lunch or afternoon tea. A pre-theatre supper is served until 7 pm. Franz Liszt once gave a concert in the Music Room, where a Guide insider enjoyed an omelette Arnold Bennett, accompanied by a schoolgirl hammering the Steinway.

Theatre Street
Norwich NR2 1RQ

T: 01603 626402
E: admin@assemblyhousenorwich.
co.uk
W: assemblyhousenorwich.co.uk

BEDROOMS: 11. All in St Mary's House extension, 6 with private garden, 1 suitable for disabled.
OPEN: all year.
FACILITIES: dining room, private dining and function rooms, civil wedding licence, in-room TV (Sky, Freeview), 1-acre grounds, public rooms wheelchair accessible, adapted toilet.
BACKGROUND MUSIC: none.
LOCATION: central, car park permits for pay-and-display.
CHILDREN: all ages welcomed (daytime children's menu).
DOGS: not allowed.
CREDIT CARDS: Amex, MC, Visa.
PRICES: per room B&B £170–£270. Fixed-price early supper £21–£25 (steak £3 supplement, side dishes £3.95).

**SEE ALSO SHORTLIST**

# NOTTINGHAM Nottinghamshire

## HART'S HOTEL

'The best place to stay in Nottingham,' is a Guide stalwart's conclusion on Tim and Stefa Hart's city hotel, in an award-winning noughties building on the castle ramparts. The Harts also own the popular Hambleton Hall, Hambleton (see entry), and here, as there, the interior design is by Stefa Hart. No residents' lounge, but there are seats by a fire in the foyer, and when the sun shines, a front courtyard and rear garden come into their own. Bedrooms have a king- or super-king-size bed, a minibar, fresh milk, L'Occitane toiletries and room service. They tend to be compact. The best are garden rooms with French doors and patio furniture for an alfresco breakfast or brunch. Since last year, sous-chef Martin Sludds has taken over the kitchen. The restaurant provides 'an attractive setting', while service proved 'very good, prompt and courteous'. Our reader had 'a very good (and very good-value) lunch – 10/10 for gazpacho and medium rare beef'. Breakfast brings pastries from the Hart's bakery, free-range eggs from Windy Ridge Farm, bacon and sausages from Dickinson & Morris of Melton Mowbray, home of the pork pie. (Robert Gower)

### 25% DISCOUNT VOUCHERS

Standard Hill
Park Row
Nottingham NG1 6GN

T: 0115 988 1900
E: reception@hartshotel.co.uk
W: hartsnottingham.co.uk

BEDROOMS: 32. 2 suitable for disabled.
OPEN: all year, restaurant closed 1 Jan.
FACILITIES: lift, reception/lobby with seating, bar, restaurant, in-room TV (Sky, Freeview), small exercise room, civil wedding licence, courtyard, garden, secure car park (£9.95), restaurant wheelchair accessible, adapted toilet.
BACKGROUND MUSIC: in bar and restaurant.
LOCATION: city centre.
CHILDREN: all ages welcomed.
DOGS: allowed in bedrooms (not unattended), public spaces (not restaurant).
CREDIT CARDS: Amex, MC, Visa.
PRICES: room only £139–£279. Breakfast £15, à la carte £37 (pre-theatre £22–£28, Sun–Thurs) plus 12.5% discretionary service charge.

# OLD HUNSTANTON Norfolk

MAP 2:A5

## THE NEPTUNE

There are just four 'immaculate' rooms at this 'wonderful' Michelin-starred restaurant in a former 18th-century coaching inn on the north Norfolk coast. And very nice they are too, with pale, unadorned walls, unfussy fabrics and white furniture. But the real star is the food from owner Kevin Mangeolles, who runs the kitchen while wife Jacki is front-of-house. His 'exquisite' modern British food is served in the neat-as-a-pin dining room with its crisp white napery – perhaps lobster tortellini with spinach and shellfish broth, followed by monkfish with Brancaster mussels and gnocchi, and Colombian chocolate marquise with clementine and Madagascan brown sugar ice cream to finish. The tasting menu provides an 'interesting and delicious introduction' to Kevin's talents. Meanwhile, service is 'attentive and friendly'. A stone's throw from the beach at Hunstanton, the Neptune makes an ideal base for exploring the area. 'Wonderful place! Amazing food, delightful owners, beautiful bedroom, excellent location. What more can I say? Go and see for yourself!'

85 Old Hunstanton Road
Old Hunstanton PE36 6HZ

T: 01485 532122
E: reservations@theneptune.co.uk
W: theneptune.co.uk

BEDROOMS: 4.
OPEN: all year, except Mon, 26 Dec, 3 weeks Jan, 1 week May, 1 week Nov.
FACILITIES: bar area, restaurant, in-room TV (Freeview), unsuitable for disabled.
BACKGROUND MUSIC: in restaurant in evening.
LOCATION: village centre, on A149.
CHILDREN: not under 10.
DOGS: not allowed.
CREDIT CARDS: Amex, MC, Visa.
PRICES: per room D,B&B £295–£330 (with tasting menu £320–£360). Set menus £47–£62, tasting menu £78 (to be taken by whole table). 1-night bookings sometimes refused Sat in high season.

# OLDSTEAD Yorkshire

MAP 4:D4

## THE BLACK SWAN AT OLDSTEAD

♔ Previous César winner

This once run-down pub up a sleepy country lane has turned into a Michelin-starred sensation, yet remains grounded by its Yorkshire roots and farming-family owners. On the edge of the North York Moors, the former drovers' inn – sturdy stone and bay windows – benefits from the rich farmland which the Banks family has worked for generations. Chef Tommy (brother James is front-of-house) and his team produce dishes that are 'traditional Yorkshire with a swirling mix of creativity and eccentricity', using ingredients largely grown or foraged locally, including some from their kitchen garden. Expect sour bread and sour butter with aged raw beef, monkfish with chanterelles and whey, damson with chicory and potato, and vegetarian menus, too, on request. While the bar is traditional with flagged floor and leather chairs, the upstairs dining room is Scandi chic with custom-made oak tables. Bedrooms, in converted stables or a village house, have soft colours, solid wood furnishings, some four-posters, plaid wool fabrics and cottagey bathrooms. 'Universally charming staff are highly professional and knowledgeable.'

Oldstead
York YO61 4BL

T: 01347 868387
E: enquiries@blackswanoldstead.co.uk
W: blackswanoldstead.co.uk

BEDROOMS: 9. 4 on ground floor in annexe wing, 5 in Ashberry House, 50 yds away.
OPEN: all year except 24–26 Dec.
FACILITIES: bar, restaurant, private dining room, in-room TV (Freeview), garden, 2-acre kitchen garden and orchard.
BACKGROUND MUSIC: in restaurant.
LOCATION: in village 7 miles E of Thirsk.
CHILDREN: not under 18 overnight, over-10s only in restaurant.
DOGS: not allowed.
CREDIT CARDS: MC, Visa.
PRICES: per room D,B&B £350–£560. Tasting menu £125 dinner, £98 Sat lunch.

# OSWESTRY Shropshire

MAP 3:B4

## PEN-Y-DYFFRYN

A morning newsletter lends a personal touch at the Hunter family's dog-friendly hotel in rolling countryside with views to the Welsh hills. It is run by Miles and Audrey Hunter with son Tommy and daughter Charlotte (sibling Henry has The Castle, Bishop's Castle, see entry). 'On arrival, we were treated to tea and scones,' writes a reader on a return visit, touched that the kitchen had baked a gluten-free scone for him. Bedrooms are in the main house and coach house, with two new luxury rooms in a garden annexe. Several have a spa bath, some a private terrace. Our reader had 'a super-king-size bed, comfy armchairs, and home-made brownies to boot'. Another added that the decor was 'a bit tired', but 'the hotel has intrinsic charm'. Guide insiders who enthused about the 'wonderful location, building and garden' were dismayed to see plastic flowers. At dinner the food was 'tasty, cooked to a high standard'. At breakfast, 'the menu is extensive, and some dishes are inventive', but one couple with small children found the service slow. (Steve Hur, John Barnes, and others)

Rhydycroesau
Oswestry SY10 7JD

T: 01691 653700
E: stay@peny.co.uk
W: peny.co.uk

BEDROOMS: 14. 4, each with patio, in coach house, 2 garden suites with patio, 1 on ground floor.
OPEN: all year except Christmas.
FACILITIES: 2 lounges, bar, restaurant, in-room TV (Freeview), 5-acre grounds (summer house, dog-walking area, fly-fishing pool).
BACKGROUND MUSIC: in evening in bar and restaurant.
LOCATION: 3 miles W of Oswestry.
CHILDREN: not under 3.
DOGS: allowed in some bedrooms, not in public rooms after 6.30 pm.
CREDIT CARDS: MC, Visa.
PRICES: per person B&B £75–£110, D,B&B £99–£145, single occupancy £99–£120. Set menu £45. 1-night bookings occasionally refused Sat.

# OXFORD Oxfordshire

## OLD BANK HOTEL

Jeremy Mogford indulges his passion for art
and literature at his luxury city-centre hotel,
where the walls are hung with works from his
collection, with a library for residents to browse.
Occupying three handsome Georgian buildings
opposite the Bodleian Library, this is a 'well-run'
boutique operation. Standards are 'reassuringly
high'. Even small double rooms have a marble
bathroom, flowers, air conditioning, a minibar,
'heavenly' toiletries, and use of a bicycle. Those
at the front look over the bustling 'High'. In
summer, convivial chatter may drift up to rooms
overlooking the Italianate courtyard garden. The
showpiece is a rooftop suite with a retractable
wall of glass, a terrace, and unrivalled views of
dreaming spires. 'Pleasant', 'appetising' brasserie
fare is served all day in Quod in the former
banking hall, at the bar, and alfresco. Daily
specials might include cod fillet, roasted salsify
and chard, with lemon beurre blanc, or root
vegetable cassoulet, kale and black beans. There is
a children's menu, and freshly squeezed and cold-
pressed juices at breakfast. The 'good, friendly
service' is praised. (See also next entry.)

92–94 High Street
Oxford OX1 4BJ

T: 01865 799599
E: reservations@oldbankhotel.co.uk
w: oldbankhotel.co.uk

BEDROOMS: 43. 1 suitable for disabled.
OPEN: all year.
FACILITIES: lift, residents' library/
bar, restaurant/bar, dining terrace,
2 meeting/private dining rooms,
in-room TV (Freeview), in-room
spa treatments, small garden, use of
bicycles, restaurant, bar wheelchair
accessible, adapted toilet.
BACKGROUND MUSIC: in restaurant and
reception area.
LOCATION: central, car park.
CHILDREN: all ages welcomed.
DOGS: allowed on terrace only.
CREDIT CARDS: Amex, MC, Visa.
PRICES: per room B&B £210–£1,500.
À la carte £35 (plus 12½% discretionary
service charge). 1-night bookings
refused weekends in peak season.

# OXFORD Oxfordshire

## OLD PARSONAGE HOTEL

Built in the 1600s for a chop-house owner and chef, this gabled stone building has long opened its oak door to paying guests. It is said that Oscar Wilde lodged here, and today's hotel still has an arty, literary vibe. The walls are hung with paintings from owner Jeremy Mogford's collection (see previous entry), and there is a 'well-stocked library' with glass doors to a terrace. Smart, contemporary bedrooms range from small doubles with a handmade bed, bespoke writing desk, and charcoal drawings of Oxford, to suites with a living and dining area. Some have a Juliet balcony or terrace. All have a marble bathroom, a walk-in shower, air conditioning and fresh flowers. Food is served from noon in the Grill Room and the courtyard garden. Typical dishes include sea bream with Cornish crab sauce, lamb rump with roast kidney, and pot-roasted red cabbage with cashew butter and apple salad. Breakfast brings smoothies, Cumberland sausage, kipper or smoked salmon. 'Most appreciated was the atmosphere throughout.' It is perfect if, like Wilde, you have the simplest tastes and are always satisfied with the best.

1 Banbury Road
Oxford OX2 6NN

T: 01865 310210
E: reservations@oldparsonage-hotel.
   co.uk
W: oldparsonagehotel.co.uk

BEDROOMS: 35. 10 on ground floor, 2 suitable for disabled.
OPEN: all year.
FACILITIES: lounge, library, bar/restaurant, in-room TV (Freeview), civil wedding licence, terrace, rear garden with summerhouse, restaurant wheelchair accessible.
BACKGROUND MUSIC: 'very light' in restaurant and bar.
LOCATION: NE end of St Giles, small car park.
CHILDREN: all ages welcomed, all-day children's menu.
DOGS: allowed on terrace only.
CREDIT CARDS: Amex, MC, Visa.
PRICES: per room B&B £210–£510. À la carte £43 (plus 12½% discretionary service charge). 1-night bookings sometimes refused peak weekends.

# PADSTOW Cornwall

MAP 1:D2

## PADSTOW TOWNHOUSE

Paul Ainsworth's all-suite bolt-hole is a perfectly seasoned accompaniment for his Michelin-starred restaurant, his café, pub and cookery school, all of which he runs with wife Emma. Culinary references at the restored Georgian town house abound, with bedrooms across three floors named after fairground sweets: ground-floor Rhubarb & Custard is a confection of rich colours and textures, and includes a painting by James Cullen, entitled Marzipan. Sensual Honeycomb, in soft greys and golds, has a hand-cast metal bed and a golden double bath tub. Toffee Apple has a separate lounge and dining area, and a double bath in oak and copper. All rooms have exclusive organic bathroom toiletries by Bloom Remedies. Downstairs there is a well-stocked kitchen pantry and honesty bar but no restaurant – guests can take breakfast or informal supper at nearby Caffè Rojano or opt for fine dining at Paul Ainsworth at No6, where raw sea bass might be followed by goose liver, wild turbot and the signature dessert, A Fairground Tale, which made it into the final of the Great British Menu in 2011.

16–18 High Street
Padstow PL28 8BB

T: 01841 550950
E: stay@padstowtownhouse.co.uk
W: paul-ainsworth.co.uk/
 padstow-townhouse

BEDROOMS: 6. 2 on ground floor.
OPEN: all year except 24–26 Dec, 2 weeks Jan, open at New Year.
FACILITIES: honesty pantry, in-room smart TV, in-room spa treatments, electric shuttle car for guest transport, on-site car park.
BACKGROUND MUSIC: in reception and kitchen pantry area.
LOCATION: in old town, 5 mins' walk from harbour.
CHILDREN: not under 16.
DOGS: not allowed.
CREDIT CARDS: MC, Visa.
PRICES: per suite B&B £300–£380. Set menu (Paul Ainsworth at No6) £85, set menu (Caffè Rojano) £30–£34.

# PADSTOW Cornwall

## THE SEAFOOD RESTAURANT

Not for nothing is this fishing port town nicknamed Padstein, with 40 catered rooms spread around six properties, but here is the restaurant-with-rooms where it all began. Rick and Jill Stein opened it in 1975 to serve fish landed almost on the doorstep. Bedrooms, styled by Jill and featuring her Porthdune toiletries, have fresh, nautical decor in soft tones of white, blue and sand. Two have a roof terrace with Adirondack chairs to sit on and enjoy the view over the Camel estuary. This is a family-friendly, dog-friendly place. Although children under three are not allowed in the restaurant, there is always Rick Stein's Café, Stein's Deli and Stein's Patisserie (pick up pasties for a picnic). There is, too, St Petroc's Bistro, where the Seafood restaurant's new head chef, Pete Murt, started 11 years ago as a kitchen porter, before working his way through the ranks, via two Michelin-starred Hibiscus in London. If you like what you eat, you can learn to make it in the cookery school. Typical dishes include grilled hake with beurre blanc, Indonesian seafood curry, or cod and chips washed down with lager – in a stein, no doubt.

Riverside
Padstow PL28 8BY

T: 01841 532700
E: reservations@rickstein.com
W: rickstein.com

BEDROOMS: 16.
OPEN: all year except 24–26 Dec.
FACILITIES: lift (to bedrooms), restaurant, in-room TV (Freeview), restaurant and toilet wheelchair accessible.
BACKGROUND MUSIC: in restaurant.
LOCATION: town centre.
CHILDREN: all ages welcomed, not under 3 in restaurant.
DOGS: allowed in some bedrooms (dog-sitting service), in conservatory at breakfast.
CREDIT CARDS: Amex, MC, Visa.
PRICES: per room B&B £165–£352, D,B&B from £235. À la carte £45, 1-night bookings refused Sat.

# PAINSWICK Gloucestershire

MAP 3:D5

## THE PAINSWICK

In one of the prettiest villages in the Cotswolds, this Palladian house overlooking the Slad valley in Laurie Lee country is a soothing escape for rattled city-dwellers. Part of the Calcot Collection (see Calcot & Spa, Tetbury; Barnsley House, Barnsley; and The Lord Crewe Arms, Blanchland), it is run 'with warm efficiency by a bright, smiling young team'. Rooms, even the 'Small' ones in the eaves, are spacious, with a contemporary, uncluttered take on the country house look, in cream and oatmeal hues. King-size beds are made up with soft linen, and there is fresh milk, fudge, biscuits, an espresso machine and digital Roberts radio. Some bathrooms have a shower over the bath, though larger ones have a roll-top, and NEOM toiletries. A loggia balcony dripping with wisteria, bar, pool room, and two large drawing rooms with log fires complete the picture. Jamie McCallum serves 'mouth-watering' modern British food in the panelled restaurant – think Cornish cod with Jerusalem artichokes, or lamb rump with black olive tapenade. Breakfasts, which include home-made crumpets and granola, are 'so good you wish you could cram in a bit more'. (KQ)

Kemps Lane
Painswick GL6 6YB

T: 01452 813688
E: enquiries@thepainswick.co.uk
W: thepainswick.co.uk

BEDROOMS: 16. 7 in garden wing, 4 in chapel wing.
OPEN: all year.
FACILITIES: bar, lounge, restaurant, games room, private dining room, in-room TV (Sky, Freeview), civil wedding licence, terrace, treatment rooms, ¾-acre garden, unsuitable for disabled.
BACKGROUND MUSIC: all day in public areas.
LOCATION: in village, 4 miles NE of Stroud.
CHILDREN: all ages welcomed, cots and fold-up beds available at extra cost (£15–£20).
DOGS: allowed by arrangement in some garden rooms, on terrace, in lounge, not in restaurant (£15 per night).
CREDIT CARDS: Amex, MC, Visa.
PRICES: per room B&B £191–£435. À la carte £43. 1-night bookings refused weekends.

# PENRITH Cumbria

MAP 4: inset C2

## ASKHAM HALL

It may have a medieval pele tower, a 17th-century topiary garden, and now a Michelin-starred restaurant, but Charles Lowther's ancestral pile also has an unpretentious, relaxed atmosphere. Stuffed full of antiques and family heirlooms, its 'shabby-chic' public rooms, where both children and dogs can roam, are comfortably cluttered with piles of books, modern art and old photographs. Expect, too, the odd frayed carpet. Large (sometimes vast) bedrooms with leaded windows and fireplace are 'decorated with flair'; the best overlook the quintessential English gardens. Some bathrooms have a marble washbasin and a roll-top bath. Richard Swale uses produce from the kitchen garden and the estate to conjure 'delightfully balanced and creative dishes' such as hand-dived scallop tartare with elderflower and rosehip, or dry-aged shorthorn beef with smoked shallot and beetroot. Meanwhile, Nico Chieze is 'an affable and attentive host' and the library's honesty bar 'made us feel we were staying at a grand house rather than a hotel'. (Robert Cooper, and others)

**25% DISCOUNT VOUCHERS**

Askham
Penrith CA10 2PF

T: 01931 712350
E: enquiries@askhamhall.co.uk
W: askhamhall.co.uk

BEDROOMS: 19. 2 suitable for disabled.
OPEN: all year except Christmas, early Jan to mid-Feb, Sun/Mon.
FACILITIES: 2 drawing rooms, snug, 3 dining rooms, in-room TV (Freeview), civil wedding licence, 12-acre grounds, outdoor swimming pool, hot tub, private function facilities, main restaurant wheelchair accessible, adapted toilet.
BACKGROUND MUSIC: in reception rooms in evening.
LOCATION: 10 mins from Penrith and junction 40 on M6.
CHILDREN: all ages welcomed, no under-10s in restaurant.
DOGS: allowed in bedrooms and public rooms, not in restaurant.
CREDIT CARDS: Amex, MC, Visa.
PRICES: per room B&B single £138–£308, double £150–£320, D,B&B £250–£420. Tasting menu £75.

# PENRITH Cumbria

MAP 4: inset C2

## THE HOUSE AT TEMPLE SOWERBY

The relaxed atmosphere and fell views make this handsome country hotel, between the Lake District and the North York Moors national park, a winner. In a quiet village in the Eden valley, the Georgian-fronted house with its walled garden combines a traditional feel with an unstuffy atmosphere. Owners Andi and Alison Sambrook have 'a way of making guests feel genuinely welcome'. 'Comfortable and quiet' bedrooms are 'immaculately presented' with striped and patterned wallpapers, elegant furniture and a contemporary bathroom. Bigger rooms have a spa bath or hydrotherapy shower, as well as extras such as digital radio and coffee machine. Chef Jack Bradley creates dishes of 'genuinely intriguing and delicious combinations', such as crab with barbecued apple and nasturtium, or hogget with ragstone cheese and pickled elderflower. The breakfast spread, readers agree, makes up for dinner's short-choice menu, including own-grown fruit smoothies, local sausages, bacon and air-dried ham. 'My eggs Benedict were excellent.' Throughout the hotel there's a 'hospitable and contented feeling'. (Simon and Mithra Tonking, and others)

**25% DISCOUNT VOUCHERS**

Temple Sowerby
Penrith CA10 1RZ

T: 01768 361578
E: stay@templesowerby.com
W: templesowerby.com

BEDROOMS: 12. 2 on ground floor, 4 in coach house.
OPEN: all year.
FACILITIES: 2 lounges, bar, restaurant, conference/function facilities, in-room TV (Freeview), 1½-acre walled garden, public rooms wheelchair accessible, adapted toilet.
BACKGROUND MUSIC: 'carefully chosen' music in restaurant in the evening.
LOCATION: village centre.
CHILDREN: all ages welcomed.
DOGS: allowed in coach house rooms and garden (not unattended).
CREDIT CARDS: Amex, MC, Visa.
PRICES: per room B&B £130–£190. Set dinner £35–£45.

# PENRITH Cumbria

MAP 4: inset C2

## TEBAY SERVICES HOTEL

A motorway services hotel with inspiring views, smart bedrooms and a friendly atmosphere? Tebay Services astonished readers. 'Actually tranquil; a miracle given its location.' 'The prices represent outstanding value for money.' 'A very welcoming hotel in a wonderful setting.' Created by the resourceful Dunning family after the M6 carved up their hill farm, the chalet-style building has smart, modern bedrooms with a 'comfortable bed, plenty of space, good lighting', and views of the surrounding countryside. There are home-made biscuits and Sedbergh Soap toiletries, too. The 'commitment to local sourcing' impressed readers, featuring strongly on menus. Food is served either in the bar or in the restaurant with 'windows the length of the room'. Portion sizes are 'generous' with beef and lamb from the family farm as well as dishes such as confit duck, and sweet potato and chilli falafel. The wine list, though, is only 'short and basic'. At 'an extremely good' breakfast, 'the scrambled eggs with smoked salmon were cooked perfectly'. Guests found the voucher for the farm shop irresistible. (Andrew Wardrop, J and JM, and others)

Orton
Penrith CA10 3SB

**T:** 01539 624351
**E:** reservations@tebayserviceshotel.com
**W:** tebayserviceshotel.com

**BEDROOMS:** 51. 1 suitable for disabled.
**OPEN:** all year except 24/25 Dec.
**FACILITIES:** lounge with log fire, bar, mezzanine, restaurant, in-room TV (Freeview), function/conference facilities, farm shop, restaurant, bar and lounge wheelchair accessible, adapted toilet.
**BACKGROUND MUSIC:** none.
**LOCATION:** 2½ miles SW of Orton.
**CHILDREN:** all ages welcomed (family rooms with bunk beds).
**DOGS:** allowed in some bedrooms (£10 per dog per night, max. 2 dogs), and in one area of lounge.
**CREDIT CARDS:** Amex, MC, Visa.
**PRICES:** per room B&B single £76–£121, double £111–£155, family room £141–£161. À la carte £30.

# PENSFORD Somerset

MAP 2:D1

## THE PIG NEAR BATH

Fallow deer roam parkland around a part-Georgian house that has been converted into one of the Pig hotels in Robin Hutson's Home Grown collection (see index). The lodge to a much grander house (of which a ruined arcade is all that remains), it received the customary shabby-chic make-over from Judy Hutson to create an air of informality, a world away from country house stuffiness. 'The staff clearly enjoy their work and are enthusiastic about the concept,' writes a Pig-fancying friend of the Guide. Atmospheric public rooms have 'plenty of seating areas and a pleasant buzz'. Bedrooms range from cosy, in the main house and coach house, to The Apple Store, an absolute pippin, set over two floors, with wood-burner, freestanding bath and monsoon showers. Menus are a feast of local and garden produce; this Pig boosts the largest kitchen garden of the litter. 'Gammon steaks were too salty, but we enjoyed hake and ray wing. Portions were enormous and the vegetables excellent.' Breakfast hit the spot, with 'a lavish buffet, the maltiest granola, fresh fruit, compotes and eggs from the estate'. (Desmond and Jenny Balmer, and others)

Hunstrete House
Pensford BS39 4NS

T: 01761 490490
E: info@thepighotel.com
W: thepighotel.com

BEDROOMS: 29. 5 in gardens, some on ground floor, 1 with wheelchair access and wet room.
OPEN: all year.
FACILITIES: 2 lounges, bar, restaurant, snug, private dining room, in-room TV (Freeview), civil wedding licence, treatment room, kitchen garden, wild flower meadow, deer park, ground floor/garden areas wheelchair accessible.
BACKGROUND MUSIC: all day in public areas.
LOCATION: 7 miles SW of Bath.
CHILDREN: all ages welcomed.
DOGS: only guide dogs.
CREDIT CARDS: Amex, MC, Visa.
PRICES: per room £170–£359. Breakfast (continental) £12, (cooked) £16, à la carte £35. 1-night bookings refused weekends, Christmas/New Year.

## PENTON Cumbria

### PENTONBRIDGE INN

♀ Previous César winner

At an isolated crossroads with uninterrupted views across the border to the Scottish hills, this former coaching inn combines a wild rural feel with unexpected luxury. Gerald and Margo Smith have injected style and warmth – slate floors, tweedy fabrics and modern art – into a traditional pub without losing its character. Bedrooms, some in the adjoining converted barn, others up a swanky glass-sided staircase, are contemporary-country, with tartan throws and headboards, rustic wooden cladding and a designer bathroom. The flowers, robes, shortbread, coffee machines and Roberts radios are 'sweet additions to a wonderfully appointed room with stunning views'. After a flurry of kitchen changes, stability has come in the form of Chris Archer, with Cottage in the Wood, Braithwaite, pedigree (see entry). Dishes such as Cartmel Valley venison with celeriac and wild mushroom, or halibut with gnocchi, use produce from the Smiths' kitchen garden at Netherby Hall. 'Delicious' breakfasts, served by 'friendly and attentive' staff, include omelettes and 'perfectly cooked poached eggs'. 'A luxurious gem in a rural setting.' (Suzi Swain, and others)

Penton CA6 5QB

T: 01228 586636
E: info@pentonbridgeinn.co.uk
W: pentonbridgeinn.co.uk

BEDROOMS: 9. 3 in converted barn, covered walkway from reception, 3 on ground floor.
OPEN: all year, restaurant closed Mon, Tues.
FACILITIES: bar, restaurant, conservatory, in-room TV (Freeview), electric charging point, bar and conservatory wheelchair accessible, adapted toilet.
BACKGROUND MUSIC: in bar and conservatory.
LOCATION: rural, 10 mins from Longtown.
CHILDREN: all ages welcomed.
DOGS: allowed in 6 bedrooms, bar and conservatory, not in restaurant.
CREDIT CARDS: Amex, MC, Visa.
PRICES: per room B&B £100–£125. Three-course à la carte dinner £50.

# PENZANCE Cornwall

MAP 1:E1

## CHAPEL HOUSE

A Guide regular gives 'five stars' this year to this B&B in a serene Georgian town house overlooking Penzance harbour. With previous incarnations as, variously, the home of the admiral who commanded the Temeraire (made famous by JMW Turner), a WW2 evacuee shelter, and the Penzance Arts Club, the house today celebrates its fine historic architecture with the best of modern comforts. The large drawing room offers a mix of sociable spaces and peaceful corners for curling up with a book; the sunny terrace is the perfect spot for a coffee or a sundowner. Individually styled bedrooms, all with a sea view, come in ocean-inspired shades of grey, green and blue, and are simply furnished with well-chosen antique, contemporary or mid-century pieces. Three rooms are open to the rafters; one has an in-room bathtub. Our regular found his room 'first class'. An 'excellent' breakfast is served in the open-plan kitchen/dining room, where a chat with owner Susan Stuart was welcomed by a guest travelling alone. At weekends, a communal kitchen supper, simply cooked from local produce, is offered. (Michael Eldridge)

Chapel Street
Penzance TR18 4AQ

T: 01736 362024
E: hello@chapelhousepz.co.uk
W: chapelhousepz.co.uk

BEDROOMS: 6.
OPEN: closed 24–29 Dec, kitchen closed for dinner Sun–Wed.
FACILITIES: drawing room, open-plan kitchen/dining area, in-room TV (Freeview), function facilities, terrace, garden, unsuitable for disabled.
BACKGROUND MUSIC: none.
LOCATION: town centre.
CHILDREN: all ages welcomed.
DOGS: allowed in bedrooms and public areas and in kitchen/dining area with consent of other guests.
CREDIT CARDS: MC, Visa.
PRICES: per room B&B single £125–£165, double £160–£220. Set dinner £27.50. 1-night bookings refused at bank holiday weekends (rooms 2, 4 and 6).

**SEE ALSO SHORTLIST**

# PENZANCE Cornwall                              MAP 1:E1

## TREREIFE

At the south-western tip of Cornwall, with views
to the sea, this handsome manor house, wrapped
in parkland and formal gardens, gives a taste of
country house living. Run by the Le Grice family
(seventh generation), the house with its Queen
Anne frontage feels more like a private stately
home than a B&B. 'The sitting room, like the
dining room, is full of antiques, lovingly cared
for and creating an atmosphere of bygone days.'
There are panelled walls hung with portraits, a
parquet-floored hall, and an oak staircase leading
to the largest bedrooms. The others are on the
ground floor, each with an individual entrance
from the courtyard. Done out in country house
style with polished wood furniture, dressing
table and perhaps a coronet bed or window seat,
most have a bath as well as a shower. The vibe
throughout is relaxed, with guests encouraged to
'treat the sitting room and the grounds as though
they were our own'; the latter include a lovely
parterre. Breakfast is 'the highlight of the visit'
with cooked dishes 'full of good local ingredients'
plus Lizzie Grice's medlar jam, courtesy of the
walled garden. (Michael Bourdeaux)

Penzance TR20 8TJ

T: 01736 362750
E: trereifepark@btconnect.com
W: trereifepark.co.uk

BEDROOMS: 4. 2 on ground floor, plus
2 self-catering apartments, and bell
tent for glamping.
OPEN: 1 Mar–end Nov.
FACILITIES: sitting room (honesty bar),
dining room, in-room TV (Freeview),
civil wedding licence, 5-acre grounds
(parterres, walled garden, woodland),
parking, unsuitable for disabled.
BACKGROUND MUSIC: none.
LOCATION: 1¼ miles SW of Penzance.
CHILDREN: all ages welcomed.
DOGS: allowed in ground-floor
bedrooms, not in public rooms
(£15 per stay).
CREDIT CARDS: Amex, MC, Visa.
PRICES: per room B&B £100–£160.
Min. 2-night stay June–Sept and for
self-catering.

**SEE ALSO SHORTLIST**

# PETWORTH Sussex

MAP 2:E3

## THE OLD RAILWAY STATION

Built in 1892 to enable the Prince of Wales to travel to Goodwood Racecourse, Petworth's railway station has been 'lovingly restored' into a 'remarkable' B&B. Owners Jennie Hudson and Blair Humphry, who took over in 2018, appear to be maintaining a first-class service. Guests are met at the original ticket window before being shown to their rooms in the original Station House or in one of four romantic Pullman carriages. Readers are enchanted by the 'pure luxury' of the Pullman rooms, redolent of a more glamorous era, with gleaming colonial-style furniture, mahogany fittings and plantation shutters. All have a spacious en suite bathroom. A full English breakfast and afternoon tea are served in the timber-panelled Waiting Room, where the high vaulted ceiling, large windows and polished wood floor date from its days as a working station. In warm weather, dining tables and parasols are set up on the platform. For dinner, Petworth's restaurants are just a five-minute drive away. It's all a long way from Clapham Junction. 'We fell in love with this place immediately' is a view echoed by many readers. (Brendan Gibb-Gray, and others)

**25% DISCOUNT VOUCHERS**

Station Road
Petworth GU28 0JF

T: 01798 342346
E: info@old-station.co.uk
W: old-station.co.uk

BEDROOMS: 10. 8 in Pullman carriages, 1 room suitable for guests with slightly restricted mobility.
OPEN: all year except 20–27 Dec.
FACILITIES: lounge/bar/breakfast room, in-room TV (Freeview), platform/terrace, 2-acre garden, public areas wheelchair accessible.
BACKGROUND MUSIC: 'soft '20s, '30s, '40s music' at breakfast.
LOCATION: 1½ miles S of Petworth.
CHILDREN: not under 10.
DOGS: not allowed.
CREDIT CARDS: MC, Visa.
PRICES: per room B&B double, house £130–£170 (single-night premium rate Fri, Sat £204), Pullman £150–£210 (single-night premium rate Fri, Sat £228–£252), reduced rates for single occupancy 'sometimes offered'.

# PICKERING Yorkshire

MAP 4:D4

## THE WHITE SWAN

Overlooking the market place, this family-run, 16th-century hotel continues to offer the coaching-inn essentials of good food, wine and comfort. It is 'well run, with a personal touch', say readers. It combines pub features – a fire-warmed snug, bar with beams, local ales – with a smarter dining room with candlesticks and polished tables. 'The hotel takes its food seriously and its wine list even more so.' Chef Darren Clemmit delivers 'honest', locally sourced food with creativity: home-made black pudding with scallops, say, or Yorkshire lamb with charred carrots. The crème brûlée is legendary. Breakfast is 'a copious buffet and plenty of cooked options', including 'a well-cooked kedgeree'. Rooms in the main building are the most characterful, with feature wallpapers, blanket throws, soft carpets and the occasional antique, and there are larger, contemporary ones in the converted stables. 'Modern, comfortable and quiet', the latter have a slate floor, and spacious bathroom. All rooms have robes, home-made biscuits and Bath House accessories. Staff are 'enthusiastic, helpful and charming'. (John Saul, David Birnie)

Market Place
Pickering YO18 7AA

T: 01751 472288
E: welcome@white-swan.co.uk
W: white-swan.co.uk

BEDROOMS: 21. 9 in annexe, on ground floor.
OPEN: all year.
FACILITIES: lounge, bar, restaurant, private dining room, bothy residents' lounge/event room, in-room TV (Freeview), small terrace (alfresco meals), 3 electric charging points, restaurant, bar and lounge wheelchair accessible, no adapted toilet.
BACKGROUND MUSIC: in bar occasionally.
LOCATION: central.
CHILDREN: all ages welcomed.
DOGS: allowed in some bedrooms, bar and lounge, not in restaurant (owners may dine with dogs in snug).
CREDIT CARDS: Amex, MC, Visa.
PRICES: per room B&B single £120–£170, double £150–£210. À la carte £36.

# PORTSCATHO Cornwall

MAP 1:E2

## DRIFTWOOD HOTEL

Fiona and Paul Robinson's New England-inspired hotel, with 'magnificent views over Gerrans Bay', ticked all the boxes for a reader this year, from the 'wonderful people' to 'food that is too good to be true'. Superior courtyard rooms in creamy hues have the best sea views, with a Juliet balcony or decked terrace. Another reader's main-house room was 'beautifully furnished, but approached through the restaurant'. Soundproofing could have been better, and how much nicer if he could have opened the large picture windows. A four-person cabin with kitchenette on the path to the 'gorgeous, secluded' hotel beach would suit a family. A change of chef sees Olly Pierrepont (from La Trompette in Chiswick, London) using seasonal Cornish produce to create such dishes as Newlyn cod with smoked ox cheek, lentils, wild garlic and morels. Tasting menus for omnivores and vegetarians must be taken by the whole table. At breakfast there are freshly squeezed juices, kedgeree, St Ewe eggs and Driftwood honey. You can order a picnic for a day on the sands, light bites or a cream tea to eat in, or on the terrace.

Rosevine
Porthscatho TR2 5EW

**T:** 01872 580644
**E:** info@driftwoodhotel.co.uk
**W:** driftwoodhotel.co.uk

**BEDROOMS:** 15. 4 accessed via courtyard, plus 2-bedroom cabin.
**OPEN:** all year except 30 Nov–18 Dec, 2–29 Jan.
**FACILITIES:** bar, restaurant, drawing room, snug, children's games room, in-room TV (Freeview), 7-acre grounds (terraced gardens, private beach, safe bathing), unsuitable for disabled.
**BACKGROUND MUSIC:** all day in restaurant and bar.
**LOCATION:** 1½ miles N of Portscatho.
**CHILDREN:** all ages welcomed, kids' supper menu (no very young children at dinner).
**DOGS:** not allowed.
**CREDIT CARDS:** MC, Visa.
**PRICES:** per room B&B £170–£310, D,B&B £250–£320. Fixed-price dinner £55, tasting menu £75. 1-night bookings refused weekends.

# RADNAGE Buckinghamshire                    MAP 2:C3

## THE MASH INN

♕ Previous César winner

It is all about earth and fire at Nick Mash's
red brick 18th-century pub, reinvented as a
restaurant-with-rooms, amid a rural community
of hamlets. Nick's family have farmed in the
Chilterns for generations, and he wants guests to
reconnect with the land. In a semi-open kitchen,
using a flame grill, Jon Parry cooks produce
picked from the kitchen garden, foraged, or
sourced from the farm, in dishes such as confit
duck leg, haricot beans and monk's beard. Fish is
delivered within 24 hours of landing. The night's
set menu might include Jerusalem artichoke soup,
pork and rhubarb, potato and black truffle, and
beeswax and buttermilk panna cotta. 'We called
in unannounced and scruffy for lunch on a busy
Sunday,' relate Guide insiders. 'Nick was very
much in evidence, helped by his son.' There was
a 'pubby atmosphere', 'a nice terrace for alfresco
dining', and 'everyone was having a good time'.
Bedrooms have a king-size bed, a shower or
freestanding bath and L:A Bruket toiletries. In the
morning, freshly baked croissants, home-made
jam, granola, porridge or buttermilk yoghurt are
brought to the bedroom door.

Horseshoe Road
Bennett End
Radnage HP14 4EB

T: 01494 482440
E: hello@themashinn.com
W: themashinn.com

BEDROOMS: 6.
OPEN: all year, closed Sun dinner, all
day Mon, Tues.
FACILITIES: snug bar and dining area,
semi-open-plan kitchen/dining room,
5-acre garden and grounds, restaurant
wheelchair accessible, adapted toilet.
BACKGROUND MUSIC: in public areas.
LOCATION: in hamlet 7 miles NW of
High Wycombe.
CHILDREN: not under 16.
DOGS: allowed in bar.
CREDIT CARDS: MC, Visa.
PRICES: per room B&B £110–£250.
Lunch Wed–Fri £25, Sun £45, set
dinner menu Wed–Sat £80.

# RAMSGILL-IN-NIDDERDALE Yorkshire

MAP 4:D3

## THE YORKE ARMS

Chef Frances Atkins is still very much at the helm of this spoiling country restaurant-with-rooms, despite new ownership; superb food and an indulgent stay are guaranteed. 'This inn remains a top place to stay and dine,' declares a regular. The creeper-covered 18th-century shooting lodge, with extensive gardens, dominates tiny Ramsgill. 'The vegetable, fruit and flower gardens are wonderful, a real joy to walk around.' Inside, antiques and squashy sofas – plus hand-painted hessian wallpaper in the dining room – are set against flagged floors and beamed ceilings, creating a 'calm, unhurried yet unstuffy' atmosphere, though 'service is seriously efficient'. Dinner is the star turn with food that's 'confident, imaginative and full of the unexpected'. Dishes might include halibut, celeriac and sea kale, or rabbit with morel and wild garlic. Refreshed rooms feature earthy colours and quirky themes: 'Brew' has teapot-patterned curtains. There are classy bathrooms and monogrammed linen, too. 'Breakfasts are as fine as one can find anywhere' – perfect fuel for walks from the doorstep. (Anthony Bradbury, HP) NOTE: As the Guide went to press, The Yorke Arms announced that it was changing to become an exclusive-use venue.

Ramsgill-in-Nidderdale
Harrogate HG3 5RL

T: 01423 755243
E: enquiries@yorke-arms.co.uk
W: theyorkearms.co.uk

BEDROOMS: 18. 4 suites in courtyard, 1 suitable for disabled.
OPEN: all year except 25 Dec, 2 weeks in Jan.
FACILITIES: lounge, bar, 2 dining rooms, 1 private dining room, in-room TV (Freeview), function facilities, 2-acre grounds, public rooms wheelchair accessible with ramps, no adapted toilet.
BACKGROUND MUSIC: in public areas.
LOCATION: centre of village.
CHILDREN: not under 12.
DOGS: allowed in some bedrooms and bar.
CREDIT CARDS: Amex, MC, Visa.
PRICES: per room D,B&B 2-course dinner £230–£375, D,B&B 8-course tasting menu £310–£455, rooms must be booked with dinner. À la carte £60, tasting menus £75–£105.

# RAVENSTONEDALE Cumbria

MAP 4:C3

## THE BLACK SWAN

♀ Previous César winner

In this small conservation village, with views to the Howgill fells, this large country pub is as much a locals' favourite as an inn with smart food and bedrooms. The substantial, late Victorian-Edwardian building, 'in a beautiful setting' with a large beer garden running down to a stream, has been energetically run by Louise Dinnes and her 'friendly and helpful' staff for 14 years. Eat in the cheerful bar, with its panelled walls, tartan carpet, dried hops, stuffed animals and open fire, or in the quieter, elegant dining room. The dinner menu of Scott Fairweather's 'delicious food' offers a creative twist on local produce; perhaps venison tartare with truffle mayo, or smoked haddock in mustard sauce, as well as staples such as beer-battered fish and chips. Breakfast is 'of high quality'. 'Spotlessly clean' bedrooms range from a four-poster suite and glamping tents to dog-friendly annexe rooms with separate entrance, to the compact and cosy. Country cottage in style, with colourful throws and patterned wallpapers, all have fresh milk and local hand-made toiletries. And, whether they have garden or village views, all are quiet.

**25% DISCOUNT VOUCHERS**

Ravenstonedale
Kirkby Stephen CA17 4NG

T: 01539 623204
E: enquiries@blackswanhotel.com
W: blackswanhotel.com

BEDROOMS: 16. 6 in annexe, 4 on ground floor, 3 suitable for disabled. Plus 3 glamping tents.
OPEN: all year.
FACILITIES: 2 bars, lounge, 2 dining rooms, free Wi-Fi in bars and lounge only, Orange mobile network only, in-room TV (Freeview), beer garden in wooded grounds, tennis/golf in village, public rooms wheelchair accessible.
BACKGROUND MUSIC: in public areas all day, but optional.
LOCATION: in village 5 miles SW of Kirkby Stephen.
CHILDREN: all ages welcomed.
DOGS: max. 3 in each of 4 ground-floor annexe rooms, not in restaurant.
CREDIT CARDS: MC, Visa.
PRICES: per room B&B single from £95, double £95–£165. À la carte £40. 1-night bookings sometimes refused.

# REEPHAM Norfolk

MAP 2:B5

## THE DIAL HOUSE

Studied eccentricity abounds at this Georgian house on the market square with most rooms styled on a geographic theme – and a hairdresser and boutique on site. 'Unashamedly quirky, but very comfortably and engagingly so,' write readers this year. 'The bedrooms are elegant', each with a record player and shared library of vinyl discs, handmade biscuits, a marble bathroom, roll-top bath and drench shower. Natural History opens on to a decked terrace. Parisian Garret has French antiques and – ooh, la-la! – a slipper bath at the foot of the bed. China, a celebration of Willow Pattern, proved 'a real treat'. Since Hannah Springham and Andrew Jones arrived in 2018 they have introduced a new cocktail bar. Andrew cooks local produce over sustainably sourced charcoal. 'The restaurant is set in a number of rooms, one hidden behind a revolving bookcase. Food was consistently good. We particularly enjoyed their Norfolk asparagus "dib dabs", mussels, and grilled fillet of cod in a delicious buttermilk and dill sauce.' The staff are 'unfailingly cheerful'. An eco picnic basket can be filled on request. (Simon and Mithra Tonking)

**25% DISCOUNT VOUCHERS**

Market Place
Reepham
Norwich NR10 4JJ

T: 01603 879900
E: info@thedialhouse.org.uk
W: thedialhouse.org.uk

BEDROOMS: 8.
OPEN: all year, restaurant closed Sun night, Mon.
FACILITIES: lounge, restaurant, private dining rooms (chef's table, 'secret room' and cellar), in-room TV (Sky), terrace, civil wedding licence, public rooms wheelchair accessible, no adapted toilet.
BACKGROUND MUSIC: in public areas.
LOCATION: on main square.
CHILDREN: all ages welcomed.
DOGS: allowed in 1 bedroom, some public rooms and in part of restaurant.
CREDIT CARDS: Amex, MC, Visa.
PRICES: per room B&B single £130–£175, double £165–£210, D,B&B £195–£240. À la carte £37. 1-night bookings refused Christmas week.

# RICHMOND Yorkshire

MAP 4:C3

## THE COACH HOUSE AT MIDDLETON LODGE

♺ Previous César winner

Minutes from the motorway, this Georgian estate feels deeply rural, with its walled garden and hundreds of acres to explore. 'A glorious setting' and very 'well cared for', readers say. James Allison and his wife, Rebecca, have turned the grounds of his family's home, designed by the 18th-century architect John Carr, into a 21st-century country retreat, complete with small spa, kitchen garden, and two restaurants. Relaxed but chic bedrooms – beams, soft colours, vintage and rustic furnishings – are spread between former stables, farmhouse and outbuildings. Some have a patio; Potting Shed rooms are the most private – one suite is a 'lovely big room with huge bathroom'. Some rooms are up steep steps – 'you need to be agile'. There is universal praise for 'excellent' food in the all-day Coach House restaurant – a huge double-height room – with dishes such as cod bouillabaisse or duck leg with chorizo cassoulet, plus vegetarian choices. There is also a taster menu-only dining room. Breakfast is a 'big, excellent buffet' with 'delicious marmalade', along with Greek omelette and huevos rancheros.

Kneeton Lane
Middleton Tyas
Richmond DL10 6NJ

T: 01325 377977
E: info@middletonlodge.co.uk
W: middletonlodge.co.uk

BEDROOMS: 45. 9 in coach house, 3 in Potting Shed, 11 in Dairy, 6 in farmhouse, 5 on ground floor, 1 suitable for disabled. 16 rooms in main house for exclusive hire only.
OPEN: all year.
FACILITIES: lounge, bar, snug, 2 restaurants, in-room TV (Sky), civil wedding licence, treatment rooms, courtyard, garden in 200-acre grounds, public rooms wheelchair accessible, adapted toilet.
BACKGROUND MUSIC: in public areas.
LOCATION: 1 mile N of village.
CHILDREN: all ages welcomed.
DOGS: allowed in some bedrooms, most public areas, one restaurant.
CREDIT CARDS: MC, Visa.
PRICES: per room B&B £190, D,B&B £270. À la carte £35, tasting menu £75.

**SEE ALSO SHORTLIST**

# RICHMOND Yorkshire

MAP 4:C3

## THE FRENCHGATE RESTAURANT & HOTEL

A Georgian town house and its 17th-century neighbour combine as a characterful hotel and restaurant, in a lovely town in Dales countryside. The lounge is furnished with carefully chosen antiques. Bedrooms have views over the small, terraced garden or down to the River Swale. Some have a Swedish power shower, others a Victorian-style roll-top or Napoli 'egg' bath, and maybe a heated marble floor. The bridal suite, with ship's timber beams, has a handmade oak four-poster and a spa bath with kinetic lighting. All rooms have a coffee machine and good toiletries. Trusted readers were greeted by owner David Todd, who sprang into action, 'carrying cases and explaining the high-tech bathroom to us'. Their bedroom, 'Panama', felt small for the big, 'very comfortable' bed. In the dining room furnished with mix-and-match oak chairs and tables, Lisa Miller wins plaudits for her use of locally sourced ingredients in such dishes as dressed Whitby crab, and roast Swaledale lamb with pickled red cabbage and carrot purée. 'Food and service at both dinner and breakfast were excellent.' (Elspeth and John Gibbon, RG)

59–61 Frenchgate
Richmond DL10 7AE

**T:** 01748 822087
**E:** info@thefrenchgate.co.uk
**W:** thefrenchgate.co.uk

**BEDROOMS:** 9, 1 on ground floor with 2 steps to en suite.
**OPEN:** all year.
**FACILITIES:** dining room, bar/terrace, lounge, in-room TV (Freeview), civil wedding licence, small garden, public rooms wheelchair accessible, adapted toilet.
**BACKGROUND MUSIC:** soft jazz in public rooms.
**LOCATION:** 200 yds NE of town square.
**CHILDREN:** all ages welcomed.
**DOGS:** not allowed.
**CREDIT CARDS:** Amex, MC, Visa.
**PRICES:** per room B&B single £98–£243, double £138–£355 (bridal/family suite). À la carte set-price menu £39.

**SEE ALSO SHORTLIST**

# RICHMOND Yorkshire

MAP 4:C3

## THE HACK & SPADE

In a hamlet west of Scotch Corner, this B&B
was formerly a tiny Georgian ale house, which
grew into a Victorian pub for labourers from the
limestone quarry. It is a Jane Eyre sort of place,
plain of face but individual and dependable
within. A Guide insider rang 'a slightly "Avon
calling" doorbell', and was welcomed by owner
Jane Ratcliffe, who showed him to one of the
tastefully styled bedrooms, with 'obviously recent'
modern bathroom. Some rooms are small, but
all have smart contemporary decor, a rainfall
shower and Arran Aromatics toiletries. Zetland
has a sofa at the foot of a super-king-size bed, a
bath and separate shower, and dales views. New
arrivals sit down at 4 pm to tea and cakes by a
log-burner, and there is a small bar should they
want something stronger. For dinner, Richmond
is a five-minute drive away (see The Frenchgate,
previous entry). In the morning, a buffet is set out
in a dining room adorned with fishing rods, and
the hostess, commended for her 'non-intrusive
sociability', cooks a locally sourced full Yorkshire.
Should you wish to send a postcard, you will find
a letterbox is set into the flank wall.

Whashton
Richmond DL11 7JL

T: 01748 823721
E: reservations@hackandspade.com
W: hackandspade.com

BEDROOMS: 5.
OPEN: all year except Christmas/New
Year, last 2 weeks Jan.
FACILITIES: small lounge and bar,
breakfast room, in-room TV
(Freeview), garden, unsuitable for
disabled.
BACKGROUND MUSIC: 'quiet spa-type
music' in the mornings.
LOCATION: 4 miles NW of Richmond.
CHILDREN: not under 7.
DOGS: not allowed.
CREDIT CARDS: MC, Visa.
PRICES: per room B&B £125–£140.

SEE ALSO SHORTLIST

# RICHMOND Yorkshire

MAP 4:C3

## MILLGATE HOUSE

This outwardly modest-looking Regency town house startles first-time visitors when they enter. Richly furnished – minimalists beware – with a profusion of clocks, silver, glass, art and antiques, it is a firm favourite among returning guests, not least for its award-winning garden. 'Our friends love it,' reports a trusted reader; 'Wonderfully eccentric,' say inspectors. Owners Tim Culkin and Austin Lynch are passionate and shrewd collectors, and not just for show. Breakfast, 'a generous buffet of fruit, cereals, delicious toast and croissants' and 'good poached egg on smoked haddock', is served with antique silver, bone-handled cutlery and Georgian teapots. The elegant dining room overlooks a small, densely planted hillside garden (open to the public April to October); the hostas, old roses, ferns and rhododendrons are spectacular. Bedrooms are spacious and comfortably traditional, more guest than hotel room, with books, fruit and fresh flowers; some have a separate sitting room. The largest, a little dark, 'but very quiet', opens right on to the garden. The location is matchless, minutes from both the River Swale and the market square.

3 Millgate
Richmond DL10 4JN

T: 01748 823571
E: millgate1@me.com
W: millgatehouse.com

BEDROOMS: 6.
OPEN: all year.
FACILITIES: hall, drawing room, dining room, in-room digital TV, garden, unsuitable for disabled.
BACKGROUND MUSIC: none.
LOCATION: town centre.
CHILDREN: all ages welcomed.
DOGS: allowed in public rooms and bedrooms (not unattended).
CREDIT CARDS: none.
PRICES: per room B&B £125–£165.

**SEE ALSO SHORTLIST**

# RICHMOND-UPON-THAMES Surrey

MAP 2:D3

## BINGHAM RIVERHOUSE

Bang on the banks of the Thames between Richmond and Petersham, this former Georgian mansion turned 'classic English hotel with a modern twist' sits in a riverside garden and terrace. It has an interesting literary past. It was here that aunt and niece lovers Katherine Bradley and Edith Cooper entertained the likes of Robert Browning, and wrote under the pseudonym of Michael Field. The next chapter is being written by mother and daughter duo Ruth and Samantha Trinder, with a nod to the past: each bedroom is named after a work by Field. The most sought-after have a river view, but a street-facing double had 'a powerful walk-in marble shower and a lovely, deep copper bath with LA-EVA products in glass bottles', reported Guide inspectors. Staff were 'affable, chatty and warm'. You can take drinks in the drawing room, and dine in the parlour or library. Steven Edwards of Hove's Etch restaurant is now overseeing the kitchen, with the focus on British food, in such dishes as guineafowl with cauliflower cheese and nasturtium. 'A veggie breakfast of delicious smashed avocado, spinach, mushrooms and tomatoes was provided on request.'

61–63 Petersham Road
Richmond-upon-Thames TW10 6UT

T: 020 8940 0902
E: be@binghamriverhouse.com
W: binghamriverhouse.com

BEDROOMS: 15.
OPEN: all year, restaurant closed Sun evening from 5.30 pm.
FACILITIES: 3 drawing room/bar/ restaurant rooms, function room, in-room TV (Freeview), civil wedding licence, terrace, ½-acre garden, complimentary use of nearby wellness centre, public rooms wheelchair accessible, adapted toilet.
BACKGROUND MUSIC: in bar and restaurant.
LOCATION: ½ mile S of centre.
CHILDREN: all ages welcomed.
DOGS: allowed with prior permission in some bedrooms (charges apply) and public areas.
CREDIT CARDS: MC, Visa.
PRICES: per room B&B £211–£364. À la carte £50. Check hotel's website for latest offers/prices.

# ROMALDKIRK Co. Durham

MAP 4:C3

## THE ROSE & CROWN

'I would love to keep this place secret – but that would be selfish.' Readers who have stayed at this 'quintessential village inn', beside a Saxon church and overlooking the green, understand this sentiment. With flagged floors, open fires, a cosy bar and panelled dining room, it offers 'a lovely blend of Old English atmosphere with modern accommodation'. Rooms are 'beautifully decorated, cosy and comfortable' and divided between more characterful ones in the main building (with window seats and exposed stone) and more contemporary, dog-friendly affairs with patio. 'Attention to detail was impressive with fresh tea and coffee delivered to the room.' Food is a highlight: Thomas Robinson, co-owner with his wife, Cheryl, comes from a long-established local farming family. Candle-lit dinners feature 'unfussy, innovative and excellent' dishes such as venison bourguignon or hake and pea fishcakes, all 'first rate, plentiful and beautifully presented'. 'Local' staff were 'dedicated to making our stay memorable' in a 'beautiful village with lots of country walks'. (David Birnie, Steven Hunter, Linda McLeod, and others)

**25% DISCOUNT VOUCHERS**

Romaldkirk
Barnard Castle DL12 9EB

T: 01833 650213
E: hotel@rose-and-crown.co.uk
W: rose-and-crown.co.uk

BEDROOMS: 14. 2 in Monk's Cottage, 5 in rear courtyard, some on ground floor, 1 suitable for disabled.
OPEN: all year except 23–28 Dec, bar menu only Mon lunchtime.
FACILITIES: lounge, bar, Crown Room (bar meals), restaurant, in-room TV (Freeview), boot room, public rooms wheelchair accessible, no adapted toilet.
BACKGROUND MUSIC: in restaurant.
LOCATION: village centre, 6 miles W of Barnard Castle.
CHILDREN: all ages welcomed, no under-8s in restaurant after 8 pm.
DOGS: allowed in bedrooms and public rooms, except restaurant.
CREDIT CARDS: Amex, MC, Visa.
PRICES: per room B&B £125–£210, D,B&B £190–£275. À la carte £35.

# ROWSLEY Derbyshire

MAP 3:A6

## THE PEACOCK AT ROWSLEY

Generations of glamorous aristocrats hang around this 17th-century manor house, gazing from gilded frames over what is today an exemplary hotel. Owned by Lord and Lady Edward Manners of Haddon Hall, it exudes traditional comfort. Readers on a return visit found their four-poster room, with views over the grounds, 'extremely well appointed', with 'elderflower cordial, elegant pictures and Chinese antique ornaments'. Front rooms overlook the road. All rooms now have air conditioning. 'They've clearly had decorators in; acres of fresh paint have been applied.' Complimentary tea in the drawing room arrived with 'the most delicious shortbread'. However, 'muzak, hélas, in all public rooms, though not as intrusive as last year'. In a dining room with Mouseman oak tables, Dan Smith's locally sourced menus include 'delicious, beautifully cooked' dishes such as lamb with pommes Anna, mint and goat's curd. There is cheaper fare in the beamed bar. After a breakfast with 'the best and lightest croissants', it's time to explore the Peak District national park, fish for trout on the estate or visit Haddon Hall and Chatsworth House. (Francine and Ian Walsh)

**25% DISCOUNT VOUCHERS**

Bakewell Road
Rowsley DE4 2EB

T: 01629 733518
E: reception@thepeacockatrowsley.com
W: thepeacockatrowsley.co.uk

BEDROOMS: 15.
OPEN: all year except 24–26 Dec, 2 weeks Jan.
FACILITIES: lounge, bar, 2 dining rooms, private dining room, in-room TV (Freeview, Apple), ½-acre garden on river, fishing rights, public areas wheelchair accessible.
BACKGROUND MUSIC: in public rooms.
LOCATION: village centre.
CHILDREN: not under 10 at weekends.
DOGS: allowed in bedrooms only, 'for small supplement'.
CREDIT CARDS: Amex, MC, Visa.
PRICES: per room B&B single £135–£150, double £215–£320, D,B&B add £69 per person. À la carte, bar £34, restaurant (Mon–Sat) £65, tasting menu (Fri and Sat) £75. 1-night bookings sometimes refused.

# RYE Sussex

## JEAKE'S HOUSE

Creeper-clad and atmospheric, Jenny Hadfield's B&B stands on the steep, cobbled main street of this medieval hilltop town. It occupies a glorious agglomeration of 17th-century merchant's house and adjacent listed buildings, including a former wool store and a chapel. Each bedroom has its own charms; the best are named after notable people associated with the house. Steep stairs lead up to Conrad Aiken (who owned the house from 1924), with an antique four-poster. Malcolm Lowry (who visited Aiken here) has a toile-draped antique four-poster, a roll-top bath and walk-in shower. You can relax by a log-burner in the parlour, and help yourself to drinks in the theatrically styled bar. Breakfast, cooked by Richard Martin, and served in the galleried former chapel, brings award-winning sausages, free-range eggs, oak-smoked haddock and smashed avocado on toast. 'We loved the deep red walls of the dining room, with old prints and two great portraits. Breakfast was one of the best ever, with devilled kidneys,' writes a trusted reader. Private parking is a 'boon'. (Richard Bright, MA, and others)

Mermaid Street
Rye TN31 7ET

T: 01797 222828
E: stay@jeakeshouse.com
W: jeakeshouse.com

BEDROOMS: 11.
OPEN: all year.
FACILITIES: parlour, bar/library, breakfast room, in-room TV (Freeview), unsuitable for disabled.
BACKGROUND MUSIC: chamber music in breakfast room.
LOCATION: central, private car park 6 mins' walk away (charge for parking permit, advance booking).
CHILDREN: not under 8.
DOGS: allowed in bedrooms, public rooms, on leads and 'always supervised', not in breakfast room.
CREDIT CARDS: MC, Visa.
PRICES: per room B&B £99–£225. 1-night bookings sometimes refused Fri/Sat.

# ST IVES Cornwall

## BLUE HAYES

What could be lovelier than to take breakfast on the terrace of Malcolm Herring's small hotel, gazing over the harbour, or to sip a Blue Hayes Colada at sunset? This is an exclusive place (no dogs, no tiny tots, no walk-ins), done out in seaside blues and creams, with the garden gate leading to the Coast Path and Porthminster Beach. Staff are 'loyal, well trained, welcoming' and intuitive. 'When we were chatting about going up to make a cup of tea, they offered to bring a tray to us in the lounge – and it didn't appear on the bill!' Bedrooms have a 'big, comfy bed, top-quality linen, enormous fluffy towels', Molton Brown toiletries, bone china, a teapot, mini-cafetière and fresh milk. One has a sea-facing balcony, one a roof terrace, one French doors to the garden. 'Sandwiches are available all day.' There are many good restaurants in town, but if you prefer to eat in, you can order a light supper, perhaps tian of smoked salmon and Cornish crab, or Trelawny cheese and asparagus tart. Breakfast includes pancakes with berries and crème fraîche, fresh-baked croissants, Cornish gammon steak or kedgeree.

**25% DISCOUNT VOUCHERS**

Trelyon Avenue
St Ives TR26 2AD

T: 01736 797129
E: bluehayes@btconnect.com
W: bluehayes.co.uk

BEDROOMS: 6.
OPEN: Mar–Oct.
FACILITIES: 2 lounges, bar, dining room, in-room TV (Freeview), small function facilities, room service, terrace, garden, parking.
BACKGROUND MUSIC: in bar and dining room only, at breakfast and supper.
LOCATION: ½ mile from centre of St Ives.
CHILDREN: not under 10.
DOGS: not allowed.
CREDIT CARDS: Amex, MC, Visa.
PRICES: per room B&B single £160–£252, double £160–£315. Supper from £17. Min. 2-night stay, but check availability.

SEE ALSO SHORTLIST

# ST IVES Cornwall

MAP 1:D1

## BOSKERRIS HOTEL

Above Carbis Bay, just far enough from the madding crowd, Jonathan and Marianne Bassett's small Edwardian hotel is the epitome of coastal style. Interiors are finished in shades of sand, sea and surf, with stripped floorboards and signature fabrics. 'The fresh and airy decor is a real plus,' writes a trusted reader, who enjoyed 'a splendid stay'. Not every bedroom has an ocean view, but all have a walk-in rainfall shower or a bath with shower over, cafetière coffee, fresh milk on request, and White Company toiletries. A twin room proved 'compact for two averagely well-fed adults' (and who wouldn't feel well fed after a cream tea on the terrace, with views to Godrevy Lighthouse?). This is, though, a small quibble. 'In the highly likely event that we return, it is the only thing I would wish different.' The staff are local, knowledgeable and helpful. 'They fell over themselves to give recommendations and make bookings.' Dinner, from a simple menu, undersells itself as 'bits and bites'. You could do very well with fish soup or dressed Newlyn crab, fish and chips, and summer pudding. (Sara Hollowell, and others)

### 25% DISCOUNT VOUCHERS

Boskerris Road
Carbis Bay
St Ives TR26 2NQ

T: 01736 795295
E: reservations@boskerrishotel.co.uk
W: boskerrishotel.co.uk

BEDROOMS: 15. 1, on ground floor, suitable for disabled.
OPEN: mid-Feb to mid-Dec, restaurant closed Sun, Mon.
FACILITIES: lounge, bar, breakfast room, supper room, in-room TV (Freeview), decked terrace, massage and reflexology treatment room, 1½-acre garden, parking, public rooms wheelchair accessible.
BACKGROUND MUSIC: 'chilled', in public rooms.
LOCATION: 1½ miles from centre (20 mins' walk), close to station.
CHILDREN: not under 10.
DOGS: not allowed.
CREDIT CARDS: Amex, MC, Visa.
PRICES: per room B&B single £127.50–£232, double £170–£310. À la carte £25. 1-night bookings usually refused in high season.

### SEE ALSO SHORTLIST

# ST MARY'S Isles of Scilly

## STAR CASTLE

The Francis family's charismatic hotel, with many historic features, continues to please regulars, mainly for its 'superb' hilltop location, genial service and tip-top seafood. 'Staying here is like being a guest at a private members' club,' one reader tells us. The star-shaped 16th-century fortress has been ingeniously converted to retain original features: a beamed and stone-walled dining room and lounge, an atmospheric bar in the dungeon, and terraces on the garrison walls. Food is 'undoubtedly the highlight of a stay' with dishes 'almost universally of excellent quality'. Locally caught seafood – lobster is a speciality – and vegetables from the kitchen garden appear on the menu as well as seared venison. Breakfast has 'splendid' choices including 'smoked haddock'. Vegans, however, may struggle. Bedrooms divide opinion: the purpose-built cottage-style rooms in the garden are considered 'wonderfully comfy with everything you could need', or 'rather dated' but 'adequate and comfortable'. Castle rooms, with sea views, have more character. The staff are 'friendly but super professional'. 'Remember to watch the sun set.'

The Garrison
St Mary's TR21 0JA

T: 01720 422317
E: info@star-castle.co.uk
W: star-castle.co.uk

BEDROOMS: 38. 27 in 2 garden wings.
OPEN: all year, B&B only Nov–mid-Feb, except New Year (full service).
FACILITIES: lounge, bar, 2 restaurants, in-room TV (Freeview), civil wedding licence, sun deck, 2-acre gardens, covered swimming pool (12 by 4 metres), vineyard, tennis, beach, golf nearby, unsuitable for disabled.
BACKGROUND MUSIC: none.
LOCATION: ¼ mile from town centre.
CHILDREN: all ages welcomed.
DOGS: allowed in garden rooms, lounge, bar, not in restaurants.
CREDIT CARDS: Amex, MC, Visa.
PRICES: per room B&B single £87–£172, double £149–£424, D,B&B single £115–£200, double £205–£480. Set menu £37–£45, à la carte £42. 1-night bookings usually refused (but call to check).

**SEE ALSO SHORTLIST**

# ST MAWES Cornwall

MAP 1:E2

## THE IDLE ROCKS

Dinghies skim beneath the 150-foot terrace of Karen and David Richards's hotel, in an enviable position overlooking the Fal estuary in a fishing village on the Roseland peninsula. First opened in 1913, it has long had a reputation for its cooking, enhanced by the arrival in 2020 of Dorian Janmaat, from Raymond Blanc's Manoir au Quat' Saisons. In a sea-facing restaurant with floor-to-ceiling windows, the short menus showcase local ingredients in such dishes as pan-seared brill, mussels and green peppercorn sauce. Bedrooms range from 'cosy' doubles with a village view and nautical-themed decor to grand sea-view rooms in soft pastels, with perhaps an emperor bed, a bath and walk-in shower. At breakfast there are freshly pressed juices, porridge with clotted cream, Cornish kipper, and smashed avocado on sourdough. Unusually for a Relais & Châteaux hotel, there was muzak playing in public areas, including the lovely terrace when a Guide inspector dropped in for a drink. This is not, then, the place for a tranquil escape, but if you like music with your moules, the Idle Rocks rocks.

Harbourside
St Mawes TR2 5AN

T: 01326 270270
E: reservations@idlerocks.co.uk
W: idlerocks.com

BEDROOMS: 19. 4 in adjacent cottage, 1 suitable for disabled.
OPEN: all year.
FACILITIES: lounge, restaurant, kids' room, boot room, in-room TV (Sky), waterside terrace, civil wedding licence, public areas wheelchair accessible, adapted toilet, parking.
BACKGROUND MUSIC: all day in public areas, except lounge.
LOCATION: central, on the harbour.
CHILDREN: all ages welcomed, under-10s not encouraged in restaurant after 8 pm.
DOGS: allowed in 2 cottage bedrooms, not in main hotel.
CREDIT CARDS: Amex, MC, Visa.
PRICES: per room B&B double £150–£405, family £250–£380. Set dinner £58, 5-course tasting menu £75. Min. 2-night stay weekends, 3 nights bank hols, 1 on D,B&B terms.

# ST MAWES Cornwall

## TRESANTON

Tumbling down cliffs overlooking Falmouth
Bay, Olga Polizzi's glowing white Tresanton
shows how to put style into a family-friendly
seaside hotel – at a price. The cluster of former
yacht clubhouse and cottages, linked by terraces,
gardens and (lots of) steps, has a Mediterranean
glow. 'Charming' bedrooms, almost all with sea
views and some with terraces, range in style from
understated country house to breezy beach chalet,
and mix contemporary and vintage furniture.
Bathrooms are 'stunning and very modern',
while an inspector loved hearing 'the sound of
waves, and little else'. Dine in the restaurant with
its outdoor terrace, or in the dog-friendly bar
with a fire for cooler days. Menus are the same
in both, strong on seafood: perhaps Porthilly
oysters, linguine with clams or monkfish with
piperade. Breakfasts 'in the sunny restaurant were
magnificent', with a generous buffet including
freshly squeezed juices and good choice of cooked
items with 'everything prettily presented. I have
never seen such perfect poached eggs.' The hotel's
popularity with locals means in daytime it's 'not
exactly peaceful. But we loved it.'

27 Lower Castle Road
St Mawes TR2 5DR

**T:** 01326 270055
**E:** info@tresanton.com
**W:** tresanton.com

**BEDROOMS:** 30. In 5 houses.
**OPEN:** all year.
**FACILITIES:** 2 lounges, bar, restaurant,
cinema, playroom, conference
facilities, in-room TV (Freeview),
civil wedding licence, terrace, ¼-acre
garden, beach club (May–Sept),
48-foot yacht, restaurant wheelchair
accessible, adapted toilet.
**BACKGROUND MUSIC:** none.
**LOCATION:** on seafront, valet parking
(car park up hill).
**CHILDREN:** all ages welcomed.
**DOGS:** allowed in some bedrooms and
in dogs' bar.
**CREDIT CARDS:** Amex, MC, Visa.
**PRICES:** per room B&B £230–£780.
Set lunch £32, à la carte £46. Min.
2-night bookings at weekends, 3-night
bookings on bank holidays.

# ST MELLION Cornwall

MAP 1:D3

## PENTILLIE CASTLE

**NEW**

A sense of space and light pervades the Corytons'
grand 17th-century family seat in a wooded estate
on the Tamar. Built in 1698, and later topped
with an embattled parapet, it is described by
owner Sammie Coryton as 'a boutique B&B',
which, says a trusted reader, 'is akin to calling
Chatsworth a manor house'. You approach via
'a long drive dotted with pheasants', to find
what feels like 'a grand private house where
the owners have gone out, having left a note
inviting you to help yourselves to everything that's
going'. The generosity is reflected in cream tea
on arrival, and large bedrooms furnished with
antiques. Dewhurst has a four-poster and works
by Wynford Dewhurst, who painted alongside
Monet. Coryton has a spectacular bathroom with
a rocking chair, roll-top bath and walk-in shower.
Formal dinners are held periodically, but the usual
form is to order a supper to heat in the Aga. 'We
had fish pie followed by fruit salad, a chilled bottle
of Muscadet from the honesty bar in the drawing
room, taken at a communal table in the kitchen.'
Even your dog will approve of that. (Robert Cooper)
NOTE: As the Guide went to press, Pentillie
Castle announced that it was changing to become
an exclusive-use venue.

Paynters Cross
St Mellion
Saltash PL12 6QD

T: 01579 350044
E: info@pentillie.co.uk
W: pentillie.co.uk

BEDROOMS: 9. 1, on ground floor,
suitable for disabled.
OPEN: all year, exclusive use Christmas
and New Year.
FACILITIES: morning room, drawing
room, dining room, guest kitchen,
in-room TV (Freeview), civil wedding
licence, 55-acre grounds, terrace,
heated outdoor pool.
BACKGROUND MUSIC: during meals.
LOCATION: near St Mellion.
CHILDREN: all ages welcomed.
DOGS: assistance dogs allowed in
downstairs area, other dogs welcome
in 3 bedrooms, games room, boot
room, grounds.
CREDIT CARDS: Amex, MC, Visa.
PRICES: per room B&B single
£175–£255, double £190–£270. (£15
discount for single occupancy). Dinner
£42 on selected dates.

# SALCOMBE Devon

MAP 1:E4

## SOAR MILL COVE HOTEL

⚜ Previous César winner

It's all about the sublime seaside setting at Keith Makepeace's family-centric, dog-friendly hotel with 'amazing views to take your breath away'. A trail leads to 'a beautiful, uncrowded beach with splendid rocks', and there is easy access to the South West Coast Path. Simple but stylish bedrooms look out to sea or over rolling National Trust countryside, from floor-to-ceiling glass doors and a private patio. It is small wonder, then, that the low-slung hotel is 'a favourite place' for many returning guests. 'I love everything about it,' writes a reader who has been going for 30 years and finds it 'like a second home'. Guide insiders with a house nearby drop in often. 'On fine days we eat our bar lunch or cream tea on a sunny terrace. Service is always good, the food original and delicious, including lovely risotto with asparagus.' In the light-filled, sea-facing dining room, Ian MacDonald's menus are big on local fish and shellfish – lobster, crab, Exe mussels – and include a vegan option. 'What more could you ask for?' 'Can't wait to go again.' (Gerald Taylor, Harriet Morris, Louisa Walker, and others)

Soar Mill Cove
Salcombe TQ7 3DS

T: 01548 561566
E: info@soarmillcove.co.uk
W: soarmillcove.co.uk

BEDROOMS: 22. 21 on ground floor.
OPEN: all year, except 2 Jan–7 Feb.
FACILITIES: lounge, bar, restaurant, coffee shop, in-room TV (Freeview), indoor spring-fed swimming pool, spa, gym, civil wedding licence, 10-acre grounds (tennis), public rooms wheelchair accessible, adapted toilet.
BACKGROUND MUSIC: in public areas.
LOCATION: 3 miles SW of Salcombe.
CHILDREN: all ages welcomed.
DOGS: allowed in all but 1 bedroom, bar, coffee shop.
CREDIT CARDS: Amex, MC, Visa.
PRICES: per room B&B £199–£429, D,B&B £299–£469. À la carte £39. 1-night bookings refused holiday weekends.

SEE ALSO SHORTLIST

# SEAHAM Co. Durham                    MAP 4:B4

## SEAHAM HALL

'A wonderful place', this Georgian mansion with a pedigree (Lord Byron was married to Anne Isabella Millbanke in the drawing room) stands in landscaped gardens overlooking Durham's heritage coast. In its time it has been a military hospital, whisky smugglers' HQ and TB sanatorium, but today it is a tip-top, cliff-top hotel with heritage, made over in contemporary, colourful style. An award-winning spa is seamlessly attached to the main building; the pool has hydrotherapy jets. Housekeeping is 'meticulous': attention to detail includes a choice of bedding. The enthusiastic young staff are 'a particular strength'. The Ada Lovelace Suite (recalling Lord Byron's daughter) has twin slipper baths in the window; garden suites have an outdoor hot tub. The dining room features gold-plated chandeliers and Damian Broom's imaginative menus: day-boat turbot with salsify cooked in dulse, and mussels; for vegans, slow-cooked sand carrots, oat and millet porridge, with smoked carrot sauce. If you prefer pan-Asian cuisine, head for Ozone in the Serenity Spa. 'We were made very welcome and were well cared for.' (AW, and others)

Lord Byron's Walk
Seaham SR7 7AG

T: 0191 516 1400
E: reservations@seaham-hall.com
W: seaham-hall.com

BEDROOMS: 21. 1 suitable for disabled.
OPEN: all year.
FACILITIES: lift, 2 lounges, bar, 2 restaurants, private dining room, conference facilities, in-room TV (Sky, BT), civil wedding licence, spa (treatment rooms, outdoor hot tubs, sun terrace, fitness suite, 20-metre heated swimming pool), 37-acre grounds (terraces, putting green), public areas wheelchair accessible, adapted toilet.
BACKGROUND MUSIC: all day in public areas.
LOCATION: 5 miles S of Sunderland.
CHILDREN: all ages welcomed.
DOGS: not allowed.
CREDIT CARDS: Amex, MC, Visa.
PRICES: per room B&B £210–£465, D,B&B £295–£555. À la carte (in restaurant) £50, vegan £40, (in Ozone) £30.

# SEAHOUSES Northumberland                    MAP 4:A4

## ST AIDAN HOTEL & BISTRO

In an enviable position overlooking the
Northumberland coast – Bamburgh Castle one
way, the Farne Islands the other – this 'friendly
and professionally run little hotel' is a coastal-
lover's treat. Bedrooms, in breezy seaside colours,
are simply furnished (some are on the cosy side)
with throws and local artwork adding warmth.
All have 'thoughtful extras, such as binoculars
for gazing out to sea' or over the harbour and
village. Young owners Rob and Tegan Tait create
a 'bright, welcoming and informal atmosphere';
Rob is from the area and has good suggestions
for walks and day-trips plus eating options
on days when the hotel's bistro is closed. For
a small operation, the latter has a surprisingly
sophisticated choice: perhaps scallops and black
pudding for a starter followed by their signature
dish of Northumbrian beef with smoked bacon
in red wine; 'well prepared and tasty'. The
interesting wine list reflects Rob's earlier career
at Hotel du Vin. Breakfast is simple but well
done: 'delicious home-made banana bread', eggs
Benedict and the full Northumbrian – providing
perfect preparation for a breezy coastal walk.
(HP, and others)

1 St Aidan's
Seahouses NE68 7SR

T: 01665 720355
E: info@staidanhotel.co.uk
W: staidanhotel.co.uk

BEDROOMS: 9. 2 in annexe.
OPEN: all year except 21–25 Dec,
3 Jan–10 Feb, bistro open Thurs–Sat
dinner.
FACILITIES: breakfast room/bistro,
bar area (honesty bar), in-room TV
(Freeview), front lawn (picnic tables),
unsuitable for disabled.
BACKGROUND MUSIC: chilled acoustic in
public rooms.
LOCATION: 300 yds from harbour,
on north side of village, with views
towards Bamburgh.
CHILDREN: not under 12.
DOGS: allowed in annexe rooms, 1 area
of breakfast room, not in bistro.
CREDIT CARDS: MC, Visa.
PRICES: per room B&B £95–£165.
À la carte £28. 1-night bookings may
be refused in summer.

# SEAHOUSES Northumberland

MAP 4:A4

## ST CUTHBERT'S HOUSE

Previous César winner

The term 'B&B' doesn't do justice to this imaginatively converted chapel with its spoiling bedrooms, breakfast feasts, and warm welcome from Jeff and Jill Sutheran. 'Jeff's friendliness turned the stay into one of pleasure.' Original features of the 19th-century chapel have been preserved; the sanctuary is now the double-height living room, complete with arched windows and cast iron pillars overlooked by a carved pulpit. Bedrooms, some on the cosy side, have a contemporary country house style with handmade, solid wood furniture, feature wallpapers, thick curtains and super-king-size beds. Only a couple have views but there's no stinting on comforts including bathrobes, coffee machines and digital radios. The Sutherans have suggestions for walks, lesser-known Northumbrian sights and evening meals. Guests also enjoyed the 'comfortable, well-lit living space' with 'an honesty bar and range of single malts'. The 'excellent' breakfasts are a tour de force, with home-made or locally sourced ingredients, and dishes including kedgeree, kippers and potato brownies in the full Northumbrian. (Robert Cooper)

**25% DISCOUNT VOUCHERS**

192 Main Street
Seahouses NE68 7UB

T: 01665 720456
E: stay@stcuthbertshouse.com
W: stcuthbertshouse.com

BEDROOMS: 6. 2 on ground floor, 1 suitable for disabled.
OPEN: all year except 'holiday periods in winter', not open Christmas/New Year.
FACILITIES: lounge, dining area, in-room TV (Freeview), public rooms wheelchair accessible.
BACKGROUND MUSIC: instrumental at breakfast.
LOCATION: less than 1 mile from harbour and village centre.
CHILDREN: 12 and upwards welcomed.
DOGS: assistance dogs only.
CREDIT CARDS: MC, Visa.
PRICES: per room B&B single £110–£130, double £130. 1-night bookings occasionally refused in high season.

# SHAFTESBURY Dorset

MAP 2:D1

## LA FLEUR DE LYS

The 'outstanding' food made from fresh local ingredients at this 'wonderful restaurant-with-rooms' on the edge of Shaftesbury's historic town centre has presumably come a long way since that served when the building operated as a girls' boarding house. Now owned by chefs Marc Preston and David Griffin-Shepherd, together with David's wife Mary, the restaurant received 'full marks' from a regular reviewer this year. Dinner, served in the traditionally styled dining room with soft lighting, might include a tart of local scallops and prawns on smoked salmon, followed by pan-fried saddle of Dorset lamb or seared loin of venison. The eight 'comfortable' bedrooms, one with a four-poster, are well equipped with fresh coffee, a selection of teas, fresh milk and home-made biscuits. Bathrooms have either a bath or shower. The only gripe from one reviewer was that it was impossible to turn off the radiator in the bedroom or open the window. Guests invariably mention both the 'helpful' hosts and 'excellent' staff who help to make this lily of the Blackmore Vale 'worthy of its entry' in the Guide yet again. (Kenneth Moore, GB)

Bleke Street
Shaftesbury SP7 8AW

T: 01747 853717
E: info@lafleurdelys.co.uk
W: lafleurdelys.co.uk

BEDROOMS: 8. 1, on ground floor, suitable for disabled.
OPEN: all year, restaurant closed Sun, lunchtime Mon and Tues.
FACILITIES: lounge, bar, dining room, conference room, in-room TV (Freeview), courtyard garden, bar and restaurant wheelchair accessible, adapted toilet.
BACKGROUND MUSIC: none, but some live music events.
LOCATION: N edge of historic town centre.
CHILDREN: all ages welcomed.
DOGS: not allowed.
CREDIT CARDS: Amex, MC, Visa.
PRICES: per room B&B single £90–£115, double £110–£195. À la carte £42, 5-course tasting menu (for whole table only) £45. 1-night bookings sometimes refused weekends in summer.

**SEE ALSO SHORTLIST**

# SHEFFIELD Yorkshire

MAP 4:E4

## BROCCO ON THE PARK

♔ Previous César winner

Behind the facade of an Edwardian villa, Scandi
chic prevails in this multi-award-winning hotel.
Owner Tiina Carr, though born in Doncaster, is
from a Finnish family. 'Immaculately presented'
bedrooms have park views, a 'large, immensely
comfortable bed', LED mood lighting, an
espresso machine, a smart TV, a monsoon rain
shower and organic toiletries. Dove has an in-
room copper bath and a balcony. Woodpecker,
though smaller, was 'light and pristine', say
Guide insiders, and was supplied with 'delicious
home-made brownies'. A fridge on the landing
with milk for each room was 'a neat touch'. In the
Neighbourhood Kitchen, or on the patio, at lunch
and dinner, small plates have a seasonal or Nordic
twist. 'The food was superb. I had a lovely chicken
dish served with a delicious leek and mushroom
sausage roll.' However, 'the highlight of the stay
was breakfast', with choices ranging from a full
English with Cumberland sausage, onion rösti
and thyme-roasted portobello mushroom to
halloumi and sweet potato hash. 'Surely one of
the best places to stay in Sheffield.' (Desmond and
Jenny Balmer, MC)

92 Brocco Bank
Sheffield S11 8RS

T: 0114 266 1233
E: hello@brocco.co.uk
W: brocco.co.uk

BEDROOMS: 8. 1 on ground floor, with
wet room, suitable for disabled.
OPEN: all year, restaurant closed most
Tues, Sun pm and Christmas Day.
FACILITIES: reception area with sofas,
award-winning restaurant with bar,
in-room smart TV, terrace (barbecue,
seating), restaurant wheelchair
accessible, adapted toilet.
BACKGROUND MUSIC: in restaurant, plus
Sunday jazz afternoons.
LOCATION: 1½ miles W of city centre.
CHILDREN: all ages welcomed (under-
3s free).
DOGS: allowed only on terrace.
CREDIT CARDS: Amex, MC, Visa.
PRICES: room only £120–£250.
Breakfast items from £3, full English
£11, 2-course lunch/dinner from £20.
Min. 2-night stay at Christmas.

# SIDLESHAM Sussex                              MAP 2:E3

## THE CRAB & LOBSTER

Birdwatchers flock to this 17th-century inn turned
restaurant-with-rooms overlooking Pagham
Harbour Nature Reserve. Recent sightings have
included spoonbills, spotted flycatchers – and a
pair of trusted Guide readers on a return visit.
Bedrooms, decorated in pastel hues, have harbour
or countryside views. Two are in adjoining Crab
Cottage, with a lounge and kitchen. If you stay at
the inn, our readers recommend Room 1, which
is excellent, with a powerful monsoon shower
over the bathtub. Room 2, reached via 'a twisty
staircase', is under the eaves and lacks headroom.
At dinner, based on locally sourced ingredients,
'the food was brilliant. I had monkfish with crab
risotto on the first night, stone bass in a mild
curry sauce the next. The puds are a delight.'
At breakfast (from 8 am on weekdays, 8.30 at
weekends), more fresh fruit would have been
appreciated. The manager, Mark Vincent, and
his staff 'provide exceptional personal service'.
Owners Sam and Janet Bakose also have The
Halfway Bridge, Lodsworth (see entry), while
chef Clyde Hollett oversees both kitchens. (Peter
Anderson, MG)

Mill Lane
Sidlesham PO20 7NB

T: 01243 641233
E: enquiries@crab-lobster.co.uk
W: crab-lobster.co.uk

BEDROOMS: 4. 2 in adjacent self-
catering Crab Cottage.
OPEN: all year.
FACILITIES: bar/dining room/snug,
in-room TV (Freeview), terrace,
small beer garden, bar and restaurant
wheelchair accessible.
BACKGROUND MUSIC: 'quiet' music in
restaurant and bar.
LOCATION: 6 miles S of Chichester.
CHILDREN: all ages welcomed.
DOGS: allowed in garden area.
CREDIT CARDS: Amex, MC, Visa.
PRICES: per room B&B single
occupancy £115–£135 (full rates apply
Fri–Sun), double £190–£320, extra
guest (Crab Cottage) £30. À la carte
£38. Min. 2-night stay at weekends.

# SIDMOUTH Devon

MAP 1:C5

## HOTEL RIVIERA

Devotees are drawn back time after time to Peter Wharton's quintessential British seafront hotel, and that is 'always a good sign', as one reader remarks this year. Another, who stayed ten years ago and 'loved it', returned to find it 'completely unchanged'. Amid a chorus of approval a lone voice calls for a little 'sympathetic modernisation'. Bedrooms vary in size, and a large, bow-fronted, sea-view room is clearly a top choice. All have room service, cut flowers, fresh milk on request. We hear high praise for the 'unfailingly friendly, attentive' staff. Chef Martin Osedo cooks classics with a modern spin, and 'dinner is an experience to look forward to'. Hits have included 'roast hake with smoked haddock fritters, cockle and prawn chowder', 'the most delectable piece of beef fillet I have had for years', and 'a monumental chocolate parfait'. Breakfast, cooked to order, includes freshly squeezed orange and grapefruit juice, fresh-baked pastries, kippers, smoked haddock, gammon and hash browns – 'excellent, as expected from our previous visit'. (Richard Creed, John Charnley)

The Esplanade
Sidmouth EX10 8AY

T: 01395 515201
E: enquiries@hotelriviera.co.uk
W: hotelriviera.co.uk

BEDROOMS: 26. None on ground floor.
OPEN: all year.
FACILITIES: small lift (not suitable for large wheelchairs), foyer, lounge, bar, restaurant, function facilities, in-room TV (Freeview), terrace, opposite beach (safe bathing), public rooms wheelchair accessible.
BACKGROUND MUSIC: in bar and restaurant, occasional live piano music in bar.
LOCATION: central, on the esplanade.
CHILDREN: all ages welcomed.
DOGS: small dogs allowed in some bedrooms, not in public rooms except foyer.
CREDIT CARDS: Amex, MC, Visa.
PRICES: per person B&B single £118–£242, double £118–£267, D,B&B add £21 per person. Set dinner £42–£46, à la carte £46.

## SNETTISHAM Norfolk

### THE ROSE & CROWN

Jeannette and Anthony Goodrich's 14th-century pub-with-rooms, with 'friendly staff' and 'fantastic food', continues to earn high praise from readers. Mark Anderson has taken over the kitchen where he teams pub classics with more exotic dishes – beer-battered haddock and chunky chips, for example, sits alongside sweet potato and chickpea harissa stew. Food is fresh and seasonal, with fish sourced from Brancaster and game from local estates. The big breakfast, whether it is a fry-up, porridge or kippers, will keep you fuelled for the day. The interiors have been refreshed: the two ground-floor bedrooms updated and some subtle improvements made to the bar. The overall feel is still rural and unpretentious, however – the Goodriches pride themselves on not using interior designers. The simple, stylish bedrooms, decorated in fresh, coastal colours, are 'comfortable', well supplied with treats: home-made biscuits, a welcome bag for dogs, toys, books and Jeannette's 'superb' guide to the local area. Expect 'bags of character' in a village setting, a couple of miles from the sea. (SJ, and others)

Old Church Road
Snettisham PE31 7LX

T: 01485 541382
E: info@roseandcrownsnettisham.co.uk
W: roseandcrownsnettisham.co.uk

BEDROOMS: 16. 2 on ground floor, 1 suitable for disabled.
OPEN: all year
FACILITIES: 3 bar areas, 2 restaurant rooms, garden room, in-room TV (Freeview), large walled garden (children's play area, climbing frame).
BACKGROUND MUSIC: low-key, mainly soft jazz in dining areas.
LOCATION: in village centre, 5 miles S of Hunstanton.
CHILDREN: all ages welcomed.
DOGS: well-behaved dogs allowed in bedrooms, bars and garden room, not in dining areas.
CREDIT CARDS: Amex, MC, Visa.
PRICES: per room B&B single £100, double £120. À la carte £35.

## SOMERTON Somerset

### THE LYNCH COUNTRY HOUSE

Crowned with a belvedere, jazz musician Roy Copeland's creeper-covered Georgian house stands in a lush, secluded spot on the edge of a market town. Two thousand trees planted 20 years ago now form woodland in grounds with a lake on which black swans glide. There are four ground-floor bedrooms in the coach house. In the main house, Kendal, under the eaves, with a double and single bed plus a campaign couch, would suit a family on manoeuvres. It has a private bathroom across the landing. Pretty in pink, Goldington has an antique oak four-poster. There is nothing slick or state of the art here; just period furniture, floral fabrics, a grand piano, and jazz memorabilia from the days when Roy Copeland played saxophone. Lynne Vincent is the 'welcoming hostess'. Breakfast, served in the lovely orangery, brings freshly squeezed orange juice, Ferme des Peupliers yogurts, Wiltshire dry-cured bacon, Irish black and white puddings, and sausages of which, they say, food writer Tom Parker Bowles speaks highly. They don't serve an evening meal but trusted readers say the food at The White Hart down the road is 'excellent' (see Shortlist).

4 Behind Berry
Somerton TA11 7PD

T: 01458 272316
E: enquiries@thelynchcountryhouse.co.uk
W: thelynchcountryhouse.co.uk

BEDROOMS: 9. 4, in coach house, on ground floor.
OPEN: all year, only coach house rooms at Christmas and New Year, no breakfast 25/26 Dec, 1 Jan.
FACILITIES: breakfast room, small sitting area, in-room TV (Freeview), ¾-acre grounds (lake), unsuitable for disabled.
BACKGROUND MUSIC: none.
LOCATION: edge of town.
CHILDREN: all ages welcomed.
DOGS: allowed (not unattended) in 1 coach house room, not in public rooms.
CREDIT CARDS: Amex, MC, Visa.
PRICES: per room B&B single £70–£95, double £80–£125, children sharing parents' room £20–£35.

**SEE ALSO SHORTLIST**

# SOUTH BRENT Devon

MAP 1:D4

## GLAZEBROOK HOUSE

Calloo! Callay! On the fringe of Dartmoor national park, this Alice-themed hotel is a veritable cabinet of curiosities, a treasure trove of wit and invention. Owners Fran and Pieter Hamman have, say Guide colleagues, 'achieved an amazing amount' since 2013 when they set about transforming the Georgian property into a simulacrum of a 19th-century collector's mansion. Public spaces include a cigar-smoking room dedicated to Churchill, where wine tastings are held. The highly individual bedrooms have handmade furniture and a luxury bathroom with 3D-effect marble tiles. Jabberwocky features mirrors fashioned from brushed-steel aircraft engines above the bed. In Tweedle Deez, with twin four-posters, a boxing glove recalls the pugilistic pair. Cheshire Cat, with illuminated coffee table and a shower for two, should make guests grin from ear to ear. In the restaurant, chefs Ben Palmer and Josh Ackland use seasonal ingredients 'all sourced within a 50-mile radius' to create classic dishes with a modern twist. 'Attentive service' at Sunday lunch accompanied 'a hefty beef roast' and locally landed fish on orzo. Reports, please.

Glazebrook
South Brent
Totnes TQ10 9JE

T: 01364 73322
E: enquiries@glazebrookhouse.com
W: glazebrookhouse.com

BEDROOMS: 9. 1, on ground floor, suitable for disabled.
OPEN: all year.
FACILITIES: reception lobby, drawing room, bar/library, whisky/gin tasting room, restaurant, Chef's Kitchen patio, in-room TV (Freeview), civil wedding licence, 3½-acre garden, parking, public rooms wheelchair accessible, adapted toilet.
BACKGROUND MUSIC: in public areas, not library or tasting room.
LOCATION: 1 mile SW of town centre.
CHILDREN: over-16s welcomed, children over 5 in restaurant only.
DOGS: not allowed.
CREDIT CARDS: Amex, MC, Visa.
PRICES: per room B&B single £164–£234, double £199–£324. À la carte £40, tasting menus (whole table only) 6/8 courses £55/£65.

# SOUTH DALTON Yorkshire

MAP 4:D5

## THE PIPE AND GLASS INN

♀ Previous César winner

A picture-perfect village inn, with Michelin-starred food plus indulgent bedrooms, keeps customers old and new more than happy. 'Brilliant, my favourite hotel.' 'My father is convinced it was one of the best meals he's had,' say readers. First impressions are of a charming yet modest coaching inn in an 'enchantingly beautiful estate village'. But James and Kate Mackenzie have blended a traditional bar – beams, exposed-brick, gleaming copper – with an elegant dining room overlooking a garden with quirky sculpture, arbours, herbarium and kitchen produce. Bedrooms – five overlook the garden, four are a five-minute walk away – have striking wallpapers, velvet-covered armchairs, sleigh or four-poster bed, and glamorous touches of red, black and silver in the decor. 'Spectacular' bathrooms have under-floor heating and twin basins; most have bath and shower. But 'the real draw' is James's cooking which is creative yet unpretentious: wild rabbit with black pudding and white-bean crumble, or halibut with cauliflower champ. 'Everything was perfect' including the 'delicious puddings'. (Sue and John Jenkinson, PA)

West End
South Dalton HU17 7PN

T: 01430 810246
E: email@pipeandglass.co.uk
W: pipeandglass.co.uk

BEDROOMS: 9. 5 in main building, 4 in converted buildings, all on ground floor, 1 suitable for disabled.
OPEN: all year except 2 weeks in Jan, no room reservations Sun and Mon.
FACILITIES: lounge, conservatory, bar, restaurant, private dining room, in-room TV (Freeview), patio (alfresco dining), garden (herbarium, kitchen garden), public rooms wheelchair accessible, adapted toilet.
BACKGROUND MUSIC: in bar and restaurant.
LOCATION: 7 miles NW of Beverley.
CHILDREN: all ages welcomed, children's menu.
DOGS: not allowed.
CREDIT CARDS: Amex, MC, Visa.
PRICES: per room B&B single £170–£220, double £200–£270. À la carte £50. Dinner usually required as part of booking.

# SOUTH LEIGH Oxfordshire                    MAP 3:E6

## ARTIST RESIDENCE OXFORDSHIRE

On the outside, it looks like a chocolate box stone thatched pub, but that belies the funky interior of this Cotswold outpost of Justin and Charlotte Salisbury's portfolio of Artist Residence properties in Brighton and London (see main entries) and Penzance (see Shortlist entry). An original fireplace with flagstone floors is complemented by bold neon art and William Morris-influenced wallpaper. A previous landlord banned 'children, mobile telephones, restaurant critics' and, it is said, vegetarians. Now, come one, come all. Food, from local farms and the kitchen garden, is served all day in a beamed bar, as well as the restaurant. There are snacks and pub classics – perhaps Gloucestershire Old Spot pork chops, Bibury rainbow trout or, for vegans, charred brassica with parsley root and herb dumpling. Rustic-chic bedrooms, some in outbuildings and a shepherd's hut, have vintage and upcycled furniture, a Roberts radio, coffee machine and Bramley toiletries. The Stables Suite, with pitched roof, super-king-size bed and in-room roll-top bath, has a log-burner and private terrace. Look in for a pint as Dylan Thomas used to do when he lived at the Manor House while writing Under Milk Wood.

Station Road
South Leigh OX29 6XN

T: 01993 656220
E: oxford@artistresidence.co.uk
W: artistresidenceoxford.co.uk

BEDROOMS: 9. 1 bedroom and 2 suites in outbuildings, Shepherd's Hut in garden.
OPEN: all year.
FACILITIES: bar, restaurant (2 dining areas, closed Sun eve), in-room TV (Freeview), large beer garden, unsuitable for disabled.
BACKGROUND MUSIC: in pub and restaurant.
LOCATION: countryside, 10 miles from Oxford, 3 miles from Witney centre.
CHILDREN: all ages welcomed.
DOGS: allowed in some rooms and public rooms (£20 per dog per night, dog beds provided).
CREDIT CARDS: Amex, MC, Visa.
PRICES: room only £135–£425. Breakfast full English £13, à la carte £28. Min. 2-night stay at weekends.

# SOUTHAMPTON Hampshire

MAP 2:E2

## THE PIG IN THE WALL

The endearing little piglet of Robin Hutson's Pig
collection occupies a crenellated Georgian house
set into the medieval city wall. Unlike its bigger
country cousin Pigs (see index), it has no kitchen
garden, no restaurant, and there is no hamming
it up with huts and hideaways – all bedrooms, in
the trademark shabby-chic style, are under one
roof, each with a larder of locally sourced snacks
to buy. They range from snug, under the eaves,
to spacious, with stand-alone roll-top bath and
walk-in monsoon shower. A ground-floor room
has a wet room and wheelchair access from the
car park. The lounge/bar/drop-in deli has squashy
leather armchairs, bare floorboards, a dresser
of vintage china, and pot herbs on scrubbed
wooden tables. Food is served from midday till
8 pm, drinks till 10.30 pm. Choices include meat
and cheese boards, salads, smoked haddock,
sausage and mash with onion gravy and greens,
spinach and ricotta ravioli, and chorizo, chickpea
and spinach stew. The Mayflower Theatre and
ferries to the Isle of Wight are a stroll away,
while Big Mama Pig, aka The Pig in the Forest,
Brockenhurst (see entry), is a half-hour drive away,

8 Western Esplanade
Southampton SO14 2AZ

T: 02380 636900
E: info@thepighotel.com
W: thepighotel.com

BEDROOMS: 12. 2 on ground floor,
1 with wet room and wheelchair
access via side door from car park.
OPEN: all year.
FACILITIES: open-plan lounge/bar/
deli counter, in-room TV (Freeview),
car park (£10 a night), public rooms
wheelchair accessible.
BACKGROUND MUSIC: in public areas.
LOCATION: close to city centre.
CHILDREN: all ages welcomed.
DOGS: not allowed.
CREDIT CARDS: Amex, MC, Visa.
PRICES: room only £140–£195.
Breakfast continental £12, cooked £16.

**SEE ALSO SHORTLIST**

# SOUTHROP Gloucestershire

MAP 2:C2

## THYME

`NEW`

A 'beautifully manicured estate which fits its billing as a village within a village', Thyme is a collection of Cotswold stone buildings with a cookery school, pub and spa interspersed with 'perfect English country gardens'. Guide inspectors loved the 'impeccable design', the hotel 'priding itself on bringing the outside in', with botanical images designed by owner Caryn Hibbert. It's farm-themed: former lambing sheds are now the cool Baa bar with life-size sheep seats. A shop is in the old piggery, the restaurant in the enormous but 'surprisingly intimate' beamed Ox Barn, with open kitchen. Here, Caryn's son Charlie creates seasonal dishes, with 'delicious bread and butter, both made on the premises'. While our inspectors' roast chicken with barley and cèpe 'was perfectly cooked', there 'isn't a huge choice'; another reader was 'disappointed that the food wasn't tastier' given the 'farm-to-fork mentality'. Country-chic rooms, in the main building and scattered around the grounds, each have 'their own style and charm' with 'nice touches – we had a complimentary decanter of home-made vermouth'. (Susan Grossman, JK, and others)

Southrop Manor Estate
Southrop
Lechlade GL7 3NX

**T:** 01367 850174
**E:** info@thyme.co.uk
**W:** thyme.co.uk

**BEDROOMS:** 32. 8 in main building, others in a lodge, garden annexe and cottages.
**OPEN:** all year, restaurant closed Sun evening–Wed lunch, pub open all week.
**FACILITIES:** drawing room, cocktail bar, restaurant, pub, in-room TV (Freeview), civil wedding licence, event space, 150-acre estate (farm, gardens, swimming pool, spa), unsuitable for disabled.
**BACKGROUND MUSIC:** in public spaces.
**LOCATION:** on large Cotswold estate N of Lechlade.
**CHILDREN:** not under 12, except for 1 cottage, younger children allowed in Ox Barn at lunchtime.
**DOGS:** only in 1 cottage, pub.
**CREDIT CARDS:** Amex, MC, Visa.
**PRICES:** per room B&B £355–£1,500. À la carte £45. 1-night bookings refused bank holiday weekends.

# STAMFORD Lincolnshire

MAP 2:B3

## THE GEORGE OF STAMFORD

Behind a Georgian facade, Lawrence Hoskins's rambling coaching inn, with beams, wood panelling and 'elegant period windows', embodies the remains of far older buildings. 'Do not go if you're looking for anything crisp, contemporary or linear,' says a reader, who relishes the inn's 'warmly welcoming, historical embrace'. From a standard room with handmade bed and contemporary furnishings to a four-poster suite with lattice window and stone fireplace, each bedroom is different. 'We had an excellent panelled room. Sheets and blankets (hurrah!) and a good bathroom,' another reader writes. When yet another complained about a lack of storage, a chest of drawers promptly arrived. Men don a jacket to dine in the Oak Room, where Mark Alsop, now promoted to chef, cooks classics and more innovative dishes. Maybe 'tempura king prawns then the best calf's liver I've had for many years'. There is more bistro-style fare in the Garden Room. You can eat in the lovely courtyard or try 'a fine-quality cheese and ham toastie' in the bar. The whole George experience 'feels like entering an older, more reliable world'. (John Barnes, IB, and others)

71 St Martins
Stamford PE9 2LB

T: 01780 750750
E: reservations@
   georgehotelofstamford.com
W: georgehotelofstamford.com

BEDROOMS: 45.
OPEN: all year.
FACILITIES: 2 lounges, 2 bars, 2 restaurants, 3 private dining rooms, business centre, in-room TV (Sky, Freeview), civil wedding licence, 2-acre grounds (courtyard, gardens), public rooms wheelchair accessible, adapted toilet.
BACKGROUND MUSIC: none.
LOCATION: ¼ mile from centre.
CHILDREN: all ages welcomed.
DOGS: allowed, not unattended in bedrooms, only guide dogs in restaurants.
CREDIT CARDS: Amex, MC, Visa.
PRICES: per room B&B single £165–£185, double £235–£400. À la carte £75 (Oak Room). 1-night bookings refused during Burghley Horse Trials.

# STANTON HARCOURT Oxfordshire          MAP 2:C2

## THE HARCOURT ARMS  `NEW`

The traditional village pub has been totally
reinvented in Witney to include not just a
restaurant and rooms, but also an upmarket deli.
Partners Alan Gleeson and Olivier Bonte wanted
to create the ultimate pub experience, and they
'do succeed' according to our inspectors. They
were 'greeted in a friendly fashion as soon as we
walked through the door', were checked in by one
of the owners, helped with luggage and shown
to a room in a 'sympathetic' extension. It had
'tweedy, heavily lined curtains, matched with an
armchair and mismatched with floral fabric on
a high, shaped headboard, fresh milk, chocolate
chip biscuits'. Wood-grain tiles in the bathroom
brought to mind a sauna cabin. 'The wet-room
shower worked well.' All rooms have a Hypnos
mattress; Blenheim, with original beams and a
four-poster, is the best. The atmospheric dining
room with wooden tables is 'topped by beams and
bottomed by old rugs on flagstones'. The menu
runs from pub staples to 'more sophisticated
dishes'. Twice-baked soufflé and blue cheese
sauce were 'perfect in piquancy'. Praise, too, for
Cornbury Park venison. Verdict: 'Early days
and all lovely.'

### 25% DISCOUNT VOUCHERS

Stanton Harcourt
Witney OX29 5RJ

T: 01865 416516
E: hello@theharcourtarms.com
W: theharcourtarms.com

BEDROOMS: 10. 1 garden room across
small rear courtyard suitable for
disabled.
OPEN: all year, kitchen closed Sun
evening.
FACILITIES: snug bar, dining bar,
restaurant, ½-acre garden, in-room
TV (Freeview), all ground floor
wheelchair accessible from parking
bays to rear, adapted toilet.
BACKGROUND MUSIC: in all public areas.
LOCATION: 6 miles SE of Witney,
4 miles SW of Eynsham.
CHILDREN: all ages welcomed.
DOGS: allowed in bar only.
CREDIT CARDS: Amex, MC, Visa.
PRICES: per room B&B (with
continental breakfast) £129–£359,
D,B&B £169–£399. À la carte £30,
breakfast charged per item, full
English £14.

# STANTON WICK Somerset

MAP 1:B6

## THE CARPENTERS ARMS

A dazzling array of hanging baskets bedecks this friendly pub-with-rooms, occupying three former miners' cottages in a Chew valley hamlet. 'It is well placed between the very no-frills and very frilly sections of the market,' write discerning readers. Part of the small Buccaneer group, it has been run by Simon Pledge for more than 20 years, with 'a good team of welcoming, smiling and well-trained staff'. There are picnic tables to the fore and a furnished patio at the side for summer drinking and dining, while a log-burner warms a bar with beams, bare-stone walls and abundant comfy seating. Bedrooms have a walk-in shower or a power shower over a bath. 'We had an airy, spacious room overlooking the rear car park. Decor was modern with some fun modern prints' and a profusion of cushions. You can eat in dining rooms, bar or alfresco. Christian Wragg's menus range from pub classics to dishes such as orange-glazed confit duck, prawn-crusted Brixham cod with mussels and wild mushroom pasta, and vegan curry. 'Breakfast was excellent' and radio blether was silenced on request. (Sue and John Jenkinson)

Wick Lane
Stanton Wick
Pensford BS39 4BX

T: 01761 490202
E: carpenters@buccaneer.co.uk
W: the-carpenters-arms.co.uk

BEDROOMS: 13.
OPEN: all year except evenings 25/26 Dec, 1 Jan.
FACILITIES: bar, snug, lounge, 2 restaurants, function room, in-room TV (Freeview), patio, secure parking, public areas wheelchair accessible, adapted toilet.
BACKGROUND MUSIC: in some areas.
LOCATION: 8 miles S of Bristol, 8 miles W of Bath.
CHILDREN: all ages welcomed (under-12s stay free, children's menu, high chairs, changing facilities available).
DOGS: allowed in bar, snug and outside areas.
CREDIT CARDS: Amex, MC, Visa.
PRICES: per room B&B single £85–£90, double £130–£140, D,B&B single £112.50–£115, double £185–£190. À la carte £37.

# STUDLAND Dorset

MAP 2:E2

## THE PIG ON THE BEACH

🏆 Previous César winner

A higgledy-piggledy 19th-century marine villa with a jumble of towers and gables gazes across Studland Bay to the chalk stacks of Old Harry Rocks. A kind of Pigwarts, it is a magical addition to Robin Hutson's Pig hotel collection (see index), cleverly styled by Judy Hutson. Her beautifully mismatched interiors contain a 17th-century Portuguese woodcut here, a red brocade lamp there. Bedrooms, with maybe a chandelier, bare floorboards and soft paint finishes, range from snug, with countryside views, to spacious, with in-room roll-top bath, monsoon shower room and sea view. More fanciful are shepherds' huts at the bottom of the garden, and thatched dovecotes in the kitchen garden, which is the lifeblood of the place. You can sink into a comfy sofa by a blazing fire, eat flatbreads from a wood-fired oven in the sunshine, or dine in the sea-view conservatory with wooden tables and potted herbs ('very informal, no two chairs alike'). The locally sourced food includes such dishes as Cornish sardines, with Isle of Wight tomatoes and garden monk's beard, or pork loin from the hotel's Saddlebacks. A path leads down to the beach.

Manor House
Manor Road
Studland BH19 3AU

T: 01929 450288
E: info@thepighotel.com
W: thepighotel.com

BEDROOMS: 23. Some on ground floor, 2 dovecot hideaways, Harry's Hut and Pig Hut in grounds, 1 suitable for disabled.
OPEN: all year.
FACILITIES: bar, lounge, snug, restaurant, private dining room, in-room TV (Freeview), civil wedding licence, 2 treatment cabins, garden, ground-floor public rooms and part of gardens wheelchair accessible.
BACKGROUND MUSIC: all day in public areas.
LOCATION: above Studland beach.
CHILDREN: all ages welcomed.
DOGS: not allowed.
CREDIT CARDS: Amex, MC, Visa.
PRICES: room only £145–£389. Breakfast £12 (continental), £16 (cooked), à la carte £35. 1-night bookings refused weekends, Christmas, New Year.

# STURMINSTER NEWTON Dorset

## PLUMBER MANOR

Standing amid flower-filled gardens, with the Devilish stream skipping through, this dog-friendly, child-friendly Jacobean manor house is traditional with a capital T. It is a family affair, having been in the same family since it was built; today it is run by Alison and Richard Prideaux-Brune, with Richard's brother Brian in the kitchen alongside chef Louis Haskell. Antique-filled rooms have a timeless air that cuts both ways. 'It does not seem to have changed since the 1980s, and many of the clientele are delighted with that,' write readers. Some who felt that it was looking too dated should rejoice that they have been refurbishing: the courtyard annexe bathrooms have been upgraded, and we hope now never to hear the word 'avocado' except in a culinary context. 'A jolly lady behind the bar served G&Ts with gusto' while, in the dining room, 'Richard was very friendly, talking tennis and golf, and checking that everyone was enjoying dinner'. The nightly-changing menu comprises 'very good if old-fashioned' dishes from, say, chicken liver pâté to a trolley of desserts, by way of fillet of beef ('really enjoyed').

**25% DISCOUNT VOUCHERS**

Sturminster Newton DT10 2AF

T: 01258 472507
E: book@plumbermanor.com
W: plumbermanor.com

BEDROOMS: 16. 10 on ground floor in courtyard, 2 suitable for disabled.
OPEN: all year except Feb.
FACILITIES: snug, bar/lounge, dining room, gallery, in-room TV (Freeview), 14-acre grounds (3-acre garden, tennis, croquet, stream), restaurant, lounge and toilet wheelchair accessible.
BACKGROUND MUSIC: none.
LOCATION: 2½ miles SW of Sturminster Newton.
CHILDREN: all ages welcomed (cots, high chairs and children's menus available).
DOGS: allowed in 4 courtyard bedrooms, not in main house.
CREDIT CARDS: Amex, MC, Visa.
PRICES: per room B&B single £120–£150, double £170–£250. Set dinner £33–£40.

# SWAFFHAM Norfolk                                     MAP 2:B5

## STRATTONS

Walk up a narrow lane between a kebab shop
and a barber's in this market town, on a sunny
afternoon, and you may be surprised to find
people enjoying tea on the lawn in front of a
Palladian villa. Strattons is full of surprises,
combining a hotel with a deli, restaurant and
housewares shop. 'The hotel has charm.' The
outré tastes of owners Les and Vanessa Scott are
everywhere in evidence. Your bedroom might
have a Jacobean four-poster, a freestanding
copper bath, a jungle mural or mermaid mosaic, a
chandelier or bowler-hat lampshades. Breakfast,
including home-made sausages, kedgeree and
'perfect' poached eggs, is served in CoCoes deli,
'an accomplished place with a happy, bustly
feeling' at the hotel gate. Throughout the
day there are quiches, tapas, legendarily good
fishcakes, 'generous' salads and home-baked
cakes. New this year is Afterfive restaurant,
launched by Vanessa Scott with chef Julia
Heatherton, drawing on local specialist suppliers
for such dishes as kiln-roast salmon risotto, ox
cheek with bacon and sage, or 'mega salad'. Take
care when you sit down in the lounge lest you
extinguish one of the house cats.

4 Ash Close
Swaffham PE37 7NH

T: 01760 723845
E: enquiries@strattonshotel.com
W: strattonshotel.com

BEDROOMS: 14. 6 in annexes, 1 on
ground floor (via entrance steps).
OPEN: all year except 1 week at
Christmas.
FACILITIES: drawing room, reading
room, restaurant, in-room TV
(Freeview), terrace, café/deli, 1-acre
garden, café wheelchair accessible.
BACKGROUND MUSIC: all day in public
areas.
LOCATION: central, parking.
CHILDREN: all ages welcomed.
DOGS: allowed in some bedrooms (£10
per day), lounges, not in restaurant.
CREDIT CARDS: Amex, MC, Visa.
PRICES: per room B&B single £99–£234,
double £159–£256. À la carte £30.
1-night bookings refused weekends,
3-night min. bank holidays.

# TALLAND-BY-LOOE Cornwall

MAP 1:D3

## TALLAND BAY HOTEL

It feels a bit as if you've fallen down Alice's rabbit hole, at this whimsical, dog-friendly hotel with a 'spectacular bay setting' by the Coast Path. In the cliff-top gardens, you might come across a fairy statue or a bench backed with a line of wooden budgies; within, it's all zebra-print sofas and a cheery grandfather clock waving to guests. 'The artwork is sometimes witty, sometimes kitsch,' comments one reader. While it is a fun place, owners Teresa and Kevin O'Sullivan are serious about hospitality. 'It is what a good hotel should be,' writes a reader who found the hotel much improved on a return visit. 'Service is excellent – they've got it just right.' Bedrooms are light and airy with, maybe, a four-poster with diaphanous drapes, and a private terrace; some have a sea view, while others are in the garden annexe. 'The room was comfortable, the food was good.' In the restaurant and conservatory brasserie Nick Hawke's locally sourced menus include a Cornish pork plate, and fresh fish and shellfish. 'Delicious nibbles in the bar set the scene for locally caught fresh haddock and chips, a dream to eat.' (Mike Craddock, and others)

Porthallow
Talland-by-Looe PL13 2JB

T: 01503 272667
E: info@tallandbayhotel.com
W: tallandbayhotel.co.uk

BEDROOMS: 23. 4 in cottages, 6 on ground floor.
OPEN: all year.
FACILITIES: lounge, bar, restaurant, brasserie/conservatory, in-room TV (Freeview), civil wedding licence, terrace, outside seating, 2-acre garden, public rooms wheelchair accessible.
BACKGROUND MUSIC: in bar and restaurant.
LOCATION: 2½ miles SW of Looe.
CHILDREN: all ages welcomed.
DOGS: in bedrooms and brasserie, not in restaurant (£15 per dog per night includes blanket, feeding mat, bowl and treats).
CREDIT CARDS: Amex, MC, Visa.
PRICES: per room B&B £130–£350, D,B&B £260–£450. À la carte £45–£55, tasting menu on request. 1-night bookings refused weekends in peak season.

# TAPLOW Berkshire                                    MAP 2:D3

## CLIVEDEN HOUSE

As you approach this glorious Italianate Thames-side summer palace designed by Charles Barry and set in 376 acres of National Trust grounds, it 'feels as if you are on the film set of Pride and Prejudice', says a Guide insider (see also Chewton Glen, New Milton). Cliveden exudes 'history in every corner, from ornate fireplaces and suits of armour, to the spectacular carved staircase'. Bedrooms, named after famous past guests, are filled with antiques. 'Buckingham, with its oak-panelled walls and fireplace, and views over the parterre to the Thames, has a bathroom that could hold a rugby team, with Carrara-marble screens behind the bath and basins.' Even Kipling, the smallest, 'has an impressive stucco ceiling'. Paul O'Neill's fine-dining menus include such dishes as roasted cod loin with crab 'lasagne', fennel and apple, and separate menus for children, vegetarians and vegans. The dining room, with its white linen and chandeliers, 'feels a little overly formal; I preferred the relaxed Astor Grill in the former stables, now beautifully done out with blue banquettes'. (JK)

Cliveden Road
Taplow SL6 0JF

T: 01628 668561
E: reservations@clivedenhouse.co.uk
W: clivedenhouse.co.uk

BEDROOMS: 47. Some on ground floor, 1 suitable for disabled.
OPEN: all year.
FACILITIES: Great Hall, bar/lounge, library, 2 restaurants, private dining rooms, in-room TV (Freeview), civil wedding licence, spa, swimming pools, 376-acre National Trust estate, public areas wheelchair accessible.
BACKGROUND MUSIC: all day in public areas.
LOCATION: 20 mins from Heathrow, 40 mins central London.
CHILDREN: all ages welcomed.
DOGS: allowed in bedrooms, public areas (excl. 1 restaurant, spa, parts of garden).
CREDIT CARDS: Amex, MC, Visa.
PRICES: per room B&B £495–£1,635, D,B&B £615–£1,755. Tasting menu £97.50, à la carte £73. 1-night bookings sometimes refused.

# TAVISTOCK Devon

MAP 1:D4

## THE HORN OF PLENTY

It's all about the views at this former 19th-century mine captain's house turned dog-friendly hotel on a hillside on the Devon/Cornwall border. The restaurant, the Italianate patio and many of the bedrooms look over five acres of gardens and the Tamar valley and beyond, to Bodmin Moor. 'Our room took full advantage of the glorious views,' relates one trusted reader. 'The setting feels very far from the madding crowd,' writes another. Inside, it's a mix of contemporary and traditional, depending whether your room is in the main house, newly built annexe or coach house where 'decor is distinctive, perhaps a little dated but all in excellent condition'. In the dining room, Ashley Wright's locally sourced dishes might be 'a bit overwrought' for some, and the approach to vegetables 'a bit nouvelle', but a regular visitor found that it 'had improved enormously, with healthy portion sizes; quality remains of the highest standard'. 'Breakfast at a window table is a delightful experience on a fine spring day.' 'The place is very well run.' (Peter Anderson, Lindsay Hunt)

Gulworthy
Tavistock PL19 8JD

T: 01822 832528
E: enquiries@thehornofplenty.co.uk
W: thehornofplenty.co.uk

**BEDROOMS:** 16. 12 in old and new coach houses (1–2 mins' walk), 7 on ground floor, 1 suitable for disabled.
**OPEN:** all year.
**FACILITIES:** lounge/bar, library, drawing room, restaurant, in-room TV (Freeview), civil wedding licence, 5-acre grounds, ground-floor public areas wheelchair accessible.
**BACKGROUND MUSIC:** occasional background music in restaurant only, 'when it's quiet'.
**LOCATION:** 3 miles SW of Tavistock.
**CHILDREN:** all ages welcomed.
**DOGS:** allowed in 12 bedrooms and library, not in restaurant or drawing room (£10 per dog per night).
**CREDIT CARDS:** MC, Visa.
**PRICES:** per room B&B single £120–£255, double £130–£295, D,B&B £215–£380. Dinner £53, tasting menu £70.

**SEE ALSO SHORTLIST**

# TEFFONT EVIAS Wiltshire

MAP 2:D1

## HOWARD'S HOUSE

This peaceful small hotel and popular restaurant in a romantic Jacobean former dower house, surrounded by country gardens, continues to delight readers. Across a quiet road, the Teffont Brook rushes by to join the River Nadder (catch a trout, and they will smoke or cure it for you). Chef Andy Britton can often be seen feeding the Legbar hens in the kitchen garden, or picking ingredients for menus that he devises with manager Simon Greenwood, one of the four owners. Specialities include game in season (maybe roast loin of venison with venison jus and chocolate oil). 'The food was ridiculously good for the price, with extras of amuse-bouche and a divine soup taster,' a reader tells us. Bedrooms, one with a four-poster, have an understated country house look. A superior room has a super-king-size bed, a seating area, coffee machine and REN toiletries. 'At night, with windows wide open, there was complete silence – wonderful.' There are 'plenty of comfy sitting areas', with open fire, and 'a lovely terrace for afternoon tea'. Another reader praises 'a delightful welcome, fine meal and excellent breakfast'. (Stuart Smith, CH)

**25% DISCOUNT VOUCHERS**

Teffont Evias
Salisbury SP3 5RJ

T: 01722 716392
E: enq@howardshousehotel.co.uk
W: howardshousehotel.co.uk

BEDROOMS: 9.
OPEN: all year except 23–27 Dec.
FACILITIES: lounge, snug, restaurant, function facilities in coach house, in-room TV (Freeview), 2-acre grounds, coach house (private function room) wheelchair accessible, adapted toilet.
BACKGROUND MUSIC: in dining room.
LOCATION: 10 miles W of Salisbury.
CHILDREN: all ages welcomed (cot, high chair).
DOGS: allowed in bedrooms (£15 charge), in public rooms except restaurant.
CREDIT CARDS: Amex, MC, Visa.
PRICES: per room B&B single £95–£120, double £150–£225, £35 for child sharing with parents. Tasting menu £80, à la carte £37–£46.50, seasonal menu £28–£33.50.

# TETBURY Gloucestershire

MAP 3:E5

## CALCOT & SPA

'We had a wonderful family holiday here. It was ideal for three generations,' writes one returning guest to this 16th-century manor house hotel, part of the Calcot Collection (see also Barnsley House, Barnsley; The Painswick, Painswick; and The Lord Crewe Arms, Blanchland). While adults steep in a hot tub in the spa courtyard, child's play is laid on in the Ofsted-registered crèche and kids' club. As well as a 12-seater cinema, there is a mini-football pitch and pirate play ship. The hotel has a 'modern, informal, country style' that is 'cosy and intimate'. Everything is easy on the eye and senses: oak and wood smoke and lavender, smart furniture, a palette of blues and milk and honey. Bedrooms, in the main house and outbuildings, which are 'grouped around attractive gardens', all have a coffee machine, mini-fridge, fresh fruit, shortbread, books and luxury toiletries. There is formal dining in The Conservatory, where menus include such dishes as Wiltshire lamb, lamb faggot, pearl barley and sand carrot. Simpler fare is served in The Gumstool Inn and alfresco. 'Little foodies' have their own menu. (Jane Bailey, and others)

Tetbury GL8 8YJ

T: 01666 890391
E: sally.barker@calcot.co
W: calcot.co

BEDROOMS: 35. 10 (for families) in cottage, 13 around courtyard, on ground floor, some suitable for disabled.
OPEN: all year.
FACILITIES: lounge, 2 bars, 2 restaurants, crèche, in-room TV (Sky, Freeview), civil wedding licence, 220-acre grounds (tennis, heated swimming pool), spa (with pool), public areas wheelchair accessible, adapted toilet.
BACKGROUND MUSIC: in restaurants.
LOCATION: 3 miles W of Tetbury.
CHILDREN: all ages welcomed.
DOGS: allowed in courtyard bedrooms, not in public rooms.
CREDIT CARDS: Amex, MC, Visa.
PRICES: per room B&B double £229–£424, D,B&B £309–£504. À la carte (Conservatory) £50, (Gumstool Inn) £35, market menu £25.

# TETBURY Gloucestershire

## THE HARE AND HOUNDS

On the doorstep of the Westonbirt Arboretum with 2,500 species of trees, and just round the corner from Highgrove, the Hare and Hounds sits in its own gardens and woodlands in a pretty corner of the Cotswolds. It has been bought from Cotswold Inns and Hotels by Fuller's (see also The Lamb Inn, Burford), but we don't expect any falling off in the standards of service and comfort that regular visitors praise. 'It provides all the requirements for a good hotel – exceptional staff, excellent service, delightful furnishings.' It has been furnished with flair, with bold colours and fabric headboards in the bedrooms, which are more traditional country house style in the Cotswold stone main building, with a contemporary feel in the coach house and in Silkwood Court, a short walk away. The Gamekeeper's Cottage even comes with its own secluded garden and hot tub. You can drink and eat in dog-friendly Jack Hare's bar (burger, fish and chips, pumpkin gnocchi, or dine in the Beaufort restaurant, on such dishes as loin of venison, suet pudding, mash, turnip and red cabbage, or pollock with bouillabaisse sauce.

Bath Road
Westonbirt
Tetbury GL8 8QL

T: 01666 881000
E: reception@hareandhoundshotel.com
W: cotswold-inns-hotels.co.uk

BEDROOMS: 42. 2 suitable for disabled, 3 in coach house, 5 in garden cottage, 12 in Silkwood Court, 1 in Gamekeeper's Cottage.
OPEN: all year.
FACILITIES: drawing room, lounges, library, bar, restaurant, private dining room, in-room TV (Freeview), civil wedding licence, gardens, woodland.
BACKGROUND MUSIC: in lounge and bar.
LOCATION: 3 miles SW of Tetbury.
CHILDREN: all ages welcomed.
DOGS: allowed by arrangement in some bedrooms, bar, garden, not in restaurant (£20 per dog).
CREDIT CARDS: Amex, MC, Visa.
PRICES: per room B&B single from £105, double £125–£305 (cottage), D,B&B £199–£379. À la carte £36.

# TETBURY Gloucestershire
MAP 3:E5

## THE ROYAL OAK

With a free jukebox, Art Deco piano, loyalty cards and children's menus, this dog-friendly 18th-century inn is truly a community hub. It's quirky, too: the bar is made from recycled church panelling and in the summer, a silver Airstream trailer dispenses garden food. The bedrooms, in a separate, 'beautifully restored' building, have a stripped-down chic, a walk-in or over-bath rain shower, and Bramley toiletries. 'We had a good-sized ground-floor room,' writes one reader after a return visit. 'If it was raining, a quick dash of a few steps would see you in the pub' with its beamed, wood-floored dining room. Here, Greek chef Stergios Pikos's short menus change seasonally and include such dishes as chickpea pancakes with lentil dhal, 'an expertly cooked steak', and sea bass. The last Monday of the month is meat-free. 'The vegetarian meal was delicious, and the strawberry patbingsu [a Korean dessert] was a highlight. A bargain at £16 per head.' The 'cheerful young staff' promote a happy atmosphere. At breakfast there are pastries from the local Hobbs House Bakery, and 'eggs Benedict were enjoyed'. (David Birnie)

1 Cirencester Road
Tetbury GL8 8EY

T: 01666 500021
E: stay@theroyaloaktetbury.co.uk
W: theroyaloaktetbury.co.uk

BEDROOMS: 6. 1 suitable for disabled.
OPEN: all year except 1 week Jan, kitchen closed Sun pm.
FACILITIES: bar, restaurant, private dining/meeting room, in-room TV (Freeview), large garden, boules, bicycle storage, bar and garden wheelchair accessible, adapted toilet.
BACKGROUND MUSIC: in bar and restaurant, free jukebox, monthly live music sessions.
LOCATION: a few mins' walk up the hill from the town centre.
CHILDREN: all ages welcomed.
DOGS: allowed throughout (no charge).
CREDIT CARDS: Amex, MC, Visa.
PRICES: per room B&B £90–£200.
À la carte £30. 1-night bookings usually refused Fri and Sat.

# THORPE MARKET Norfolk                    MAP 2:A5

## THE GUNTON ARMS

Ivor Braka has indulged his passion for art at
his pub-with-rooms set in a deer park near the
north Norfolk coast. Arriving on a blustery
day, our inspectors were blown away by Sol
LeWitt's white breeze-block pyramid sculpture,
which is 'beautiful to gaze at', or to graze at if
you are a deer. They received a warm welcome
and a guided tour. Fires blazed in 'two large,
comfortable lounges'. Works on display ranged
from Tracey Emin neons and Paula Rego prints to
tasteful oil portraits in keeping with the antique
furniture. Bedrooms (including one once used
by Lillie Langtry, with a slipper bath) have been
individually designed. 'Ours was large, with
views over the park from three front windows,
antique Anglepoise lamps, blankets, no duvet.'
Braka's partners, Simone and Stuart Tattersall,
are front-of-house and (Mark Hix-trained) chef
respectively. In three dining rooms, the menu
uses locally sourced produce in such dishes as crab
pasta and venison sausages. In the Elk Room,
adorned with massive elk antlers, steaks are
cooked over fire. It's mighty, meaty, raunchy, rock
and roll, and 'unique and fascinating'.

Cromer Road
Thorpe Market NR11 8TZ

T: 01263 832010
E: office@theguntonarms.co.uk
W: theguntonarms.co.uk

BEDROOMS: 16. 4 in coach house on
ground floor, 4 suites in converted
barn house, 1 suitable for disabled.
OPEN: all year except 25 Dec, half day
31 Dec.
FACILITIES: 3 restaurants, 3 lounges,
bar, TVs in bar and lounges, set in
privately owned 1,000-acre game
estate, public rooms wheelchair
accessible, adapted toilet.
BACKGROUND MUSIC: in bar area.
LOCATION: 5 miles from Cromer,
4 miles from North Walsham.
CHILDREN: all ages welcomed.
DOGS: allowed in 5 bedrooms, public
rooms, not in Elk Room.
CREDIT CARDS: Amex, MC, Visa.
PRICES: per room B&B single £85–£310,
double £95–£320. À la carte from £35.
Min. 2-night stays on Sat.

# TISBURY Wiltshire

## THE BECKFORD ARMS

With Beckford Phoenix ale on tap, 'top-quality' cooking, and bedrooms with Welsh blankets and seagrass floor covering, this sophisticated pub at the edge of the Fonthill Estate in the Nadder valley is the perfect synthesis of traditional and contemporary. It is a winning formula that owners Dan Brod and Charlie Luxton have since applied at The Talbot Inn, Mells, and The Lord Poulett Arms, Hinton St George (see entries). Our inspectors' large double had 'a freestanding bathtub with brass fittings, claw feet and a lovely view' towards the estate, a 'compact' shower room, hooks and wooden hangers but no wardrobe. Extras include fresh milk, chocolate cake, and an emergency kit with toothpaste and razor. Two adults-only lodges are a stroll away. New chef Richie Peacock uses local and home-grown ingredients in everything from pub classics such as pork pie with home-made chutney to day-boat fish and vegan dishes. The wine list is 'a delight', and guests can also stroll into the village to the owners' wine shop for a tasting, then get a lift back. Morning brings 'good croissants' and home-smoked salmon.

Fonthill Gifford
Tisbury SP3 6PX

T: 01747 870385
E: info@beckfordarms.com
W: beckfordarms.com

BEDROOMS: 10. 2 in lodges on the Fonthill Estate.
OPEN: all year except 25 Dec.
FACILITIES: sitting room (sometimes Sunday classic-movie nights), bar, restaurant, private dining room, in-room TV (Freeview), function facilities, 1-acre garden.
BACKGROUND MUSIC: in public areas all day.
LOCATION: in village, 1 mile N of Tisbury.
CHILDREN: all ages welcomed, no children in lodges.
DOGS: allowed in 1 bedroom and public areas.
CREDIT CARDS: MC, Visa.
PRICES: per room B&B £95–£130 (lodges £175–£195), D,B&B £150–£230. À la carte £40. 1-night bookings usually refused weekends.

**SEE ALSO SHORTLIST**

# TITCHWELL Norfolk

MAP 2:A5

## TITCHWELL MANOR

Twitchers are in their element at Titchwell, with an RSPB nature reserve just up the road – but so too are foodie couples, beach-seeking families and dogs, who can eat with their owners in the casual Eating Rooms. The former Victorian farmhouse, set a little back from the road, has views across fields and glistening marshes to the sea. Inside, there is a spirit of exuberance and some bold design, which you'll get a taste of if you have tea by the fire in the jazzy sitting room. Some bedrooms have stripes, florals, vintage furniture, perhaps a statement headboard, while others in annexes have a cool, pale coastal palette. The Potting Shed has a remote-controlled log-burner, and an in-room roll-top bath. Two signature rooms have a hot tub. In the conservatory, owner Eric Snaith and head chef Chris Mann use local and foraged ingredients in such dishes as brill, oyster and horseradish sauce, quail egg and baked potato mash. On their last visit, our inspectors were especially impressed by breakfast, with home-made granola, Dingley Dell sausages, and avocado on sourdough toast. 'We loved the thick yogurt with a tangy berry compote.'

**25% DISCOUNT VOUCHERS**

Titchwell
Brancaster PE31 8BB

T: 01485 210221
E: info@titchwellmanor.com
W: titchwellmanor.com

BEDROOMS: 26. 12 in herb garden, 3 in stables, 1 in Potting Shed, 18 on ground floor, 2 suitable for disabled.
OPEN: all year.
FACILITIES: lounge, bar, conservatory, restaurant, in-room TV (Freeview), civil wedding licence, in-room treatments, ¼-acre walled garden, public rooms wheelchair accessible, adapted toilet.
BACKGROUND MUSIC: in restaurant and bar.
LOCATION: off A149 between Burnham Market and Hunstanton.
CHILDREN: all ages welcomed.
DOGS: allowed in some rooms, bar, not lounge or restaurant (£15 per dog per night).
CREDIT CARDS: Amex, MC, Visa.
PRICES: per room B&B £140–£325. À la carte £42. 1-night bookings occasionally refused.

# TITLEY Herefordshire

MAP 3:C4

## THE STAGG INN

⚘ Previous César winner

At the meetings of two ancient drovers' roads, close to the Welsh border, Steve and Nicola Reynolds's rural village dining-pub-with-rooms has been a foodie destination for more than 20 years. Step inside and you will find a cosy local, its beams festooned with hops and novelty jugs. The menu is chalked up on a board with no pretension, although Steve's cooking, using local ingredients, is exemplary. Almost everything is made on the premises, including the crisps, served with vinegar foam. Typical dishes include Springfield chicken breast with coppa, Puy lentils and potato dauphinoise. There is a separate menu of vegan and vegetarian dishes, and one for kids. Breakfast is good, too: 'I love the home-made marmalade.' Bedrooms above the pub have character, but can be noisy on a big Stagg night. For quiet, go for one at the Georgian-cum-Victorian vicarage a quarter of a mile away, with a garden and croquet lawn. They are traditionally furnished in the style of a private home, and Winterton has an in-room slipper bath. All the rooms have fresh milk, ground coffee, and a minibar of drinks at pub prices.

**25% DISCOUNT VOUCHERS**

Titley
Kington HR5 3RL

T: 01544 230221
E: reservations@thestagg.co.uk
W: thestagg.co.uk

BEDROOMS: 6. 3 at The Vicarage (300 yds).
OPEN: all year except 24–26 Dec, 1 Jan, 1 week Jan/Feb, 1 week June, 2 weeks Nov, every Sun eve, Mon, Tues.
FACILITIES: sitting room (Vicarage), bar, dining room, small outside seating area (pub), in-room TV (Freeview), 1½-acre garden (Vicarage).
BACKGROUND MUSIC: none.
LOCATION: on B4355 between Kington and Presteigne.
CHILDREN: all ages welcomed.
DOGS: allowed in pub bedrooms, public rooms.
CREDIT CARDS: Amex, MC, Visa.
PRICES: per room B&B £100–£140. À la carte £37, vegetarian/vegan £27.50. 1-night bookings occasionally refused bank holiday weekends.

# TORQUAY Devon

MAP 1:D5

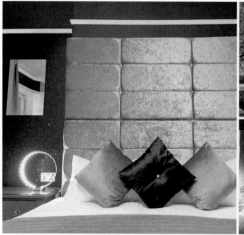

## THE 25 BOUTIQUE B&B  **NEW**

When readers tell us that Andy and Julian
Banner-Price's award-winning, adults-only
B&B would knock the spots off many a more
prestigious hotel, we take notice. Certainly it
deserves promotion to a full entry, for attention to
detail and sheer exuberance. A rainbow-striped
male mannequin floor lamp in reception sets the
tone. Among the 'unbelievably stylish' bedrooms,
ground-floor Torre has zebra stripes, Oddicombe
a giant gerbera mural, and Broadsands a slipper
bath and power shower. A fluffy swan in a
coronet, apparently named Simon, graces a wall
in the sitting room of newly revamped Shoalstone,
with its theatre lighting and huge rain shower
head. Extras include smart controls, mood
lighting, a coffee machine, a fridge, home-made
treats and Elemis toiletries. The comfy drawing
room surprises by being so in keeping with the
house's Edwardian origins. The hosts 'go out of
their way to be helpful'. Guests are plied with
cake on arrival, and the breakfast menu is 'worthy
of a five-star hotel', with free-range eggs, locally
farmed pork sausages, kippers, smoked salmon,
or the full Devon. Fawltless Towers.

## 25% DISCOUNT VOUCHERS

25 Avenue Road
Torquay TQ2 5LB

T: 01803 297517
E: stay@the25.uk
W: the25.uk

BEDROOMS: 6.
OPEN: Feb–end Oct.
FACILITIES: drawing room, dining
room, in-room smart TV (movies on
demand), patio, parking.
BACKGROUND MUSIC: at breakfast.
LOCATION: 5 mins' walk from the sea,
20 mins' walk from town.
CHILDREN: not under 17.
DOGS: not allowed.
CREDIT CARDS: Amex, MC, Visa.
PRICES: per room B&B single £99–£179,
double £129–£199. Min. stay of 2 or 3
nights may apply at certain times.

**SEE ALSO SHORTLIST**

# THE GOOD HOTEL GUIDE 2021

Use this voucher to claim a 25% discount off the normal price for bed and breakfast at hotels with a `25% DISCOUNT VOUCHERS` sign on the Guide entry. You must request a voucher discount at the time of booking and present this voucher on arrival. Further details and conditions overleaf. *Valid to 6th October 2021.*

**25%**
DISCOUNT
VOUCHER

---

# THE GOOD HOTEL GUIDE 2021

Use this voucher to claim a 25% discount off the normal price for bed and breakfast at hotels with a `25% DISCOUNT VOUCHERS` sign on the Guide entry. You must request a voucher discount at the time of booking and present this voucher on arrival. Further details and conditions overleaf. *Valid to 6th October 2021.*

**25%**
DISCOUNT
VOUCHER

---

# THE GOOD HOTEL GUIDE 2021

Use this voucher to claim a 25% discount off the normal price for bed and breakfast at hotels with a `25% DISCOUNT VOUCHERS` sign on the Guide entry. You must request a voucher discount at the time of booking and present this voucher on arrival. Further details and conditions overleaf. *Valid to 6th October 2021.*

**25%**
DISCOUNT
VOUCHER

---

# THE GOOD HOTEL GUIDE 2021

Use this voucher to claim a 25% discount off the normal price for bed and breakfast at hotels with a `25% DISCOUNT VOUCHERS` sign on the Guide entry. You must request a voucher discount at the time of booking and present this voucher on arrival. Further details and conditions overleaf. *Valid to 6th October 2021.*

**25%**
DISCOUNT
VOUCHER

---

# THE GOOD HOTEL GUIDE 2021

Use this voucher to claim a 25% discount off the normal price for bed and breakfast at hotels with a `25% DISCOUNT VOUCHERS` sign on the Guide entry. You must request a voucher discount at the time of booking and present this voucher on arrival. Further details and conditions overleaf. *Valid to 6th October 2021.*

**25%**
DISCOUNT
VOUCHER

---

# THE GOOD HOTEL GUIDE 2021

Use this voucher to claim a 25% discount off the normal price for bed and breakfast at hotels with a `25% DISCOUNT VOUCHERS` sign on the Guide entry. You must request a voucher discount at the time of booking and present this voucher on arrival. Further details and conditions overleaf. *Valid to 6th October 2021.*

**25%**
DISCOUNT
VOUCHER

**CONDITIONS**

1. Hotels with a **25% DISCOUNT VOUCHERS** sign have agreed to give readers a discount of 25% off their normal bed-and-breakfast rate.
2. One voucher is good for the first night's stay only, at the discounted rate for yourself alone or for you and a partner sharing a double room.
3. Voucher acceptance is subject to room availability. Hotels have discretion, and may decline to accept a voucher reservation if they expect to be busy at the full room price.
4. Hotels accepting 25% discount vouchers are correct at time of going to press. To confirm whether a hotel accepts 25% discount vouchers, see the hotel's entry on the Guide's website: **goodhotelguide.com**

**CONDITIONS**

1. Hotels with a **25% DISCOUNT VOUCHERS** sign have agreed to give readers a discount of 25% off their normal bed-and-breakfast rate.
2. One voucher is good for the first night's stay only, at the discounted rate for yourself alone or for you and a partner sharing a double room.
3. Voucher acceptance is subject to room availability. Hotels have discretion, and may decline to accept a voucher reservation if they expect to be busy at the full room price.
4. Hotels accepting 25% discount vouchers are correct at time of going to press. To confirm whether a hotel accepts 25% discount vouchers, see the hotel's entry on the Guide's website: **goodhotelguide.com**

**CONDITIONS**

1. Hotels with a **25% DISCOUNT VOUCHERS** sign have agreed to give readers a discount of 25% off their normal bed-and-breakfast rate.
2. One voucher is good for the first night's stay only, at the discounted rate for yourself alone or for you and a partner sharing a double room.
3. Voucher acceptance is subject to room availability. Hotels have discretion, and may decline to accept a voucher reservation if they expect to be busy at the full room price.
4. Hotels accepting 25% discount vouchers are correct at time of going to press. To confirm whether a hotel accepts 25% discount vouchers, see the hotel's entry on the Guide's website: **goodhotelguide.com**

**CONDITIONS**

1. Hotels with a **25% DISCOUNT VOUCHERS** sign have agreed to give readers a discount of 25% off their normal bed-and-breakfast rate.
2. One voucher is good for the first night's stay only, at the discounted rate for yourself alone or for you and a partner sharing a double room.
3. Voucher acceptance is subject to room availability. Hotels have discretion, and may decline to accept a voucher reservation if they expect to be busy at the full room price.
4. Hotels accepting 25% discount vouchers are correct at time of going to press. To confirm whether a hotel accepts 25% discount vouchers, see the hotel's entry on the Guide's website: **goodhotelguide.com**

**CONDITIONS**

1. Hotels with a **25% DISCOUNT VOUCHERS** sign have agreed to give readers a discount of 25% off their normal bed-and-breakfast rate.
2. One voucher is good for the first night's stay only, at the discounted rate for yourself alone or for you and a partner sharing a double room.
3. Voucher acceptance is subject to room availability. Hotels have discretion, and may decline to accept a voucher reservation if they expect to be busy at the full room price.
4. Hotels accepting 25% discount vouchers are correct at time of going to press. To confirm whether a hotel accepts 25% discount vouchers, see the hotel's entry on the Guide's website: **goodhotelguide.com**

# TUDDENHAM Suffolk

MAP 2:B5

## TUDDENHAM MILL

Swans glide, willows weep, and the great brick chimney no longer belches smoke at this 18th-century watermill, now a smart, modern hotel. The bar still features the waterwheel, the mill's gearing apparatus is on show in the beamed dining room, and some of the 'impressive' bedrooms have direct access to the millstream through fold-back glass doors. Most rooms, with Italian-designed furniture, a Philippe Starck bath, six-foot bed (no twins), home-baked cookies and fresh milk, are in separate annexes. Alternatively, two of the 'cute, hobbity huts', aka Meadow Nooks, 'in an idyllic setting', have a terrace with a hot tub. Readers found theirs 'immaculately clean and simple', and enjoyed 'a restful night's sleep'. There are light bites in the bar, but the big draw is the dining room where chef/patron Lee Bye keeps his nose to the grindstone, cooking creative dishes – maybe locally shot game, or bream with bouillabaisse and salsa verde. 'The restaurant deserves its reputation', and staff show an 'unforced generosity of spirit'. At breakfast there is 'good variety, with everything served at table'. (David Verney, and others)

High Street
Tuddenham
Newmarket IP28 6SQ

T: 01638 713552
E: info@tuddenhammill.co.uk
W: tuddenhammill.co.uk

BEDROOMS: 21. 18 in 2 separate buildings, 12 on ground floor, 6 in pods in meadow, 2 with hot tub, 1 suitable for disabled.
OPEN: all year.
FACILITIES: bar/snug, restaurant, function rooms, in-room TV (Freeview), civil wedding licence, treatment room, 12-acre meadow.
BACKGROUND MUSIC: in bar, reception and restaurant.
LOCATION: in village, 8 miles NE of Newmarket.
CHILDREN: all ages welcomed (kids' menu and half portions).
DOGS: allowed in some bedrooms (£25 a night), and in bar.
CREDIT CARDS: MC, Visa.
PRICES: per room B&B £195–£415, D,B&B £255–£475. À la carte £47, tasting menu £70. Min. 2-night stay at weekends.

# ULLSWATER Cumbria

MAP 4: inset C2

## HOWTOWN HOTEL

It's traditional with a capital T at the 'delightfully old-fashioned' Howtown, with dinner gong, no in-room TVs, and extremely limited Wi-Fi. Owned by the Baldry family for more than 120 years, this creeper-covered former farmhouse, in an enviable position on Ullswater, has a welcoming clutter of warming pans, Toby jugs and chintz. It is full of quirky charm, offering 'traditional high standards with a very personal touch'. Mrs Baldry's, no less. Large, comfortable bedrooms with no lock come with blankets, not duvets. In the bathroom is Imperial Leather soap; 'bring your own shampoo'. At the dinner gong, it's down to the cosy red-velvet and stained-glass bar before a four-course meal of 'excellent but never fancy' classic dishes such as Stilton soufflé and chateaubriand in red-wine sauce. The duck-egg-blue dining room is a treat of silver cutlery and polished-wood tables. Next morning, tea is brought to your room. 'A perfect base for a weekend, with walks from the door and a snug base to return to.' (Martin Bailey, and others)

Ullswater
Penrith CA10 2ND

T: 01768 486514
E: editor@goodhotelguide.com
W: howtown-hotel.com

BEDROOMS: 15. 2 in annexe, plus 4 self-catering cottages.
OPEN: 27 Mar–1 Nov.
FACILITIES: 3 lounges, TV room, 2 bars, dining room, tea room, Wi-Fi in cottages and tea room only, 2-acre grounds, 200 yds from lake (private foreshore, fishing), walking, sailing, climbing, riding, golf nearby, restaurant wheelchair accessible, toilet not adapted.
BACKGROUND MUSIC: none.
LOCATION: 4 miles S of Pooley Bridge, bus from Penrith station 9 miles.
CHILDREN: all ages welcomed.
DOGS: allowed in some bedrooms (£4 per night charge), not in public rooms.
CREDIT CARDS: MC, Visa.
PRICES: per person B&B £66–£83, D,B&B £105–£122. Dinner £39.

# UPPER SLAUGHTER Gloucestershire

## LORDS OF THE MANOR

⚜ Previous César winner

This 17th-century manor house of honeyed Cotswold stone looks every bit the smart country house hotel. Inside, all is relaxed and informal, with board games in the lounge and Hunter wellies by the entrance. It has been owned by the Munir family since the late 1990s. Passionate collectors, they have added artwork and decorative pieces to the interiors where traditional decor (button-back armchairs, pleated pelmets, floral wallpaper) meets quirky contemporary style. Bedrooms are in the main house and the attached converted barn and granary. Lords rooms are the largest – one has a colonial four-poster bed, another a bay window overlooking the gardens – but all offer a laid-back, luxurious feel, with embroidered silk throws, coffee- and tea-making facilities plus elderflower pressé and Damana toiletries. There are two restaurants: the fine-dining Atrium and the less formal Dining Room. Menus, including an imaginative vegan menu and a vegetarian tasting menu, are created by chef Charles Smith; service is 'confident and assured'. 'We had a very good time and hope to return,' says one recent guest. (Rosemary Melling)

Upper Slaughter GL54 2JD

T: 01451 820243
E: reservations@lordsofthemanor.com
W: lordsofthemanor.com

BEDROOMS: 26. 16 in granary and stables, 1 on ground floor.
OPEN: all year.
FACILITIES: lounges, bar, 2 restaurants, library, games room, in-room TV (Freeview), civil wedding licence, terrace, 8-acre grounds, some public rooms wheelchair accessible, no adapted toilet.
BACKGROUND MUSIC: in lounge bar and restaurant.
LOCATION: in village, 2 miles N of Bourton-on-the-Water.
CHILDREN: all ages welcomed.
DOGS: allowed in some bedrooms, public rooms, not restaurant (£30 a night).
CREDIT CARDS: Amex, MC, Visa.
PRICES: per room B&B £155–£510, D,B&B £280–£640. À la carte £45, tasting menu £95. 1-night bookings refused mid-summer Sat.

# UPPINGHAM Rutland

MAP 2:B3

## LAKE ISLE

Satisfied diners have been coming for years to this restaurant-with-rooms in the heart of the pretty market town. 'In all the time it has existed we have never had a less than perfect evening meal,' writes a fan. Owned by Richard and Janine Burton, the Grade II listed, 18th-century whitewashed building sits right on the High Street. Bedrooms mix traditional and contemporary, with pale-painted furniture, bold-striped wallpapers and button-back armchairs. Some have a bathroom with whirlpool bath. They may be on the cosy side – 'a smallish room but plenty big enough' – though 'beds are really comfy, and they have all the extras'. Besides, point out readers, 'the reason you stay at Lake Isle is the food'. Exciting and imaginative dishes might include grilled sea bream with samphire and oysters, or guineafowl with sherried lentils and black pudding crumb, served in 'an attractive room looking out at the High Street'. Breakfast keeps up the standards; no cold buffet but a 'proper feast' with 'each course brought to our table'. (John and Elspeth Gibbon, CH, and others)

16 High Street East
Uppingham LE15 9PZ

T: 01572 822951
E: info@lakeisle.co.uk
W: lakeisle.co.uk

BEDROOMS: 12. 2 in cottages.
OPEN: all year, restaurant closed Sun night, Mon lunch, bank holidays.
FACILITIES: bar, restaurant, in-room TV (Freeview), small car park, unsuitable for disabled.
BACKGROUND MUSIC: in restaurant.
LOCATION: town centre.
CHILDREN: all ages welcomed.
DOGS: allowed in courtyard bedrooms, not in public areas.
CREDIT CARDS: Amex, MC, Visa.
PRICES: per room B&B single £75–£85, double £90–£120, D,B&B single £114–£124, double £167–£197. À la carte £39.

# VENTNOR Isle of Wight

MAP 2:E2

## HILLSIDE

On a steep hillside under St Boniface Down, this 'thatched but imposing' Georgian hotel is a labour of love for Danish owner Gert Bach. 'There are sea views from most bedrooms, and from manicured gardens, made for sitting down with a cup of tea or something stronger,' writes a Guide insider. The style is Scandi, 'stripped-back chic, with pale oak floors, white walls, splashes of colour in blankets, and bold artwork'. A family of pig statues welcomes you at the door; the host welcomes you within. 'Gert greeted us every time we returned, and lingered to chat when serving dinner and breakfast,' others relate. All bedrooms have a Vispring bed, Danish lighting and modern artwork, but no kettle; teas and coffees are served downstairs and charged for. From 5 to 8 pm the brasserie serves cakes, drinks and simple fare such as soup and quiches, made from locally sourced and home-grown ingredients. 'The food is well cooked and presented', but there are more exciting options downtown. An 'especially good breakfast' brings 'delicious home-made breads, cold meats and fish', new-laid eggs from the hens. (JK, and others)

**25% DISCOUNT VOUCHERS**

151 Mitchell Avenue
Ventnor PO38 1DR

T: 01983 852271
E: mail@hillsideventnor.co.uk
W: hillsideventnor.co.uk

**BEDROOMS:** 12. Plus self-catering apartment.
**OPEN:** all year.
**FACILITIES:** restaurant, 2 lounges, conservatory, in-room TV (Freeview), terrace, 5-acre garden (vegetable garden, sheep, beehives), close to tennis club, golf, unsuitable for disabled.
**BACKGROUND MUSIC:** in restaurant in evening.
**LOCATION:** above village centre.
**CHILDREN:** not under 12.
**DOGS:** not allowed.
**CREDIT CARDS:** MC, Visa.
**PRICES:** per room B&B single £123–£163, double £146–£226, apartment £186–£302. Brasserie, 2 courses £15. Min. 2-night bookings preferred.

# VENTNOR Isle of Wight

MAP 2:E2

## THE ROYAL HOTEL

Lawns run down to the pool in sub-tropical gardens 'which, with their climbing geraniums, are magnificent' at this cliff-top hotel overlooking the esplanade. 'From the genuine reception to the moment we leave the hotel, we feel valued and cared for in this fast-paced life,' say readers, hinting at a timeless air within. And yes, it is more cocktails and piano than boutique-chic. The bedrooms vary in size and aspect. Some have a country house feel, with antiques; others are more contemporary. Sea and garden views command a premium. 'Ours was, as usual, just right, and we had everything we could need,' write trusted readers. 'The staff are very kind, attentive and capable. Our reservation was dealt with perfectly, our ferries booked and a parking space reserved.' New chef Ben Chamberlain is developing the menus while retaining such favourites as lamb sausages and day-boat fish with beurre blanc. 'The Gallybagger cheese soufflé is something special!' There is a separate menu for vegetarians and vegans. Remember, too, to take afternoon tea, as Queen Victoria often did, perhaps on the Geranium Terrace. (Eric and Mary Woods, and others)

Belgrave Road
Ventnor PO38 1JJ

T: 01983 852186
E: enquiries@royalhoteliow.co.uk
W: royalhoteliow.co.uk

BEDROOMS: 51. 1 suitable for disabled.
OPEN: all year.
FACILITIES: lift, lounge, bar, 2 restaurants, conservatory, function rooms, in-room TV, civil wedding licence, spa treatment rooms, terrace, 2-acre grounds, outdoor heated pool, public areas/toilet wheelchair accessible, six electric charging points.
BACKGROUND MUSIC: in public areas, pianist on peak-season weekends.
LOCATION: short walk from centre.
CHILDREN: all ages welcomed.
DOGS: allowed in some bedrooms, not in restaurants.
CREDIT CARDS: Amex, MC, Visa.
PRICES: per room B&B single £115–£135, double £170–£305, D,B&B add £35 per person. Dinner £40, tasting menu £50. Min. 2-night stays on peak weekends.

# VERYAN-IN-ROSELAND Cornwall

MAP 1:D2

## THE NARE

♔ Previous César winner

'The Nare's description of itself as "the country house hotel by the sea" sums it up nicely. It is so comfortable, in a somewhat old-fashioned way,' writes a regular visitor to Toby Ashworth's much-loved hotel. He adds that everything is 'as welcoming, friendly and helpful as ever'. Sub-tropical gardens, which flourish around the hotel above dog-friendly Carne Beach, are home to an outdoor pool (there is an indoor one too). Sea-facing bedrooms and suites have floor-to-ceiling windows and a balcony or terrace, while country-view rooms have their own charm. The styling is traditional, with artwork and antiques, comfy seating, a writing desk, fresh flowers, and Penhaligon toiletries. At 4 pm, by long tradition, a Cornish cream tea is served, and an early supper is offered to children. You can eat in The Quarterdeck restaurant, on the terrace, or in the silver-service dining room, with a 'wonderfully retro' hors d'oeuvre trolley, and flame grills from the gueridon. Chef Brett Camborne-Paynter's menus have something for everyone – maybe a steak, seaweed gnocchi or line-caught turbot with langoustine emulsion. (Peter Govier)

Carne Beach
Veryan-in-Roseland TR2 5PF

T: 01872 501111
E: stay@narehotel.co.uk
W: narehotel.co.uk

BEDROOMS: 41. Some on ground floor, 1 in cottage, 5 suitable for disabled.
OPEN: all year.
FACILITIES: lift, lounge, drawing room, sun lounge, gallery, study, bar, library, light lunch room, 2 restaurants, conservatory, in-room TV (Sky, Freeview), gym, indoor and outdoor swimming pools, 2-acre grounds, 2 boats, tennis, public rooms wheelchair accessible, adapted toilet.
BACKGROUND MUSIC: none.
LOCATION: S of Veryan.
CHILDREN: all ages welcomed.
DOGS: allowed in bedrooms, gardens, not in public areas.
CREDIT CARDS: Amex, MC, Visa.
PRICES: per room B&B £328–£925, D,B&B £370–£970. Fixed-price dinner £50, tasting menu £60, à la carte £50.

# WADEBRIDGE Cornwall

MAP 1:D2

## TREWORNAN MANOR   NEW

The River Amble flows past the hamlet a mile
from Wadebridge where a Grade II listed manor
house is now a 'first-rate' B&B, promoted to
a full entry following persuasive reports from
readers. Inside, Paul and Lesley Stapleton have
created what 'feels like a mixture of farmhouse
meets boutique hotel'. 'We were immediately
impressed,' write visitors who stayed when
dining chez Nathan Outlaw in Port Isaac. 'Paul
was welcoming and there were lovely-looking
cakes and scones set out as a treat.' Smart
bedrooms have an emperor bed. Finisterre,
accessed from the courtyard, has a lounge and a
bath with walk-in shower. Less expensive Lundy
has 'lovely views from a window seat, interesting
furniture, a very unusual bathroom with excellent
shower and a rope connected to the bell tower
above – proper history'. Extras include 'cafetière
coffee, milk in a fridge along the corridor, and
home-made flapjacks'. There is an honesty bar
in the lounge, and 'we loved the library-themed
snug room'. An 'exceptional breakfast' brings
blueberry pancakes with clotted cream, a full
Cornish with hog's pudding. (Kevin and Victoria
Seymour, and others)

Trewornan Bridge
Wadebridge PL27 6EX

T: 01208 812359
E: enquiries@trewornanmanor.co.uk
W: trewornanmanor.co.uk

BEDROOMS: 7. 2 in courtyard annexe,
1 on ground floor.
OPEN: all year.
FACILITIES: lounge, snug, dining room,
in-room TV (Freeview), civil wedding
licence, 8-acre gardens.
BACKGROUND MUSIC: in dining room,
lounge at breakfast and evening.
LOCATION: 1 mile N of Wadebridge.
CHILDREN: not under 14.
DOGS: not allowed.
CREDIT CARDS: MC, Visa.
PRICES: per room B&B double
£135–£225.

# WAREHAM Dorset

MAP 2:E1

## THE PRIORY

The old-fashioned charms of this former 16th-century priory in beautiful cottage gardens sloping down to the River Frome in the centre of Wareham are not lost on readers, who conclude that 'the hotel is a delight'. Bedrooms are deliciously different, from one on the ground floor with a walk-in drencher shower to another with river views, up steep stairs in the eaves, full of crooked character. Steps away, a room in the Boathouse was 'beautifully decorated and appointed. Its location by the river is rather special.' Ground-floor Boathouse suites also have French doors to a veranda. The drawing room may be 'rather dated', but the restaurant is in a light, modern conservatory. Here, Stephan Guinebault's cooking 'maintains its high standard'. Typical choices include Portland crab salad, Devon Farm beef fillet or wild mushroom risotto. Background music is 'gentle and pleasant', service 'excellent, friendly and attentive'. 'Going for a long, bracing walk by the coast after a Priory breakfast, then back for tea, scones and the fire makes for an excellent winter's day.' (Max Lickfold, BB, and others)

### 25% DISCOUNT VOUCHERS

Church Green
Wareham BH20 4ND

T: 01929 551666
E: admin@theprioryhotel.co.uk
W: theprioryhotel.co.uk

BEDROOMS: 17. Some on ground floor, 4 suites in Boathouse, 1 suitable for disabled.
OPEN: all year.
FACILITIES: sitting room, drawing room, snug bar, 2 dining rooms, in-room TV (Freeview), spa treatments, 4½-acre gardens (croquet, river frontage, moorings, fishing), restaurant wheelchair accessible.
BACKGROUND MUSIC: pianist in drawing room Sat evenings 'and special occasions'.
LOCATION: town centre.
CHILDREN: not under 14.
DOGS: not allowed.
CREDIT CARDS: Amex, MC, Visa.
PRICES: per room B&B single £176–£304, double £220–£380, D,B&B double £295–£455. Fixed-price dinner £55. 1-night bookings refused high season, peak weekends.

# WELLS Somerset

MAP 2:D1

## STOBERRY HOUSE

♔ Previous César winner

'Superbly positioned, with stunning views to the cathedral and the Somerset country beyond, Glastonbury Tor in the distance.' Set in beautiful gardens and parkland, Frances and Tim Meeres Young's 18th-century coach house is run as an extra-special B&B. Bedrooms, each individually styled, one with a four-poster, are dressed to the nines. 'Our room was The Studio, a spacious self-contained cottage with a huge bed, a well-equipped bathroom with heated floor, a sunny table and chairs outside.' Extras included 'bottles of wine, chocolates, apples, a coffee machine and copious documentation about the house, garden and city'. Other readers were less keen on the self-catering Gatehouse Cottage, which, they felt, 'needed a bit of a make-over'. There are spaces for guests to relax inside and out, perhaps with a cream tea. 'Presiding over everything is Frances with a team of friendly young women.' A lavish breakfast buffet in the 'bright and light' orangery includes smoothies, cold meats, Mere smoked trout, Somerset cheeses and home-made jams. Cooked dishes, charged extra, must be ordered the night before. (Edward Mirzoeff, and others)

---

**25% DISCOUNT VOUCHERS**

Stoberry Park
Wells BA5 3LD

T: 01749 672906
E: stay@stoberry-park.co.uk
W: stoberryhouse.co.uk

BEDROOMS: 7. 1 in studio cottage, 2 in the gatehouse cottage.
OPEN: all year except 2 weeks over Christmas and New Year.
FACILITIES: 3 sitting rooms (1 with pantry), breakfast room/orangery, in-room TV (Freeview), 6½-acre garden in 25 acres of parkland.
BACKGROUND MUSIC: none.
LOCATION: outskirts of Wells.
CHILDREN: allowed for exclusive use and hire of the house, if children are old enough to have their own room.
DOGS: not allowed.
CREDIT CARDS: Amex, MC, Visa.
PRICES: per room B&B (continental; £5.50 cooked) single £85, double £95–£168. À la carte £35 (pre-ordered). 1-night bookings sometimes refused weekends during high season.

# WEST HOATHLY Sussex

MAP 2:E4

## THE CAT INN

♥ Previous César winner

'This is one of the best, if not the best-run inn we've ever stayed at.' 'Fabulous! Absolutely fabulous!' We hear praise this year as warm as the welcome at this tile-hung, 16th-century village pub. Owner Andrew Russell held a management role at nearby Gravetye Manor, East Grinstead (see entry), and is 'the most amazing host'. Bedrooms have a simple, cottage-cum-contemporary look, a coffee machine, fresh milk and Bramley toiletries. 'We had a room overlooking the church, with every comfort.' Logs burn merrily in a bar hung with pewter mugs, where Harvey, the spaniel, rules the roost (it may be called the Cat Inn but it is very dog-friendly). Walls are hung with carefully chosen modern paintings: 'Andrew has a fine appreciation of art.' You can order sandwiches and pub classics, or more adventurous, 'absolutely delicious' dishes from Alex Jacquemin's menus, which use organic produce from The Cat's own market garden, where chickens forage and fertilise. 'Breakfasts were outstanding, with fresh strawberries and raspberries.' (Simon Rodway, Embry Rucker)

### 25% DISCOUNT VOUCHERS

North Lane
West Hoathly RH19 4PP

T: 01342 810369
E: thecatinn@googlemail.com
W: catinn.co.uk

BEDROOMS: 4.
OPEN: all year except Christmas, restaurant open New Year's Eve and lunch on New Year's Day.
FACILITIES: bar, 3 dining areas, in-room TV (Freeview), terrace (alfresco meals), restaurant wheelchair accessible.
BACKGROUND MUSIC: none.
LOCATION: in village.
CHILDREN: not under 7 (unless 'well-behaved').
DOGS: allowed in bedrooms, bar, specific dining area (£10 a night).
CREDIT CARDS: Amex, MC, Visa.
PRICES: per room B&B double £130–£165 (single occupancy rates available on request). À la carte £28.

# WHITEWELL Lancashire                          MAP 4:D3

## THE INN AT WHITEWELL

There is an outdoorsy, tally-ho vibe about Charles
Bowman's rural inn on the banks of the River
Hodder, with views to the Forest of Bowland.
With its stone-flagged flooring, mullioned
windows, hunting prints, stags' heads, stuffed
game birds and 'copious supply of umbrellas',
it brings forth colourful reports from readers.
Bedrooms are furnished with antiques, perhaps
a four-poster or Savoir bed, an open fire or
longcase clock. They are spacious, though one
had a bathroom 'designed for a very thin giant'. A
coach house room, up a steep slope, had a ground-
floor bathroom and 'effectively a suite' above,
with a Victorian canopy bath, 'an extraordinary
museum piece'. 'The food is outstanding, both
in the bar and the restaurant. Especially good
were the queen scallops in garlic, to say nothing
of lobster bisque and lamb with white beans and
parsley mash.' 'Grouse was available, this being a
grouse-shooting area, and we soon got the hang of
waiting in the bar for the specials board to appear.'
'One rings down for complimentary tea when
one wakes in the morning – what a luxury!' (John
Saul, Rodney and Mary Milne-Day, and others)

Whitewell
Clitheroe BB7 3AT

T: 01200 448222
E: reception@innatwhitewell.com
W: innatwhitewell.com

BEDROOMS: 23. 4 in coach house, 150 yds,
2 on ground floor.
OPEN: all year.
FACILITIES: 3 bars, restaurant,
boardroom, private dining room,
in-house wine shop, spa treatments,
in-room TV (Freeview), civil wedding
licence, 5-acre grounds (wild-flower
meadow, large river terrace with
tables), 7 miles' fishing (ghillie
available), main bar, hall, reception
wheelchair accessible, adapted toilet.
BACKGROUND MUSIC: none.
LOCATION: 6 miles NW of Clitheroe.
CHILDREN: all ages welcomed.
DOGS: allowed in bedrooms, public
rooms, not in main dining room.
CREDIT CARDS: MC, Visa.
PRICES: per room B&B single £99–£185,
double £137–£256. À la carte £40.

# WHITLEY Wiltshire

MAP 2:D1

## THE PEAR TREE INN    NEW

There is a great sense of fun at this 17th-century village pub, now run as a bar-and-restaurant-with rooms by Jackie Cosens and Adrian Jenkins – she the life and soul front-of-house, he the chef. The 'wonderful inn, set in secluded grounds', enters the Guide this year at the urging of a reader. Named after pear varieties, the bedrooms are 'comfortable and styled to reflect a modern take on a farmhouse'. Some have a wall of Cole & Son's 'Woods and Pears' wallpaper or a frame from a Desperate Dan or Dennis the Menace comic strip. Dog-friendly annexe rooms have outdoor access via French doors. A family suite has a king-size bed, a 'quirky snug', two single beds on a mezzanine, and a private terrace. 'Our daughter was enchanted by her own space.' All rooms have fresh milk, home-made biscuits and Bramley toiletries. Produce from local farmers and growers, fish from British waters, and free-range, traceable meat appear in such dishes as River Fowey mussels; chargrilled dry-aged steak; and grilled cauliflower on white-bean mash with kale pesto and kibbled onions. Breakfast is 'top-notch'. (Nicola Gray)

Top Lane
Whitley
Melksham SN12 8QX

T: 01225 704966
E: hello@peartreewhitley.co.uk
W: peartreewhitley.co.uk

BEDROOMS: 8. 4 in converted barn, 1 suitable for disabled.
OPEN: all year.
FACILITIES: bar/snug, 2 dining rooms, garden (alfresco dining), in-room TV (terrestrial), parking, restaurant wheelchair accessible, adapted toilet.
BACKGROUND MUSIC: in restaurants and bar.
LOCATION: in the heart of the village.
CHILDREN: all ages welcomed (free cot, extra bed £15).
DOGS: in barn annexe bedrooms, bar and Garden Room restaurant (not Sun Room), £12.50 a night.
CREDIT CARDS: Amex, MC, Visa.
PRICES: per room B&B £95–£150, D,B&B £145–£200. À la carte £30. 1-night bookings refused Fri and Sat.

# WINCHESTER Hampshire

MAP 2:D2

## THE OLD VINE

As Winchester Cathedral sits atop its massive, round-arched Norman crypt, so this nearby Georgian building that is now run as a pub-with-rooms was built over a 14th-century basement tavern. 'Wonderfully situated', it has cathedral views. A vine scrambles up the front wall, while within is an atmospheric beamed bar, where sandwiches are served. In the restaurant, the menu – strong on Hampshire produce – runs the gamut of pub classics and such dishes as lamb tagine, seabass with salsa verde, and vegan chickpea and lentil curry. It is perhaps more pub than gastro, a reader tells us, but it is served by 'friendly, efficient young staff'. The bedrooms are named after designers and styled accordingly. Nina Campbell has two queen-size mahogany sleigh beds and her delicate 'Peony Place' wallpaper. Osborne & Little, overlooking the cathedral green, has Victorian antiques, a king-size, mahogany four-poster, Osborne & Little fabrics, a coffee machine and fridge with fresh milk. The Design House Cathedral Suite, with king-size sleigh bed, can accommodate a foldaway bed for a third guest.

**25% DISCOUNT VOUCHERS**

8 Great Minster Street
Winchester SO23 9HA

T: 01962 854616
E: reservations@oldvinewinchester.com
W: oldvinewinchester.com

BEDROOMS: 6. Self-contained 2-bed apartment, with garage, in annexe.
OPEN: all year except Christmas Day.
FACILITIES: bar, restaurant, in-room TV (Freeview), parking permits, restaurant and bar wheelchair accessible, but not toilets.
BACKGROUND MUSIC: in bar.
LOCATION: town centre, permits supplied for on-street parking.
CHILDREN: all ages welcomed, no under-6s in restaurant or in bar at night.
DOGS: only in bar.
CREDIT CARDS: Amex, MC, Visa.
PRICES: per room B&B single £120–£160, double £140–£200. Set menu (2/3 courses) £25 residents only, à la carte £30.

# WINDERMERE Cumbria

MAP 4: inset C2

## CEDAR MANOR

A 'beautifully intimate hotel', a five-minute drive from Windermere, Cedar Manor garners nothing but praise from readers for its luxurious bedrooms, thoughtful touches and spot-on service. 'The setting is beautiful, the accommodation is excellent, the staff and food are wonderful.' Bedrooms have a contemporary country house style with striking wallpapers and fabrics, Herdwick wool carpets, bespoke wood furniture and great attention to detail. 'Our lovely room had a great bed and was well furnished and quiet.' Another reader adds: 'The REN products and fine bedlinens, robes, thick towels, and welcome chocolates were a lovely touch.' There's a short evening lounge menu including cheese and meat platters; otherwise the hotel provides a list of local eateries, with helpful notes. If you want to indulge beforehand, the afternoon tea is 'a splendid balance of savoury and sweet selections'. Breakfast includes a Cumbrian Grill, 'probably the best cooked hotel breakfast I have had'. Throughout, the 'fantastic, friendly' staff under friendly owners Jonathan and Caroline Kaye provide a 'flawless service'. (Steve and Sue Rowes, DB, and others)

---

**25% DISCOUNT VOUCHERS**

Ambleside Road
Windermere LA23 1AX

T: 01539 443192
E: info@cedarmanor.co.uk
W: cedarmanor.co.uk

**BEDROOMS:** 10. 1 split-level suite in coach house.
**OPEN:** all year except 13–26 Dec, 3–21 Jan.
**FACILITIES:** 2 lounges, restaurant, in-room TV (Freeview), patio, ¼-acre garden, unsuitable for disabled.
**BACKGROUND MUSIC:** 'very quiet', at mealtimes, in lounge and restaurant.
**LOCATION:** 5-min. walk from town centre.
**CHILDREN:** not under 10.
**DOGS:** not allowed.
**CREDIT CARDS:** Amex, MC, Visa.
**PRICES:** per room B&B single £125–£425, double £145–£475, Min. 2-night stay at weekends and bank holidays.

# WINDERMERE Cumbria

MAP 4: inset C2

## GILPIN HOTEL AND LAKE HOUSE

This luxurious country house hotel (Relais & Châteaux) offers 'indulgent' rooms, Michelin-starred dining, spacious grounds, legions of staff, and 'comfort in all the right places'. The Cunliffe family, who have owned it since 1988, 'keep making it better every year', say fans. In 2020 this means new, extravagantly large spa lodges: bold glass-and-wood affairs with circular bath, private garden and spa. These are in addition to smaller spa lodges overlooking a pond and Scandi-style garden suites, and contemporary rooms in the Edwardian house. Six Lake House rooms, in a former fishing lodge on a 100-acre estate half a mile away, have exclusive access to a 20-metre pool and spa. Dining is a choice between Michelin-starred HRiSHi, which offers Modern British cuisine with an Asian twist, such as Cartmel Valley wild duck with spiced pumpkin chutney, and the 'funky' Gilpin Spice with its pan-Asian small and large plates, and more modest prices. Come here to relax in the gardens, the 'swanky' bar, the 'wonderfully restful' sitting room, or around Lake House's private woodland and lake. (ST)

Crook Road
Windermere LA23 3NE

T: 01539 488818
E: hotel@thegilpin.co.uk
W: thegilpin.co.uk

BEDROOMS: 36. 6 garden suites, 10 spa lodges, 6 in Lake House (½ mile away), 1 room suitable for disabled.
OPEN: all year.
FACILITIES: Gilpin Hotel: bar, lounge, 2 restaurants, patio, 22-acre grounds, public rooms wheelchair accessible, adapted toilet. Lake House: lounge, conservatory, spa (heated pool), 100-acre grounds; in-room TV (Sky), civil wedding licence.
BACKGROUND MUSIC: in restaurants.
LOCATION: on B5284, 2 miles SE of Windermere.
CHILDREN: not under 7.
DOGS: allowed in 2 bedrooms, not in public rooms.
CREDIT CARDS: Amex, MC, Visa.
PRICES: per room B&B £295–£795, D,B&B £385–£885. Set dinner £70, à la carte £35–£75, tasting menus £40–£95. Min. 2-night stay at weekends.

# WINGHAM Kent

## THE DOG AT WINGHAM

Every Dog has its day, and Marc Bridgen's canine-friendly gastropub-with-rooms has been garnering awards since his family took it on in 2016. The ancient building stands shoulder-on to the Canterbury–Sandwich road in a pretty village. The bedrooms, styled by Marc's mother, Marilyn, are 'attractively decorated, with plain-coloured walls, glam touches and statement headboards'. All have a Hypnos bed and a bathroom with walk-in shower. A suite has an antique four-poster. Our inspectors had a room at the rear, and noted the singing of pipes in a room above in the afternoon, but at night all was quiet. Chef Samuel McClurkin works with local suppliers to source the best ingredients, but reaches out as far as the Isle of Lewis for smoked salmon and black pudding. A 'comfortable lounge bar' has walls hung with doggy artwork, and a checked carpet (houndstooth, naturally). In the restaurant, 'the service matches the wonderful food', readers write. To give you a flavour, maybe roast hogget loin and pressed breast with rosemary and red wine sauce. Our verdict: 'Winning value for money.' (JC, VC, and others)

**25% DISCOUNT VOUCHERS**

Canterbury Road
Wingham
Canterbury CT3 1BB

T: 01227 720339
E: info@thedog.co.uk
W: thedog.co.uk

BEDROOMS: 8.
OPEN: all year, kitchen closes 5 pm Sun.
FACILITIES: lounge bar, restaurant bar, dining room, garden room, terrace (alfresco dining), in-room TV (Freeview), civil wedding licence, golf packages, monthly dining club, unsuitable for disabled.
BACKGROUND MUSIC: in bar and restaurant, live music events.
LOCATION: in village 7 miles E of Canterbury.
CHILDREN: all ages welcomed.
DOGS: welcomed throughout.
CREDIT CARDS: Amex, MC, Visa.
PRICES: per room B&B single £80–£280, double £90–£280. À la carte £40 (vegan £38, 24 hours' notice).

# WOLD NEWTON Yorkshire

MAP 4:D5

## THE WOLD COTTAGE

Enviably placed between the North York Moors, the Yorkshire Wolds and the coast, this Georgian manor house offers elegant rooms, restful views and a warm welcome. Katrina and Derek Gray emphasise that it's their home, not a hotel. 'It's exactly that ambience which makes the place attractive,' says one guest. Set amid mature trees and landscaped gardens, including terraces and a pond, the handsome red brick house overlooks farmland. Gracious interiors of sash windows and high ceilings include a sitting room with a real fire and 'tasteful' art, and an elegant dining room with wine-red walls and a polished-wood table for shared breakfasts. The menu – including porridge, locally smoked haddock with poached egg, Yorkshire ham and cheese, plus home-made bread – should outweigh any unease at communal eating. Bedroom choices range from traditional with antiques and silky drapes – one has a four-poster – to more contemporary, where neutral colours are jazzed up with a tartan-covered armchair or a bold throw. Most have a bath and shower; all have robes and fresh milk. Go to walk, birdwatch or just relax.

### 25% DISCOUNT VOUCHERS

Wold Newton
Driffield YO25 3HL

T: 01262 470696
E: katrina@woldcottage.com
W: woldcottage.com

BEDROOMS: 6. 2 in converted barn, 1 on ground floor, 2 self-catering cottages.
OPEN: all year.
FACILITIES: lounge, dining room, in-room TV (Freeview), 3-acre gardens (croquet) in 240-acre grounds (farmland, woodland), public rooms wheelchair accessible.
BACKGROUND MUSIC: at breakfast in dining room.
LOCATION: just outside village.
CHILDREN: all ages welcomed.
DOGS: not allowed.
CREDIT CARDS: MC, Visa.
PRICES: per person B&B £55–£90, family room £135–£200. 1-night bookings refused weekends in summer.

# WOOTTON COURTENAY Somerset

MAP 1:B5

## DUNKERY BEACON COUNTRY HOUSE

This Edwardian hunting lodge with a veranda from which to gaze out to the highest point on Exmoor, or at the starry black sky, is today a 'delightful, well-managed' hotel, run by owners John and Jane Bradley. Much has changed since the days when 20 single rooms were let exclusively to male shooting enthusiasts. Bedrooms are furnished in smart contemporary style. A 'comfortable, spacious', dog-friendly ground-floor suite proved to be 'right up to date with all the 21st-century gadgets: music system, DVD-player and a vast TV screen (rather large for the sitting area!)'. One bedroom has a sunken bath with a shower over, another a mahogany sleigh bed. All are supplied with a cafetière, fresh milk and Keiji toiletries. In the Coleridge restaurant, John Bradley uses produce from Somerset suppliers, and from their own and local gardens, in such dishes as poached supreme of salmon with linguine, white wine and herb sauce, and sprouting broccoli. Jane, front-of-house, spent 15 years with venerable wine merchant Berry Bros. & Rudd. 'Service was impeccable.' Breakfast brings an 'excellent choice'.

---

**25% DISCOUNT VOUCHERS**

Wootton Courtenay TA24 8RH

T: 01643 841241
E: info@dunkerybeaconaccommodation.co.uk
W: dunkerybeaconaccommodation.co.uk

BEDROOMS: 8. 1 on ground floor.
OPEN: mid-Feb–27 Dec, restaurant Wed–Sat pm (only Fri, Sat in winter), Sun lunch.
FACILITIES: lounge, restaurant, breakfast room, free Wi-Fi in most bedrooms, in-room TV (Freeview), limited mobile phone reception, ¾-acre garden, unsuitable for disabled.
BACKGROUND MUSIC: in restaurant in evening.
LOCATION: 4 miles SW of Dunster.
CHILDREN: not under 10.
DOGS: allowed in 2 suites (£5 per night, max. 2 dogs), not in public rooms.
CREDIT CARDS: MC, Visa.
PRICES: per room B&B £85–£169. À la carte £37. 1-night bookings refused Fri/Sat and on all stays in peak season (but check for late availability).

# YARM Yorkshire                    MAP 4:C4

## JUDGES

ⓥ Previous César winner

Shrouded from the world by rolling gardens and wooded dells and with 'impeccably maintained grounds', this creeper-covered Victorian country house was once a retreat for circuit judges. 'The building's history adds to its charm,' writes one reader, who was married there. Public rooms, including a clubby bar and elegant drawing room, are 'splendid, a fire glowing in the entrance hall'. Bedrooms are comfortably traditional with striped and toile de Jouy wallpapers, armchairs, some with a four-poster. Readers appreciated touches such as 'fresh fruit and sherry replenished every day', even 'a television in the bathroom'. 'The excellent dinner preceded by delicious canapés in the lounge beside a blazing fire' might include fillet of beef with onion crumb and red wine or halibut with chorizo dauphine. There are vegan and vegetarian options, and bistro dishes. 'Professional and very friendly staff' are consistently praised. 'When we left, it was the cheerful general manager, Tim Howard, who brought round our car and put our luggage within it,' writes a trusted reader. (Anthony Bradbury, Joanne Vickers, GD, AC, and others)

**25% DISCOUNT VOUCHERS**

Kirklevington Hall
Kirklevington
Yarm TS15 9LW

T: 01642 789000
E: reception@judgeshotel.co.uk
W: judgeshotel.co.uk

BEDROOMS: 21. Some on ground floor.
OPEN: all year.
FACILITIES: lounge, bar, restaurant, private dining room, in-room TV (Freeview), function facilities, business centre, civil wedding licence, 36-acre grounds (paths, running routes), access to local spa and sports club, unsuitable for disabled.
BACKGROUND MUSIC: Radio 4 at breakfast, classical background music in restaurant.
LOCATION: 1½ miles S of centre.
CHILDREN: all ages welcomed.
DOGS: guide dogs only.
CREDIT CARDS: Amex, MC, Visa.
PRICES: per room B&B single £105–£205, double £145–£225, D,B&B double £220–£300. À la carte £50.

# YORK Yorkshire

MAP 4:D4

## MIDDLETHORPE HALL & SPA

Overlooking the racecourse and surrounded by gardens and parkland, this gem of a William and Mary house with its 'stunning exterior' feels deeply rural yet is just over a mile from York. Staying here is 'absolutely super' according to one guest and, with its grand drawing room and library, and wood-panelled dining room, it feels like a minor stately home – indeed, it was given to the National Trust in 2008. Bedrooms, split between the main hall and converted stable block and cottages, are country house in style with antiques, patterned wallpapers, blankets and eiderdowns. Everything is top quality, including the fresh flowers, fruit and home-made biscuits. Canapés before dinner are taken in the drawing room, with its 'deep sofas, and roaring fire'. The meal itself is a four-course affair of Modern British dishes – crab ravioli with sea vegetables, perhaps, or beef fillet with oxtail bonbons and rounded off with Yorkshire rhubarb with parkin and stem ginger. Breakfast offers 'excellent molten scrambled egg, freshly squeezed juice and leaf tea'. A pampering stay. (Richard Morgan-Price, and others)

Bishopthorpe Road
York YO23 2GB

T: 01904 641241
E: info@middlethorpe.com
W: middlethorpe.com

BEDROOMS: 29. 17 in courtyard, 2 in cottage, 1 suite suitable for disabled.
OPEN: all year.
FACILITIES: hall, drawing room, library, 2 dining rooms, bar, 2 private dining rooms, in-room TV (Freeview), civil wedding licence, 20-acre grounds, spa (10 by 6 metre indoor swimming pool), public rooms wheelchair accessible, no adapted toilet.
BACKGROUND MUSIC: none.
LOCATION: 1½ miles S of centre.
CHILDREN: not under 6.
DOGS: allowed in garden suites and cottage only, by prior arrangement.
CREDIT CARDS: Amex, MC, Visa.
PRICES: per room B&B £132–£539, D,B&B from £218. 6-course tasting menu £75, à la carte £60.

**SEE ALSO SHORTLIST**

# YORK Yorkshire

## THE PARISI HOTEL   `NEW`

In a buzzy area of the city, ten minutes from the Minster, this Victorian rectory hides an 'unexpectedly cool and colourful, stylish hotel', says a Guide insider. Run by sisters Sophie and Maria Scott, who have a 'good eye for design', it feels part art gallery – paintings crowd walls – and part members' club because of its relaxed atmosphere. 'Guests start chatting in the sitting room over a bottle of wine (bring your own).' With books and wood-burning stove, mid-century sofas and colour-block walls, this room, like elsewhere, mixes retro and contemporary. Bedrooms might pair an antique desk with a simple wardrobe, Anglepoise lamps with Ercol armchairs. One sports a yellow four-poster and blue walls. Standard rooms are small but all have 'decent extras such as coffee machine and fresh milk'. Bathrooms, most with bath and shower, have quality products. Breakfast, in a glazed-roof room filled with plants, is 'a joy, the choice delicious', from poached pears to smoked salmon and scrambled eggs, plus Dad's home-made marmalade. After sight-seeing, chill in the courtyard garden before dining in one of the neighbourhood eateries. (HP)

51 St Denys Road
York YO1 9QD

T: 01904 658815
E: info@theparisi.com
W: theparisi.com

BEDROOMS: 11, 1 on ground floor.
OPEN: open all year except 23–27 Dec, 3 weeks in Jan.
FACILITIES: sitting room/library, breakfast room, in-room TV (Freeview), courtyard garden, unsuitable for disabled.
BACKGROUND MUSIC: at breakfast in dining room (Radio 2).
LOCATION: central York.
CHILDREN: over-7s welcomed.
DOGS: not allowed.
CREDIT CARDS: Amex, MC, Visa.
PRICES: per room B&B £99–£239. Min. 2-night stay bank holidays, race days, some weekends.

SEE ALSO SHORTLIST

## ZENNOR Cornwall

MAP 1:D1

### THE GURNARD'S HEAD

You drive over moors on a near-deserted road to reach Charles and Edmund Inkin's relaxed, informal dining-pub-with-rooms on Cornwall's Atlantic coast. (The brothers also own two sister establishments – see The Old Coastguard, Mousehole, and The Felin Fach Griffin, Felin Fach, Wales.) A trusted reader battled his way through swirling mists, down 'surely one of the most beautiful coastal roads in England', and, stepping inside, 'was greeted by a roaring log fire and warmly welcomed'. 'My bedroom was small but done out in modern taste, with a luxurious shower, a genuinely interesting selection of books', a Roberts radio but no TV. All rooms have Bramley toiletries and fresh flowers. Food is served in the shabby-chic bar, restaurant and snug, or alfresco on sunny days. Max Wilson sources local, sustainable ingredients for his imaginative menus. 'The meals were superb, with home-baked breads, delicious starters of mackerel or cauliflower and horseradish soup, and outstanding fish from Newlyn.' After breakfast – 'a particular highlight' – you can set out to walk the nearby Coast Path. 'Magical wild unspoilt Cornwall at its best.' (Mike Craddock, C and ES, S and JJ)

Treen
Zennor
St Ives TR26 3DE

T: 01736 796928
E: enquiries@gurnardshead.co.uk
W: gurnardshead.co.uk

BEDROOMS: 7.
OPEN: all year except 24/25 Dec.
FACILITIES: bar, restaurant, lounge area, 3-acre garden (alfresco dining), public areas wheelchair accessible.
BACKGROUND MUSIC: Radio 4 at breakfast, selected music at other times, in bar and restaurant.
LOCATION: 7 miles SW of St Ives, on B3306.
CHILDREN: all ages welcomed.
DOGS: allowed (water bowls, towels and biscuits provided).
CREDIT CARDS: MC, Visa.
PRICES: per room B&B single £110–£165, double £135–£200. Set menus £22–£28, à la carte £28. 1-night bookings refused weekends occasionally.

# SCOTLAND

Scottish Highlands

# ARDUAINE Argyll and Bute

MAP 5:D1

## LOCH MELFORT HOTEL

In 17 acres of gardens and beach on the Argyll coast, Calum and Rachel Ross's hotel drinks in the views across Asknish Bay and the island-studded Sound of Jura. The house was built in the late 1890s by James Arthur Campbell, who started the adjacent Arduaine Garden, now owned by the National Trust for Scotland, and best seen at rhododendron time. All but five bedrooms are sea facing. Dog-friendly rooms in an annexe have a private terrace; rooms above have a balcony. The styling is simple and contemporary: 'not luxurious but very comfortable, and adequately equipped', writes a reader, who found this 'a very pleasant place to stay'. All rooms have Highland Soap toiletries. You can dine in the restaurant, or more simply in the bistro. New chef Richard Young sources food from local suppliers – West Coast langoustine, crab, scallops, game in season – in such dishes as seafood chowder, and roast loin of Mull venison with rosemary jus. 'Good food at breakfast and dinner,' says our reader, who notes that this is a 'good place to stop en route to Oban and its ferries'. There's wild swimming off a sandy beach, too. (Tony Hall)

Arduaine
Oban PA34 4XG

**T:** 01852 200233
**E:** reception@lochmelfort.co.uk
**W:** lochmelfort.co.uk

**BEDROOMS:** 30. 20 in annexe, 10 on ground floor, 2 suitable for disabled.
**OPEN:** all year except Mon–Wed Nov–Mar, 3 weeks Dec/Jan, open Christmas/New Year.
**FACILITIES:** sitting room, library, bar/bistro, restaurant, in-room TV (terrestrial), wedding facilities, 17-acre grounds, public rooms wheelchair accessible.
**BACKGROUND MUSIC:** in restaurant and bistro.
**LOCATION:** 19 miles S of Oban.
**CHILDREN:** all ages welcomed.
**DOGS:** allowed in 6 bedrooms (£10 per dog per night), not in public rooms, except bistro.
**CREDIT CARDS:** Amex, MC, Visa.
**PRICES:** per room B&B single £60–£150, double £70–£200, D,B&B double £144–£274. À la carte £40.

# ARINAGOUR Argyll and Bute

MAP 5:C1

## COLL HOTEL

**NEW**

Seafaring readers anchored at Arinagour to seek a shower and dinner at the social hub of 'a beautiful island with spectacular beaches, dark-sky park and wonderful wildlife'. It gains a full entry this year, with the addition of a 'modern but sympathetic' extension, including spacious bar areas, and a restaurant with views to Mull and the Treshnish isles. 'We were met enthusiastically and told they indeed had a shower room for non-residents. Towels were thrust into our hands and we were directed to a large wet room. Brilliant!' The Oliphant family have poured heart and soul into Coll's only hotel since the '60s, and 'deserve every success'. Bedrooms (three with garden access) are unfussy and immaculate, with a luxury bed and home-baked treats. The menus showcase local produce – creel-caught lobster and crab, fish landed in Oban, grass-fed lamb. 'We enjoyed fish soup, delicately cooked Gigha halibut with cherry tomato, spinach and Parmesan risotto with rocket (outstanding).' Breakfast brings Loch Fyne kippers, Cumberland sausage or haggis, before a day's dolphin-spotting or a visit to the RSPB reserve. (David Birnie, MC)

**25% DISCOUNT VOUCHERS**

Arinagour
Isle of Coll PA78 6SZ

**T:** 01879 230334
**E:** info@collhotel.com
**W:** collhotel.com

**BEDROOMS:** 10.
**OPEN:** all year, Christmas and New Year house parties only.
**FACILITIES:** lounge bar, public bar, restaurant, residents' lounge and dining room, in-room TV (Freeview), garden, helipad, bicycles, extension room wheelchair accessible.
**BACKGROUND MUSIC:** none.
**LOCATION:** village centre.
**CHILDREN:** all ages welcomed (children stay free, except for food).
**DOGS:** allowed in bar areas, not in restaurant or bedrooms.
**CREDIT CARDS:** MC, Visa.
**PRICES:** per room B&B £90–£165. À la carte from £25.

# ARISAIG Highland

MAP 5:C1

## ARISAIG HOUSE

**NEW**

Set into the sheltering hillside overlooking Loch nan Uamh and the Moidart coast, a Victorian Arts and Crafts shooting lodge is run as a 'magical' hotel with 'amazing gardens and grounds'. The original house, designed by Philip Webb, burnt down in 1935 and was altered in the rebuilding, but the designed landscape is little changed, and specimen trees stand tall. If the first impression on stepping inside is 'somewhat austere', this is dispelled by a warm welcome and a wealth of 'interesting furniture and paintings'. The spacious bedrooms have a loch view, soft paint finishes or toile de Jouy wallpaper, and fresh flowers. They are not state of the art – 'no phone and no TV' – but restful. 'Our room was huge and very comfortable, with a good bathroom and large bed.' There are drawing rooms in which to relax, while at lunch and dinner Sarah Winnington-Ingram cooks with produce from local suppliers and the walled garden – shellfish, venison, lamb from the hill. You can breakfast on eggs from the hotel's ducks and hens before discovering the cave that sheltered Bonnie Prince Charlie on his last night on these shores. (Diana Goodey)

**25% DISCOUNT VOUCHERS**

Beasdale
Arisaig PH39 4NR

**T:** 01687 450730
**E:** enquiries@arisaighouse.co.uk
**W:** arisaighouse.co.uk

**BEDROOMS:** 14. None on ground floor.
**OPEN:** 1 Apr–31 Oct.
**FACILITIES:** drawing room, morning room, bar, dining room, billiard room, 19-acre gardens and woodlands (alfresco dining), free Wi-Fi on ground floor and in some bedrooms, wedding facilities, restaurant wheelchair accessible.
**BACKGROUND MUSIC:** evenings in dining room and drawing room.
**LOCATION:** 30 miles W of Fort William, 2 miles E of Arisaig village.
**CHILDREN:** all ages welcomed.
**DOGS:** allowed in all areas except dining room.
**CREDIT CARDS:** Amex, MC, Visa.
**PRICES:** per room B&B £210–£255. Fixed-price dinner £45.

# AULDEARN Highland

MAP 5:C2

## BOATH HOUSE

♀ Previous César winner

Hotel grounds don't get much more 'exquisite' than at Don and Wendy Matheson's 'beautiful if unadorned' Georgian mansion, sitting amid 22 acres of lawns, meadows and woodland. This year two eco lodges are being added by the trout lake. Boath is, though, just off the Inverness–Aberdeen road, so 'sometimes traffic noise is audible in the house', with its Ionic columns and art gallery. Trusted readers were greeted by the manager, the owners' son, Sam, and shown to a room with a coffee machine, shortbread and fresh milk. The style and comfort pleased them – less so a reader who found the look of rugs on bare boards 'a bit barn like'. One room has twin slipper baths, another an antique French bed. Dinner, served by 'charming, engaging and knowledgeable' staff, features produce from the 'well-kept' walled garden and local suppliers. A meal of foie gras, venison and chocolate tart was 'well up to the high standards expected here'. You can eat more informally in (or outside) the Kale Yard café, which has a wood-fired pizza oven. At breakfast there is freshly squeezed orange juice, smoked fish or the full works. (John Holland, DB)

Auldearn
Nairn IV12 5TE

**T:** 01667 454896
**E:** info@boath-house.com
**W:** boath-house.com

**BEDROOMS:** 11. 2 in cottages (50 yds), 1 suitable for disabled, 2 self-catering eco lodges. Plus 2 in separate B&B at owners' house.
**OPEN:** all year.
**FACILITIES:** 2 lounges, whisky bar/library, restaurant with private dining annexe, in-room TV (Freeview), civil wedding licence, 22-acre parkland, public rooms and café wheelchair accessible, step up to toilet.
**BACKGROUND MUSIC:** soft in dining room.
**LOCATION:** 2 miles E of Nairn.
**CHILDREN:** all ages welcomed, no under-8s at dinner.
**DOGS:** allowed in some bedrooms, not in public rooms.
**CREDIT CARDS:** Amex, MC, Visa.
**PRICES:** per room B&B £220–£290. Set dinner £45.

# BALLANTRAE Ayrshire

MAP 5:E1

## GLENAPP CASTLE

With sweeping views of Ailsa Craig and the Mull of Kintyre, Paul and Poppy Szkiler's Scottish Baronial-style castle hotel balances a 'stunning, grand building' with 'relaxed luxury'. A returning reviewer hoped it would be 'as good as last time' and 'needn't have worried'. The grounds are 'extensive and kept to the very highest standards'. Bedrooms have a sea or garden aspect; a 'large, spotlessly clean and well-appointed' ground-floor room had both. Housekeeping is 'immaculate'. All have antique furniture, sofa, armchairs, and super-king-size bed; some have a separate sitting room, and many have a fire. Bathrooms are stocked with Penhaligon toiletries. Drinks and canapés are a 'tasty' precursor to chef Ian Bennett's 'delicious' menus. The roast breast of Goosnargh duck with butternut squash purée and roasted couscous wins high praise from diners, as do the 'range, presentation and flavour' of vegetarian dishes. Breakfast is 'beautifully presented' and includes 'home-made jams and freshly baked bread'. So good, indeed, that guests may find it hard to tear themselves away. (Carol Bulloch, RG)

Ballantrae KA26 0NZ

T: 01465 831212
E: info@glenappcastle.com
W: glenappcastle.com

BEDROOMS: 17. 7 on ground floor, 1 suitable for disabled, lift to public rooms on first floor.
OPEN: all year.
FACILITIES: lift, drawing room, library, 2 dining rooms, wedding facilities, in-room TV (Freeview), 36-acre grounds (walled gardens, woodland, lake, tennis, croquet), boat for charter, access to local spa, public rooms wheelchair accessible.
BACKGROUND MUSIC: occasional pianist during meals and tea.
LOCATION: 2 miles S of Ballantrae.
CHILDREN: all ages welcomed.
DOGS: allowed in some bedrooms, not in public rooms.
CREDIT CARDS: Amex, MC, Visa.
PRICES: per room B&B £415–£699, D,B&B £550–£799. À la carte £55.

# BALQUHIDDER Stirling

## MONACHYLE MHOR

It feels gloriously remote, down a single-track road in an 'amazing location' overlooking lochs and hills, but this farmhouse turned restaurant-with-rooms is 'sophisticated and stylish'. Recommended as 'an idyllic stop to escape from the world, dine well, and go for walks', it was the childhood home of Tom Lewis, who now runs the property with his wife, Lisa May, with a passion for good food and an eye for design. Bedrooms range from cosily rustic with blanket throws, exposed-stone walls and bright colours, to sprawling affairs with wood floors, designer lighting and egg-shaped bath. There's a three-storey tree 'pod' as well as a self-catering wagon and cabin in the grounds. After a day outdoors, return to the 'candlelit and cosy' lounge. Drinks in the bar, with its funky Italian stools, are followed by a dinner featuring 'exquisite Scottish food' largely sourced from their farm and garden, which might include Peterhead mackerel, kohlrabi remoulade, salsa verde and Monachyle Blackface lamb, Jerusalem artichoke, wild garlic. Guests are looked after by 'an enthusiastic and proud team'. (Brian Whitten, and others)

Balquhidder
Lochearnhead FK19 8PQ

**T:** 01877 384622
**E:** monachyle@mhor.net
**W:** monachylemhor.net

**BEDROOMS:** 17. 4 on ground floor, 9 in courtyard, 1 in modular three-storey 'pod', 1 suitable for disabled. Plus self-catering wagon and cabin.
**OPEN:** all year.
**FACILITIES:** lounge, living room, bar, conservatory restaurant, in-room TV, wedding facilities, function facilities, garden, 2,000-acre estate (foraging, wild swimming, water sports), public rooms wheelchair accessible.
**BACKGROUND MUSIC:** all day in public areas.
**LOCATION:** 4 miles off the A84, down a single-track lane skirting Loch Voil.
**CHILDREN:** all ages welcomed.
**DOGS:** allowed in 3 bedrooms, bar and lounge.
**CREDIT CARDS:** Amex, MC, Visa.
**PRICES:** per room B&B £195–£360. Set menu £65, seasonal tasting menu £85.

# BLAIRGOWRIE Perth and Kinross                    MAP 5:D2

## KINLOCH HOUSE

Highland cattle in their jaunty headgear graze
fields around this creeper-swagged Victorian
country house (Relais & Châteaux), where the
Allen family provide 'a masterclass' in hotel-
keeping, bringing 'perfection in every respect'.
A drive swooshes up to the door, and within are
panelled walls, oil paintings, the odd stag's head
or bristle of antlers. The hosts 'allow their guests
to fully relax and enjoy the beautiful furnishings
and lovely antiques'. Bedrooms range from the
tolerably large to positively huge suites with a
spacious bathroom. All are supplied with Arran
Aromatics products. Stripes, checks and florals
abound without being strident. Swags and
pelmets frame views of gardens, countryside and
Marlee Loch. You can pick up a book from the
library, sink into a sofa by the fire in a lounge or
bar and, when the grandfather clock says it's time,
sip a local single malt. Steve MacCallum's nightly-
changing menus make the most of Perthshire
meat and game, wild salmon and produce from
the walled kitchen garden. At breakfast, the
sausages, bread and jams are all made in-house.
'What a beautiful place to stay!'

Dunkeld Road
Blairgowrie PH10 6SG

**T:** 01250 884237
**E:** reception@kinlochhouse.com
**W:** kinlochhouse.com

**BEDROOMS:** 15. 4 on ground floor.
**OPEN:** all year except 2 weeks from
mid-Dec, open for New Year.
**FACILITIES:** bar, lounge, drawing
room, conservatory, dining room,
private dining room, in-room TV
(Freeview), wedding facilities, 28-acre
grounds, public areas on ground
floor wheelchair accessible, toilet not
adapted.
**BACKGROUND MUSIC:** none.
**LOCATION:** 3 miles W of Blairgowrie,
on A923.
**CHILDREN:** all ages welcomed, not
under 6 in restaurant at dinner.
**DOGS:** not allowed.
**CREDIT CARDS:** Amex, MC, Visa.
**PRICES:** per room B&B £210–£360. Set
dinner £58. 1-night bookings refused
busy periods.

# BRAEMAR Aberdeenshire

MAP 5:C2

## THE FIFE ARMS  NEW

If the annual Braemar Gathering had not put the village on the map, this dramatic reinvention of a many-gabled coaching inn by Swiss art dealers Iwan and Manuela Wirth would surely do so. Designer Russell Sage has had his own Highland fling, filling the interiors with artwork, installations and Victoriana in celebration of the area and luminaries with links to it. A Picasso hangs in the drawing room. A Monarch of the Glen has been stuffed and instated in the dining room, where you can admire a geometric mural by Guillermo Kuitca as you order from Tim Kensett's beautifully judged menus, which include loin of Highland venison, birch-seared salmon or salt-baked celeriac. There is pub grub in The Flying Stag. Bedrooms range from sumptuous Royal Suites worthy of Victoria herself with, perhaps, a carved oak four-poster and copper bath, to croft rooms with a cabin bed, ideal for a solo guest or very close couple. At breakfast, stoke up on wood-fired kippers, organic eggs, Stornoway black pudding, smoked baked beans and tattie scones, before visiting Balmoral or exploring the Cairngorms national park.

Mar Road
Braemar AB35 5YN

T: 01339 720200
E: mail@thefifearms.com
W: thefifearms.com

BEDROOMS: 46.
OPEN: all year.
FACILITIES: bar, drawing room, library, in-room TV (terrestrial), pub, restaurant, 2 meeting rooms, 2-acre gardens, spa.
BACKGROUND MUSIC: in public spaces.
LOCATION: in town centre.
CHILDREN: all ages welcomed (children's menus, family and interconnecting rooms).
DOGS: in some bedrooms, pub.
CREDIT CARDS: Amex, MC, Visa.
PRICES: per room B&B £250–£1,200. À la carte £46 (dining room), £30 (Flying Stag pub).

# CHIRNSIDE Scottish Borders

## CHIRNSIDE HALL

You will find abundant wildlife to photograph around Christian Korsten's Victorian country house in the Scottish Borders. It is 'a substantial mansion with the main rooms facing south across farmlands to the Cheviot hills', report trusted readers whose attic room was 'rather dark' but had 'beautiful views from two small windows'. It was spacious, with a good bed, a large bathroom with a bath and walk-in shower, and plenty of storage space. Some rooms have a four-poster, all have wool carpets and luxury toiletries. The style is traditional, with antique pieces. The lounge has deep sofas, while, in a dual-aspect dining room, the four-course, nightly-changing menu might include loin of roe deer from the estate, langoustine tortellini, and a vegetarian option (although plant-eaters will avert their eyes from the stags' and boars' heads that stare glassily from walls). 'The food was very good, with local produce.' Breakfast brings local black pudding and haggis, and Eyemouth kippers. Service is warm and informal: 'The waitress was very friendly – her favourite expression was "okey-dokey".' (Elspeth and John Gibbon)

Chirnside
Duns TD11 3LD

**T:** 01890 818219
**E:** reception@chirnsidehallhotel.com
**W:** chirnsidehallhotel.com

**BEDROOMS:** 10.
**OPEN:** all year.
**FACILITIES:** 2 lounges, dining room, private dining room/library/conference rooms, in-room TV (Freeview), billiard room, wedding facilities, 1½-acre grounds, lounges and restaurant wheelchair accessible.
**BACKGROUND MUSIC:** 'easy listening' in public areas.
**LOCATION:** 1½ miles E of Chirnside, NE of Duns.
**CHILDREN:** all ages welcomed.
**DOGS:** allowed in some bedrooms, not in public rooms.
**CREDIT CARDS:** Amex, MC, Visa.
**PRICES:** per room B&B single £105, double £190, D,B&B single £140, double £260. À la carte £40.

## THE COLINTRAIVE HOTEL

On a no-through road in a small village with spectacular views across the Kyles of Bute, this former shooting lodge is today a 'thoroughly recommended' dining pub-with-rooms-and-moorings. New owners Clare Banner and Joe Burnett, along with Maggie the tabby cat, extend a warm welcome. Bedrooms now have a fridge and a contemporary bathroom. There are sea views from the Bute and Attenborough rooms, the latter favoured by the late Sir Richard. Ardentraive, with country views, can sleep up to four. A log fire burns in the friendly bar, where snacks are served all day. From the dining room you can watch cattle grazing at the water's edge as you order from daily menus composed by chef Joe, who worked for the stellar Angela Hartnett in London. Local ingredients shine in such dishes as Isle of Bute onglet, or Gigha halibut with sea herbs, borlotti beans and almond chimichurri. 'We were offered a place at their Burns Night supper, which was a great success, and met nearly all the locals.' Wildlife spotters thrill to the sight of deer and red squirrels, eagles, seals and basking sharks. (Paul Hogarth)

Colintraive PA22 3AS

**T:** 01700 841207
**E:** enquiries@colintraivehotel.com
**W:** colintraivehotel.com

**BEDROOMS:** 4.
**OPEN:** all year except 25 Dec, restaurant closed Mon lunch.
**FACILITIES:** lounge, bar, restaurant, games room, in-room TV (Freeview), wedding facilities, small beer garden, yacht moorings, public rooms on ground floor wheelchair accessible, no adapted toilet.
**BACKGROUND MUSIC:** in public areas; occasional live music.
**LOCATION:** in village, 20 miles W of Dunoon.
**CHILDREN:** all ages welcomed.
**DOGS:** allowed in bedrooms, public rooms, not in restaurant.
**CREDIT CARDS:** Amex, MC, Visa.
**PRICES:** per room B&B single £89–£160, double £99–£185. À la carte £55.

# COLONSAY Argyll and Bute

MAP 5:D1

## THE COLONSAY

The island's only hotel is set on a hillside above the harbour, and has sweeping views across the bay to Jura. It has been the hub of village life since 1750. Painted in soothing blues and greens and furnished with deep sofas and wood-burning stoves, it has the look and feel of a welcoming, well-ordered home. The manager, Grace Johnston, maintains the peaceful atmosphere by keeping things low-key and friendly. Bedrooms, each named after a local location, are understated but nicely done, and have well-chosen contemporary oak furniture and fabrics by Colefax & Fowler, Designers Guild and Pierre Frey. Ardskenish, the largest, has views over the harbour; Port Lobh (with exclusive use of the bathroom down the hall) is the smallest, and looks out towards Colonsay church. Dinner is served anywhere you like, though the dining room, with its crisp white napery and floor-to-ceiling windows, is as good a place as any to tuck into Anthony Orr's seasonally changing menu focusing on local and Scottish ingredients, simply cooked. In the busy bar there are island beers on tap as well as a selection of local and mainland artisan gins.

Isle of Colonsay PA61 7YU

T: 01951 200316
E: hotel@colonsayholidays.co.uk
W: colonsayholidays.co.uk

**BEDROOMS:** 9.
**OPEN:** mid-Mar–Nov, Christmas, New Year.
**FACILITIES:** conservatory, 2 lounges, log room, bar, restaurant, free Wi-Fi on ground floor, in-room TV (Sky), 1-acre grounds, ground-floor public rooms wheelchair accessible, adapted toilet.
**BACKGROUND MUSIC:** in bar sometimes.
**LOCATION:** 400 yds W of harbour.
**CHILDREN:** all ages welcomed.
**DOGS:** allowed in 2 bedrooms, public rooms except restaurant.
**CREDIT CARDS:** MC, Visa.
**PRICES:** per room B&B single £85–£95, double £130–£190. Pre-ferry set menus £19–£25 Mon, Thurs, Fri, Sat, à la carte £30.

# CONTIN Highland

MAP 5:C2

## COUL HOUSE

A private road leads to this singular Georgian mansion in lovely gardens and grounds, with ancient trees, a pitch-and-putt area, and a fairy trail through the rhododendrons for children. Susannah and Stuart Macpherson bought it as a hotel in 2003 sight unseen, and have been refining it ever since. Bedrooms, with muted decor, range from small doubles to a junior suite with a large bed and chesterfield sofa bed, mood lighting, a roll-top tub with TV, and a separate walk-in rainforest shower. The most sought-after have mountain views; the hotel is on the doorstep of the North Coast 500 driving route. Every bathroom is now connected to the pressurised water system for a good spritz. Public rooms have ornate plaster ceilings, arches, columns, antiques, blazing fires, and a sea of patterned carpet. In the octagonal dining room, Garry Kenley's seasonally changing menus cater to all tastes, with such dishes as Mongolian fire pot vegetable stir fry, fish of the day or loin of venison with rabbit sausage. You can eat more simply in the dog-friendly lounge (soup, sandwiches). Breakfast is 'excellent and promptly served'.

Contin
Strathpeffer IV14 9ES

T: 01997 421487
E: stay@coulhouse.com
W: coulhouse.com

**BEDROOMS:** 21. 4 on ground floor, 1 suitable for disabled.
**OPEN:** all year except 23–26 Dec.
**FACILITIES:** lounge bar, drawing room, hall, restaurant, in-room smart TV, wedding/conference facilities, 8-acre grounds (9-hole pitch-and-putt), ground floor wheelchair accessible, adapted toilet.
**BACKGROUND MUSIC:** in lounge bar and restaurant.
**LOCATION:** 17 miles NW of Inverness.
**CHILDREN:** all ages welcomed.
**DOGS:** allowed in some bedrooms, all public rooms except restaurant (£9.50 per night).
**CREDIT CARDS:** Amex, MC, Visa.
**PRICES:** per room B&B double £130.50–£385 (single occupancy rates on application). À la carte £39. 1-night bookings refused New Year.

# CRAIGHOUSE Argyll and Bute                    MAP 5:D1

## JURA HOTEL

There are glorious views across Small Isles Bay
from the McCallum family's hotel, restaurant
and pub, in the only village, on the only road,
on this remote, beautiful island. Despite the lack
of competition, it maintains high standards.
The location is 'truly fabulous', with frequent
sightings of the red deer that vastly outnumber
humans. Spruced-up bedrooms and suites have
a 'superb modern bathroom' or shower room.
Two are supplied with bathrobes for a flit to a
separate private bathroom. The decor is simple,
with soft-hued paint finishes. There is TV in
one of the lounges and, now, Wi-Fi throughout.
Stuart Russell cooks pub fare and more complex
dishes, using local ingredients such as venison,
langoustine and Islay crab. Breakfast brings
home-baked sourdough, kippers or 'fat pancakes
with crispy bacon and maple syrup'. If funds
are tight, £5 will buy you a pitch for a small tent
on the lawn. If £1,080 is burning a hole in your
pocket, you can, alternatively, spend a night at the
Quadrangle on the new Ardfin golfing estate, but
you'll miss out on an authentic taste of friendly
community life.

Craighouse
Isle of Jura PA60 7XU

**T:** 01496 820243
**E:** hello@jurahotel.co.uk
**W:** jurahotel.co.uk

**BEDROOMS:** 17. 15 en suite, 2 with
private bathroom.
**OPEN:** all year except Christmas and
New Year.
**FACILITIES:** bar, TV lounge, restaurant,
outdoor eating area, picnic benches,
wedding facilities (events shack),
public areas wheelchair accessible, no
adapted toilet.
**BACKGROUND MUSIC:** all day in bar and
restaurant.
**LOCATION:** in village, opposite Small
Isles Bay, 300 yds from passenger
ferry terminal, 7 miles from car-ferry
terminal.
**CHILDREN:** all ages welcomed.
**DOGS:** allowed in pub only.
**CREDIT CARDS:** MC, Visa.
**PRICES:** per room B&B single £70–£80,
double £110–£150. À la carte £35.

# DUNVEGAN Highland

MAP 5:C1

## THE THREE CHIMNEYS AND THE HOUSE OVER-BY

In the remote north of Skye, a whitewashed stone crofter's cottage overlooking Loch Dunvegan, with views to the peaks of Harris and North Uist, is home to an ambitious restaurant-with-rooms. Smart, contemporary, ground-floor suites in the next-door House Over-By have a sea view and direct garden access, a king-size bed, and extras including fresh milk and home-baked treats to go with the espresso machine, as well as Temple Spa products. Five rooms have steps to a seating area; one, with a wet room, is suitable for a wheelchair-user and/or a family. Since taking the helm, Gordon Campbell Gray (see also The Pierhouse, Port Appin) has replaced the bathrooms, which now have a walk-in rain shower. There is a lounge with a modern log-burner, where guests can enjoy a malt whisky or cocktail. Chef Scott Davies still showcases the finest ingredients, locally grown, raised, shot, fished or foraged. A new menu allows diners to pick and mix such dishes as roasted Sconser scallop, fermented fennel and squid ink dashi; Skye red deer or Isle of Lewis woodcock; apple, miso, doughnut and cider crème. At breakfast, everything possible is home made.

Colbost
Dunvegan
Isle of Skye IV55 8ZT

**T:** 01470 511258
**E:** eatandstay@threechimneys.co.uk
**W:** threechimneys.co.uk

**BEDROOMS:** 6. All on ground floor (5 split-level) in separate building, 1 suitable for disabled.
**OPEN:** all year except 20 Dec–late Jan.
**FACILITIES:** lounge/breakfast room (House Over-By), restaurant, in-room TV (Freeview), wedding facilities, garden on loch, restaurant and lounge wheelchair accessible, adapted toilet.
**BACKGROUND MUSIC:** in lounge and restaurant, 'for different moods and times of day'.
**LOCATION:** 5 miles W of Dunvegan.
**CHILDREN:** all ages welcomed.
**DOGS:** not allowed.
**CREDIT CARDS:** Amex, MC, Visa.
**PRICES:** per room B&B double £365, triple £465 (no charge for child under 8, sharing). Dishes £6–£45, kitchen table tasting dinner £110.

# EDINBURGH

MAP 5:D2

## 94DR

'My only disappointment was that my stay had to come to an end,' says a more than satisfied guest at this personable guest house on Southside's Dalkeith Road. A beautiful entrance hall with Victorian floor tiles, fresh flowers and an elegant velvet sofa set the tone for Paul Lightfoot and John MacEwan's boutique B&B. Downstairs, the cool, sophisticated decor is enlivened by bold artwork. The lounge library has an 'eclectic selection of titles' plus an honesty bar. Upstairs, the bedrooms, each named after a Scottish whisky, are comfortable and well appointed, some with original features. Those at the front have views of Salisbury Crags and Arthur's Seat; those at the back overlook the garden to the Pentland hills beyond. Distinctly decadent bathrooms have power shower, under-floor heating, waffle robes and White Company toiletries. Breakfast is taken in the 'comfortable' conservatory where service is 'prompt and attentive'. Paul's home-made granola, dressed with honey, apricot and vanilla, is 'delicious'. He also rustles up a cracking cooked breakfast. (RB)

**25% DISCOUNT VOUCHERS**

94 Dalkeith Road
Edinburgh EH16 5AF

T: 0131 662 9265
E: stay@94dr.com
W: 94dr.com

BEDROOMS: 6.
OPEN: all year except 25/26 Dec (ring to check Jan 2021 opening times).
FACILITIES: lounge with honesty bar, drawing room, breakfast room, in-room TV (BT, Freeview, Netflix), walled garden, bicycles available to borrow, pop-up dining event twice a month.
BACKGROUND MUSIC: during the day in guest lounge.
LOCATION: A 20-min. walk or a 10-min. bus journey to all amenities.
CHILDREN: 3 and upwards welcomed.
DOGS: not allowed.
CREDIT CARDS: MC, Visa.
PRICES: per room B&B £150–£200. Min. 2-night stay weekends Mar–Oct, 4-night stay at New Year.

**SEE ALSO SHORTLIST**

# EDINBURGH

## PRESTONFIELD

Wrapped in parkland, this gleaming white country house that is only ten minutes from the city centre takes luxury to hedonistic levels, with lavish decorations and indulgent service. The 17th-century mansion, with its shuttered windows and carved ceilings, exudes 'an air of gorgeous splendour'. Owned by James Thomson, Prestonfield is a glamorous mix of rich colours, antiques, tapestries, gilded portraits and glinting crystal. Intimate rooms with brocade sofas are perfect places to enjoy afternoon tea, and if it's warm, you can sit on the terrace. 'Magnificent' bedrooms come with velvets, antiques, darkly patterned wallpapers, rococo mirrors, and perhaps a Gothic day bed or silver chariot bath. Treats include fruit, complimentary champagne and 'a real bed with sheets and blanket'. 'Dinner was excellent, in a gorgeous room with amazing decor.' The menu might include duck and wood pigeon terrine followed by stone bass with tempura mussels. Vegans are catered for, and the wine list is weighty. 'Excellent' breakfasts run from omelettes and smashed avocado to the full Scottish with haggis. (John Barnes)

Priestfield Road
Edinburgh EH16 5UT

**T:** 0131 225 7800
**E:** reservations@prestonfield.com
**W:** prestonfield.com

**BEDROOMS:** 23. 1, on ground floor, suitable for disabled.
**OPEN:** all year.
**FACILITIES:** lift, 2 drawing rooms, sitting room, library, whisky bar, restaurant, private dining rooms, in-room TV (Sky), wedding facilities, terraces, tea house, 20-acre grounds, public rooms wheelchair accessible, adapted toilet.
**BACKGROUND MUSIC:** 'when suitable' in public areas.
**LOCATION:** next to Royal Holyrood Park.
**CHILDREN:** all ages welcomed.
**DOGS:** allowed in bedrooms, public rooms and park, not in restaurant (£25 per dog per night).
**CREDIT CARDS:** Amex, MC, Visa.
**PRICES:** per room B&B £355–£655, D,B&B £435–£725. Set 3-course dinner £40, à la carte £55.

**SEE ALSO SHORTLIST**

# EDINBURGH

## 24 ROYAL TERRACE NEW

There is modern art everywhere in the chichi bar at this boutique hotel in William Playfair's palace-fronted Georgian terrace. The changing exhibitions are very much what it's all about, giving guests the chance to appreciate art in lavish surroundings. The 16 bedrooms are colourfully stylish too, with designer fabric, oversized headboards and a mix of contemporary and period furniture. They range from singles overlooking the back garden, with smart TV and a bathroom with HD BluCube speakers, to junior suites with a large seating area. Two superior doubles – one with views to the Firth of Forth – have an in-room roll-top bath. Breakfast, served until noon and charged separately, brings a choice of a continental buffet and cooked dishes. These include waffles with berries and maple syrup, scrambled egg with smoked Scottish salmon, an exceptional vegan full Scottish with meatless haggis, and Cointreau hot chocolate, cafetière or espresso coffee and superior teas. They also offer soups, sandwiches and sharing boards, but you'll need to venture out for a full evening meal.

24 Royal Terrace
Edinburgh EH7 5AH

**T:** 0131 297 2424
**E:** reservations@24royalterrace.com
**W:** 24royalterrace.co.uk

**BEDROOMS:** 16. 1 on ground floor, plus 2 studio apartments.
**OPEN:** all year.
**FACILITIES:** bar, in-room smart TV, terrace, garden (outdoor tables), unsuitable for disabled.
**BACKGROUND MUSIC:** in public areas.
**LOCATION:** east of city centre.
**CHILDREN:** all ages welcomed.
**DOGS:** allowed in public rooms and garden.
**CREDIT CARDS:** Amex, MC, Visa.
**PRICES:** room £159–£400. Continental breakfast £9, cooked breakfast £15. 1-night bookings refused Aug, New Year, special events.

**SEE ALSO SHORTLIST**

# EDINBURGH

## 23 MAYFIELD

This family-run B&B, in a detached Victorian house a mile from the city centre, is nothing short of outstanding, say readers. Built in 1868, the house retains many original features, such as beautiful cornicing and stained-glass windows. Owners Ross and Kathleen Birnie, who 'show clear pride in and enjoyment of their work', have given the public rooms the feel of a gentleman's club, with leather seating, Georgian chess board, honesty bar and a vast selection of old and rare books. Bedrooms are 'in keeping with the ambience of the house'; there are king-size beds, solid mahogany furniture and handmade furnishings, plus fresh coffee and cafetière, a selection of teas and Border Biscuits. Several rooms have a four-poster bed; all have a modern bathroom with Noble Isle toiletries. Readers report no traffic noise in the bedrooms on the ground floor or those in the middle of the house. At breakfast Ross's smile 'lit up the room' as he served a Caledonian feast of local eggs, haggis, Stranraer sausages, black pudding and clootie dumpling. Lighter dishes include cereal and porridge topped with malt whisky. (RG, and others)

23 Mayfield Gardens
Edinburgh EH9 2BX

T: 0131 667 5806
E: info@23mayfield.co.uk
W: 23mayfield.co.uk

BEDROOMS: 7, 1 on ground floor.
OPEN: all year except Christmas.
FACILITIES: club room, breakfast room, in-room smart TV (Freeview), terrace, garden, parking.
BACKGROUND MUSIC: at breakfast.
LOCATION: 1 mile S of city centre.
CHILDREN: aged 3 and over welcomed.
DOGS: not allowed.
CREDIT CARDS: MC, Visa.
PRICES: per room B&B £110–£230. Usually 2-night min. stay but check availability.

**SEE ALSO SHORTLIST**

# ELIE Fife

## THE SHIP INN

Rachel and Graham Bucknall run a happy ship
indeed at this village pub-with-rooms on the
beach, with view across the Firth of Forth. Guide
inspectors, arriving on a wet November day,
found the place buzzing, 'but we were greeted
warmly, checked in' and shown to a dog-friendly
ground-floor room with white-painted shutters
and a bathroom with walk-in shower. 'The bed
was enormous, dressed in white linen with a
simple woollen throw.' Admiral room, with bath
and shower, is large enough to take an extra bed,
and has a window seat from which to watch
the pub's cricket team playing on the sands. All
rooms have coastal style, nautical knick-knacks,
an espresso machine and Siabann toiletries.
Food is served in the bar, with its log fires, and
in the upstairs restaurant. Chef Mat Majer's
menus champion local produce in such dishes
as monkfish with chickpea, saffron and tomato
stew, haddock and chips or, for vegans, spiced
cauliflower with sweet potato, pickles, tahini
dressing, pomegranate and mint. 'The staff in the
restaurant were delightful.' The Bucknalls also
have The Bridge Inn at Ratho (see Shortlist entry).

The Toft
Elie KY9 1DT

**T:** 01333 330246
**E:** info@shipinn.scot
**W:** shipinn.scot

**BEDROOMS:** 6.
**OPEN:** all year, except Christmas Day.
**FACILITIES:** bar, restaurant, beach bar,
in-room TV (Freeview), wedding
facilities, beer garden/terrace.
**BACKGROUND MUSIC:** in public areas.
**LOCATION:** in town, on the bay.
**CHILDREN:** all ages welcomed.
**DOGS:** in bar, downstairs restaurant,
2 bedrooms (£15 per stay).
**CREDIT CARDS:** MC, Visa.
**PRICES:** per room B&B £100–£220.
À la carte £35 (vegetarian/vegan £27).
1-night bookings refused at New Year.

# GAIRLOCH Highland

MAP 5:B1

## SHIELDAIG LODGE

Once a Victorian hunting lodge, this 'unpretentious' hotel makes the most of both its history and its West Highland geography on the banks of Loch Gairloch. Deer stalking, fishing and falconry are all on offer on the 26,000-acre estate. Inside, among a 'splendid aroma of peat, whisky and leather', are deep leather sofas, log fires, tartan and tweed furnishings and more than 250 whiskies in the bar. Chef Jerome Prodanu's daily-changing menus have an equally Scottish flavour, incorporating estate lamb, venison and beef as well as locally caught seafood and produce from the lodge's own vegetable garden. Readers were very happy with their 'Cape Wrath oysters and sweet North Uist scallops with black pudding and supreme of duck'. The wine list is 'good'. 'Seal spotting at dinner and breakfast was a real treat.' Upstairs, 'large and comfortable' bedrooms are country-Caledonian in style: a tartan headboard here, a stag-print cushion there. Some have sweeping views of the loch, others overlook the garden. 'A fantastic location, excellent staff and very good food.' (John Barnes, David Birnie)

Badachro
Gairloch IV21 2AN

T: 01445 741333
E: reservations@shieldaiglodge.com
W: shieldaiglodge.com

BEDROOMS: 12.
OPEN: all year.
FACILITIES: lounge, library, bar, restaurant, snooker/private dining room, in-room TV (Freeview), wedding facilities, garden, 26,000-acre estate (tennis, fishing, red deer stalking, falconry centre, motor boat for charter), public areas wheelchair accessible.
BACKGROUND MUSIC: in lounge, bar and restaurant.
LOCATION: 4¼ miles S of Gairloch.
CHILDREN: all ages welcomed.
DOGS: not allowed.
CREDIT CARDS: Amex, MC, Visa.
PRICES: per room B&B single £95–£170, double £130–£350. Set menu £44.50, tasting menu (on request) £69.

# GLASGOW

## GRASSHOPPERS

A recent guest describes this modern, style-conscious and budget-friendly penthouse hotel, next to Glasgow Central Station, as a 'great find'. From the less-than-promising entrance, a lift whisks guests up six floors to a Scandi-meets-urban eyrie of dove-grey and white with pale oak floors, contemporary furniture and soft lighting, there to be greeted by its 'very welcoming' owner, Barrie Munn. A corridor leads to the bedrooms, either overlooking the rooftops of Union Street or the station's glazed roof. Stylishly simple bedrooms have large casement windows (with blackout curtains), handmade wallpaper and plump duvet. Pod-like bathrooms are compact but have a powerful shower and Arran Aromatics toiletries. There is a small bar in the sitting room. Breakfast, a feast of bacon and eggs, fresh fruit and yogurt as well as porridge, cheeses and cold meats, is served in The Kitchen where home-made cakes, sausage rolls and tea and coffee are freely available. Our reviewer ordered the 'modestly priced' suppers in advance, and found them 'very pleasant'. 'We thoroughly enjoyed our stay,' he enthuses. (Michael Blakely)

87 Union Street
Glasgow G13 TA

T: 0141 222 2666
E: info@grasshoppersglasgow.com
W: grasshoppersglasgow.com

BEDROOMS: 29.
OPEN: all year except 4 days Christmas.
FACILITIES: breakfast/supper room, sitting room with small bar, in-room TV (Sky).
BACKGROUND MUSIC: none.
LOCATION: by Central Station.
CHILDREN: all ages welcomed, cots and extra beds (request at time of booking).
DOGS: allowed.
CREDIT CARDS: Amex, MC, Visa.
PRICES: per room B&B single £70–£108, double £90–£148. À la carte £17.

**SEE ALSO SHORTLIST**

# GLENFINNAN Highland

MAP 5:C1

## GLENFINNAN HOUSE HOTEL

You can almost hear the skirling of pipes as you gaze across Loch Shiel from Jane MacFarlane's waterside mansion to the Glenfinnan Monument and distant Ben Nevis. Topped by a lone Highlander, the monument recalls the doomed 1745 Jacobite rebellion, and few vistas are more emotive than this one. Manja and Duncan Gibson have been manager and chef at the hotel since 2002, and staff are 'courteous and helpful'. Readers this year stayed in a room with a four-poster and a loch view, and loved the 'stunning location'. All bedrooms have mahogany and oak furniture and rich fabrics but no key, TV or telephone. Garden-view rooms have a spa bath. Lounges have antiques, blazing fires, and artwork on a Jacobite theme. You can eat in a bar bristling with antlers, or in the dining room – perhaps pan-fried monkfish with tomato, basil and courgette risotto or sausages, either venison or vegan. 'Dinner in the bar was delicious, and I felt my vegetarian needs were met wonderfully.' After breakfast there are 'glorious walks', and Harry Potter fans can ride the steam train across the famous Glenfinnan Viaduct. (Justine Rogan, and others)

Glenfinnan
Fort William PH37 4LT

**T:** 01397 722235
**E:** availability@glenfinnanhouse.com
**W:** glenfinnanhouse.com

**BEDROOMS:** 14.
**OPEN:** 26 Mar–17 Oct.
**FACILITIES:** drawing room, bar/lounge, playroom, restaurant, wedding facilities, 1-acre grounds (play area), unsuitable for disabled.
**BACKGROUND MUSIC:** Scottish in bar and restaurant.
**LOCATION:** 15 miles NW of Fort William.
**CHILDREN:** all ages welcomed.
**DOGS:** allowed in bedrooms and some public rooms, not in restaurant or drawing room.
**CREDIT CARDS:** Amex, MC, Visa.
**PRICES:** per room B&B single £130–£250, double £150–£270. À la carte £25–£40.

**SEE ALSO SHORTLIST**

# GRANTOWN-ON-SPEY Highland

## CULDEARN HOUSE

On the edge of the Cairngorms national park, William and Sonia Marshall's bay-fronted Victorian house looks on to a tract of the ancient woodlands that surround Grantown-on-Spey. It is more 'fine guest house' than hotel, say readers. When our inspectors last visited, they found 'an atmosphere of comfort and warmth', the six bedrooms done in eclectic country house style (dual-aspect Craigievar has some fine antiques). The Marshalls are welcoming hosts: 'We had a very pleasant room, and interesting chats with the man of the house.' Guests gather for drinks before dinner in a lounge 'with family photos on the sideboard'. Sonia Marshall's nightly-changing menus, which some readers report are 'more akin to home cooking than fine dining', are a showcase of local ingredients: free-range eggs, humanely reared beef and fish from the Moray coast. 'The meat and game were so tender and full of flavour.' At breakfast there is 'lovely fruit salad, home-made marmalade, and a good choice of cooked dishes', including haggis. Fishing, shooting, golf, wildlife-watching and whisky tours can be arranged.

Woodlands Terrace
Grantown-on-Spey PH26 3JU

**T:** 01479 872106
**E:** enquiries@culdearn.com
**W:** culdearn.com

**BEDROOMS:** 6. 1 on ground floor, with wet room, suitable for disabled.
**OPEN:** all year except Feb, Mar, Christmas (open New Year).
**FACILITIES:** drawing room, dining room, in-room TV (Freeview), ¾-acre garden, public rooms wheelchair accessible.
**BACKGROUND MUSIC:** none.
**LOCATION:** edge of town (within walking distance).
**CHILDREN:** 10 and upwards welcomed, younger children by arrangement.
**DOGS:** only guide dogs.
**CREDIT CARDS:** Amex, MC, Visa.
**PRICES:** per room B&B single £125–£150, double £160–£180. Fixed-price dinner £48.

# GRANTOWN-ON-SPEY Highland

MAP 5:C2

## THE DULAIG

Hens roam the landscaped gardens of this B&B, a stroll from a town set amid ancient woodlands on the edge of the Cairngorms national park. The Edwardian house was designed by Alexander Marshall Mackenzie, after he completed London's Waldorf Hotel. It is 'a wonderful place', a reader writes. Carol and Gordon Bulloch are 'fantastic hosts who cannot do enough to make you comfortable'. New arrivals are welcomed with tea and home-baked scones in the drawing room, which 'looks on to the beautiful garden, with lots of life (wild and tame!)'. The bedrooms have Arts and Crafts or Art Nouveau furniture. One has a double-ended slipper bath with over-bath rain shower, one a spa bath with shower over, while dual-aspect Shapland has a large walk-in shower with body jets. All rooms have a mini-fridge, under-floor bathroom heating, luxury toiletries and a daily surprise cake. Breakfast brings porridge, heather honey, kipper and horseradish fishcakes, a full Scottish with haggis, and, of course, new-laid eggs. You can order a packed lunch for a day's fishing on the Spey. 'We really enjoyed our stay. Haste us back!' (Valerie Anderson)

Seafield Avenue
Grantown-on-Spey PH26 3JF

T: 01479 872065
E: enquiries@thedulaig.com
W: thedulaig.com

BEDROOMS: 3.
OPEN: all year except Christmas, New Year.
FACILITIES: drawing room, dining room, in-room TV (Freesat), 1½-acre garden (pond, summer house), veranda, parking (garage for motorbikes and bicycles), not suitable for disabled.
BACKGROUND MUSIC: quiet Scottish music at breakfast 'with guests' permission'.
LOCATION: 600 yards from Grantown-on-Spey.
CHILDREN: not under 12.
DOGS: only assistance dogs allowed.
CREDIT CARDS: Amex, MC, Visa.
PRICES: per room B&B single £140–£160, double £180–£200.

# GULLANE East Lothian

MAP 5:D3

## THE BONNIE BADGER

A half-hour drive from Edinburgh, Tom and Michaela Kitchin have turned the old Golf Inn, in a village on the Firth of Forth, into a chic gastropub-with-rooms. The same 'nature-to-plate' values apply here as at the Michelin-starred Kitchin on Edinburgh's Leith waterfront, but dishes as simple as egg and chips and fish pie sit alongside more elaborate meals such as Borders lamb with haggis and potato terrine on seasonal menus devised by Tom and chef Matthew Budge. The Stables dining room, with its exposed roof timbers and sandstone walls, is as impressive as the food. So is the stripped-back decor elsewhere, which has been given a cool contemporary look by Swedish Michaela. Bedrooms, in the inn and two cottages, are done in tones of sand and teal inspired by the Lothian countryside, with eye-twizzling 'thistle' wallpaper by designer Mairi Helena. Each has a marble bathroom with walk-in shower. Guests receive turn-down treats of hot chocolate and nibbles. Breakfast brings a full Scottish, avocado and poached eggs, or a bacon roll. 'We shall certainly return,' say readers who enjoyed 'a super evening meal'. (LAM)

Main Street
Gullane EH31 2AB

T: 01620 621111
E: info@bonniebadger.com
W: bonniebadger.com

BEDROOMS: 13. 5 in adjacent cottages.
OPEN: all year.
FACILITIES: bar, restaurant, outside dining room, garden room, private dining room, garden area, in-room TV (Sky), wedding facilities, bar and restaurant wheelchair accessible, adapted toilet.
BACKGROUND MUSIC: in public areas.
LOCATION: centre of village.
CHILDREN: all ages welcomed, children's menu.
DOGS: allowed in specific bedrooms (£25 a night), in restaurant and pub area.
CREDIT CARDS: Amex, MC, Visa.
PRICES: per room B&B £195–£420 (£300–£595 around key golf event days). À la carte £40, early set dinner (5–6.30 pm) £19–£26.

# GULLANE East Lothian

MAP 5:D3

## GREYWALLS

A mere ha-ha separates this Arts and Crafts Edwardian house from Muirfield golf course. Designed by Sir Edwin Lutyens, it is surrounded by gardens attributed to Gertrude Jekyll. It has been 'beautifully furnished' by the Weaver family, in country house style, with antiques and artwork of the period. You can have a drink on the lawn overlooking the 18th green, take tea in the tiny Summer House Tea Room, or relax by the fire with a book from the library. Bedrooms, some in cottages, range from a 'caddie's closet' single to a premier double with a deep, freestanding bath and steam shower. Most rooms are spacious, and have a view of golf course or gardens, perhaps a bath and walk-in shower, dual-aspect windows and an original fireplace. 'The staff are courteous, welcoming; they could not be more helpful.' An all-day menu is served in the bar, and there is fine dining in one of four rooms, where chef Ryan McCutcheon's locally sourced menus might include seared North Atlantic cod with oyster gnocchi and nettle velouté. Breakfast brings free-range eggs, and grilled kipper with scallop butter. (EAS)

Muirfield
Gullane EH31 2EG

**T:** 01620 842144
**E:** gm@greywalls.co.uk
**W:** greywalls.co.uk

**BEDROOMS:** 23. 4 on ground floor, 6 in cottages 100 yds from main house.
**OPEN:** all year.
**FACILITIES:** bar/lounge, drawing room, library, restaurant, in-room TV (Freeview), wedding facilities, function facilities, spa treatments, 6-acre garden, Summer House Tea Room.
**BACKGROUND MUSIC:** none, pianist on Fri, Sat pm.
**LOCATION:** 20 miles E of Edinburgh.
**CHILDREN:** all ages welcomed, travel cots provided.
**DOGS:** allowed in cottage bedrooms, not in public rooms.
**CREDIT CARDS:** Amex, MC, Visa.
**PRICES:** per room B&B single £95–£430, double £325–£450. Market menu £45, vegetarian £40, à la carte £55.

# INVERGARRY Highland

MAP 5:C2

## GLENGARRY CASTLE HOTEL

**NEW**

On the shore of Loch Oich, this rambling baronial Victorian house has its own castle ruins in its extensive wooded grounds – Invergarry Castle is said to have hosted Bonnie Prince Charlie after the Battle of Culloden. Guests can stay in splendour in 'a glorious building with splendid staircases', run by the MacCallum family for 60 years. Step into the hall to find a sofa by a blazing fire, walls hung with landscape paintings and a totemic stag's head. Bedrooms range from a modest single to a luxurious four-poster room with loch views. 'Ours was magnificent, with sheets and blankets and an amazing, long bath,' writes a reader. Guests order drinks at reception to enjoy in the muzak-free, 'large and wonderful lounges'. At dinner, tables are 'beautifully laid', with silverware and fine china, for a limited-choice menu of such dishes as game terrine with red onion marmalade, saddle of rabbit stuffed with wild mushrooms and, for vegans, pearl barley risotto. After a breakfast kipper, you can play tennis, row or fish on the loch, or visit romantic Eilean Donan Castle. (John Barnes)

Invergarry PH35 4HW

**T:** 01809 501254
**E:** castle@glengarry.net
**W:** glengarry.net

**BEDROOMS:** 26.
**OPEN:** 26 Mar–1 Nov.
**FACILITIES:** library, lounge with bar service, in-room TV (Freeview), 60-acre grounds (gardens, woodlands, tennis, rowing boats, castle ruins).
**BACKGROUND MUSIC:** none.
**LOCATION:** on A82, 1 mile S of A87 junction in Invergarry.
**CHILDREN:** all ages welcomed, not in deluxe bedrooms (3–12 years £25, over-12s £50 in parents' room, children's supper by arrangement).
**DOGS:** allowed in some bedrooms and hall, not in deluxe rooms, lounge or library.
**CREDIT CARDS:** Amex, MC, Visa.
**PRICES:** per room single £100, double £150–£290. Fixed-price dinner £38.

# INVERKEILOR Angus                              MAP 5:D3

## GORDON'S

Readers are charmed by the warm welcome
they receive from hostess Maria Watson and the
'outstanding food' created by Garry, her son,
at this restaurant-with-rooms in a Victorian
terrace house in a village close to the North Sea
coast. It was opened in 1986 by Maria with her
husband, Gordon, but on his death in 2016, Garry
took over as chef. There are just five bedrooms,
each with its own emphatic style. Thistle has
Timorous Beasties' Grand Thistle wallpaper, a
roll-top bath and separate shower. The spacious
annexe, Courtyard Suite, 'smart, spotless and very
comfortable', has a freestanding roll-top bath
and a shower room. Garry's nightly-changing
five-course menus offer a choice of two dishes at
each course. For instance, North Sea halibut with
chorizo, couscous, coriander and curry vinaigrette
or Angus roe deer loin in pistachio crust with
confit shoulder, butter bean cassoulet and girolle
jus: 'fine ingredients lovingly prepared'. 'The wine
list was balanced and provided excellent choices.'
Breakfast, with freshly squeezed orange juice and
a full Scottish with Stornoway black pudding,
does not disappoint. (J and JN, S and AM)

Main Street
Inverkeilor DD11 5RN

T: 01241 830364
E: gordonsrest@aol.com
W: gordonsrestaurant.co.uk

BEDROOMS: 5. 1 on ground floor in
courtyard annexe.
OPEN: all year (incl. 25 and 31 Dec),
closed Jan, Mon and Tues in summer,
Sun–Tues 31 Oct–31 Mar.
FACILITIES: lounge, restaurant, in-room
TV (terrestrial), small garden and
patio, only restaurant wheelchair
accessible.
BACKGROUND MUSIC: in restaurant.
LOCATION: in hamlet, 6 miles NE of
Arbroath.
CHILDREN: over-12s welcomed (no
family rooms).
DOGS: not allowed.
CREDIT CARDS: MC, Visa.
PRICES: per room B&B £110–£165.
Fixed-price dinner £69.

# IONA Argyll and Bute

MAP 5:D1

## ARGYLL HOTEL

Set amid the splendid isolation of a sparsely
populated Hebridean island, this small 19th-
century hotel is a few minutes' walk from the
ferry, and has magnificent views across the
Sound of Iona to Mull. To limit the hotel's impact
on its surroundings, owners Wendy and Rob
MacManaway and Katy and Dafydd Russon
run things as sustainably as possible. Food really
matters here; the kitchen is, they say, 'at the heart
of what we do'. Meat and fish come from local
and ethical sources: fruit, vegetables and salads
are grown mainly in the organic garden; bread,
pastries and cakes are all made on the premises.
Dinner might include pan-seared Isle of Mull
scallops or roast loin of Iona hogget followed by
rhubarb, stem ginger and honeycomb cranachan.
The cosy rooms tend to be compact, with pine
furniture, and oatmeal and pale blue furnishings;
some have sea views, while others overlook the
garden. The largest room has an exposed stone
wall and wood-burning stove (you can also ask
reception for a hot-water bottle). There is plenty
of space to relax downstairs, perhaps by the fire
in the North Lounge, or in the sunshine in the
Sun Lounge.

**25% DISCOUNT VOUCHERS**

Isle of Iona PA76 6SJ

**T:** 01681 700334
**E:** reception@argyllhoteliona.co.uk
**W:** argyllhoteliona.co.uk

**BEDROOMS:** 17. 7 in linked extension.
**OPEN:** early Mar to early Nov.
**FACILITIES:** 3 lounges (1 with TV),
conservatory, dining room, free Wi-Fi
in public areas, wedding facilities,
seafront lawn, organic vegetable
garden, lounges/dining room
wheelchair accessible, unadapted
toilet, one step up.
**BACKGROUND MUSIC:** modern Scottish,
'gentle' jazz, country music in dining
room.
**LOCATION:** village centre.
**CHILDREN:** all ages welcomed, under-
4s free.
**DOGS:** up to 2 'well-behaved' dogs
allowed in bedrooms, not in dining
room or sun lounge.
**CREDIT CARDS:** MC, Visa.
**PRICES:** per room B&B single £80–£85,
double £100–£210. À la carte £35.
1-night bookings often refused (ring
to check).

# KILBERRY Argyll and Bute

## KILBERRY INN

'It's always good to be back,' write readers returning to David Wilson and Clare Johnson's restaurant-with-rooms in a former croft. It stands on a quiet, scenic coastal road with views to the Inner Hebrides. 'We were greeted by David with a big hug.' Bedrooms, surrounding a gravelled courtyard, are appropriately simple. Each has a Hypnos bed, a walk-in shower and its own entrance (open the door and smell the roses and herbs in raised beds). Thoughtful touches include fresh milk and home-made shortbread, books and magazines. 'This year, the snug has been turned into a home cinema showing Ealing comedies.' A red telephone box just outside is labelled 'The Wee Bar' (not an invitation to misuse it, but possibly the world's smallest bar). At night, Clare cooks a 'fantastic' three-course dinner, served in a room with exposed stone walls and, on dreich days, a roaring fire. One reader found it all so 'totally romantic' that he 'proposed on the spot to my now wife'. Breakfast for such loved-up couples brings porridge, Kintyre eggs, Skipness smoked salmon, Stornoway black pudding and tattie scones. (Tony Hall, GC)

Kilberry
Tarbert PA29 6YD

T: 01880 770223
E: relax@kilberryinn.com
W: kilberryinn.com

BEDROOMS: 5. All on ground floor.
OPEN: Tues–Sun mid-Mar–end Sept, Tues–Sat Oct, Fri/Sat Nov/Dec, New Year (closed Christmas).
FACILITIES: restaurant, snug (wood-burning stove), variable Wi-Fi, in-room TV (Freeview), small garden.
BACKGROUND MUSIC: in restaurant at dinner.
LOCATION: 16 miles NW of Tarbert, on B8024.
CHILDREN: not under 12.
DOGS: allowed by arrangement in 2 bedrooms, not in public rooms.
CREDIT CARDS: MC, Visa.
PRICES: per room D,B&B single £160, double £250. À la carte £37. 1-night bookings sometimes refused holiday weekends.

# KILLIECRANKIE Perth and Kinross        MAP 5:D2

## KILLIECRANKIE HOTEL

Trusted readers again 'strongly endorse' this 'wonderful' country house hotel, which is 'kind and welcoming to children, families and adults alike'. The whitewashed former dower house overlooks the stunning, wooded Pass of Killiecrankie carved out by the River Garry. 'It is personally run by Henrietta Fergusson, ably supported by her excellent team, with truly fine food and wine.' A sense of 'Scottish heritage' runs through everything, from the tartans in a 'splendidly decorated dining room' and the plaid-clad waiting staff, to a whisky menu (including a very local, smoky Blair Athol). 'It is a joy to watch the great variety of birds on the numerous feeders which can be seen from the bar and breakfast room.' Traditionally styled, 'good and comfortable' bedrooms have shortbread, and cut flowers from brimming herbaceous borders, which are 'a delight in summer'. Mark Easton's modern cooking features such ingredients as Perthshire lamb and Aberdeen Angus beef. The 'mind-boggling wine list' is supervised by an 'expert sommelier'. Also appreciated: the 'blessed absence of background music'. (Stephen and Pauline Glover, KF)

Killiecrankie
Pitlochry PH16 5LG

**T:** 01796 473220
**E:** enquiries@killiecrankiehotel.co.uk
**W:** killiecrankiehotel.co.uk

**BEDROOMS:** 10. 2 on ground floor.
**OPEN:** 19 Mar–3 Jan.
**FACILITIES:** sitting room, bar with conservatory, dining room, breakfast conservatory, in-room TV (Freeview), 4½-acre grounds (gardens, woodland), public areas wheelchair accessible.
**BACKGROUND MUSIC:** none.
**LOCATION:** in hamlet 3 miles W of Pitlochry.
**CHILDREN:** all ages welcomed.
**DOGS:** allowed in bar and some bedrooms (not unattended), not in sitting or dining rooms.
**CREDIT CARDS:** Amex, MC, Visa.
**PRICES:** per person B&B from £135, subject to availability, per room D,B&B single £170–£180, double £290–£350 (deduct £65 for single occupancy of a double room). Set dinner £45. 1-night bookings sometimes refused weekends.

# KINGUSSIE Highland

## THE CROSS AT KINGUSSIE

♤ Previous César winner

Amid the wooded mountain scenery of the
Cairngorms national park, a Victorian tweed mill
once driven by the rocky, rushing Gynack Burn
lives on as a restaurant-with-rooms. More power
to owners Celia and Derek Kitchingman, say
trusted readers. This is 'the best hotel we stayed
in on a Highland tour', writes one. 'We were
knocked out,' another concurs. 'We had a room
with a small balcony overlooking the fast-flowing
burn, and could lie in bed with the doors open,
listening to the soothing rush of water.' 'Ours
was a modern attic room. The bed was really
comfortable, the shower excellent, the towels were
of high quality.' There are two cosy lounges, one
with a log-burner. You can take a cream tea on
the terrace and watch as red squirrels raid the bird
feeders. In the beamed stone dining room, David
Skiggs's menus are a showcase for local produce.
George Gow's lamb and wild venison were 'the
best meat dishes either of us had tasted this year'. At
breakfast, 'not quite in the same league', there are
free-range eggs, freshly squeezed juice, Mr Gow's
bacon and sausages, smoked fish and freshly
baked croissants. (Colin Bradshaw, John Holland)

Ardbroilach Road
Kingussie PH21 1LB

T: 01540 661166
E: relax@thecross.co.uk
W: thecross.co.uk

BEDROOMS: 8.
OPEN: Tues–Sat, Feb–early Jan, closed
Christmas but open for New Year.
FACILITIES: 2 lounges, restaurant,
in-room TV (Freeview), 4-acre
grounds (terraced garden, woodland),
restaurant wheelchair accessible.
BACKGROUND MUSIC: none.
LOCATION: 440 yds from village centre.
CHILDREN: all ages welcomed.
DOGS: not allowed.
CREDIT CARDS: Amex, MC, Visa.
PRICES: per room B&B £130–£180,
D,B&B £220–£270. Set 3-course dinner
£55, 6-course tasting menu £65.

# KIRKBEAN Dumfries and Galloway

MAP 5:E2

## CAVENS

Jane and Angus Fordyce demonstrate 'a rare combination of relaxed professionalism and high standards', says a visitor to their Georgian country house. It stands in extensive grounds near the Solway coast, Criffel hill a solitary backdrop. 'We were made to feel very much at home.' Fires burn in public rooms filled with period furniture, walls adorned with portraits of the Oswald family, the original owners. A painting of Mrs Oswald and a highly irreverent ode to her by Robert Burns are displayed in Oswald Room, with a light-filled sitting room with a sofa bed. Spacious, dual-aspect Criffel has a super-king-size bed, a seating area, a bath and separate shower. Large ground-floor Solway has a comfy sofa, garden access, a bath and walk-in shower. All rooms are well furnished and have fine china and locally made biscuits. Angus cooks a short three-course dinner of local meat and fish. 'The food was first class; we both particularly enjoyed the perfectly cooked rib-eye steak.' Breakfast offers local sausages and locally smoked salmon. (Colin Arthur, F and DT)

Kirkbean
Dumfries DG2 8AA

**T:** 01387 880234
**E:** enquiries@cavens.com
**W:** cavens.com

**BEDROOMS:** 6. 1 on ground floor.
**OPEN:** Mar–Nov, exclusive use by groups at New Year.
**FACILITIES:** 2 sitting rooms, dining room, wine cellar, meeting facilities, in-room TV (Freeview), 10-acre grounds.
**BACKGROUND MUSIC:** light classical all day in 1 sitting room, dining room.
**LOCATION:** in village.
**CHILDREN:** all ages welcomed.
**DOGS:** allowed by arrangement, not in public rooms or unattended in bedrooms.
**CREDIT CARDS:** MC, Visa.
**PRICES:** per room D,B&B single £232, double £290–£350, family £370–£390. Dinner £35 for non-residents. 1-night bookings may be refused Easter, bank holidays.

# KYLESKU Highland

MAP 5:B2

## KYLESKU HOTEL

♆ Previous César winner

Ferries no longer skim across Loch Glendhu to
Kylestrome, but you can still watch the day's catch
being landed on the slipway, from Tanja Lister
and Sonia Virechauveix's 17th-century coaching
inn turned award-winning hotel. It is 'remote, but
well worth the drive', writes a reader. 'The design
is relaxed and modern and works well,' relates
another. Pristine bedrooms are painted in restful
pastels. The best are balcony rooms in a modern
annexe, Willie's Hoose. 'Our room had a stunning
view of the loch, which one could watch for ages
as the light changed.' There are mesmerising
views, too, from the dining room, bar and decked
terrace. Tommy Barney, who trained under
the previous chef, now heads the kitchen. A
Highlander from toque to toe, he specialises in
locally grown, fished and foraged ingredients and
dishes – Loch Glendhu mussels, seafood platter,
king scallops, kedgeree and crispy seaweed, rare-
breed burger. Croft-grown produce appears on a
vegetarian menu. 'Breakfast was also excellent.'
You can order a picnic for a day's seal-spotting,
and use drying facilities on your return. (Simon
James, RG, and others)

Kylesku IV27 4HW

**T:** 01971 502231
**E:** info@kyleskuhotel.co.uk
**W:** kyleskuhotel.co.uk

**BEDROOMS:** 11. 4 in annexe, 1 suitable
for disabled.
**OPEN:** mid-Feb–end Nov, ring to
enquire about Christmas and
New Year.
**FACILITIES:** lounge, bar, restaurant,
in-room TV (Freeview), small garden
(tables for outside eating), area of
lounge and dining room wheelchair
accessible, toilet not adapted.
**BACKGROUND MUSIC:** from 10 am, in
bar and half the dining area.
**LOCATION:** 10 miles S of Scourie.
**CHILDREN:** all ages welcomed.
**DOGS:** allowed in bedrooms (£15 a
night to a max. £60 a stay), public
rooms.
**CREDIT CARDS:** MC, Visa.
**PRICES:** per room B&B single £85–£130,
double £130–£200, family £160–£190.
À la carte £45.

# MUTHILL Perth and Kinross                    MAP 5:D2

## BARLEY BREE

A red-stone 19th-century inn in a conservation village took on a new lease of life in 2007 when Fabrice and Alison Bouteloup hung out the flower baskets and opened their restaurant-with-rooms. Fabrice spent boyhood summers on his grandmother's farm in France and is passionate about provenance and Slow Food. Alison brings wine expertise to the party. They love to welcome families, and provide a children's menu. A log-burner blazes in a 'characterful' beamed dining room, where a small thicket of antlers hints at a penchant for game. Indeed, facilities are available to guests who want to shoot more than the breeze. Expect such dishes as rump of venison, savoy cabbage, baby onion and smoked pancetta. 'As ever, dinner was a real treat, with attentive but light-touch service,' write readers on a fourth visit. Walls are hung with works by marine sculptor Sam MacDonald. In hot weather you can dine alfresco. Most of the traditionally furnished bedrooms have a shower. The best ones, with shower and roll-top bath, looks out to Muthill's salient landmark, a 12th-century Romanesque church tower. 'Everything was excellent.' (Simon James, RL)

6 Willoughby Street
Muthill PH5 2AB

T: 01764 681451
E: info@barleybree.com
W: barleybree.com

BEDROOMS: 6.
OPEN: all year except 24–26 Dec, various dates throughout year (see website), restaurant closed Mon, Tues.
FACILITIES: lounge bar, restaurant, in-room TV (Freeview), small terrace and lawn, drying facilities, gun cupboard, restaurant wheelchair accessible, toilet not adapted.
BACKGROUND MUSIC: none.
LOCATION: village centre.
CHILDREN: all ages welcomed, cot, baby-changing, children's menu.
DOGS: assistance dogs only.
CREDIT CARDS: Amex, MC, Visa.
PRICES: per room B&B single from £80, double £99–£160, D,B&B £155–£399 (on certain dates). À la carte £45.

# OBAN Argyll and Bute

## THE MANOR HOUSE

'A haven of comfort and good food,' writes one regular reviewer of this small hotel on Oban Bay. Built for the Duke of Argyll in the 18th century, the stone manor house is also the former home of one Admiral HC Otter who painted Bible texts on the rocks of Lorne, and had the words 'Jehovah Shammah' carved above the back door. The building's listed status means that bedrooms are fairly cosy, but all offer 'really good furnishings' and 'lovely views', particularly those overlooking the harbour and bay, where otters of the marine variety, as well as basking seals and a variety of birdlife, may be spotted (binoculars are provided). Bathrooms are compact but well stocked with large bottles of Molton Brown toiletries. Chef Mandy Todd joined the team in 2019 and her eclectic daily-changing menu mixes Scottish ingredients with more exotic flavours picked up on her travels. An 'excellent dinner' might include a goat's cheese mousse followed by harissa-marinated lamb, or perhaps scallops with pork cheeks. 'Friendly staff' and a 'good breakfast' complete the picture. (Tony Hall)

Gallanach Road
Oban PA34 4LS

T: 01631 562087
E: info@manorhouseoban.com
W: manorhouseoban.com

BEDROOMS: 11. 1 on ground floor.
OPEN: all year except 24–26 Dec.
FACILITIES: lounge, bar, restaurant, in-room TV (Freeview), wedding facilities, 1½-acre grounds, private car park, deep-water mooring, access to nearby gym and golf.
BACKGROUND MUSIC: traditional in bar and restaurant.
LOCATION: ½ mile from centre.
CHILDREN: not under 12.
DOGS: allowed in bedroom by arrangement, not unattended, not in public rooms.
CREDIT CARDS: Amex, MC, Visa.
PRICES: per room B&B £140–£295, D,B&B £230–£393. Set dinner (5 courses) £49, à la carte £45.

# PEAT INN Fife

## ⚲ THE PEAT INN

César award: Scottish restaurant-with-rooms of the year

Lending its name to the hamlet that grew up around it, this former coaching inn turned restaurant-with-rooms held Scotland's first Michelin Star in 1987. It has been owned since 2006 by Katherine and (chef) Geoffrey Smeddle, and regained that coveted star in 2010. Guide inspectors who arrived in the evening reported a friendly welcome. 'The cheery lady at reception kindly moved her car to make space for us to park.' They were shown to one of the suites in a separate building (all but one are split level). It was 'pretty and light, with silver-sprigged wallpaper and botanical prints'. A mezzanine lounge had tea and coffee facilities, 'sherry, apples, home-made brownies', and a view of grazing sheep and alpacas. Drinks were served in a lounge with a log fire, while one of three dining rooms had 'Mad Men-esque decor with orange and teal menus and cushions'. A tasting menu included 'a beautiful smoked trout and caviar plate', halibut gravadlax, pork cheek and more. 'Each dish tasted and looked wonderful.' Breakfast in the suite was 'also fantastic'. '"Continental" doesn't do it justice.'

Peat Inn
Cupar KY15 5LH

**T:** 01334 840206
**E:** stay@thepeatinn.co.uk
**W:** thepeatinn.co.uk

**BEDROOMS:** 8. All suites, on ground floor in annexe, 7 split-level, 1 suitable for disabled.
**OPEN:** all year except 1 week Christmas, 1 week Jan, open from 28 Dec for New Year, restaurant closed Sun/Mon.
**FACILITIES:** lounge in restaurant, in-room TV (terrestrial), ½-acre garden, restaurant wheelchair accessible, adapted toilet.
**BACKGROUND MUSIC:** in restaurant.
**LOCATION:** 6 miles SW of St Andrews.
**CHILDREN:** all ages welcomed, no under-7s at dinner, no under-14s unaccompanied in suite.
**DOGS:** not allowed.
**CREDIT CARDS:** Amex, MC, Visa.
**PRICES:** per room B&B single £220–£245, double £240–£265. À la carte £65, tasting menu £78.

# PITLOCHRY Perth and Kinross

MAP 5:D2

## THE GREEN PARK

♥ Previous César winner

Ironwork sculptures adorn the wide lawn that borders Loch Faskally at the McMenemie family's extended Victorian country house, along with waterside seating areas. The hotel's ambience is timeless and inclusive. Wildlife spotters are encouraged to pick up binoculars, and to jot down sightings in a nature diary that lives on the piano in the main lounge. There is a 9-hole golf course and, indoors, a jigsaw puzzle always on the go. Activity breaks of the gentler kind include cryptic crossword puzzles, Scrabble and creative writing. From 11 am, the sideboard is set with vacuum flasks of coffee, tea and biscuits, and in the afternoon, home-baked cakes come out. Scottish-themed artwork adorns public spaces. Before dinner, guests mingle over complimentary sherry. After 18 years in the kitchen, Richard Murray has stepped up as head chef. Trusted readers enjoyed a 'delicious, succulent fillet of Orkney salmon with a sweet pepper salad and new potatoes'. Most bedrooms – in the main house and purpose-built wings – overlook the loch. Some have a balcony; 16 are on the accessible ground floor. (RG, JT)

### 25% DISCOUNT VOUCHERS

Clunie Bridge Road
Pitlochry PH16 5JY

T: 01796 473248
E: bookings@thegreenpark.co.uk
W: thegreenpark.co.uk

**BEDROOMS:** 51. 16 on ground floor, 1 suitable for disabled.
**OPEN:** all year except Christmas.
**FACILITIES:** 2 lifts, lounge bar, main lounge, sun lounge, in-room TV (BT, Freeview), 3-acre garden, public areas wheelchair accessible.
**BACKGROUND MUSIC:** none.
**LOCATION:** ½ mile N of town centre.
**CHILDREN:** all ages welcomed.
**DOGS:** allowed in bedrooms, not in public rooms.
**CREDIT CARDS:** MC, Visa.
**PRICES:** per person B&B £92–£102, D,B&B £103–£128 (no supplement for singles). Set dinner £30.

### SEE ALSO SHORTLIST

# PITLOCHRY Perth and Kinross                    MAP 5:D2

## KNOCKENDARROCH HOTEL

♀ Previous César winner

Pitlochry's renowned Festival Theatre was born in 1951 in the grounds of this Victorian mansion, run today as a welcoming hotel by Struan and Louise Lothian. Bedrooms are traditionally furnished, with Scottish art, perhaps a wall of statement wallpaper, floral and plaid accents, a balcony or dual-aspect windows, views of woodland and mountains. Suites have a coffee machine, a drinks cooler, smart TV. We hear praise for a 'polite European receptionist' and 'prompt service'. Barely had a Guide trusty sunk into a leather armchair by a roaring log fire than 'canapés of smoked haddock mousse and haggis were brought'. A cabinet is stocked with more than 50 malt whiskies. A lounge menu offers light lunches, while in the dining room Nick Imrie's nightly-changing menus include such dishes as assiette of seafood, braised feather blade of Highland beef, and a creative veggie option. At breakfast there are free-range eggs, Perthshire sausages, smoked haddock. Summer packages include a pre-theatre dinner and transport across the river to catch, as it might be, Private Lives or The Pasadena Roof Orchestra. (Robert Gower, and others)

---

**25% DISCOUNT VOUCHERS**

Higher Oakfield
Pitlochry PH16 5HT

T: 01796 473473
E: bookings@knockendarroch.co.uk
W: knockendarroch.co.uk

BEDROOMS: 14. 2 on ground floor.
OPEN: Feb–early Dec.
FACILITIES: 2 lounges, restaurant, in-room TV (Freeview), 2-acre wooded garden, bicycle storage, car park (electric charging points), unsuitable for disabled.
BACKGROUND MUSIC: in restaurant in evening.
LOCATION: central.
CHILDREN: not under 10.
DOGS: not allowed.
CREDIT CARDS: Amex, MC, Visa.
PRICES: per room B&B £175–£345, D,B&B £225–£395. Set dinner £49. 1-night bookings sometimes refused Sat.

**SEE ALSO SHORTLIST**

# PITLOCHRY Perth and Kinross

MAP 5:D2

## RIVERWOOD

You can gaze out at the River Tay over breakfast at Ann and Alf Berry's Arts and Crafts-style B&B in wooded grounds on the edge of a conservation village. It is a 'fabulous place', says a trusted reader. The interior is immaculate: remove your shoes, please, before coming in from a day's fishing for brown trout on their private stretch of river, enjoying a complimentary round of golf on the Strathtay course just minutes' walk away, or spotting red squirrels and pheasant in bosky glades. There are two double bedrooms upstairs. At ground level, two junior suites have glass doors to a private patio, while two suites have a seating area or lounge and doors to decking. All have a super-king-size bed, a coffee machine and mini-fridge, a smart bathroom with under-floor heating and Scottish Fine Soaps products. The palette is mainly white and grey with some clever use of darker shades. On some nights a home-cooked dinner of the best local ingredients is served – maybe beef fillet or lamb cutlets, salmon or sea bass. A 'great breakfast' brings fresh fruit salad, potato rösti, Perthshire bacon and Dunkeld smoked salmon. (Tony Hall)

Strathtay
Pitlochry PH9 0PG

**T:** 01887 840751
**E:** info@riverwoodstrathtay.com
**W:** riverwoodstrathtay.com

**BEDROOMS:** 6. 4 suites on ground floor.
**OPEN:** 6 Feb–14 Dec, dinner available on selected days (check website).
**FACILITIES:** lounge/dining room, library, in-room TV (Freeview), 4½-acre grounds (lawns, woodland, fishing), complimentary access to nearby golf course.
**BACKGROUND MUSIC:** 'easy listening' in dining room at mealtimes.
**LOCATION:** in village, 9½ miles SW of Pitlochry.
**CHILDREN:** not under 12.
**DOGS:** not allowed.
**CREDIT CARDS:** MC, Visa.
**PRICES:** per room B&B £120–£155, D,B&B (on selected nights) £190–£230 (single occupancy rates on request). 1-night bookings sometimes refused in peak season.

**SEE ALSO SHORTLIST**

# PORT APPIN Argyll and Bute

MAP 5:D1

## THE AIRDS HOTEL

☙ Previous César winner

A 'lovely mix of quiet seaside, stunning hillside and island life' can be found here, by Loch Linnhe, and within easy reach of Glasgow and Edinburgh. A reader returning after 30 years found everything at Shaun and Jenny McKivragan's former ferry inn 'excellent although expensive'. Decked out in designer fabrics by Zoffany, Colefax & Fowler and Designers Guild, with Frette linen and Bulgari toiletries, bedrooms vary in style but all are 'beautifully peaceful'. Most offer magnificent views of the loch and the Morvern mountains; those with no view are larger. Drinks and canapés by the fire are followed by dinner in a 'bright dining room with an excellent view of the sea'. Here, new chef Matthew Price's seasonal menus are a celebration of local ingredients, including 'superb seafood and game'. Afterwards, perhaps a wee dram in the whisky bar. Breakfast offers everything from 'porridge, fruits, yogurt and compote' to a 'range of cooked options and lashings of tea of our choice'. Staff are 'charming and very courteous' and there is a selection of wellies to borrow for a walk to the lighthouse at low tide. (John Barnes, Peter Foster)

Port Appin PA38 4DF

T: 01631 730236
E: airds@airds-hotel.com
W: airds-hotel.com

**BEDROOMS:** 11. 2 on ground floor, plus 2 self-catering cottages.
**OPEN:** all year, restaurant closed Mon/Tues Nov–end Jan (open Christmas and New Year).
**FACILITIES:** 2 lounges, conservatory, whisky bar, restaurant, wedding facilities, in-room TV (Freeview), spa treatments, ½-acre garden, unsuitable for disabled.
**BACKGROUND MUSIC:** none.
**LOCATION:** 20 miles N of Oban.
**CHILDREN:** all ages welcomed, no under-8s in dining room in evening (children's high tea).
**DOGS:** allowed in bedrooms (not unattended) and conservatory.
**CREDIT CARDS:** Amex, MC, Visa.
**PRICES:** per room D,B&B single £285–£535, double £335–£570. Set dinner £64, seasonal tasting menu £95.

# PORT APPIN Argyll and Bute

## THE PIERHOUSE

Situated 'well off the beaten track', this former
home of a piermaster is a 'relaxed and friendly'
lochside bolt-hole, known for its seafood
restaurant. Converted in 1992, the hotel is now
owned by international hotelier Gordon Campbell
Gray, who has given it a gentle nip and tuck.
The individually styled bedrooms have either a
loch- or cliff-facing view, though one guest was
underwhelmed by the 'immediate view of the
car park' from a ground-floor room. The decor
is kept simple, perhaps with 'a touch of tartan'.
The super-comfortable beds are equally plain, just
'white linen and a beige knitted throw'. In the
evening, guests can enjoy a drink in the Ferry bar
before tucking into dinner cooked by new chef
Michael Leathley. His seafood-rich menu is based
on the freshest local produce, including lobster
from a Pierhouse creel, Loch Linnhe langoustine,
Loch Creran oysters and West Coast scallops.
Service is 'good and helpful'. The 'great' breakfast
is 'efficiently served', with a buffet as well as a
cooked menu that includes scrambled eggs with
Loch Fyne smoked salmon and Inverawe kippers.
(Diana Goodey, M and PB)

Port Appin PA38 4DE

T: 01631 730302
E: reservations@pierhousehotel.co.uk
W: pierhousehotel.co.uk

BEDROOMS: 12.
OPEN: all year except 24–26 Dec.
FACILITIES: residents' snug, lounge,
bar, restaurant, private dining room,
in-room TV (Freeview), wedding
facilities, sauna, in-room spa
treatments, terrace, yacht moorings,
unsuitable for disabled.
BACKGROUND MUSIC: in bar and
restaurant.
LOCATION: in village, 20 miles N of
Oban.
CHILDREN: all ages welcomed (cots,
high chairs).
DOGS: well-behaved dogs allowed in
2 bedrooms (not unattended, £15 per
night), not in public rooms.
CREDIT CARDS: Amex, MC, Visa.
PRICES: per room B&B £125–£295
(single occupancy of cliff-facing
room, Sun–Thurs, Nov–Mar, £85).
À la carte £42.

# PORTPATRICK Dumfries and Galloway    MAP 5:E1

## KNOCKINAAM LODGE

'A stiff walk from Portpatrick along the cliffs' brings you to Sian and David Ibbotson's Victorian hunting lodge overlooking the Irish Sea. It is a 'very comfortable, spacious house', write readers, while the best bedrooms offer 'Churchillian levels of luxury'. Indeed, you can book the room in which Churchill slept when he and Eisenhower planned the D-Day landings here. It has a sleigh bed and a century-old enamelled-concrete soaking bath. Rooms have a sea or garden view, perhaps a half-tester bed or a separate lounge. All have posh toiletries. The scones with afternoon tea by the fire are 'dangerously tempting', not to speak of 120-plus malt whiskies. Long-serving chef Tony Pierce changes his tasting menus each day, and you will want to be on form for his modern Scottish fare. Local and home-grown ingredients appear in such dishes as grilled, salted Ayrshire cod with mussels and greenhouse tomato emulsion, or roast canon of Galloway lamb with a rosemary-scented jus. The 'polished service' and all-round professionalism also win praise. In all, 'I can't recommend it highly enough,' another reader declares. (Peter Foster, DL)

### 25% DISCOUNT VOUCHERS

Portpatrick DG9 9AD

**T:** 01776 810471
**E:** reservations@knockinaamlodge.com
**W:** knockinaamlodge.com

**BEDROOMS:** 10.
**OPEN:** all year.
**FACILITIES:** 2 lounges, bar, restaurant, in-room TV (Freeview), wedding facilities, 20-acre grounds (garden, beach), public areas wheelchair accessible.
**BACKGROUND MUSIC:** in restaurant in evening.
**LOCATION:** 3 miles S of Portpatrick.
**CHILDREN:** all ages welcomed, no under-12s in dining room, children's high tea provided.
**DOGS:** allowed in some bedrooms, grounds, not in public rooms.
**CREDIT CARDS:** Amex, MC, Visa.
**PRICES:** per person D,B&B single £200–£345, double £165–£240. Set lunch £40 (Sun £35). 1-night bookings refused certain weekends, Christmas, New Year.

# PORTREE Highland

MAP 5:C1

## VIEWFIELD HOUSE

Set in 20 acres of woodland garden just outside
Portree, 'relaxing' Viewfield House has the look
and feel of a much-loved family home. And so
it is, with generations of the Macdonald family
having added their own stamp to the late 19th-
century building, including colonial memorabilia
and a veritable menagerie of taxidermy in the hall.
Iona Macdonald Buxton and her husband, Jasper,
offer 'large and comfortable' bedrooms over
three floors, many with views across the Sound
of Raasay. They are reassuringly traditional, with
pretty wallpapers of birds and flowers, brass beds
in some rooms, antique furniture and shelves of
hardbacks. More contemporary accommodation
is available in the converted stables. A hearty
breakfast menu includes porridge, haddock,
smoked salmon and the full Scottish. Viewfield
House no longer serves formal evening meals, but
instead offers a lighter option of soup, cheeseboard,
charcuterie and vegan platters. There are several
good restaurants in Portree. Salty sea dogs, take
note: the hotel has its own yacht, which can be
booked for half-day trips to see Skye at its very
best – from the water. (A and EW)

Viewfield Road
Portree
Isle of Skye IV51 9EU

**T:** 01478 612217
**E:** info@viewfieldhouse.com
**W:** viewfieldhouse.com

**BEDROOMS:** 13. 1 on ground floor
(suitable for disabled), 2 in adjacent
converted stables.
**OPEN:** Apr–Oct.
**FACILITIES:** drawing room, morning/
TV room, dining room, 20-acre
grounds (croquet, swings), public
rooms wheelchair accessible.
**BACKGROUND MUSIC:** none.
**LOCATION:** S side of Portree.
**CHILDREN:** all ages welcomed.
**DOGS:** allowed in bedrooms, not in
public rooms.
**CREDIT CARDS:** MC, Visa.
**PRICES:** per person B&B £82–£100.
Light dinner £15.50. 1-night bookings
only on application in high season.

**SEE ALSO SHORTLIST**

# RANNOCH STATION Perth and Kinross          MAP 5:D2

## MOOR OF RANNOCH – RESTAURANT & ROOMS

♉ Previous César winner

The phrase 'in the middle of nowhere' takes on real meaning when you step down from the overnight sleeper for a stay at Scott and Stephanie Meikle's remote restaurant-with-rooms. It stands in a vast, empty landscape of lochs and lochans, with views to the mountains of Glen Coe and treeless Rannoch Forest. Guide readers arrived disgruntled four hours late, but 'our spirits lifted when Scott Meikle was on the platform to greet us and carry our bags'. Coffee in 'the lovely warm lounge with a well-stocked bar, books and board games' proved yet more reviving. A dual-aspect corner bedroom afforded 'views across the wild moor, and soon a group of deer congregated below us'. People come here for the dark skies and stark beauty, away from the digital chatter of the modern world. Rooms have a decanter of malt whisky, chocolates and home-baked biscuits. At night, Steph's cooking 'absolutely delights'. A dinner of 'hot crusted herring, Gigha halibut, jellies and brown-bread ice cream, plus an ample cheeseboard' proved 'outstanding'. 'Next morning, porridge with Drambuie awaited us.' (Anthony Bradbury, GB)

Rannoch Station PH17 2QA

T: 01882 633238
E: info@moorofrannoch.co.uk
W: moorofrannoch.co.uk

BEDROOMS: 5.
OPEN: Thurs–Mon until 23 Nov 2020, 11 Feb–23 Nov 2021.
FACILITIES: lounge, bar, conservatory dining room, no Wi-Fi or TV, unsuitable for disabled.
BACKGROUND MUSIC: none.
LOCATION: on a single-track, dead-end road, 40 miles W of Pitlochry.
CHILDREN: all ages welcomed.
DOGS: welcomed in all areas of the hotel.
CREDIT CARDS: Amex, MC, Visa.
PRICES: per room B&B £180–£195. Set meal £49.

# ST OLA Orkney Islands

MAP 5:A3

## THE FOVERAN

Stunning sea views accompany the food at this 'welcoming' restaurant-with-rooms, where the dining room overlooks the sheltered waters of Scapa Flow and the southern Orkney Islands. It is a family affair, run by Paul and Helen Doull, in the kitchen and front-of-house, with Paul's brother Hamish and Hamish's wife, Shirley, in charge of maintenance and administration. Simple, 'spotless' ground-floor bedrooms have Scottish fabrics, neutral decor and Duck Island toiletries. In the dining room, with its watery, big-sky views through floor-to-ceiling windows, a handwoven tapestry is by cousin Leila Thomson. Paul works with local, seasonal, traceable, sustainable produce – the distinctive, seaweed-grazed North Ronaldsay lamb, Orkney beef and shellfish – to create short menus of such dishes as baked fillet of sole, smoked olive and lemon tapenade, and fillet steak topped with caramelised onions and haggis under a puff-pastry lattice, with whisky cream sauce. Breakfast brings salted porridge, home-baked bannock, Orkney sausages, salmon smoked by Jollys of Kirkwall with buttery scrambled eggs, or a vegetarian full Scottish. Reports, please.

Kirkwall
St Ola KW15 1SF

**T:** 01856 872389
**E:** info@thefoveran.com
**W:** thefoveran.com

**BEDROOMS:** 8. All on ground floor, 1 single with private bathroom across hall.
**OPEN:** Apr–early Oct, by arrangement at other times, restaurant closed variable times Apr, Oct.
**FACILITIES:** lounge, restaurant, in-room TV, 12-acre grounds (private rock beach), restaurant wheelchair accessible, adapted toilet.
**BACKGROUND MUSIC:** local/Scottish traditional in restaurant.
**LOCATION:** 3 miles SW of Kirkwall.
**CHILDREN:** all ages welcomed.
**DOGS:** not allowed.
**CREDIT CARDS:** MC, Visa.
**PRICES:** per room B&B single from £85, double £125–£140, D,B&B (for dinner up to £30) single from £113, double from £180. À la carte £37. 1-night bookings refused May–Sept (phone to check).

# SANQUHAR Dumfries and Galloway                    MAP 5:E2

## BLACKADDIE HOUSE

The River Nith ripples past the garden of Jane
and Ian McAndrew's old manse and gastronomic
destination, in a rolling landscape with views to
the Lowther hills. Bedrooms are 'kept to a high
standard'. A self-contained suite has French doors
to a riverside patio. Dual-aspect Grouse has a
large four-poster, a spa bath and rainfall shower.
All rooms have home-made shortbread, tablet,
Scottish mineral water and fresh fruit. 'Our room
was spacious, newly decorated, with a vast, most
comfortable bed,' readers write. 'The staff are
attentive and helpful.' But it is Ian McAndrew's
cooking that is acclaimed above all. 'From the
salmon-and-cucumber mousse appetiser, it was
obvious we were in for an absolute treat.' A
nightly-changing menu, with either/or choices,
might include pan-roast cod fillet on smoked
haddock chowder; the tasting menu, seared loin
of roe deer, eryngii mushroom, duxelles, buttered
cabbage and roast shallot. 'Even the onion ice
cream palate-cleanser really hit the mark.' If you
visit, do send us your own report from the world's
oldest post office. (DCM, MA, PK)

Blackaddie Road
Sanquhar DG4 6JJ

**T:** 01659 50270
**E:** ian@blackaddiehotel.co.uk
**W:** blackaddiehotel.co.uk

**BEDROOMS:** 7. Plus two 2-bed self-
catering cottages, 1 suitable for
disabled.
**OPEN:** all year except 24–27 Dec.
**FACILITIES:** bar, restaurant, breakfast/
function room, library, conservatory,
in-room TV (Freeview), wedding
facilities, 2-acre grounds, cookery
school, fishing, parking, public rooms
wheelchair accessible.
**BACKGROUND MUSIC:** in public areas.
**LOCATION:** outskirts of village.
**CHILDREN:** all ages welcomed.
**DOGS:** allowed in most bedrooms
(£10 per night), public rooms, not in
restaurant.
**CREDIT CARDS:** Amex, MC, Visa.
**PRICES:** per room B&B single
£115–£240, double £135–£260. Fixed-
price menu £65, tasting menu £75/£90
(6/8 courses).

# SCARISTA Western Isles

MAP 5:B1

## SCARISTA HOUSE

✿ Previous César winner

There are few more remote hotels in the Guide than this Georgian former manse, in a 'spectacular' setting between a white-sand beach and heather-clad mountains. Run by Patricia Martin and her husband, Tim, it is a welcoming place, where new arrivals are greeted with a pot of leaf tea, home-baked cake and scones. Lounges have a cosy, 'lived-in' feel, with 'squashy sofas' and a real fire. Three of the bedrooms are in an annexe. Lily has a super-king-size bed, a bookshelf bedhead stocked with Penguin classics, and an anteroom in which to sit and watch the sunset. The decor may be a mite dated, but there is praise for a 'wonderful, spotless bathroom' with a bath to wallow in and a powerful overhead shower. Dinner is composed of organic, wild and home-produced ingredients. A typical menu: Uist crab tart; navarin of Lewis lamb; fresh figs, brown-bread ice cream and langues de chat. At breakfast there is Ayrshire bacon, Stornoway sausages, Inverawe kipper, Salar smoked salmon, eggs from the house hens when they are laying. Then a visit to one of the island's tweed weavers is a must.

Scarista
Isle of Harris HS3 3HX

**T:** 01859 550238
**E:** stay@scaristahouse.com
**W:** scaristahouse.com

**BEDROOMS:** 6. 3 in annexe.
**OPEN:** 9–30 Nov 2020, Mar–mid-Oct.
**FACILITIES:** drawing room, library, 2 dining rooms, Wi-Fi not available in some bedrooms, wedding facilities, 1-acre garden, unsuitable for disabled.
**BACKGROUND MUSIC:** none.
**LOCATION:** 15 miles SW of Tarbert.
**CHILDREN:** all ages welcomed.
**DOGS:** allowed in bedrooms and 1 public room.
**CREDIT CARDS:** Amex, MC, Visa.
**PRICES:** per room B&B single £165–£180, double £233–£250. Set dinner £49.50–£57. Advance 1-night bookings refused.

# SCOURIE Highland

MAP 5:B2

## EDDRACHILLES HOTEL

This 'ideally situated' hotel, which offers shoreside views of Badcall Bay, with its bobbing fishing boats, and Quinag mountain beyond, continues to win warm praise from readers. The 18th-century house stands in one of Europe's last great wildernesses, almost beyond the reach of a phone signal, so switch off and relax. Guests love the personal attention from owners Fiona and Richard Trevor. 'Everyone, young and old, was made to feel very welcome,' wrote one after a family celebration. There are six sea-facing bedrooms, while four overlook a courtyard garden. They are traditionally furnished and supplied with good Scottish toiletries. 'Our bedroom offered a comfortable bed and everything we, as outdoor people, needed,' a trusted correspondent told us. The lounge/bar and restaurant are, similarly, bigger on comfort than style. There is 'a lovely conservatory area where afternoon cakes were served at no extra charge'. Evening meals offered 'great locally sourced food'. As we go to press the hotel is between chefs, but we expect continuity, not change. (James Barclay, Edward Jackson, Howard and Stephanie Bunyan, and others)

Badcall Bay
Scourie IV27 4TH

T: 01971 502080
E: info@eddrachilles.com
W: eddrachilles.com

BEDROOMS: 10. 4 ground-floor rooms.
OPEN: 28 Mar–1 Nov.
FACILITIES: large reception, bar/lounge, sun lounge, restaurant, free (slow) Wi-Fi in public areas, in-room TV (Freeview), wedding facilities, 3-acre grounds, parking, public rooms wheelchair accessible.
BACKGROUND MUSIC: in public areas 3–10.30 pm, not in restaurant, sun lounge.
LOCATION: 2 miles S of Scourie, on the North Coast 500 route.
CHILDREN: all ages welcomed.
DOGS: well-behaved dogs allowed in bedrooms, public rooms (one part of restaurant, subject to 'three barks' rule), £10 per stay.
CREDIT CARDS: MC, Visa.
PRICES: per room B&B single £100–£125, double £120–£165. Set dinner £33–£39.

**SEE ALSO SHORTLIST**

# SLEAT Highland

## KINLOCH LODGE

♔Previous César winner

With views to take the breath away, this former hunting lodge owned by Lord and Lady Macdonald stands on the shores of Loch Na Dal at the foot of densely wooded Kinloch hill. Managed by daughter Isabella, it exudes that 'air of confidence of a place that knows what it is doing and does it well'. In the past two years, interiors have been given a fresher look, while public rooms retain their charm, with family portraits and heirlooms. 'Luxurious' bedrooms are individually styled, some with antiques, some more contemporary, maybe with French doors or a bath under a window. Suites, in a more recent extension, will suit a family. All have a king-size bed and L'Occitane toiletries. In the dining room, local ingredients shine in such dishes as fillet of sea trout, pearl barley, seafood sauce. Roux protégé Marcello Tully has been here since 2007 and holds workshops. Breakfast brings fresh orange juice, home-baked scones, South Uist smoked salmon and kedgeree. A ghillie offers not just fishing, but foraging and bushcraft lessons. 'All in all, a most rewarding experience, albeit one that comes at a price.' (DG, and others)

Sleat
Isle of Skye IV43 8QY

T: 01471 833333
E: reservations@kinloch-lodge.co.uk
W: kinloch-lodge.co.uk

BEDROOMS: 19. 10 in North Lodge, 9 in South Lodge, 3 on ground floor, 1 suitable for disabled.
OPEN: all year.
FACILITIES: 3 drawing rooms, whisky bar, dining room, in-room TV (Sky), wedding facilities, cookery courses, 'huge' grounds on edge of loch, public rooms wheelchair accessible.
BACKGROUND MUSIC: gentle classical in dining room.
LOCATION: on shore of Loch Na Dal on east coast of Skye, not far off A851.
CHILDREN: all ages welcomed.
DOGS: in bedrooms only, and not unattended.
CREDIT CARDS: MC, Visa.
PRICES: per person, B&B £130–£210, D,B&B £150–£250. Set dinner (5 courses) £85, tasting menu (7 courses) £95.

# SPEAN BRIDGE Highland

MAP 5:C2

## SMIDDY HOUSE

'Every visit exceeds expectations,' writes a fan of Robert Bryson and Glen Russell's restaurant-with-rooms in a village dubbed 'the crossroads to the Highlands'. It stands at an actual crossroads, but double-glazing screens out traffic noise. The old blacksmith's workshop, a separate stone bothy, now sleeps four. It has a spiral staircase to a mezzanine, a fridge, bath and shower. In the main house, some bedrooms are small, but all are individually furnished and 'lovely'. Our inspectors' street-facing room was 'welcoming, fresh and well cared for', with handmade toiletries. Rear-facing Tobermory has a distant view of Aonach Mòr in the Nevis range. The lounge and dining room are homely and quirky, with clocks, ornaments and accolades for excellence on display. Robert is the perfect host, welcoming new arrivals with tea, cake and conversation. Glen's menus include locally caught fish and shellfish, 'tender, very tasty' and beautifully cooked venison from a neighbouring estate, naturally reared Highland beef and lamb, and vegetarian options, all 'cooked and served to perfection'. (Philip Bright, and others)

Roy Bridge Road
Spean Bridge PH34 4EU

**T:** 01397 712335
**E:** enquiry@smiddyhouse.com
**W:** smiddyhouse.com

**BEDROOMS:** 5, 1 suite in adjacent cottage.
**OPEN:** all year except 25/26, 31 Dec, restaurant closed Mon all year, Sun, Tues, Wed, Jan–Mar.
**FACILITIES:** garden room, restaurant, in-room TV (Freeview), parking.
**BACKGROUND MUSIC:** in restaurant.
**LOCATION:** 9 miles N of Fort William.
**CHILDREN:** not under 7.
**DOGS:** not allowed.
**CREDIT CARDS:** MC, Visa.
**PRICES:** per room B&B single £105, double £120–£245. Set dinners £34.50–£40.

# STRACHUR Argyll and Bute                    MAP 5:D1

## THE CREGGANS INN

The sunsets are something to behold from this whitewashed inn at Creggans Point, on the east shore of Loch Fyne, with views to the Kintyre mountains. Run as a hotel since the mid-1800s, and today owned by Gill and Archie MacLellan, it was once owned by Sir Fitzroy Maclean, believed to be Ian Fleming's inspiration for James Bond. Traditionally furnished side-facing bedrooms are fine, but it is well worth paying more for a window on the loch – after all, you only live twice! One spacious top-floor room has pretty toile de Jouy wallpaper and fabrics; all rooms have Scottish Fine Soaps toiletries. Downstairs, house dogs Hector and Boo snooze by a log fire. The bar holds a range of single malts, including The MacPhunn, developed by Sir Fitzroy. In the bistro, Irvine McArthur's locally sourced dishes might include Loch Fyne scallops, pan-fried lamb rump, and maybe chickpea, aubergine and kale curry. At breakfast there is porridge with cream and a wee dram, a full Scottish with tattie scone and Stornoway black pudding, but surely Loch Fyne smoked fish is the choice to make – or pay an extra £8 and have the lot.

Strachur PA27 8BX

T: 01369 860279
E: info@creggans-inn.co.uk
W: creggans-inn.co.uk

BEDROOMS: 14.
OPEN: all year, except Christmas.
FACILITIES: 2 lounges, bar, dining room, bistro, in-room TV (Freeview), 2-acre grounds, moorings for guests arriving by boat.
BACKGROUND MUSIC: all day in bar.
LOCATION: in village.
CHILDREN: all ages welcomed, under-14s sharing with parents, £15.
DOGS: allowed in bedrooms (not unattended) and in bar, not in other public rooms (£7.50 per dog per night, max 1 large or 2 small per room).
CREDIT CARDS: Amex, MC, Visa.
PRICES: per room B&B double £140–£200. À la carte £30.

# STRATHTUMMEL Perth and Kinross

MAP 5:D2

## THE INN AT LOCH TUMMEL

A great leap of imagination carried Alice and Jade Calliva from a Croydon flat to the 18th-century coaching inn with spectacular views across the loch to Schiehallion, the local Munro. The inn was derelict when the Callivas bought it in March 2016. Today it is a rustic-chic haven, a 'welcoming and calming place', writes a recent guest. Bedrooms are decorated in muted shades, with contemporary and antique furniture, perhaps a dress rail in place of a wardrobe, and toile de Jouy curtains. Each room has a new king- or super-king-size bed, a power shower; all but one have a bath. They are supplied with Scottish toiletries, home-made shortbread and a wee dram. 'The free whisky in the room was much enjoyed.' The blue-painted, loch-facing library/breakfast room is the place to sink into a sofa and read, while the side terrace with wood-fired oven has come together since last year. 'Very good food at both breakfast and dinner' is sourced from local suppliers; it includes Dunkeld hand-made beef burgers, Shetland mussels, or a vegan option. Resident dogs Maggie, Mabel and Maude will welcome your four-legged friend. (DG)

**25% DISCOUNT VOUCHERS**

Queens View
Strathtummel
Pitlochry PH16 5RP

**T:** 01882 634317
**E:** info@theinnatlochtummel.com
**W:** theinnatlochtummel.com

**BEDROOMS:** 6. 2, on ground floor, suitable for disabled.
**OPEN:** all year, but closed Christmas and Jan (except the few days before New Year), Mon, Tues.
**FACILITIES:** snug, bar, library, breakfast room, free Wi-Fi in communal areas, large garden and patio, wedding facilities, ground-floor bar and snug wheelchair accessible, no adapted toilet.
**BACKGROUND MUSIC:** in bar/restaurant and library.
**LOCATION:** 10 miles W of Pitlochry.
**CHILDREN:** usually not under 5.
**DOGS:** allowed throughout (£10 per dog per night).
**CREDIT CARDS:** MC, Visa.
**PRICES:** per room B&B £105–£155. À la carte £35. 1-night bookings refused peak weekends.

# STRONTIAN Highland

MAP 5:C1

## KILCAMB LODGE

You need to take a ferry crossing before traversing a mountain pass and a deep glen to arrive at this 'superb country house in a remote and extraordinary setting' with a private beach on a loch shore with mountain views. The part Georgian, part Victorian lodge has smart country-style bedrooms, some more contemporary with bright tartans, big headboard and window seat. 'My loch-facing room was really a suite, and had gorgeous views.' 'Standard' rooms can be small, report readers, and light sleepers should check if close to the kitchens. There is a choice of formal dining room – white napery, rich-red wallpapers – and the modish brasserie, serving perhaps roast venison with haggis cannelloni or grilled lemon sole with Isle of Mull mussels. While general praise is for the 'delicious food, especially the home-made bread at dinner', one reviewer was unhappy with the meal and found the room rate high. The good service and warm welcome, though, gain praise: 'Where do they find such a polished team in such a remote location?' (James Steward, and others)

**25% DISCOUNT VOUCHERS**

Strontian PH36 4HY

T: 01967 402257
E: enquiries@kilcamblodge.co.uk
W: kilcamblodge.co.uk

BEDROOMS: 11.
OPEN: all year, 'some closures in Nov, Dec, Jan', restaurant closed Mon/Tues Nov–Jan.
FACILITIES: drawing room, lounge/bar, restaurant, brasserie, in-room TV (Freeview), wedding facilities, 22-acre grounds, bar, brasserie, restaurant wheelchair accessible, toilet not adapted.
BACKGROUND MUSIC: at dinner.
LOCATION: edge of village.
CHILDREN: all ages welcomed.
DOGS: allowed in 5 bedrooms, not in public rooms.
CREDIT CARDS: MC, Visa.
PRICES: per room B&B single £160–£200, double £180–£385, D,B&B £260–£445. Tasting menu £78, à la carte £44. 1-night bookings refused Christmas, New Year, Easter.

# TARLAND Aberdeenshire                                MAP 5:C3

## DOUNESIDE HOUSE

The feeling of a family home pervades this hotel in brimming gardens on the edge of the Cairngorms national park. Bequeathed to the MacRobert Trust, the house was originally bought as a holiday retreat by Sir Alexander MacRobert, who transformed it in the Scottish Revival style. Lovely Edwardian interiors are filled with possessions and children's portraits. Spacious bedrooms have period furnishings. More eclectic rooms are in cottages and apartments. There is a health club, a tennis court, children's play park, and croquet on an infinity lawn. Trusted readers found their ground-floor apartment room 'excellent for dogs, with a good drying porch and well-designed shower room'. Afternoon tea in the bar brought 'tempting sweet flans', while in the conservatory restaurant, David Butters's use of local and home-grown ingredients, in such dishes as venison loin with poached brambles and beetroot jus, was 'absolutely first rate – each course mouth-watering'. But 'beware the muzak!' Breakfast brings organic porridge with crystallised pistachios, lime honey and crème fraîche, peat-smoked haddock and a full vegan. (Robert Gower, and others)

Tarland AB34 4UL

**T:** 01339 881230
**E:** manager@dounesidehouse.co.uk
**W:** dounesidehouse.co.uk

**BEDROOMS:** 23. 9 in cottages, plus 4 apartments in Casa Memoria, 2 cottages suitable for disabled.
**OPEN:** all year.
**FACILITIES:** bar, wine bar, piano lounge, library, conservatory restaurant. in-room Smart TV (Freeview), wedding facilities, health centre (indoor pool, all-weather tennis court), 17-acre grounds, public areas wheelchair accessible, adapted toilet.
**BACKGROUND MUSIC:** in bar and restaurant.
**LOCATION:** 7 miles NW of Aboyne.
**CHILDREN:** all ages welcomed.
**DOGS:** allowed in cottages and apartments, not in main building.
**CREDIT CARDS:** MC, Visa.
**PRICES:** per room B&B £174–£314. Set dinner £35–£45, tasting menu (Thurs–Sat) £80.

# THURSO Highland

MAP 5:B2

## FORSS HOUSE

**NEW**

The River Forss loops around this late Georgian Highland retreat in wooded grounds, today a dog-friendly hotel that is ideal for anglers, with shooting, stalking and hiking also on offer. You enter through a castellated extension built in 1930 by one Major Radclyffe, hunter and falconer, to house his trophies. The warmth that lies within owes much to Anne Mackenzie, the 'charming, diminutive lady of the house', and life and soul since 1989. She is still here to advise why you must have a 'teardrop' of water with your whisky, but Nicholas Gorton is the manager. Main house bedrooms range from cosy to colossal. There are others in the River House and Fishing Lodge annexes. A reader was shown to a 'huge bedroom overlooking the slightly wild gardens', with 'red and green floral decor' and 'very comfortable red sofa'. The bathroom had 'a vast bath, more like a swimming pool, with a shower over'. At dinner, a short menu includes such dishes as Caithness beef fillet and ox cheek, Scrabster cod with smoked mussels, and a vegan option. 'The food was superb,' other readers pronounce. (Chris Elliott, and others)

Forss
Thurso KW14 7XY

**T:** 01847 861201
**E:** stay@forsshousehotel.co.uk
**W:** forsshousehotel.co.uk

**BEDROOMS:** 14. 3 on ground floor, 6 in neighbouring annexes, 1 suitable for disabled.
**OPEN:** all year.
**FACILITIES:** bar, dining room, breakfast room, lounge, in-room TV (Freeview), meeting room, wedding facilities, 19-acre grounds with river and waterfall.
**BACKGROUND MUSIC:** in public areas breakfast and evening.
**LOCATION:** 5 miles W of Thurso.
**CHILDREN:** all ages welcomed (under-5s free).
**DOGS:** allowed in Sportsmen's Lodges and bar.
**CREDIT CARDS:** Amex, MC, Visa.
**PRICES:** per room B&B £165–£215. Fixed-price 3-course dinner £47.50, 6-course tasting menu £65.

# TORRIDON Highland

MAP 5:C1

## THE TORRIDON

**NEW**

Far-flung Torridon hosts an extreme Scottish triathlon, but there are gentler pursuits for guests at this resort hotel, a 'baronial pile' on a wooded estate at the head of Loch Torridon. Approached by a single-track road, it entails 'a long drive, especially if you are coming from south of the border, but, my goodness, it is a worthwhile trip!' writes a reader. Wildlife-watching, mountain biking, archery, Munro-bagging, stargazing and gastronomic grazing are all on offer. Contemporary bedrooms, some much more colourful than others, have a Victorian-style bathroom; many have spectacular loch and mountain views. 'Our room was small but special in many ways, with an excellent bed, two good armchairs, good lighting and a marble bathroom.' Fires blaze in public rooms, the 'service at your armchair is swift and friendly'. In 1887 restaurant, Paul Green's menus are a paean to Highland produce, with locally shot game, langoustine from the loch, fruit and vegetables from the kitchen garden, and meat from the Highland cattle and Tamworth pigs on the farm. There are cheaper, family-friendly rooms and pub grub at the Inn. (Steven Parsons)

Annat
by Achnasheen
Torridon IV22 2EY

**T:** 01445 791242
**E:** info@thetorridon.com
**W:** thetorridon.com

**BEDROOMS:** 18. 1 deluxe suite in adjacent cottage, 1, on ground floor, suitable for disabled.
**OPEN:** all year except Jan, Mon–Wed Nov–Mar.
**FACILITIES:** ramp, lift, drawing room, library, whisky bar, dining room, wedding facilities, 58-acre gardens.
**BACKGROUND MUSIC:** classical at night in dining room.
**LOCATION:** on W coast, 10 miles SW of Kinlochewe.
**CHILDREN:** all ages welcomed.
**DOGS:** in cottage suite and inn only.
**CREDIT CARDS:** Amex, MC, Visa.
**PRICES:** per room B&B £185–£995. Fixed-price 3-course dinner £65. 1-night bookings sometimes refused.

# ULLAPOOL Highland

MAP 5:B1

## THE CEILIDH PLACE

With bookshop and bar, coffee shop, restaurant and events space, the Urquhart family's hotel in a fishing village on Loch Broom hums with activity. Opened in 1970 by the late actor Robert Urquhart, it began as a café in a boatshed, where musicians could sing for their supper. Subsuming surrounding cottages, it grew and diversified, and now has characterful bedrooms, each with a Roberts radio, well-thumbed paperbacks, no TV. Readers on a third visit had 'a large, modern twin room at the back, with lots of clunky wood but a rooftop view'. Those on a budget bunk down in the Clubhouse across the car park. 'There's free tea and coffee to be made in the upstairs lounge', with library, pantry and piano. 'We used the honesty bar to save queuing downstairs.' Scott Morrison's eclectic menus are 'bistro style, which suits us fine'. Typical choices include wild venison pie, chickpea, spinach and sweet potato tagine, and Loch Broom langoustine. At breakfast there is porridge, kippers, a full Scottish or full veggie. The bar has been refurbished since last year – not that anyone was complaining. (C and PB)

### 25% DISCOUNT VOUCHERS

12–14 West Argyle Street
Ullapool IV26 2TY

**T:** 01854 612103
**E:** stay@theceilidhplace.com
**W:** theceilidhplace.com

**BEDROOMS:** 13. 10 with facilities en suite, 3 sharing bathroom and shower room, plus 11 in Clubhouse (max. 32 guests).
**OPEN:** all year except from 3 Jan for 3 weeks.
**FACILITIES:** bar, lounge, café/restaurant, bookshop, conference/function facilities, wedding facilities, 2-acre garden, public areas wheelchair accessible.
**BACKGROUND MUSIC:** in public areas.
**LOCATION:** village centre (car park).
**CHILDREN:** all ages welcomed, no charge for under-5s, £30 a night for 5–10s.
**DOGS:** allowed throughout (not unattended in bedroom), £12 per dog per stay.
**CREDIT CARDS:** MC, Visa.
**PRICES:** per room B&B £132–£180 (rooms in Clubhouse £24–£32 per person). À la carte £30.

# WALKERBURN Scottish Borders

MAP 5:E2

## WINDLESTRAW

John and Sylvia Matthews's keen 'eye for detail' has lifted this convivial restaurant-with-rooms to the 'top range of small establishments' since they took it over in 2015. The six well-proportioned bedrooms in this 'stunning' Edwardian manor house overlook the verdant Tweed valley and are a happy marriage of period features – the Grand bedroom has an Edwardian bathtub – and modern luxuries, including 'extremely comfortable' beds and contemporary bathrooms, some with a freestanding slipper bath, all with White Company toiletries. Downstairs, the light, elegant public rooms have a 'peaceful ambience' with open fires, 'good art and excellent furnishings'. Chef Stu Waterston's fine-dining menu changes daily and features home-grown and local produce, such as one reader's 'perfectly cooked rack of lamb' and four Scottish cheeses 'in peak condition', followed by 'sinfully moreish' puds. The wine list, though 'smallish', is 'reasonably priced' and well chosen. Breakfast includes home-made soda bread, full Scottish fry-up and impeccable omelettes. Windlestraw comes 'highly' recommended. More reports, please.

Galashiels Road
Walkerburn EH43 6AA

T: 01896 870636
E: stay@windlestraw.co.uk
W: windlestraw.co.uk

BEDROOMS: 6.
OPEN: all year except mid-Dec to mid-Feb.
FACILITIES: bar, sunroom, lounge/restaurant, in-room TV (Freeview), wedding facilities, 2-acre landscaped garden, parking.
BACKGROUND MUSIC: none.
LOCATION: in Walkerburn, 8 miles east of Peebles.
CHILDREN: all ages welcomed.
DOGS: allowed in bedrooms (not unattended), public rooms, not restaurant, £10 per dog per night.
CREDIT CARDS: MC, Visa.
PRICES: per room B&B £190–£300. 5-course set menu £70.

# WALES

Snowdonia

## HARBOURMASTER HOTEL

The quayside setting of this bright-blue hotel in the original harbourmaster's house is pretty special, with a feel of Brittany about it. Inside, it's just as lovely. 'When entering the hotel you feel you have opened a treasure chest,' writes one reader after an 'amazing' weekend. Once known as The Red Lion, it is now a local hub 'buzzing with people'. The service is 'excellent, always delivered with a warm smile'. Smart bedrooms are spread over three adjacent buildings. All those in the main house have a sea view. Serious 'attention to detail' includes Frette bedlinen, Melin Tregwynt blanket, fresh milk, and Molton Brown toiletries. Warehouse rooms are spacious, with a 'super-stylish' bathroom. Aeron Queen has a balcony, a velvet sofa, minibar and freestanding zinc bath. In the restaurant, Ludo Dieumegard's cooking is a showcase for locally farmed and fished produce – perhaps pan-roast cod with Jerusalem artichoke, hispi cabbage and salsa verde. At breakfast there is the full Welsh with Penlan bacon, local sausages and laver bread; avocado sourdough, Welsh rarebit. 'The food was fabulous.' (FT, and others)

Pen Cei
Aberaeron SA46 0BT

T: 01545 570755
E: info@harbour-master.com
W: harbour-master.com

BEDROOMS: 13. 4 in warehouse, 2 in cottage, 1 suitable for disabled.
OPEN: all year except 24–26 Dec, drinks only (from 2 pm) on Boxing Day.
FACILITIES: lift (in warehouse), bar, restaurant, in-room TV (Freeview), small terrace, restaurant and bar wheelchair accessible.
BACKGROUND MUSIC: all day in bar and restaurant.
LOCATION: central, on the harbour.
CHILDREN: 5 and upwards welcomed, must have own room.
DOGS: only guide dogs.
CREDIT CARDS: Amex, MC, Visa.
PRICES: per room B&B single £110–£270, double £120–£280, D,B&B double £180–£325. Set dinner £30–£38, à la carte £38. 1-night bookings refused most weekends, min. 2-night stay for D,B&B rate.

## TREFEDDIAN HOTEL

It may have a four-star rating, but there is nothing too swanky about this child-friendly, dog-friendly hotel overlooking Cardigan Bay, across the road from dunes, golf links and white-sand beach. It has been in the Cave-Browne-Cave family for more than a century and has a strong following among Guide readers. 'It is the ideal family hotel, with enough space to avoid children if you want peace and quiet,' writes one. More than half of the individually styled bedrooms have a sea view, some have a balcony. One room has a four-poster, and many are spacious, with a palette of sand, sea and surf. Rear-facing rooms are cooler and quieter, with a view of the garden and countryside. Activities include tennis and putting (with sailing and pony trekking to hand), while there are lounges, a playroom and library for wet days as well as an indoor pool. Smart-casual dress is expected at dinner, when 'good food, with plenty of choice' includes such dishes as steamed paupiette of Dover sole with prawn mousse and cardinal sauce, and aubergine and chickpea tagine. 'It remains a favourite with our family, aged 88 to 12.' (Dorothy Brining)

Tywyn Road
Aberdovey LL35 0SB

T: 01654 767213
E: info@trefwales.com
W: trefwales.com

BEDROOMS: 59. 1 suitable for disabled.
OPEN: all year except 8 Dec–12 Jan.
FACILITIES: lift, lounge bar, study, family lounge, adult lounge, restaurant, games room (snooker, table tennis), in-room TV (Freeview), indoor swimming pool, beauty salon, 15-acre grounds (lawns, tennis, putting green), most public rooms wheelchair accessible, adapted toilet.
BACKGROUND MUSIC: none.
LOCATION: ¼ mile N of Aberdovey.
CHILDREN: all ages welcomed.
DOGS: allowed in library, some bedrooms (£12 per night).
CREDIT CARDS: MC, Visa.
PRICES: per person B&B £90–£115, D,B&B £106–£132 (per night for min. 2-night stay, but check for 1-night availability; longer stay discounts). Fixed-price dinner £28.

## THE ANGEL HOTEL

Previous César winner

Whether you stay in the Victorian lodge in Abergavenny Castle grounds, in the former stables, or in the main building, William Griffiths's Georgian coaching inn on the edge of the Brecon Beacons continues to impress. Guide insiders endorse last year's award of a César, noting 'many good things', from 'best reading lights ever' to a weather forecast delivered to your room, with advice on the next day's activities. Bedrooms have neutral decor, contemporary furnishing, and a Villeroy & Boch or Fired Earth bathroom. Staff are 'exceptionally helpful, willing and cheery'. William's gallery-owner mother selects the artwork for public rooms, while the hotel bakery provides cakes for afternoon tea. You can dine in the Foxhunter bar or more formally in the Oak Room, where menus cater to all, including children and vegans. 'At dinner a pianist played. We had delicious asparagus and lemon sole goujons.' Alternatively, at sister establishment The Walnut Tree, veteran chef Shaun Hill holds a Michelin star. Breakfast, served until 11 am, brings smoothies, smoked fish, local sausages, a full vegan or full vegetarian. (A and CR, and others)

15 Cross Street
Abergavenny NP7 5EN

**T:** 01873 857121
**E:** info@angelabergavenny.com
**W:** angelabergavenny.com

**BEDROOMS:** 35. 2 in adjacent mews, and 4 cottages.
**OPEN:** all year except 24–27 Dec.
**FACILITIES:** lift, lounge, bar, tea room, restaurant, private function rooms, bakery, in-room TV (Freeview), civil wedding licence, courtyard, public rooms wheelchair accessible, adapted toilet.
**BACKGROUND MUSIC:** in restaurant and tea room, pianist in restaurant Fri and Sat dinner.
**LOCATION:** town centre.
**CHILDREN:** all ages welcomed.
**DOGS:** allowed in the Foxhunter bar and courtyard.
**CREDIT CARDS:** Amex, MC, Visa.
**PRICES:** per room B&B £139–£259, À la carte £45. 1-night bookings sometimes refused.

## PORTH TOCYN HOTEL

'I would love to keep it to myself, but I thought I should share the good news. This place rocks.' Praise indeed for this postwar coastal hotel in a 'glorious location overlooking Cardigan Bay'. With 71 years in the business, and the fourth generation now fully involved, the Fletcher-Brewer family know how to keep their guests happy. Expect 'great service, really good food, perfect bedrooms and bathrooms'. 'Our country-view room was large and uncluttered, with a super-king-size bed, house martins flashing by the bay window.' There was no hospitality tray, but tea or coffee could be delivered. Public rooms are furnished with antiques. For families there is a games room, high teas or light suppers. Lunch and afternoon tea can be served on the terrace. Dinner, cooked by Louise Fletcher-Brewer and Darren Shenton-Morris, 'was unfailingly superb', with special praise for Thai fishcakes and pan-fried pork loin with chargrilled pineapple and bubble and squeak. 'The whole atmosphere was warm and inviting. We would be happy to stay again.' (Arabella Cornelius, Alan and Edwina Williams, and others)

Bwlchtocyn
Abersoch LL53 7BU

T: 01758 713303
E: bookings@porthtocynhotel.co.uk
W: porthtocynhotel.co.uk

BEDROOMS: 17. 3 on ground floor, 1 shepherd's hut, 1 self-catering cottage.
OPEN: 2 weeks before Easter–early Nov.
FACILITIES: sitting rooms, children's snug, small bar, dining room, in-room TV (Freeview), 20-acre grounds (outdoor swimming pool, 10 by 6 metres, heated May–end Sept, tennis), call to discuss wheelchair access.
BACKGROUND MUSIC: none.
LOCATION: 2 miles outside village.
CHILDREN: all ages welcomed, no under-6s at dinner.
DOGS: allowed in bedrooms, not in restaurant or some public rooms.
CREDIT CARDS: MC, Visa.
PRICES: per room B&B single from £90, double £125–£210. À la carte £38, fixed-price dinner £42–£49. 1-night bookings occasionally refused at weekends.

## GWESTY CYMRU

'We would certainly go back,' say Guide readers, after a stay at Huw and Beth Roberts's small hotel looking out over the Victorian promenade and Cardigan Bay. Bedrooms are individually styled, each with a signature colour to reflect an aspect of the landscape. 'Room 8, at the top, had slate stone walls, a large bed, sofa and a sea view. The bathroom was beautifully done.' Bay-view rooms are clear favourites, except in a heatwave, when those who opt for the cheaper, air-conditioned back rooms have the last laugh. In the restaurant, chef Padrig Jones's approachable menus are big on local produce. 'We had dinner twice, excellent both times, but the breakfast Scotch egg, with a taste of Bloody Mary, stood out.' The staff are 'friendly and helpful, recommending a local chippy and warning about aggressive seagulls'. But never mind the gulls: in autumn and winter, as the sun dips below the horizon, take a ringside seat on the apron of lawn to witness a swirling cloud of starlings performing their incredible air show. Parking is difficult, so leave the car behind if you can. (SA Mathieson, A and EW, and others)

19 Marine Terrace
Aberystwyth SY23 2AZ

**T:** 01970 612252
**E:** info@gwestycymru.co.uk
**W:** gwestycymru.co.uk

**BEDROOMS:** 8. 2 on ground floor.
**OPEN:** all year except 21 Dec–8 Jan, restaurant closed for lunch Tues.
**FACILITIES:** small bar area, restaurant, seafront terrace, in-room TV (Freeview), unsuitable for disabled.
**BACKGROUND MUSIC:** 'easy listening' all day in reception and restaurant.
**LOCATION:** central, on seafront.
**CHILDREN:** no under-5s, all ages welcomed at lunch.
**DOGS:** not allowed.
**CREDIT CARDS:** MC, Visa.
**PRICES:** per room B&B single £70–£80, double £90–£150, family £150–£160. À la carte £36, fixed-price menu £16–£20.

**SEE ALSO SHORTLIST**

## ♥COES FAEN

César award: green hotel of the year

On the edge of Snowdonia, with 30 acres of gardens overlooking the Mawddach estuary, lies one of the most innovative, eco-friendly hotels in the UK. Within a lodge that originally housed waiting staff and stables, owners Sara and Richard Parry-Jones have carried out what led our inspectors on their last visit to enthuse: 'Such design, style and architectural detail, such a brilliant site and such hospitable hosts are extremely rare.' The entrance with glass staircase in the hillside and trickling water takes the breath away. Space, natural light and technology have all been exploited to the full. Each room has a unique feature – a secluded terrace with cedar hot tub; a handcrafted wooden bath; a widescreen cinema. New this year, the Mawddach Suite, reached by an ancient tunnel, has a lounge with cocktail bar and views of the Cader Idris range. There is stabling for your horse, but although there is a dog-friendly room no puppies are allowed – human or canine. On four nights a week Wayne Scarlet cooks such Tuscan-inspired dishes as ravioli of local crab, pappardelle with wild boar ragout, and vegan options. 'A brilliant project.'

Barmouth LL42 1TE

T: 01341 281632
E: croeso@coesfaen.co.uk
W: coesfaen.co.uk

BEDROOMS: 7. 1, on ground floor with patio, suitable for disabled, 1 in annexe.
OPEN: all year except Christmas, New Year, dinner served Wed–Sat.
FACILITIES: entrance hall, snug, dining room, in-room TV (Freeview), 15-acre woodland garden, stable, restaurant and bar wheelchair accessible.
BACKGROUND MUSIC: in public areas.
LOCATION: 1 mile E of town centre.
CHILDREN: not under 18.
DOGS: 'clean, well-behaved dogs (no puppies)' allowed in 1 bedroom and stables by arrangement, not in public rooms, dog-sitting available.
CREDIT CARDS: Amex, MC, Visa.
PRICES: per room B&B single £175–£305, double £195–£325. Set dinner £45–£55.

## LLWYNDU FARMHOUSE

Amid sheep-grazed pastures, this 16th-century
farmhouse at the foot of the Rhinog mountains
has glorious views over Cardigan Bay to the Llyn
peninsula. Since moving here in 1985, Peter and
Paula Thompson have created an unpretentious,
welcoming guest house. Interiors have exposed
timbers, inglenooks and amusing quirks such as
a walk-in wardrobe with a sea view. Bedrooms
are in the farmhouse and a converted hay barn
and granary. Two sea-facing house rooms have
a four-poster. A family room in the granary has
its own access. Guests gather for drinks in the
lounge before dinner is served in the atmospheric
old hall. A member of Slow Food UK, Peter
Thompson cooks an impressive nightly-changing
menu of local produce in season, with imaginative
choices at each course – maybe Welsh Black
beef, salt marsh lamb, free-range pork, mackerel,
mussels, crab … Children's portions or high tea
are available on request. Let them know if you
are vegetarian. Breakfast brings award-winning
sausages, dry-cured bacon, and salmon from
a Pembrokeshire smokery. Afterwards, 'there
are beautiful walks and bicycle rides up the
Mawddach estuary'.

### 25% DISCOUNT VOUCHERS

Llanaber
Barmouth LL42 1RR

T: 01341 280144
E: intouch@llwyndu-farmhouse.
co.uk
W: llwyndu-farmhouse.co.uk

BEDROOMS: 6. 3 in granary, 1 on ground
floor.
OPEN: all year except Christmas,
restaurant closed Sun and Wed.
FACILITIES: lounge, restaurant, in-room
TV (Freeview), ¼-acre garden in
4-acre grounds.
BACKGROUND MUSIC: 'occasionally and
on demand' in dining room.
LOCATION: 2 miles N of Barmouth.
CHILDREN: all ages welcomed.
DOGS: not allowed.
CREDIT CARDS: MC, Visa.
PRICES: per room B&B £115–£126.
Set dinner £25–£30 (2 or 3 courses).
1-night bookings refused July/Aug.

# BRECHFA Carmarthenshire

MAP 3:D2

## TY MAWR

The red kites that soar above the Cothi valley have a bird's-eye view of Brechfa Forest – perfect for hiking and biking – and of this rustic 16th-century country house hotel on its margin, with the River Marlais running by. It was taken over in late 2019 by Paul Bennett and Melissa Hurley, who have begun a programme of gentle, practical upgrading, while preserving the relaxed ethos. The bedrooms are not fancy, but have comfy seating and all the usual extras. Some have works by Welsh artist Nigel Wood, drawing inspiration from the surrounding landscape. Guide regulars found their ground-floor room, with a comfortable super-king-size bed, ideal for their dog; there is no extra charge for four-legged visitors. In the dining room, divided from the breakfast room by a large stone fireplace, Paul's concise, changing three-course dinner menus include such dishes as a casserole of Himalayan salt-aged beef with chestnut and braised shallot, while a plant-based menu is promised. There is a cosy lounge with plenty of seating, a log-burning stove and exposed stone walls. Reports, please.

Brechfa SA32 7RA

T: 01267 202332
E: info@wales-country-hotel.co.uk
W: wales-country-hotel.co.uk

BEDROOMS: 6. 2 on ground floor, 1 with private access.
OPEN: all year.
FACILITIES: sitting room, bar, breakfast room, restaurant, in-room TV (Freeview), 1-acre grounds.
BACKGROUND MUSIC: classical in restaurant during dinner.
LOCATION: village centre.
CHILDREN: 10 and upwards welcomed.
DOGS: allowed in bedrooms (no charge), sitting room and bar, not in restaurant or breakfast room (biscuits, bowls, and information on local walks provided).
CREDIT CARDS: Amex, MC, Visa.
PRICES: per room B&B single £80, double £115–£130, D,B&B single £100, double £160–£175. Set dinner £25–£30. 1-night bookings occasionally refused.

## THE COACH HOUSE

Drawn back for a sixth visit to the annual
Baroque Music Festival in this market and
minster town, trusted readers found everything 'as
good as before' at Kayt and Hugh Cooper's eco-
aware B&B. 'Hugh helped to unload our luggage
before bringing tea and some very good bara
brith (fruit loaf).' Behind the facade of a 19th-
century coaching inn, the house is contemporary
and smart. Bedrooms, painted in muted, natural
shades, have a coffee machine, fresh milk in
a minibar fridge, and Cole & Lewis toiletries.
Brychan mini-suite has a sofa, a bath and separate
walk-in shower. Even the smallest 'classic' rooms
are not poky. 'We were grateful to have such a
comfortable room to return to during two days
of torrential rain.' A variety of restaurants and
pubs are a stroll away. Breakfast brings a wide
choice, served to the unobtrusive strains of harp
music, and includes Glamorgan vegetarian
sausages, pikelets, local free-range eggs, laver
bread, and porridge with Welsh honey. Guests
can order a packed lunch before setting out to
explore the Brecon Beacons national park. (Jill
and Mike Bennett)

12 Orchard Street
Llanfaes
Brecon LD3 8AN

T: 01874 640089
E: reservations@coachhousebrecon.
com
W: coachhousebrecon.com

BEDROOMS: 6.
OPEN: all year except 1 week over
Christmas (open New Year).
FACILITIES: reading room, breakfast
room, lounge (with drink service),
in-room TV (Freeview), garden,
drying room, secure bicycle storage,
unsuitable for disabled.
BACKGROUND MUSIC: classical or Welsh
harp music in breakfast room.
LOCATION: ½ mile from town centre.
CHILDREN: 15 and upwards welcomed.
DOGS: not allowed.
CREDIT CARDS: MC, Visa.
PRICES: per room B&B single £79–£155,
double £84–£160, 1-night bookings
usually refused Fri and Sat Mar–Oct.

# CAERNARFON Gwynedd

## PLAS DINAS COUNTRY HOUSE

'Wow! This is the most wonderful country house,'
writes a reader. You don't need to be a fan of
the Netflix series The Crown to appreciate this
former home of the Armstrong-Jones family,
regularly visited by Princess Margaret and with
a collection of royal memorabilia. It dates from
the mid-1600s, but is substantially Victorian.
New owners Daniel and Annie Perks have
refurbishment in hand, so we reserve judgment
on the decor of the drawing room, which our
inspector found a bit of a mixture. Bedrooms are
more harmonious, and the views to Snowdonia
positively sing. Snowdon room is hung with
some of his original signed photographs. Princess
Margaret has a four-poster and a roll-top bath
for two. Mount has views to the Menai Strait. All
have Molton Brown products, home-made fudge
and biscuits. In the Gun Room, Daniel ap Geraint,
a former award-winning restaurateur, cooks 'food
to die for'. 'Dinner was divine.' 'The atmosphere
created by the staff and owners is wonderful.' Our
inspector's breakfast was a bit of a curate's egg,
but on this, too, we wait to hear more. (Tracey
Blessed, Deborah Meadows, TC, and others)

**25% DISCOUNT VOUCHERS**

Bontnewydd
Caernarfon LL54 7YF

T: 01286 830214
E: info@plasdinas.co.uk
W: plasdinas.co.uk

BEDROOMS: 10, 1 on ground floor.
OPEN: all year except Christmas,
restaurant closed Sun, Mon.
FACILITIES: drawing room, restaurant,
private dining room, in-room TV
(Freeview), civil wedding licence,
15-acre grounds, parking.
BACKGROUND MUSIC: in drawing room
and dining room.
LOCATION: 5-min. drive S of town.
CHILDREN: over-10s welcomed.
DOGS: pets allowed in bedrooms and in
drawing room (not food service areas)
at additional charge by arrangement.
CREDIT CARDS: Amex, MC, Visa.
PRICES: per room B&B £119–£249. Set
dinner £48. 1-night bookings refused
New Year's Eve.

# CARDIGAN Ceredigion

## CAEMORGAN MANSION

It's easier being green when you stay with environmentally aware hosts Beverley and David Harrison-Wood in their 19th-century mansion a short drive from Cardigan Bay. Under-floor heating and hot water throughout is supplied by a biomass boiler, while solar panels help cut down on electricity usage. Trusted readers received 'a warm and friendly welcome from Beverley, who showed us the house geography'. Three of the immaculate bedrooms – one with balcony – are on the second floor. Our reader had first-floor Cenarth, with 'John Lewis furniture' and a chandelier, but wasn't a fan of the 'blue LED bulbs in the bedside lamps'. The slate-walled bathroom had 'an elliptical basin with fountain tap, sitting on a Doric column', and a body-jet shower. All rooms have thick-pile carpet, a coffee machine, fresh milk and eco-friendly toiletries. In the dining room with its central wood-burning stove, David's menu includes such dishes as Welsh lamb cutlets with red wine, rosemary and shallot sauce. Ingredients are sourced locally for maximum freshness and minimum food miles.

Caemorgan Road
Cardigan SA43 1QU

T: 01239 613297
E: guest@caemorgan.com
W: caemorgan.com

BEDROOMS: 5.
OPEN: all year except Christmas and New Year, restaurant closed Sun.
FACILITIES: bar and restaurant (for residents only), in-room TV (Freeview), function facilities, 2-acre gardens.
BACKGROUND MUSIC: none.
LOCATION: ½ mile N of town centre.
CHILDREN: not under 15.
DOGS: assistance dogs only.
CREDIT CARDS: MC, Visa.
PRICES: per room B&B £99–£130. À la carte £38. 1-night bookings often refused peak weekends.

# CRICKHOWELL Powys

MAP 3:D4

## GLIFFAES

'We have always loved the house and gardens and river views,' say Guide regulars of this 'very friendly' hotel in the heart of the Brecon Beacons national park. Susie and James Suter are the third generation of her family to run the hotel, where a day's fishing on the River Usk might be followed by an ample afternoon tea (sandwiches and home-made cakes) on the terrace or perhaps a leisurely game of croquet. Readers value the traditional touches, such as the 'turn-down service' and the 'wonderful old-fashioned lounges'. Period features in the bedrooms are complemented by modern luxuries, such as White Company bedlinen, Vispring beds and Noble Isle toiletries. Some bedrooms have a Delft-tiled fireplace; others a wisteria-clad balcony. In the dining room, chef Karl Cheetham produces 'imaginative' cuisine with a local flavour: roasted haunch of wild venison, perhaps, or mushroom, leek and spinach pudding. One reader thought the menu would be improved by some simpler choices. Breakfast includes locally smoked kippers and French toast made from traditional bara brith. 'A very well-run hotel.' (F Kuhlmann, and others)

**25% DISCOUNT VOUCHERS**

Gliffaes Road
Crickhowell NP8 1RH

T: 01874 730371
E: calls@gliffaes.com
W: gliffaeshotel.com

BEDROOMS: 23. 4 in cottage, 1 on ground floor suitable for disabled.
OPEN: all year except New Year and Jan.
FACILITIES: 2 sitting rooms, conservatory, bar, dining room, in-room TV, civil wedding licence, 33-acre garden (tennis, croquet, private fishing on River Usk), public rooms wheelchair accessible.
BACKGROUND MUSIC: in bar in the evening.
LOCATION: 3 miles W of Crickhowell.
CHILDREN: all ages welcomed.
DOGS: not allowed indoors (free kennels available).
CREDIT CARDS: Amex, MC, Visa.
PRICES: per room B&B single £145–£209, double £155–£325, D,B&B double £231–£401. À la carte £38–£40. 1-night bookings refused high-season weekends.

## THE OLD VICARAGE

Ideally situated for exploring Powis Castle or foodie Ludlow, this red brick Victorian vicarage stands back from the winding A484 in the Welsh Marches, looking over rolling pastures to the Shropshire hills. It has been run as a B&B since 2006 by owners Helen and Tim Withers, who welcome new arrivals with tea in the drawing room. The bedrooms, each named after a nearby river, are traditionally styled and furnished. Mule has a five-foot double bed and blue toile de Jouy wallpaper. Severn suite has two double bedrooms with a shared bathroom between. Teme, the largest room, has a six-foot double bed that can be made up as twins. The large garden is home to a wildlife pond, vegetable beds and hens. If you wish to eat in, you can order a meze plate, or sit down to a three-course dinner of local and organic produce, which might include free-range chicken with peperonata, sweet potato mash and purple-sprouting broccoli. At breakfast there is a buffet, laver bread omelette and hot-smoked salmon with scrambled new-laid eggs.

### 25% DISCOUNT VOUCHERS

Dolfor
Newtown SY16 4BN

T: 07753 760054
E: mail@theoldvicaragedolfor.co.uk
W: theoldvicaragedolfor.co.uk

**BEDROOMS:** 4.
**OPEN:** all year except last 3 weeks Dec, dining room closed Sun.
**FACILITIES:** drawing room, dining room, in-room TV (Freeview), 1½-acre garden, unsuitable for disabled.
**BACKGROUND MUSIC:** none.
**LOCATION:** 3 miles S of Newtown.
**CHILDREN:** all ages welcomed, under-2s free.
**DOGS:** not allowed.
**CREDIT CARDS:** Amex, MC, Visa.
**PRICES:** per room B&B single £70–£90, double £95–£120, family £112–£150 (cot £10). Meze plate £12, set 3-course dinner £25. 1-night bookings refused bank holidays and Royal Welsh Show week.

# DOLGELLAU Gwynedd

## FFYNNON

Up narrow Love Lane in a town under Cader
Idris, this dark-stone Victorian rectory-turned-
hotel makes a stylish base for a trip to Snowdonia.
The bedrooms all have a touch of theatre.
Dual-aspect Aimee has a corbeille bed, seating
areas with views over the garden, and a spa bath
with overhead shower. Annis has an oriental
theme. Sydney has a carved mahogany bed, an
in-room slipper bath and a shower room. The
experience, which includes an outdoor hot tub,
is 'eccentric, even surreal', but wholly a pleasure.
A fire burns within an ornate surround in a cosy
lounge with honesty bar. German-born chef/
proprietor Bernhard Lanz and his wife, Angela,
'couldn't have been nicer', say Guide insiders.
Bernhard rolled up his sleeves to resolve a
plumbing problem while Angela fixed the Wi-Fi.
In the dining/breakfast room Bernhard cooks
a short menu of beautifully presented, locally
sourced dishes such as chargrilled pork medallions
with apple sage sauce and market vegetables. A
generous breakfast brings a buffet and the full
Welsh, setting you up to explore the national park.

Love Lane
Dolgellau LL40 1RR

T: 01341 421774
E: info@ffynnontownhouse.com
W: ffynnontownhouse.com

BEDROOMS: 6.
OPEN: all year, restaurant closed
Sun–Wed.
FACILITIES: sitting room, dining room,
study/hall, butler's pantry, in-room
TV (Freeview), garden (secluded
outdoor hot tub), parking.
BACKGROUND MUSIC: all day in sitting
room and dining room.
LOCATION: town centre.
CHILDREN: all ages welcomed ('baby
pack' free of charge), beds for 2–16
years £25 a night.
DOGS: not allowed.
CREDIT CARDS: MC, Visa.
PRICES: per room B&B single £110–
£160, double £160–£220. Set dinner
£28–£50, à la carte £35. Min. 2-night
stay at weekends and bank holidays.

**SEE ALSO SHORTLIST**

# DOLYDD Gwynedd                                    MAP 3:A3

## Y GOEDEN EIRIN

Sandwiched between Snowdonia and the
Menai estuary, this B&B in a converted granite
cowshed celebrates both its Welsh heritage and
its eco credentials. Alongside slate and timber,
wool blankets and fleeces are in-room recycling
instructions, solar panels and even an electric car
charging point. Guests receive a warm Welsh
welcome from Eluned Rowlands who, together
with her late husband, John, ran the place for a
time as a restaurant before later opening a B&B. A
portrait in the beamed dining room by Sir Kyffin
Williams is of the great Welsh dramatist John
Gwilym Jones, from whose short story collection
Y Goeden Eirin (The Plum Tree) the house takes
its name. The Rowlandses were friends with both
men, and a love of literature and art is apparent
in shelves lined with books, and the prints up the
staircase. There are four plum trees now in the
grounds, where two bedrooms are set in renovated
outbuildings. When our inspectors visited, they
had the house room, with its own small entrance
hall, alcove dressing room and bathroom. An
Aga-cooked breakfast of local produce is served at
the kitchen table. Reports, please.

Dolydd
Caernarfon LL54 7EF

T: 01286 830942
E: eluned.rowlands@tiscali.co.uk
W: ygoedeneirin.co.uk

BEDROOMS: 3. 2 on ground floor in
annexe 3 yds from house.
OPEN: all year except Christmas/New
Year.
FACILITIES: breakfast room, lounge,
in-room TV (Freeview), 20-acre
pastureland, electric car charging
point.
BACKGROUND MUSIC: none.
LOCATION: 3 miles S of Caernarfon.
CHILDREN: not under 10.
DOGS: well-behaved dogs in annexe
bedrooms and public rooms by prior
arrangement.
CREDIT CARDS: none, cash or cheque
payment requested on arrival.
PRICES: per room B&B single from £65,
double £90–£100. 1-night bookings
refused in peak summer.

# EGLWYSWRW Pembrokeshire

MAP 3:D2

## AEL Y BRYN

♛ Previous César winner

Year after year we receive rave reviews from readers extolling both house and hosts at Robert Smith and Arwel Hughes's modern, single-storey B&B with beautifully tended gardens, gazing out to the Preseli hills. 'We have never met such charming and interesting hosts.' 'Simply the best B&B we have ever stayed in,' read typical reports. The bedrooms, all with fresh milk in a mini-fridge, are decorated in restful shades, with contemporary furnishings, and big windows to make the most of both the light and the vistas. A suite, with a huge walk-in shower, opens on to a private patio. 'Our bedroom had wonderful views over the wildlife pond to Carningli, which dominates the skyline above Newport.' The conservatory is the place to sit and watch the sunset or to marvel at the stars in a bat-black sky. On some nights, by prior arrangement, guests can sit down to a dinner of 'locally sourced quality food, with freshly picked vegetables from the garden that go to make a culinary delight'. The 'no charge for corkage is much appreciated'. (Bob and Jean Henry, Rosemary and Michael Globe, and others)

Eglwyswrw
Crymych SA41 3UL

T: 01239 891411
E: stay@aelybrynpembrokeshire.co.uk
W: aelybrynpembrokeshire.co.uk

BEDROOMS: 4. All on ground floor.
OPEN: all year except Christmas/New Year.
FACILITIES: library, music room, dining room, conservatory (telescope), in-room TV (Freeview), courtyard, 2½-acre garden (wildlife pond, stream, bowls court), public rooms wheelchair accessible.
BACKGROUND MUSIC: none.
LOCATION: ½ mile N of Eglwyswrw.
CHILDREN: not under 16.
DOGS: not allowed.
CREDIT CARDS: Amex, MC, Visa.
PRICES: per room B&B single £90–£120, double £110–£150. Set dinner £26–£30. 1-night bookings refused bank holidays.

# FELIN FACH Powys

## THE FELIN FACH GRIFFIN

♥ Previous César winner

Dogs love this dining-pub-with-rooms, between the Black mountains and the Brecon Beacons, as much as their two-legged friends do. It is, our readers agree, a wonderful place. Launched in 2000 by Charles Inkin, it set the tone for two further ventures, The Old Coastguard, Mousehole, and The Gurnard's Head, Zennor (see entries), which he runs with brother Edmund. All have a relaxed ambience and values of sustainability and support for the community. The bedroom style is smart casual, with Welsh blankets, flowers, a Roberts radio, home-baked biscuits, books and Bramley toiletries – no goggle-box, no UHT milk. You can eat in any of a series of small rooms, one with an Aga, where resident canines Max and Lottie might be seen warming themselves. Lunch and supper bring such dishes as oak-smoked salmon fishcakes, Middle White sausages with mash and greens, or gnocchi with peas and girolles. You can have your own dog with you at one table – or under the table in the Tack Room, if no one objects. Breakfast includes fruit from the kitchen garden, apple juice from the Usk valley, and home-made soda bread.

### 25% DISCOUNT VOUCHERS

Felin Fach
Brecon LD3 0UB

T: 01874 620111
E: fran@eatdrinksleep.ltd.uk
W: felinfachgriffin.co.uk

BEDROOMS: 7.
OPEN: all year except 24/25 Dec.
FACILITIES: bar, dining rooms, limited mobile signal, 3-acre garden (kitchen garden, alfresco dining), bar/dining room wheelchair accessible, adapted toilet.
BACKGROUND MUSIC: Radio 4 at breakfast, 'selected music' afternoon and evening.
LOCATION: 4 miles NE of Brecon, in village on A470.
CHILDREN: all ages welcomed, child's camp bed £15, travel cot no charge.
DOGS: allowed in bedrooms, in bar and Tack Room, but not in restaurant, bowls, towels, biscuits supplied.
CREDIT CARDS: MC, Visa.
PRICES: per room single B&B £116–£146, double £142–£182, D,B&B single £156–£176, double £202–£242. À la carte £33, set supper £29.

# FISHGUARD Pembrokeshire

MAP 3:D1

## THE MANOR TOWN HOUSE

Above the harbour in a seaside town with spectacular views over Cardigan Bay to the Preseli hills, this Georgian town house B&B is all that the smart street front promises – and more. Helen and Chris Sheldon are 'perfect hosts'. 'We arrived late from the [Rosslare] ferry, and they made us very welcome,' writes a reader this year. Bedrooms have contemporary decor, with perhaps bright fabric headboards and the occasional well-chosen antique, as well as vegan Noble Isle toiletries and an honesty hamper of Welsh treats. Two superior sea-view rooms can sleep a family. Airy lounges with wood floor and earthy hues are hung with works by Welsh artists. A cream tea can be taken by a log-burning stove or, when the sun shines, on the rear terrace, with its views over the fishing-boat-bobbing harbour where, 50 years ago, Hollywood descended to film Under Milk Wood. A generous breakfast buffet, organic eggs and hand-made sausages fixes you up to walk the Pembrokeshire Coast Path that runs below; take a packed lunch. 'We had a delightful stay, one of many over the years,' another reader affirms. (Mary Milne-Day, David Humphreys)

11 Main Street
Fishguard SA65 9HG

**T:** 01348 873260
**E:** info@manortownhouse.com
**W:** manortownhouse.com

**BEDROOMS:** 6.
**OPEN:** all year except 23–28 Dec.
**FACILITIES:** 2 lounges, breakfast room, in-room TV (Freeview), small walled garden, unsuitable for disabled.
**BACKGROUND MUSIC:** classical in breakfast room.
**LOCATION:** town centre.
**CHILDREN:** all ages welcomed.
**DOGS:** very small dogs in one bedroom, not in dining areas.
**CREDIT CARDS:** MC, Visa.
**PRICES:** per room B&B single £80–£105, double £110–£145. 1-night bookings sometimes refused peak weekends.

# GLYNARTHEN Ceredigion                        MAP 3:D2

## PENBONTBREN

♔ Previous César winner

Richard Morgan-Price and Huw Thomas are personable hosts at their dog-friendly B&B with a difference, in gardens and grounds with views to the Preseli hills. Readers are unanimous in their praise for the 'generous and warm welcome' and the 'fine eye for detail'. Suites, in converted stables, barn and granary, have a garden terrace and a sitting room with a minibar, fresh milk in a fridge, an espresso machine and Welsh cakes. The separate Garden Room is smaller, with no sitting room, but it has a terrace with a covered pergola. Such spacious accommodation is ideal for guests wishing to stay longer than one night, to explore the nearby beaches and Ceredigion countryside or to walk the Coast Path. In the morning, tables are set with fine china and fresh flowers, for an 'excellent breakfast' of freshly squeezed juice, Agen prunes, porridge, the full Welsh or local smoked salmon, smoked haddock or cockles, bacon and laver bread with a poached egg. For dinner there are restaurants not far away, or you might eat a picnic supper alfresco and wait as night falls and stars spangle the Bible-black sky.

**25% DISCOUNT VOUCHERS**

Glynarthen
Llandysul SA44 6PE

T: 01239 810248
E: contact@penbontbren.com
W: penbontbren.com

BEDROOMS: 6. 5 in annexe, 1 in garden, 3 on ground floor, 1 family suite, 1 suitable for disabled.
OPEN: all year except 24–26 Dec.
FACILITIES: breakfast room, in-room TV (Freeview), 7-acre grounds (croquet lawn), bike storage, public rooms wheelchair accessible, adapted toilet.
BACKGROUND MUSIC: none.
LOCATION: 5 miles N of Newcastle Emlyn.
CHILDREN: all ages welcomed.
DOGS: allowed in some bedrooms, not in breakfast room.
CREDIT CARDS: Amex, MC, Visa.
PRICES: per room B&B single £85–£110, double £100–£120, family £140. 1-night bookings sometimes refused weekends.

# HARLECH Gwynedd

MAP 3:B3

## CASTLE COTTAGE

At the top of one of the world's steepest streets, Glyn and Jacqueline Roberts's restaurant-with-rooms occupies two 16th-century buildings above Edward I's formidable castle (faint hearts, take the High Street route). Guide readers were welcomed by chef/patron Glyn, 'a natural in the hospitality business'. The focus is very much on food, but the 'excellent' bedrooms have 'comfort as well as charm', contemporary decor and modern oak furniture contrasting with original features. Some have a bath with shower over, others a bath and shower, and perhaps a view of sea, castle or Mount Snowdon. They are supplied with biscuits and fresh milk. Drinks and 'delicious' canapés are served in a beamed bar with a log-burning fire. 'The menus are seasonal, and preference is given to local produce, from the sea as well as the farm' – maybe duet of Welsh beef, or goujons of sole in herb and almond crust. At dinner, any reservations about loud music in the bar and elaborate menu descriptions were 'routed by the quality of the meal'. Don't be late for your breakfast kipper; check-out is at 10.30 am. (SM, AM, and others)

---

### 25% DISCOUNT VOUCHERS

Y Llech
Harlech LL46 2YL

T: 01766 780479
E: glyn@castlecottageharlech.co.uk
W: castlecottageharlech.co.uk

**BEDROOMS:** 7. 4 in annexe, 2 on ground floor.
**OPEN:** Open Thurs–Sat in mid-Feb and March, Wed–Sat April–Oct.
**FACILITIES:** bar/lounge, restaurant, in-room TV (Freeview), unsuitable for disabled.
**BACKGROUND MUSIC:** in bar and restaurant at mealtimes.
**LOCATION:** town centre.
**CHILDREN:** all ages welcomed.
**DOGS:** not allowed.
**CREDIT CARDS:** MC, Visa.
**PRICES:** per room B&B single £85–£125, double £130–£175. Set menus £39–£42, tasting menu £45.

# LAMPETER Ceredigion

## THE FALCONDALE

Sweeping views across the Teifi valley are just
one reason why this Grade II listed Italianate
villa is a popular choice for weddings. Standing
in seclusion a mile outside town, it was designed
by Thomas Talbot Bury, an associate of AWN
Pugin, and originally named, in Welsh, Valley
of the Kestrel. Now owned by Lisa Hutton and
Derek Parton, it offers 'the very quintessence of
a warm welcome and a good bed in the country'.
The bedrooms are individually designed and
spacious. One has a modern four-poster, and an
iron-lace Juliet balcony from which to admire
the azaleas in their pomp. All rooms have period
furniture, perhaps a wall of statement wallpaper,
a cafetière, a teapot, home-made shortbread
and Temple Spa toiletries. Chef Tony Schum
favours local Welsh produce for daily updated
menus that might include a platter of seafood
from Cardigan Bay, venison loin, or a veggie
Glamorgan sausage with Perl Las (a blue cheese)
sauce. There are 'comfortable public rooms', an
in-house beauty therapist should you wish to be
sugared or shellacked, and wonderful walks along
the Ceredigion Coast Path or in the Cambrian
mountains. (RG)

Falcondale Drive
Lampeter SA48 7RX

T: 01570 422910
E: info@thefalcondale.co.uk
W: thefalcondale.co.uk

BEDROOMS: 17.
OPEN: all year.
FACILITIES: lift (to some bedrooms),
bar, 3 lounges, conservatory,
restaurant, in-room TV (Freeview),
civil wedding licence, beauty
treatment room, terrace, 14-acre
grounds, restaurant and ground floor
wheelchair accessible, adapted toilet.
BACKGROUND MUSIC: in restaurant and
lounges.
LOCATION: 1 mile N of Lampeter.
CHILDREN: all ages welcomed.
DOGS: allowed (£10 per night) in
bedrooms, public areas, not restaurant.
CREDIT CARDS: MC, Visa.
PRICES: per room B&B single
£100–£205, double £135–£230,
D,B&B double (min. 2 nights)
£199–£294. À la carte £50, fixed-price
3-course menu £32, 7-course tasting
menu £67.50.

# LLANDRILLO Denbighshire

MAP 3:B4

## TYDDYN LLAN

The views roll out over the Vale of Edeyrnion to the Berwyn mountains, and provide a backdrop for the 'superb' food served in this restaurant-with-rooms. The extended Georgian ducal hunting lodge is owned by Susan and Bryan Webb; it's here that Bryan, a chef for more than 40 years, cooks in harmony with the seasons, adapting dishes for children, and catering to vegans and vegetarians with notice. A night's tasting menu might include risotto with truffles, wild bass with laver bread and butter sauce, Goosnargh duck breast and faggot with confit potato, cider and apple sauce. 'The matching of ingredients shows flair, and the balance of courses leaves you feeling satisfied and not over full.' Traditionally styled bedrooms are 'well furnished and comfortable'. Even standard rooms have home-made biscuits; early-morning tea or coffee arrives on request. Better rooms have a cafetière and Gilchrist & Soames toiletries. The Garden Suite has patio doors on to a secluded private garden. Breakfast brings freshly squeezed juices, local farm apple juice, lavender honey, dry-cured Welsh bacon and smoked salmon.

### 25% DISCOUNT VOUCHERS

Llandrillo
Corwen LL21 0ST

T: 01490 440264
E: info@tyddynllan.co.uk
W: tyddynllan.co.uk

BEDROOMS: 13. 3 with separate entrance, 1, on ground floor, suitable for disabled.
OPEN: all year except Mon/Tues, and last 2 weeks of Jan, restaurant closed Wed/Thurs lunch.
FACILITIES: 2 lounges, bar, 2 dining rooms, in-room TV (Freeview), no mobile signal, civil wedding licence, 3-acre garden, public rooms wheelchair accessible.
BACKGROUND MUSIC: none.
LOCATION: 5 miles SW of Corwen.
CHILDREN: all ages welcomed.
DOGS: allowed in some bedrooms (£10 per night), not in public rooms.
CREDIT CARDS: Amex, MC, Visa.
PRICES: per room B&B £190–£320, D,B&B £320–£450. Set dinner £70, tasting menus £85–£95, à la carte £70. 1-night bookings refused Christmas.

# LLANDUDNO Conwy                                    MAP 3:A3

## BODYSGALLEN HALL AND SPA

Set in 220 acres of parkland, this antique-filled
Elizabethan mansion has plenty to impress, from
the oak-panelled hall and 13th-century tower to
the modern spa and 'lovely' gardens. 'We much
enjoyed the splendidly furnished public rooms,
the hall, lounge and library with bound volumes
of Punch,' write trusted readers. 'The view from
the dining room to Snowdonia is remarkable.'
As you would expect in a Grade I listed building,
there is no lift to the country-style bedrooms,
some with a four-poster. 'Our superior double
was reached by 34 steps, and was huge, with an
enormous bed. The bathroom, down a flight of
steps, had all one might reasonably desire.' Some
rooms are in cottages overlooking the 17th-
century parterre, and in converted outbuildings.
Food service was slow even at breakfast, though it
brought 'ultimately admirable kippers', and 'the
staff were universally friendly'. When booking a
package, be sure you know what is offered. 'The
£50 dinner allowance covered two courses but not
three.' The cooking is ambitious, but at the time of
writing a change of chef is imminent, so we await
reports. (Anthony Bradbury, and others)

The Royal Welsh Way
Llandudno LL30 1RS

T: 01492 584466
E: info@bodysgallen.com
W: bodysgallen.com

**BEDROOMS:** 31. 16 in cottages, 1 suitable
for disabled.
**OPEN:** all year, restaurant closed Mon
and Tues lunch.
**FACILITIES:** hall, drawing room,
library, bar, dining room, in-room TV
(Freeview), civil wedding licence, 220-
acre park (gardens, croquet, tennis),
spa (swimming pool), ground floor
wheelchair accessible.
**BACKGROUND MUSIC:** none.
**LOCATION:** 2 miles S of Llandudno
and Conwy.
**CHILDREN:** no under-6s in hotel, or
under-8s in spa.
**DOGS:** allowed in some cottages by
prior arrangement.
**CREDIT CARDS:** Amex, MC, Visa.
**PRICES:** per room B&B single
£190–£450, double £215–£510, D,B&B
double £290–£600. À la carte £66.
1-night bookings sometimes refused.

**SEE ALSO SHORTLIST**

# LLANGAMMARCH WELLS Powys

MAP 3:D3

## LAKE COUNTRY HOUSE HOTEL & SPA

Mock Tudor meets the Tyrol with a colonial twist at Jean-Pierre Mifsud's former hunting and fishing lodge in wooded grounds overlooking a trout lake, with 9-hole golf course, and the River Irfon running through. An architectural gallimaufry, it is 'as eccentric and as lovely as ever', a hotelier reader assures us this year. Downstairs are comfy lounges filled with antiques and chandeliers, jumbled sofas, a log-burner, books and board games. Up a creaky staircase are traditional bedrooms, perhaps with an antique dresser, wall hangings and canopy bed. Suites in a purpose-built lodge have a more contemporary look, with a lounge, double doors to the grounds, and a separate shower and bath. In the dining room, chef Joe Bartlett's menus for omnivores and vegetarians include such dishes as loin of venison, onion bread sauce, game chips and chard, or pumpkin and sage pithivier, smoky mash, buttered greens and chestnuts. At breakfast there is a full Welsh, kippers and smoked haddock, before a day's fishing or a visit to the spa that pampered Kaiser Wilhelm II in 1912. (Richard Morgan-Price, PH)

---

**25% DISCOUNT VOUCHERS**

Llangammarch Wells LD4 4BS

T: 01591 620202
E: info@lakecountryhouse.co.uk
W: lakecountryhouse.co.uk

**BEDROOMS:** 32. 12 suites in adjacent lodge, 7 on ground floor, 1 suitable for disabled.
**OPEN:** all year.
**FACILITIES:** lounge, bar, restaurant, breakfast room, in-room TV (Freeview), spa (15-metre swimming pool), civil wedding licence, 50-acre grounds (tennis, trout lake, 9-hole golf course), public rooms wheelchair accessible.
**BACKGROUND MUSIC:** none.
**LOCATION:** 8 miles SW of Builth Wells.
**CHILDREN:** all ages welcomed, no under-8s in spa.
**DOGS:** allowed (£15 per dog per night), not in main lounge, dining room, spa.
**CREDIT CARDS:** Amex, MC, Visa.
**PRICES:** per room B&B single from £115, double £130–£260, D,B&B (min. 2 nights) £195–£340. Fixed-price dinner £47.50.

# LLANTHONY Monmouthshire

MAP 3:D4

## LLANTHONY PRIORY HOTEL

Soaring arches frame views of the Black mountains and the Vale of Ewyas at this ruined 12th-century Augustinian abbey with a hotel in the former prior's lodgings. Incorporating the Grade I listed south-west tower, it was remodelled in the 18th century, possibly by the poet Walter Savage Landor, who bought the abbey in 1803 and unwittingly caused the worst damage since the Dissolution. Owners Victoria and Geoff Neal have introduced some of the comforts that the modern hotel guest expects, while respecting the unique historic character of the property. Four bedrooms are in the tower, accessed by a spiral staircase. They have antique furniture, a four-poster or half-tester bed, and share two shower rooms on the first floor. The three remaining bedrooms have their own shared bathroom. In this remote, romantic setting there is no Wi-Fi, no mobile phone signal and, by choice, no TV. There is a cosy bar in the undercroft, and hearty fare in a dining room with open fire and vaulted ceiling. After tucking into spicy bean goulash, fish pie or beef casserole, you can step outside to marvel at the stars.

Llanthony
Abergavenny NP7 7NN

T: 01873 890487
E: llanthonypriory@btconnect.com
W: llanthonyprioryhotel.co.uk

BEDROOMS: 7. All with shared showers/bathrooms.
OPEN: Fri–Sun (Nov–Mar), Tues–Sun (Apr–Oct), 27 Dec–1 Jan, closed Mon except bank holidays.
FACILITIES: lounge, bar, dining room, no Wi-Fi, mobile phone signal or TV, extensive grounds (including priory ruins), unsuitable for disabled.
BACKGROUND MUSIC: none.
LOCATION: 10 miles N of Abergavenny.
CHILDREN: over-4s welcomed in family rooms.
DOGS: not allowed.
CREDIT CARDS: MC, Visa.
PRICES: per room B&B single £75–£80, double £95–£100. À la carte £20.

# LLYSWEN Powys

## LLANGOED HALL

Expect art and architecture at this 'really grand' Jacobean mansion set in gardens and parkland in the Wye valley, with views to the Black mountains. Restored and redesigned by Clough Williams-Ellis before he worked on Portmeirion, it houses the 'fabulous' art collection of the late Sir Bernard Ashley (widower of the designer Laura Ashley), who bought the hall in 1987. Original works by Whistler, Sickert and Augustus John are on display. Bedrooms, some with original Laura Ashley fabrics, have Noble Isle toiletries, robes, slippers, a decanter of Madeira, home-made flapjacks, and 24-hour room service. A trusted Guide reader was very happy with her 'comfortable and well-furnished' North Wing room, and its 'excellent bathroom'. Staff are 'in plentiful supply', friendly and fleet. The ambience is 'most welcoming'. Head chef Sam Bowser draws inspiration from the organic kitchen garden to create his menus. Choose five, seven or nine courses, of such dishes as smoked pork, black garlic and bacon purée with maple-glazed salsify; for vegans, artichoke teriyaki with sorrel. Breakfast brings free-range eggs, and honey from the bees. (MC)

Llyswen
Brecon LD3 0YP

**T:** 01874 754525
**E:** reception@llangoedhall.com
**W:** llangoedhall.co.uk

**BEDROOMS:** 23.
**OPEN:** all year.
**FACILITIES:** great hall, morning room, library, bar/lounge, restaurant, billiard room, function rooms, in-room TV (Freeview), civil wedding licence, 17-acre gardens and parkland, unsuitable for disabled.
**BACKGROUND MUSIC:** in restaurant, during functions, pianist on special occasions.
**LOCATION:** 12 miles NE of Brecon.
**CHILDREN:** all ages welcomed.
**DOGS:** allowed in 2 bedrooms, £25 per night, not in public rooms. Heated kennels (no charge) available.
**CREDIT CARDS:** MC, Visa.
**PRICES:** per room B&B single £147–£937, double £160–£950, D,B&B £270–£1,050. Tasting menu £55, £75, £95.

# NARBERTH Pembrokeshire

## THE GROVE OF NARBERTH

♦ Previous César winner

Jacobean splendour meets Arts and Crafts elegance at this gleaming white hotel, set in a leafy glade outside one of Pembrokeshire's prettiest market towns. Owners Neil and Zoë Kedward have created a luxurious country retreat with a Welsh aesthetic. Local crafts and textiles are mixed with richly coloured Persian rugs, antique furniture and modern pieces; a colour scheme echoes the landscape's gentle hues. Bedrooms and suites are a mix of traditional – ornate fireplaces, textured wallpapers and perhaps a double-ended stand-alone bathtub – and contemporary. Some have a four-poster bed, others a half-tester, and one has triple-aspect views and a vaulted ceiling. Dinner, served in the relaxed Artisan Rooms or the more formal Fernery, is Douglas Balish's celebration of the best of Welsh ingredients, such as lamb from the Preseli hills, fish from local fishermen, and vegetables and fruit from the hotel's kitchen gardens. Afternoon tea may be taken either in the restaurant or on the terrace, perhaps after taking one of the walking trails through the hotel's extensive grounds.

Molleston
Narberth SA67 8BX

T: 01834 860915
E: reservations@grovenarberth.co.uk
W: thegrove-narberth.co.uk

**BEDROOMS:** 26. 12 in cottages in grounds, 1 suitable for disabled.
**OPEN:** all year.
**FACILITIES:** 3 lounges, bar, 4 restaurant rooms, in-room TV (Sky), in-room spa treatments, civil wedding licence, 26-acre grounds, ground floor wheelchair accessible, adapted toilet.
**BACKGROUND MUSIC:** in public areas.
**LOCATION:** 1 mile S of Narberth.
**CHILDREN:** all ages welcomed, no under-12s in Fernery.
**DOGS:** allowed in some bedrooms and lounge, the Snug dining room.
**CREDIT CARDS:** MC, Visa.
**PRICES:** per room B&B £125–£665, D,B&B £368–£778. Tasting menu £69–£105, à la carte (Artisan Rooms) £40. 1-night bookings refused at peak times.

**SEE ALSO SHORTLIST**

# NEWPORT Pembrokeshire

## CNAPAN

'How could a simple family home on a narrow, bustling high street possibly work as a popular guest house? Step inside Cnapan and you quickly find out.' A reader this year thoroughly endorses our inspector's approval for Judith and Michael Cooper's 'outstanding' B&B in a Georgian house within a conservation area. Bedrooms have original features, neutral decor, contemporary furnishings and modern bathroom fittings. A family room has a double bed with a single in an adjoining room. Rooms at the back overlook the secluded garden. Front rooms may experience some traffic noise, but enjoy views of St Mary's church, the Norman castle and Carningli mountain. All have art by local artists, wool blankets and Mason & Miller bath products. A breakfast of 'fresh produce, beautifully cooked', brings a full Welsh or full vegetarian, oak-smoked salmon, vegan chickpea and apricot patties, kippers and more, with 'everything piping hot'. The Coopers no longer offer an evening meal, but will recommend good local restaurants. 'This is how a B&B should be run – warm, friendly and helpful.' (Helen Harvey, RG)

East Street
Newport SA42 0SY

T: 01239 820575
E: enquiry@cnapan.co.uk
W: cnapan.co.uk

BEDROOMS: 5. Includes 1 family room. Plus self-catering cottage.
OPEN: all year except Christmas and holiday in Feb and early March (ring or check website for dates).
FACILITIES: sitting room, bar, in-room TV (Freeview), small garden.
BACKGROUND MUSIC: none.
LOCATION: town centre.
CHILDREN: all ages welcomed.
DOGS: not allowed.
CREDIT CARDS: MC, Visa.
PRICES: per room B&B single £65–£80, double £85–£98, family room (sleeps 3) £100–£115. Dinner for parties of 18 or more by arrangement. 1-night bookings sometimes refused weekends at peak times.

# NEWPORT Pembrokeshire

MAP 3:D1

## LLYS MEDDYG

♀ Previous César winner

Near the edge of town, a walk from the beach, this 19th-century town house is a popular restaurant with smart contemporary rooms – and a rather chic yurt. It is 'a small hotel with big appeal', a reader writes. Colourful potted pansies and a warm welcome from owners Ed and Lou Sykes created an instant good impression when our inspector last called. Main-house bedrooms have views to Carningli mountain or Newport Bay. Three are in a mews in the garden. All have a king-size bed, a Welsh throw, works by local artists, a mini-fridge with local milk, and organic toiletries. Glampers will love the yurt with its under-floor heating. 'We were fortunate to have a large room with enormous bathroom – worth the exercise climbing to the top of the house and then descending to the Cellar bar for an excellent meal.' You can eat in the ground-floor dining room, or alfresco, but the cellar, with log-burner, is cosiest. An imaginative menu of local produce includes wood-fired steaks, fish and vegan dishes, with ingredients foraged by Ed. At breakfast there is home-made jam and their own cold-smoked salmon. (Michael and Patricia Blanchard)

East Street
Newport SA42 0SY

**T:** 01239 820008
**E:** info@llysmeddyg.com
**W:** llysmeddyg.com

**BEDROOMS:** 8. 1 on ground floor, 3 in mews annexe, plus a yurt.
**OPEN:** all year, restaurant closed Mon, Tues (Nov–Apr).
**FACILITIES:** bar, lounge, restaurant, kitchen garden dining area (open in summer holidays), in-room TV (Freeview), civil wedding licence, garden, unsuitable for disabled.
**BACKGROUND MUSIC:** in bar and dining room.
**LOCATION:** central.
**CHILDREN:** all ages welcomed.
**DOGS:** allowed in 3 annexe bedrooms, bar, on lead in garden.
**CREDIT CARDS:** MC, Visa.
**PRICES:** per room B&B single £80–£145, double £120–£160, family from £210. À la carte £35. 1-night bookings refused some Saturdays.

# PENALLY Pembrokeshire

MAP 3:E1

## PENALLY ABBEY

**NEW**

There is plenty to please the eye here: a lovely Georgian-Gothic house with romantic cusped windows and glorious views across Carmarthen Bay to Caldey Island. It is, readers say, an 'immensely likeable place'. Bedrooms have a restful palette, with perhaps a wall of toile de Jouy 'Le Temple de Jupiter' wallpaper, a headboard emblazoned with birds, or a kelim to add colour and movement. A four-poster room has a lovely ogee-headed window to frame the vista. 'Double-aspect Room 3 was gorgeous, spacious and well lit. The bathroom was large with an excellent shower and separate bath.' Dog-friendly first-floor rooms in a converted coach house have a balcony with tables and chairs. 'We could happily have spent our entire holiday at the hotel being looked after by their lovely staff,' wrote one correspondent. The bar is an architectural gem, while in the restaurant short menus of locally sourced ingredients include such dishes as pan-fried sea bass with charred broccoli. A medieval ruin in the grounds was possibly the chantry chapel of the eponymous abbey. (Sally Mehalko, DG, SH)

Penally
Tenby SA70 7PY

T: 01834 843033
E: info@penally-abbey.com
W: penally-abbey.com

BEDROOMS: 12. 4 in coach house, 2 on ground floor.
OPEN: all year except first 2 weeks of Jan.
FACILITIES: drawing room, bar, sunroom, restaurant, function room, in-room TV (Freeview), civil wedding licence, in-room treatments, terrace, 1-acre lawns.
BACKGROUND MUSIC: 'very gentle' in bar and restaurant.
LOCATION: 1½ miles SW of Tenby.
CHILDREN: all ages welcomed.
DOGS: allowed in coach house bedrooms (not unattended), bar, sunroom, not in restaurant.
CREDIT CARDS: MC, Visa.
PRICES: per room B&B £165–£265. À la carte £45 (vegetarian £35). 1-night bookings refused only at Christmas and major sporting event weekends.

# PENARTH Vale of Glamorgan

MAP 3:E4

## RESTAURANT JAMES SOMMERIN

♀ Previous César winner

There are great views over the esplanade to the Bristol Channel and the Art Deco pier pavilion from Louise and James Sommerin's Michelin-starred restaurant-with-rooms. Occupying a quirky Victorian, gabled, timbered, balconied terrace, it is 'the place to go to in south Wales if you like fancy food', writes a trusted reader. A sea-view room is an obvious choice, but all rooms are bright, smart and contemporary, with an 'elegant and efficient' bathroom. 'There are no frills, though I was delighted to be brought delicious, freshly baked Welsh cakes when I had just arrived,' reports one reader. As you dine, you can watch James Sommerin and his brigade at work beyond the long serving counter. 'The cooks, some of whom served us at the table, were young and enthusiastic.' The food is 'fairly complicated, but everything was excellent'. Clear, unpretentious menu descriptions make no grand claims for wild sea bream, samphire, ginger and artichoke, or Welsh lamb, coconut, butternut squash, cumin and mint – the proof is in the eating. Breakfast includes 'a full Welsh with laver bread and vegetarian options'. (Catrin Treadwell, Jonathan Rose)

The Esplanade
Penarth CF64 3AU

T: 029 2070 6559
E: info@jamessommerinrestaurant.
   co.uk
W: jamessommerinrestaurant.co.uk

BEDROOMS: 9. 1 suitable for disabled.
OPEN: all year except Mon/Tues, 24–26 Dec, 1 Jan, restaurant closed 26 Dec, 1 Jan.
FACILITIES: bar, restaurant, private dining room, in-room TV (Freeview), restaurant and bar wheelchair accessible, adapted toilet.
BACKGROUND MUSIC: in bar and restaurant.
LOCATION: on the esplanade.
CHILDREN: well-behaved children of all ages welcomed.
DOGS: not allowed.
CREDIT CARDS: MC, Visa.
PRICES: per room B&B £190–£210, D,B&B £280–£300 (for 2 people, Sun/Wed/Thurs). Tasting menus 6–9 courses £75–£95, chef's table 14 courses, £150, à la carte £53 (not Fri or Sat).

**SEE ALSO SHORTLIST**

# PWLLHELI Gwynedd

MAP 3:B2

## PLAS BODEGROES

On the remote Llyn peninsula, Gunna and
Chris Chown's Georgian country house, in a
magical woodland setting, is run as a much-
loved restaurant-with-rooms, offering 'good
food, a relaxed atmosphere, peace and quiet, and
a beautifully maintained garden in an area of
outstanding natural beauty'. In spring, wisteria
drapes the veranda, before more than 100 old
rose varieties come into bloom. Bedrooms are
tastefully furnished, and have milk in a minibar,
and a cafetière. Readers liked their room
overlooking the kitchen garden, with 'a king-size
bed, armchairs and a coffee table, home-made
shortbread', but weren't as fond of the wet room
shower with squeegee mop. Having taken a step
back, Gunna once again runs front-of-house,
while Hugh Bracegirdle cooks a three-course
dinner of home-grown and local produce, Welsh
Black beef, mountain and salt marsh lamb and
responsibly sourced fish. 'We particularly enjoyed
monkfish with shallots and bacon, and peppered
venison with a wee venison pie.' Snowdonia is on
the doorstep, Blue Flag beaches close by.

Nefyn Road
Efailnewydd
Pwllheli LL53 5TH

T: 01758 612363
E: info@bodegroes.co.uk
W: bodegroes.co.uk

**BEDROOMS:** 10. 2 in courtyard cottage.
**OPEN:** all year except Christmas,
3 Jan–6 Feb, restaurant closed for
dinner Sun and Mon.
**FACILITIES:** lounge, bar, breakfast
room, restaurant, in-room TV
(Freeview), 5-acre grounds (courtyard
garden), restaurant wheelchair
accessible, adapted toilet.
**BACKGROUND MUSIC:** none.
**LOCATION:** 1 mile W of Pwllheli.
**CHILDREN:** all ages welcomed.
**DOGS:** allowed in some bedrooms for
'a nominal charge', not in public
rooms.
**CREDIT CARDS:** MC, Visa.
**PRICES:** per room B&B single
£110–£130, double £130–£170. Fixed-
price dinner £49. 1-night bookings
sometimes refused bank holidays.

# ST DAVIDS Pembrokeshire

MAP 3:D1

## TWR Y FELIN HOTEL

A Georgian windmill sits at the heart of Wales's
first contemporary arts hotel, on the edge of
the UK's smallest city, a stroll from Caerfai
Bay. More than 100 original works by British
and international artists are on display. 'No-
expense-spared' bedrooms showing 'care and
attention to detail', in the mill and Oriel Wing,
have a chocolate-and-cream palette. Some have
a terrace or Juliet balcony, a bath and separate
shower. There are panoramic views from the
observatory above the showpiece Tower Suite. A
20-room annexe should open any time soon. In the
restaurant, chef Sam Owen's menus include such
locally sourced dishes as halibut with cockles and
laver bread. No dogs are allowed, as the hotel is
hypoallergenic, but even so one reader suffered
a severe adverse reaction to 'paintings with
women bleeding from their eyebrows', the work
of street artist Charles Uzzell-Edwards, aka
'Pure Evil'. Accompanied by less shock value are
Marcus Oleniuk's photographs of the St Davids
peninsula and Ann Goodfellow's beautiful
ceramic sculptures. Breakfast has 'a Welsh
flavour'. (MC, and others)

**25% DISCOUNT VOUCHERS**

Caerfai Road
St Davids SA62 6QT

T: 01437 725555
E: stay@twryfelinhotel.com
w: twryfelinhotel.com

BEDROOMS: 21. Some on ground floor,
some in separate wing, 1 suitable for
disabled, 20 more in purpose-built
annexe scheduled to be available soon.
OPEN: all year.
FACILITIES: bar, restaurant, lounge, in-
room TV (Sky), landscaped grounds,
civil wedding licence, car charging
points, public areas wheelchair
accessible, adapted toilet.
BACKGROUND MUSIC: in public areas.
LOCATION: a few hundred yards from
centre of St Davids.
CHILDREN: not under 12.
DOGS: not allowed.
CREDIT CARDS: Amex, MC, Visa.
PRICES: per room B&B £210–£380,
D,B&B £280–£440. À la carte £52.
Normally 2-night min. stay Fri and
Sat, but check for 1-night availability.

**SEE ALSO SHORTLIST**

# SKENFRITH Monmouthshire

MAP 3:D4

## THE BELL AT SKENFRITH

On the banks of the River Monnow lies this characterful boutique retreat fashioned from a 300-year-old coaching inn, all flagstone floors and beams. There are lovely riverside views and walks; dog owners will be pleased to find an outdoor shower for their pets, who are welcomed in the Dog and Boot bar. The setting does have its disadvantages as The Bell was unfortunately badly affected by recent flooding, and needed to dry out. Each of the 11 contemporary bedrooms is named after a different brown trout fishing fly. Tups Indispensable, for instance, has a double-ended bath (in-room); Whickham's Fancy has a separate sitting room overlooking the river. In the dining room, chef Joseph Colman's 'excellent' food is imbued with Celtic flavours. Readers enjoyed a 'first-class' Brecon fillet steak with 'imaginative vegetables', and 'top-hole' Welsh cheeses served at room temperature ('hooray'). A reasonably priced wine list offers an extensive choice of wines by the glass as well as a more indulgent section. 'Delightful young staff' and a 'warm and efficient welcome', comments one satisfied guest. (KJ Salway)

**25% DISCOUNT VOUCHERS**

Skenfrith NP7 8UH

T: 01600 750235
E: reception@skenfrith.co.uk
W: skenfrith.co.uk

BEDROOMS: 11.
OPEN: all year.
FACILITIES: bar, restaurant, Wine Room (for reading, relaxing, private dining), Dog and Boot bar, in-room TV (BT, Freeview), 2-acre grounds (terrace, garden), restaurant, bar and terrace wheelchair accessible, adapted toilet.
BACKGROUND MUSIC: 'intermittently' in bar and restaurant.
LOCATION: 9 miles W of Ross-on-Wye.
CHILDREN: all ages welcomed.
DOGS: well-behaved dogs allowed in bedrooms and Dog and Boot bar, Pooch Parlour dog shower in garden with towels.
CREDIT CARDS: MC, Visa.
PRICES: per room B&B £150–£250, D,B&B £190–£290. À la carte £43. 1-night bookings refused Sat.

# TREMADOG Gwynedd                        MAP 3:B3

## PLAS TAN-YR-ALLT    **NEW**

Surrounded by gardens and ancient woodland, with views over the Glaslyn estuary to the Rhinog mountains, this late Georgian villa-turned-B&B revels in its rich history. Bedrooms are named after notable past residents – William Madocks, who built the house; Percy Bysshe Shelley, who spent a year here completing Queen Mab; and Mary Hilda, who was born at the Plas, and whose nephew Clough Williams-Ellis was responsible for a mural, 'The Triumph of Neptune'. Luxuries include an Italian espresso machine, a mini-fridge, fresh flowers, and a bathroom with heated slate floor. You can lie in a four-poster in dual-aspect Madocks Room and hear the steam trains on the Ffestiniog railway chuffing across the sea wall that was also his creation. A cream tea is served in the drawing room, with 'sumptuous furnishings', a baby grand and drinks globe, or on the veranda. Breakfast, cooked by owners Howard Mattingley and Mark White, brings 'a nice selection of cereals and juices followed by a choice of items freshly cooked to order'. Readers are full of praise for the 'excellent accommodation with convivial hosts'. (Ian Morgan, Andrew Billingsley, and others)

Tremadog
Porthmadog LL49 9RG

T: 01766 514591
E: info@plastanyrallt.co.uk
W: plastanyrallt.co.uk

BEDROOMS: 3.
OPEN: all year except 3rd week of Dec to 1 Jan.
FACILITIES: drawing room, dining room, 40-acre grounds, in-room TV (Freeview), unsuitable for disabled.
BACKGROUND MUSIC: in drawing room and dining room.
LOCATION: just above the village of Tremadog.
CHILDREN: not under 16.
DOGS: not allowed.
CREDIT CARDS: MC, Visa.
PRICES: per room B&B £104–£144. 1-night bookings refused bank holidays, weekends and at peak times.

# TYWYN Gwynedd                    MAP 3:B3

## DOLFFANOG FAWR

Few guest houses have as magnificent a mise en scène as this one in Snowdonia, set among pretty lawned gardens, with views across sheep-filled pastures to Tal-y-llyn lake and Cader Idris. The 18th-century farmhouse is run by Alex Yorke and Lorraine Hinkins, who have decorated their four simple but stylish bedrooms in neutral colours, with artwork by local artists and cosy throws from a nearby woollen mill. Rooms at the front have garden views framed by the Dyfi and Tarren hills, those at the back look towards the lake. If other guests agree, dogs are welcome in the lounge, which is home to a wide variety of books, maps, and has a fire on chilly days. The set dinner menu 'is a delight and not to be missed', with a 'well-chosen wine list' and 'modest mark-up'. A communal breakfast brings sausages, eggs and bacon, cooked any way you like, or perhaps toast made from freshly baked bread with home-made jam. Outside, the garden attracts a wide variety of birds, including the great spotted woodpecker and the siskin. Red kites, buzzards and peregrine falcons can occasionally be seen; cuckoos call in the valley in late spring.

Tal-y-llyn
Tywyn LL36 9AJ

T: 01654 761247
E: info@dolffanogfawr.co.uk
W: dolffanogfawr.co.uk

BEDROOMS: 4. 1 reached by covered walkway.
OPEN: Mar–Oct, dinner served Thurs–Sat.
FACILITIES: lounge, dining room, in-room TV (Freeview), 1-acre garden (hot tub), unsuitable for disabled.
BACKGROUND MUSIC: none.
LOCATION: by lake, 10 miles E of Tywyn.
CHILDREN: not under 10.
DOGS: allowed by arrangement, in bedrooms (not unattended) and lounge 'if other guests don't mind', not in dining room.
CREDIT CARDS: MC, Visa.
PRICES: per room B&B single £90–£120, double £110–£120. À la carte £28 (2% surcharge if paying by credit card). 1-night bookings often refused.

# WHITEBROOK Monmouthshire

## THE WHITEBROOK

It would be easy to miss Chris and Kirsty Harrod's Michelin-starred restaurant-with-rooms, tucked away above a single-track road in a Wye valley hamlet – but miss it and you'd miss out. Chris worked for Raymond Blanc at Le Manoir aux Quat'Saisons, Great Milton (see entry), 'but this is an experience of a different kind'. As well as sourcing produce as locally as possible, Chris forages for herbs and plants from pennywort to hogweed, and incorporates them in his dishes. They might include squab pigeon, cauliflower, forced rhubarb, charred kale and wild chervil, or Crown Prince pumpkin, buttermilk, purple sprouting broccoli and three-cornered garlic. The rooms are 'functional rather than overtly luxurious', painted in pale shades, with a modern bathroom, a double-ended bath and walk-in shower as well as organic toiletries. One, with views of the valley and eponymous brook, has a sleigh bed; another, overlooking the garden, has a stone wet room. Welsh cake and fresh milk offered on arrival are nice touches; the tea is from Cornwall. But the food is the big attraction. 'This man must be in line for two stars.'

Whitebrook NP25 4TX

T: 01600 860254
E: info@thewhitebrook.co.uk
W: thewhitebrook.co.uk

BEDROOMS: 8.
OPEN: all year, except 24 Dec (rooms), 25/26 Dec, 1 Jan, 2 weeks in Jan, restaurant closed Mon, Tues, and Wed lunch.
FACILITIES: lounge/bar, restaurant, in-room TV (Freeview), terrace, 1-acre garden, restaurant and women's toilet wheelchair accessible.
BACKGROUND MUSIC: 'chill-out' in restaurant and lounge.
LOCATION: 6 miles S of Monmouth.
CHILDREN: all ages welcomed, over-8s only in restaurant on weekdays, over-16s only at weekends.
DOGS: only guide dogs allowed.
CREDIT CARDS: Amex, MC, Visa.
PRICES: per room B&B £140–£235, D,B&B £330–£425. 8-course dinner £95, fixed-price lunch £47–£60.

# CHANNEL ISLANDS

La Corbière lighthouse, Jersey

# HERM

## THE WHITE HOUSE

With no cars, and white sandy beaches, this tiny island paradise has just one hotel. But there is no hint of complacency here – nor telephones, TVs or even clocks, except those on 'the new radios in the bedrooms'. Alight from the ferry from Guernsey, and a tractor will collect your bags to be delivered to your room in the main hotel or one of the surrounding cottages. Some have a balcony, others have French doors to the pool, and most have a sea view, while nine overlook the garden. The style is slightly dated, with nautical colours of pale blue, white and sand (time truly has stood still here). Alone on the second floor, the Crow's Nest family suite is ideal for sunset watching. If you forget your flip-flops or bucket and spade, Herm's shop can supply it, but pity chef Krzysztof Janiak if he runs out of ingredients for his ambitious menus in the Conservatory restaurant. Modern British dishes with German and French accents might include salt- and sugar-cured salmon rolled in activate charcoal, with preserved pumpkin and salted popcorn. Brasserie fare is available in the turquoise-painted Ship Inn.

Herm GY1 3HR

T: 01481 750075
E: reservations@herm.com
W: herm.com

BEDROOMS: 40. 23 in cottages, some on ground floor.
OPEN: early Apr–early Nov.
FACILITIES: 3 lounges, 2 bars, 2 restaurants, conference room, 1-acre gardens (tennis), 7-metre outdoor swimming pool, wheelchair access to island difficult.
BACKGROUND MUSIC: in the Ship Inn.
LOCATION: by harbour, ferry from Guernsey (20 mins).
CHILDREN: all ages welcomed.
DOGS: allowed in 2 bedrooms (£20 per dog per night), reception lounge, garden, bars, with restrictions.
CREDIT CARDS: MC, Visa.
PRICES: per room B&B single £70–£199, double £145–£284, D,B&B single £96–£225, double £197–£336, Crow's Nest £325–£370. Set dinner £38, à la carte £29.

# LITTLE SARK Sark

MAP 1: inset E6

## ❦LA SABLONNERIE

César award: island hotel of the year

'Paradise,' write readers on their 'umpteenth' stay at this rose-smothered, whitewashed hotel on a tiny, car-free island. Established by the Perrée family in 1948, and today run by the 'charming and helpful' Elizabeth Perrée, it centres on a 400-year-old farmhouse, and down the years has spilled over into neighbouring cottages. Past guests include Vivien Leigh and Laurence Olivier. This is a romantic place, which you reach via a scenic isthmus by horse-drawn carriage. Newly redecorated interiors are old-fashioned in the best sense, with antiques, rough-plastered walls and exposed beams. 'Delightful' bedrooms have a rustic simplicity. A fire burns in the lounge on chilly days. In summer, you can have a cream tea or dine in the flower-filled garden. Colin Day uses locally farmed and fished ingredients in such dishes as seafood platter, lobster with ginger and lime, spring lamb with Madeira sauce and wild mushrooms. At breakfast there is Sark honey from the bees that gorge on the blazing gorse. Experiences including a dip in tidal Venus Pool, boat trips, puffin-spotting and stargazing linger in the memory. (JB)

Little Sark GY10 1SD

T: 01481 832061
E: reservations@sablonneriesark.com
W: sablonneriesark.com

BEDROOMS: 22. Some in nearby cottages.
OPEN: mid-Apr–Oct.
FACILITIES: 3 lounges, 2 bars, restaurant, Wi-Fi by arrangement, civil wedding licence, 1-acre garden (tea garden/bar, croquet), unsuitable for disabled.
BACKGROUND MUSIC: classical/piano in bar.
LOCATION: Little Sark, via boat from Guernsey (guests will be met at the harbour on arrival).
CHILDREN: all ages welcomed.
DOGS: allowed at hotel's discretion in some bedrooms, not in public rooms.
CREDIT CARDS: MC, Visa.
PRICES: per room B&B £97.50–£195. Set menus £35, à la carte £55.

# ST BRELADE Jersey

MAP 1: inset E6

## THE ATLANTIC HOTEL

It's all about the seaside at this luxury hotel designed to resemble a 1930s ocean liner, where readers this year had a 'wonderful, relaxing stay'. On a headland overlooking St Ouen's Bay, with landscaped gardens and outdoor pool, it has full-height windows to show off the view, contemporary artwork drawing inspiration from sea and sand, and a restaurant serving sublime seafood. Those bedrooms without a sea view overlook the golf course, and all rooms have a marble bathroom, 24-hour room service, fresh fruit and a daily newspaper. A ground-floor Executive Suite had a minibar fridge with Jersey milk, good tea but instant coffee. The kitchen is the bailiwick of executive chef Will Holland. In the Ocean restaurant, 'tasty amuse-bouche', scallops and John Dory were 'top drawer'. Both the tasting menu and tasting room proved less of a hit, though Jersey potato with Winchester cheese and onion ash was rated highly. Breakfast in bed brought 'proper fresh orange juice' and bacon in a 'wonderful' sourdough roll. A happy ship, then, 'with some great staff, lovely views and tasty food'. (Kevin and Victoria Seymour)

Le Mont de la Pulente
St Brelade JE3 8HE

T: 01534 744101
E: info@theatlantichotel.com
W: theatlantichotel.com

BEDROOMS: 50. Some on ground floor.
OPEN: all year except 4 weeks Jan–Feb.
FACILITIES: lift, lounge, library, cocktail bar, restaurant, private dining room, fitness centre, in-room TV (Sky), civil wedding licence, 10-acre garden (tennis, indoor and outdoor heated swimming pools, 10 by 5 metres), public rooms wheelchair accessible, no adapted toilet.
BACKGROUND MUSIC: in restaurant, lounge and cocktail bar in evenings.
LOCATION: 5 miles W of St Helier.
CHILDREN: all ages welcomed.
DOGS: guide dogs only.
CREDIT CARDS: Amex, MC, Visa.
PRICES: per room B&B single £130–£450, double £150–£460. Market menu £55, à la carte £72, tasting menu £85.

**SEE ALSO SHORTLIST**

# ST PETER Jersey

MAP 1: inset E6

## GREENHILLS COUNTRY HOUSE HOTEL

Guests returning to the Seymour family's hotel, tucked away amid Jersey's tranquil Green Lanes, are greeted each year by the same smiling faces. 'The staff really make it,' says a fan. Carmelita Fernandes is 'a magnificent manager. There is a real sense of teamwork and desire to serve the guests.' A 'beautiful old granite house' with beams and log fires, which dates from 1674, is flanked by newer wings 'very much in keeping' with the style. A bedroom overlooking the flower-filled courtyard garden was 'quite large, decorated in soft greys and greens'. It had a 'fairly small bathroom with very good walk-in shower', and White Company toiletries. Superior Plus rooms, with French doors to the garden, have an espresso machine and a mini-fridge. Chef Lukasz Pietrasz, in his 11th year here, uses local produce in such dishes as sea bass with crab linguine and fennel ceviche. 'The food was both excellent and value for money.' Breakfast brings local apple juice and 'very good cooked items'. You might take afternoon tea alfresco, or lounge by the small pool. 'On our last night I took a dip at 10 pm – gorgeous!' (Andrew Kleissner)

Mont de l'École
St Peter JE3 7EL

T: 01534 481042
E: reservations@greenhillshotel.com
W: seymourhotels.com

BEDROOMS: 33. 10 on ground floor, 1 suitable for disabled.
OPEN: all year except 23 Dec–mid-Feb.
FACILITIES: 2 lounges, bar, restaurant, garden, terrace, in-room TV, civil wedding licence, outdoor heated swimming pool, access to leisure club at sister hotel, public rooms wheelchair accessible, adapted toilet.
BACKGROUND MUSIC: in public areas.
LOCATION: 8 miles NW of St Helier.
CHILDREN: all ages welcomed.
DOGS: allowed in 4 ground-floor bedrooms on request (£10 per dog per night), not in public areas, but assistance dogs 'always welcome'.
CREDIT CARDS: Amex, MC, Visa.
PRICES: per room B&B £109–£233. Fixed-price dinner £31.50–£39.50, à la carte £50.

# ST PETER PORT Guernsey

MAP 1: inset E5

## LA FREGATE

There is a sea view from every bedroom in this extended 18th-century manor house, made over in contemporary hotel style, with the emphasis more on modern leisure and business than olde worlde charm. The bedrooms are styled in beige, aqua and peach, in an understated way that does not upstage the views. Two are singles; doubles have a queen-size bed. Some bay-view rooms have a balcony, while deluxe rooms in a new wing have floor-to-ceiling windows and a balcony or terrace. All have bleached wood furniture, comfortable seating, room service and twice-daily housekeeping. The harbour feels very near when seen through the windows, but it's a bit of a hike back up a pretty path from the town, although worth visiting, we are assured. You can eat in a light-filled dining room or, better yet, on the terrace, above tiered gardens and rooftops, gazing out at Sark and Herm. The à la carte menu reprises the classics, with extensive use of local produce, especially fish and shellfish. For instance, Guernsey crab, prawns and avocado, oysters, seafood Thermidor, chateaubriand, duck à l'orange, steak tartare and crêpe Suzette. Reports, please.

Beauregard Lane
Les Cotils
St Peter Port GY1 1UT

T: 01481 724624
E: enquiries@lafregatehotel.com
W: lafregatehotel.com

BEDROOMS: 22.
OPEN: all year.
FACILITIES: lounge/bar, restaurant, lift, private dining/function rooms, in-room TV (Freeview), terrace (alfresco dining), ½-acre terraced garden, unsuitable for disabled.
BACKGROUND MUSIC: in bar.
LOCATION: hilltop, 5 mins' walk from centre.
CHILDREN: all ages welcomed.
DOGS: guide dogs only.
CREDIT CARDS: Amex, MC, Visa.
PRICES: per room B&B single £105, double £210–£265, suite £465.
À la carte £50.

**SEE ALSO SHORTLIST**

# ST SAVIOUR Jersey

MAP 1: inset E6

## LONGUEVILLE MANOR

A sense of history pervades this 14th-century manor house, festooned with wisteria, which sits in landscaped grounds in a wooded valley. You can dine in the wood-panelled Great Hall, sit by medieval fireplaces, stroll in the Victorian garden. A Ship of Theseus, altered over the centuries, it is now run by third-generation owners Malcolm and Patricia Lewis as a luxury food and spa hotel with outdoor pool (Relais & Châteaux). The 'charming' staff are long serving under the 'hands-on' manager, Pedro Bento. Bedrooms are a mix of the antique and contemporary, one with beams from the Spanish Armada, another in a turret. One reader's suite had 'a lovely, comfortable bed', a 'huge bath', and a shower which, 'if on full blast was like being in the ring with Tyson'. Chef Andrew Baird uses produce from local suppliers and the kitchen garden to create such dishes as loin of venison, braised red cabbage, glazed apple, blackberry, salt-baked celeriac and hazelnuts. The wine cellar holds 4,000 bottles. 'We had the tasting menu with shedloads of wine, beautifully executed, faultless.' (Richard Morgan-Price)

Longueville Road
St Saviour JE2 7WF

T: 01534 725501
E: info@longuevillemanor.com
W: longuevillemanor.com

BEDROOMS: 30. 8 on ground floor, suite in cottage.
OPEN: all year except 4–21 Jan.
FACILITIES: lift, 2 lounges, cocktail bar, 2 dining rooms, in-room smart TV, conference facilities, civil wedding licence, spa, 18-acre grounds (croquet, tennis, outdoor heated pool), public areas wheelchair accessible.
BACKGROUND MUSIC: in bar and restaurant.
LOCATION: 1½ miles E of St Helier.
CHILDREN: all ages welcomed.
DOGS: allowed, not in restaurant.
CREDIT CARDS: Amex, MC, Visa.
PRICES: per room B&B £200–£575, D,B&B £310–£685. Fixed-price menu £55. tasting menu £100, à la carte £75. 1-night bookings refused weekends, bank holidays.

# IRELAND

Roundstone, nr Clifden, Connemara

# BAGENALSTOWN Co. Carlow

MAP 6:C6

## LORUM OLD RECTORY

Previous César winner

If the locally made grandfather clock in the hall is the beating heart of this Victorian rectory-turned-B&B in the Barrow river valley, hostess Bobbie Smith is the life and soul. With daughter Rebecca, Bobbie welcomes guests into her childhood home, filled with antiques, squashy sofas, fresh-cut flowers, pewter mugs, brassware, fringed lamps, paintings and prints. All four bedrooms, with views of the Blackstairs mountains, have period furniture, home-made biscuits, a shower room with power shower. A spacious dual-aspect bedroom, painted a dreamy blue, has a carved four-poster, an original fireplace, and a bookcase full of well-thumbed novels. Dinner is served communally by candlelight in a crimson dining room, with cabinets of crystal and china, watched by Frans Hals's eternally smiling cavalier. Readers abandoned plans to eat out, preferring to stay in every night for a dinner cooked by Bobbie, a member of chefs' group Euro-Toques Ireland, using local, home-grown organic ingredients. The full Irish breakfast provides ballast for a day's cycling, walking, fishing, a round of golf, or croquet on the lawn.

**25% DISCOUNT VOUCHERS**

Kilgreaney
Bagenalstown R21 RD45

T: 00 353 59 977 5282
E: bobbie@lorum.com
W: lorum.com

BEDROOMS: 4.
OPEN: Feb–end Nov.
FACILITIES: drawing room, study, dining room, snug, 1-acre garden (croquet) in 18-acre grounds, wedding facilities, unsuitable for disabled.
BACKGROUND MUSIC: none.
LOCATION: 4 miles S of Bagenalstown on R705 to Borris.
CHILDREN: aged 16 and over welcomed.
DOGS: by arrangement, not on furniture or in dining room.
CREDIT CARDS: MC, Visa.
PRICES: per room B&B single €130, double €180–€200. Set dinner €50.

# BALLINGARRY Co. Limerick

MAP 6:D5

## THE MUSTARD SEED AT ECHO LODGE

This 'splendid' heritage hideaway in Ballingarry, where staff 'fall over each other to be helpful', is popular with Guide readers. The unusual name was born when a previous owner brought the established Mustard Seed restaurant to the Victorian house more than 20 years ago. Today, the hotel is painted in rich, warm colours with framed prints on the walls, and is home to bowls of fresh flowers, and a jumble of gumboots by the front door. In the kitchen is Angel Pirev, whose menus are lovingly created from the best seasonal ingredients. The food, served in twin Georgian dining rooms, is 'good and sufficiently unusual to make us want to try everything', though one regular reviewer could have done without the background music. Bedrooms, some in the main house with its hand-carved oak staircase, others in a separate wing, ooze country house charm, with antique furniture and designer furnishings. Many rooms have lush valley views; some have French doors on to the manicured gardens. Breakfast is a leisurely affair, and can be taken on the terrace, weather permitting. 'We could not have done better.' (Paul Hogarth, and others)

Ballingarry V94 EHN8

T: 00 353 69 68508
E: info@mustardseed.ie
W: mustardseed.ie

BEDROOMS: 16. 1, on ground floor, suitable for disabled.
OPEN: all year except 24–26 Dec, 3 weeks from mid-Jan.
FACILITIES: entrance hall, library, restaurant, sunroom, in-room TV (terrestrial), wedding facilities, 12-acre grounds, restaurant and public rooms wheelchair accessible, adapted toilet.
BACKGROUND MUSIC: in restaurant.
LOCATION: in village, 18 miles SW of Limerick.
CHILDREN: all ages welcomed.
DOGS: 'well-behaved' pets welcome, in designated bedrooms (not unattended), not in public rooms.
CREDIT CARDS: Amex, MC, Visa.
PRICES: per person B&B €95–€170, D,B&B €129–€199. Twilight Dinner (4 courses) €49, Classic Dinner (4 courses) €66.

# BALLYCASTLE Co. Mayo

MAP 6:B4

## STELLA MARIS

A sea view was a prerequisite when the British
Admiralty built this Victorian coastguard's
HQ, complete with gun turrets, overlooking
Bunatrahir Bay on the rugged coast of County
Mayo. Run as a hotel by Frances Kelly-
McSweeney for the past 20 years, it opens for
just five months, from May till September, when
guests can sit in the 100-foot sun lounge – literally,
the standout feature – and gaze over the Atlantic
to Downpatrick Head sea stack, and across rolling
countryside. Behind lies an enfilade of public
rooms, painted in shades of peach and sage, with
shiny polished floors, good antiques and open
fires. Bedrooms – most of them sea-facing – have
period furniture and old-fashioned charm (no tea-
making facilities). Frances determines the night's
short menu according to what is available. The
simple, modern Irish fare includes soups, meat
and day-boat fish – maybe John Dory with lemon
and capers, or fillet of prime Irish Hereford beef,
balsamic onion purée, Cashel Blue cream. Golfers
must be torn between courses at Enniscrone and
Carne in Belmullet, 40 minutes' drive away.

Ballycastle

**T:** 00 353 96 43322
**E:** info@stellamarisireland.com
**W:** stellamarisireland.com

**BEDROOMS:** 11. 1, on ground floor,
suitable for disabled.
**OPEN:** 1 May–30 Sept, restaurant
closed Mon evening.
**FACILITIES:** lounge, bar, restaurant,
conservatory, in-room TV (Freeview),
2-acre grounds, public rooms
wheelchair accessible, adapted toilet.
**BACKGROUND MUSIC:** none.
**LOCATION:** 1½ miles W of Ballycastle.
**CHILDREN:** not under 5.
**DOGS:** not allowed.
**CREDIT CARDS:** MC, Visa.
**PRICES:** per room B&B single €90–€110,
double €150–€195. À la carte €40.

# BALLYMOTE Co. Sligo

MAP 6:B5

## TEMPLE HOUSE

The anticipation builds as you follow a half-mile drive through sheep-grazed pastures to Roderick and Helena Perceval's 18th-century classical mansion, remodelled in 1864. In an age when Capability Brown was laying out parkland for English aristocrats, complete with picturesque ruin, the Percevals had the real thing: a crumbling Knights Templar castle, which stands beside a mile-long lake, beyond Italianate terraced gardens. Grand though it might be, this is a family home, filled with antiques and ancestral portraits. 'Twins' bedroom has matching half-tester beds. Dual-aspect 'Half Acre' is simply vast. 'Maple' has the original furniture from 1864, 'Porch' a 14-foot wardrobe. At night, children enjoy a kitchen supper, before adult guests gather in the morning room for drinks, then sit down in a house-party atmosphere to a four-course dinner that will include such choices as Andrala Farm pork belly, with scallops, and cod with a tempura oyster, trout caviar, cauliflower purée and nori beurre blanc. Breakfast brings Irish apple juice, compote of rhubarb from the walled garden, home-made soda bread and a full Irish.

**25% DISCOUNT VOUCHERS**

Temple House Demesne
Ballymote F56 NN50

**T:** 00 353 71 918 3329
**E:** stay@templehouse.ie
**W:** templehouse.ie

**BEDROOMS:** 7. Plus 3 non-B&B reserved for house parties.
**OPEN:** Apr–mid-Nov.
**FACILITIES:** morning room, dining room, vestibule, table tennis room, wedding facilities, 1½-acre garden on 1,000-acre estate, water sports on site.
**BACKGROUND MUSIC:** none.
**LOCATION:** 12 miles S of Sligo.
**CHILDREN:** all ages welcomed, kitchen supper for those 3–12.
**DOGS:** not allowed.
**CREDIT CARDS:** MC, Visa.
**PRICES:** per room B&B single €125–€145, double €179–€219. Set dinner €59.

# BALLYVAUGHAN Co. Clare

MAP 6:C4

## GREGANS CASTLE HOTEL

♢ Previous César winner

This 'epitome of Irish country house hospitality' overlooks Galway Bay, in the dramatic Burren landscape, said to have been the inspiration for Tolkien's Lord of the Rings. Owned and managed by Simon Haden and Frederieke McMurray, the 18th-century manor house exudes 'style and comfort', with thoughtful touches that include 'candles lit in public spaces as dusk falls'. Bedrooms are 'ample and comfortable', decorated in a neutral palette enlivened by splashes of green, blue and turquoise. Rooms overlook the garden, the bay or the mountains; some have a private garden. All have a selection of books, original artwork and Bamford toiletries, plus bathtub and shower. Chef Robbie McCauley's cooking is thought 'first rate'; one reviewer called dinner 'outstanding – culminating in the best grouse I have eaten'. Other dishes might include East Clare venison or wild Irish halibut. The extensive wine list includes 'very acceptable wine by the glass'. Breakfast brings a good choice of hot and cold options, with almost everything sourced from local suppliers. (Richard Parish)

Gragan East
Ballyvaughan H91 CF60

T: 00 353 65 707 7005
E: stay@gregans.ie
W: gregans.ie

BEDROOMS: 21. 7 on ground floor, 1 suitable for disabled.
OPEN: mid-Feb–early Dec, restaurant closed Mon, Thurs (bistro food available).
FACILITIES: drawing room, bar, dining room, 15-acre grounds (ornamental pool, croquet), wedding facilities, public areas wheelchair accessible, no adapted toilet.
BACKGROUND MUSIC: all day in bar, mealtimes in dining room.
LOCATION: 3½ miles SW of Ballyvaughan.
CHILDREN: all ages welcomed.
DOGS: allowed in some ground-floor bedrooms, not in public rooms.
CREDIT CARDS: Amex, MC, Visa.
PRICES: per room B&B €240–€515, D,B&B €389–€655. Set menu and à la carte €79, tasting menu €100. 1-night bookings sometimes refused Sat, bank holidays.

# CASTLEHILL Co. Mayo

MAP 6:B4

## ENNISCOE HOUSE

'More comfortable home than guest house', this classic Georgian house stands in deep countryside at the foot of Nephin mountain. It has been owned by the same family since the 1790s: Susan Kellett and her son, DJ, now preside over the shabby-chic jumble of inherited antiques, ancestral portraits and heritage ephemera. Bedrooms, reached via an elliptical grand staircase, are spacious, filled with vintage furniture and a selection of hardback books. The grandest rooms, at the front, have a canopy or four-poster bed, swagged curtains, and views of park and lake. Rooms in the older part of the house overlook the garden, and have slightly more modest furnishings, but are no less comfortable. Downstairs, there are two sitting rooms with open fire; the more formal one is decorated in the style of a grand country house, with original silk Adam design wallpaper. The former library is 'the perfect spot for a G&T', before a 'slap-up dinner' made from fresh, seasonal produce, organic vegetables and fruit from the garden, and honey from its beehives.

## 25% DISCOUNT VOUCHERS

Castlehill
Ballina F26 EA34

**T:** 00 353 96 31112
**E:** mail@enniscoe.com
**W:** enniscoe.com

**BEDROOMS:** 6. Plus self-catering units behind house.
**OPEN:** Apr–Oct, New Year.
**FACILITIES:** 2 sitting rooms, dining room, free Wi-Fi in public rooms, some bedrooms, wedding facilities, 3-acre garden in 30-acre grounds.
**BACKGROUND MUSIC:** occasionally in public areas.
**LOCATION:** 2 miles S of Crossmolina, 12 miles SW of Ballina.
**CHILDREN:** all ages welcomed.
**DOGS:** allowed in certain bedrooms, public rooms, not dining room.
**CREDIT CARDS:** MC, Visa.
**PRICES:** per person B&B €95–€135, D,B&B €135–€175. Set menu €50.

# CASTLELYONS Co. Cork

MAP 6:D5

## BALLYVOLANE HOUSE

A house-party atmosphere prevails at Jenny and Justin Green's Italianate mansion set amid romantic gardens and parkland. Built in 1728 and remodelled in the 1870s, this is, say the hosts, not quite hotel, guest house or B&B, but a lived-in home, filled with an accretion of possessions – antiques, portraits, saggy sofas, hunting trophies and snoozing dogs in front of blazing fires. Each bedroom has its own character, perhaps a Victorian bath encased in mahogany, with an enamel jug for a makeshift shower. Views through tall sash windows are of terraced gardens, ancient woodlands, trout lakes and the far Galtee mountains. A coffee machine and Bluetooth speaker nod to modernity, but there is no TV, just a transistor radio, home-made elderflower cordial, Ribena, and chocolate. New chef Olive Brennan cooks a communal dinner of home-reared or locally farmed, fished and foraged produce, fruit and vegetables from the walled garden, wild salmon from their beats on the River Blackwater, and rare breed pork. Children have a ball, with tractor trailer rides, trampolines, a tree house, high tea, animals to feed and eggs to collect.

### 25% DISCOUNT VOUCHERS

Castlelyons
Fermoy P61 FP70

T: 00 353 25 36349
E: info@ballyvolanehouse.ie
w: ballyvolanehouse.ie

BEDROOMS: 6. Plus 'glamping' tents May–Sept.
OPEN: all year, closed Mon, Tues, Wed in winter except for group bookings, Christmas/New Year (self-catering only).
FACILITIES: hall, drawing room, garden hall (honesty bar), dining room, wedding facilities, barn (table tennis), 80-acre grounds (15-acre garden, croquet, tennis, trout lakes).
BACKGROUND MUSIC: none.
LOCATION: 22 miles NE of Cork.
CHILDREN: all ages welcomed.
DOGS: allowed, but kept on lead during shooting season July–Jan.
CREDIT CARDS: MC, Visa.
PRICES: per room B&B single €200, double €200–€260, glamping €160–€185. Set dinner €65.

# CLIFDEN Co. Galway

MAP 6:C4

## THE QUAY HOUSE

♈ Previous César winner

There's personality aplenty at this family-run B&B 'stuffed with antiques and curios' in a former Georgian harbourmaster's house and three of its neighbours, overlooking Owenglin estuary. You will find clocks, working and broken, here a Buddha, there a Cupid, portraits in gilt frames, bovine horns, antlers, 'family photos everywhere'. The family in question are the Foyles: Julia and Paddy, who make warm, outgoing hosts, while son Toby runs sister property Blue Quay Rooms. Elegant bedrooms with gilt-framed mirrors and sometimes a four-poster or half-tester have a harbour view, perhaps a Juliet balcony or terrace. 'It's all very homely and casual without being sloppy'; housekeeping is rigorous. 'After we left, my wife and I discovered we had both gone round our large and very comfortable room trying to find dust, and couldn't,' writes a reader this year. Everyone has a tale of some little extra kindness; Julia is a fount of local knowledge while the breakfasts are first rate. 'Large top-class resort hotels can do a bigger spread, but there was ample choice and everything was outstandingly good. We intend to go back.' (Richard Hall)

Beach Road
Clifden H71 XF76

T: 00 353 95 21369
E: res@thequayhouse.com
W: thequayhouse.com

BEDROOMS: 16. 3 on ground floor, 1 suitable for disabled, 7 studios (6 with kitchenette) in annexe.
OPEN: end Mar–end Oct.
FACILITIES: 2 sitting rooms, breakfast conservatory, in-room TV (Freeview), small garden, fishing, sailing, golf, riding nearby, breakfast room and public areas wheelchair accessible.
BACKGROUND MUSIC: none.
LOCATION: on harbour, 8 mins' walk from centre.
CHILDREN: all ages welcomed.
DOGS: not allowed.
CREDIT CARDS: MC, Visa.
PRICES: per room B&B single €100–€120, double €170–€185. 1-night bookings may be refused bank holiday weekends.

**SEE ALSO SHORTLIST**

# CLIFDEN Co. Galway

MAP 6:C4

## SEA MIST HOUSE

Just off the scenic Connemara Loop, this B&B
has been in the same family for three generations,
giving it a rich, lived-in patina and making guests
feel it is 'like staying with friends'. Extensive
renovations have been carried out since Sheila
Griffin's grandfather purchased the property
more than a century ago, but many of its elegant
Georgian features remain. Two cosy sitting
rooms, one quieter, are furnished with old and
new pieces. Original artwork collected over the
generations cover the walls. Polished tables are
stacked with well-thumbed books. Upstairs (with
a peaceful reading nook halfway), bedrooms are
spacious with high ceilings, antique furniture
and charming window seats. Bathrooms have
shower only. Sheila is a 'relaxed host', 'warm and
hospitable'. Breakfast, taken in a large, light-
filled conservatory overlooking the flower-filled
garden, comes courtesy of mainly local producers:
a full Irish, perhaps, or smoked salmon from the
Connemara Smokehouse topped with scrambled
eggs from the owner's own hens and herbs from
the garden. 'The vegan breakfasts are wonderful.'

Seaview
Clifden H71 NV63

T: 00 353 95 21441
E: sheila@seamisthouse.com
W: seamisthouse.com

BEDROOMS: 4.
OPEN: mid-Mar–end Oct.
FACILITIES: 2 sitting rooms,
conservatory dining room, mini-
library, ¾-acre garden, unsuitable
for disabled.
BACKGROUND MUSIC: none.
LOCATION: just down from the main
square, on the edge of town.
CHILDREN: not under 4.
DOGS: not allowed.
CREDIT CARDS: MC, Visa.
PRICES: per room B&B €80–€110.

SEE ALSO SHORTLIST

# CLONES Co. Monaghan

MAP 6:B6

## HILTON PARK

The ancestral domain of the Madden family for almost three centuries, this grand Italianate mansion stands in pleasure grounds on an accredited wildlife estate. 'It is not a hotel,' they say, but a private home to which they have been entertaining guests for 30 years. Today, Johnny and Lucy Madden have handed over the hosts' role to ninth-generation Fred and Joanna, who extend a welcome with tea and fresh-baked cakes. 'The entrance hall, with its deer heads and large candles, makes an impressive impact' as you step inside to find beautiful antiques, portraits, books and fresh flowers. Your bedroom might have a four-poster or half-tester bed, and a lake view through eight-foot windows. 'My bathroom had a freestanding bath with striking blue feet, a hand-held shower attachment, and vintage radiator.' Dinner brings produce from the walled garden, lamb, venison and fish from the estate. After a breakfast of organic yogurt, home-made granola and butcher's sausages, you can play a round of golf on the 18-hole course, fish or swim in the lakes, spot pine martens, red squirrels, otters and rare honeybees.

Clones H23 C582

T: 00 353 47 56007
E: mail@hiltonpark.ie
W: hiltonpark.ie

BEDROOMS: 6.
OPEN: Mar–mid-Dec, groups only at Christmas/New Year.
FACILITIES: 3 drawing rooms, study, breakfast room, dining room, games room, billiard room, free Wi-Fi (in public areas), wedding facilities, 600-acre grounds (3 lakes for fishing and wild swimming, golf course, croquet).
BACKGROUND MUSIC: occasionally in dining room.
LOCATION: 4 miles S of Clones.
CHILDREN: all ages welcomed, children's high tea.
DOGS: not allowed in house.
CREDIT CARDS: MC, Visa.
PRICES: per room B&B €210–€240, extra bed €40–€50 (under-3s stay free). Set dinner €65.

# DRINAGH Co. Wexford

MAP 6:D6

## KILLIANE CASTLE
## COUNTRY HOUSE AND FARM

If murder holes in a 15th-century fortified tower hint at a want of hospitality, the welcome in the adjacent stone farmhouse could not be warmer. Jack and Kathleen Mernagh are the owners of both buildings, bought by Jack's father in 1920, and the house is very much a family home. Son Paul manages the hotel side, while his wife, Patrycja, charms guests front-of-house and runs the kitchen. The property sits at the heart of a dairy farm, in gardens with a tennis court, croquet lawn, golf pitch-and-putt course and driving range. A reader, greeted with tea and home-baked biscuits, found a fire burning merrily in the elegant lounge. Bedrooms, supplied with spring water from an artesian well, have bucolic views of grazing cattle. In summer, Patrycja will cook dinner, including soup, a salad of home-grown produce, and maybe a choice of slow-cooked beef or locally landed fish. At breakfast there is a 'fabulous' buffet, eggs from the farm, Duncannon smoked salmon, home-baked soda bread, and honey from the hives. 'A gem,' say fans. 'A beautiful place with great hosts' and handy for the Rosslare ferry.

**25% DISCOUNT VOUCHERS**

Drinagh Y35 E1NC

T: 00 353 53 915 8885
E: info@killianecastle.com
W: killianecastle.com

BEDROOMS: 10. 2 in former stable block.
OPEN: mid-Feb–mid-Dec.
FACILITIES: lounge (honesty bar), snug, dining room, in-room TV (Freeview), garden, grounds (nature trail, tennis, croquet, pitch and putt, 300-metre driving range), 230-acre dairy farm, unsuitable for disabled.
BACKGROUND MUSIC: in dining room and reception.
LOCATION: 1½ miles S of Drinagh.
CHILDREN: all ages welcomed.
DOGS: allowed in grounds, not indoors.
CREDIT CARDS: MC, Visa.
PRICES: per room B&B single €85–€95, double €125–€155, D,B&B double €190–€225. Set 3-course dinner €45.

# DUBLIN

MAP 6:C6

## THE WILDER TOWNHOUSE `NEW`

22 Adelaide Road
Dublin 2

T: 00 353 1 969 6598
E: stay@thewilder.ie
W: www.thewilder.ie

Frankie and Josephine Whelehan have transformed a Victorian red brick property a short walk from St Stephen's Green into a chic city-centre bolt-hole. This was once a refuge for retired governesses and 'bewildered women', who would be still more disconcerted if they could see the modern art adorning the walls, the air-conditioned bedrooms, the espresso machine, fridge and Parisian bath products that are standard issue. 'What a metamorphosis!' writes a Guide inspector. 'Any vestige of institutional gloom has been dispelled by a stunning combination of white paint, bold paintings, eccentric antiques, a touch of chintz and bright velvet and the most luxurious of beds and bathrooms.' From 'shoebox' rooms with a rainforest shower, to suites with a seating area and luxury bathroom, all have quirky touches and well-chosen Irish literature. This is an adult hotel, not one for families. Craft gins are served in the Gin and Tea Rooms, while 'excellent light meals as well as delicious breakfasts' can be taken in 'a charming room opening on to a flowery terrace'.

BEDROOMS: 42. Some suitable for disabled (contact hotel directly).
OPEN: all year.
FACILITIES: Gin and Tea Rooms, Garden Room, terrace, in-room TV (terrestrial), 8 parking spaces.
BACKGROUND MUSIC: in lobby and bar.
LOCATION: near St Stephen's Green.
CHILDREN: all ages welcomed, but not an ideal place for children.
DOGS: not allowed.
CREDIT CARDS: Amex, MC, Visa.
PRICES: per room €130–€500. Continental breakfast €14.50, continental and a cooked dish €19.50.

**SEE ALSO SHORTLIST**

# GLASLOUGH Co. Monaghan

MAP 6:B6

## CASTLE LESLIE

The claim that Clan Leslie 'can trace its ancestry back to Attila the Hun' might give you pause, but fear not: the warmest Irish welcome awaits at this baronial-style Victorian pile on a 1,000-acre estate with three lakes and an equestrian centre. The architect was pre-Raphaelite painter Sir John Leslie – his elder brother, Charles, having planned an Irish Château de Chambord before choking to death on a fish bone – and is filled with heirlooms gathered on a Grand Tour. Heritage bedrooms all come with a colourful story. One has the first plumbed bath in Ireland, another a bathroom in an oversized doll's house, while not one but two were 'used by John Betjeman whenever he stayed'. The furnishings are as lavish as the accompanying tales. Rooms in The Lodge, by the riding stables, have a balcony or private courtyard. You can relax in vast drawing rooms, one with a grand piano and Della Robbia fireplace, enjoy country cooking and the craic in Conor's bar, or such refined dishes as quenelle crab, crispy Morteau sausage and oyster leaves in Snaffles restaurant. There is no TV, but, frankly, who needs it?

Glaslough H18 FY04

T: 00 353 47 88100
E: info@castleleslie.com
W: castleleslie.com

BEDROOMS: 70 bedrooms. 50 in Lodge (2 suitable for disabled), self-catering cottages.
OPEN: all year except 16–27 Dec.
FACILITIES: drawing rooms, bar, breakfast room, restaurant, conservatory, billiard room, library, private dining rooms, cinema, some in-room TV, wedding facilities, spa (outdoor hot tub), equestrian centre, 14-acre gardens on 1,000-acre estate, public areas wheelchair accessible.
BACKGROUND MUSIC: in public areas of Lodge.
LOCATION: 7 miles NE of Monaghan.
CHILDREN: all ages welcomed.
DOGS: allowed on estate, not in Castle, Lodge.
CREDIT CARDS: Amex, MC, Visa.
PRICES: per room B&B €155–€210. 6-course dinner €68. 1-night bookings sometimes refused.

# GOREY Co. Wexford

MAP 6:D6

## MARLFIELD HOUSE

Built for the Earls of Courtown, this Regency-style, 19th-century dower house has been run as an 'absolutely lovely' hotel by the Bowe family for more than 40 years. It stands in landscaped grounds, domain of George, the peacock, with a lake, woodland walks and 'well-tended topiary'. Interiors are filled with antiques, oil paintings and cut flowers. Country house-style bedrooms range from cosy to state rooms. All have rich fabrics, a marble bathroom, Floris toiletries, robes and slippers, fresh fruit. The French Room has period furniture and French doors to a circular terrace. As we go to press, lakeside pavilion rooms are due to open. The kitchen garden supplies the fine-dining Conservatory restaurant and Duck Terrace café (steaks, salads, flatbreads, with Middle Eastern and Asian influences). Our inspector chose the former and went through the card, from amuse-bouche to pudding, noting quality ingredients 'expertly cooked'. A typical dish: pan-fried hake, spinach, chicken skin crisp, oyster mushroom. Children will enjoy playing in a tree house, petting ponies and feeding the chickens that supply the eggs for an 'excellent' breakfast.

Courtown Road
Gorey Y25 DK23

T: 00 353 53 942 1124
E: margaret@marlfieldhouse.ie
W: marlfieldhouse.com

BEDROOMS: 19. 8 on ground floor.
OPEN: 1 Feb–9 Jan. Conservatory restaurant Fri and Sat dinner, Sun lunch (ring hotel for additional seasonal openings/closures).
FACILITIES: reception hall, drawing room, library/bar, 2 restaurants, in-room TV (Freeview, Virgin), wedding facilities, 36-acre grounds (tennis, croquet).
BACKGROUND MUSIC: in library/bar, restaurant.
LOCATION: 1 mile E of Gorey.
CHILDREN: all ages welcomed.
DOGS: in bedroom and grounds by arrangement, subject to conditions, not in public rooms.
CREDIT CARDS: Amex, MC, Visa.
PRICES: per room B&B €224–€700, D,B&B €278–€728. Set dinner (5-courses ) €64, à la carte €45.

# HOLYWOOD Co. Down

MAP 6:B6

## RAYANNE HOUSE

Nothing is done by halves at Conor and Bernie
McClelland's B&B, occupying a Victorian
merchant's house with views across Belfast lough.
Our inspectors praised a 'wholehearted, eccentric
and endearing combination of old-fashioned
lavishness and contemporary standards'. Not
only the architectural features, but also murals
and some of the ornaments are original to the
house, on which the McClellands have put their
own stamp. The Rory McIlroy bedroom has a
golf-themed bathroom with grass-effect tiles and
a shower with grab handle fashioned from one
of McIlroy's clubs. The Honeymoon Suite has
a balcony, from which the occupants must have
watched the Titanic sail out of the Harland and
Wolff shipyard. On certain dates, chef Conor
honours the occasion by recreating the last nine-
course dinner served to first-class passengers. On
other selected nights there is a tasting menu. An
award-winning breakfast includes such offerings
as prune soufflé on a purée of green figs; organic
eggs with Parmesan breadsticks wrapped in
Parma ham; and French toast with Clonakilty
black and white pudding and apple compote.

60 Demesne Road
Holywood BT18 9EX

T: 028 9042 5859
E: info@rayannehouse.com
W: rayannehouse.com

BEDROOMS: 10. 1, on ground floor,
suitable for disabled.
OPEN: all year, 'limited service'
Christmas/New Year.
FACILITIES: 2 lounges, dining room,
conference facilities, wedding
facilities, 1-acre grounds, public rooms
wheelchair accessible, adapted toilet.
BACKGROUND MUSIC: light jazz in
dining room.
LOCATION: ½ mile from Holywood
town centre, 6 miles NE of Belfast.
CHILDREN: all ages welcomed.
DOGS: may be allowed by prior
arrangement.
CREDIT CARDS: Amex, MC, Visa.
PRICES: per room B&B single
£100–£120, double £135–£160, family
£160–£165. Dinner, 7-course tasting
menu on certain nights, £65 (10%
service added).

# LAHINCH Co. Clare

MAP 6:C4

## MOY HOUSE

What appears on approach to be a white-painted bungalow with a belvedere turns out to be a Georgian country house hotel on a hillside overlooking Lahinch Bay. But then, Moy House is full of surprises, not least an original well in the bathroom of a suite with its own conservatory. The property had long stood empty when Antoin O'Looney transformed it into a hotel 20-odd years ago. Public rooms are characterful and inviting, with antiques, fresh flowers and an honesty bar. Bedrooms, most with a sea view, mix contemporary and traditional furnishings. The master bedroom has a seating area and original fireplace. All rooms have L'Occitane toiletries. Chef Matthew Strefford works with produce from Moy House's own farm and garden, and from local fishermen, to devise supper and tasting menus. Perhaps a simple shepherd's pie from the one, pan-fried hake with garden vegetables and herb risotto from the other. Breakfast brings 'fantastic sausages', farm eggs and smoked salmon. 'Our visit here was a delight.' One of the first guests to stay here in 2001, a trusted reader, still has fond memories of the place. (PH, SM)

Lahinch

T: 00 353 65 708 2800
E: info@moyhouse.com
W: moyhouse.com

BEDROOMS: 9. 4 on ground floor.
OPEN: Apr–end Oct, restaurant closed Sun, Mon.
FACILITIES: drawing room, library, restaurant, in-room TV (Freeview), wedding facilities, 15-acre grounds, unsuitable for disabled.
BACKGROUND MUSIC: in restaurant at mealtimes.
LOCATION: 2 miles outside Lahinch.
CHILDREN: all ages welcomed.
DOGS: not allowed.
CREDIT CARDS: Amex, MC, Visa.
PRICES: per room B&B €165–€395. À la carte €40, tasting menu (Tues–Sat) €65.

# LETTERFRACK Co. Galway

MAP 6:C4

## ROSLEAGUE MANOR

'We returned after five years, and everything
lived up to our recollection,' says one trusted
reviewer of this salmon-pink Georgian manor
house overlooking Ballinakill Bay in wild
Connemara. Glorious sea and garden views are
complemented by a lived-in country house style,
with a grandfather clock, gilt-framed mirrors and
hunting prints. Drawing rooms are warmed by
open fires and there is a light and airy Victorian-
style conservatory. Our reader was upgraded
to a 'genuinely enormous' room – this was
'unnecessary but nice'. All bedrooms are spacious,
and contain antique furniture and paintings, with
'comfortable reading chairs' as well as books and
fresh flowers. 'Great' food, such as Cleggan Bay
crab claws and Irish Hereford beef fillet, is served
in the period-style dining room where children
are permitted but 'do not disturb'. Breakfast
consists of an 'enormous buffet' – be sure to leave
room for the 'delicious stewed rhubarb' – perhaps
before embarking on one of the many local or
more distant walks. 'We recommended it to a
friend – who loved it.' (Ben Twist)

Letterfrack

T: 00 353 95 41101
E: info@rosleague.com
W: rosleague.com

BEDROOMS: 21. 2 on ground floor.
OPEN: mid-Mar–mid-Nov.
FACILITIES: 2 drawing rooms,
conservatory/bar, dining room,
in-room TV (Freeview), wedding
facilities, 25-acre grounds (tennis).
BACKGROUND MUSIC: none.
LOCATION: 7 miles NE of Clifden.
CHILDREN: all ages welcomed.
DOGS: 'well-behaved' dogs allowed.
CREDIT CARDS: MC, Visa.
PRICES: per room B&B single €106–
€147, double €193–€253. Set dinner
€36–€55, à la carte €42. Min. 2-night
stay at bank holiday weekends.

# LIMERICK Co. Limerick

MAP 6:D5

## NO. 1 PERY SQUARE

It's hard to believe that this boutique hotel, in a Grade 1 listed town house, at the corner of one of Ireland's most perfectly preserved Georgian terraces, was once a youth hostel. Now owned by Patricia Roberts, it is home to period pieces, chandeliers and elegant decor. You can take afternoon tea in the drawing room overlooking the Victorian People's Park with its bandstand and gazebos. Upstairs, instead of dormitories, there are four bedrooms with tall sash windows, antiques, a roll-top bath and monsoon shower. At the top of the house there is a two-bedroom suite with a lounge and kitchenette. Smaller, contemporary bedrooms, with a monsoon shower, plus a basement spa, are around the corner in a purpose-built block, linked via former rates offices. First-floor Sash restaurant will provide guests with 'a fine dinner'; classic dishes with a twist showcase local and kitchen-garden ingredients. For example, stout-glazed beef, parsnip mash, sticky dates and braised leeks. Brunch and an all-day menu of soups, small plates, platters, salads, fish and burgers are served in the Long Room bar/lounge.

Georgian Quarter
1 Pery Square
Limerick

T: 00 353 61 402402
E: info@oneperysquare.com
W: oneperysquare.com

BEDROOMS: 20. 3 suitable for disabled.
OPEN: all year except 24–26 Dec.
FACILITIES: lift, lounge/bar, drawing room, restaurant, private dining room, in-room TV (Freeview), wedding facilities, small kitchen garden, terrace, basement spa, deli/wine shop, parking, public rooms wheelchair accessible.
BACKGROUND MUSIC: in restaurant and lounge.
LOCATION: central.
CHILDREN: all ages welcomed.
DOGS: only assistance dogs allowed.
CREDIT CARDS: Amex, MC, Visa.
PRICES: per room B&B single from €135, double €165–€318. Set dinner (Sash restaurant) €49, à la carte (Long Room) €30.

# LISDOONVARNA Co. Clare                    MAP 6:C4

## SHEEDY'S

The small town 'wraps itself around' Martina
and John Sheedy's peachy yellow hotel, on a
hilltop with 'lovely' views of Clare 'to catch the
heart off guard and blow it open', as the poet
Seamus Heaney puts it. The Sheedy family
started farming here in the 1700s, and John's
grandmother, Alice, first opened the door to
paying guests in the 1930s. 'Martina gave us such
a warm greeting,' related a Guide inspector. 'We
were shown about, then up to our room, with
the promise of a pot of tea in a sunny spot in the
lobby once we'd settled in.' Bedrooms have 'a
mix of antiques and sympathetic contemporary
pieces', Gilchrist & Soames toiletries, books
and magazines. Junior suites come with a large
seating area, a bath and walk-in power shower.
Downstairs, 'a crackling fire' burned in a lounge
with 'squashy sofas and a lovely display of
flowers'. John Sheedy sources produce from local
farmers, fishers, crofters and foragers for his
dinner menus. At breakfast artisanal sausages,
home-made preserves, 'moreish sourdough'
and organic porridge provide ballast for an
exploration of the Cliffs of Moher or the stark
moonscape of the Burren.

Lisdoonvarna V95 NH22

T: 00 353 65 707 4026
E: info@sheedys.com
W: sheedys.com

BEDROOMS: 11. 5 on ground floor.
OPEN: Easter–end Sept, restaurant
closed Tues/Wed dinner in Apr, Sun
only from May onwards.
FACILITIES: sitting room/library, sun
lounge, bar, restaurant, in-room TV
(Freeview), ½-acre garden, restaurant
wheelchair accessible, adapted toilet.
BACKGROUND MUSIC: 'easy listening' at
breakfast, light jazz at dinner.
LOCATION: 20 miles SW of Galway.
CHILDREN: over-12s welcomed.
DOGS: not allowed.
CREDIT CARDS: MC, Visa.
PRICES: per room B&B €160–€200,
D,B&B €220–€280. À la carte €60.
1-night bookings refused weekends
in Sept.

# LONGFORD Co. Longford

MAP 6:C5

## VIEWMOUNT HOUSE

♛ Previous César winner

This elegant 17th-century country house set among orchards and beautifully designed gardens 'ticks every box' for readers. After receiving 'the warmest welcome' from Beryl Kearney and husband James, our regular reviewer was shown to his ground-floor suite where he immediately felt 'very much at home'. Bedrooms are traditional, with an emphasis on comfort, and boast large windows, period features, antique furniture, fresh flowers and original fireplaces. Many overlook the 'lovely' grounds, which include an enchanting Japanese garden. Bathrooms are 'immaculate'. The spacious candlelit VM restaurant is housed in the old stables; its continuing popularity with locals is proof of its good food. Here 'very well-trained' staff serve chef Marcio Laan's classic French dishes with a modern twist, such as 'a tiny sphere of pork with a crisp coating and touch of chilli'. Breakfast, cooked and served by Beryl, includes a local twist on eggs Benedict or muffins with Irish potato pancakes, accompanied by the 'most delicious smoked bacon I can remember'. 'My stay was memorable and all for the right reasons.' (TL)

---

**25% DISCOUNT VOUCHERS**

Dublin Road
Longford N39 N2X6

T: 00 353 43 334 1919
E: info@viewmounthouse.com
W: viewmounthouse.com

BEDROOMS: 12. 7 in modern extension, some on ground floor, 1 suitable for disabled.
OPEN: all year except 25 Oct–4 Nov, restaurant open Wed–Sat for dinner, Sun lunch, closed 24–27 Dec.
FACILITIES: reception room, library, sitting room, breakfast room, restaurant, in-room TV (Freeview), wedding facilities, 4-acre grounds, breakfast room and restaurant wheelchair accessible, adapted toilet.
BACKGROUND MUSIC: in restaurant.
LOCATION: 1 mile E of town centre.
CHILDREN: all ages welcomed.
DOGS: not allowed.
CREDIT CARDS: Amex, MC, Visa.
PRICES: per room B&B €170–€190. D,B&B €280–€310. Set dinner €60, early bird dinner €35.

# MAGHERALIN Co. Armagh

## NEWFORGE HOUSE

♔ Previous César winner

In mature gardens and 50 acres of pasture on the edge of the village, Louise and John Mathers's creeper-clad Georgian mansion is an elegant home from home. Such is the hospitality that John was awarded a British Empire Medal for it in 2018. 'We did not meet Louise,' writes a reader after a night's stay, 'but John and the staff could not have made us more welcome.' The family has been here for six generations, and the antiques reflect the history, as do the original wood and tiled floors. Bedrooms have cut flowers, fresh milk, leaf tea, a cafetière and home-made treats; one has a four-poster and an original fireplace in the bathroom, while another has a half-tester. After drinks in the drawing room, guests sit down at 8 pm to a dinner cooked by John with local and home-grown produce. An either/or choice might bring rib-eye of beef dry-aged in a Himalayan salt chamber, or fish landed at Kileel. 'Lovely place to stay and the food was outstanding,' writes another reviewer. At breakfast there is an Ulster fry with award-winning sausages, and eggs from the hens that live the life of Reilly in the orchard. (Paul Hogarth, Sally Mehalko)

58 Newforge Road
Magheralin BT67 0QL

T: 028 9261 1255
E: enquiries@newforgehouse.com
W: newforgehouse.com

BEDROOMS: 6.
OPEN: Feb–mid-Dec, restaurant closed Sun/Mon evenings.
FACILITIES: drawing room, dining room, in-room TV (Freeview), wedding facilities, 2-acre gardens (vegetable garden, wild-flower meadow, orchard, woodland) in 50 acres of pastureland, unsuitable for disabled.
BACKGROUND MUSIC: in dining room.
LOCATION: edge of village, 20 miles SW of Belfast.
CHILDREN: 10 and over welcomed.
DOGS: not allowed.
CREDIT CARDS: MC, Visa.
PRICES: per room B&B single £95–£145, double £140–£215, D,B&B double £238–£313. À la carte £49.

# MOUNTRATH Co. Laois

MAP 6:C5

## ⚜ROUNDWOOD HOUSE

César award: Irish hotel of the year

There's plenty of personality alongside the period furniture at this 18th-century Irish country house in parkland at the foot of the Slieve Bloom mountains: a library in the double-height stables is dedicated to the history of the evolution of civilisation, and dinner is served with a serenade from the 'singing chef'. Main-house bedrooms have glorious views through tall sash windows; rooms in the 17th-century Yellow House are more cottage style. A twin has mismatched wooden beds, toile de Jouy wallpaper and a crammed bookcase. Owners Hannah and Paddy Flynn have a relaxed style: when readers arrived late, 'the staff came to our room to tell us dinner would not be until 8.15 pm, giving us time to enjoy our very good G&T while showering and changing'. The meal is worth waiting for: Paddy, who has been joined in the kitchen by Ted Pegg, who manages the kitchen garden, has considerable 'culinary expertise'. Dishes might include curried soup, lamb loin with blueberry sauce, and a raspberry lemon pie. 'The evening was so enjoyable, with the best dinner we've had in a long time.' There's a bonus, too: breakfast is served until 11 am.

**25% DISCOUNT VOUCHERS**

Mountrath R32 TK79

T: 00 353 57 873 2120
E: info@roundwoodhouse.com
W: roundwoodhouse.com

BEDROOMS: 10. 4 in Yellow House.
OPEN: all year except 24–26 Dec.
FACILITIES: drawing room, dining room, study, library, wedding facilities, 18-acre grounds, parking, unsuitable for disabled.
BACKGROUND MUSIC: none.
LOCATION: 3 miles N of village.
CHILDREN: all ages welcomed, travel cots, no charge for under-5s sharing with parents, €30 for over-5s, children's supper.
DOGS: not allowed.
CREDIT CARDS: Amex, MC, Visa.
PRICES: per room B&B single €110, double €170, triple €200. Set supper of soup, cheese and dessert €25, 4 courses €60.

# MULTYFARNHAM Co. Westmeath

MAP 6:C5

## MORNINGTON HOUSE

Home to the O'Hara family since 1858, this Irish country manor house with its gardens and wooded grounds lies just outside the village, in a landscape of rolling hills and ancient forests. Anne and Warwick O'Hara first opened their doors to guests in 1986. 'The house loves people,' they say – and so, clearly, do they. Our inspector was much impressed by their hospitality and conversation. A stay begins with tea and cakes by the fire in an elegant dual-aspect drawing room with framed family photos on a grand piano, the wallpaper dating from 1896, when the building was substantially altered. The spacious bedrooms have period furniture, pretty fabrics, high ceilings, tall sash windows, fresh-cut flowers. A cooked breakfast, ordered the night before, is served at the dining-room table, with home-made bread and jams. They no longer offer dinner, but there is a well-liked gastropub in Multyfarnham, which is also home to a Franciscan abbey with life-size Stations of the Cross in the garden. Anglers can spend days fishing on loughs Derravaragh and Owel. There are golf courses nearby, and horse riding can be arranged.

**25% DISCOUNT VOUCHERS**

Multyfarnham N91 NX92

T: 00 353 44 937 2191
E: stay@mornington.ie
W: mornington.ie

BEDROOMS: 4.
OPEN: 9 Apr–31 Oct (and for groups in Nov).
FACILITIES: drawing room, dining room, free Wi-Fi in reception and some bedrooms, 50-acre grounds (¾-acre garden, croquet, bicycle hire), converted stables (meetings, weddings, events), unsuitable for disabled.
BACKGROUND MUSIC: none.
LOCATION: 9 miles NW of Mullingar.
CHILDREN: welcomed by arrangement only.
DOGS: not allowed.
CREDIT CARDS: Amex, MC, Visa.
PRICES: per room B&B single €105, double €160.

# NEWPORT Co. Mayo

MAP 6:B4

## NEWPORT HOUSE

**NEW**

'It was like going back into the past and being treated like guests in a private home' for a reader this year after a stay at Kieran Thompson's Georgian mansion overlooking the estuary and quay on Clew Bay. And it is for being 'old-fashioned but in a charming, relaxing way' that it gains full-entry status this year. 'Bookings are taken by phone', not online. Interiors are filled with antiques and paintings, shelves crammed with vintage books. A 'spacious room in the main house' had no tea-making facilities, but a request for a cup of tea on arrival brought 'an elegant tray laden with silverware and home-made cakes and shortbread, which we ate by the fire in one of the drawing rooms'. It all feels very warm and personable. At dinner 'we heard many returning guests being greeted by name and offered their favourite drink'. The food is 'uniformly delicious', featuring venison as well as locally caught fish and shellfish: perhaps Clew Bay oysters, Lough Furnace wild salmon. With fishing rights on the river and Lough Beltra, anglers are in their element. (Felicity Taylor)

**25% DISCOUNT VOUCHERS**

Newport F28 F243

T: 00 353 98 41222
E: info@newporthouse.ie
W: newporthouse.ie

BEDROOMS: 14. 4 in courtyard, 2 on ground floor.
OPEN: early Apr–early Oct.
FACILITIES: bar, drawing room, sitting room, dining room, Wi-Fi only in reception and some bedrooms, in-room TV, 15-acre grounds, walled garden, private fishery, bicycle hire.
BACKGROUND MUSIC: none.
LOCATION: in village, 7 miles N of Westport.
CHILDREN: all ages welcomed.
DOGS: allowed in courtyard bedrooms, not in public rooms.
CREDIT CARDS: Amex, MC, Visa.
PRICES: per person B&B €125–€140, D,B&B €193–€208. À la carte €62, 5-course set dinner €68.

# OUGHTERARD Co. Galway

## CURRAREVAGH HOUSE

A house-party atmosphere prevails at this
country house in 180 acres of grounds on Lough
Corrib, built in 1842 and run as a sporting lodge
by owner Henry Hodgson's great grandfather
from 1890. Little changes from year to year, and
why should it? Readers find it 'reassuring, cosy,
undemanding'. Old-fashioned bedrooms have
fresh flowers, water from the spring, and views
over wooded grounds to the lough or Benlevy.
There are no room keys, and just one TV, in the
study. Tea and home-baked cakes are served in
the drawing room. At 8 pm guests sit down at
separate tables for a four-course, locally sourced
dinner cooked by Henry's wife, Lucy, who
trained with Prue Leith. It might feature dishes
such as Skeaghanore duck, Jerusalem artichoke,
fermented plum, carrots, port and anise. Breakfast
includes freshly squeezed orange juice, soda
bread, croissants, local sausages, bacon and honey-
roast ham. No frappu-cappu-latte here; coffee
arrives in a 1950s Cona flask over a methylated
spirit flame. You can order a picnic, spend the day
fishing for brown trout, walk the grounds or take
your pick of golf courses.

Oughterard

T: 00 353 91 552312
E: mail@currarevagh.com
W: currarevagh.com

BEDROOMS: 10.
OPEN: 11 Mar–30 Nov.
FACILITIES: sitting room/library,
drawing room, dining room, 180-acre
grounds (lakeshore, fishing, ghillies
available, boating, tennis, croquet),
golf, riding nearby, unsuitable for
disabled.
BACKGROUND MUSIC: none.
LOCATION: 4 miles NW of Oughterard.
CHILDREN: aged 6 and upwards
welcomed.
DOGS: allowed in 1 bedroom, not in
public rooms.
CREDIT CARDS: MC, Visa.
PRICES: per person B&B single
occupancy €100–€120, double
€80–€95, D,B&B (double) €120–€145.
Set dinner €50.

# RATHMULLAN Co. Donegal

MAP 6:B5

## RATHMULLAN HOUSE

Built for a bishop in about 1760, Rathmullan House has been a beacon of Donegal hospitality since the early '60s. Happily situated on the banks of Lough Swilly (guests can step from the hotel's garden straight on to a sandy beach), the house has been in the same family for 60 years, and is today run by Mark and Mary Wheeler. The 34 spacious bedrooms are homely rather than fashion conscious, with a smattering of antiques, and 'crisp white sheets and artisan woollen blankets' on the beds. Some have a balcony or patio. Downstairs, comfortable sitting rooms with open fires overlook the manicured lawn rolling down to the lough. A Victorian walled garden provides much of the produce for the Cook & Gardener restaurant where chef Abdul Muhib Azad's modern Irish menus are locally inspired. Dinner might be pan-seared fillet of hake landed in Greencastle or steamed mussels from Mulroy Bay. Milleens, Cooleeney and Cashel Blue are all regulars on the Irish cheese plate. Stone-baked pizzas and Irish craft beers are available in the Tap Room in the old cellar of the house. The breakfast is 'delightful'.

Rathmullan F92 YA0F

T: 00 353 74 915 8188
E: reception@rathmullanhouse.com
W: rathmullanhouse.com

BEDROOMS: 34. Some on ground floor.
OPEN: open all year except 24–27 Dec, 6 Jan–6 Feb.
FACILITIES: bar, 2 lounges, library, TV room, playroom, cellar bar/pizza parlour, restaurant, in-room TV (terrestrial), wedding facilities, 15-metre heated indoor swimming pool, 7-acre grounds (tranquillity garden, walled kitchen garden, croquet), restaurant, lounges wheelchair accessible.
BACKGROUND MUSIC: none.
LOCATION: ½ mile N of village.
CHILDREN: all ages welcomed.
DOGS: allowed in bedrooms, not in public rooms.
CREDIT CARDS: Amex, MC, Visa.
PRICES: per person B&B €80–€145. D,B&B €120–€190. À la carte €50. 1-night bookings refused Sat and public holidays.

# RIVERSTOWN Co. Sligo                          MAP 6:B5

## COOPERSHILL

You get Irish country house living at its best at
Simon and Christina O'Hara's Georgian ancestral
home, where fallow deer roam the 500-acre
estate, with its woodland walks and a river for
fishing. New arrivals receive a warm welcome
with fresh-baked scones by a log fire in a sitting
room full of paintings and Irish Georgian
furniture. The traditional decor continues in
the bedrooms, one with a king-size canopy bed,
another with twin four-posters. Four corner
rooms have dual-aspect windows, some with a
river view. 'It's so tranquil, no TV or radio.' On
cold days your electric blanket will be switched
on by one of the friendly staff, 'invariably called
Mary', the owners joke. Christina cooks a
daily-changing menu of local, home-grown and
foraged produce including rack of lamb with
wild garlic and basil pesto or Atlantic black sole
in a white wine sauce. Breakfast sets you up to
explore WB Yeats country: fresh orange juice,
new-laid eggs, home-baked potato bread, honey
from a bee-loud glade. 'I will arise and go there,'
writes a reader – or, more prosaically, 'We would
return.' (Sally Mehalko)

Riverstown F52 EC52

T: 00 353 71 916 5108
E: reservations@coopershill.com
W: coopershill.com

BEDROOMS: 7.
OPEN: Apr–Oct, off-season house
parties by arrangement.
FACILITIES: front hall, drawing room,
dining room, snooker room, wedding
facilities, 500-acre estate (garden,
tennis, croquet, woods, farmland,
river with trout fishing), unsuitable
for disabled.
BACKGROUND MUSIC: none.
LOCATION: 11 miles SE of Sligo.
CHILDREN: all ages welcomed.
DOGS: not allowed.
CREDIT CARDS: MC, Visa.
PRICES: per room B&B single
occupancy €151–€175, double
€234–€260, D,B&B double €352–€378.
Set dinner €59.

# SHANAGARRY Co. Cork

MAP 6:D5

## BALLYMALOE HOUSE

Fifty-seven years after Myrtle Allen opened a restaurant in her home on her husband's farm, her values are still articles of faith at this legendary country house hotel. Myrtle died in 2018, but 'her spirit lingers', say readers. Peter Loughnane, the new general manager, now helps Myrtle's daughter Fern with running the hotel, while Fern's sister-in-law Darina runs the cookery school and organic farm outside Shanagarry. From breads baked early each morning, to fruit and vegetables from the walled garden, as much as possible is home-produced. Dervilla O'Flynn composes her menus according to what arrives fresh in the kitchen on the day, finalising dinner choices after fish is delivered in the afternoon (typical dishes: monkfish with garden herbs; pork braised in Normandy cider). Breakfast brings kippers, the famous freshly baked bread and Ballymaloe eggs. Bedrooms, in the main house and in garden and courtyard annexes, have country house decor, a mix of period and contemporary furniture, and fresh-cut flowers. Three new bedrooms have been added this year as Myrtle's legacy continues to grow. (Mary Milne-Day)

### 25% DISCOUNT VOUCHERS

Shanagarry P25 Y070

T: 00 353 21 465 2531
E: res@ballymaloe.ie
W: ballymaloe.ie

BEDROOMS: 32. 12 in adjacent building, 4 on ground floor with wheelchair access.
OPEN: all year, except 24–26 Dec, Mon–Thurs in Jan.
FACILITIES: drawing room, bar, 2 TV rooms, conservatory, restaurant, private dining, wedding facilities, 6-acre gardens, tennis, 5-hole golf course, outdoor swimming pool (10 by 4 metres), cookery school, café/kitchen shop, restaurant wheelchair accessible.
BACKGROUND MUSIC: none.
LOCATION: 20 miles E of Cork.
CHILDREN: all ages welcomed.
DOGS: not allowed.
CREDIT CARDS: Amex, MC, Visa.
PRICES: per room B&B single from €150, double €280–€440. Set dinner, 5 courses (Mon–Sat) €80, Sun night buffet €70.

# SHORTLIST

Old Swan, Minster Lovell

LONDON

# BATTY LANGLEY'S

A one-off, this eccentric hotel in gentrified
Spitalfields commemorates the novelists,
politicians and silk merchants of the area, along
with its petty thieves, tarts and vagabonds. In two
artfully restored 18th-century buildings, Peter
McKay and Douglas Blain fuse Georgian 'Grand
Taste' and sybaritic comforts. A wood-panelled
sitting room, with plush sofas, cosy nooks and
an honesty bar, offers a tranquil escape from the
City nearby. In the bedrooms, crushed velvet
bedspreads and goose down-filled pillows sit
comfortably with vintage fittings; bathrooms
might have a throne loo or a 'bathing machine'.
Breakfast, delivered to the room, has yogurt,
fruit, granola, pastries and bagels. (Underground:
Liverpool Street)

MAP 2:D4
12 Folgate Street
London E1 6BX
T: 020 7377 4390
W: battylangleys.com

BEDROOMS: 29. 1 suitable for disabled.
OPEN: all year.
FACILITIES: lift, library, parlour,
lounge, meeting rooms, in-room TV
(Freeview), small courtyard.
BACKGROUND MUSIC: none.
LOCATION: 5 mins' walk from
Liverpool Street Underground and
rail stations.
CHILDREN: all ages welcomed.
DOGS: assistance dogs only.
CREDIT CARDS: Amex, MC, Visa.
PRICES: per room £159–£1,200.
Breakfast £11.

LONDON

# BERMONDSEY SQUARE HOTEL

In buzzy Bermondsey, this zestful hotel offers
good-value accommodation in a bright, modern
setting. The snappily designed bedrooms vary
in size: some rooms interconnect or have a sofa
bed to accommodate a family; spacious top-floor
suites have a private terrace and expansive views
stretching to the Shard. On the ground floor,
the open-space lounge and restaurant are open
to freelancers, students and office workers, who
come for the shared workspace and all-day British
menu; a patio on the square opens for dining in
fine weather. The hotel is alcohol free: glasses are
provided for guests who bring their own, to have
in their room. Breakfast has smoothies, avocado
on toast, and more. (Underground: London
Bridge, Bermondsey)

MAP 2:D4
Bermondsey Square
London SE1 3UN
T: 020 7378 2450
W: bermondseysquarehotel.co.uk

BEDROOMS: 90. 4 suitable for disabled.
OPEN: all year.
FACILITIES: lift, open-plan lounge/
restaurant/co-working space, meeting
rooms, in-room TV (Freeview),
terrace.
BACKGROUND MUSIC: in public spaces.
LOCATION: 15 mins' walk from London
Bridge Underground and rail stations.
CHILDREN: all ages welcomed.
DOGS: allowed in some bedrooms,
public areas.
CREDIT CARDS: Amex, MC, Visa.
PRICES: per room B&B from £120.
À la carte £30.

**NEW**

LONDON
# THE BUXTON

Victorian social reformer and brewer Sir Thomas Fowell Buxton lends his name to this modish gastropub in Spitalfields. He would no doubt approve of its vintage styling, sustainable values and selection of local beer. Each of the compact, neatly designed bedrooms has a curated selection of books; handwoven artworks, rugs and blankets made by local weavers offset otherwise-plain decoration. Guests can ascend to the roof terrace for 360-degree views across the East End and the City, or head down to the trendy bar and bistro, for friendly service and seasonally changing British-European menus. Whitechapel Gallery and Brick Lane are around the corner. (Underground: Aldgate East, Whitechapel)

MAP 2:D4
42 Osborn Street
London  E1 6TD
T: 020 7392 2219
W: thebuxton.co.uk

BEDROOMS: 15.
OPEN: all year except 22 Dec–1 Jan.
FACILITIES: pub/bistro, in-room TV, rooftop garden terrace, eating and drinking areas wheelchair accessible.
BACKGROUND MUSIC: all day in public areas.
LOCATION: 2 mins' walk from Aldgate East Underground station.
CHILDREN: all ages welcomed.
DOGS: allowed in pub only.
CREDIT CARDS: Amex, MC, Visa.
PRICES: per room B&B (continental) £100–£125. À la carte £25.

LONDON
# CHARLOTTE STREET HOTEL

Wide, striped awnings jauntily shelter the café tables lined up outside this Firmdale hotel, close to Soho and the West End theatres. Step inside to find an unabashed embrace of colour and contemporary British art (the hotel's design was inspired by the Bloomsbury set). A lounge and library are inviting, with log-burning fires and plenty of space to sit; a well-stocked honesty bar tempts. Thoughtfully equipped bedrooms are bold and bright, and vary in size; some can be connected to accommodate a group. At lunch and dinner in the lively restaurant, modern British dishes might include seared scallops, crab fritters, cauliflower purée, cucumber jelly, plus pastas, salads and grills. (Underground: Goodge Street)

MAP 2:D4
15–17 Charlotte Street
London  W1T 1RJ
T: 020 7806 2000
W: charlottestreethotel.com

BEDROOMS: 52. 1 suitable for disabled.
OPEN: all year.
FACILITIES: bar/restaurant, drawing room, library, in-room TV (Freeview), civil wedding licence, cinema, gym.
BACKGROUND MUSIC: in restaurant and bar.
LOCATION: 5 mins' walk to Goodge Street Underground station.
CHILDREN: all ages welcomed.
DOGS: allowed 'on a case-by-case basis'.
CREDIT CARDS: Amex, MC, Visa.
PRICES: per room from £350. Breakfast £18, set menu (2 courses) £22.50, (3 courses) £25, à la carte £45.

LONDON

# ECCLESTON SQUARE HOTEL

High-spec technology fuses with 'domesticated heaven' at this smart Pimlico hotel, on a tranquil garden square within easy reach of a major travel hub. 'Comfortable' bedrooms in the Georgian building, some with a patio or a balcony, have a monochrome palette and high-tech, yet intuitive, features: a 'digital concierge' on a tablet, smart-glass shower walls, an adjustable bed with massage settings. Rooms are equipped with a capsule coffee machine; pots of tea are freshly brewed and delivered on request. Guests also receive a smartphone loaded with local information and free mobile Internet. Throughout, 'super-friendly' staff maintain an 'impeccable' standard. Neighbourhood eateries abound. (Underground: Victoria)

MAP 2:D4
37 Eccleston Square
London  SW1V 1PB
T: 020 3503 0692
W: ecclestonsquarehotel.com

BEDROOMS: 39. Plus 2-bed Town House with patio garden.
OPEN: all year.
FACILITIES: drawing room, cocktail lounge, in-room TV (Sky), parking discounts.
BACKGROUND MUSIC: in public areas.
LOCATION: 5 mins' walk from Victoria Underground and rail stations.
CHILDREN: not under 13.
DOGS: not allowed.
CREDIT CARDS: Amex, MC, Visa.
PRICES: per room B&B from £180.

LONDON

# THE FIELDING

'Remarkably quiet' considering its prime position in bustling Covent Garden, this small hotel with a pretty, plant-decked Georgian exterior is a 'good-value' option in an ideal central location. Henry Fielding, the novelist and one-time local magistrate, lends his name. Audience and cast members of the Royal Opera House, across the street, like it for its well-turned-out but modest bedrooms, and reliable staff. Each 'excellently lit' room has tea and coffee, slippers and an eye mask, plus a well-equipped shower room (two rooms have a bath). No breakfast is provided, but there's plenty of choice in the surrounding streets – just ask the 'helpful staff' at reception. (Underground: Covent Garden)

MAP 2:D4
4 Broad Court
London  WC2B 5QZ
T:  020 7836 8305
W: thefieldinghotel.co.uk

BEDROOMS: 25. Some, on ground floor, wheelchair accessible, plus 1- and 4-bed apartments in adjoining building.
OPEN: all year.
FACILITIES: in-room TV (Freeview), free access to nearby spa and fitness centre.
BACKGROUND MUSIC: none.
LOCATION: 3 mins' walk to Covent Garden Underground station.
CHILDREN: all ages welcomed.
DOGS: not allowed.
CREDIT CARDS: Amex, MC, Visa.
PRICES: per room single £125, double £205–£229.

## LONDON
# 54 QUEEN'S GATE

Close to the museums, the Royal Albert Hall and Hyde Park, this intimate hotel (part of the Bespoke Hotels group) occupies one in a row of white-painted Edwardian town houses. Within the modishly refurbished Grade II listed building, serene, modern bedrooms are each dedicated to a renowned Londoner (Pankhurst, Eliot, Elgar, etc), and made comfortable with air conditioning, dressing gowns and slippers, a coffee machine and a minibar of soft drinks. (Front-facing rooms may have some traffic noise.) Breakfast is in a bright, airy room; a full English is freshly cooked. After a day out, the stylish lounge, bar and terrace are lulling retreats. Plentiful restaurant choice nearby. (Underground: South Kensington)

MAP 2:D4
54 Queen's Gate
London SW7 5JW
T: 020 7761 4000
W: 54queensgate.com

BEDROOMS: 24.
OPEN: all year.
FACILITIES: bar, lounge, terrace, in-room TV.
BACKGROUND MUSIC: none.
LOCATION: 10 mins' walk from South Kensington Underground station.
CHILDREN: not under 16.
DOGS: not allowed.
CREDIT CARDS: Amex, MC, Visa.
PRICES: per room from £209.

**NEW**

## LONDON
# GEORGIAN HOUSE HOTEL

In turns style-conscious and spellbinding, this modern Pimlico hotel holds surprises for wizards and Muggles alike. Bright and contemporary accommodation in varying sizes – from small single rooms to spacious family apartments – is spread out between the main, Grade II listed building and two town houses nearby. Harry Potter fans of all ages might prefer wizard-themed basement 'chambers' in the main house: accessed via a hidden door in a bookcase, they reveal (faux) stained-glass windows, velvet drapes, trunks and tapestries. A café/bar serves breakfast, drinks, snacks, sandwiches and an enchanting afternoon tea. Stairs are steep; cheerful staff will help with luggage. (Underground: Victoria, Pimlico)

MAP 2:D4
35–39 St George's Drive
London SW1V 4DG
T: 020 7834 1438
W: georgianhousehotel.co.uk

BEDROOMS: 63. Some on ground floor, 18 in nearby town houses.
OPEN: all year.
FACILITIES: reception, café/bar (closed Sun eve), breakfast room, private meeting/function room, 2-person 'cinema', in-room TV.
BACKGROUND MUSIC: in café/bar.
LOCATION: 10 mins' walk from Victoria Underground and rail stations.
CHILDREN: all ages welcomed.
DOGS: not allowed.
CREDIT CARDS: MC, Visa.
PRICES: per room B&B £95–£450.

## LONDON
# GOOD HOTEL

Tied up in Royal Victoria Dock, near ExCel London, this floating hotel offers contemporary accommodation 'with a cause' – the charitable business channels profits into local and international social initiatives. With communal tables and cushion-filled nooks, a spacious open-plan, industrial-style work/lounge area on the ground floor has freelancers and budding entrepreneurs in mind; after a day's toil, guests take in the sunset from the AstroTurfed rooftop. Most of the minimalist-chic bedrooms overlook the water of the Docklands; corner rooms have two bathrooms, including one for wheelchair users. Mediterranean-style light bites, served all day, follow the continental breakfast buffet. (DLR: Royal Victoria)

MAP 2:D4
Western Gateway
London E16 1FA
T: 020 3637 7401
W: goodhotellondon.com

BEDROOMS: 148. 4 suitable for disabled.
OPEN: all year.
FACILITIES: lift, bar, library/lounge, restaurant, meeting rooms, rooftop terrace, 24-hour concierge service, bicycle hire.
BACKGROUND MUSIC: in public spaces.
LOCATION: 5 mins' walk from Royal Victoria DLR station.
CHILDREN: all ages welcomed.
DOGS: only assistance dogs allowed in bedrooms, other dogs on lead in public areas.
CREDIT CARDS: Amex, MC, Visa.
PRICES: per room from £109. Breakfast £12.50, à la carte £29.

**NEW**

## LONDON
# THE GYLE

A short pace from the Eurostar terminal, this zany hotel is in a row of 19th-century town houses on a leafy public square. An undercurrent of Scottishness runs through the modern bedrooms: oak flooring and vintage mirrors are spruced up with Scottie dog cushions, tartan textiles and, in places, sporrans on the wall. Some rooms, in the basement, have a decadent sunken bath; others have a private balcony overlooking the inner courtyard. Complimentary hot drinks are available all day in the moss-walled lounge. Greet the day with a continental buffet of meats and cheeses, home-baked breads and pastries; at gloaming, choose among fine single malts, regional wines and craft beers. (Underground: King's Cross, St Pancras)

MAP 2:D4
16–18 Argyle Square
London WC1H 8AS
T: 020 3301 0333
W: thegyle.co.uk

BEDROOMS: 33. Some on ground floor.
OPEN: all year.
FACILITIES: bar/lounge, in-room smart TV, interior courtyard.
BACKGROUND MUSIC: in bar/lounge.
LOCATION: 5 mins' walk from King's Cross St Pancras Underground and rail stations.
CHILDREN: all ages welcomed.
DOGS: allowed.
CREDIT CARDS: Amex, MC, Visa.
PRICES: per room B&B £147–£309.

LONDON

# HAM YARD HOTEL

The leafy rooftop garden at this arty, design-conscious Soho hotel provides a tranquil escape in an animated neighbourhood. A Tony Cragg sculpture greets visitors in the courtyard; inside, vibrant fabrics, quirky furniture and the latest works from an international roster of artists serve up Kit Kemp's signature Firmdale Hotels look. There's top-to-bottom allure, from that beehive-lined residents-only roof terrace to a buzzy basement bar; in between, the well-stocked library and vast restaurant have afternoon teas and leisurely meals. Elegant bedrooms take in city or courtyard views through floor-to-ceiling windows. A cinema, a spa and a 1950s bowling alley are striking features. (Underground: Piccadilly Circus)

MAP 2:D4
1 Ham Yard
London W1D 7DT
T: 020 3642 2000
W: hamyardhotel.com

BEDROOMS: 91. 6 suitable for disabled.
OPEN: all year.
FACILITIES: lift, bar, restaurant, drawing room, library, meeting rooms, spa, gym, in-room TV (Freeview), civil wedding licence, rooftop terrace and garden, valet parking (charge).
BACKGROUND MUSIC: in bar.
LOCATION: 3 mins' walk from Piccadilly Circus Underground station.
CHILDREN: all ages welcomed.
DOGS: allowed 'on a case-by-case basis'.
CREDIT CARDS: Amex, MC, Visa.
PRICES: per room from £498. Breakfast from £15, à la carte £42, 3-course pre-theatre menu £24.

LONDON

# HAYMARKET HOTEL

A gleeful mix of vintage furnishings and modern artwork defines this 'elegant, sophisticated' Firmdale hotel in the heart of Theatreland. The library and buzzy conservatory are made for relaxation; in the basement, the glamorous swimming pool area is 'more bar than spa'. 'Lovely' bedrooms, each with their own style, have 'a very comfortable bed'; larger rooms and suites can accommodate extra beds or cots to suit a family. Guests in the Townhouse have their own front door and direct access to the main hotel. Eat updated bistro dishes in the restaurant, or on the terrace when the weather's fine; 'breakfast is top quality'. The South Bank is within 'easy walking distance'. (Underground: Piccadilly Circus)

MAP 2:D4
1 Suffolk Place
London SW1Y 4HX
T: 020 7470 4000
W: haymarkethotel.com

BEDROOMS: 50. Some suitable for disabled, plus 5-bed town house.
OPEN: all year.
FACILITIES: lift, lobby, library, conservatory, bar, restaurant, in-room TV, civil wedding licence, indoor swimming pool, gym.
BACKGROUND MUSIC: in bar and restaurant.
LOCATION: 5 mins' walk to Piccadilly Circus Underground station.
CHILDREN: all ages welcomed.
DOGS: allowed 'on a case-by-case basis'.
CREDIT CARDS: Amex, MC, Visa.
PRICES: per room B&B from £390. 3-course set menu £19.95, à la carte £40.

## LONDON
## HOTEL 41

Overlooking Buckingham Palace, this chic, discreet hotel on the fifth floor of a historic building gives guests the royal treatment. A pre-arrival questionnaire ensures residents' preferences are met (pillow firmness, a humidifier, yoga mat, etc) in the smart black-and-white bedrooms; other perks include home-made treats and season-specific bathrobes. Pampering is bolstered by a butler, a champagne trolley and an invitation to 'plunder the pantry' of freshly baked breads, pastries, cold meats, cheeses and desserts in the clubby lounge. Sister hotel The Rubens, within the same building, takes care of lunch and dinner. A pet concierge guarantees dogs are nobly treated, too. Part of the Red Carnation group. (Underground: Victoria)

MAP 2:D4
41 Buckingham Palace Road
London  SW1W 0PS
T: 020 7300 0041
W: 41hotel.com

BEDROOMS: 30. Some suitable for disabled, if requested.
OPEN: all year.
FACILITIES: lounge, in-room TV (Sky), room service, butler and chauffeur service, free access to nearby spa and gym.
BACKGROUND MUSIC: in public areas.
LOCATION: 5 mins' walk from Victoria Underground and rail stations.
CHILDREN: all ages welcomed.
DOGS: allowed in bedrooms, public rooms.
CREDIT CARDS: Amex, MC, Visa.
PRICES: per room B&B from £365.

## LONDON
## H10 LONDON WATERLOO

A complimentary glass of cava – a nod to the hotel group's Spanish origins – welcomes guests to this good-value hotel within walking distance of the National Theatre and the South Bank. Floor-to-ceiling windows in the understated modern bedrooms (some small) have 'good double glazing' to protect from outside noise; the best rooms have a panorama of the city. There are cocktails in the lobby bar, and newspapers and magazines in the lounge; the restaurant serves Mediterranean fare with a Spanish flourish. Kick-start the day with 'excellent' cooked dishes and a 'considerable' breakfast buffet; wind down in the evening with fine views of London's skyline from the eighth-floor Waterloo Sky bar. (Underground: Waterloo)

MAP 2:D4
284–302 Waterloo Road
London  SE1 8RQ
T: 020 7928 4062
W: hotelh10londonwaterloo.com

BEDROOMS: 177. Some suitable for disabled.
OPEN: all year.
FACILITIES: lifts, 2 bars, restaurant, in-room TV, public areas wheelchair accessible, adapted toilet.
BACKGROUND MUSIC: in public areas.
LOCATION: 10 mins' walk from Waterloo Underground station.
CHILDREN: all ages welcomed.
DOGS: assistance dogs allowed.
CREDIT CARDS: Amex, MC, Visa.
PRICES: per room B&B from £192.
À la carte £30.

LONDON

# KNIGHTSBRIDGE HOTEL

All is serene at this handsome 1860s town house hotel, just minutes from Hyde Park. Firmdale Hotels co-owner Kit Kemp combines statement pieces, antique prints and earthy tones in its cosy sitting areas. A striking oversized headboard and good bedside lighting feature in the bright, spacious bedrooms; front rooms overlook verdant Beaufort Gardens. A short all-day room-service menu stands in lieu of a restaurant, offering the likes of chestnut and wild mushroom linguini. For young guests: a special menu, a London activity book, and milk and cookies at bedtime. Guests exhausted by the museums and crowds in nearby South Kensington can recover with cocktails and in-room beauty treatments. (Underground: Knightsbridge)

MAP 2:D4
10 Beaufort Gardens
London  SW3 1PT
T: 020 7584 6300
W: knightsbridgehotel.com

BEDROOMS: 44.
OPEN: all year.
FACILITIES: drawing room, library, in-room TV (Freeview), room service.
BACKGROUND MUSIC: in public areas.
LOCATION: 10 mins' walk from Knightsbridge Underground station.
CHILDREN: all ages welcomed.
DOGS: small dogs allowed by arrangement.
CREDIT CARDS: Amex, MC, Visa.
PRICES: per room from £432. Breakfast £18.

LONDON

# THE LALIT

A former grammar school for boys near Tower Bridge has been overlaid with Indian opulence to make a classy hotel. It is one of a large, privately owned portfolio. The neoclassical building's panelled walls, large windows and stone fireplaces are embellished with chandeliers, carved screens and exotic flowers. More privilege than penance, the Headmaster's Room is a clubby space for champagne and cognac; Baluchi restaurant has contemporary Indian cuisine in the majestic assembly hall. Embroidered headboards adorn the wood-floored bedrooms and suites; marble bathrooms are supplied with bathrobes, slippers and Indo-French toiletries. In the spa: a choice of Eastern or Western treatments. (Underground: London Bridge)

MAP 2:D4
181 Tooley Street
London  SE1 2JR
T: 020 3765 0000
W: thelalit.com

BEDROOMS: 70. 4 suitable for disabled.
OPEN: all year.
FACILITIES: 2 bars, restaurant, bread bar, tea lounge, in-room TV, terrace, gym, spa.
BACKGROUND MUSIC: on low level in public spaces.
LOCATION: 10 mins' walk to London Bridge Underground and rail stations.
CHILDREN: all ages welcomed.
DOGS: only assistance dogs allowed.
CREDIT CARDS: Amex, MC, Visa.
PRICES: per room B&B from £259.

LONDON

# THE LASLETT

A style-conscious place occupying five white stucco Victorian houses, this modern hotel draws inspiration from its eclectic locality. Equal parts coffee house, drinking hole, library and art gallery, the bar and lounges showcase collaborations with designers and artists, all with the relaxed vibe of a neighbourhood hang-out. Chic, pleasingly spare bedrooms are made personal with Penguin classics, artworks and vintage curios; all have a neat bathroom supplied with bathrobes and high-end toiletries. In the Henderson bar, named after one of the founding fathers of the Notting Hill Carnival, knock elbows with locals who've dropped in for healthy brunches, all-day eats, nibbles and cocktails. (Underground: Notting Hill Gate)

MAP 2:D4
8 Pembridge Gardens
London W2 4DU
T: 020 7792 6688
W: living-rooms.co.uk

BEDROOMS: 51. 3 suitable for disabled, 2 split-level single rooms.
OPEN: all year.
FACILITIES: lift, bar/restaurant, in-room TV (Sky), front terrace, room service, complimentary passes to local gym, discounts at nearby restaurants.
BACKGROUND MUSIC: all day in public areas.
LOCATION: next to Notting Hill Gate Underground station.
CHILDREN: all ages welcomed.
DOGS: small dogs allowed by arrangement.
CREDIT CARDS: Amex, MC, Visa.
PRICES: per room B&B from £277. À la carte £42.

LONDON

# LIME TREE HOTEL

A peaceful retreat, Charlotte and Matt Goodsall's Belgravia hotel occupies twin Georgian town houses within walking distance of some of the city's most popular tourist spots. Major refurbishment in 2020 has resulted in a collection of smart bedrooms and a laid-back café that serves breakfast, light lunches, savoury treats and home-made cakes till teatime. Bright bedrooms vary in size, shape and layout, but all retain their original high ceiling, cornicing and sash windows; crisp linens and natural toiletries come as standard. Upper-floor rooms are up several flights of stairs; staff are on hand to help with luggage. A lounge has guidebooks and magazines; a neat, compact garden is at the back. (Underground: Victoria)

MAP 2:D4
135–137 Ebury Street
London SW1W 9QU
T: 020 7730 8191
W: limetreehotel.co.uk

BEDROOMS: 28.
OPEN: all year.
FACILITIES: lounge, restaurant, in-room TV (Freeview), meeting facilities, small garden.
BACKGROUND MUSIC: 'quiet' in lounge, restaurant.
LOCATION: 5 mins' walk from Victoria Underground and rail stations.
CHILDREN: not under 5.
DOGS: only assistance dogs allowed.
CREDIT CARDS: Amex, MC, Visa.
PRICES: per room B&B £125–£340. 1-night bookings sometimes refused Sat and peak periods.

LONDON

# THE MAIN HOUSE

Visitors can live like a local at this eclectic
Victorian house close to Portobello Road, in
chic, characterful Notting Hill. Each spacious,
uncluttered suite occupies an entire floor, and
has a tasteful mix of mellow wood, white walls,
antique furnishings and artwork. Well supplied
for city exploration, each room is equipped with
maps and guidebooks, umbrellas and a mobile
phone; freshly brewed organic tea or French
coffee may be taken in the room or on the terrace.
Breakfast is at a nearby deli or artisan bakery,
where a discounted price is available upon
brandishing a Main House key. Guests have
access to a private health club nearby; the hostess
has heaps of local tips to share. (Underground:
Notting Hill Gate)

MAP 2:D4
6 Colville Road
London W11 2BP
T: 020 7221 9691
W: themainhouse.co.uk

BEDROOMS: 4.
OPEN: all year.
FACILITIES: in-room TV (Freeview),
roof terrace, airport chauffeur service,
2-hour London tour, DVD library, use
of pool, gym at private club.
BACKGROUND MUSIC: none.
LOCATION: 10 mins' walk from Notting
Hill Gate Underground station.
CHILDREN: well-behaved children
welcomed, on request.
DOGS: not allowed.
CREDIT CARDS: MC, Visa.
PRICES: per room £130–£180 (3-night
min. stay), discounts at local
restaurants.

LONDON

# ROSEATE HOUSE

A stroll from Hyde Park, this elegant hotel is
spread over three mid-19th-century town houses,
a comfortable, homely atmosphere between them.
The classically decorated public spaces have
period furnishings and oil paintings; traditionally
styled bedrooms look on to the tree-lined street
or a private mews. Rooms vary in size – the four-
poster suite has its own sitting room – but all have
an antique desk and an easy chair; well-supplied
limestone shower- or bathrooms have robes,
slippers and high-end toiletries. There's a short
menu of modern European dishes, plus cocktails
and a large selection of whiskies, in the restaurant
and bar; breakfast can be taken in the bedroom.
(Underground: Paddington, Lancaster Gate)

MAP 2:D4
3 Westbourne Terrace
London W2 3UL
T: 020 7479 6600
W: roseatehotels.com/london/
   roseatehouse

BEDROOMS: 48.
OPEN: all year.
FACILITIES: lift, bar, restaurant, in-
room TV, business/function facilities,
terrace, garden, parking.
BACKGROUND MUSIC: in reception, bar
and restaurant during the day.
LOCATION: 5 mins' walk from
Paddington and Lancaster Gate
Underground stations.
CHILDREN: all ages welcomed.
DOGS: allowed in bedrooms only.
CREDIT CARDS: Amex, MC, Visa.
PRICES: per room B&B from £233.

LONDON

## ST JAMES'S HOTEL AND CLUB

In a quiet Mayfair cul-de-sac, this sophisticated hotel (Althoff Collection) houses silkily decorated bedrooms, a Michelin-starred restaurant, and a plush, velvet-seated bistro and bar. Down panelled corridors, works of fine art are hung throughout the former diplomats' club; a shortcut leads directly to Green Park. Bedrooms are kitted out with state-of-the-art technology, though the luckiest guests might simply turn their gaze outward: many of the rooms have their own balcony, and views over neighbourhood rooftops. Meals may be taken in the bistro or refined Seven Park Place restaurant; in the morning, 'wellness breakfasts' include green smoothies, almond-milk porridge and quinoa crumpets. (Underground: Green Park)

MAP 2:D4
7–8 Park Place
London  SW1A 1LS
T: 020 7316 1600
W: stjameshotelandclub.com

BEDROOMS: 60. 2 on ground floor, some suitable for disabled.
OPEN: all year.
FACILITIES: lounge, bar/bistro, restaurant (closed Sun, Mon), 4 private dining rooms, in-room TV, civil wedding licence, function rooms.
BACKGROUND MUSIC: in public areas.
LOCATION: 5 mins' walk from Green Park Underground station.
CHILDREN: all ages welcomed.
DOGS: not allowed.
CREDIT CARDS: Amex, MC, Visa.
PRICES: per room B&B from £350. À la carte (bistro) £45, 2- or 3-course menus (restaurant) £65–£75, tasting menu (restaurant) £95.

LONDON

## SOUTH PLACE HOTEL

'Distinctly cool', this City hotel is liked for its 'friendly staff', 'beautiful rooms' and 'tasty breakfasts'. Designed with playful flair by Terence Conran, it's a buzzy, after-work haunt of business types. Take your pick of eating places: sophisticated seafood in the Michelin-starred Angler restaurant; updated British classics in the Chop House; cocktails and snacks in the glamorous bars. 'Quiet, truly relaxing' bedrooms are decorated with original artwork and bespoke furniture; well-equipped bathrooms have a deep tub or walk-in shower. A morning paper arrives with breakfast – perhaps coconut granola, sweetcorn pancakes, eggs many ways. 'Recommended 100 per cent.' (Underground: Liverpool Street, Moorgate)

MAP 2:D4
3 South Place
London  EC2M 2AF
T: 020 3503 0000
W: southplacehotel.com

BEDROOMS: 80. 4 suitable for disabled.
OPEN: all year, restaurant closed Sat lunch, Sun.
FACILITIES: lift, 4 bars, 2 restaurants, residents' lounge, in-room TV (Sky, Freeview), civil wedding licence, meeting rooms, gym, spa, garden.
BACKGROUND MUSIC: in public areas, live DJ weekends in bars.
LOCATION: 5 mins' walk from Liverpool Street Underground and rail stations.
CHILDREN: all ages welcomed.
DOGS: small- and medium-size dogs allowed in rooms, bars, assistance dogs in restaurant.
CREDIT CARDS: Amex, MC, Visa.
PRICES: per room B&B £220–£830. À la carte (Chop House) £37, à la carte (Angler restaurant) £75, tasting menus (Angler restaurant) £70–£100.

**NEW**

ALDRINGHAM Suffolk
# FIVE ACRE BARN

'A model of hospitality', this 'pleasingly modern, minimalist' B&B close to the Suffolk coast has won awards for its contemporary design. 'Bruce Badrock and David Woodbine are charming, excellent hosts who work hard to make sure everything is pretty perfect,' say trusted readers in 2020. In a shingle-clad extension, light-filled suites (all mezzanine, bar one) have 'interesting art' and pops of colour; patio doors open on to a decked terrace, with a wildflower garden just beyond. 'Well-designed and comfortable', the sitting area, dining room and kitchen are in the original barn, where complimentary tea and cake are served every afternoon. 'Exceptional' breakfasts include 'perfectly cooked' hot options.

MAP 2:B6
Aldeburgh Road
Aldringham IP16 4QH
T: 07788 424642
W: fiveacrebarn.co.uk

BEDROOMS: 5. All in extension, 1 suitable for disabled.
OPEN: all year, occasionally wholly booked as holiday rental.
FACILITIES: sitting room, dining room/kitchen, in-room TV, 5-acre grounds.
BACKGROUND MUSIC: at breakfast 'as required'.
LOCATION: 2½ miles N of Aldeburgh.
CHILDREN: not under 12.
DOGS: allowed in 3 bedrooms, public areas.
CREDIT CARDS: Visa.
PRICES: per room B&B single £95–£155, double £135–£195. 2-night min. stay Fri, Sat nights.

ALFRISTON Sussex
# DEANS PLACE

In large grounds on the banks of the Cuckmere river, this extensively enlarged old farmhouse is a fine base for country walks and cream teas. Bedrooms vary in size, from compact doubles to larger rooms with expansive views over 'beautifully cared-for' gardens. Refurbishment continues: more bedrooms received a welcome rejuvenation (eye-catching wallpapers, more modern furnishings) this year. In good weather, take afternoon tea on the terrace; when the temperature dips, retreat to a spot by the log fire in the bar. Dinner brings a 'well-balanced' menu of modern British dishes, in either the refined restaurant (Thurs–Sat) or the cosy bar (Sun–Wed). At breakfast: 'enormous' portions of 'good traditional stuff'.

MAP 2:E4
Seaford Road
Alfriston BN26 5TW
T: 01323 870248
W: deansplacehotel.co.uk

BEDROOMS: 36. 1 suitable for disabled.
OPEN: all year, pre-bookings only over Christmas, New Year.
FACILITIES: bar, restaurant, function rooms, in-room TV (Freeview), civil wedding licence, terrace, 4-acre garden, heated outdoor swimming pool (May–Sept).
BACKGROUND MUSIC: in bar and dining room, occasional live jazz at Sun lunch.
LOCATION: Alfriston village, 3 miles from the coast and walking distance of South Downs.
CHILDREN: all ages welcomed.
DOGS: allowed in some bedrooms, public rooms, not in restaurant.
CREDIT CARDS: MC, Visa.
PRICES: per room B&B £89–£255, D,B&B £129–£308. À la carte £43.

**ALFRISTON** Sussex

# WINGROVE HOUSE

Friendly staff create a relaxing atmosphere at this 'charming' restaurant-with-rooms in a picturesque village in the South Downs national park. A colonial-style veranda wraps around the 19th-century house; there are heated, all-weather terraces and, inside, a cosy lounge with an open fire. Chic bedrooms, some in an ancient malthouse, mix neutral hues and tweedy fabrics; several have a terrace or balcony; most have verdant views. Footfall from above may be noticeable. Chef Mathew Comben's 'top-quality' modern British dishes are served in the bright, 'well-decorated' restaurant, candlelit at night. Inspired by seasonal, local produce, menus might include Sussex smokie bonbons; loin of venison, mini-pithivier.

MAP 2:E4
High Street
Alfriston  BN26 5TD
T: 01323 870276
W: wingrovehousealfriston.com

BEDROOMS: 16. 5 on ground floor, plus 3-bed pet-friendly cottage.
OPEN: all year.
FACILITIES: lounge/bar, restaurant, private dining room, in-room TV (Freeview), terrace, walled garden, restaurant wheelchair accessible.
BACKGROUND MUSIC: in restaurant.
LOCATION: at the end of the village High Street, 20 mins' drive from Glyndebourne.
CHILDREN: welcomed in restaurant, not overnight.
DOGS: not in bedrooms, 'although well-behaved dogs are welcome on the terrace'.
CREDIT CARDS: Amex, MC, Visa.
PRICES: per room B&B £100–£225. À la carte £34.

**NEW**

**ALNMOUTH** Northumberland

# THE RED LION INN

Opposite the parish church in a pretty village on the Aln estuary, this traditional 18th-century coaching inn is 'clearly a popular local watering hole'. The wood-panelled bar entices with real ales and beers from regional artisan brewers; locally sourced, 'reasonably priced' pub fare (perhaps baked goat's cheese; steak and ale pie, home-made chips) is served by 'friendly' staff. 'Tasteful, well-appointed' first-floor bedrooms have modern oak furniture, a 'very comfortable' bed, a smart bathroom. Along with 'an elementary buffet', breakfast, ordered the night before, delivers 'trencher portions of beautifully cooked scrambled eggs and good toast'. A sheltered beer garden takes in scenic views over the water.

MAP 4:A4
22 Northumberland Street
Alnmouth  NE66 2RJ
T: 01665 830584
W: redlionalnmouth.com

BEDROOMS: 7. 4 in annexe.
OPEN: all year.
FACILITIES: bar, restaurant, in-room TV (Freeview), beer garden.
BACKGROUND MUSIC: in bar, restaurant, live music events throughout the year.
LOCATION: in village centre.
CHILDREN: all ages welcomed.
DOGS: allowed in bar area, not in restaurant, bedrooms.
CREDIT CARDS: MC, Visa.
PRICES: per room B&B single £90–£140, double £110–£160. 2-night min. stay at weekends, except in quiet period Jan–Mar.

**NEW**

AMBLESIDE Cumbria
# RIVERSIDE BED & BREAKFAST

On a quiet lane, opposite a 'delightful, babbling' river, Richard and Diney Standen's 'superior' B&B is an 'easy and pleasant' walk from Ambleside. The large Victorian house has sofas in a light-filled lounge, a blazing fire in the wood-burner, wines and 'interesting' spirits in the honesty bar, plus 'every imaginable' area map and guidebook. 'Reasonably priced' accommodation, with views of the garden, river or Loughrigg Fell, have 'quality linens', coffee, tea and biscuits; fluffy towels and local toiletries in the immaculate bathrooms. 'Breakfast is a highlight': the orange juice is freshly squeezed; the bread, freshly baked. Let Diney press upon you a slice of home-baked cake before you head off on a walk.

MAP 4: inset C2
Under Loughrigg
Ambleside LA22 9LJ
T: 015394 32395
W: riverside-at-ambleside.co.uk

BEDROOMS: 6.
OPEN: all year except 15 Dec–1 Feb.
FACILITIES: lounge, breakfast room, in-room smart TV, 2 terrace areas, garden.
BACKGROUND MUSIC: none.
LOCATION: ¾ mile W of Ambleside.
CHILDREN: not under 10.
DOGS: not allowed.
CREDIT CARDS: MC, Visa.
PRICES: per room B&B £120–£140. 2-night min. stay.

AMBLESIDE Cumbria
# ROTHAY MANOR

Jamie and Jenna Shail's manor house hotel dates to 1823, but its tastefully refreshed style and ambitious cooking place it squarely in the 21st century. Individually decorated bedrooms, including a newly refurbished suite, are equipped with bathrobes, a coffee machine and Fairtrade tea; the best rooms have a balcony overlooking the landscaped gardens, the wooded grounds and the fells beyond. In the fine-dining restaurant, chef Daniel McGeorge's dishes are 'a class act'; the laid-back lounge has simpler fare. Guests have complimentary use of a local health club in town. Easy lake walks and hilly hikes are within reach – especially ideal for doggy companions, who are made very welcome inside the hotel and out.

MAP 4: inset C2
Rothay Bridge
Ambleside LA22 0EH
T: 015394 33605
W: rothaymanor.co.uk

BEDROOMS: 19. 2 in bungalow in the grounds, 1 suitable for disabled.
OPEN: all year except 3–22 Jan.
FACILITIES: bar, lounge, drawing room, restaurant (3 dining areas), in-room TV (Sky), civil wedding licence, 2-acre landscaped gardens (croquet), public rooms wheelchair accessible.
BACKGROUND MUSIC: all day in bar, lounge and restaurant.
LOCATION: ¼ mile SW of Ambleside.
CHILDREN: all ages welcomed.
DOGS: allowed in 4 bedrooms, public rooms, separate area of restaurant.
CREDIT CARDS: Amex, MC, Visa.
PRICES: per room B&B £130–£350, D,B&B £215–£460. À la carte £55, 5- and 9-course tasting menus. 1-night bookings normally refused Sat, bank holidays.

ANGMERING Sussex

# THE LAMB AT ANGMERING

'The welcome is warm; the staff, unfailingly smiley; the ambience, lively; and the food, very good' at the Newbon family's revived village pub on the edge of the South Downs national park. Locals and tourists come to the oak-floored bar and smart, informal restaurant for Sussex brews, Sunday roasts and 'delicious' gastropub dishes – perhaps a 'particularly flavoursome shellfish bisque'. A fire burns in the inglenook fireplace in winter; in good weather, the terrace overlooking St Nicholas Gardens is just the spot for an alfresco meal. 'Comfortably furnished' modern bedrooms have simple country charm in their florals and plaids; some can accommodate an extra bed for a child. Breakfast is cooked to order.

MAP 2:E3
The Square
Angmering BN16 4EQ
T: 01903 774300
W: thelamb-angmering.com

BEDROOMS: 8. 1 on ground floor with private entrance.
OPEN: all year, restaurant closed 25 Dec.
FACILITIES: bar, restaurant, in-room TV (Freeview), terrace, garden.
BACKGROUND MUSIC: 'quiet music' in public spaces.
LOCATION: in village, 15 miles E of Chichester.
CHILDREN: all ages welcomed, not in bar area after 9 pm.
DOGS: allowed in pub, on terrace.
CREDIT CARDS: MC, Visa.
PRICES: per room B&B £99–£215. À la carte £30.

ARMSCOTE Warwickshire

# FUZZY DUCK

Like ducks to water, locals flock to this stylish 18th-century coaching inn, drawn to its modern country comforts and 'extremely good' food. Head chef Andrew Edwards's modern British fare might include twice-baked cheese soufflé or comforting classics such as garlic-roasted chicken, truffle fries. Staying guests are cosseted with high-quality linens and woollen throws in 'minimalist' bedrooms; bathrooms are supplied with robes and complimentary goodies from the owners' beauty company, Baylis & Harding. Two rooms, ideal for a family, have a loft bed tucked in above the bathroom. After breakfast – cooked-to-order dishes accompany the cold buffet – borrow guidebooks and wellies for a countryside ramble.

MAP 3:D6
Ilmington Road
Armscote CV37 8DD
T: 01608 682635
W: fuzzyduckarmscote.com

BEDROOMS: 4.
OPEN: all year, except Sun evening from 5 pm, all day Mon.
FACILITIES: bar, restaurant, snug, in-room smart TV (Freeview), civil wedding licence, 1-acre garden.
BACKGROUND MUSIC: in public areas.
LOCATION: 9 miles S of Stratford-upon-Avon.
CHILDREN: all ages welcomed.
DOGS: allowed.
CREDIT CARDS: Amex, MC, Visa.
PRICES: per room B&B from £117. À la carte £32.

ARNSIDE Cumbria

# NUMBER 43

Lesley Hornsby's personably run B&B, in a tall
Victorian house, gazes across the estuary to
the Lakeland fells – and the hostess provides
binoculars to take it all in. The bay window of
the bright, art-hung sitting room is a tranquil
spot to savour the view, along with a tipple from
the honesty bar. On the first and second floors,
bedrooms and suites decorated in calming hues
provide homely comforts: biscuits, posh teas,
freshly ground coffee; milk in the mini-fridge;
spoiling toiletries. Breakfast, fresh and local, is a
feast: home-made granola, dry-cured back bacon,
Cumberland sausage; Buck's Fizz on Sundays. A
suntrap in the afternoon and evening, the compact
terrace affords a wide panorama over the water.

MAP 4: inset C2
The Promenade
Arnside LA5 0AA
T: 01524 762119
w: no43.org.uk

BEDROOMS: 5.
OPEN: all year.
FACILITIES: lounge, dining room,
in-room TV (Freeview), terrace.
BACKGROUND MUSIC: at breakfast.
LOCATION: village centre, on The
Promenade.
CHILDREN: allowed in some bedrooms.
DOGS: not allowed.
CREDIT CARDS: MC, Visa.
PRICES: per room B&B £125–£195.
2-night min. stay at weekends, 3-night
min. stay on bank holidays.

ASTHALL Oxfordshire

# THE MAYTIME INN

Recently refreshed, this 'delightful, friendly' 17th-
century coaching inn retains its authentic country
air. Creepers climb up the front of the mellow
stone building; in the rear, a large garden has an
outdoor gin bar, a boules pitch and fine views over
the rolling countryside. 'Comfortable, beautifully
converted' bedrooms, in the main building and
around the courtyard, enjoy a serenade of the
burbling Windrush stream. In the popular bar, all
17th-century stonework and old timbers, locals
and visitors choose from a 'good selection' of gins,
ales and ciders; the kitchen sends out seasonal
rustic dishes and pub classics. With bread from
the local bakery and coffee from an artisanal
roaster nearby, breakfast is 'top-notch'.

MAP 2:C2
Asthall OX18 4HW
T: 01993 822068
w: themaytime.com

BEDROOMS: 6. All on ground floor.
OPEN: all year except 25 Dec.
FACILITIES: bar, restaurant, in-room
TV (Freeview), large terrace, garden
with outdoor bar, boules pitch.
BACKGROUND MUSIC: in bar and
restaurant.
LOCATION: 2 miles from Burford.
CHILDREN: all ages welcomed (under-
18s must be accompanied by an adult).
DOGS: allowed in public areas, not in
bedrooms.
CREDIT CARDS: MC, Visa.
PRICES: per room B&B single £85–£160,
double £95–£160, D,B&B £135–£200.
À la carte £25–£30.

AYSGARTH Yorkshire
## STOW HOUSE

Phil and Sarah Bucknall's stone-built Victorian rectory is on the edge of the village, with the green sweep of the Yorkshire Dales all around. A playful, welcoming place, the B&B is filled with contemporary art, books and the crackling fire of several wood-burners. Bedrooms are an eclectic mix of period furniture and modern pieces, exposed timbers and Wensleydale views. They're all different: an antique dresser here, a red-painted cast-iron bath there. Bolton Castle is a four-mile yomp from the door – and the hostess's made-to-order cocktails are the perfect pick-me-up after a hike. Morning light floods the breakfast room, where freshly squeezed juice, home-baked bread and local produce are the order of the day.

MAP 4:C3
Aysgarth DL8 3SR
T: 01969 663635
W: stowhouse.co.uk

BEDROOMS: 7. 1 on ground floor.
OPEN: all year except 23–28 Dec.
FACILITIES: sitting room (honesty bar), snug, dining room, in-room TV (Freeview), 2-acre grounds.
BACKGROUND MUSIC: none.
LOCATION: 7 miles from Leyburn, 9 miles from Hawes.
CHILDREN: all ages welcomed.
DOGS: well-behaved dogs allowed in 5 bedrooms, public rooms.
CREDIT CARDS: MC, Visa.
PRICES: per room B&B £115–£185. 2-night min. stay on weekends May–Sept.

BAINBRIDGE Yorkshire
## YOREBRIDGE HOUSE

There's no cause for truancy at this former Victorian school and headmaster's house, in a pretty Dales village on the River Ure. Owners Charlotte and David Reilly have adorned indulgent bedrooms with items collected from their foreign travels – Caribbean seashells, say, or a bedhead fashioned from an antique Moroccan window. Some rooms have a private terrace and a hot tub worthy of California. Afternoon tea is worth the trip to the Master's Room; in the romantic, candlelit dining room, chef Dan Shotton's 'excellent, well-presented' modern dishes (perhaps Yorkshire heritage pork, pig cheek, turnip) make liberal use of produce from local suppliers. 'We love the atmosphere – laid-back luxury without pretensions.'

MAP 4:C3
Bainbridge DL8 3EE
T: 01969 652060
W: yorebridgehouse.co.uk

BEDROOMS: 12. Some on ground floor suitable for disabled, 4 in schoolhouse, plus The Barn suite in village, 5 mins' walk.
OPEN: all year.
FACILITIES: lounge, bar, garden room, restaurant, in-room TV (Sky), civil wedding licence, 5-acre grounds.
BACKGROUND MUSIC: all day in public areas.
LOCATION: outskirts of Bainbridge.
CHILDREN: all ages welcomed.
DOGS: allowed in 2 rooms, by arrangement.
CREDIT CARDS: MC, Visa.
PRICES: per room B&B from £220, D,B&B from £340. 3-course menu £60, tasting menu £80.

BAINTON Yorkshire
# WOLDS VILLAGE

Rooms and a restaurant are joined by a tea shop, an art gallery, and a craft and gift shop on Sally and Chris Brealey's Georgian farmstead in the Yorkshire Wolds. A family project, the complex has involved three generations over more than two decades. Soundproofed bedrooms are in a barn traditionally built using reclaimed bricks and pantiles; extensively researched decor in each heralds a different historic period, from Tudor to Art Deco. The restaurant and tea room serve country classics (salads, pies, a 'ploughman's feast') made with local produce. Along a meandering trail in the surrounding woods, a whimsical art collection includes a massive mosaic dragon, toadstool seats and a teddy bears' picnic.

MAP 4:D5
Manor Farm
Bainton YO25 9EF
T: 01377 217698
W: woldsvillage.co.uk

BEDROOMS: 7. 3 on ground floor, 1 suitable for disabled.
OPEN: all year except 2 weeks from 28 Dec.
FACILITIES: lounge, bar, restaurant, in-room TV (Freeview), art gallery, 6-acre grounds.
BACKGROUND MUSIC: in restaurant.
LOCATION: 6 miles W of Driffield.
CHILDREN: all ages welcomed.
DOGS: allowed in outside courtyard.
CREDIT CARDS: Amex, MC, Visa.
PRICES: per room B&B single £70, double £100. À la carte £25.

BARNSLEY Gloucestershire
# THE VILLAGE PUB

The hub of a pretty Cotswolds village, this mellow-stone pub-with-rooms (Calcot Collection) is liked for its stylish accommodation and relaxed nature. Spruced-up bedrooms, accessed via a separate entrance from the pub, range in size from snug to capacious. Very smart, they have books, magazines and a capsule coffee machine, plus, perhaps, a claw-footed bath in the country-chic bathroom. Light sleepers might request a room away from the road. Seasonal classics are a mainstay of the pub menu; in the morning, the breakfast spread includes home-made jams, home-baked bread, Burford Brown eggs. Residents have access, too, to the Rosemary Verey-designed grounds of sister hotel Barnsley House, nearby (see main entry).

MAP 3:E6
Barnsley GL7 5EF
T: 01285 740421
W: thevillagepub.co.uk

BEDROOMS: 6.
OPEN: all year.
FACILITIES: bar, restaurant, in-room TV (Freeview), courtyard.
BACKGROUND MUSIC: in bar, restaurant.
LOCATION: on the B4425 Cirencester to Bibury road, 4 miles NE of Cirencester town.
CHILDREN: all ages welcomed.
DOGS: allowed in bedrooms, public areas.
CREDIT CARDS: Amex, MC, Visa.
PRICES: per room B&B £114–£209, D,B&B £194–£264. À la carte £40.

**NEW**

BARTLOW Cambridgeshire

# THE THREE HILLS

Its name may derive from the Roman burial mounds nearby (the largest in Europe), but there's nothing dispiriting about this 17th-century Grade II listed inn close to Cambridge. Immaculately modernised, the pub and restaurant are a family-friendly community hub. There are upgraded bar classics to be eaten, perhaps in a cosy spot next to the log-burner; more sophisticated dishes in the oak-beamed orangery; on the covered garden patio, alfresco treats from the outdoor chargrill and pizza oven. For overnight guests, rustic-chic bedrooms are equipped with a Roberts radio, a capsule coffee machine and fine toiletries; a snug library has settle-in sofas, and books to borrow. A circular walk leads to the ancient tumuli.

**25% DISCOUNT VOUCHERS**

MAP 2:C4
Dean Road
Bartlow  CB21 4PW
T: 01223 890500
W: thethreehills.co.uk

BEDROOMS: 6. 4 in rear annexe, 2 on ground floor suitable for disabled.
OPEN: all year.
FACILITIES: bar, snug/library, restaurant (closed Sun evening, all day Mon), in-room smart TV (Freeview), function facilities, large patio, garden (with rabbits, chickens and guinea pigs in pets' corner), meadow.
BACKGROUND MUSIC: soft music (light jazz) in bar, restaurant.
LOCATION: in a small village, 12 miles SE of Cambridge.
CHILDREN: all ages welcomed.
DOGS: allowed in 4 annexe rooms, bar, snug.
CREDIT CARDS: Amex, MC, Visa.
PRICES: per room B&B £100–£130, D,B&B £190–£210. À la carte £42.

BATH Somerset

# GROVE LODGE

With crystal chandeliers, velvet sofas and whimsical wallcoverings, Mary and Giovanni Baiano's Georgian villa interweaves old-world charm with a touch of flamboyance. Spacious suites on the upper floors each have a private drawing room; large windows overlook the verdant front garden and countryside. Rooms are thoughtfully supplied with a coffee machine, fruit, home-made biscotti and fudge; breakfast, elegantly served in the suite, includes home-made marmalade, jams and granola, plus hot potato cakes with the full English. The hospitable Anglo-Italian owners offer a complimentary pick-up service (by arrangement) for guests arriving by train or bus. NOTE: As the Guide went to press, Grove Lodge announced that it was closing.

**25% DISCOUNT VOUCHERS**

MAP 2:D1
11 Lambridge
Bath  BA1 6BJ
T: 01225 310860
W: grovelodgebath.co.uk

BEDROOMS: 3 suites.
OPEN: Feb–Dec.
FACILITIES: in-room TV (Freeview), large front garden.
BACKGROUND MUSIC: none.
LOCATION: 1¾ miles from Bath Spa station.
CHILDREN: not under 12.
DOGS: not allowed.
CREDIT CARDS: Amex, MC, Visa.
PRICES: per room B&B single £100–£120, double £160–£250. 1-night bookings sometimes refused at weekends.

BATH Somerset

# HARINGTON'S HOTEL

A genial atmosphere fills this style-conscious boutique hotel, on a quiet cobbled street in the heart of the city. Well-equipped bedrooms are spread across three upper floors – there's no lift, but friendly staff help with luggage. Each room (some are compact) has tea- and coffee-making facilities, plus oversized towels and a power shower; vividly patterned wallpaper and quirky design touches add whimsy. A blanket, towel and treats are provided for doggy companions. Light lunches and afternoon teas are served in the lounge; in the bar, cocktails and Bath ales. Breakfast has bacon butties, pancakes, leaf teas. A plus: the private hot tub (extra charge) in the secluded courtyard – a contemporary take on the thermal baths.

MAP 2:D1
8–10 Queen Street
Bath BA1 1HE
T: 01225 461728
W: haringtonshotel.co.uk

BEDROOMS: 13. Plus self-catering town house and apartments.
OPEN: all year except 25/26 Dec.
FACILITIES: lounge, breakfast room, café/bar, in-room TV (Freeview), room service, conference room, small courtyard with hot tub, secure pre-bookable parking nearby (extra charge).
BACKGROUND MUSIC: in public areas.
LOCATION: city centre.
CHILDREN: all ages welcomed.
DOGS: allowed.
CREDIT CARDS: Amex, MC, Visa.
PRICES: per room B&B £70–£198.
2-night min. stay some weekends.

BATH Somerset

# PARADISE HOUSE

'Our welcome couldn't have been more solicitous, the young staff more charming, nor the house on a sunny day any lovelier,' say regular Guide readers this year of David and Annie Lanz's peaceful B&B. It sits across the River Avon from the town, in 'surely just about the best private terraced garden in Bath'. The Georgian drawing room has an open fire in cool weather, and 'spectacular views over the city and hills' through floor-to-ceiling windows; contemporary and period-style bedrooms each have an 'excellent' bed, and a powerful shower in the modern bathroom. 'We particularly liked the Venetian window in our capacious bathroom.' Praiseworthy breakfasts, with good veggie options, are 'speedily cooked'.

MAP 2:D1
86–88 Holloway
Bath BA2 4PX
T: 01225 317723
W: paradise-house.co.uk

BEDROOMS: 12. 4 on ground floor, 3 in annexe.
OPEN: all year except 3 days over Christmas.
FACILITIES: drawing room, breakfast room, in-room TV (Freeview), ½-acre garden, parking.
BACKGROUND MUSIC: Classic FM all day in public areas.
LOCATION: 15 mins' downhill walk to the centre.
CHILDREN: all ages welcomed.
DOGS: not allowed.
CREDIT CARDS: Amex, MC, Visa.
PRICES: per room B&B £150–£260.
2-night min. stay at weekends.

BATH Somerset

## THE ROSEATE VILLA

In 'pretty gardens', overlooking Henrietta Park, this peaceful villa formed from two Victorian houses is 'within walking distance of everything'. The 'friendly welcome' from 'delightful' manager Jean-Luc Bouchereau includes 'a generous tea' with home-baked cake (and a box of treats for doggy guests); all around are well-chosen antiques and interesting prints. Smartly decorated bedrooms — some snug, others generously sized — are stocked with home-made shortbread and fresh milk. In the chic new bar, morning coffees and afternoon teas give way to custom cocktails in the evening; breakfast brings Buck's Fizz paired with, perhaps, compotes, croissants and 'proper kippers'. Sister hotel Roseate House is in London (see Shortlist entry).

MAP 2:D1
Henrietta Road
Bath BA2 6LX
T: 01225 466329
W: roseatehotels.com/bath/
    theroseatevilla/

BEDROOMS: 21. 2-room suite on lower ground floor.
OPEN: all year.
FACILITIES: bar, breakfast/dining room, in-room TV, small garden, terrace, parking.
BACKGROUND MUSIC: 'soft' radio in breakfast room.
LOCATION: 3 mins' walk from the city centre, by Henrietta Park.
CHILDREN: all ages welcomed.
DOGS: allowed, if more than 10 months old.
CREDIT CARDS: Amex, MC, Visa.
PRICES: per room B&B from £181.

**NEW**

BEADNELL Northumberland

## BEADNELL TOWERS

Coast and countryside are brought inside this Grade II listed, 18th-century building in a seaside village noted for watersports and wide beaches. Following top-to-bottom refurbishment, the 'attractively decorated' hotel has playful displays throughout: vintage suitcases and Bakelite telephones in reception; nautical gear, more industrial than twee. Sophisticated bedrooms are each different: some have a terrace; others interconnect to accommodate a family; four can be supplied with bedding and treats for an accompanying pup. On the ground floor, an L-shaped bar leads to the wood-floored restaurant — both 'clearly popular with locals and tourists' — where 'friendly, willing, if sometimes inexperienced, staff' serve up 'honest pub fare'.

MAP 4:A4
The Wynding
Beadnell NE67 5AY
T: 01665 721211
W: beadnelltowers.co.uk

BEDROOMS: 18. 5 on ground floor.
OPEN: all year.
FACILITIES: bar, lounge, restaurant, in-room TV, private dining room, terrace.
BACKGROUND MUSIC: in dining area.
LOCATION: in Beadnell, 800 yards from the beach.
CHILDREN: all ages welcomed.
DOGS: allowed in 4 bedrooms, bar.
CREDIT CARDS: MC, Visa.
PRICES: per room B&B £129–£259. À la carte £30.

BELPER Derbyshire

# DANNAH FARM

Busy hens are the only neighbours at Joan and Martin Slack's 'charming, welcoming' B&B, on a 150-acre working farm in the Derbyshire Dales. Spacious bedrooms with space to sit are decked out 'with all the luxury trimmings'; three suites have a terrace with a private outdoor hot tub. Guests may also book, for private use, the neat 'spa cabin' and outdoor hot tub hidden behind a screen of trees, in a secluded spot in the garden. Supper platters of meats, cheeses, fish, salads and pudding can be ordered in advance; alternatively, the hosts can recommend local eateries and arrange transport, if requested. With just-laid farmyard eggs and thick slices of home-baked bread, the 'plentiful' breakfast is a 'delicious' start to the day.

MAP 2:A2
Bowmans Lane
Belper DE56 2DR
T: 01773 550273
W: dannah.co.uk

BEDROOMS: 8. 4 in adjoining converted barn, 3 on ground floor.
OPEN: all year except Christmas.
FACILITIES: 2 sitting rooms, dining room, meeting room, in-room TV (Freeview), large walled garden, outdoor hot tub, parking.
BACKGROUND MUSIC: none.
LOCATION: 2 miles from Belper.
CHILDREN: all ages welcomed.
DOGS: allowed in some bedrooms.
CREDIT CARDS: MC, Visa.
PRICES: per room B&B single £95–£110, double £165–£295. In-room supper platter £19.95. 2-night min. stay Fri, Sat.

BEXHILL-ON-SEA Sussex

# COAST

Piero and Lucia Mazzoni bring 'warm' Italian hospitality to the British seaside at their 'impeccably decorated' B&B. Styled in modern, minimalist greys and whites, the Edwardian villa is made lively with occasional pops of colour: red wingback chairs, clusters of yellow flowers. Genteel bedrooms (some compact) have little luxuries: biscuits, a capsule coffee machine and a silent fridge; in the under-floor-heated bathroom, a cascade shower, fluffy towels and high-end toiletries. The best room has a whirlpool bath, and a private sea-view balcony. Breakfast includes fresh fruit, home-baked bread, a vegetarian full English, and pancakes with crème fraîche and maple syrup. The De La Warr Pavilion is close by.

MAP 2:E4
58 Sea Road
Bexhill-on-Sea TN40 1JP
T: 01424 225260
W: coastbexhill.co.uk

BEDROOMS: 5.
OPEN: all year.
FACILITIES: lounge, breakfast room, in-room TV (Freeview, Sky), secure bicycle storage.
BACKGROUND MUSIC: none.
LOCATION: town centre, 100 yards from the seafront.
CHILDREN: not under 5.
DOGS: not allowed.
CREDIT CARDS: Amex, MC, Visa.
PRICES: per room B&B single £85–£118, double £99–£135. 1-night bookings sometimes refused weekends and high season.

BEXHILL-ON-SEA Sussex

# THE DRIFTWOOD

Coolly contemporary behind its gunmetal-grey facade, this design-conscious hotel and restaurant is steps from the seafront and the De La Warr Pavilion. Natural timbers and exposed brick walls give the Victorian town house much character; the open kitchen in the ground-floor brasserie-style restaurant turns out Asian-influenced dishes (Chinese pork and cabbage dumplings; Malaysian beef rendang). Upstairs, bedrooms in heritage colours have a large bed dressed with peppy cushions and throws; a walk-in shower in a modern bathroom. Pleasing extras: bathrobes and slippers, a coffee machine, a mini-fridge with fresh milk, water and beer. Breakfast, perhaps French toast with a mixed berry compote, is cooked to order.

MAP 2:E4
40 Sackville Road
Bexhill-on-Sea  TN39 3JE
T:  01424 732584
W:  thedriftwoodbexhill.co.uk

BEDROOMS: 6.
OPEN: all year.
FACILITIES: restaurant, in-room TV.
BACKGROUND MUSIC: none.
LOCATION: in town centre.
CHILDREN: all ages welcomed.
DOGS: not allowed.
CREDIT CARDS: Amex, MC, Visa.
PRICES: per room £99–£139. 1-night bookings refused weekends.

BIBURY Gloucestershire

# THE SWAN

'What a setting!' Creeper-covered and wood fire-warmed, this busy 17th-century coaching inn (now owned by Fuller's) stands on the banks of the River Coln, in a quaint village William Morris described as the most beautiful in England. River, village or courtyard views pour in to the light, country-style bedrooms; cottage suites in the pretty garden are ideal for larger groups. There's a choice of dining areas: gastropub fare is served under antler chandeliers in the dog-friendly bar and courtyard; the brasserie has modern European cooking, perhaps Bibury trout. Afternoon tea may be taken inside or out; in clement weather, find a spot for sunning in the hotel's delightful riverside garden across the lane.

MAP 3:E6
Bibury  GL7 5NW
T:  01285 740695
W:  fullers.co.uk/hotels

BEDROOMS: 22. Some on ground floor, 4 in adjacent garden cottages.
OPEN: all year.
FACILITIES: lift, lounge, bar, brasserie, in-room TV (Freeview), ½-acre garden, civil wedding licence, function facilities.
BACKGROUND MUSIC: 'subtle' in public spaces.
LOCATION: village centre.
CHILDREN: all ages welcomed.
DOGS: well-behaved dogs allowed in bar, lounge, garden, some bedrooms.
CREDIT CARDS: Amex, MC, Visa.
PRICES: per room B&B £170–£405, D,B&B £240–£475. À la carte (brasserie) £36.

BIRMINGHAM Warwickshire

# THE HIGH FIELD TOWN HOUSE

Run in conjunction with The High Field gastropub next door, this white-fronted Victorian villa in upmarket Edgbaston has the feel of a 'boutique country house'. A coded entry system leads to a homely sitting room with vases of fresh flowers, complimentary newspapers and a capsule coffee machine; something a little stronger may be found in the honesty bar. Well-chosen antiques and retro furnishings fill the bedrooms. Bright and modern, each room has its own style; some are large enough to accommodate a family. Pop across the driveway when hunger strikes: along with cocktails and bubbly, elevated pub grub includes the likes of harissa roast aubergine, chickpeas, pomegranate; chicken Milanese, garlic and sage butter.

## 25% DISCOUNT VOUCHERS

MAP 3:C6
23 Highfield Road
Birmingham B15 3DP
T: 0121 647 6466
W: highfieldtownhouse.co.uk

BEDROOMS: 12. 1 suitable for disabled.
OPEN: all year, except 24/25 Dec.
FACILITIES: sitting room, bar, restaurant in adjacent building (wheelchair accessible), in-room TV (Freeview), private dining, terrace, garden, parking.
BACKGROUND MUSIC: in sitting room.
LOCATION: 10 mins' drive from city centre.
CHILDREN: all ages welcomed.
DOGS: allowed in pub, not in bedrooms.
CREDIT CARDS: Amex, MC, Visa.
PRICES: per room B&B £115–£210.
À la carte £35, 2-course early dining menu (12 pm–6 pm) £14.75.

BISHOPSTONE Wiltshire

# HELEN BROWNING'S ROYAL OAK

On the edge of the Wiltshire Downs, this quirky, affable dining pub-with-rooms stands on an organic farm, a vision of food ethics pioneer Helen Browning. Regular returnees laud the 'excellent, friendly' staff and the well-established pub (Arkell's Brewery), where visitors tuck in to real ales, organic wines and generous, scrupulously sourced meals. Set around a sunny courtyard, well-equipped, modern-rustic bedrooms are 'clean, comfortable, and warm when necessary'; residents also have an inviting lounge stocked with books, hot drinks, a record player and a collection of LPs. 'Plenty of walks' from the door: cross woodland and orchards; roam across hills or wildflower valleys; visit the farm's pigs, sheep and cattle.

## 25% DISCOUNT VOUCHERS

MAP 3:E6
Cues Lane
Bishopstone SN6 8PP
T: 01793 790481
W: helenbrowningsorganic.co.uk

BEDROOMS: 12. All in annexe, 100 yards from pub, 1 suitable for disabled.
OPEN: all year.
FACILITIES: lounge, pub (2 dining areas), meeting/function room, in-room TV (Freeview), ½-acre garden (rope swing, Wendy house, 'flighty hens'), parking.
BACKGROUND MUSIC: occasionally, in public spaces.
LOCATION: on an organic farm, in village, 7 miles E of Swindon, 10 miles from Marlborough.
CHILDREN: all ages welcomed.
DOGS: allowed in 3 bedrooms, in public rooms 'at our discretion'.
CREDIT CARDS: MC, Visa.
PRICES: per room B&B £85–£160.
À la carte £32.

BLACKPOOL Lancashire

## NUMBER ONE ST LUKE'S

Mark and Claire Smith have run their well-liked South Shore B&B for a decade and a half, and their experience shows. Spacious, individually decorated bedrooms in the red-brick detached house each have a king-size bed and plenty of perks: snacks and drinks, a music system and wide TV, a power shower and spa bath in the bathroom. A large conservatory overlooks the garden; outside, there are sun loungers, a hot tub and a putting green. A universal electric car charging point is for guests' use. Fill up on a 'full Blackpool' at breakfast before heading out to explore: the famous promenade and Pleasure Beach are minutes away on foot. (See also sister hotel Number One South Beach, next entry.)

MAP 4:D2
1 St Luke's Road
Blackpool FY4 2EL
T: 01253 343901
W: numberoneblackpool.com

BEDROOMS: 3.
OPEN: all year.
FACILITIES: dining room, conservatory, in-room TV (Freeview), garden (putting green), parking.
BACKGROUND MUSIC: none.
LOCATION: 2 miles S of town centre.
CHILDREN: not under 4.
DOGS: by prior arrangement.
CREDIT CARDS: Amex, MC, Visa.
PRICES: per person B&B £60–£140.
1-night bookings occasionally refused weekends.

BLACKPOOL Lancashire

## NUMBER ONE SOUTH BEACH

Steps from the promenade, this friendly small hotel is close to many of the town's attractions. It is owned by Janet and Graham Oxley, and Claire and Mark Smith (see also Number One St Luke's, previous entry). Colourful bedrooms are individually decorated with flair; the best have a balcony to take in the sea views. Each room is kitted out with thoughtful extras (lint roller, sewing kit, shoehorn, etc) and smart technological touches such as remote-controlled lighting, a waterproof TV by the spa bath, and a walk-in power shower. Golf enthusiasts may look forward to tee time: the games room has an indoor golf simulator. Breakfast features all the favourites, including vegetarian options. Tram and bus stops are close by.

**25% DISCOUNT VOUCHERS**

MAP 4:D2
4 Harrowside West
Blackpool FY4 1NW
T: 01253 343900
W: numberonesouthbeach.com

BEDROOMS: 14. Some suitable for disabled.
OPEN: all year except 26–31 Dec.
FACILITIES: lift, lounge, bar, restaurant, games room, in-room TV (Freeview), meeting/conference facilities, parking.
BACKGROUND MUSIC: quiet classical music in bar and lounge.
LOCATION: 2½ miles S of town centre.
CHILDREN: not under 5.
DOGS: assistance dogs only.
CREDIT CARDS: Amex, MC, Visa.
PRICES: per room B&B £85–£174.
À la carte £28.35, Sun lunch £18.95.
1-night bookings generally refused Sat in high season.

BOURNEMOUTH Dorset

## THE GREEN HOUSE

Ethical hospitality is a priority at this 'friendly, really special' hotel, in a handsome Victorian villa close to the seafront. From the community vegetable garden and sustainably sourced furnishings to the solar panels and beehives on the roof, a green ethos has been built in to the place. Smart bedrooms (some snug) are decorated in pleasing, earthy tones; they have 'crisp' organic bed linens, 'soft pillows' and 'proper fluffy Fairtrade-cotton towels'. 'We were delighted we weren't provided with pointless single-use-plastic toiletry bottles.' The Arbor restaurant serves food all day; naturally, chef Andy Hilton's unfussy modern menus use organic, Fairtrade and locally sourced ingredients. The result: 'delicious'.

MAP 2:E2
4 Grove Road
Bournemouth BH1 3AX
T: 01202 498900
W: thegreenhousehotel.com

BEDROOMS: 32. 1 suitable for disabled.
OPEN: all year.
FACILITIES: lift, bar, restaurant, in-room TV (Freeview), civil wedding licence, private event facilities, 1-acre garden, terrace, parking.
BACKGROUND MUSIC: in public areas.
LOCATION: 5 mins' walk from beach, 10 mins' walk from town centre.
CHILDREN: all ages welcomed, not in restaurant after 7 pm.
DOGS: not allowed.
CREDIT CARDS: Amex, MC, Visa.
PRICES: per room B&B from £119, D,B&B from £179. À la carte £35. 1-night bookings refused Sat in peak season.

BRADFORD-ON-AVON Wiltshire

## TIMBRELL'S YARD

By the footpath skirting the Avon, this popular bar/restaurant-with-rooms occupies a Grade II listed building in a 'delightful' town. Snacks, small plates, refined pub food and dry-aged steaks are plied in the industrial-style dining areas throughout the day; the 'excellent' bar has a wide selection of craft spirits, local ales and ciders. Outdoor seating in the courtyard 'is a plus'. Along a maze of stairs and corridors, voguish bedrooms (many facing the river) have modern textiles, reclaimed furniture and wonky floors; split-level suites (with 'steep, polished steps') are fitted with deep window seats. Part of the Stay Original Company; see also The Swan, Wedmore, and The White Hart, Somerton (Shortlist entries).

MAP 2:D1
49 Saint Margaret's Street
Bradford-on-Avon BA15 1DE
T: 01225 869492
W: timbrellsyard.com

BEDROOMS: 17.
OPEN: all year.
FACILITIES: bar, restaurant, private dining room, in-room TV (Freeview), river-facing terrace.
BACKGROUND MUSIC: in public spaces 'to suit time and ambience'.
LOCATION: centre of Bradford-on-Avon, 3-min. walk from railway station.
CHILDREN: all ages welcomed.
DOGS: allowed in bedrooms, bar.
CREDIT CARDS: MC, Visa.
PRICES: per room B&B from £115. À la carte £34.

BREEDON ON THE HILL Leicestershire

# BREEDON HALL

There's a warm, unassuming country feel at Charles and Charlotte Meynell's listed Georgian manor house, in the centre of a village in the National Forest. Standing in a well-cared-for garden behind high brick walls, the elegantly restored home has a fire-warmed drawing room and a clutch of bedrooms decorated with character. B&B guests choose among rooms with handsome old beams or, perhaps, a roll-top bath overlooking the lawn. No keys are provided: 'It's a family home, and feels like one,' the hosts say. Breakfast brings fresh fruit, home-made granola, marmalade and jams, and eggs from the house's hens; local pub grub is as near as the end of the drive. Historic market towns Melbourne and Ashby-de-la-Zouch are close.

MAP 2:A2
Breedon on the Hill DE73 8AN
T: 01332 864935
W: breedonhall.co.uk

BEDROOMS: 5. Plus 3 self-catering cottages.
OPEN: all year except Sun, 'sometimes' in Feb and Mar, first two weeks July, Christmas and New Year.
FACILITIES: drawing room, dining room, snug, in-room TV (Freeview), civil wedding licence, 1-acre grounds, parking.
BACKGROUND MUSIC: none.
LOCATION: village centre.
CHILDREN: preferably not under 12, 'but we may make exceptions upon request'.
DOGS: well-behaved dogs allowed in bedrooms, public rooms (resident dog).
CREDIT CARDS: Amex, MC, Visa.
PRICES: per room B&B £95–£165.
1-night bookings refused on popular June weekends.

**NEW**

BRIGHTON Sussex

# BRIGHTONWAVE

One in a row of Victorian town houses, a five-minute stroll from the pier, this Kemptown B&B has some 'lovely little touches' that please appreciative guests. Richard Adams and Simon Throp are the helpful, informative owners. Some of the crisp, contemporary bedrooms may be compact, but each room is 'very clean, and has everything you need': bottles of water, tea- and coffee-making facilities, chocolates. One room has a private patio garden with seating; another, a Juliet balcony. Works by local artists decorate the lounge, where guests have books to borrow, and access to a laptop and printer. Cooked-to-order breakfasts are served till 10.30 am on the weekend; a continental breakfast may be taken in the room.

MAP 2:E4
10 Madeira Place
Brighton BN2 1TN
T: 01273 676794
W: brightonwave.com

BEDROOMS: 8.
OPEN: all year except Christmas.
FACILITIES: lounge, in-room TV (Freeview).
BACKGROUND MUSIC: none.
LOCATION: in Kemptown, just off the seafront.
CHILDREN: not under 14.
DOGS: not allowed.
CREDIT CARDS: Amex, MC, Visa.
PRICES: per room B&B £70–£180.
2-night min. stay at weekends.

## BRIGHTON Sussex

# PASKINS

Within the East Cliff conservation area, the Marlowe family's characterful Kemptown B&B has long been a bastion of sustainable living. Spread across two buildings on the quiet street of 19th-century town houses, the 'comfortable' bedrooms range in size from snug singles to a large four-poster room. Each has an imaginative Art Deco feel and a modern shower room stocked with cruelty-free toiletries. A creative flair takes over at breakfast, where choices include home-made vegetarian sausages, bagels from a local baker, and duck eggs with toast soldiers. The owners' daughter, Claudia, and her partner, Charlotte, who manage the B&B, have helpful local tips to offer. Brighton Pier is a ten-minute seafront walk away.

MAP 2:E4
18–19 Charlotte Street
Brighton BN2 1AG
T: 01273 601203
W: paskins.co.uk

BEDROOMS: 19.
OPEN: all year except 21–27 Dec.
FACILITIES: dining room, in-room TV (Freeview), parking vouchers (£10 for 24 hours).
BACKGROUND MUSIC: 1920s/1930s music at breakfast.
LOCATION: just off the seafront.
CHILDREN: all ages welcomed.
DOGS: allowed (not unattended) in some bedrooms, by arrangement.
CREDIT CARDS: Amex, MC, Visa.
PRICES: per room B&B £60–£190. Discounts for Vegetarian Society, Vegan Society and Amnesty International members. 1-night bookings refused Sat.

## BRIGHTON Sussex

# A ROOM WITH A VIEW

Steps from the beach in arty Kemptown, this 'immaculately presented' Regency house is a bright, modern B&B where guests receive a 'cheerful, friendly' welcome. 'It's small, but so comfortable', with an appealing decor and pictures of the town by local artists. Most of the airy bedrooms look over the sea and down to the pier. Each, with light wood floors, has its own style; 'thoughtful' comforts include biscuits, a capsule coffee machine, a mini-fridge, even earplugs in the bedside drawer. In the bathroom or walk-in wet room: 'fluffy towels and dressing gowns'. The 'excellent' breakfast is a highlight: blueberry pancakes, perhaps, or 'highly recommended double eggs Benedict'. Free parking can be pre-arranged.

MAP 2:E4
41 Marine Parade
Brighton BN2 1PE
T: 01273 682885
W: aroomwithaviewbrighton.com

BEDROOMS: 10. 1 on ground floor.
OPEN: all year.
FACILITIES: lounge, breakfast room, in-room smart TV, parking.
BACKGROUND MUSIC: 'gentle' in breakfast room.
LOCATION: on the seafront.
CHILDREN: not under 12.
DOGS: not allowed.
CREDIT CARDS: Amex, MC, Visa.
PRICES: per room B&B £140–£295.

BRISLEY Norfolk

# THE BRISLEY BELL

From lively quiz nights and Friday-evening cricket matches to afternoon tea and board games by the inglenook fireplace, this red-tiled 17th-century inn facing the village common has all the traits of a buzzy local landmark. It is owned and run by Norfolk-bred Amelia Nicholson and Marcus Seaman, who restored the old pub and extended it to include stylish modern bedrooms in converted barns, set in a spread of lawns and landscaped gardens. Served across a series of dining areas, the pub menu lists English favourites tweaked with French techniques (perhaps pheasant breast, roast cauliflower, chorizo fricassee). Nature trails, country estates and the north Norfolk heritage coastline are within easy reach.

MAP 2:B5
The Green
Brisley NR20 5DW
T: 01362 705024
w: thebrisleybell.co.uk

BEDROOMS: 6. All on ground floor in converted barns, 1 suitable for disabled.
OPEN: all year except 24–26 Dec, limited pub hours 25/26 Dec.
FACILITIES: bar, snug, restaurant (closed Mon), garden room, in-room TV (Freeview), 2-acre garden, croquet lawn.
BACKGROUND MUSIC: none, except for live music events.
LOCATION: just outside village.
CHILDREN: all ages welcomed.
DOGS: welcomed in 2 bedrooms, bar, snug, garden.
CREDIT CARDS: MC, Visa.
PRICES: per room B&B £78–£191. À la carte £30–£35.

BRIXHAM Devon

# HARBOUR VIEW

Overlooking the colour and activity of the working harbour in a busy fishing town, this 'modest' B&B, in the former harbour master's house, is run by 'helpful, considerate' host Stephen King. 'It's exceptional value for such a pleasant, comfortable spot.' Straightforward bedrooms on the top three floors may be 'small, but they're spotless', and have all the essentials: tea- and coffee-making facilities, an alarm clock radio, controllable central heating; 'a comfy bed and a good shower'. The two top-floor rooms are ideal for a family or group. In the morning, a 'fabulous' full English breakfast is served in 'any combination, cooking style and quantity you like'. Steps, opposite, lead down to the quayside.

MAP 1:D5
65 King Street
Brixham TQ5 9TH
T: 01803 853052
w: harbourviewbrixhamandb.co.uk

BEDROOMS: 8.
OPEN: all year.
FACILITIES: open-plan breakfast room/ sitting area, in-room TV, courtyard, pre-bookable harbourside parking (charge).
BACKGROUND MUSIC: none.
LOCATION: on Brixham's inner harbour.
CHILDREN: all ages welcomed.
DOGS: allowed in 2 bedrooms.
CREDIT CARDS: Amex, MC, Visa.
PRICES: per room B&B £64–£109. 3-night min. stay in high season, 1-night bookings refused weekends all year.

BROADWAY Worcestershire

# THE OLIVE BRANCH

Pam Talboys runs her 'beautifully appointed' B&B on a quiet cul-de-sac in this honey-hued village. Well-equipped bedrooms in the Grade II listed Cotswold stone building have country cottage charm, plus 'a comfy bed, decent storage space and a small but lavishly provisioned bathroom'. The cosy sitting room has books to borrow, and a wood burner for cool days; in fine weather, the enclosed rear garden is a particularly pleasant place to be – with or without a tipple from the honesty bar. 'First-rate breakfasts', taken in the front parlour with its original stone flags, are a feast of home-baked breads and muesli bars; local jam, marmalade and honey; yogurts and cheeses. Planning a day out? The hostess is a repository of local information.

**25% DISCOUNT VOUCHERS**

MAP 3:D6
78 High Street
Broadway WR12 7AJ
T: 01386 853440
W: theolivebranch-broadway.com

BEDROOMS: 7. Some on ground floor, 1 suitable for disabled.
OPEN: all year except 25–27 Dec.
FACILITIES: lounge, breakfast room, in-room TV, ¼-acre garden, gazebo, 'easy parking', dining room and lounge wheelchair accessible.
BACKGROUND MUSIC: in lounge, breakfast room.
LOCATION: in village centre.
CHILDREN: all ages welcomed.
DOGS: not allowed.
CREDIT CARDS: MC, Visa.
PRICES: per room B&B single £110–£125, double £130–£150. 1-night bookings generally refused weekends in high season.

BROOK Hampshire

# THE BELL INN

Flagstone floors, old beams and open fires at this 18th-century coaching inn make fine bones for the smart tweeds and bright wall coverings of its updated country interior. In a quiet New Forest hamlet, the red brick building has been in the Eyre family since 1782; under the same ownership are two adjoining golf courses. Ranging from snug to capacious, individually decorated bedrooms include interconnecting rooms to accommodate a family. In the farmhouse-style restaurant, and on picnic tables in the garden, modern dishes might include Lymington crab or pork chops from New Forest pigs; the bar menu lists comfort foods and a splendid collection of gins. Next day, there's 'good choice', with gluten-free options, at breakfast.

MAP 2:E2
Brook SO43 7HE
T: 023 8081 2214
W: bellinn-newforest.co.uk

BEDROOMS: 28. Some interconnecting, 8 on ground floor.
OPEN: all year.
FACILITIES: bar, lounge, 2 dining rooms, in-room TV (Freeview), civil wedding licence, beer garden (games, boules pitch), patio, parking.
BACKGROUND MUSIC: all day in bar.
LOCATION: 1 mile from Junction 1 of the M27, on the edge of the New Forest.
CHILDREN: all ages welcomed.
DOGS: allowed in some bedrooms, bar, public rooms, not in dining room.
CREDIT CARDS: MC, Visa.
PRICES: per room B&B single from £84, double £109–£199. À la carte £30. 2-night min. stay Fri/Sat.

 **NEW**

MAP 1:B6
1 High Street
Bruton BA10 0AB
T: 01749 813030
W: numberonebruton.com

**BRUTON** Somerset

# NUMBER ONE BRUTON

In a cool, arty town, Aled and Claudia Rees have crafted this voguish hotel and farm-to-table restaurant from a medieval inn, forge and string of cottages. Restored original features lend much character to the creatively decorated bedrooms: rich colours, aged flooring and vintage furnishings in the main house; high vaulted ceilings in the forge; exposed beams and an Arts and Crafts influence in the dog-friendly cottages. In all rooms: a truckle of Cheddar cheese and crackers, local cider and fresh fruit, essential-oil toiletries. At lunch and dinner, chef Merlin Labron-Johnson's much-praised cooking is served in the stylishly stripped-back restaurant; a substantial farmhouse breakfast with home-made jams compounds the treats.

BEDROOMS: 12. 4 in forge, 3 in cottages.
OPEN: all year.
FACILITIES: sitting room (honesty bar), restaurant (closed Sun night–Wed lunch), in-room TV, ¼-acre courtyard garden.
BACKGROUND MUSIC: none.
LOCATION: at one end of the High Street.
CHILDREN: all ages welcomed.
DOGS: allowed in cottage rooms, not in restaurant.
CREDIT CARDS: MC, Visa.
PRICES: per room B&B £130–£220. Set dinner menu £54. 2-night min. stay preferred at weekends.

MAP 2:B4
High Street
Buckden PE19 5XA
T: 01480 812300
W: thegeorgebuckden.com

**BUCKDEN** Cambridgeshire

# THE GEORGE

In a 'quaint village', this 19th-century coaching inn carries on a tradition of hosting travellers journeying between York and London along the Great North Road. It has been owned and run by Anne and Richard Furbank for nearly 20 years. 'The hotel bustles in a calm way all day', as locals find much to please: the 'popular' family-friendly restaurant, for bar bites and heartier modern British dishes; the terrace, for alfresco meals and drinks; the owners' womenswear shop next door, for a fashionable update. Accommodation is in straightforward, rather traditional bedrooms with a 'clean, modern' bathroom, bathrobes and spoiling toiletries. At breakfast: omelettes, a pancake stack, grilled kippers; 'excellent coffee'.

BEDROOMS: 12. 3 suitable for disabled.
OPEN: all year.
FACILITIES: lift, bar, lounge, restaurant, private dining rooms, in-room TV (Freeview), civil wedding licence, courtyard.
BACKGROUND MUSIC: in public areas.
LOCATION: ¼ mile from centre.
CHILDREN: all ages welcomed.
DOGS: allowed in some public areas, not in bedrooms, only guide dogs in restaurant.
CREDIT CARDS: Amex, MC, Visa.
PRICES: per room B&B £80–£150, D,B&B £150–£210. À la carte £35.

## BUCKFASTLEIGH Devon
# KILBURY MANOR

Meadowland leads down to the River Dart from Julia and Martin Blundell's peaceful countryside B&B, in a 17th-century Devonshire longhouse within easy reach of Dartmoor national park. Lush wisteria fronts the white-painted building in season; all year round, contemporary country-style bedrooms are a comfortable place to lay your head. Choose between B&B accommodation in the main house or converted barn: each room is supplied with coffee, tea, hot chocolate, locally bottled water; all-natural toiletries. Wake to a breakfast spread including home-made preserves and compotes, then stretch your legs around the flower borders, pond and fruit trees in the grounds, or on any of the rural walks, virtually from the door.

MAP 1:D4
Colston Road
Buckfastleigh TQ11 0LN
T: 01364 644079
W: kilburymanor.co.uk

BEDROOMS: 4. 2 in converted stone barn across the courtyard, plus a 1-bed cottage.
OPEN: all year.
FACILITIES: breakfast room, in-room TV (Freeview), 4-acre grounds, courtyard, bicycle and canoe storage.
BACKGROUND MUSIC: 'gentle classical music played at low level' in breakfast room.
LOCATION: 1 mile from Buckfastleigh centre.
CHILDREN: not under 8.
DOGS: not allowed.
CREDIT CARDS: MC, Visa.
PRICES: per room B&B £75–£105. 2-night min. stay Apr–Sept.

## BURFORD Oxfordshire
# BAY TREE HOTEL

A wisteria-festooned arch frames the entry to this prettily refurbished hotel, forged from a row of 17th-century honey-hued houses. It retains its flagstone floors, ancient beams, galleried staircase and huge open fireplaces, though the 'immaculate' modern bedrooms (in an attractive mix of florals, checks, tweeds and hunting-themed fabrics) have been brought well up to date with 'good lighting' and a 'comfortable bed'. Guests with a dog should ask for one of the garden rooms, which have direct outdoor access. There are local ales, light meals and board games in the bar; in the restaurant, well-crafted modern British cuisine. Now part of the Fuller's portfolio; see also The Swan, Bibury (Shortlist entry).

MAP 3:D6
Sheep Street
Burford OX18 4LW
T: 01993 822791
W: fullers.co.uk/hotels

BEDROOMS: 21. 2 adjoining garden rooms on ground floor.
OPEN: all year.
FACILITIES: library, bar, restaurant, in-room TV (Freeview), civil wedding licence, function facilities, patio, walled garden.
BACKGROUND MUSIC: 'subtle' in public areas.
LOCATION: 5 mins' walk from Burford High Street.
CHILDREN: all ages welcomed.
DOGS: well-behaved dogs allowed in some bedrooms, public rooms except restaurant.
CREDIT CARDS: Amex, MC, Visa.
PRICES: per room B&B £139–£310, D,B&B £209–£380. À la carte £43.

**BURLEY** Hampshire

# BURLEY MANOR

Overlooking a deer park, in an open New Forest landscape, this Victorian verderer's manor house is today a restful hotel with a popular restaurant and a cosy duo of spa treatment rooms. Country-chic bedrooms range from snug to capacious; 'spacious' garden suites have a private terrace with seating, and steps leading down to the lawn and swimming pool. An 'unusual, eclectic' menu lists 'excellent' Mediterranean-inspired small and sharing plates – local beets, feta, hazelnut; sumac pork cheeks, squash, nduja. There's 'plenty of choice' at breakfast: 'a good selection of fruit and yogurts; jams in personal pots; good-quality breads'. 'Extra points, too, for adding hollandaise sauce, on request, to our poached eggs.'

MAP 2:E2
Ringwood Road
Burley BH24 4BS
T: 01425 403522
W: burleymanor.com

BEDROOMS: 40. Some in garden wing, 2 suitable for disabled.
OPEN: all year, 'house party retreats' over Christmas, New Year.
FACILITIES: drawing room, lounge/bar, 3 dining rooms (1 conservatory), conference facilities, in-room TV, civil wedding licence, treatment rooms, 8-acre grounds, heated outdoor pool (Jul–Sept), parking.
BACKGROUND MUSIC: in public rooms.
LOCATION: 7 mins' walk from Burley village.
CHILDREN: all ages welcomed at lunch, no under-13s overnight.
DOGS: allowed in most bedrooms, public rooms, not in restaurant.
CREDIT CARDS: MC, Visa.
PRICES: per room B&B £149–£334. À la carte £35. 2-night min. stay on weekends.

**BURRINGTON** Devon

# NORTHCOTE MANOR HOTEL & SPA

Deep in the Taw valley, Jean-Pierre Mifsud's wisteria-hung 18th-century manor house is a 'very comfortable' hideaway surrounded by orchards and woodlands. 'Accommodating' staff run the place to 'high standards'. There are books to borrow and 'great log stoves' by deep sofas; a modern spa has treatments for lazy days. Snug or spacious, traditional or modern, with terrace or garden views, bedrooms have 'all the necessities'. Stay in for dinner: chef Richie Herkes's tasting menu is 'unmissable'. Next day, keep an eye out for the resident roe deer in the extensive grounds. Fly fishing can be arranged. Sister hotel The Lake Country House Hotel & Spa is in Llangammarch Wells, Wales (see main entry).

MAP 1:C4
Burrington EX37 9LZ
T: 01769 560501
W: northcotemanor.co.uk

BEDROOMS: 16. 5 in extension, 1 suitable for disabled.
OPEN: all year.
FACILITIES: lounge/bar, snug, restaurant, in-room TV (Freeview), civil wedding licence, spa (steam room, sauna, hot tub, 12.5-metre swimming pool, gym, treatment rooms, lounge/café area), 20-acre grounds.
BACKGROUND MUSIC: classical in public areas after midday.
LOCATION: 3 miles S of Umberleigh.
CHILDREN: all ages welcomed, not under 9 in restaurant at dinner.
DOGS: allowed in some bedrooms, not in 1 lounge, restaurant.
CREDIT CARDS: Amex, MC, Visa.
PRICES: per room B&B £180–£290, D,B&B £270–£360. À la carte £49.50, 6-course tasting menu £65.

## BURY ST EDMUNDS Suffolk
## THE NORTHGATE

Minutes from Bury's ancient abbey, two Victorian town houses have been transformed into a glamorous spot in town. Order a cocktail from the slick, 'well-stocked' bar before tucking in to the 'ambitious' menu in the handsome restaurant. Here, sustainably sourced regional produce informs the modern dishes and seasonal small plates – perhaps confit salsify, pickled shallot, fresh truffle; Middle White pork loin, spiced apple. In fine weather, the large terrace makes 'an excellent venue'. The spacious, creamy-hued bedrooms are 'nicely furnished' with French-inspired pieces; garden-facing rooms are quietest. Part of the Chestnut group; see also The Westleton Crown, Westleton, and The Ship at Dunwich (Shortlist entries).

MAP 2:B5
Northgate Street
Bury St Edmunds IP33 1HP
T: 01284 339604
W: thenorthgate.com

BEDROOMS: 10.
OPEN: all year.
FACILITIES: bar/lounge, restaurant, private function room, in-room TV (Freeview), garden, terrace, parking.
BACKGROUND MUSIC: in public areas.
LOCATION: 6 mins' walk from town.
CHILDREN: all ages welcomed.
DOGS: allowed in 1 bedroom, in public rooms except chef's table.
CREDIT CARDS: Amex, MC, Visa.
PRICES: per room B&B £155–£295. À la carte £40.

## CAMBRIDGE Cambridgeshire
## GONVILLE HOTEL

Overlooking verdant Parker's Piece, this large, family-owned hotel is a short walk to colleges, shops and cafés. Appreciative guests like the 'delightful, helpful staff' and cheerful public spaces. Air-conditioned bedrooms range from neat 'classic' rooms to sumptuous floral-themed rooms with a seating area, some with French doors that open on to the garden. Choose to eat in the 'bright, pleasant' brasserie, or the well-regarded fine-dining restaurant, where weekly-changing dinner menus are served Tuesday to Saturday. Breakfast has an 'enormous buffet'; cooked dishes are 'as large in quantity as one would wish'. On-site parking (paid) is a bonus. Pick-ups and drop-offs in the hotel's Bentley can be pre-arranged.

MAP 2:B4
Gonville Place
Cambridge CB1 1LY
T: 01223 366611
W: gonvillehotel.co.uk

BEDROOMS: 84. Some on ground floor, some suitable for disabled, 8 in Gresham House within the grounds.
OPEN: all year.
FACILITIES: lift, bar, lounge, 2 restaurants, in-room TV (Freeview), spa beauty treatments, parking (£15 council charge), bicycles to borrow.
BACKGROUND MUSIC: in public areas, live jazz in bar on Fri, Sat evenings.
LOCATION: city centre.
CHILDREN: all ages welcomed.
DOGS: allowed in some bedrooms, reception area.
CREDIT CARDS: Amex, MC, Visa.
PRICES: per room B&B £200–£320. Set dinner (Cotto restaurant) £70–£75, à la carte (Atrium brasserie) £50.

**CARBIS BAY Cornwall**

# THE GANNET INN

In a pretty village that slopes down to the bay, this 'friendly' spot has 'the feel of a boutique hotel, with extra-special touches'. Thick armchairs cluster in comfortable groups, some by the wood-burner, in the spacious bar; in the smart dining areas, guests sit down to hearty grills, classic Cornish fare and Sunday lunches. The bedrooms are 'lovely': styled in hues inspired by sand, sea and sky, they range in size from cosy to family friendly. Some have views of spectacular seascapes. A short walk down the hill, guests may use the spa and swimming pool at sister property, Carbis Bay Hotel, before stepping on to the Blue Flag beach; here, too, is the St Ives branch line for the short train ride into town.

MAP 1:D1
St Ives Road
Carbis Bay  TR26 2SB
T: 01736 795651
W: gannetstives.co.uk

BEDROOMS: 16.
OPEN: all year.
FACILITIES: lounge/bar (darts, pool table), restaurant, in-room TV, civil wedding licence, terrace, yacht charter.
BACKGROUND MUSIC: in public areas.
LOCATION: 1 mile from St Ives.
CHILDREN: all ages welcomed.
DOGS: only assistance dogs allowed.
CREDIT CARDS: Amex, MC, Visa.
PRICES: per room B&B £180–£365.

**CHATTON Northumberland**

# CHATTON PARK HOUSE

In spring, a wealth of daffodils lines the drive to Paul and Michelle Mattinson's 'most welcoming' Georgian house, which stands in neat gardens that stretch towards a spread of Northumberland countryside. There's much to appreciate in each season, from the open fire in the leather-armchaired lounge, to the restful strolls around the grounds. Adult-only B&B accommodation is in large, garden-facing bedrooms on the first floor. Each room has thoughtful extras (tea- and coffee-making facilities, a mini-fridge, fluffy bathrobes); two have a separate lounge. Generous breakfasts, with oak-smoked local kippers and locally made jams, are ordered in advance. Castles, gardens and the coast are within reach.

MAP 4:A3
New Road
Chatton  NE66 5RA
T: 01668 215507
W: chattonpark.com

BEDROOMS: 4. Plus 2-bed self-catering lodge with private garden.
OPEN: Easter–31 Oct.
FACILITIES: sitting room, breakfast room, in-room TV (Sky, Freeview), 4-acre grounds, parking.
BACKGROUND MUSIC: none.
LOCATION: ½ mile from Chatton.
CHILDREN: not allowed.
DOGS: not allowed.
CREDIT CARDS: Amex, MC, Visa.
PRICES: per room B&B single £99–£139, double £149–£249. 1-night bookings sometimes refused.

CHELTENHAM Gloucestershire
# THE BRADLEY

Period features, paintings and objets d'art fill the de Savary family's elegant B&B, in a Georgian town house in the fashionable Montpellier district. The spacious, gracious lounge, with its sink-into-me sofas, has fresh flowers, books, newspapers and board games; there's tea and home-baked cake to be had – by the fire, when the weather calls for it – and a tipple or two from the honesty bar. Treats await in the bedrooms, too – sloe gin, nibbles, fresh milk, robes and fine toiletries. Every room is different: some are cosy and contemporary; others, rather more plush; three have a private balcony or patio. Breakfast has plenty of choice, from mixed-berry waffles to veggie sausages and a whole smoked kipper.

MAP 3:D5
19 Royal Parade Mews
Cheltenham GL50 3AY
T: 01242 519077
W: thebradleyhotel.co.uk

BEDROOMS: 10. 2 garden rooms.
OPEN: all year.
FACILITIES: lounge (honesty bar), breakfast room, conservatory, in-room TV (Freeview), small garden, parking permits (£5 per day).
BACKGROUND MUSIC: in breakfast room, lounge.
LOCATION: in the Montpellier quarter.
CHILDREN: not under 12.
DOGS: welcomed in some rooms.
CREDIT CARDS: Amex, MC, Visa.
PRICES: per room B&B £105–£400.

CHELTENHAM Gloucestershire
# BUTLERS

'Enjoyable, quirky and good value', Paul Smyth and Shaun Bailey's butler-themed B&B occupies a 19th-century gentleman's residence, 'an easy walk' to the promenade and the Montpellier district. Large, traditionally decorated bedrooms bear the name of a famous butler (Jeeves, Hudson, Brabinger, etc), and are just as gracefully turned out as their namesake: each has a hospitality tray, 'pleasing antiques', and a 'gleaming bathroom' with a powerful shower. There are books and newspapers in the lounge; the small garden is a pleasant place to sit in warm weather. Breakfast, which can be taken on the roof terrace, has a short menu of favourites: home-made oat porridge, Scotch pancakes, smoked salmon, eggs any way.

**25% DISCOUNT VOUCHERS**

MAP 3:D5
Western Road
Cheltenham GL50 3RN
T: 01242 570771
W: butlers-hotel.co.uk

BEDROOMS: 8.
OPEN: all year except Christmas.
FACILITIES: drawing room, breakfast room, in-room TV (Freeview), roof terrace, ¼-acre garden, parking.
BACKGROUND MUSIC: quiet radio in the morning.
LOCATION: 15 mins' stroll to the promenade or Montpellier.
CHILDREN: not under 9.
DOGS: not allowed.
CREDIT CARDS: MC, Visa.
PRICES: per room B&B single £60–£75, double £85–£120. 2-night min. stay during weekends and festivals.

**NEW**

CHELTENHAM Gloucestershire

# COTSWOLD GRANGE HOTEL

Between town and racecourse, Nirav and Dhruti Sheth's conveniently situated hotel is in a fine stone mansion in leafy Pittville. Built in the 1830s, the building retains its original high ceilings, cantilevered staircase and decorative mouldings. Individually decorated bedrooms range from home-away-from-home (with pretty prints and cushions) to wholly dramatic (with a carved-wood four-poster bed). Supplied with tea- and coffee-making facilities, they vary in size; some have space to accommodate a family of three. The bijou bar is a stylish spot for a drink; in good weather, sit and sip on the terrace bordered by pleached ornamental pear trees. The shops, restaurants and cafés in town are a 15-minute walk away.

MAP 3:D5
Pittville Circus Road
Cheltenham  GL52 2QH
T: 01242 515119
W: cotswoldgrangehotel.co.uk

BEDROOMS: 20.
OPEN: all year except Christmas.
FACILITIES: bar, breakfast room, in-room TV (Freeview), terrace, front and rear gardens.
BACKGROUND MUSIC: in bar, breakfast room.
LOCATION: in Pittville.
CHILDREN: all ages welcomed.
DOGS: in some bedrooms, bar.
CREDIT CARDS: Amex, MC, Visa.
PRICES: per room B&B single £70–£125, double £80–£250. 1-night bookings refused May–Oct.

CHELTENHAM Gloucestershire

# NO. 131

Across from Imperial Gardens, this trio of well-restored Georgian town houses forms an alluring whole: one modish, metropolitan hotel with a smart restaurant, two lively bars and a collection of very-voguish bedrooms. Recent refurbishment and expansion has brought The House and King's House, on either side of the original villa, into the fold; from capacious family suites to snug hideaways, each cool, contemporary room has its own character. In public spaces hung with striking artworks from the likes of David Hockney, Banksy and Peter Blake, partake in all-day brunches, small- or large-plate lunches, dinners early or late; inspired cocktails and some 400 gins make fine accompaniment. Part of The Lucky Onion group (see also next entry).

MAP 3:D5
131 Promenade
Cheltenham  GL50 1NW
T: 01242 822939
W: no131.com

BEDROOMS: 36. 11 in No. 131, 8 in The House, 17 in King's House.
OPEN: all year.
FACILITIES: drawing room, lounge, 2 bars, snug, restaurant, private dining rooms, cheese and wine room, games room, in-room TV (Freeview), 3 terraces, parking.
BACKGROUND MUSIC: all day in public areas.
LOCATION: in the Montpellier district, close to the town centre.
CHILDREN: all ages welcomed.
DOGS: allowed on terraces only.
CREDIT CARDS: Amex, MC, Visa.
PRICES: per room B&B from £120. À la carte £35.

CHELTENHAM Gloucestershire

## NO. 38 THE PARK

Easy-going cool seeps through this Georgian town house in a leafy corner of Pittville, close to Cheltenham Racecourse. Repurposed furniture, modern lighting and original artworks lend the public spaces character. Warmed by a log fire when the temperature dips, the lounge has deep sofas made for curling up in with a drink and a biscuit from the help-yourself cookie jar. Smartly styled bedrooms (some snug) set their own tone, with a claw-footed bath here, or an original fireplace there. All rooms have a king-size bed, decent robes, good toiletries and a capsule coffee machine. Large-choice breakfasts include porridge with honeycomb, or avocado and poached eggs on sourdough toast. Part of The Lucky Onion group (see also previous entry).

MAP 3:D5
38 Evesham Road
Cheltenham GL52 2AH
T: 01242 822929
W: no38thepark.com

BEDROOMS: 13. 1, on ground floor, suitable for disabled.
OPEN: all year.
FACILITIES: sitting room, open-plan kitchen/restaurant, private dining room, in-room Apple TV (Sky), small courtyard garden, limited parking.
BACKGROUND MUSIC: all day in public areas.
LOCATION: 10 mins' walk from town centre.
CHILDREN: all ages welcomed, not in restaurant.
DOGS: allowed in bedrooms, public rooms except restaurant.
CREDIT CARDS: Amex, MC, Visa.
PRICES: per room B&B £130–£295. 1-night bookings sometimes refused weekends in high season.

CHESTER Cheshire

## THE CHESTER GROSVENOR

Grand from every direction, this 'very smart' Grade II listed hotel is in a 'central location that can hardly be bettered if you're keen to be in the thick of things'. 'The service is second to none,' say trusted readers this year, 'and charming staff greet you wherever you meet them.' 'Exceptionally comfortable, very quiet' bedrooms – some modern, some more traditional – have 'a comfy bed, proper seating and excellent lighting'; 'every amenity' is provided ('but why not complimentary bottled water?'). Informal brunches, lunches and dinners are served in the 'likeable', light-filled brasserie; in chef Simon Radley's Michelin-starred restaurant, modern à la carte and tasting menus are very fine indeed.

MAP 3:A4
Eastgate
Chester CH1 1LT
T: 01244 324024
W: chestergrosvenor.com

BEDROOMS: 79. 1 suitable for disabled.
OPEN: all year except 24/25 Dec.
FACILITIES: lift, drawing room, lounge, bar, brasserie, restaurant, meeting/private dining rooms, in-room TV (Sky, Freeview), civil wedding licence, function facilities, spa, 'convenient' parking.
BACKGROUND MUSIC: in public areas.
LOCATION: in city centre.
CHILDREN: all ages welcomed, not under 12 in bar and restaurant.
DOGS: not allowed.
CREDIT CARDS: Amex, MC, Visa.
PRICES: per room B&B from £155. Tasting menu (restaurant) £69 or £99, à la carte (brasserie) £45.

**CHESTER** Cheshire

# ODDFELLOWS

A sense of fun persists at this 'great, quirky' hotel in the centre, which was once the meeting place for a society of misfits and artists – the Odd Fellows in question. Typewriters chase up the walls of the neoclassical building in places, while wickerwork hares prepare for a boxing match; a colourful zaniness spills through the public spaces and out to the AstroTurfed terrace, popular with lively gatherings and weddings. Bedrooms in the main house and a modern annexe are just as comfortably eccentric, perhaps with a circular bed, or twin roll-top baths under the eaves. Imaginative, uncomplicated dishes are served throughout the day in the restaurant, the 'secret garden' and the flamboyant lounge bar.

MAP 3:A4
20 Lower Bridge Street
Chester CH1 1RS
T: 01244 345454
w: oddfellowschester.com

BEDROOMS: 18. 14 in annexe, 1 suitable for disabled, plus self-catering apartments nearby.
OPEN: all year except Christmas Day.
FACILITIES: bar, lobby, restaurant, private dining room, in-room TV, civil wedding licence, terrace, garden.
BACKGROUND MUSIC: in public spaces.
LOCATION: in city centre.
CHILDREN: all ages welcomed.
DOGS: not allowed.
CREDIT CARDS: Amex, MC, Visa.
PRICES: per room B&B £130–£299. À la carte £34.

**CHICHESTER** Sussex

# CHICHESTER HARBOUR HOTEL & SPA

Bright modern artworks and cheery design fill this contemporary hotel, in a freshly refurbished Grade II* listed building within the city's Roman walls. In the public areas, original features such as a grand staircase, marble fireplaces and huge sash windows have been finely restored; colourful, individually styled bedrooms retain leafy or cathedral views. Take pre-dinner drinks in the Art Deco bar before pulling up a seat in the new Ship restaurant for chef Alex Aitken's local-produce-packed brasserie dishes (grilled south-coast-landed fish; New Forest mushroom risotto). The subterranean spa has a hydrotherapy pool, gym, steam room and treatments; for days out, the hotel can arrange picnics and bicycle hires.

MAP 2:E3
North Street
Chichester PO19 1NH
T: 01243 778000
w: harbourhotels.co.uk/chichester

BEDROOMS: 36. Plus 1-bedroom cottage.
OPEN: all year.
FACILITIES: bar, restaurant, orangery, private dining room, in-room TV, civil wedding licence, business facilities, spa, gym, terrace, limited parking, restaurant wheelchair accessible.
BACKGROUND MUSIC: in public areas.
LOCATION: within the city walls.
CHILDREN: all ages welcomed.
DOGS: assistance dogs allowed.
CREDIT CARDS: Amex, MC, Visa.
PRICES: per room B&B from £155, D,B&B from £205. Set dinner £12.75, à la carte £30. 2-night min. stay at peak times and public holidays.

CHIDDINGFOLD Surrey

# THE CROWN INN

On the corner of the village green, this 'lovely' country inn has been extending a hospitable welcome to pilgrims and travellers for centuries. Constructed in 1441, the timber-framed building is full of 'traditional character'. Local tipples are served in the popular bar amid medieval carvings, 'massive beams', stained-glass windows and inglenook fireplaces; in the oak-panelled restaurant, traditional fare is attentively served. Well-appointed bedrooms, all sloping floors and antique furnishings, have chic toiletries and a digital radio; across the courtyard, two rooms open on to a private garden. Breakfast, served till 11 am on the weekend, has good cooked choices and a buffet of morning-baked pastries.

MAP 2:D3
The Green
Chiddingfold GU8 4TX
T: 01428 682255
W: thecrownchiddingfold.com

BEDROOMS: 8.
OPEN: all year.
FACILITIES: bar, snug, restaurant, in-room TV (Sky, Freeview), private dining, 2 small courtyard gardens, large terrace, parking, public rooms wheelchair accessible.
BACKGROUND MUSIC: in public spaces.
LOCATION: 20 mins from Guildford.
CHILDREN: all ages welcomed.
DOGS: allowed in bar and lounge, not in bedrooms.
CREDIT CARDS: Amex, MC, Visa.
PRICES: per room B&B £130–£220. À la carte £28.

CHURCH STRETTON Shropshire

# VICTORIA HOUSE

Diane Chadwick is the 'wonderfully energetic, helpful' hostess at this 'splendid' town-centre B&B within walking distance of the Shropshire hills. The Victorian town house has 'well-priced, convenient' accommodation in 'comfortable' bedrooms, each 'tastefully decorated' with artworks and antique pieces that lend much character. Guests appreciate the hostess's generous touch and eye for detail: each bedroom is supplied with bathrobes and toiletries, teas, coffee, hot chocolate, sherry and biscuits. Light lunches and sweet treats may be taken in the cosy, on-site café, Jemima's Kitchen. Served in a garden-facing room, breakfast, with freshly baked pastries and sausages from locally reared pigs, is 'superb'.

**25% DISCOUNT VOUCHERS**

MAP 3:C4
48 High Street
Church Stretton SY6 6BX
T: 01694 723823
W: victoriahouse-shropshire.co.uk

BEDROOMS: 6.
OPEN: all year.
FACILITIES: seating area, breakfast room, café/tea room (open 9.30 am to 4 pm Tues–Sun), in-room TV (Freeview), walled garden, pay-and-display parking (deducted from hotel bill or permits supplied).
BACKGROUND MUSIC: in breakfast room and café.
LOCATION: in town centre.
CHILDREN: all ages welcomed.
DOGS: allowed in some bedrooms, café.
CREDIT CARDS: Amex, MC, Visa.
PRICES: per room B&B single £66–£84, double £87–£104. 1-night bookings refused bank holiday weekends.

COLERNE Wiltshire

# LUCKNAM PARK

Approach this 18th-century mansion, exulting in 500 acres of parkland and gardens, down a mile-long avenue of lime and beech trees: what awaits is 'very grand and lovely'. There are an arboretum and a rose garden to wander through; trails to explore, on horseback if desired; cookery classes for all tastes. In a walled garden, the award-winning spa has swimming pools and treatments galore. Young visitors aren't neglected: they have sports and pony rides, indoor and outdoor play areas. At mealtimes, choose between chef Hywel Jones's Michelin-starred fine dining restaurant and the informal modern brasserie. Then rest up for another day, in one of the elegant bedrooms – they range in size from snug to spacious.

MAP 2:D1
Colerne  SN14 8AZ
T: 01225 742777
W: lucknampark.co.uk

BEDROOMS: 43. Some in courtyard, 1 suitable for disabled, plus a 3-bed and a 4-bed cottage.
OPEN: all year, restaurant closed Mon, Tues.
FACILITIES: drawing room, library, restaurant, brasserie, in-room TV, civil wedding licence, spa, indoor pools, outdoor hydrotherapy and saltwater plunge pools, terrace, tennis, croquet, football pitch, equestrian centre, 5-acre grounds within 500 acres of parkland.
BACKGROUND MUSIC: in public areas.
LOCATION: 7 miles W of Chippenham.
CHILDREN: all ages welcomed.
DOGS: allowed in 4 bedrooms, part of brasserie.
CREDIT CARDS: Amex, MC, Visa.
PRICES: per room B&B £414–£1,714, D,B&B £588–£1,888. 2-night min. stay at weekends.

CORNWORTHY Devon

# KERSWELL FARMHOUSE

Named after the wells and cress beds fed by nearby springs, Nichola and Graham Hawkins's B&B is enfolded by their small working farm. The well-renovated 400-year-old longhouse is decorated with antiques, contemporary artwork and farmhouse furnishings; freshly cut flowers are a charming touch. The old milking parlour, as well as housing the honesty bar, exhibits the work of contemporary ceramicists, glassmakers, painters and photographers. Spacious bedrooms have a wide bed and all the essentials, plus thoughtful extras: teas and ground coffee, fluffy bathrobes, novels and magazines. Farm-fresh breakfasts include eggs Benedict or Royale, and a full Devon with bacon and sausages from home-reared pigs.

MAP 1:D4
Cornworthy  TQ9 7HH
T: 01803 732013
W: kerswellfarmhouse.co.uk

BEDROOMS: 5. 2 in adjacent barns, 1 on ground floor.
OPEN: Mar–mid-Dec.
FACILITIES: sitting room, 2 dining rooms, art gallery, in-room TV (Freeview), 14-acre grounds, parking.
BACKGROUND MUSIC: none.
LOCATION: 4 miles S of Totnes, 4 miles N of Dartmouth.
CHILDREN: not under 12.
DOGS: not allowed.
CREDIT CARDS: none accepted.
PRICES: per room B&B single £90–£125, double £120–£160. 2-night min. stay Apr–end Sept, unless a single night becomes available.

## CORSHAM Wiltshire

# THE METHUEN ARMS

Handsome and historic, this buzzy pub-with-rooms has character to spare. It is owned by the Butcombe Brewery. The conscientiously restored Georgian coaching inn, down the High Street from Corsham Court of Poldark fame, has a voguish appeal, with tweed cushions, heritage hues, and botanical prints above plush sofas; tables are set up for alfresco eating in good weather. Chef Leigh Evans's cooking is acclaimed for good reason: here, garden produce is harvested for such dishes as roasted hake, garlic spinach, vegetable bhaji; beetroot risotto. Some of the spacious, recently refurbished bedrooms can accommodate a family. At breakfast, fresh pastries, home-made granola, fruit and compotes accompany interesting cooked options.

MAP 2:D1
2 High Street
Corsham SN13 0HB
T: 01249 717060
W: themethuenarms.com

BEDROOMS: 19. 5 in annexe, some on ground floor.
OPEN: all year, restaurant closed Sun evening from 6 pm.
FACILITIES: bar, restaurant, private dining rooms, in-room TV (Freeview), garden, courtyard, parking, bar and restaurant wheelchair accessible.
BACKGROUND MUSIC: in bar, dining areas.
LOCATION: 8 miles NE of Bath.
CHILDREN: all ages welcomed.
DOGS: allowed in 7 bedrooms, bars, casual dining area, courtyard.
CREDIT CARDS: Amex, MC, Visa.
PRICES: per room B&B £120–£220. À la carte £35.

## COVENTRY Warwickshire

# BARNACLE HALL

A tranquil haven with a 'warm welcome' lies beyond the old oak door of Rose Grindal's 'charming' 16th-century farmhouse. Three miles from the M6, a 20-minute drive from Coventry, it feels a world away from both. The house has low doorways, characterful beams, nooks and crannies, the whole standing within lush gardens swaddled by surrounding fields. Steps of varying heights betray its age, but the spacious, traditionally decorated bedrooms have all the modern essentials: a flat-screen TV, a radio alarm, individually controlled central heating. They also come with a generous hospitality tray and fresh flowers. Breakfast caters for all, with fresh fruit and cereal, as well as hot dishes cooked to order.

MAP 3:C6
Shilton Lane
Coventry CV7 9LH
T: 02476 612629
W: barnaclehall.co.uk

BEDROOMS: 3.
OPEN: all year except Christmas, New Year.
FACILITIES: sitting room, dining room, in-room TV (Freeview), patio, garden.
BACKGROUND MUSIC: none.
LOCATION: 7 miles NE of Coventry, SE of Nuneaton.
CHILDREN: all ages welcomed.
DOGS: assistance dogs allowed.
CREDIT CARDS: none accepted.
PRICES: per room B&B single £50–£60, double £75–£85.

COVENTRY Warwickshire
## COOMBE ABBEY

Its past as a 12th-century Cistercian abbey bestows 'character, eccentricity and individuality at its best' on this atmospheric hotel, which stands amid a 'well-maintained' country park and 'superb' formal gardens. 'I felt as if I were on a movie set,' one reader reported in 2020. The building's grand interiors include a carved stone pulpit, and a series of confessional booths in the high-vaulted lobby. Gloriously furnished 'bed chambers' may have a canopy bed; well-designed bathrooms (perhaps hidden behind a bookcase) sport a Victorian bath or a richly tiled shower. Sweet and savoury afternoon teas and classic menus are served in the conservatory restaurant, where candles are lit at night. A popular events venue.

MAP 3:C6
Brinklow Road
Coventry CV3 2AB
T: 02476 450450
W: coombeabbey.com

BEDROOMS: 121. 16 on ground floor, 1 suitable for disabled.
OPEN: all year.
FACILITIES: lift, bar, restaurant, private dining rooms, in-room TV, wedding/conference facilities, terrace, 500-acre grounds (gardens, parkland, historic woodland), parking (£5 per day).
BACKGROUND MUSIC: in public spaces.
LOCATION: 5 miles from city centre, in Coombe Country Park.
CHILDREN: all ages welcomed.
DOGS: not allowed.
CREDIT CARDS: Amex, MC, Visa.
PRICES: per room B&B £89–£289, D,B&B from £154. À la carte £48.

CRAYKE Yorkshire
## THE DURHAM OX

For centuries, this 'friendly, well-run' village pub-with-rooms has hosted visitors following an ancient Celtic trail to York. Today, with owners Michael and Sasha Ibbotson at the helm, a 'personal but unfussy touch' ensures guests, and their dogs, continue to feel taken care of. In the busy dining areas, stone flags, wood panelling and inglenook fireplaces provide a 'delightfully decorated' backdrop to the 'excellent', 'carefully prepared' food. Most of the neat bedrooms are in stone-built farm cottages behind the pub. 'Reading was easy in our comfy, well-lit room. Excellent coffee, too.' On clear days, soak in the 'superb' views over the Vale of York. Maps are available to borrow, for gentle strolls and serious hikes alike.

MAP 4:D4
Westway
Crayke YO61 4TE
T: 01347 821506
W: thedurhamox.com

BEDROOMS: 6. 5 in converted farm cottages, 3 on ground floor, 1 suite accessed via external stairs. Plus 3-bed self-catering cottage in village.
OPEN: all year.
FACILITIES: 3 bars, restaurant, private dining room, in-room TV (Freeview), function facilities, 2-acre grounds, parking.
BACKGROUND MUSIC: in pub and restaurant.
LOCATION: 3 miles E of Easingwold town centre.
CHILDREN: all ages welcomed.
DOGS: allowed in public areas, most bedrooms.
CREDIT CARDS: Amex, MC, Visa.
PRICES: per room B&B single £100–£150, double £120–£150, D,B&B £180–£205. À la carte £35.

DARTMOUTH Devon

# STRETE BARTON HOUSE

'The warmth of the welcome' inspired guests to write to us this year about Stuart Litster and Kevin Hooper's 'superbly decorated' B&B, in a village on the South West Coast Path. Large sofas in the lounge of the Jacobean manor house allow space to enjoy the hosts' good cheer and home-baked cake, while marvelling at the views across Start Bay. Contemporary bedrooms have 'pristine bedding', fresh flowers, biscuits and a beverage tray; 'windows open to let in sea air and birdsong'. 'Comprehensive' breakfasts include fresh fruit, local yogurts and 'beautifully cooked and presented' hot dishes. The pine-fringed bay around Blackpool Sands, 20 minutes' walk away, is an area of outstanding natural beauty.

MAP 1:D4
Totnes Road
Dartmouth  TQ6 0RU
T: 01803 770364
W: stretebarton.co.uk

BEDROOMS: 6. 1 in cottage annexe.
OPEN: Feb–Oct.
FACILITIES: sitting room, breakfast room, library, in-room TV (Freeview), ⅓-acre garden.
BACKGROUND MUSIC: none.
LOCATION: 5 miles W of Dartmouth.
CHILDREN: not under 8.
DOGS: allowed in cottage suite.
CREDIT CARDS: Amex, MC, Visa.
PRICES: per room B&B £105–£175. 1-night bookings sometimes refused in high season.

DELPH Lancashire

# THE OLD BELL INN

'Quite an appearance.' An illuminated display of gin bottles on glass shelves greets visitors to Philip Whiteman's 'well-kept, traditional' inn, in a scenic village outside Manchester. The Gin Emporium, a Guinness World Record breaker, has over 1,100 types. The 18th-century coaching house also shelters a busy bar ('all polished brass, shiny bottles, hard-working staff'), an informal brasserie serving 'excellent meals', and a cosy restaurant that's popular for its imaginative menus. 'Clean, workaday bedrooms' are well equipped (quieter ones are at the rear). To escape the throng, overnight guests may use a first-floor conservatory lounge. At breakfast: pastries, freshly squeezed orange juice, hearty cooked options.

MAP 4:E3
Huddersfield Road
Delph  OL3 5EG
T: 01457 870130
W: theoldbellinn.co.uk

BEDROOMS: 18. 4 in extension.
OPEN: all year.
FACILITIES: bar, lounge, brasserie, restaurant, in-room TV (Freeview), function facilities, terrace, parking, restaurant wheelchair accessible.
BACKGROUND MUSIC: in public areas.
LOCATION: 5 miles from Oldham.
CHILDREN: all ages welcomed.
DOGS: not allowed.
CREDIT CARDS: Amex, MC, Visa.
PRICES: per room B&B single £75–£85, double £120–£150. À la carte £32.

DIDMARTON Gloucestershire

## THE KING'S ARMS

Embracing its rural roots, this traditional inn cosies up deep in the Cotswold countryside. Hunker down in the heritage-hued pub: there are old photos on the walls and candlesticks on tables; a log fire is lit when the temperature dips. In the main building and renovated stables, cottage-style bedrooms (think equestrian paintings and sheepskin rugs) are named after prize-winning hounds from the local hunt. Doggy guests receive a bed and a bottle of dog beer; their human companions have tea, coffee, biscuits and eco-friendly toiletries. British dishes in the restaurant feature game sourced from neighbouring estates, plus daily blackboard specials. In summer, pizzas are cooked in a wood-fired oven in the garden.

MAP 3:E5
The Street
Didmarton GL9 1DT
T: 01454 238245
w: kingsarmsdidmarton.co.uk

BEDROOMS: 6. Plus 2 self-catering cottages.
OPEN: all year.
FACILITIES: 2 bars, restaurant, private dining room, garden (boules), main pub and restaurant wheelchair accessible.
BACKGROUND MUSIC: in pub.
LOCATION: in village.
CHILDREN: all ages welcomed.
DOGS: allowed in bedrooms, public areas.
CREDIT CARDS: MC, Visa.
PRICES: per room B&B from £127.50. À la carte £33.

DODDINGTON Kent

## THE OLD VICARAGE

On the edge of a Kent Downs village, Claire Finley's elegant Georgian B&B stands in well-maintained gardens with views over rolling countryside. The Grade II listed house retains period features dating back to 1656 while maintaining a modern country-house aesthetic, with squashy sofas, original art, statement flower arrangements and the occasional antique. Large suites overlook the garden or 11th-century churchyard next door. One has a roll-top bath; another, a living room with an open fire. Served in a bright, airy room, traditional English breakfasts use locally sourced produce. The hostess has a heap of eating places to recommend, from good country pubs to Michelin-approved eateries nearby.

MAP 2:D5
Church Hill
Doddington ME9 0BD
T: 01795 886136
w: oldvicaragedoddington.co.uk

BEDROOMS: 5. All suites, 2 in adjacent cottage.
OPEN: all year except 22 Dec–5 Jan.
FACILITIES: entrance hall, drawing room, breakfast room, in-room TV, ¼-acre garden.
BACKGROUND MUSIC: none.
LOCATION: on the edge of the village, 6 miles from Sittingbourne railway station.
CHILDREN: not under 3.
DOGS: allowed in coach house.
CREDIT CARDS: MC, Visa.
PRICES: per room B&B single £75–£120, double £105–£140.

DODDISCOMBSLEIGH Devon

## THE NOBODY INN

Down narrow, winding country lanes, Sue Burdge's inn is so much the model of an olde-worlde Devon pub that it 'could have been created by a set designer'. There's a 'good, welcoming ambience' in the 'beguiling' bar, with beams, brasses and blazing log-burner, the counter 'stacked with bottles and barrels of every kind of drink imaginable'. The building's age results in a range of bedroom sizes, from very small (four-foot bed, separate bathroom) to reasonably spacious, with 'a big, comfortable bed'. A decanter of sherry is a nice touch. Off the varied menu, in the restaurant: steak and ale pie or something more ambitious, perhaps venison roll, beetroot fondant, hassleback potatoes, juniper jus.

MAP 1:C4
Doddiscombsleigh EX6 7PS
T: 01647 252394
W: nobodyinn.co.uk

BEDROOMS: 5.
OPEN: all year except 25 Dec (open for lunchtime drinks), restaurant closed Sun, Mon, but bar menu available.
FACILITIES: 2 bars, restaurant, free Wi-Fi ('improving but may be patchy'), in-room TV (Freeview), garden, patio, parking, dining room wheelchair accessible, no adapted toilet.
BACKGROUND MUSIC: none.
LOCATION: in village, 8 miles SW of Exeter.
CHILDREN: not under 5.
DOGS: allowed, on lead, in bar only.
CREDIT CARDS: MC, Visa.
PRICES: per room B&B single £59–£90, double £79–£110, D,B&B single £79–£105, double £110–£140.
À la carte £32.

**NEW**

DOVER Kent

## THE WHITE CLIFFS HOTEL

In a tranquil village on St Margaret's Bay, there's 'a very sincere welcome' and 'good community spirit' to be had at Gavin Oakley's 'comfortable, quietly efficient' hotel. The clutch of classically Kentish timber-clad buildings houses 'warm, spotless' bedrooms in all shapes and sizes, from 'tiny' boltholes to family apartments. Simple and homely, they're 'just right, with everything we needed', say readers this year: crisp cotton linens, soft wool furnishings and natural bath products, plus tea and coffee from local producers. In the laid-back bar and restaurant, a short, seasonal menu includes fish and shellfish straight off the boats, and meat and vegetables from local farms; sourdough pizzas, too, in the summertime.

**25% DISCOUNT VOUCHERS**

MAP 2:D5
High Street
Dover CT15 6AT
T: 01304 852229
W: thewhitecliffs.com

BEDROOMS: 18. 9 in surrounding buildings, 2 apartments in mews cottages, 1 suitable for disabled.
OPEN: all year.
FACILITIES: bar, lounge, dining room, in-room TV (Freeview), parking, bar and dining room wheelchair accessible.
BACKGROUND MUSIC: in bar, occasionally.
LOCATION: 10 mins' drive from port of Dover.
CHILDREN: all ages welcomed.
DOGS: allowed.
CREDIT CARDS: Amex, MC, Visa.
PRICES: per room B&B single £90–£150, double £130–£190. À la carte £30.

DUNWICH Suffolk

## THE SHIP AT DUNWICH

'Unpretentious and friendly', this creeper-covered
inn is close to the unspoiled salt marshes of
Dunwich Heath and the RSPB reserves at Dingle
Marshes and Minsmere. Once a smugglers' haunt,
the red-brick building has a nautical-themed
bar and three neat, rustic dining areas, where
the daily-changing specials often include freshly
caught oysters, lobster or crab. An ancient fig tree
and an old fishing boat watch over the sheltered
courtyard and beer garden. The bedrooms, some
snug, have a simple country charm. The best
have expansive marsh views; some, in converted
outbuildings, are 'perfect for dogs'. Part of the
Chestnut group; see also The Northgate, Bury
St Edmunds, and The Westleton Crown,
Westleton (Shortlist entries).

MAP 2:B6
St James Street
Dunwich  IP17 3DT
T:  01728 648219
W:  shipatdunwich.co.uk

BEDROOMS: 16. 4 on ground floor
in converted stables, 1 suitable for
disabled.
OPEN: all year.
FACILITIES: bar, restaurant (3 dining
areas), in-room TV (Freeview, smart
TV in family rooms), courtyard, large
beer garden.
BACKGROUND MUSIC: none.
LOCATION: a few hundred yards from
Dunwich beach.
CHILDREN: all ages welcomed.
DOGS: warmly welcomed inside and
out.
CREDIT CARDS: MC, Visa.
PRICES: per room B&B £95–£165,
D,B&B £125–£195. À la carte £25–£30.
2-night min. stay at weekends in
peak season.

DURHAM Co. Durham

## FORTY WINKS GUEST HOUSE
## & RESIDENCE

'A treasure trove', Debbie and Nigel Gadd's
theatrically decorated, four-storey Edwardian
house is in 'a great situation', on a quiet cobbled
street, a short walk from the town centre. The
'up-to-date' bedrooms, in calming, serene hues,
have organic teas, a coffee machine, 'excellent
lighting', and 'instant hot water' in the bathroom.
Rooms at the front gaze across woods to the
Norman castle; take in churchyard views at the
back. 'Our beautiful, well-equipped first-floor
suite had splendid cathedral views.' NOTE: As
the Guide went to press, Forty Winks announced
that it was closing.

### 25% DISCOUNT VOUCHERS

MAP 4:B4
40 South Street
Durham  DH1 4QP
T:  0191 386 8217
W:  fortywinksdurham.co.uk

BEDROOMS: 8.
OPEN: all year except 24–27 Dec.
FACILITIES: dining room, study,
in-room TV (Freeview), courtyard,
public parking (charge).
BACKGROUND MUSIC: classical music at
breakfast.
LOCATION: a short walk from the city
centre.
CHILDREN: not under 16.
DOGS: not allowed.
CREDIT CARDS: Amex, MC, Visa.
PRICES: per room B&B £110–£195.

## EAST WITTON Yorkshire

## THE BLUE LION

Offering an 'utterly authentic' slice of rural Wensleydale hospitality, Paul and Helen Klein have been running their 'sophisticated' 18th-century inn for 30 years. The former coaching house is liked for its 'good atmosphere': there are log fires, settles, 'pleasant, knowledgeable staff', and many locals (whose dogs get a bowl of water) enjoying hand-pumped ales. In the bar and candlelit restaurant, 'well-executed comfort food' might include cassoulet of Yorkshire duck confit, Morteau sausage, roasted tomato and white beans, served with sourdough and sauerkraut. Country-style bedrooms, 'spotlessly clean and comfortable', occupy the main building and converted outbuildings. Breakfast sees you through to lunch.

MAP 4:C4
Main Road
East Witton DL8 4SN
T: 01969 624273
w: thebluelion.co.uk

BEDROOMS: 15. 9 in courtyard annexe.
OPEN: all year.
FACILITIES: 2 bars, 2 dining areas, private dining room, in-room TV (Freeview), 1-acre garden, parking, restaurant, bar wheelchair accessible.
BACKGROUND MUSIC: none.
LOCATION: in village, 4½ miles from Leyburn.
CHILDREN: all ages welcomed.
DOGS: allowed in bar, garden, some bedrooms.
CREDIT CARDS: MC, Visa.
PRICES: per room B&B £99–£155, D,B&B £145–£195. À la carte £43.95. 1-night bookings occasionally refused Sat nights.

## EASTBOURNE Sussex

## THE GRAND HOTEL

'Like an ocean liner', this great, white Victorian edifice gazes over the water from the seafront of the resort town. 'All is glamorous' inside the grand hotel (Elite Hotels): there are 'spacious public rooms, long corridors with patterned carpets, lofty ceilings and arched windows'. Throughout, too, 'such kind staff' and a family-friendly feel – 'how nice to see children'. Traditionally styled bedrooms and suites have towelling robes, an espresso machine, high-end toiletries, 24-hour room service. 'Our first morning, breakfast was brought on a trolley with fold-out flaps – very civilised.' There's tea to be had in the great hall or on the terrace; two restaurants to choose from at lunch and dinner. Breakfast is 'excellent'.

MAP 2:E4
King Edwards Parade
Eastbourne BN21 4EQ
T: 01323 412345
w: grandeastbourne.com

BEDROOMS: 152. 1 suitable for disabled.
OPEN: all year, Mirabelle closed Sun, Mon, first 2 weeks Jan.
FACILITIES: lifts, 5 lounges, bar, 2 restaurants, function facilities, in-room TV (BT, Freeview), civil wedding licence, large terrace, spa/health club (indoor and outdoor pools), 2-acre garden, public areas wheelchair accessible.
BACKGROUND MUSIC: in lounges, live music at weekends.
LOCATION: on the seafront, outside the centre.
CHILDREN: all ages welcomed.
DOGS: allowed in bedrooms.
CREDIT CARDS: Amex, MC, Visa.
PRICES: per room B&B single £120–£690, double £150–£694. Set dinner £46 (Mirabelle), £42 (Garden).

## EDENBRIDGE Kent
# HEVER CASTLE B&B

The comforts are fit for a queen at this sumptuous B&B, in the Tudor-style Edwardian wings of double-moated 13th-century Hever Castle. The childhood home of ill-fated Anne Boleyn stands in a spread of award-winning gardens; bedrooms are in the richly decorated Aster and Anne Boleyn wings, where moulded ceilings, grand chimney pieces and rich tapestries heighten the grandeur. Every room is different: choose one with a gold chaise longue, or one with a four-poster bed; all are supplied with tea- and coffee-making facilities, and spoiling toiletries in a bathroom of limestone or marble. Breakfast, a lavish affair, is served in each wing's own dining room. Residents have free access to the castle and grounds.

MAP 2:D4
Edenbridge TN8 7NG
T: 01732 861800
W: www.hevercastle.co.uk

BEDROOMS: 28. Some on ground floor, some suitable for disabled, plus self-catering Medley Court cottage.
OPEN: all year except 25 and 31 Dec.
FACILITIES: lounge, billiard room, in-room TV (Sky, Freeview), civil wedding licence, courtyard garden, tennis court, 625-acre grounds, parking.
BACKGROUND MUSIC: none.
LOCATION: 1½ miles from Hever station.
CHILDREN: all ages welcomed.
DOGS: not allowed.
CREDIT CARDS: Amex, MC, Visa.
PRICES: per room B&B £180–£335. 'Dine and stay' events on selected dates throughout the year.

## EDINGTON Wiltshire
# THE THREE DAGGERS

Red brick on the outside, country cool and craft-beery on the inside, this 'impressive' pub-with-rooms serves as a village hub – and then some. The enterprise consists of a lively restaurant, a buzzy, award-winning microbrewery, a well-stocked deli/farm shop, a hillside spa barn, and a clutch of 'splendid' bedrooms to fall in to at the end of the day. Through it all, the staff are 'warm, engaging and fuss-free'. Choose among rooms newly refurbished in 2020, each supplied with fresh flowers, natural toiletries, and fluffy towels warmed on towel rails. For extra lounging about, a comfy residents' lounge has a generous stash of drinks and snacks. Need a pair of wellies for a walk? They're there to borrow, too.

MAP 2:D1
47 Westbury Road
Edington BA13 4PG
T: 01380 830940
W: threedaggers.co.uk

BEDROOMS: 3.
OPEN: all year.
FACILITIES: residents' living room/kitchen, bar, dining area, private dining room, in-room TV (Freeview), civil wedding licence, garden (direct access to village park), spa barn, microbrewery, farm shop.
BACKGROUND MUSIC: in the pub.
LOCATION: 10 mins' drive from Westbury.
CHILDREN: all ages welcomed.
DOGS: allowed in bedrooms, public rooms.
CREDIT CARDS: Amex, MC, Visa.
PRICES: per room B&B £120–£160. À la carte £40.

EGHAM Surrey

# THE RUNNYMEDE ON THAMES HOTEL AND SPA

An idyllic spot for messing about in boats, this Thames-side hotel and spa is 'so very relaxing'. The 1970s building is enlivened with quirky touches: retro decor, oversized deckchairs, toy ducks in the lounge. Clean-cut bedrooms in a variety of sizes have 'every amenity'; those facing the river take in 'spectacular' views. Quieter rooms are away from the road. Choose to eat buffet-style overlooking the water, or à la carte in the airy Lock Bar & Kitchen – a riverside terrace is open for alfresco eating in good weather. Breakfast has 'extensive choice'. Plenty of diversion is available: 'endless treatment opportunities' in the spa; riverboat picnics; hiking trails that lead to Windsor Park.

MAP 2:D3
Windsor Road
Egham  TW20 0AG
T: 01784 220600
W: runnymedehotel.com

BEDROOMS: 180. 2 suitable for disabled.
OPEN: all year, Leftbank restaurant closed Sun evening, The Lock Bar & Kitchen closed for lunch Mon–Thurs, Sat.
FACILITIES: lounge, 2 restaurants, in-room TV (Freeview), civil wedding licence, indoor and outdoor pools, 12-acre grounds, parking.
BACKGROUND MUSIC: in public areas.
LOCATION: on the banks of the River Thames, in town 5 miles SE of Windsor.
CHILDREN: all ages welcomed.
DOGS: allowed in some bedrooms, by prior arrangement, not in public areas.
CREDIT CARDS: Amex, MC, Visa.
PRICES: per room B&B £161.50–£275. À la carte (Lock) £35, buffet (Leftbank) £29–£32.

FAIRFORD Gloucestershire

# THE BULL HOTEL

Facing the market square in a Cotswolds town known for its fine 'wool church', this stone-built 15th-century building has variously hosted a monks' chanting-house, a post office and a coaching inn. Today an updated pub and hotel (part of the Barkby Group), it has a stone-walled bar with exposed timbers, local cask ales and plush seating by a crackling fire. Rustic pub staples in the stylish dining areas are given a modern touch in dishes such as double Gloucester cheese soufflé; chicken Milanese, garlic roasties, salsa verde. Staying guests choose among contemporary country-style bedrooms decorated with vintage finds and wool throws. Fishing enthusiasts appreciate the hotel's private stretch of the River Coln.

MAP 3:E6
Market Place
Fairford  GL7 4AA
T: 01285 712535
W: thebullhotelfairford.co.uk

BEDROOMS: 21.
OPEN: all year.
FACILITIES: bar, lounge, morning room, 3 dining rooms, function facilities, in-room TV (Freeview), terraces, private fishing rights.
BACKGROUND MUSIC: in bar, dining rooms.
LOCATION: in village centre.
CHILDREN: all ages welcomed.
DOGS: in 1 bedroom, bar.
CREDIT CARDS: Amex, MC, Visa.
PRICES: per room B&B £100–£220. À la carte £35.

FALMOUTH Cornwall
# THE GREENBANK

Soothing sounds of the sea, boats bobbing on the
water, 'magnificent' vistas across the harbour
– life on the water's edge doesn't come much
closer. 'Attractively furnished', this large hotel
is an amalgam of modern additions to the oldest
hotel in the historic maritime town. Florence
Nightingale stayed here; her name can still be
seen in the guest book displayed in reception.
Coastal light floods in to contemporary public
spaces; fresh-faced bedrooms and suites have
harbour-facing seating, and colours of sea and sky.
Food is served all day in the restaurant – perhaps
local fish with lemon dill butter; in the dog-
friendly Working Boat pub, find hearty portions,
Sunday roasts and a home brew. Step straight on
to a boat from the hotel's pontoons.

MAP 1:E2
Harbourside
Falmouth  TR11 2SR
T:  01326 312440
W:  greenbank-hotel.co.uk

BEDROOMS: 61.
OPEN: all year.
FACILITIES: lift, ramps, bar, pub,
restaurant, lounge, in-room TV, civil
wedding licence, spa treatments.
BACKGROUND MUSIC: in bar, restaurant.
LOCATION: on Falmouth harbour.
CHILDREN: all ages welcomed.
DOGS: allowed in 9 bedrooms, pub, not
in restaurant, bar.
CREDIT CARDS: Amex, MC, Visa.
PRICES: per room B&B £109–£359,
D,B&B £159–£409. 1-night bookings
sometimes refused.

FALMOUTH Cornwall
# HIGHCLIFFE

'Beautifully decorated, a little quirky', Vanessa
and Simon Clark's Victorian town house
lies between the town and the seafront. The
contemporary B&B brims with eclectic features
and lively colours. High-ceilinged, imaginatively
designed bedrooms share a 'boutiquey' look and
thoughtful amenities; some offer sweeping views
of the sun rising over the harbour. Breakfast
includes daily specials, perhaps wilted spinach
and garlic mushrooms on organic toast; home-
made rösti with a poached egg. For 'Idle Birds',
a comprehensive breakfast hamper (home-made
granola, plus hot scrambled eggs and grilled
bacon) can be left outside the room. The 'superb
hosts' offer helpful advice on local eating and
drinking spots.

MAP 1:E2
22 Melvill Road
Falmouth  TR11 4AR
T:  01326 314466
W:  highcliffefalmouth.com

BEDROOMS: 8.
OPEN: early Jan–early Dec.
FACILITIES: lounge, breakfast room,
in-room TV (Freeview), parking.
BACKGROUND MUSIC: occasionally in
dining room.
LOCATION: 5 mins' walk from town
and harbour.
CHILDREN: not under 8.
DOGS: not allowed.
CREDIT CARDS: MC, Visa.
PRICES: per room B&B single £50–£70,
double £72–£165. 1-night bookings
refused May–Oct.

## FALMOUTH Cornwall
# THE ROSEMARY

'Fabulous' views stretch across Falmouth Bay from Lynda and Malcolm Cook's relaxing B&B. The 'friendly' hosts welcome guests with a drink and home-baked cake, and provide tips on what to see and do in the area. 'Shipshape' bedrooms on the first and second floors of the Edwardian town house are well supplied with filtered water, biscuits, fresh milk for hot drinks, toiletries and fluffy bathrobes; sea-view rooms have binoculars, too. Take a Cornish cream tea in the lounge; in sunshine, sit on the deck in the 'beautiful' rear garden. Breakfast has 'first-class' choices: home-made preserves, local cheese, a Cornish cooked. Ask for a picnic hamper before embarking on a coastal ramble or a trip to the beach.

MAP 1:E2
22 Gyllyngvase Terrace
Falmouth TR11 4DL
T: 01326 314669
W: therosemary.co.uk

BEDROOMS: 8.
OPEN: 4 Jan–mid-Dec (call for winter availability).
FACILITIES: lounge, bar, breakfast room, in-room TV (Freeview), garden, sun deck.
BACKGROUND MUSIC: none.
LOCATION: 200 yards from beach and seafront, 10 mins' walk from town.
CHILDREN: all ages welcomed.
DOGS: allowed in some bedrooms by arrangement (not unattended), on a lead in lounge, bar and garden.
CREDIT CARDS: MC, Visa.
PRICES: per room B&B single £60–£75, double £80–£120. 2-night min. stay preferred in high season.

## FAR SAWREY Cumbria
# CUCKOO BROW INN

The views stretch over lakeland countryside from this unpretentious 18th-century inn, atop a hill in a pretty village between Lake Windermere and Hawkshead. Past the gabled entrance, fuss-free hospitality's the draw here: it's a dog- and family-friendly spot where, the owners say, 'muddy boots are welcome'. Garlands of hops and old photographs decorate the convivial, wood burner-warmed bar and dining room, where local ales and hearty pub fare are served; in former stables, sofas, games and a log-burning stove create a cosy retreat. Most of the modern, simply styled bedrooms are in an annexe attached to the main building; family rooms have a screened-off area for children. Hiking and cycling trails abound.

MAP 4: inset C2
Far Sawrey LA22 0LQ
T: 015394 43425
W: cuckoobrow.co.uk

BEDROOMS: 14. Some on ground floor.
OPEN: all year.
FACILITIES: lobby, bar, dining room, games room/lounge, in-room TV (Freeview), terrace, small garden.
BACKGROUND MUSIC: in bar, lounge, games room.
LOCATION: village centre.
CHILDREN: all ages welcomed.
DOGS: allowed in bedrooms, public rooms.
CREDIT CARDS: MC, Visa.
PRICES: per room B&B £110–£150, D,B&B from £150.

FERRENSBY Yorkshire

## THE GENERAL TARLETON

'A relaxing place to enjoy good food, good service and a good night's sleep', this revamped 18th-century coaching inn with views across open countryside is owned and run by chef/patron John Topham and his wife, Claire. 'The food is the main reason to stay here,' report guests this year, 'with much use of locally sourced ingredients in unexpectedly delicious combinations.' Sit by the log fire in the lounge, then retire to one of the modern bedrooms. 'Warm, comfortable and well fitted out', they are stocked with 'tasty' home-made biscuits. 'Reasonable prices, too.' The restaurant-with-rooms is well placed to break up trips between Scotland and England; Harrogate, York and the Dales are an easy drive away.

MAP 4:D4
Boroughbridge Road
Ferrensby  HG5 0PZ
T: 01423 340284
W: generaltarleton.co.uk

BEDROOMS: 13.
OPEN: all year, no accommodation 24–26 Dec, 1 Jan.
FACILITIES: bar, cocktail lounge, atrium, restaurant, private dining room, in-room TV (Freeview), parking.
BACKGROUND MUSIC: in public areas.
LOCATION: 4 miles from Knaresborough.
CHILDREN: all ages welcomed.
DOGS: not allowed.
CREDIT CARDS: Amex, MC, Visa.
PRICES: per room B&B single from £89, double from £129. À la carte £35.

FOLKESTONE Kent

## ROCKSALT

Jutting over the harbour, this cleanly contemporary, dark-timber-and-glass restaurant offers striking Channel views, an 'imaginative' menu, and stylish, loft-like bedrooms for sleeping off the feast. The much-praised cooking features Kentish produce, and fish caught off the south-east coast; meals may be taken on the open deck on a balmy day. The day's haul might include barbecued monkfish, or lamb tagine, spiced pear couscous, spinach. A minute away, above the Smokehouse, a sister restaurant, industrial-chic bedrooms with stripped-back brick walls, an antique bed and a trim, modern wet room have a glimpse of the water (binoculars provided). A continental breakfast hamper is delivered to the room in the morning.

MAP 2:E5
4–5 Fish Market
Folkestone CT19 6AA
T: 01303 212070
W: rocksaltfolkestone.co.uk

BEDROOMS: 4.
OPEN: all year, closed Mon Oct–Mar, restaurant closed Sun, Mon Oct–Mar.
FACILITIES: bar, restaurant, terrace, in-room TV (BT), on-street parking.
BACKGROUND MUSIC: in restaurant.
LOCATION: by the harbour.
CHILDREN: all ages welcomed.
DOGS: not allowed.
CREDIT CARDS: Amex, MC, Visa.
PRICES: per room B&B (continental) £110–£140. À la carte £40, cooked breakfast £10.

FONTMELL MAGNA Dorset

## THE FONTMELL

The village stream runs between the dog-friendly bar and the bookshelf-lined restaurant of this stylishly updated roadside inn, in a peaceful rural setting between Shaftesbury and Blandford Forum. Guests and regulars rub shoulders over craft beers, weekly-changing ales and home-made sausage rolls in the bar; in the dining room, the much-lauded menu uses fish delivered daily from Brixham, meat from the pub's own rare-breed pigs, and locally grown fruit and vegetables. The pizza oven in the garden is fired up in the summer. Bedrooms on the first floor are pleasingly decorated, perhaps with a bay-window reading nook, or a roll-top bath under sloped ceilings. Hearty breakfasts; packed lunches.

MAP 2:E1
Crown Hill
Fontmell Magna SP7 0PA
T: 01747 811441
W: thefontmell.com

BEDROOMS: 6.
OPEN: all year.
FACILITIES: bar, restaurant, in-room TV (Freeview), large garden.
BACKGROUND MUSIC: in public areas.
LOCATION: 5 miles S of Shaftesbury.
CHILDREN: all ages welcomed.
DOGS: allowed in some bedrooms, public rooms.
CREDIT CARDS: Amex, MC, Visa.
PRICES: per room B&B £105–£200. À la carte £30.

FOWEY Cornwall

## THE OLD QUAY HOUSE

Dazzling estuary views and a friendly welcome await at this 'marvellously situated' quayside hotel. The Victorian building, once the refuge of seamen, has been transformed with 'tastefully rejuvenated' public spaces. Classic British fare with a Cornish twist is served in the informal restaurant or out on the 'beautiful terrace' overlooking the water. Sleep in 'a superb, comfy bed' in one of the 'clean, fresh, contemporary' bedrooms; thoughtful touches include 'fluffy towels', biscuits and bottled water, books and local guides, umbrellas and raincoats. A fridge on the landing has jugs of fresh milk. After a wake-up call of seagulls and lapping sea, 'delicious' breakfasts are served in the sun-drenched restaurant.

MAP 1:D3
28 Fore Street
Fowey PL23 1AQ
T: 01726 833302
W: theoldquayhouse.com

BEDROOMS: 13.
OPEN: all year.
FACILITIES: open-plan lounge, bar, restaurant, in-room TV (Freeview), civil wedding licence, terrace, parking permits supplied, bar, lounge and restaurant wheelchair accessible.
BACKGROUND MUSIC: in public areas.
LOCATION: town centre.
CHILDREN: not under 12.
DOGS: not allowed.
CREDIT CARDS: Amex, MC, Visa.
PRICES: per room B&B £199–£399, D,B&B £279–£479. Set dinner £37.50 (2 courses), £45 (3 courses).

### GILSLAND Cumbria

# THE HILL ON THE WALL

Come teatime, guests arriving at Elaine Packer's farmhouse B&B are welcomed with hot drinks and home-made cake. The Georgian building, which overlooks Hadrian's Wall near Birdoswald, is filled with 'every comfort': its traditionally decorated bedrooms are supplied with glossy magazines, bathrobes, freshly ground cafetière coffee, a biscuit barrel and chocolates. On cool days, browse the library by the wood-burning stove; when the weather's fine, sit in the 'beautiful' walled garden and watch the light change over the North Pennines and the Lakeland fells beyond. 'So peaceful.' Ordered the night before, breakfast brings 'gigantic portions' of home-cooked Northumbrian fare. Packed lunches available (£6).

MAP 4:B3
The Hill
Gilsland  CA8 7DA
T:  016977 47214
W: hillonthewall.co.uk

BEDROOMS: 3. 1 on ground floor.
OPEN: Mar–Oct.
FACILITIES: lounge, breakfast room, in-room TV (Freeview), 1-acre garden, terrace, parking, secure bicycle storage.
BACKGROUND MUSIC: none.
LOCATION: 1 mile W of Gilsland on the B6318.
CHILDREN: not under 10.
DOGS: not allowed.
CREDIT CARDS: MC, Visa for online bookings only.
PRICES: per room B&B from £90.

### GOATHLAND Yorkshire

# FAIRHAVEN COUNTRY GUEST HOUSE

Head straight out on to the moors from Peter and Sarah Garnett's 'very comfortable' Edwardian guest house in a scenic village. Return by steam locomotive to Goathland station – a stand-in for Hogsmeade in the Harry Potter films. The hosts provide a welcoming pot of tea and home-made cake in the large lounge; there are games and books, and an open fire in cool weather. Simply styled, homely bedrooms with 'beautiful moorland views' are 'well stocked' with hot drinks and biscuits; fresh milk and filtered water are in the dining-room fridge. 'Superb' breakfasts include daily specials – baked spiced plums with home-made granola and Greek yogurt, say. The front terrace and rear garden catch the sunset.

## 25% DISCOUNT VOUCHERS

MAP 4:C5
The Common
Goathland  YO22 5AN
T:  01947 896361
W: fairhavencountryguesthouse.co.uk

BEDROOMS: 9. 1 with separate private bathroom.
OPEN: all year except 1 week over Christmas.
FACILITIES: lounge, dining room, in-room TV (Freeview), front terrace, large garden, parking, secure bicycle storage, dinner available on certain evenings in winter, all year for parties of 6 or more.
BACKGROUND MUSIC: during breakfast.
LOCATION: close to the North York Moors steam railway, 8 miles from Whitby.
CHILDREN: all ages welcomed.
DOGS: not allowed.
CREDIT CARDS: MC, Visa.
PRICES: per room B&B single £47–£71, double £90–£112.

## GRANGE-IN-BORROWDALE Cumbria
# BORROWDALE GATES

Broad views and the promise of walks from the door draw guests to this traditional Lakeland hotel with up-to-date facilities. 'Tranquil, well-appointed' bedrooms gaze over the Borrowdale valley and the surrounding fells. Many rooms have a balcony, or patio access to the garden; all have a refreshment tray, bathrobes, a digital library of magazines and newspapers via a smart phone or tablet. On inclement days, the lounge's picture windows provide immersive valley views without your moving a muscle. A showcase for Cumbrian produce (Borrowdale trout, fell-bred Herdwick lamb), the restaurant has 'superb food for all, including vegetarians'. 'Breakfast sustains fell walkers through a long day.'

MAP 4: inset C2
Grange-in-Borrowdale CA12 5UQ
T: 01768 777204
W: borrowdale-gates.com

BEDROOMS: 25. Some on ground floor.
OPEN: all year except Jan.
FACILITIES: lift, open-plan bar, dining room and lounge (log fire), reading room, in-room TV, wedding facilities (exclusive use only), 2-acre grounds, terrace.
BACKGROUND MUSIC: none.
LOCATION: 5 miles from Keswick, in the heart of the Borrowdale valley.
CHILDREN: all ages welcomed.
DOGS: allowed in 3 bedrooms, not in dining room, bar, lounge.
CREDIT CARDS: MC, Visa.
PRICES: per room B&B single £107, double £156–£232, D,B&B single £140, double £222–£298. À la carte £44.

## GRANGE-OVER-SANDS Cumbria
# CLARE HOUSE

'A big hit' with returning guests, the Read family's 'wonderfully old-fashioned' hotel is praised for its 'superb service, excellent food and very friendly staff'. The comfortably furnished Victorian house has well-appointed bedrooms, 'equally good' bathrooms. Morning coffee, light lunches and afternoon tea can be enjoyed in the lounges, which have open fires and views of the bay, or in the 'well-tended' garden. At dinner, Andrew Read and Mark Johnston's 'beautifully presented' dishes might include pork tenderloin, roast cauliflower, rösti potato; perhaps warm orange cake with marmalade ice cream to follow. Served on linen-dressed tables, varied breakfasts bring banana-and-berry pancakes, smoked haddock or Spanish-style eggs.

**25% DISCOUNT VOUCHERS**

MAP 4: inset C2
Park Road
Grange-over-Sands LA11 7HQ
T: 015395 33026
W: clarehousehotel.co.uk

BEDROOMS: 18. 1 on ground floor suitable for disabled.
OPEN: mid-Mar–mid-Dec.
FACILITIES: 2 lounges, dining room, in-room TV (Freeview), 1-acre grounds, parking.
BACKGROUND MUSIC: none.
LOCATION: in village.
CHILDREN: all ages welcomed.
DOGS: only assistance dogs allowed.
CREDIT CARDS: MC, Visa.
PRICES: per person D,B&B £108–£117.

GRASMERE Cumbria

## THE YAN AT BROADRAYNE

'Refreshingly different.' On a hillside flanked by grazing Herdwick sheep – 'a beautiful setting' – this 17th-century barn and cluster of old outbuildings have been reinvented as a contemporary hotel and bistro. It's a hands-on family affair, run by Jess Manley; her husband, Will (the chef); and Jess's parents, Dave and Sally Keighley. Uncluttered modern bedrooms styled in tones of grey all have fell views; they have a 'basic' hospitality tray and space to sit, plus thoughtful touches ('useful charging sockets, good reading lights'). Among the 'adventurous' dishes in the 'Alpine lodge-style' bistro: a 'memorable' fancy fish selection platter. Nearby, the 555 bus (Kendal–Grasmere) makes a car 'almost unnecessary'.

MAP 4: inset C2
Broadrayne Farm
Grasmere LA22 9RU
T: 015394 35055
w: theyan.co.uk

BEDROOMS: 7. Plus self-catering cottages.
OPEN: all year except 4–22 Jan.
FACILITIES: lounge, bar/bistro, in-room TV (Freeview), drying room, bicycle storage.
BACKGROUND MUSIC: 'chilled' in bistro.
LOCATION: close to A591, 1 mile N of Grasmere.
CHILDREN: all ages welcomed.
DOGS: allowed in 2 rooms (1 dog per room), on lead in public spaces.
CREDIT CARDS: MC, Visa.
PRICES: per room £100–£220. Breakfast £10, à la carte £30. 2-night min. stay.

GREAT LANGDALE Cumbria

## THE OLD DUNGEON GHYLL

For over 300 years, this unpretentious, dog-friendly inn has been sought out by weary travellers, walkers and climbers, including some of Britain's greatest mountaineers. In a 'glorious setting', at the head of the Great Langdale valley, it is managed for the National Trust by Jane and Neil Walmsley. Visitors value it for the 'willing, helpful staff', 'reasonably priced accommodation', and chance to digitally detox. Most of the simple, 'country-style' rooms have dramatic views of the fells. The popular Hikers' bar (one-time cow stalls) dishes up 'straightforward pub food'; home-baked treats accompany morning coffee or afternoon tea in the lounge. Walking routes are readily provided; packed lunches can be arranged.

MAP 4: inset C2
Great Langdale LA22 9JY
T: 015394 37272
w: odg.co.uk

BEDROOMS: 12.
OPEN: all year except 24–26 Dec.
FACILITIES: residents' bar and lounge, dining room, bar, free Wi-Fi in public areas and some bedrooms, 1-acre garden, drying room, parking.
BACKGROUND MUSIC: live music most Wed evenings.
LOCATION: 5 miles from Hawkshead.
CHILDREN: all ages welcomed.
DOGS: allowed in bedrooms, public areas, not in dining room.
CREDIT CARDS: MC, Visa.
PRICES: per room B&B single £62.50, double from £125. À la carte £25. 2-night min. stay on weekends.

## HALIFAX Yorkshire
# SHIBDEN MILL INN

Opposite Red Beck, the stream that once powered its machinery, a former mill in the wooded Shibden valley draws locals and visitors with its many comforts. The past at Max Heaton's refurbished 17th-century inn is still redolent in the bustling, oak-beamed bar, where guests sample Shibden Mill's own brew by a vast open hearth. Jolly bedrooms are individually styled, and supplied with bathrobes, teas and coffee. There are gingham and floral prints in one; in another, a deep velvet sofa at the foot of a half-tester bed. Chef Will Webster's ambitious, Yorkshire-inspired menus have surprises: miso-glazed cod, roasted cauliflower purée, mussels, morels; in the summer, the Shack in the garden serves up alfresco grub.

MAP 4:D3
Shibden Mill Fold
Halifax HX3 7UL
T: 01422 365840
W: shibdenmillinn.com

BEDROOMS: 11.
OPEN: all year except 25/26 Dec, 1 Jan.
FACILITIES: bar, lounge, restaurant, private dining rooms, in-room TV (Freeview), small conference facilities, patio, 2-acre garden, parking, complimentary access to local health club.
BACKGROUND MUSIC: in main bar, restaurant.
LOCATION: 2 miles from Halifax town centre.
CHILDREN: all ages welcomed.
DOGS: allowed in bar.
CREDIT CARDS: Amex, MC, Visa.
PRICES: per room B&B single £95–£220, double £100–£265, D,B&B £188–£259. À la carte £35.

## HARROGATE Yorkshire
# THE WEST PARK HOTEL

Across from the Stray's 200 acres of open parkland, this Victorian coach house with flower-bedecked balconies is an alluring town-centre hotel. Seasonal menus of fresh fish and seafood, sharing platters and grills are served in the brasserie, bold and buzzy with a zinc-topped bar and sea-green leather banquettes; in clement weather, the courtyard opens for alfresco dining. Well-appointed bedrooms (quieter ones at the rear) are supplied with teas and a coffee machine; spacious duplex suites have a lounge and dining area, and access to the roof terrace. There's plenty of choice at breakfast, from organic granola and fresh berries to salt beef and a potato rösti. Part of the Provenance Inns & Hotels group.

MAP 4:D4
19 West Park
Harrogate HG1 1BJ
T: 01423 524471
W: thewestparkhotel.com

BEDROOMS: 25. Some suitable for disabled.
OPEN: all year.
FACILITIES: bar, brasserie, meeting/private dining rooms, in-room TV (Freeview), large walled terrace, adjacent NCP car park, pay and display street parking.
BACKGROUND MUSIC: in public areas.
LOCATION: town centre.
CHILDREN: all ages welcomed.
DOGS: well-behaved dogs allowed in some bedrooms, bar.
CREDIT CARDS: Amex, MC, Visa.
PRICES: per room B&B £134–£254, D,B&B £194–£314. À la carte £35.

**NEW**

HASTINGS Sussex

## THE LAINDONS

In a handsome Grade II listed Georgian coaching house, a stroll from the sea, Malcolm and Karen Twist have created a seasidey look in their modern B&B. Bright, light and perky, the spacious, high-ceilinged bedrooms have quality linens on a bed handcrafted from reclaimed timber, plus a period fireplace, padded window seat or chaise longue. Home-made biscuits, ground coffee and organic teas – even earplugs to combat seagull squawks – are welcome extras. The hosts bake their own bread and roast their own coffee for breakfast in the conservatory: maple-blueberry pancakes and crispy bacon, say, a full English or a yogurt-granola-compote jar, along with a freshly made juice or smoothie to kick-start the day.

MAP 2:E5
23 High Street
Hastings TN34 3EY
T: 01424 437710
W: thelaindons.com

BEDROOMS: 5. Plus 2 with shared bathroom.
OPEN: all year except 24–26 Dec, first 2 weeks Jan.
FACILITIES: drawing room (honesty bar), breakfast room, in-room TV (Freeview).
BACKGROUND MUSIC: gentle background music in public areas at breakfast.
LOCATION: in the heart of the Old Town.
CHILDREN: not under 10.
DOGS: not allowed.
CREDIT CARDS: MC, Visa.
PRICES: per room B&B single £120, double £140–£175. 2-night min. stay at weekends Apr–Sept.

**NEW**

HAWKHURST Kent

## THE QUEEN'S INN

A royal welcome is granted at this eclectically revived 16th-century coaching inn, in a historic Wealden village on the Kent/Sussex border. Against an old-meets-new backdrop of beams, brick walls, velvet wingback chairs and plush banquettes, Kentish wines, ales and ciders headline the drinks list in the bar; hungry visitors have a choice of dining areas. Chef and co-owner Sally-Anne Day's smart, rustic restaurant has grilled steaks and a varied, modern menu; the industrial-chic Charcoal Kitchen's the place for nibbles, pizzas, and meat and fish from the charcoal oven. Staying guests choose among creatively decorated bedrooms with some lush additions: coffee and tea, home-made brownies, botanical toiletries.

MAP 2:E4
Rye Road
Hawkhurst TN18 4EY
T: 01580 754233
W: thequeensinnhawkhurst.co.uk

BEDROOMS: 7.
OPEN: all year.
FACILITIES: bar, snug, 3 dining areas, in-room TV, function facilities, front patio.
BACKGROUND MUSIC: in bar, restaurant.
LOCATION: in village, within the High Weald Area of Outstanding Natural Beauty.
CHILDREN: all ages welcomed.
DOGS: allowed in bar, one area of restaurant.
CREDIT CARDS: Amex, MC, Visa.
PRICES: per room B&B single £95–£160, double £110–£175. À la carte £32.50. 2-night min. stay at weekends.

HEACHAM Norfolk

# HEACHAM HOUSE

Rebecca and Robert Bradley's red brick Victorian house overlooks the village duck pond, a 15-minute stroll from the wide sands and salt marshes of north Norfolk's 'sunset coast'. B&B accommodation is in pretty bedrooms supplied with bathrobes and facecloths, fresh milk and home-baked biscuits; a posy of garden blooms makes a cheery welcome. There's home-baked bread, home-made granola, local honey and freshly ground coffee at breakfast; specials might include buttermilk pancakes, or roast tomatoes and halloumi on brioche. The enthusiastic hosts can offer advice on stately homes, seal safaris and plenty more in between. RSPB Snettisham and Titchwell are close; walking and cycling routes start from the door.

MAP 2:A4
18 Staithe Road
Heacham PE31 7ED
T: 01485 579529
W: heachamhouse.com

BEDROOMS: 3.
OPEN: all year except Christmas, New Year.
FACILITIES: sitting room, breakfast room, in-room TV (Freeview), garden, parking, bicycle storage.
BACKGROUND MUSIC: none.
LOCATION: centre of village, 3 miles from Hunstanton.
CHILDREN: not under 14.
DOGS: not allowed.
CREDIT CARDS: none accepted.
PRICES: per room B&B single from £75, double £95–£105. 1-night bookings refused weekends, Easter–Oct.

HELMSLEY Yorkshire

# THE FEATHERS

Hunt for mice at this hotel, restaurant and coffee shop: the carved-wood trademark of Arts and Crafts figure Robert Thomas, the Mouseman of Kilburn, runs on pillars, window sills and bar counter within the two adjoining buildings on the bustling market square. Downstairs are low ceilings, an open fire, craft beers and ciders (many from local breweries); hungry guests have their pick of grazing boards, grilled meats, seasonal dishes and pub classics. Modern bedrooms decked out in plush fabrics are supplied with bottled water and tea- and coffee-making facilities; superior rooms have a super-king-size bed and space to sit. Part of the Coaching Inn group; see also The Feathers, Ledbury, and The Talbot Hotel, Oundle (Shortlist entries).

MAP 4:C4
Market Place
Helmsley YO62 5BH
T: 01439 770275
W: feathershotelhelmsley.co.uk

BEDROOMS: 25. 2 on ground floor.
OPEN: all year.
FACILITIES: 2 bars, restaurant, lounge, in-room TV (Freeview), civil wedding licence, function facilities, courtyard.
BACKGROUND MUSIC: in public spaces.
LOCATION: on market square.
CHILDREN: all ages welcomed.
DOGS: allowed in some bedrooms, bar, courtyard, not in restaurant.
CREDIT CARDS: Amex, MC, Visa.
PRICES: per room B&B single from £60, double £80–£180. À la carte £35.

## HERTFORD Hertfordshire
# NUMBER ONE PORT HILL

In a pleasant market town, Annie Rowley's artful B&B teems with vintage glassware, sculptures and 'an unbelievable collection' of objects. The Georgian town house, featured in Pevsner's guide to Hertfordshire, has 'immaculately kept' bedrooms: two are cosy; one's large, with a French gilt bed, and a raised boat bath in the bathroom. Plentiful extras include Belgian hot chocolate, sweet and savoury snacks, bathrobes and 'eclectic' reading material. Traffic noise is muted by 'very good' double glazing. Breakfast, with freshly ground coffee and home-made preserves, is taken communally, or in the shade of the ancient wisteria in the walled garden. A fine dinner is available some nights; eating places are close by.

MAP 2:C4
1 Port Hill
Hertford  SG14 1PJ
T: 01992 587350
W: numberoneporthill.co.uk

BEDROOMS: 3.
OPEN: all year except Christmas.
FACILITIES: drawing room, in-room TV (Sky, Freeview), front and back gardens, limited street parking.
BACKGROUND MUSIC: none.
LOCATION: 5 mins' walk from town centre.
CHILDREN: not under 12 ('though exemptions may be made, if discussed, for younger children').
DOGS: not allowed.
CREDIT CARDS: MC, Visa.
PRICES: per room B&B £130–£160. Dinner £45 (dependent on number of guests).

## HEXHAM Northumberland
# BATTLESTEADS

'The many "green" features of this hotel are laudable,' say Guide readers of the 'colourful, interesting grounds', 'amazing' dark sky observatory and sustainable approach at Dee and Richard Slade's rural hotel. 'Comfortable' bedrooms in the main building (part of an 18th-century farmstead) and in wood-built lodges at the back vary in size. Some may be 'on the small side, though adequate', while others, in the lodges, are 'vast'. Modern menus in the restaurant use locally sourced produce and the bounty from the kitchen garden and new mushroom farm; at breakfast, find smoked haddock and salt-cured kippers from the on-site smokery. Not far: Hadrian's Wall, and 'the majestic flow' of the North Tyne river.

MAP 4:B3
Wark-on-Tyne
Hexham  NE48 3LS
T: 01434 230209
W: battlesteads.com

BEDROOMS: 22. 4 on ground floor, 5 in lodge, 2 suitable for disabled.
OPEN: all year except 25 Dec.
FACILITIES: bar, dining room, in-room TV (Freeview), civil wedding licence, function facilities, drying room, 2-acre grounds (walled garden, kitchen garden, dark sky observatory).
BACKGROUND MUSIC: in bar, restaurant.
LOCATION: 12 miles N of Hexham.
CHILDREN: all ages welcomed.
DOGS: allowed in public rooms, some bedrooms (resident dog).
CREDIT CARDS: Amex, MC, Visa.
PRICES: per room B&B from £125, D,B&B from £170. À la carte £33.

HEXHAM Northumberland

## THE BEAUMONT

Facing the park, in the heart of the historic market town, this contemporary town house hotel is run with 'energy and commitment to high standards'. The Victorian building has undergone considerable refurbishment in recent years; its smart, open-plan bar/lounge/restaurant on the ground floor – with its fine, modern panelling, pleasingly mismatched fabrics, colourful local artwork and 'interesting, varied' menu – is a fitting place to take in the owners' ambitions. Spread over three floors, bedrooms are supplied with essential-oil toiletries and a hospitality tray with filtered water, tea, coffee and biscuits. (Ask for one of the brightly redecorated rooms for an extra dose of style.) 'Breakfast is splendid, too.'

MAP 4:B3
Beaumont Street
Hexham NE46 3LT
T: 01434 602331
W: thebeaumonthexham.co.uk

BEDROOMS: 33. 1 suitable for disabled.
OPEN: all year.
FACILITIES: open-plan bar/lounge/restaurant, in-room TV, function facilities.
BACKGROUND MUSIC: in bar, restaurant.
LOCATION: in town centre.
CHILDREN: all ages welcomed.
DOGS: allowed in designated public areas only, not in bedrooms.
CREDIT CARDS: Amex, MC, Visa.
PRICES: per room B&B £113–£156, D,B&B £163–£200. À la carte £30.

HITCHIN Hertfordshire

## THE FARMHOUSE AT REDCOATS

Undulating countryside spreads around this well-restored old farmhouse and its outbuildings, whose many characterful original features date back to the 15th century. The hotel and restaurant, part of the Nye family's Anglian Country Inns, have comfortable sitting areas, warming fires in myriad nooks and crannies, and pleasingly quirky touches. Bedrooms spread across the main house, converted stables and a Grade II listed barn each have their own style. On bare-wood tables in the conservatory restaurant, foraged finds and farm-to-fork produce, some from the kitchen garden, are cooked alongside seasonal game. Two bars dispense real ales, wine and cocktails. Hearty farmhouse breakfasts greet the day.

MAP 2:C4
Redcoats Green
Hitchin SG4 7JR
T: 01438 729500
W: farmhouseatredcoats.co.uk

BEDROOMS: 27. 8 in converted stables and coach house, 15 in Grade II listed barn conversion across the yard, some on ground floor.
OPEN: all year.
FACILITIES: 2 bars, lounge, conservatory restaurant, 3 private dining rooms, in-room TV (Freeview), civil wedding licence, 4-acre grounds, parking.
BACKGROUND MUSIC: 'subtle' in public areas.
LOCATION: 9 mins' drive from Stevenage.
CHILDREN: all ages welcomed.
DOGS: well-behaved dogs allowed in stable rooms.
CREDIT CARDS: Amex, MC, Visa.
PRICES: per room B&B £110–£170, D,B&B £185–£225. À la carte £33.

## HOLKHAM Norfolk
# THE VICTORIA INN

Close to 'one of the most beautiful, isolated beaches', this genteelly refurbished pub on the Earl of Leicester's Holkham estate is 'perfect for exploring the north Norfolk coast'. Enthusiastic staff welcome locals, tourists and their dogs to the open-plan bar, where hunting trophies and taxidermied wildfowl are displayed; in the dining rooms, local produce (beef from the estate; shellfish, fish and samphire from local waters) dictates the daily specials on the unfussy menu. Bedrooms and family-friendly suites in country-cottage hues have a few antiques and plenty of perks, including a mini-fridge with complimentary drinks. A plus, for Ancient House residents: a walled rose garden, for the sun and the scent.

MAP 2:A5
Park Road
Holkham NR23 1RG
T: 01328 711008
W: victoriaatholkham.co.uk

BEDROOMS: 20. 10 in Ancient House, opposite, 1 on ground floor suitable for disabled.
OPEN: all year.
FACILITIES: bar, lounge, restaurant with conservatory extension, in-room TV, garden.
BACKGROUND MUSIC: in public areas.
LOCATION: on the Holkham estate, 1¾ miles W of Wells-next-the-Sea.
CHILDREN: all ages welcomed.
DOGS: allowed in inn bedrooms, bar, restaurant, not in Ancient House.
CREDIT CARDS: MC, Visa.
PRICES: per room B&B from £125.
À la carte £35.

## HOLT Norfolk
# BYFORDS

At the heart of a 'bustling' market town, a higgledy-piggledy building, said to be Holt's oldest, houses this all-day café and store with 'very comfortable' accommodation and a lively holiday atmosphere. A winding staircase at the back of the deli leads up to bedrooms newly revamped with character. Every room has its own style (and some can accommodate a family), but all have vintage furnishings on stripped-wood floors; an entertainment system; home-made biscuits, fresh milk and water. In the refurbished conservatory eating area, the comprehensive menu includes dishes such as oven-baked parmesan-crusted chicken, plus sharing platters, salads and pizzas. Picnic items, and more, are in the deli.

MAP 2:A5
1–3 Shirehall Plain
Holt NR25 6BG
T: 01263 711400
W: byfords.org.uk

BEDROOMS: 16. Plus self-catering apartment.
OPEN: all year.
FACILITIES: café/bar, deli, in-room TV (Sky), terrace, private secure parking.
BACKGROUND MUSIC: in café.
LOCATION: in town centre.
CHILDREN: all ages welcomed.
DOGS: not allowed.
CREDIT CARDS: Amex, MC, Visa.
PRICES: per room B&B £165–£235.

HUDDERSFIELD Yorkshire

# THE THREE ACRES INN & RESTAURANT

In Pennine countryside, this 'friendly' roadside drovers' inn has 'detour-worthy food'; 'tremendous views to all sides' are nearly as impressive. It is owned by Neil Truelove and his son, Tom. Bedrooms, spread across the main building and garden cottages, are 'comfortable, clean and functional, with an agreeable bed'; some can accommodate a family. Locals join residents in the 'civilised' dining room for head chef Tom Davies's 'high-quality' seasonal cooking – perhaps forest mushrooms, crispy egg, truffle; braised Bolster Moor ox cheek, roast garlic pomme purée, glazed carrots. Vegetarians have their own menu. The day starts well: home-made muesli, home-baked sourdough, local bacon and sausage.

MAP 4:E3
Roydhouse
Huddersfield HD8 8LR
T: 01484 602606
W: 3acres.com

BEDROOMS: 17. 1 suitable for disabled, 8 in annexe.
OPEN: all year except evenings 25 and 26 Dec, midday 31 Dec, evening 1 Jan.
FACILITIES: bar, restaurant, in-room TV (Freeview), civil wedding licence, small function/private dining facilities, terraced garden.
BACKGROUND MUSIC: in bar, restaurant.
LOCATION: in hamlet, 6 miles from Huddersfield town centre.
CHILDREN: well-behaved children welcomed.
DOGS: not allowed.
CREDIT CARDS: Amex, MC, Visa.
PRICES: per room B&B single £60–£125, double £90–£175. À la carte £50.

HURLEY Berkshire

# HURLEY HOUSE

'The ambience and superb staff are a feature' of this modern hotel in the Chiltern hills, close to a pretty stretch of the Thames Path. Another feature: its well-regarded restaurant, a sophisticated space (sleek wood panelling, leather banquettes, oversized artwork) where the 'excellent' menu includes steaks grilled on the charcoal Josper. Eat alfresco in fine weather – the wide terraces have heated awnings – or opt for a lighter meal in the smartly rustic, slate-floored bar. Styled in creams and greys, urbane bedrooms have up-to-date comforts such as air conditioning and under-floor heating; efficient insulation subdues noise from the adjacent busy road. At breakfast: a 'good choice' of cooked dishes.

MAP 2:D3
Henley Road
Hurley SL6 5LH
T: 01628 568500
W: hurleyhouse.co.uk

BEDROOMS: 10. Some suitable for disabled.
OPEN: all year, restaurant closed Sun evenings.
FACILITIES: bar, snug, restaurant, private dining room, in-room TV (Freeview), function facilities, civil wedding licence, spa treatment room, large terrace, electric car charging points.
BACKGROUND MUSIC: in public areas until 11 pm, plus live music at Sun lunch and on selected evenings.
LOCATION: 5 miles E of Henley-on-Thames, 10 miles NW of Windsor.
CHILDREN: all ages welcomed.
DOGS: allowed in bar area.
CREDIT CARDS: Amex, MC, Visa.
PRICES: per room B&B £170–£325. À la carte £45.

**IRONBRIDGE** Shropshire

## THE LIBRARY HOUSE

Books line the sitting-room shelves at Sarah and Tim Davis's 'beautifully decorated' B&B in the heart of the historic town – an apt scene for a Grade II listed Georgian town house that was once the village library. Fittingly, writers lend their names to the neat bedrooms. Chaucer opens on to a garden terrace; high-ceilinged Eliot overlooks the River Severn; spacious Milton has a large bed and a reading corner. In each: waffle robes, fresh milk, a hot-water bottle. A log-burner blazes in the sitting room when the temperature dips; in good weather, take tea in the terraced garden. Breakfast, with home-made marmalade, is served at linen-topped tables. Ironbridge Gorge, a UNESCO World Heritage site, is close.

MAP 3:C5
11 Severn Bank
Ironbridge TF8 7AN
T: 01952 432299
W: libraryhouse.com

BEDROOMS: 3.
OPEN: all year.
FACILITIES: sitting room, breakfast room, in-room TV (Freeview), courtyard, mature garden, passes for local car parks.
BACKGROUND MUSIC: none.
LOCATION: town centre.
CHILDREN: not under 13.
DOGS: not allowed.
CREDIT CARDS: MC, Visa.
PRICES: per room B&B single £75–£95, double £100–£140.

**NEW**

**KELLING** Norfolk

## THE PHEASANT

On a 2,000-acre estate of woods and parkland, this traditional hotel is a tranquil country retreat. Most of the classically styled bedrooms (some dog friendly) are on the ground floor; interconnecting rooms are ideal for a family or a group. A coffee machine and spoiling toiletries come as standard; bathrobes and slippers, too, in superior rooms. Take tea on the lawn on a fine day; at lunch and dinner, sample local and estate-grown produce in the restaurant or orangery, perhaps an oxtail ravioli or a beetroot and roasted vegetable Wellington. A varied breakfast (home-made granola, omelettes, Cley smoked kipper, etc) provides ample fuel for discovering north Norfolk's coastal walks and nature reserves.

MAP 2:A5
Coast Road
Kelling NR25 7EG
T: 01263 588382
W: pheasanthotelnorfolk.co.uk

BEDROOMS: 32. 24 on ground floor, 1 suitable for disabled.
OPEN: all year.
FACILITIES: bar/lounge, restaurant, orangery, private dining room, in-room TV, civil wedding licence, terrace, 2½-acre garden, public rooms wheelchair accessible.
BACKGROUND MUSIC: in public areas.
LOCATION: 3½ miles NE of Holt.
CHILDREN: all ages welcomed.
DOGS: welcomed in 4 bedrooms, bar, orangery, not in restaurant.
CREDIT CARDS: Amex, MC, Visa.
PRICES: per room B&B single £130–£190, double £190–£250, D,B&B £245–£305. À la carte £35. 2-night min. stay at weekends July–Aug, bank holidays.

KESWICK Cumbria
# LYZZICK HALL

Unparalleled fell views and 'capable, obliging staff' are found at this family-friendly spot on the lower slopes of Skiddaw. The early Victorian hotel has been owned by the Fernandez family, now co-owners with the Lake family, for 35 years. 'Well-equipped' bedrooms all overlook the landscaped gardens; most also take in the 'stunning scenery' of the fells. Browse books and magazines, or play a board game, in the fire-warmed lounges; the spa and indoor swimming pool are a welcome retreat after a day's sightseeing or mountain hike. At mealtimes, there are 'excellent' British dishes, 'divine desserts' and 'whatever the children fancy'. Breakfast has no buffet, but 'plenty of choice'. Many walks from the door.

MAP 4: inset C2
Underskiddaw
Keswick CA12 4PY
T: 017687 72277
w: lyzzickhall.co.uk

BEDROOMS: 28. 1 on ground floor.
OPEN: early Feb–New Year, except 24–26 Dec.
FACILITIES: bar, 2 lounges, orangery, restaurant, in-room TV (Freeview), 10-metre heated indoor swimming pool, spa facilities, 4-acre grounds.
BACKGROUND MUSIC: 'discreet' in public areas.
LOCATION: 2 miles N of Keswick.
CHILDREN: all ages welcomed.
DOGS: allowed in 1 bedroom, grounds if supervised at all times.
CREDIT CARDS: MC, Visa.
PRICES: per room B&B £150–£238, D,B&B £230–£318. À la carte £40.

KIDLINGTON Oxfordshire
# THE BELL AT HAMPTON POYLE

George Dailey's honey-stone roadside inn, north of Oxford, is a popular village hub where locals come for the 'excellent' cooking – and where farther-flung guests settle in for 'a very nice stay'. A wood stove sits on a large stone hearth in the flagstone-floored pub; in the restaurant, diners watch pizzas, chargrilled local meats and upgraded pub classics being prepared in the open kitchen. 'Comfortable', clean-cut bedrooms, each stocked with fluffy towels and organic toiletries, are above the bar and in an adjacent cottage with sloped ceilings and characterful low beams. They vary in size and layout, so ring ahead if you have particular needs. Blenheim Palace and Bicester Village are not far away.

MAP 2:C2
11 Oxford Road
Kidlington OX5 2QD
T: 01865 376242
w: thebelloxford.co.uk

BEDROOMS: 9. 5 in cottage, 1 on ground floor suitable for disabled.
OPEN: all year.
FACILITIES: bar, restaurant, snug, in-room TV (Freeview), function facilities, terrace, parking.
BACKGROUND MUSIC: in bar and restaurant.
LOCATION: 10 miles N of Oxford, 7 miles E of Woodstock.
CHILDREN: all ages welcomed (no extra beds or facilities).
DOGS: allowed in bar, not in bedrooms.
CREDIT CARDS: Amex, MC, Visa.
PRICES: per room B&B single £95–£130, double £120–£175. À la carte £35, 2-course set menu (Mon–Thurs, 6 pm–7 pm) £12.50.

KING'S LYNN Norfolk

# BANK HOUSE

In a 'fine waterfront setting', this 'distinguished' Georgian bank turned town hotel is a sought-after spot for locals, who gather in its popular bar and brasserie. It is owned by the Goodrich family (see The Rose & Crown, Snettisham, main entry). Bedrooms vary in size and layout: call ahead to discuss best options. Most rooms have a river view; all have pampering toiletries, 'good-quality magazines', a 'well-researched guide' of local hotspots. (Quirky touches like a bathtub in the bedroom and a partially partitioned-off bathroom were less appreciated by some Guide readers this year.) Modern brasserie classics are served across the varied dining areas; breakfast is 'simple and straightforward'. Parking can be 'difficult'.

**25% DISCOUNT VOUCHERS**

MAP 2:A4
King's Staithe Square
King's Lynn  PE30 1RD
T: 01553 660492
W: thebankhouse.co.uk

BEDROOMS: 12.
OPEN: all year except Christmas Day.
FACILITIES: bar, 3 dining rooms, meeting/function rooms, vaulted cellars for private functions, in-room TV (Freeview), riverside terrace, courtyard, all public rooms wheelchair accessible, adapted toilet.
BACKGROUND MUSIC: from mid-morning onwards, in public areas (but 'turned off on demand').
LOCATION: on the quayside.
CHILDREN: all ages welcomed.
DOGS: allowed in Counting House, bar, terrace, 2 bedrooms.
CREDIT CARDS: Amex, MC, Visa.
PRICES: per room B&B single £85–£120, double £115–£220. À la carte £32.

KINGSBRIDGE Devon

# THURLESTONE HOTEL

'Thoroughly dependable, yet stylish in an old-fashioned way', this family-friendly hotel has been run with care by the Grose family for more than 120 years. Approached by lanes 'resplendent with wildflowers', it lies in 19 acres of sub-tropical gardens on the South Devon National Trust coastline. 'Stunning' widescreen views are found in most of the well-equipped bedrooms; family rooms have a bunk bed, or extra space for a cot or additional bed. The terrace café and 16th-century village inn serve real ales and fresh seafood; in the smart Trevilder restaurant, the menu lists 'good classic stuff'. Rock pools are five minutes away; a plethora of on-site diversions includes croquet, tennis, a nine-hole golf course and a spa.

MAP 1:D4
Kingsbridge  TQ7 3NN
T: 01548 560382
W: thurlestone.co.uk

BEDROOMS: 65. 2 suitable for disabled.
OPEN: all year.
FACILITIES: lift, lounge, bar, restaurant, poolside café, village pub, in-room TV (Sky), civil wedding licence, function facilities, terrace, spa, outdoor heated swimming pool, tennis, 9-hole golf course, children's club during school holidays.
BACKGROUND MUSIC: none.
LOCATION: 4 miles SW of Kingsbridge.
CHILDREN: all ages welcomed.
DOGS: allowed in some bedrooms, not in public rooms.
CREDIT CARDS: Amex, MC, Visa.
PRICES: per room B&B from £235. À la carte £40, tasting menu £70. 2-night min. stay.

KINGSWEAR Devon

# KAYWANA HALL

Across the estuary from Dartmouth, in hillside woodland, Tony Pithers and Gordon Craig's ultra-modern B&B is in a 1960s Le Corbusier-inspired 'butterfly house' – one of four in Devon. In this adults-only space, the atmosphere is intimate and discreet. Sleek, light-filled bedrooms decorated with abstract art each have their own entrance and private terrace with outdoor seating (some reached via steep steps). Well equipped, they have a mini-fridge, an iPod dock, an espresso machine and home-made sweet treats. Breakfast, in an open-plan room overlooking the swimming pool, might start with freshly squeezed juices, locally baked bread and fruit compote; eggs Benedict, home-made vegetarian sausages or other cooked dishes follow.

MAP 1:D4
Higher Contour Road
Kingswear TQ6 0AY
T: 01803 752200
w: kaywanahall.co.uk

BEDROOMS: 4.
OPEN: May–end Sept.
FACILITIES: kitchen/breakfast room, free Wi-Fi in bedrooms, in-room TV (Freeview), 12-acre grounds, 9-metre outdoor swimming pool (heated in summer months), parking.
BACKGROUND MUSIC: none.
LOCATION: 5 mins from Dartmouth via ferry.
CHILDREN: not accepted.
DOGS: only assistance dogs allowed.
CREDIT CARDS: MC, Visa.
PRICES: per room B&B £195–£245. 2-night min. stay.

KNARESBOROUGH Yorkshire

# NEWTON HOUSE

There's 'plenty of Yorkshire friendliness' at Denise Carter's 'good-value' B&B, in the centre of a 'fascinating town to explore'. 'Well-appointed' bedrooms (some spacious; one, a 'tiny but perfectly adequate' single room) in the 18th-century house are traditionally decorated; each has its own little library and a hospitality tray. Guests may help themselves to local beers, spirits or soft drinks in the well-stocked honesty bar. In the evening, light bites such as soup or an omelette might be 'rustled up'; the hostess can recommend nearby eateries for more substantial fare. Home-made sourdough bread, jams and compotes are a worthy part of 'slow-food' breakfasts that 'set you up for the day'. A bonus: on-site parking.

MAP 4:D4
5–7 York Place
Knaresborough HG5 0AD
T: 01423 863539
w: newtonhouseyorkshire.com

BEDROOMS: 12. 2 on ground floor suitable for disabled, 2 in converted stables.
OPEN: all year.
FACILITIES: sitting room (honesty bar), dining room, in-room TV (Freeview), small courtyard garden (wildlife area), parking.
BACKGROUND MUSIC: Classic FM at breakfast.
LOCATION: town centre, 4 miles from Harrogate.
CHILDREN: all ages welcomed.
DOGS: allowed in 2 stable block rooms with outside access, not in public rooms.
CREDIT CARDS: Amex, MC, Visa.
PRICES: per room B&B single £70–£110, double £95–£145. 1-night bookings generally refused weekends.

**NEW**

## KNUTSFORD Cheshire
# THE COURTHOUSE

On the main road through town, the historic courtrooms and judges' lodgings of this 'imposing', iconic Grade II listed building have been transformed into a style-conscious hotel, restaurant and grand events venue. In 'deep Georgian hues', high-ceilinged bedrooms hold reminders of the past – trunk-style furniture here, a cheval mirror there, bone china cups and saucers. Among the thoughtful perks: home-made cookies, a coffee machine, a hot water bottle. Under a splendid domed ceiling in the 'truly stunning' former Crown Court, diners pass judgment on cocktails and wholesome modern British food. A revamp of the restaurant and rooftop gardens is underway. Part of the small, family-run Flat Cap group of Cheshire hotels.

MAP 3:A5
Toft Road
Knutsford WA16 0PB
T: 01565 743333
w: thecourthousecheshire.com

BEDROOMS: 9.
OPEN: all year.
FACILITIES: bar, restaurant, in-room smart TV, wedding/function facilities, rooftop garden.
BACKGROUND MUSIC: in restaurant.
LOCATION: in town centre.
CHILDREN: all ages welcomed.
DOGS: allowed.
CREDIT CARDS: Amex, MC, Visa.
PRICES: per room B&B from £159.
À la carte £35.

## LANCHESTER Co. Durham
# BURNHOPESIDE HALL

Christine Hewitt is the 'attentive, welcoming' hostess at this Grade II* listed house, in extensive gardens surrounded by acres of farmland and forest. Engineer William Hedley, inventor of Puffing Billy, once lived here. Today, 'good-value' B&B accommodation is in 'clean, quiet and comfortable' traditionally decorated bedrooms in the main house, adjoining farmhouse and cottage. Inside, find open fires, pictures and photos, and country views through sash windows; outside, trails lead to the river and the Lanchester Valley Railway Path. Home-made, home-reared, home-grown fare features at a 'lovely' breakfast; dinner may be requested in advance. Well placed for Durham. 'We recommend it without hesitation.'

MAP 4:B4
Durham Road
Lanchester DH7 0TL
T: 01207 520222
w: burnhopeside-hall.co.uk

BEDROOMS: 13. 5 in adjoining farmhouse, 3 in cottage in the grounds.
OPEN: all year, except when booked for exclusive use.
FACILITIES: sitting room, dining room, library, billiard room, in-room TV (Freeview), 475-acre grounds; farmhouse rooms have a sitting room, dining room; cottages have a sitting room where breakfast can be served; all with log fires.
BACKGROUND MUSIC: none.
LOCATION: 5 miles NW of Durham.
CHILDREN: all ages welcomed.
DOGS: welcomed (resident dogs).
CREDIT CARDS: Amex, MC, Visa.
PRICES: per room B&B single £70–£85, double £100–£120. Dinner, by arrangement, £40.

LANGHAM Norfolk

## THE HARPER

Bubbled up in a former glassblowing workshop, Sam Cutmore-Scott's contemporary country hotel is a fusion of informality and understated luxury. Inside the meticulously renovated flint-and-brick building, iron, copper and slate form an appealing backdrop for modern artworks and boldly coloured furnishings. Sit down to seafood suppers and local specialities in the dining room; small and sharing plates in the bar; alfresco eats around the courtyard's fire pit. Clean-cut modern bedrooms have a heated oak floor; treats include a coffee machine and a fridge stocked with pre-made cocktails. Relax in the spa, or embark on a day out – hampers and suggested walking or cycling routes are enthusiastically provided.

MAP 2:A5
North Street
Langham NR25 7DH
T: 01328 805000
W: theharper.co.uk

BEDROOMS: 32. Some on ground floor, 2 suitable for disabled.
OPEN: all year.
FACILITIES: bar, lounge, dining room, games room, in-room smart TV, spa (12 by 5 metre indoor swimming pool, spa bath, sauna, steam room, treatments), decked courtyard, complimentary bicycle hire.
BACKGROUND MUSIC: in public spaces.
LOCATION: 2 miles S of Blakeney, within the Norfolk Coast Area of Outstanding Natural Beauty.
CHILDREN: all ages welcomed, not under 16 in spa.
DOGS: allowed in ground-floor bedrooms, in bar, games room, not in dining areas.
CREDIT CARDS: MC, Visa.
PRICES: per room B&B £175–£390. À la carte £45. 2-night min. stay at weekends.

LAVENHAM Suffolk

## THE SWAN HOTEL & SPA

Formed from a trio of timber-framed 15th-century buildings, this swish hotel and spa in the heart of the medieval village is 'so cosy and welcoming'. Modern country-style bedrooms in a variety of sizes (some accessed via 'picturesque corridors with ups and downs and twists and turns') retain characterful features such as old beams, mullioned windows or an inglenook fireplace; they are well supplied with all the essentials, including bathrobes and upmarket toiletries. Guests have a choice of dining areas: light bites in the Airmen's bar; 'excellent' British favourites in the garden-facing brasserie; refined dishes in the Gallery restaurant. Part of The Hotel Folk; see also The Crown, Woodbridge (Shortlist entry).

MAP 2:C5
High Street
Lavenham CO10 9QA
T: 01787 247477
W: theswanatlavenham.co.uk

BEDROOMS: 45. 1 suitable for disabled.
OPEN: all year.
FACILITIES: 3 lounges, bar, brasserie, restaurant, in-room TV (Freeview), civil wedding licence, private dining/function facilities, spa (treatment rooms, sauna, steam room, outdoor hydrotherapy pool), terrace, garden, parking.
BACKGROUND MUSIC: occasionally in public areas.
LOCATION: in village.
CHILDREN: all ages welcomed.
DOGS: in some bedrooms, bar, lounge, garden, not in restaurants.
CREDIT CARDS: Amex, MC, Visa.
PRICES: per room B&B £119–£295, D,B&B £189–£365. À la carte £40.

LEATHERHEAD Surrey

# BEAVERBROOK

In a sweep of Surrey parkland, this late Victorian mansion has been transformed into a lavish, art-filled hotel with a multitude of mod cons, and several to spare. It was once the rural retreat of press baron Lord Beaverbrook, who hosted parties and pow-wows here throughout the mid-20th century; its illustrious past is reflected in bedrooms named after celebrated visitors. Find a spot to call your own in the well-stocked library or fashionably old-world bar; take afternoon tea on the terrace; soak in the countryside views from the swimming pool in the holistic spa. There's a choice of bedrooms, some family- and dog-friendly, in three buildings across the estate; a trio of restaurants, too, caters for varying tastes.

MAP 2:D4
Reigate Road
Leatherhead  KT22 8QX
T: 01372 227670
W: beaverbrook.co.uk

BEDROOMS: 35. 11 in Garden House, 6 in coach house, 1 suitable for disabled.
OPEN: all year.
FACILITIES: bar, snug, lounge, 3 restaurants, library, cinema, in-room TV (Sky), civil wedding licence, indoor and outdoor swimming pools, 470-acre grounds, walled garden, woodlands, lake, cookery school, kids' club.
BACKGROUND MUSIC: in restaurant, bar.
LOCATION: 2 miles from town centre.
CHILDREN: all ages welcomed.
DOGS: welcomed in some bedrooms, public spaces.
CREDIT CARDS: Amex, MC, Visa.
PRICES: per room B&B £420–£1,550. À la carte (Garden House restaurant) £55. 2-night min. stay on Sat, bank holidays, Christmas, New Year's Eve.

LEDBURY Herefordshire

# THE FEATHERS

A striking landmark in the centre of the market town, this refreshed hotel occupies two black-and-white-timbered Tudor buildings with many original features: exposed ancient beams, leaded windows, a centuries-old staircase. Individually decorated bedrooms are furnished in 'a somewhat quirky style'; the best are spacious, with a sitting area, perhaps a four-poster bed. Small plates, sharing platters and brasserie dishes (grilled fillet of hake, say, or celeriac tarte tatin) can be eaten in the restaurant, dog-friendly bar or lounge; in the courtyard when the weather allows. 'Good choice' at breakfast. Part of the Coaching Inn group; see also The Feathers, Helmsley, and The Talbot Hotel, Oundle (Shortlist entries).

MAP 3:D5
25 High Street
Ledbury  HR8 1DS
T: 01531 635266
W: feathersledbury.co.uk

BEDROOMS: 20. 1 suite in cottage, plus self-catering apartments.
OPEN: all year.
FACILITIES: bar, lounge, restaurant, coffee house, in-room TV (Freeview), civil wedding licence, function facilities, courtyard garden, parking.
BACKGROUND MUSIC: none.
LOCATION: town centre.
CHILDREN: all ages welcomed.
DOGS: allowed in bedrooms, most public areas, not in restaurant.
CREDIT CARDS: Amex, MC, Visa.
PRICES: per room B&B £80–£254. À la carte £34. 1-night bookings sometimes refused weekends.

## LEVENS Cumbria

# HARE AND HOUNDS

Becky and Ash Dewar run their family-friendly village pub in the Lyth valley, an unspoilt area characterised by damson orchards, green pastures and broad-leaved woodlands. Within the 16th-century hostelry, visitors mingle with regulars in the beamed bar and bright restaurant: here, cask ales and locally produced spirits accompany comforting pub classics (burgers, pizzas, grills) and more modern dishes – courgette and artichoke fritters, say. Upstairs, and in a spacious barn annexe, contemporary country-style bedrooms have welcome extras: home-made brownies, ground coffee, Cumbrian-made toiletries. The Lake District is close, but there are knolls and fells to walk right in the neighbourhood.

MAP 4: inset C2
Church Road
Levens LA8 8PN
T: 015395 60004
W: hareandhoundslevens.co.uk

BEDROOMS: 5. 1 in barn annexe.
OPEN: all year, no accommodation 24/25 Dec.
FACILITIES: pub, residents' lounge, restaurant, in-room TV (Freeview), ½-acre beer garden, parking.
BACKGROUND MUSIC: in pub and restaurant.
LOCATION: in village.
CHILDREN: all ages welcomed.
DOGS: allowed in 1 bedroom, pub, garden, not in restaurant.
CREDIT CARDS: Amex, MC, Visa.
PRICES: per room B&B £70–£185. À la carte £50 for 2 people. 2-night min. stay for weekends booked 1 month in advance.

## LEWANNICK Cornwall

# COOMBESHEAD FARM

In meadows and woodland, this rustic guest house and restaurant attract a convivial clientele, who come for the 'stupendous' farm-to-fork cooking and handsomely countrified bedrooms. The whole, in a centuries-old farmhouse and surrounding barns, is run by chef Tom Adams, with 'delightful, enthusiastic young staff'. Home-smoked, -cured and -pickled ingredients are paired with organic Cornish produce and locally foraged food in the 'feasting barn'. Bedrooms, simple and comfortable, have views stretching across to Dartmoor. Four new rooms in a converted barn were planned as the Guide went to press. With kombuchas and smoothies, breakfast, naturally, is a feast. On-site sourdough bakery; monthly bread workshops.

MAP 1:D3
Lewannick PL15 7QQ
T: 01566 782009
W: coombesheadfarm.co.uk

BEDROOMS: 9. 1 with adjoining bunk-bedroom, 4 in converted barn, 1 suitable for disabled.
OPEN: all year except Jan, restaurant closed Mon–Wed.
FACILITIES: living room, lounge, library, dining room, kitchen, bakery, 66-acre grounds, parking.
BACKGROUND MUSIC: in evening in living room, dining room and kitchen.
LOCATION: in village, 3 miles from A30, 6 miles from Launceston.
CHILDREN: not under 16, except at Sunday lunch.
DOGS: allowed in grounds only, on a lead, not in guest house, restaurant.
CREDIT CARDS: Amex, MC, Visa.
PRICES: per room B&B £180–£195. Set dinner £70.

LICHFIELD Staffordshire

# SWINFEN HALL

Entered through a magnificent hall with a hand-carved ceiling and balustraded minstrels' gallery, the Wiser family's 'imposing', ethically run Georgian manor is a 'very grand', yet 'relaxing', experience, thanks to 'friendly' staff. Spacious bedrooms with 'lovely views' over the estate grounds are decorated in period or more modern style; all have thoughtful additions (home-made flapjacks, a thermos of fresh milk). On a fine day, take tea on the terrace overlooking the gardens and deer park; in hunker-down weather, find a seat by the log fire in the cocktail lounge. At dinner, à la carte and tasting menus in the oak-panelled restaurant focus on home-grown and -reared produce; the bar has more casual options.

MAP 2:A2
Swinfen
Lichfield  WS14 9RE
T: 01543 481494
W: swinfenhallhotel.co.uk

BEDROOMS: 17.
OPEN: all year except Christmas Day evening, Boxing Day, restaurant closed Sun, Mon evenings (bar menu available).
FACILITIES: bar, lounge, cocktail lounge, restaurant, private dining rooms, in-room TV (Sky), civil wedding licence, 100-acre grounds (formal gardens, walled kitchen garden, courtyard garden, deer park, meadows, woodland), parking, public rooms wheelchair accessible.
BACKGROUND MUSIC: in public areas.
LOCATION: 2 miles S of Lichfield, just off the A38.
CHILDREN: all ages welcomed.
DOGS: not allowed.
CREDIT CARDS: Amex, MC, Visa.
PRICES: per room B&B single £125–£335, double £150–£375. À la carte £50.

LINCOLN Lincolnshire

# BRIDLEWAY BED & BREAKFAST

A trot up the bridleway reaches this 'excellent' B&B, in a rural setting next to an oak wood. It is run by Jane Haigh, an artist, who provides a 'lovely welcome': afternoon tea, home-made scones, clotted cream; advice on local restaurants; even a lift into Lincoln, nearby. Country-cosy rooms in converted stables have their own entrance; inside are calming hues, mellow wood, bathrobes and daily baked treats. 'Magnificent' breakfasts in the conservatory include fresh fruit salad, Aga-cooked porridge and pancakes, and a wide range of hot dishes, using eggs from Jane's hens; a continental hamper, with warm pastries, can be delivered to the room. Borrow wellies and the family dogs for walks. Stabling provided.

**25% DISCOUNT VOUCHERS**

MAP 4:E5
Riseholme Gorse
Lincoln  LN2 2LY
T: 01522 545693
W: bridlewaybandb.co.uk

BEDROOMS: 4. All on ground floor in converted outbuildings.
OPEN: Jan–mid-Dec.
FACILITIES: conservatory, in-room TV (Freeview), ½-acre grounds, 2 stables, manège, paddock for guests' horses.
BACKGROUND MUSIC: none, unless requested.
LOCATION: 3½ miles from Lincoln.
CHILDREN: not under 16.
DOGS: only assistance dogs allowed.
CREDIT CARDS: Amex, MC, Visa.
PRICES: per room B&B single £79–£110, double £93–£140. 1-night bookings refused weekends, high season.

## LITTLE ECCLESTON Lancashire

# THE CARTFORD INN

For centuries, this quirky coaching inn by the bridge over the River Wyre has looked across the rural panorama to the Bowland fells. Today, it is owned by Julie and Patrick Beaumé, who have added a community art gallery and an agreeably rustic deli to the boutiquey bedrooms, lively pub and well-regarded restaurant. The modern bedrooms (two refurbished this year) are bold and bright, with eclectic touches; most overlook the winding river. Two imaginatively decorated cabins, each with a split-level bedroom, spacious lounge and river-view balcony, stand in landscaped grounds. Relish Lancastrian produce cooked with a Gallic tweak at lunch and dinner; pick up a snack from the farm shop for the journey home.

MAP 4:D2
Cartford Lane
Little Eccleston PR3 0YP
T: 01995 670166
W: thecartfordinn.co.uk

BEDROOMS: 16. Some in riverside annexe, 1 suitable for disabled, 2 cabins in grounds.
OPEN: all year except 24–28 Dec, restaurant closed Mon lunch, except bank holidays.
FACILITIES: bar, restaurant, in-room TV (Freeview), function facilities, deli/coffee shop, riverside terrace, garden, parking.
BACKGROUND MUSIC: in public areas.
LOCATION: 8 miles E of Blackpool, easily reached from M6 and M55.
CHILDREN: all ages welcomed (some time restrictions in bar, restaurant).
DOGS: not allowed.
CREDIT CARDS: Amex, MC, Visa.
PRICES: per room B&B single £80–£150, double £130–£250, D,B&B from £180. À la carte £33.

## LIVERPOOL Merseyside

# HOPE STREET HOTEL

In the buzzing heart of the city, opposite the Philharmonic Hall, this contemporary hotel in a former Victorian carriage works is 'ideally placed' for exploring the many cultural venues in a creative neighbourhood. Its 'airy, modern' spaces have a stripped-back style, all exposed brick walls, pitch pine beams and vintage iron supports. Varying in size, minimalist bedrooms range from snug double rooms to rooftop suites with a hot tub terrace and 'wonderful views' of city landmarks. Further extension has added more rooms, plus a sleek spa and a cinema. From breakfast till late, 'delicious' modern British dishes are served in the restaurant; in the bar, sharing platters and easy eats pair with made-to-order cocktails.

MAP 4:E2
40 Hope Street
Liverpool L1 9DA
T: 0151 709 3000
W: hopestreethotel.co.uk

BEDROOMS: 150. 2 suitable for disabled.
OPEN: all year.
FACILITIES: lift, bar, 2 lounges, restaurant, private dining rooms, in-room TV (Sky, Freeview), civil wedding licence, spa (treatment rooms, indoor swimming pool, indoor/outdoor vitality pool), gym, cinema, limited parking nearby (charge).
BACKGROUND MUSIC: in public spaces.
LOCATION: city centre.
CHILDREN: all ages welcomed.
DOGS: allowed in some bedrooms, public areas, bar side of restaurant.
CREDIT CARDS: Amex, MC, Visa.
PRICES: per room B&B £105.50–£508.50, D,B&B £134.50–£537.50. À la carte £41.

**LIVERPOOL Merseyside**

## LOCK & KEY

Lush botanical wallpapers and voluptuous velvets cut a dash at this wildly welcoming, freshly converted Georgian town house hotel in the city centre. 'Superb', seductively dark-toned bedrooms (some snug) each have a marble-clad shower room with a rainfall shower; larger rooms are also supplied with cocktail chairs and a drinks trolley. In the speakeasy-style bar and restaurant, bare brick walls and light-bulb pendants set the tone for hours-long brunches, themed cocktails, pizzas and pastas, and wind-down nightcaps. Fear not the hipster: 'The big attraction here,' say trusted readers in 2020, whose young-at-heart 90-year-old father loved the place, 'are the wonderful staff and the atmosphere they create.'

MAP 4:E2
15–17 Duke Street
Liverpool L1 5AP
T: 0151 909 8766
W: lockandkeyhotels.com

BEDROOMS: 14. 1 on ground floor.
OPEN: all year.
FACILITIES: bar/restaurant, in-room smart TV.
BACKGROUND MUSIC: in bar/restaurant.
LOCATION: in the Ropewalks district.
CHILDREN: all ages welcomed.
DOGS: not allowed.
CREDIT CARDS: Amex, MC, Visa.
PRICES: per room £70–£249. Brunch £6–£8.50 (served 8 am–3 pm).

**LOOE Cornwall**

## THE BEACH HOUSE

Tea and a home-baked treat greet arriving visitors at Rosie and David Reeve's laid-back B&B overlooking Whitsand Bay. Three bedrooms face the sea; two access the garden. Each is simply decorated, 'spotlessly clean', and supplied with bathrobes, slippers, bottles of Cornish water, and a hospitality tray with fresh milk. In the morning, the buffet is a spread of cereals, fresh fruit, muffins and yogurt; hot cooked dishes, ordered the night before, include French toast, pancakes and Cornish sausages. A sandy beach with rock pools to explore is steps away; the South West Coast Path, which runs in front of the house, leads, past smugglers' caves, to Polperro. The hosts have ready local knowledge to share.

MAP 1:D3
Marine Drive
Looe PL13 2DH
T: 01503 262598
W: thebeachhouselooe.co.uk

BEDROOMS: 5.
OPEN: all year except Christmas.
FACILITIES: garden room, breakfast room, in-room TV (Freeview), terrace, ½-acre garden, beach opposite, spa treatments, parking.
BACKGROUND MUSIC: classical radio in breakfast room.
LOCATION: ½ mile from centre.
CHILDREN: not under 16.
DOGS: only assistance dogs allowed.
CREDIT CARDS: MC, Visa.
PRICES: per room B&B £85–£135. 2-night min. stay.

LUDLOW Shropshire

# THE CHARLTON ARMS HOTEL

A ten-minute walk, over the stone bridge, from Ludlow Castle, this 'good-value' pub-with-rooms stands above the River Teme, its large terrace taking in 'the enjoyable panorama of the town'. It is owned by Cedric and Amy Bosi, who encourage a cheery atmosphere in the popular bar and restaurant. The traditional bar 'heaves' with locals and visitors, here for the well-cooked modern dishes and pub classics; the landlord's French roots are revealed in a 'good' fish soup served with croutons and rouille. 'Well-appointed' bedrooms, some snug, are up the stairs; three newly added rooms each have a river-view balcony. In the morning, ask for the papers over a breakfast of local sausages and Clun Valley eggs.

MAP 3:C4
Ludford Bridge
Ludlow SY8 1PJ
T: 01584 872813
W: thecharltonarms.co.uk

BEDROOMS: 12.
OPEN: all year except Christmas, New Year.
FACILITIES: bar, lounge, snug, restaurant, in-room TV, terrace.
BACKGROUND MUSIC: all day in bar, restaurant.
LOCATION: by Ludford Bridge, 11-min. walk to town centre.
CHILDREN: all ages welcomed.
DOGS: allowed in bar, lounge, snug.
CREDIT CARDS: MC, Visa.
PRICES: per room B&B single £100–£160, double £100–£200. À la carte £28.

LUDLOW Shropshire

# THE CLIVE ARMS

A 2019 makeover gave this 18th-century building a string of smart bedrooms and a modern, open-plan bar and restaurant, ten minutes' drive from Ludlow. It is part of the Earl of Plymouth's Oakly Park estate. Individually styled rooms in the main building and rear courtyard are supplied with pleasing extras: ground coffee, loose-leaf teas, locally baked biscuits; a choice of pillows. Guests sensitive to traffic noise (an A road runs close by) should call to discuss their best options. In the 'field-to-fork' restaurant, seasonal menus reflect the freshest produce from the hotel's walled garden and the surrounding farms. Steps away: the Ludlow Farmshop, a hive of cheesemaking, butchering, preserving and cooking.

MAP 3:C4
Bromfield
Ludlow SY8 2JR
T: 01584 856565
W: theclive.co.uk

BEDROOMS: 17. 14 in courtyard annexe, some on ground floor, 1 suitable for disabled.
OPEN: all year.
FACILITIES: bar, lower bar, restaurant, snug, private dining room, in-room TV (Freeview), conference room, courtyard, beer garden.
BACKGROUND MUSIC: in public areas.
LOCATION: 4 miles NW of Ludlow.
CHILDREN: all ages welcomed.
DOGS: allowed in public rooms, some bedrooms.
CREDIT CARDS: Amex, MC, Visa.
PRICES: per room B&B from £144. À la carte £28–£40.

LUPTON Cumbria

## THE PLOUGH

Ideally placed for exploring the Lake District and
the Yorkshire Dales, this laid-back roadside inn,
in an 18th-century hostelry, has a modern rustic
look: wide wooden tables and mismatched chairs,
a wood-burning stove, sheepskin-covered bar
stools under oak beams. Locals and visitors come
for well-considered pub classics (duck and damson
sausages; roast cod loin) with good vegetarian
and vegan options. Graceful country bedrooms
have pale-painted furniture, squashy armchairs, a
digital radio and a coffee machine; perhaps a brass
bed or a vast beamed bathroom with a slipper
bath. Ideal for a family, the top-floor suite has two
bedrooms and glorious views over Farleton Knott.
Good cooked choices at breakfast.

MAP 4: inset C2
Cow Brow
Lupton  LA6 1PJ
T: 015395 67700
w: theploughatlupton.co.uk

BEDROOMS: 6.
OPEN: all year, no accommodation
24/25 Dec.
FACILITIES: lounge, bar, restaurant,
variable Wi-Fi signal, in-room TV
(Freeview), civil wedding licence,
terrace, garden, restaurant wheelchair
accessible, parking.
BACKGROUND MUSIC: in reception, bar
and restaurant.
LOCATION: 1 mile off junction 36, M6,
4 miles from Kirkby Lonsdale.
CHILDREN: all ages welcomed.
DOGS: allowed in most bedrooms, bar.
CREDIT CARDS: MC, Visa.
PRICES: per room B&B from £85,
D,B&B from £115. À la carte £30.

LYME REGIS Dorset

## DORSET HOUSE

'Top class in all respects', Lyn and Jason Martin's
Grade II listed Regency B&B overlooking the
Jurassic coast is pleasing inside and out. An
honesty bar adds to the attraction of the snug
(fire-warmed in cool weather); on fine days,
guests may have breakfast on the veranda. On the
first floor, handsome modern bedrooms each have
their own style and charm, plus a host of extras:
freshly ground coffee and artisanal tea, locally
baked treats, fluffy bathrobes, British-made
toiletries. Through large sash windows, three
of the rooms have sea views beyond the town's
rooftops. The Aga-fresh breakfast is 'excellent',
with locally roasted coffee, home-made granola
and sourdough, and organic sausages and bacon.

**25% DISCOUNT VOUCHERS**

MAP 1:C6
Pound Road
Lyme Regis  DT7 3HX
T: 01297 442055
w: dorsethouselyme.com

BEDROOMS: 5.
OPEN: all year except Christmas.
FACILITIES: snug, breakfast room,
reception, in-room TV (Freeview),
veranda, paid parking nearby.
BACKGROUND MUSIC: in breakfast room.
LOCATION: 300 yards from town centre.
CHILDREN: all ages welcomed.
DOGS: not allowed.
CREDIT CARDS: Amex, MC, Visa.
PRICES: per room B&B single £85–£175,
double £95–£185. 1-night bookings
usually refused.

**NEW**

LYME REGIS Dorset

# GREENHILL HOUSE

'If Lyme Regis is the pearl of the Dorset coast, then this beautiful B&B is surely one of its diamonds.' Overlooking Lyme Bay, Sara and Ed Hollway's 'restful, relaxing' 1930s home gives 'a blissful experience'. 'Everything has been carefully thought out to provide the utmost comfort and convenience': there are maps, books, jigsaw puzzles and board games in the sitting room; 'top-quality design, with a hint of the '30s, executed with panache and a touch of humour' in the well-equipped bedrooms. Bountiful breakfasts are served in a 'lovely' dining room or the 'delightful' garden, where the views to Golden Cap and the Jurassic Coast are 'sublime'. The walk back from town is steep – let the bus or a taxi take the strain.

MAP 1:C6
Somers Road
Lyme Regis  DT7 3EX
T: 01297 445497
W: greenhillhousebandb.co.uk

BEDROOMS: 3.
OPEN: all year except 20–29 Dec.
FACILITIES: sitting room, dining room, in-room TV (Freeview), ½-acre garden.
BACKGROUND MUSIC: none.
LOCATION: on a hillside, above the town.
CHILDREN: all ages welcomed (although there are no special facilities).
DOGS: not allowed.
CREDIT CARDS: not accepted.
PRICES: per room B&B single £130–£155, double £150–£175.

MALVERN WELLS Worcestershire

# THE COTTAGE IN THE WOOD

High in the Malvern hills, this refurbished Georgian dower house has 'stunning' views over the Severn valley. A years-long makeover, completed in 2020, has resulted in contemporary public spaces in shades of grey, and a collection of smart, up-to-date bedrooms that range from snug to spacious. Floor-to-ceiling windows in the wood-floored restaurant (popular with groups) afford views of a rural panorama that stretches to the Cotswolds – a fine backdrop for the modern dishes, including vegan and gluten-free options, at lunch and dinner. Casual meals and drinks may also be taken alfresco on the new terrace, all the better to soak in the fresh air. Close by: country lanes, historic market towns, the Elgar route.

MAP 3:D5
Holywell Road
Malvern Wells  WR14 4LG
T: 01684 588860
W: cottageinthewood.co.uk

BEDROOMS: 32. 4 in Beech Cottage, 19 in coach house, 10 on ground floor, 1 suitable for disabled.
OPEN: all year.
FACILITIES: bar, restaurant, meeting room, in-room TV (Freeview), covered terrace, 8-acre grounds, parking, public rooms wheelchair accessible, adapted toilet.
BACKGROUND MUSIC: 'quiet, relaxing music' in bar, restaurant.
LOCATION: 4 miles from Malvern Wells.
CHILDREN: all ages welcomed.
DOGS: allowed in some bedrooms, not in public rooms.
CREDIT CARDS: Amex, MC, Visa.
PRICES: per room B&B £119–£229, D,B&B £189–£299. À la carte £40.

## MANCHESTER
# THE COW HOLLOW HOTEL

Once industrial, now simply 'in', the city's lively Northern Quarter is a fitting spot for this Victorian textile warehouse-turned-hip hotel. Fronted by a cool cocktail bar, the boutiquey venue is owned by Mujtaba and Amelia Rana, who have kept the metal staircases and exposed brick, and added indoor greenery and modern style. Clean-cut, contemporary bedrooms have up-to-date tech (a smart TV; a Netflix subscription); rainfall showers and high-end toiletries are standard. Complimentary treats include Prosecco and nibbles in the evening; milk and cookies later. A breakfast bag of granola, juice, fruit and a pastry is delivered to the room in the morning. No restaurant, but popular eateries are close by.

MAP 4:E3
57 Newton Street
Manchester M1 1ET
T: 0161 228 7277
W: cowhollow.co.uk

BEDROOMS: 16.
OPEN: all year except 25/26 Dec.
FACILITIES: cocktail bar, in-room TV (Freeview, Netflix).
BACKGROUND MUSIC: in cocktail bar.
LOCATION: in the Northern Quarter.
CHILDREN: all ages welcomed (sharing with one adult, max. room occupancy of 2).
DOGS: not allowed.
CREDIT CARDS: Amex, MC, Visa.
PRICES: per room B&B £99–£299.

## MANCHESTER
# DIDSBURY HOUSE

Between two parks, this refurbished Victorian villa with sophisticated accommodation is within easy reach of the city. It is part of the small Eclectic Hotels group (see also Eleven Didsbury Park, next entry). A voguish B&B, it was designed with a boutique mindset: vintage prints and statement wallpaper, tempered by fresh flowers, books, open fires and sink-into sofas; at the top of a staircase, an impressive stained-glass window. Tasteful bedrooms, some set over two levels, retain original high windows and delicate cornices; among up-to-date amenities are a butler tray with fresh milk, perhaps a roll-top bath or two. There are afternoon teas and aperitifs to be had; on the weekend, breakfast is served until noon.

MAP 4:E3
Didsbury Park
Manchester M20 5LJ
T: 0161 448 2200
W: didsburyhouse.co.uk

BEDROOMS: 27. Some on ground floor, 1 suitable for disabled.
OPEN: all year.
FACILITIES: bar, 2 lounges, breakfast room, in-room TV (Sky), civil wedding licence, meeting/function facilities, heated walled terrace.
BACKGROUND MUSIC: in public areas, volume adjusted to suit the atmosphere and time of day.
LOCATION: 6 miles from Manchester city centre and airport, easy access to M60.
CHILDREN: all ages welcomed.
DOGS: not allowed.
CREDIT CARDS: Amex, MC, Visa.
PRICES: per room £120–£300. Breakfast £16.

## MANCHESTER
# ELEVEN DIDSBURY PARK

A retreat from the city, the large walled garden of this suburban Victorian town house is an inviting place to hang loose. Rattan swings are suspended from beams; on the lawn or under the covered terrace, sun loungers, hammocks and a sofa await. Squashy sofas encourage the laid-back atmosphere in the sitting room. Individually decorated, modern bedrooms are spread over three floors; the best, a split-level suite, has a veranda leading to the garden. In all rooms: spa-worthy toiletries, a minibar, a butler tray with fresh milk. Breakfast is in the bright conservatory. The city centre and airport are a short train-ride or drive away. Part of the Eclectic Hotels group; see also Didsbury House (previous entry).

MAP 4:E3
11 Didsbury Park
Manchester M20 5LH
T: 0161 448 7711
W: elevendidsburypark.com

BEDROOMS: 20. 1, on ground floor, suitable for disabled.
OPEN: all year.
FACILITIES: 2 lounge/bars, in-room TV (Sky), veranda, walled garden, wedding/conference facilities, parking.
BACKGROUND MUSIC: all day in public areas.
LOCATION: 6 miles from Manchester city centre and airport, easy access to M60.
CHILDREN: all ages welcomed.
DOGS: not allowed.
CREDIT CARDS: Amex, MC, Visa.
PRICES: per room £150–£300. Breakfast £16.

## MARAZION Cornwall
# THE GODOLPHIN

'If hotels had personalities, this one would be a cheerful extrovert.' Across the causeway from St Michael's Mount, this bright, south-facing restaurant-with-rooms shares the energy of its 'young and enthusiastic' staff. 'Tactfully modernised and enlarged', it is decorated with uplifting coastal colours and local artwork. 'Smart, modern' bedrooms face the village or the sea; the view over Mount's Bay is worth the upgrade. 'Our sea-view balcony was sunny from lunchtime on.' Caught-that-day seafood is a highlight of the short, 'fresh, tasty' menu served in the breezy restaurant and beachfront terrace ('a pity the menu doesn't change more regularly'). Breakfast includes sweet waffles, a full Cornish and a veggie shakshuka.

MAP 1:E1
West End
Marazion TR17 0EN
T: 01736 888510
W: thegodolphin.com

BEDROOMS: 10. Some suitable for disabled.
OPEN: all year.
FACILITIES: 2 bars, split-level dining area, in-room TV (Freeview), wedding/function facilities, 2 terraces, parking, dining room wheelchair accessible.
BACKGROUND MUSIC: in public areas, occasional live acoustic music.
LOCATION: 4 miles E of Penzance.
CHILDREN: all ages welcomed.
DOGS: allowed in 2 bedrooms, designated dining area, on terrace.
CREDIT CARDS: MC, Visa.
PRICES: per room B&B £100–£295. À la carte £30.

## MARCHAM Oxfordshire
## B&B RAFTERS

Come behind the stone wall to find this inviting B&B, on the edge of an Oxfordshire village within reach of historic houses, Cotswold communities and the city of dreaming spires. It is warmly run by Sigrid Grawert, who has helpful local information to share. Modern bedrooms (one with a private balcony) are equipped with teas, coffee, a cool drink and fluffy robes; on the landing are honesty-box soft drinks and snacks, and a capsule coffee machine. The suntrap garden has space to sit. In the morning, an award-winning breakfast is taken at the large communal table: freshly squeezed orange juice, home-baked sourdough bread, home-made marmalade and jams, a superb porridge menu. Special diets are catered for.

MAP 2:C2
Abingdon Road
Marcham OX13 6NU
T: 01865 391298
W: bnb-rafters.co.uk

BEDROOMS: 4.
OPEN: all year except Christmas, New Year.
FACILITIES: breakfast room, in-room smart TV (Freeview), garden, parking.
BACKGROUND MUSIC: none.
LOCATION: 3 miles W of Abingdon, 10 miles S of Oxford.
CHILDREN: not under 11.
DOGS: not allowed.
CREDIT CARDS: MC, Visa.
PRICES: per room B&B single £64–£69, double £95–£139. 2-night min. stay on bank holiday weekends.

## MARGATE Kent
## SANDS HOTEL

A short seafront stroll from the Turner Contemporary gallery, Nick Conington's 'smart', modern hotel is a welcome part of Margate's renaissance. The 'attractively refurbished' Victorian building preens by the beach, with 'huge windows that provide a great opportunity for sunset watching'. Some of the sea-facing bedrooms have a private balcony; others look towards the Old Town, its vintage shops and cafés. The 'lovely' first-floor dining room leads to a terrace for alfresco meals when the weather is fine. On the menu: modern European dishes, with vegan and vegetarian options. Take breakfast with a view over the bay; rise-and-shine choices include buttermilk pancakes, grilled kippers and a full Kentish.

MAP 2:D5
16 Marine Drive
Margate CT9 1DH
T: 01843 228228
W: sandshotelmargate.co.uk

BEDROOMS: 20. 1 suitable for disabled.
OPEN: all year.
FACILITIES: lift, bar, restaurant, in-room TV (Freeview), civil wedding licence, balcony terrace, seasonal rooftop bar, ice-cream parlour, public areas wheelchair accessible.
BACKGROUND MUSIC: in public areas.
LOCATION: town centre.
CHILDREN: all ages welcomed.
DOGS: allowed, not in restaurant.
CREDIT CARDS: Amex, MC, Visa.
PRICES: per room B&B £140–£200, D,B&B £200–£260. À la carte £35.

## MATLOCK BATH Derbyshire
## HODGKINSON'S HOTEL

Zoe and Chris Hipwell's personable small hotel has 'superb' views, across the rooftops of the historic spa village, towards limestone cliffs and the River Derwent. The terraced gardens have space to sit; inside the Georgian town house, most of the restored features (ornate glasswork, a tiled entrance hall, the wood-and-glass bar) date to the ownership of Victorian wine merchant Job Hodgkinson, who stored his wares in the Roman-era cave. Some of the traditionally furnished bedrooms have river views; all are supplied with beverage-making facilities and a clock radio. One room with a pull-out couch and space for an extra bed is ideal for a family. Modern European dishes are served in the intimate restaurant. 'Excellent walks' from the door.

MAP 3:B6
150 South Parade
Matlock Bath  DE4 3NR
T: 01629 582170
W: hodgkinsons-hotel.co.uk

BEDROOMS: 8.
OPEN: all year except Christmas week, restaurant closed Sun, Mon eve, except on bank holidays and for guests who have pre-booked.
FACILITIES: sitting room, restaurant with bar, in-room TV (Freeview), terraced garden, limited parking (road parking nearby).
BACKGROUND MUSIC: radio (daytime), 'lounge, easy listening' (evening) in public areas and restaurant.
LOCATION: centre of village, 1 mile from Matlock and Cromford.
CHILDREN: all ages welcomed.
DOGS: allowed in some bedrooms, lounge, not in restaurant.
CREDIT CARDS: MC, Visa.
PRICES: per room B&B £95–£165, D,B&B £151–£221. Set dinner £28 (2 courses), £32 (3 courses).

## MEVAGISSEY Cornwall
## PEBBLE HOUSE

High above the 14th-century fishing village, Andrea and Simon Copper's sleekly designed, child-free retreat offers a stunning seascape, which stretches across Mevagissey Bay to historic Chapel Point and beyond. Clean-cut, modern bedrooms, all with wide, floor-to-ceiling windows, bring the outside in. One has a private patio with seating; another, a Juliet balcony. Light lunches, Cornish cream teas and the host's award-winning breakfasts (home-made granola and soda bread; a choice of seven cooked dishes) are served in the open-plan breakfast room/lounge; in fine weather, sit on the terrace and bask in 180-degree sea views. Picnics can be ordered to take out on the South West Coast Path, steps away.

MAP 1:D2
Polkirt Hill
Mevagissey  PL26 6UX
T: 01726 844466
W: pebblehousecornwall.co.uk

BEDROOMS: 5. 1 on ground floor with private terrace.
OPEN: Feb–early Nov, exclusive-use self-catering over Christmas, New Year.
FACILITIES: lounge/breakfast room, in-room TV (Freeview, Sky in some rooms), terrace, small functions, parking.
BACKGROUND MUSIC: in breakfast room.
LOCATION: on South West Coast Path, 10 mins' walk to Mevagissey, 16 miles E of Truro.
CHILDREN: not allowed, except for self-catering bookings.
DOGS: not allowed.
CREDIT CARDS: Amex, MC, Visa.
PRICES: per room B&B £175–£225.

MEVAGISSEY Cornwall

# TREVALSA COURT

'Charm and dependability make this a comfortable, unpretentious place to stay,' reports a regular returnee to John and Susan Gladwin's cliff-top hotel on the outskirts of Mevagissey. The 1930s house stands in sub-tropical gardens – 'a wonderful place to unwind, take a cream tea, or begin the stroll down to the private beach'. Inside, find a panelled dining room, a small bar, and a sitting room with books and games. All but two bedrooms have 'fabulous' sea views. In the restaurant, seafood and local farm produce show up on menus of small plates and modern British dishes. The cooking is 'always reliable', though guests this year wished for more variety. And while 'service can be slow', the food is 'worth waiting for'.

MAP 1:D2
School Hill
Mevagissey  PL26 6TH
T: 01726 842468
W: trevalsa-hotel.co.uk

BEDROOMS: 15. 4 on ground floor.
OPEN: mid-Feb–late Nov (phone to check if open at Christmas, New Year).
FACILITIES: lounge, bar, restaurant, in-room TV (Freeview), 2-acre garden, summer house, public rooms wheelchair accessible.
BACKGROUND MUSIC: all day in bar.
LOCATION: on cliff-top, at edge of village.
CHILDREN: all ages welcomed.
DOGS: allowed in bedrooms, not in restaurant, in other public rooms with consent of other guests.
CREDIT CARDS: Amex, MC, Visa.
PRICES: per room B&B single from £70, double £125–£295. À la carte £35. 1-night bookings refused high season.

**NEW**

MINSTER LOVELL Oxfordshire

# OLD SWAN

'Everyone's idea of a Cotswold pub', this 600-year-old inn is one of the oldest buildings in a picturesque village of thatched houses on the River Windrush. Outside is a spread of gardens, wildflower meadows and woodland; inside, cosy nooks, log fires, flagstone floors and sturdy beams form a characterful backdrop for pie-and-pint evenings, or cocktails, seasonal specials and pub classics (artichoke risotto, ewe's curd; Hobgoblin-battered haddock). Well-ordered bedrooms, some able to accommodate a family, have rustic charm in their plaid throws and cushions; bathrobes, slippers and upmarket toiletries are welcome extras. Guests may use the tennis and spa facilities at sister hotel Minster Mill, across the road.

MAP 3:E6
Minster Lovell  OX29 0RN
T: 01993 862512
W: oldswan.co.uk

BEDROOMS: 15. 6 on ground floor, plus 3-bed cottage.
OPEN: all year.
FACILITIES: ramps, bar, restaurant, in-room TV (Freeview), terrace, 65-acre grounds, bicycle hire.
BACKGROUND MUSIC: none.
LOCATION: in village 3 miles W of Witney, 15 miles from Oxford.
CHILDREN: all ages welcomed.
DOGS: in some bedrooms, bar.
CREDIT CARDS: Amex, MC, Visa.
PRICES: per room B&B £110–£250, D,B&B £210–£350. À la carte £32. 2-night min. stay some weekends.

MORECAMBE Lancashire

# THE MIDLAND

In a 'superb position' overlooking Morecambe
Bay, this 'Art Deco wonder' was restored to its
former glory by the small English Lakes group.
'The joy is the long dining room' of the 'lovely'
Sun Terrace restaurant, which follows the curve
of the building. Every table has a 'wonderful'
sea view through huge windows, but draw your
gaze inside, too: 'the food is excellent; the wine
list, extensive; and the staff are keen to please'.
Up a 'charming' spiral staircase (or reached via
a compact lift), curved corridors lead to urbane
modern bedrooms, many with a view over the sea.
Mornings, 'the breakfast buffet is plentiful; the
whisky offering with porridge, a nice touch'. Ideal
for the Isle of Man ferry from Heysham.

MAP 4:D2
Marine Road West
Morecambe LA4 4BU
T: 01524 424000
W: englishlakes.co.uk/the-midland

BEDROOMS: 44. 2 suitable for disabled.
OPEN: all year.
FACILITIES: lift, lounge, bar, restaurant,
in-room TV, function rooms, civil
wedding licence, lawns, parking.
BACKGROUND MUSIC: '1930s/1950s
music' in lounge.
LOCATION: overlooking Morecambe
Bay, steps from the stone jetty.
CHILDREN: all ages welcomed.
DOGS: well-behaved dogs allowed, not
in restaurant.
CREDIT CARDS: Amex, MC, Visa.
PRICES: per room B&B £128–£460,
D,B&B £186–£518. À la carte £31.
1-night bookings refused Sat.

MORPETH Northumberland

# ST MARY'S INN

'Friendly, attentive' staff encourage a 'jovial,
relaxed' feel at this updated pub-with-rooms, in
a 'cleverly renovated' former hospital building.
It stands on the edge of a new housing estate in
a small village south of Morpeth. Bedrooms are
styled with a mix of modern furnishings and
antique pieces. 'Ours was uncluttered, clean and
bright, with a well-lit bathroom and a generous
supply of toiletries.' In the 'heaving' bar, try the
pub's own locally brewed ale; there's 'quality
cooking', with 'good' vegetarian options, in the
restaurant. Breakfast, healthy or hearty, is served
in a high-ceilinged room 'flooded with light'.
Jesmond Dene House, Newcastle upon Tyne (see
main entry), is under the same ownership.

MAP 4:B4
St Mary's Lane
Morpeth NE61 6BL
T: 01670 293293
W: stmarysinn.co.uk

BEDROOMS: 11. 1 suitable for disabled.
OPEN: all year.
FACILITIES: lift, 4 bar areas, dining
room, private dining rooms, in-room
TV (Freeview), grassed area at front.
BACKGROUND MUSIC: 'easy listening' in
bar and dining areas.
LOCATION: 2½ miles W of Stannington.
CHILDREN: all ages welcomed.
DOGS: allowed in 1 bedroom, bar, not
in restaurant.
CREDIT CARDS: Amex, MC, Visa.
PRICES: per room B&B £99–£119,
D,B&B £129–£159. À la carte £27.

MULLION Cornwall
## POLURRIAN ON THE LIZARD

A path leads from this cliff-top hotel to a stretch of private beach on the west of the Lizard peninsula – just one of several vantage points to take in the stunning coastal views. A relaxed, airy retreat in a 'wonderful position', the hotel appeals to guests of all ages, with tennis, kayaking, spa treatments and yoga sessions alongside a host of child-friendly activities during the holidays. Many of the neat, modern bedrooms face the water; some accommodate a family. In the restaurant, informal, Mediterranean-inspired dishes make the best of Cornish ingredients, much sourced from within a 20-mile radius. Borrow wellies, fishing nets, and buckets and spades; come back in time for an award-winning cream tea.

MAP 1:E2
Polurrian Road
Mullion TR12 7EN
T: 01326 240421
W: polurrianhotel.com

BEDROOMS: 41. Some on ground floor, 1 suitable for disabled. Plus four 3-bedroom self-catering villas.
OPEN: all year.
FACILITIES: lift, bar, lounge, snug, restaurant, in-room TV, civil wedding licence, function facilities, cinema, games room (table football, table tennis), spa, indoor pool, 9-metre outdoor pool (Apr–Sept), 12-acre grounds, terrace, tennis court, climbing frame.
BACKGROUND MUSIC: in public areas.
LOCATION: in village.
CHILDREN: all ages welcomed.
DOGS: allowed in some bedrooms, not in restaurant.
CREDIT CARDS: Amex, MC, Visa.
PRICES: per room B&B from £119, D,B&B from £159.

NEWQUAY Cornwall
## THE HEADLAND HOTEL

Above Fistral beach, the Armstrong family's child- and dog-friendly hotel basks in 'spectacular views' of the ocean and one of Cornwall's surfing hotspots. The in-house Surf Sanctuary teaches kitesurfing and stand-up paddleboarding, but the impressive Victorian building and new Aqua Club offer less adventurous diversions, too: six swimming pools, indoors and out; a host of treatments in the luxury spa; buckets and spades for the beach; games, books and DVDs for rainy days. Most of the bedrooms (some with a balcony) have coastal hues and views. Day or night, varied menus and venues – on the waterfront terrace, in the sophisticated Samphire restaurant, or poolside – highlight Cornish produce in season.

MAP 1:D2
Headland Road
Newquay TR7 1EW
T: 01637 872211
W: headlandhotel.co.uk

BEDROOMS: 95. 1 suitable for disabled, plus 39 self-catering cottages in the grounds.
OPEN: all year.
FACILITIES: 5 lounges, bar, 4 restaurants, in-room TV (Freeview), civil wedding licence, conference/event facilities, 10-acre grounds, spa, gym, aqua club (indoor and outdoor heated swimming pools, sun terrace).
BACKGROUND MUSIC: in restaurants.
LOCATION: on a headland overlooking Fistral beach.
CHILDREN: all ages welcomed.
DOGS: allowed in bedrooms, public rooms, not in restaurants.
CREDIT CARDS: Amex, MC, Visa.
PRICES: per room B&B single £80–£425, double £140–£525, D,B&B £176–£561. À la carte £36.

NEWQUAY Cornwall

# LEWINNICK LODGE

Atop the craggy Pentire headland, this cliff-edge hotel dispenses exhilarating views and the soothing sounds of the Atlantic. Sleek and stylish inside, it has a laid-back atmosphere and environmentally friendly principles. Most bedrooms take in a vista that stretches towards Towan Head and Fistral Beach. Each has a large bed, home-made biscuits, binoculars and a digital radio; in the bathroom are robes, organic toiletries, perhaps a slipper bath. In the 'busy, informal' restaurant and bar, and on the wide terrace above the waves, produce from local fishermen and farmers are featured in such unfussy dishes as pan-roasted Cornish pollock, squid and chickpea stew, mussels. Good walks from the door.

MAP 1:D2
Pentire Headland
Newquay TR7 1QD
T: 01637 878117
W: lewinnicklodge.co.uk

BEDROOMS: 17. Some suitable for disabled.
OPEN: all year.
FACILITIES: lift, bar, lounge, snug, restaurant, in-room smart TV (Sky, Freeview), in-room spa treatments, terraced beer garden, parking, Tesla electric car charging points.
BACKGROUND MUSIC: all day in public spaces.
LOCATION: Pentire headland.
CHILDREN: all ages welcomed.
DOGS: allowed in some bedrooms, bar, terrace, not in restaurant.
CREDIT CARDS: MC, Visa.
PRICES: per room B&B £120–£300.
À la carte £29.50. 1-night bookings sometimes refused high season.

NORTHALLERTON Yorkshire

# CLEVELAND TONTINE

Travellers have long stopped at this Georgian hostelry, which skirts the North York moors. Today's visitors like the former coaching inn for its 'friendly' staff and the 'very good' food served in the 'busy' restaurant. Well-appointed, 'well-lit' bedrooms, some more boldly styled than others, may have a four-poster bed or a freestanding bath; some have views towards distant hills. Afternoon tea may be taken on the garden terrace or in the morning room; breakfast has 'good choice'. The hotel stands on an 'unusual site' close to two A roads, but 'its double glazing works well, and we heard no traffic noise', report Guide readers this year. Part of the Provenance Inns group; see The Carpenters Arms, Felixkirk (main entry).

MAP 4:C4
Staddlebridge
Northallerton DL6 3JB
T: 01609 882671
W: theclevelandtontine.com

BEDROOMS: 7.
OPEN: all year.
FACILITIES: bar, lounge, morning room, bistro, in-room TV (Freeview), room service, function facilities, garden, parking.
BACKGROUND MUSIC: in public rooms.
LOCATION: 8 miles NE of Northallerton.
CHILDREN: all ages welcomed.
DOGS: allowed in bar, lounge.
CREDIT CARDS: Amex, MC, Visa.
PRICES: per room B&B £95–£195.
Set menu £21.95 (2 courses), £24.95 (3 courses), à la carte £36.

NORWICH Norfolk

## NORFOLK MEAD

'Perfect peace and quiet' drifts across 'lush grounds' to James Holliday and Anna Duttson's 'splendid', wisteria-hung Georgian house by the River Bure. The relaxed atmosphere is thanks, in part, to 'informal, attentive' staff; spa treatments and cosy nooks do the rest. 'Well-equipped bedrooms' have uplifting decor; some have a private balcony or terrace. 'Our room was spacious and light, with its own seating area.' The summer houses and cottages, which can accommodate four or six people, suit groups. Eat well: 'beautifully fresh and elegantly presented' dishes at dinner; home-made marmalade, 'excellent black pudding, sausages and smoked bacon' at breakfast. The hotel's day boat is available for hire.

MAP 2:B5
Church Loke
Norwich NR12 7DN
T: 01603 737531
W: norfolkmead.co.uk

BEDROOMS: 16. 2 cottages, 3 in summer houses.
OPEN: all year.
FACILITIES: lounge, bar, snug, restaurant, private dining rooms, in-room TV (Freeview), civil wedding licence, 2 beauty treatment rooms, 8-acre grounds, walled garden, fishing lake, day boat hire.
BACKGROUND MUSIC: in public areas.
LOCATION: about 20 mins' drive from Norwich.
CHILDREN: all ages welcomed.
DOGS: allowed in some bedrooms in grounds, not in main building.
CREDIT CARDS: MC, Visa.
PRICES: per room B&B £135–£360. À la carte £40.

NORWICH Norfolk

## 38 ST GILES

'Well placed' for city exploration, this luxury B&B, in a grand 18th-century house, is within walking distance of the Theatre Royale and the central marketplace. Most of the bedrooms and suites are up the stairs; all have fine linens, good toiletries, teas and a coffee machine. They range in size ('our "cosy" room really was small, with a bijou shower room'); the best are huge, with space to sit, perhaps even a glamorous bathroom. An 'elegant' breakfast is served at tables 'beautifully laid with bone china'. Start with freshly squeezed juice, plus yogurt and berries, or home-made granola; crème fraîche pancakes, and eggs scrambled, poached or fried are cooked to order. Paid parking is on a neighbouring road.

MAP 2:B5
38 St Giles Street
Norwich NR2 1LL
T: 01603 662944
W: 38stgiles.co.uk

BEDROOMS: 12. 1 on ground floor, 4 in apartment and town house.
OPEN: all year except 24–28 Dec.
FACILITIES: breakfast room, lounge, in-room TV (Freeview), courtyard garden, limited private parking (advance booking, £15 per day).
BACKGROUND MUSIC: at breakfast.
LOCATION: central.
CHILDREN: all ages welcomed.
DOGS: not allowed.
CREDIT CARDS: MC, Visa.
PRICES: per room B&B single £105–£210, double £130–£260, town house (2 doubles) from £275, apartment (2 doubles) from £300.

OUNDLE Northamptonshire
## LOWER FARM

Adjoining their small arable farm, the Marriott family has converted a series of outbuildings into homely B&B rooms. Robert Marriott and his brother, John, run the farm; Caroline Marriott is the 'friendly, accommodating' hostess. Surrounded by fields and fresh air, simply decorated bedrooms occupy the former milking parlour and stables arranged around a courtyard with seating; several rooms may be connected to suit a family. The hearty farmhouse breakfast might include porridge with fresh cream, a farmer's butty, and steak and eggs (a speciality) – ideal for tackling walking and cycling tracks from the door, including the Nene Way footpath, which runs through the farm. The village pub is a short stroll away.

MAP 2:B3
Main Street
Oundle PE8 5PU
T: 01832 273220
W: lower-farm.co.uk

BEDROOMS: 10. All on ground floor, 1 suitable for disabled.
OPEN: all year.
FACILITIES: breakfast room, in-room TV (Freeview), courtyard garden, parking.
BACKGROUND MUSIC: radio 'if guests wish' in breakfast room.
LOCATION: at one end of the village, 3 miles from Oundle.
CHILDREN: all ages welcomed.
DOGS: allowed in 2 bedrooms, not in public rooms.
CREDIT CARDS: Amex, MC, Visa.
PRICES: per person B&B £55–£90.

**NEW**

OUNDLE Northamptonshire
## THE TALBOT HOTEL

Charm and character – perhaps even a queenly ghost – have been passed down through the centuries at this handsome Grade I listed building in a market town on the River Nene. Today a sympathetically updated hotel, it retains a large window and staircase believed to have come from the medieval castle of Fotheringhay, nearby. Classically furnished bedrooms vary in size, from single rooms to family-friendly suites; all are supplied with tea, coffee, bottled water and biscuits. Grazing plates and uncomplicated dishes (seared sea bream, Israeli couscous, say) from the restaurant may be eaten alfresco in the pretty garden. Part of the Coaching Inn group; see also The Feathers, Helmsley, and The Feathers, Ledbury (Shortlist entries).

MAP 2:B3
New Street
Oundle PE8 4EA
T: 01832 273621
W: thetalbot-oundle.com

BEDROOMS: 34. Some on ground floor.
OPEN: all year.
FACILITIES: lounge, bar, coffee house, restaurant, in-room TV (Freeview), civil wedding licence, conference/ function facilities, courtyard, garden, parking.
BACKGROUND MUSIC: in public areas.
LOCATION: in town centre.
CHILDREN: all ages welcomed.
DOGS: allowed in bedrooms, lounge, bar, not in restaurant.
CREDIT CARDS: Amex, MC, Visa.
PRICES: per room B&B £105–£239. À la carte £35.

**PAKEFIELD** Suffolk

## THE HOG HOTEL

Uncurl in comfort in this recently renovated hotel in an old maritime village on the Suffolk coast. Family-owned and friendly, it supports hedgehog conservation. Clean-cut bedrooms (some with their own entrance) are kitted out in restful shades and abstract prints; they have a drench shower and Suffolk-made organic toiletries in the bathroom. Casual meals (salads, sandwiches, burgers) are served in the spruce bar; on Friday and Saturday evenings, the restaurant has a monthly-changing menu of local favourites and specialities from around the world. On a fine day, step in to the garden, where little Hog 'hotels' shelter hedgehog guests, then wander a little further to see the colourful huts on the beach.

MAP 2:B6
41 London Road
Pakefield NR33 7AA
T: 01502 569805
W: thehoghotel.co.uk

BEDROOMS: 16. 1 suite suitable for disabled.
OPEN: all year, restaurant open 6 pm–10 pm Fri, Sat.
FACILITIES: bar, restaurant, in-room smart TV, function facilities, conservatory, terrace, garden.
BACKGROUND MUSIC: in public areas.
LOCATION: in village, 2 miles S of Lowestoft.
CHILDREN: all ages welcomed.
DOGS: welcomed in some bedrooms, not in main hotel, bar, restaurant.
CREDIT CARDS: Amex, MC, Visa.
PRICES: per room B&B £110–£230. À la carte £32.

**PENZANCE** Cornwall

## ARTIST RESIDENCE CORNWALL

On a sloping street behind the harbour, this 17th-century house run with 'lovely' staff brims with 'intriguing artwork' and vintage flourishes. Typical of Justin and Charlotte Salisbury's eclectic hotel collection (see also main entries for Artist Residence in London, Brighton and South Leigh), the shabby chic bedrooms – including ones that can accommodate a dog or a family – are mildly eccentric, mightily different. Some are small, with a modern shower room; one is huge, with a log-burner-warmed sitting area; others, in between, have hand-painted murals across walls and ceilings. At brunch, lunch and dinner, 'tasty' seasonal meals and a smokehouse menu draw diners to the informal, 'quirky' Cornish Barn.

MAP 1:E1
20 Chapel Street
Penzance TR18 4AW
T: 01736 365664
W: artistresidence.co.uk

BEDROOMS: 22. Plus 3-bedroom cottage in grounds.
OPEN: all year.
FACILITIES: bar, restaurant, in-room TV (Freeview), terrace, beer garden.
BACKGROUND MUSIC: in public areas.
LOCATION: town centre.
CHILDREN: all ages welcomed.
DOGS: allowed in some bedrooms, restaurant.
CREDIT CARDS: Amex, MC, Visa.
PRICES: per room £85–£350. Breakfast £4–£10.50, à la carte £35. 1-night stay sometimes refused weekends.

PENZANCE Cornwall
# VENTON VEAN

Original art and vintage furnishings complement the Victorian stained-glass panels and fireplaces at Philippa McKnight and David Hoyes's intimate B&B next to Penlee Park. Spacious bedrooms in contemporary hues, some with painted floorboards, have a king-size bed and thoughtful extras: refreshments, bathrobes, eco-friendly toiletries. An airy sitting room has plenty of books. Breakfasts keep food miles low and creativity high: guests wake to home-made jams, compotes and yogurt; perhaps smoked fish from Newlyn or Mexican tortillas with hot salsa and fried eggs. Vegan and vegetarian diets are willingly catered for. The lush garden is full of unusual plants; the seafront and town centre are close by.

MAP 1:E1
Trewithen Road
Penzance  TR18 4LS
T: 01736 351294
W: ventonvean.co.uk

BEDROOMS: 5. 1 with adjoining single room, suitable for a family.
OPEN: all year except 25/26 Dec.
FACILITIES: sitting room, dining room, in-room smart TV, garden.
BACKGROUND MUSIC: at breakfast in dining room.
LOCATION: 7 mins' walk from the centre of Penzance and Penzance seafront.
CHILDREN: not under 5.
DOGS: not allowed.
CREDIT CARDS: MC, Visa.
PRICES: per room B&B single £75–£95, double £85–£105. 2-night bookings preferred in peak season (May–Sept).

PORLOCK WEIR Somerset
# LOCANDA ON THE WEIR

La dolce vita beckons from chef/patron Pio Catemario di Quadri's restaurant-with-rooms, in a coastal hamlet within Exmoor national park. Run with his wife, Cindy, in a bay-windowed Victorian house above the harbour, it combines Italian brio with country house comfort. With a view of the sea, the welcoming lounge has comfy sofas, drinks and snacks, books to browse; a blazing fire on cold days. Comfort rises to the first-floor bedrooms, each individually styled with interesting pictures; some have a window seat for taking in the bay views. In the evening, candlelight sets the scene for Pio's exhilarating cuisine: lightly pickled beetroot, feta, pomegranate; shoulder of Exmoor spring lamb 'lavished in ancient spices'.

MAP 1:B5
Porlock Weir  TA24 8PB
T: 01643 863300
W: locandaontheweir.co.uk

BEDROOMS: 5.
OPEN: all year, restaurant closed Tues eve in high season.
FACILITIES: bar/lounge, restaurant, free Wi-Fi in public areas, in-room TV (Freeview), front garden, public rooms wheelchair accessible.
BACKGROUND MUSIC: none.
LOCATION: within Exmoor national park, in a coastal hamlet on the South West Coast Path.
CHILDREN: not under 12.
DOGS: allowed in 3 bedrooms, in lounge, restaurant if well-behaved.
CREDIT CARDS: MC, Visa.
PRICES: per room B&B single £115–£210, double £125–£220, D,B&B £205–£300. À la carte £45, set menu £40. 2-night min. stay on Fri and Sat, May–Sept.

RAMSGATE Kent
## ALBION HOUSE

A wrought-iron balcony wraps round Ben and Emma Irvine's beautifully restored hotel, in a Regency building overlooking the beach and Royal Harbour. In the past, it hosted politicians, actors, even Princess Victoria, who stayed while recuperating from an illness. A sense of grandeur remains today, in its high ceilings, ornate cornices and carved fireplaces. Elegant public spaces have mirrors, plants, walls painted deep heritage shades; a lounge is a 'welcoming' spot. Softly styled bedrooms, some high up in the eaves, are supplied with bathrobes, teas and coffee. (A busy road at the front may affect light sleepers.) Sea views are assured in Townley's restaurant, where 'pleasant, personable staff run the show'.

MAP 2:D6
Albion Place
Ramsgate CT11 8HQ
T: 01843 606630
W: albionhouseramsgate.co.uk

BEDROOMS: 14. 1 suitable for disabled.
OPEN: all year.
FACILITIES: 2 lounges, bar/restaurant, snug, in-room TV (Freeview), private dining room, electric bicycle hire.
BACKGROUND MUSIC: all day in public spaces.
LOCATION: above Ramsgate Main Sands beach.
CHILDREN: all ages welcomed.
DOGS: allowed in bedrooms, public rooms.
CREDIT CARDS: MC, Visa.
PRICES: per room B&B £80–£300, D,B&B £129–£385. À la carte £60. 1-night bookings refused weekends in July, Aug.

RAMSGATE Kent
## THE FALSTAFF

'A lovely seaside escape', two 'tastefully refurbished' Regency town houses, on a quaint street near the harbour, combine to make this 'buzzy, welcoming' bar and restaurant-with-rooms. 'It has really found its level as a friendly local,' say trusted readers in 2020, as visitors drop in for a real ale, or coffee and cake by the wood-burning stove. Heritage hues, vintage furnishings and fine prints characterise the neat bedrooms, each 'spotless' and stocked with 'nice, fluffy towels, good bedlinen, good toiletries'. There are summer barbecues in the large, sunny garden; takeaway snacks from the deli. Dine on 'terrific gastropub food at reasonable prices'; in the morning, 'the delicious breakfast has plenty of choice'.'

MAP 2:D6
16–18 Addington Street
Ramsgate CT11 9JJ
T: 01843 482600
W: thefalstafframsgate.com

BEDROOMS: 8. Plus 2 self-catering apartments.
OPEN: all year, restaurant closed Mon, Tues.
FACILITIES: bar, restaurant, deli, in-room TV (Freeview), garden, parking, bicycle storage.
BACKGROUND MUSIC: in bar, restaurant.
LOCATION: in town, a minute's walk to the seafront.
CHILDREN: all ages welcomed.
DOGS: allowed in some bedrooms, parts of bar, restaurant.
CREDIT CARDS: Amex, MC, Visa.
PRICES: per room B&B £100–£165.

REETH Yorkshire

# CAMBRIDGE HOUSE

'Marvellous hosts' Robert and Sheila Mitchell offer 'perfect comfort' at their Swaledale B&B, on the outskirts of a rural village surrounded by far-reaching countryside panoramas. In an area popular with walkers and cyclists, the 'thoughtful' owners provide bicycle storage and a drying room along with other 'splendid facilities' for active sorts. South-facing bedrooms with 'superb views' are supplied with hot drinks and dressing gowns; all but a single room have a bath and shower. Afternoon tea and home-made cake are served in the conservatory; the lounge has wines and local beers in the honesty bar, and a log fire in winter. Breakfast is 'a great start to the day'; 'very good' packed lunches can be provided.

MAP 4:C3
Arkengarthdale Road
Reeth  DL11 6QX
T: 01748 884633
W: cambridgehousereeth.co.uk

BEDROOMS: 5.
OPEN: Feb–mid-Dec.
FACILITIES: lounge, dining room, conservatory, in-room TV (Freeview), small garden, terrace, parking.
BACKGROUND MUSIC: none.
LOCATION: 500 yards from centre of Reeth.
CHILDREN: not under 12.
DOGS: 1 well-behaved dog allowed, by arrangement, in bedroom (not unattended), conservatory.
CREDIT CARDS: MC, Visa.
PRICES: per room B&B single £80–£100, double £95–£115. 'Limited availability' of 1-night bookings Apr–Sept.

RICHMOND Yorkshire

# EASBY HALL

On a country lane outside Richmond, this stone-built Georgian house is the stuff rural ruminations are made of. Surrounded by acres of gardens, including a woodland walk, an orchard, a breezy paddock and the tranquil ruins of Easby Abbey, Karen and John Clarke provide luxurious B&B accommodation in their sumptuously decorated home. Spacious suites, in a separate wing from the main house, each have a huge bed; a log-burner or open fire; a champagne fridge. Afternoon tea in the drawing room is a relaxed affair. Breakfast, served at a time to suit the guest, has home-made compotes and preserves of garden fruit; local bacon; eggs from resident hens. The historic market town is a short riverbank walk away.

MAP 4:C3
Easby
Richmond  DL10 7EU
T: 01748 826066
W: easbyhall.com

BEDROOMS: 3. 1 suitable for disabled, plus 2-bed self-catering cottage.
OPEN: all year.
FACILITIES: drawing room, breakfast room, in-room TV (Freeview), 4-acre gardens, paddocks, loose boxes and stables for horses.
BACKGROUND MUSIC: none.
LOCATION: less than 2 miles E of Richmond.
CHILDREN: all ages welcomed.
DOGS: obedient, house-trained dogs allowed in bedrooms and in public rooms, 'provided other guests don't object'.
CREDIT CARDS: none accepted.
PRICES: per room B&B £180.

RIPLEY Surrey

## BROADWAY BARN

In the centre of a historic village, Mindi McLean's B&B is in a 'beautifully and tastefully restored' 200-year-old barn that wins praise from Guide readers – not least for the 'eggs Benedict made right'. 'Engaging, thoughtful and attentive, Mindi charmed us,' say guests this year. 'Exquisitely furnished' bedrooms are equipped with little luxuries: dressing gowns, slippers, flowers and home-made shortbread. Wake to a morning feast taken in the conservatory overlooking the small walled garden. With a spread of home-baked breads, home-made jams and granola, and house-recipe chipolatas, 'the breakfast is a fitting end to an amazing stay'. 'Very easy access' to Guildford, Woking and other Surrey towns.

MAP 2:D3
High Street
Ripley GU23 6AQ
T: 01483 223200
W: broadwaybarn.com

BEDROOMS: 4. Plus self-catering flat and cottages.
OPEN: all year.
FACILITIES: conservatory sitting room/breakfast room, in-room TV (Freeview), small garden.
BACKGROUND MUSIC: 'subtle' at breakfast.
LOCATION: village centre.
CHILDREN: not under 12.
DOGS: not allowed.
CREDIT CARDS: Amex, MC, Visa.
PRICES: per room B&B £130.

ST ALBANS Hertfordshire

## SOPWELL HOUSE HOTEL

In extensive grounds, the former home of Lord Louis Mountbatten is today a 'well-run' hotel with contemporary bedrooms, cosseting suites, a choice of eating and drinking spaces, and a sleek spa. Bedrooms in the extended 300-year-old manor house are 'practical and well furnished, with all the amenities'; upmarket mews suites are in landscaped gardens in a gated compound. The 'bustling' brasserie has classic bistro dishes ('seemingly something for everyone'); more formal, modern British dinners are taken in the restaurant (Wed–Sat). Besides the state-of-the-art spa, several walled gardens provide space for relaxation and reflection. 'Plentiful' breakfasts are 'nicely served, with freshly squeezed orange juice'.

MAP 2:C3
Cottonmill Lane
St Albans AL1 2HQ
T: 01727 864477
W: sopwellhouse.co.uk

BEDROOMS: 128. 16 mews suites.
OPEN: all year, restaurant open Wed–Sat for dinner, Sun lunch.
FACILITIES: cocktail lounge, bar, 2 restaurants, sitting room, meeting and conference facilities, in-room TV (Sky, BT), civil wedding licence, spa, indoor pool, gym, 12-acre grounds.
BACKGROUND MUSIC: in lobby and restaurants.
LOCATION: 1½ miles from the city centre and rail station.
CHILDREN: over-12s welcomed, not in spa or swimming pool.
DOGS: not allowed.
CREDIT CARDS: Amex, MC, Visa.
PRICES: per room B&B £179–£799, D,B&B £229–£849. À la carte £45.

## ST AUSTELL Cornwall
# LOWER BARNS

Off a single-track road amid tranquil farmland, Janie and Mike Cooksley's quirky B&B on the Roseland peninsula is a joyous burst of artistry, colour and all-round cheer. Each well-equipped bedroom is unlike another: one has its own stone-built sauna; another, a Romani caravan parked by the front door; some have a conservatory or private courtyard. In the wildflower garden, fairy lights decorate the Shack, where informal dinners, arranged in advance, are served. Local producers supply the ingredients – perhaps fish straight off the boat at Mevagissey harbour. Breakfast brings home-baked muffins, farm sausages and a juice of the day; guests in three garden suites have breakfast delivered to the room.

MAP 1:D2
Bosue
St Austell PL26 6EU
T: 01726 844881
W: lowerbarns.co.uk

BEDROOMS: 8. 4 in the grounds, 1 suitable for disabled.
OPEN: all year.
FACILITIES: conservatory breakfast room, dining room, in-room TV (BT), civil wedding licence, small function facilities, garden, in-room spa treatments, outdoor hot tub, parking.
BACKGROUND MUSIC: at guests' request.
LOCATION: 7 miles SW of St Austell, 1 mile past Lost Gardens of Heligan.
CHILDREN: all ages welcomed.
DOGS: allowed in 1 suite, with own bedding.
CREDIT CARDS: MC, Visa.
PRICES: per room B&B £130–£180, D,B&B £230–£280. 2-course set dinner £50 (BYOB). 2-night min. stay at weekends.

## ST IVES Cornwall
# HEADLAND HOUSE

A tranquil retreat from the bustle of nearby St Ives, Mark and Fenella Thomas's chic Edwardian house stands on a steep hill above Carbis Bay. Well-equipped bedrooms share a smart, airy style, but are otherwise individual. A garden room has loungers on a private deck; in another, beach views are best admired from a broad window seat; yet another, while compact, has a freestanding roll-top bath in a spacious bathroom. Home-made cake is delivered to the room each afternoon; in clement weather, borrow a book or a magazine from the lounge to read in a garden hammock, or sip a complimentary aperitif. Hearty Cornish breakfasts (including a weekly special) kick-start the day with a view across the water.

MAP 1:D1
Headland Road
St Ives TR26 2NS
T: 01736 796647
W: headlandhousehotel.co.uk

BEDROOMS: 9. 3 off the courtyard garden.
OPEN: Apr–mid-Oct.
FACILITIES: lounge, conservatory breakfast room, in-room TV (Freeview), large front garden, sun deck, parking.
BACKGROUND MUSIC: none.
LOCATION: 1½ miles from St Ives centre, 5 mins from Carbis Bay beach.
CHILDREN: not under 15.
DOGS: allowed in bedrooms, public rooms.
CREDIT CARDS: MC, Visa.
PRICES: per room B&B £95–£170. 2-night min. stay preferred.

ST IVES Cornwall
# TREVOSE HARBOUR HOUSE

Styled in a palette of blues and whites, Angela
and Olivier Noverraz's 'beautifully appointed'
1850s mid-terrace house, a short stroll from the
harbourside, is 'a delight'. Vintage finds and
upcycled furniture mix easily with original art
by St Ives artists; a neat terrace has seating for
a sunny day. Beyond the snug, with its books to
borrow and honesty-bar cocktails to mix, serene
bedrooms have a large bed and organic toiletries.
Most rooms have views of the harbour and the
bay; a spacious split-level annexe room has a
separate seating area. There's plenty of choice
at breakfast, where local, in-season produce is
highlighted: Cornish cheeses, smoked fish from St
Mawes, home-made granola and preserves.

MAP 1:D1
22 The Warren
St Ives  TR26 2EA
T:  01736 793267
W:  trevosehouse.co.uk

BEDROOMS: 6. 1 in rear annexe.
OPEN: late Mar–Nov.
FACILITIES: snug, breakfast room, in-
room TV (BT), in-room treatments,
terrace, limited parking close by.
BACKGROUND MUSIC: in snug.
LOCATION: town centre.
CHILDREN: not under 12.
DOGS: not allowed.
CREDIT CARDS: Amex, MC, Visa.
PRICES: per room B&B £170–£295.
2-night min. stay.

ST LEONARDS-ON-SEA Sussex
# THE CLOUDESLEY

Holistic therapist, photographer and award-
winning gardener Shahriar Mazandi brings
his diverse talents to this modern B&B, a short
walk from the seafront. His home has an eclectic
feel: the drawing rooms are stocked with art,
gardening and photography books; the walls are
hung with his photographs. Serene bedrooms,
decorated with original works of art, have a
large bed and a compact shower room; no TV,
but plenty to read. Served in the bright dining
room or on the sunny bamboo terrace, breakfast
has much choice, including vegan options and an
impressive omelette menu (spinach and cheese;
sausage, sage and courgette; seasonal berries and
Armagnac). In-room massages and reflexology
treatments are available.

## 25% DISCOUNT VOUCHERS

MAP 2:E4
7 Cloudesley Road
St Leonards-on-Sea  TN37 6JN
T:  07507 000148
W:  thecloudesley.co.uk

BEDROOMS: 4.
OPEN: all year.
FACILITIES: dining room, 2 sitting
rooms, honesty bar, in-room spa
treatments, ¼-acre garden, patio.
BACKGROUND MUSIC: none.
LOCATION: 10 mins from St Leonards-
on-Sea town centre.
CHILDREN: well-behaved children
accepted.
DOGS: not allowed.
CREDIT CARDS: MC, Visa.
PRICES: per room B&B £75–£135.
2-night min. stay preferred at
weekends.

ST LEONARDS-ON-SEA Sussex

# ZANZIBAR INTERNATIONAL HOTEL

'Splendidly quirky' and 'utterly relaxed',
Max O'Rourke's seafront hotel brims with an
'interesting collection' of curios from far-flung
lands. The distinctive bedrooms are set over
several floors, and overlook the tropical garden or
the sea. Decorated to reflect different destinations,
they come in a 'huge variety': streamlined Japan,
with a low, king-size bed, has a deep-soak spa
bath; Antarctica is dazzlingly white, with floor-to-
ceiling windows and 'wonderful sea views'. 'The
busy road in front quietens at night.' A beachy bar
offers cocktails and water views. Breakfast comes
with newspapers, plus suggestions for eateries and
outings. Stretch your legs: Hastings Old Town is a
half-hour's beachfront walk away.

MAP 2:E4
9 Eversfield Place
St Leonards-on-Sea  TN37 6BY
T: 01424 460109
W: zanzibarhotel.co.uk

BEDROOMS: 8. 1 on ground floor.
OPEN: all year.
FACILITIES: bar, breakfast room,
in-room TV (Freeview), Zen garden,
parking.
BACKGROUND MUSIC: 'quiet' in bar.
LOCATION: on the seafront, 650 yards
W of Hastings pier.
CHILDREN: not under 5.
DOGS: allowed in bedrooms, public
areas.
CREDIT CARDS: Amex, MC, Visa.
PRICES: per room B&B £99–£295.

ST MARTIN'S Isles of Scilly

# KARMA ST MARTIN'S

Steps from the powdery white beach, this friendly,
laid-back hotel (the only hotel on the island)
has panoramic views across to Teän Sound
and Tresco. Light, contemporary bedrooms in
the low-built building have books and vintage
furnishings; large bay windows gaze over the
ocean. Four-legged companions are made just as
welcome: they have a bowl and blanket, can relish
a dish from the Kanine Kitchen, then toast their
good fortune with some 'Pawsecco'. For their
human companions, lobster rolls and platters of
freshly caught seafood are menu mainstays in the
restaurant, or alfresco in the sub-tropical garden.
Spa treatments are available; more active sorts
might hire a day boat or snorkel with seals.

MAP 1: inset C1
Lower Town
St Martin's  TR25 0QW
T: 01720 422368
W: karmastmartins.com

BEDROOMS: 30. 12 on ground floor,
5 suitable for disabled.
OPEN: Easter–end Oct.
FACILITIES: bar, restaurant, 2 lounges,
in-room TV (Freeview), civil wedding
licence, treatment room, games room
for children, 7-acre grounds.
BACKGROUND MUSIC: jazz in bar,
restaurant, muted on request.
LOCATION: 2 mins' walk from Lower
Town Quay.
CHILDREN: all ages welcomed.
DOGS: dogs allowed in upper dining
room, some bedrooms.
CREDIT CARDS: Amex, MC, Visa.
PRICES: per room B&B £150–£600,
D,B&B £230–£680. À la carte £50.

ST MARY'S Isles of Scilly

## ST MARY'S HALL HOTEL

In sub-tropical gardens, minutes from two of Hugh Town's sandy beaches, this privately owned hotel is liked for its 'unfailingly friendly, efficient' staff. Roger Page is the 'knowledgeable, helpful' manager. Airy bedrooms in the extended town house vary in size, though all have a large bed, high-end toiletries, and home-made biscuits on a well-stocked tray. Family-friendly suites, most with a galley kitchenette, accommodate up to four guests. At lunch and dinner, choose from local seafood, and meat from the owners' rare-breeds farm; at breakfast, find freshly squeezed juice, and eggs from St Mary's hens. Picnics and packed lunches can be arranged for guests keen on exploring the neighbouring islands.

MAP 1: inset C1
Church Street
St Mary's TR21 0JR
T: 01720 422316
W: stmaryshallhotel.co.uk

BEDROOMS: 27.
OPEN: mid-Mar–mid-Oct.
FACILITIES: 2 lounges, bar, 2 restaurants, in-room TV (Freeview), garden.
BACKGROUND MUSIC: in public areas.
LOCATION: 5 mins' walk from town centre, 10 mins' walk from quay.
CHILDREN: all ages welcomed.
DOGS: allowed in ground-floor suites, public rooms.
CREDIT CARDS: MC, Visa.
PRICES: per room single £99–£245, double £179–£327, D,B&B double £223–£371. À la carte £45.

ST TUDY Cornwall

## THE ST TUDY INN

In a 'chocolate-box village' on the River Camel, this 17th-century inn is today a 'beautifully decorated' restaurant-with-rooms 'with not a hair out of place'. Pared-back bedrooms in a converted barn are decorated in soft modern greys, with 'well-chosen' furnishings. Extras include a coffee machine, fresh milk and sweet treats, plus natural toiletries in the well-designed bathrooms (some are snug). Real ales, fine wines or cocktails by an open fire in the old bar precede modest portions of creative rustic cuisine from the 'nicely varied' menu. After breakfast ('our avocado on sourdough, and eggs and asparagus were lovely, though the buffet was a bit sparse'), head to the coast or set off for Bodmin Moor.

MAP 1:D3
St Tudy PL30 3NN
T: 01208 850656
W: sttudyinn.com

BEDROOMS: 4. All in converted barn annexe, 2 on ground floor.
OPEN: all year, bar and dining room closed Sun eve, Mon.
FACILITIES: bar, dining room, in-room smart TV, terrace.
BACKGROUND MUSIC: in restaurant.
LOCATION: village centre.
CHILDREN: all ages welcomed.
DOGS: allowed by arrangement in 1 bedroom, bar, not in dining room.
CREDIT CARDS: Amex, MC, Visa.
PRICES: per room B&B £150–£165, D,B&B £210–£225. À la carte £30. 2-night min. stay at weekends.

SALCOMBE Devon

# SALCOMBE HARBOUR HOTEL

It's not just the 'stupendous view', but 'the whole ambience' that guests find appealing about this Victorian hotel and spa on Salcombe's tranquil estuary. The soothing bedrooms have a pleasing maritime feel, with stripes and shades of blue; most have huge estuary-facing windows, a balcony and binoculars to fully take in the panorama. A classy extra: ice and lemon slices are delivered to the room each evening, to complement gin and sherry from complimentary decanters. Devon produce and the day's catch are served in the restaurant and on the sunny terraces; for a day out, ask about picnic hampers stocked with goodies. Harbour Hotels in Chichester and Southampton (see Shortlist entries) are sisters.

MAP 1:E4
Cliff Road
Salcombe TQ8 8JH
T: 01548 844444
W: salcombe-harbour-hotel.co.uk

BEDROOMS: 50. Some on ground floor, suitable for disabled.
OPEN: all year.
FACILITIES: bar/lounge, restaurant, in-room TV (Freeview), civil wedding licence, spa, private moorings.
BACKGROUND MUSIC: in public areas.
LOCATION: town centre.
CHILDREN: all ages welcomed.
DOGS: allowed in some bedrooms, on lead on terrace, not in public rooms.
CREDIT CARDS: Amex, MC, Visa.
PRICES: per room B&B £129–£460, D,B&B £179–£510. À la carte £50. 1-night bookings sometimes refused.

SALCOMBE Devon

# SOUTH SANDS

A wide, beach-facing terrace reaches across this 'informal', family-friendly hotel, in a sheltered cove just outside the centre of the busy sailing town. Breezy bedrooms, including spacious suites with a kitchen and a balcony or patio, have seaside touches (seascape paintings; a seagull sculpture); those at the front have sea views. Preprandials on the terrace might be followed by fresh-as-can-be fish and shellfish, and seasonal West Country dishes off an all-day menu. Coastal paths start from the back door; the National Trust garden Overbeck's is up the hill. Leave the car where you've parked it: the most delightful way to reach the town centre is via sea tractor down South Sands beach to meet the passenger ferry.

MAP 1:E4
Bolt Head
Salcombe TQ8 8LL
T: 01548 845900
W: southsands.com

BEDROOMS: 27. Some on ground floor, 1 suitable for disabled, 5 suites with separate entrance.
OPEN: all year.
FACILITIES: bar, restaurant, in-room TV (Freeview), civil wedding licence, terrace, bar and restaurant wheelchair accessible.
BACKGROUND MUSIC: in public areas.
LOCATION: on South Sands beach, 1½ miles from Salcombe town centre.
CHILDREN: all ages welcomed.
DOGS: allowed in some bedrooms, bar, half the restaurant.
CREDIT CARDS: MC, Visa.
PRICES: per room B&B £95–£595. À la carte £45. 1-night bookings refused weekends in peak season.

SALISBURY Wiltshire

# LEENA'S GUEST HOUSE

A 15-minute riverside stroll from the cathedral, 'excellent, helpful hosts' Gary and Edith Heikki Street provide good-value B&B accommodation in their 'first-rate' guest house. Flower borders front the modest Edwardian home; within are traditionally decorated, 'comfortably appointed' rooms. Each of the 'immaculate' bedrooms is supplied with coffee- and tea-making facilities, plus a sweet treat; bathrooms have recently been refurbished. Appreciative guests speak of the 'imaginative breakfasts – they're not just the usual fry-up'. Besides yogurts and fruits (including, in season, raspberries and redcurrants from the garden), the menu has hot-smoked salmon and a choice of omelettes; special diets are catered for.

MAP 2:D2
50 Castle Road
Salisbury SP1 3RL
T: 07814 897907
W: www.leenasguesthouse.co.uk

BEDROOMS: 5. 1 on ground floor.
OPEN: May–Nov.
FACILITIES: lounge, breakfast room, in-room TV (Freeview), garden, parking.
BACKGROUND MUSIC: ambient, 'from kitchen when chef is cooking', during breakfast.
LOCATION: 12 mins' walk via riverside footpaths to town centre and Salisbury cathedral.
CHILDREN: all ages welcomed.
DOGS: not allowed.
CREDIT CARDS: none accepted.
PRICES: per room B&B single £85–£99, double £95–£115. 2-night min. stay.

SCARBOROUGH Yorkshire

# PHOENIX COURT

In a 'great central location' within walking distance of the town, Donna and Mike Buttery's personably run guest house overlooks the surf-licked sands of North Bay. Many of the spacious bedrooms in the twin Victorian town houses have sweeping sea views through large windows; two rooms can accommodate a family. Improvements continue: several rooms were redecorated in 2020, and most have a new orthopaedic bed. Mornings, choose a locally smoked kipper or the host's cooked-to-order hot breakfast (vegetarian and vegan diets catered for). Out the front door, step on to the cliff tops and easily access paths down to the seafront. Packed lunches (£6) are ordered the day before. A bonus: the private car park.

MAP 4:C5
8–9 Rutland Terrace
Scarborough YO12 7JB
T: 01723 501150
W: phoenixcourt.co.uk

BEDROOMS: 12. 1 on ground floor.
OPEN: Mar–Oct.
FACILITIES: lounge (honesty bar), breakfast room, in-room TV (Freeview), drying facilities, parking.
BACKGROUND MUSIC: local radio in breakfast room.
LOCATION: 10 mins' walk from the town centre and South Bay.
CHILDREN: all ages welcomed.
DOGS: not allowed.
CREDIT CARDS: MC, Visa.
PRICES: per room B&B single £45–£75, double £60–£80, family £80–£95. 2-night min. stay at weekends.

**NEW**

SEDBERGH Cumbria
## THE BLACK BULL

'A great deal of care and attention' has gone into this sleekly revamped 17th-century inn, in a small, book-loving town at the foot of the Howgill fells. It is owned and run by chef/patron Nina Matsunaga and her husband, James Ratcliffe, a Dales native. Wood flooring and dark banquettes pair with pots of moss and fern on the tables in the bar and restaurant; at mealtimes, modern, Asian-inspired field-to-fork dishes (perhaps Howgill Herdwick lamb loin, crapaudine beetroot, scarlet elf cup) 'burst with bold flavours'. Upstairs, serene bedrooms have locally made wool blankets and photographs of the surrounding landscape; high-spec bathrooms with see-through glass walls are stocked with essential-oil toiletries.

**25% DISCOUNT VOUCHERS**

MAP 4:C3
44 Main Street
Sedbergh LA10 5BL
T: 015396 20264
W: theblackbullsedbergh.co.uk

BEDROOMS: 18.
OPEN: all year.
FACILITIES: bar, restaurant, in-room TV, 1-acre garden, bar and restaurant wheelchair accessible.
BACKGROUND MUSIC: in public spaces.
LOCATION: in town centre, close to M6 (Junction 37).
CHILDREN: all ages welcomed.
DOGS: in 3 bedrooms, bar, not in restaurant.
CREDIT CARDS: Amex, MC, Visa.
PRICES: per room B&B single £112.50–£172, double £125–£205. À la carte £34. 1-night bookings refused Sat in high season.

SEDBERGH Cumbria
## THE MALABAR

At the foot of the Howgill fells, in the far western Dales, Fiona and Graham Lappin's stylish, rural B&B is surrounded by glorious scenery. Glorious, too, is the welcome: guests are greeted with home-baked scones and a menu of 12 loose-leaf teas. The restored 18th-century cattle barn houses chic, spacious rooms with original oak beams; warm colours and block-print fabrics reflect the owners' time spent in India and south-east Asia – as does the lassi at breakfast. Taken in the dining room or in the garden at a time to suit, breakfast offers home-baked bread, seasonal juices, local specials. A generous home-cooked dinner of bang-in-season produce is served during the week; Friday meals have an Indian influence.

MAP 4:C3
Garths
Sedbergh LA10 5ED
T: 015396 20200
W: themalabar.co.uk

BEDROOMS: 6. 2 on ground floor, 1 family suite with private entrance.
OPEN: all year.
FACILITIES: bar, sitting room, dining room, in-room TV (Freeview), ⅓-acre garden, parking.
BACKGROUND MUSIC: in public areas during afternoon tea and in the evenings.
LOCATION: 2 miles W of Sedbergh.
CHILDREN: all ages welcomed.
DOGS: allowed in 1 suite, public rooms 'if other guests are happy with it'.
CREDIT CARDS: MC, Visa.
PRICES: per room B&B £120–£240, D,B&B (Mon–Fri) £180–£320. 1-night bookings sometimes refused Easter, Christmas, New Year, bank holiday weekends.

SEDGEFORD Norfolk

# MAGAZINE WOOD

The wild Norfolk coast is minutes away from the rustic luxury of Pip and Jonathan Barber's chic countryside B&B. Each spacious, elegant suite has its own entrance and terrace; inside are a large bed and mood lighting, plus a deep bath and separate shower in the bathroom. Thoughtful extras add to the cocoon: books, DVDs and binoculars are provided; a tablet computer serves as an online concierge, to summon breakfast, download a newspaper or create a bespoke itinerary. The day begins 'anytime': a well-stocked cupboard contains muesli, cereals, fruits and croissants; milk and organic yogurts are in the fridge. Cooked breakfasts (charged extra) are ordered the night before. A dining pub is within walking distance.

MAP 2:A5
Peddars Way
Sedgeford  PE36 5LW
T: 01485 750740
W: magazinewood.co.uk

BEDROOMS: 3. All on ground floor, 2 in converted barn.
OPEN: all year except Christmas.
FACILITIES: in-room TV (on-demand movies), in-room spa treatments, 3-acre grounds, parking.
BACKGROUND MUSIC: none.
LOCATION: 5 miles from Hunstanton.
CHILDREN: infants welcomed.
DOGS: allowed (not unattended) in 1 bedroom.
CREDIT CARDS: MC, Visa.
PRICES: per room B&B (continental) £105–£149. Cooked breakfast £7.50. 2-night min. stay most weekends.

SHAFTESBURY Dorset

# THE GROSVENOR ARMS

Traces of the 17th century survive in this coaching inn-turned-hotel, rebuilt in the early 1800s by Earl Grosvenor. Visitors in 2020 were impressed by their 'vast' bedroom and equally 'huge' bathroom, with a freestanding bath; less impressive were some signs of wear and tear – 'but we understand refurbishment is ongoing'. In the buzzing restaurant, 'clearly popular with locals', the 'very good food' from a locally sourced menu might include flat-iron chicken or squash-stuffed rotolo pasta. A lone diner reported spotty service at a recent dinner, although 'breakfast was excellent'. Stoke up on Old Spot sausage, smoky beans and hash browns for the climb up Gold Hill, immortalised in Sir Ridley Scott's Hovis ad.

MAP 2:D1
The Commons
Shaftesbury  SP7 8JA
T: 01747 850580
W: grosvenorarms.co.uk

BEDROOMS: 16. 2 first-floor rooms accessible by lift, with no further steps.
OPEN: all year.
FACILITIES: lift to first floor only, bar, lounge, restaurant, conservatory, private dining room, ballroom, in-room smart TV (Freeview), courtyard garden, parking permit, bar and restaurant wheelchair accessible, adapted toilet.
BACKGROUND MUSIC: in bar.
LOCATION: town centre, 1-min. walk from Gold Hill.
CHILDREN: all ages welcomed.
DOGS: allowed in bedrooms, bar, conservatory, not in restaurant.
CREDIT CARDS: Amex, MC, Visa.
PRICES: per room B&B £105–£240, D,B&B £140–£275. À la carte £35.

SHANKLIN Isle of Wight

# HAVEN HALL

In award-winning landscaped gardens that look out to sea, Arielle and David Barratt's cliff-top Edwardian house is a five-minute stroll down the coastal path to the beach on Sandown Bay. The hands-on owners, who live in a separate wing, run their island guest house with a gracious spirit. Carefully chosen period furnishings give the bedrooms and suites Arts and Crafts character; nearly all the rooms have views over the water. Head outside: the swimming pool and grass tennis court in the tranquil grounds are ideal for active sorts. Mornings, French doors in the breakfast room open to the patio and flowerbeds – a cheery sight to accompany the spread of fruits, cereals, breads, jams and home-made compotes.

**25% DISCOUNT VOUCHERS**

MAP 2:E2
5 Howard Road
Shanklin PO37 6HD
T: 07914 796494
W: havenhallhotel.com

BEDROOMS: 14. 1, on ground floor, suitable for disabled, 7 available for self-catering.
OPEN: all year.
FACILITIES: bar, lounge, dining room, in-room TV (Freeview), civil wedding licence, outdoor pool (heated May–Sept), grass tennis court, croquet, 2-acre grounds.
BACKGROUND MUSIC: none.
LOCATION: on E side of island, overlooking the English Channel.
CHILDREN: not under 12.
DOGS: welcomed in 3 bedrooms.
CREDIT CARDS: Amex, MC, Visa.
PRICES: per room B&B £420–£950. 1-night bookings sometimes refused on bank holidays, weekends in high season.

SHANKLIN Isle of Wight

# RYLSTONE MANOR

Above Sandown Bay, Mike and Carole Hailston's 'delightfully relaxing' island B&B enjoys a 'lovely' setting: it stands within the perimeter of public gardens, with steps leading down to the seafront. There's plenty of space inside the 19th-century gentleman's residence, where the bar and homely sitting rooms sport rich hues, period furnishings and leaded windows. Some of the traditionally styled bedrooms offer glimpses of the sea through leafy trees; one has a four-poster bed; another, a window seat perfect for looking over the Chine. A secluded private garden surrounds the house. The Hailstons are founts of Isle of Wight information, and can point out the easy walk to the shops and restaurants in Old Shanklin.

**25% DISCOUNT VOUCHERS**

MAP 2:E2
Rylstone Gardens
Shanklin PO37 6RG
T: 01983 862806
W: rylstone-manor.co.uk

BEDROOMS: 8.
OPEN: Feb–early Nov.
FACILITIES: drawing room, bar/lounge, dining room, in-room TV (Freeview), terrace, ¼-acre garden in 4-acre public gardens.
BACKGROUND MUSIC: none.
LOCATION: in Shanklin Old Village.
CHILDREN: not under 16.
DOGS: only assistance dogs allowed.
CREDIT CARDS: MC, Visa.
PRICES: per room B&B single £110–£130, double £135–£165, D,B&B double £193–£223. 3-night min. stay June–Aug 'unless space allows'.

SHEFFORD WOODLANDS Berkshire

# THE PHEASANT INN

Wooden settles, old photographs and, yes, the odd stuffed pheasant add to the appealing character of this revamped sheep drover's inn, which overlooks a wide spread of the Berkshire Downs. Amid quirky prints, shelves of books to borrow, and vintage leather bar stools, locals and visitors easily find a place to roost. Overnighters fall in to one of the smart bedrooms, each supplied with cafetière coffee, quality teas and fresh milk; natural toiletries and towelling robes in the shower- or bathroom. Served on bare-wood tables, elevated pub food (treacle-cured trout; mushroom Wellington) includes vegan options; breakfast has plenty of choice. The North Wessex Downs, all around, are a walker's wonderland.

MAP 3:E6
Ermin Street
Shefford Woodlands RG17 7AA
T: 01488 648284
W: thepheasant-inn.co.uk

BEDROOMS: 11.
OPEN: all year.
FACILITIES: bar, restaurant, private dining room, in-room TV (Sky), courtyard, garden, parking.
BACKGROUND MUSIC: in public areas.
LOCATION: 9½ miles NW of Newbury.
CHILDREN: all ages welcomed.
DOGS: allowed in bedrooms, public rooms, by arrangement.
CREDIT CARDS: Amex, MC, Visa.
PRICES: per room B&B £115–£150. À la carte £28.

SHERBORNE Dorset

# THE EASTBURY HOTEL & SPA

A 'lovely' walled garden gives a country house air to this small hotel in the heart of a historic market town. The 'pleasant retreat' has been restored to its Edwardian splendour by Peter and Lana de Savary. 'Comfortable, well-furnished' bedrooms are supplied with bathrobes and slippers, teas, coffees and home-made biscuits. In the garden, five new green-roofed suites, all dog friendly, each have a private terrace. Afternoon teas and brasserie dishes are served in the bar and lounge, or on the terrace, in good weather; in the evening, chef Matthew Street's creative fine-dining and tasting menus are a high point. To soothe body and soul: a spa with a hydrotherapy pool and hot tub; Sherborne Abbey, just steps away.

MAP 2:E1
Long Street
Sherborne DT9 3BY
T: 01935 813131
W: theeastburyhotel.co.uk

BEDROOMS: 26. 5 in walled gardens, 4 with external access, 2 suitable for disabled, 8 wheelchair accessible.
OPEN: all year.
FACILITIES: bar/dining room, morning room, drawing room, library, private dining room, in-room TV (Freeview), wedding/function facilities, spa (hydrotherapy pool, outdoor hot tub), terrace, 1-acre walled garden, parking, electric car charging point.
BACKGROUND MUSIC: in bar, restaurant.
LOCATION: town centre.
CHILDREN: all ages welcomed.
DOGS: allowed in 9 bedrooms, lounges, part of restaurant.
CREDIT CARDS: Amex, MC, Visa.
PRICES: per room B&B £115–£375, D,B&B £154–£453. À la carte £39.

SHERBORNE Dorset

## THE KINGS ARMS

Hands-on chef/patron Sarah Lethbridge and her husband, Anthony, run this 'very friendly' stone-walled country pub in a pretty village four miles from Sherborne. Local artwork (all for sale) hangs in the public spaces; in the snug, where a wood-burning stove is lit in cool weather, a stack of the day's newspapers is ready for flipping through. Local ales and 'great' ciders in the bar pair nicely with the updated pub grub served in the smart dining room: warm mackerel escabeche, perhaps, or roast lamb rump, black olive polenta. Staying guests have a choice of colourful, individually styled bedrooms. Each has a marble wet room, with a rainfall shower and towelling bathrobes; some overlook the croquet lawn and garden.

MAP 2:E1
North Street, Charlton Horethorne
Sherborne DT9 4NL
T: 01963 220281
w: thekingsarms.co.uk

BEDROOMS: 10. 1 suitable for disabled.
OPEN: all year, limited service over Christmas, New Year.
FACILITIES: lift, snug, bar, restaurant, in-room TV (Freeview), terrace, garden, free use of local sports centre, discounts at Sherborne Golf Club, parking.
BACKGROUND MUSIC: none.
LOCATION: in village, 4 miles NE of Sherborne.
CHILDREN: all ages welcomed.
DOGS: allowed in bar.
CREDIT CARDS: MC, Visa.
PRICES: per room B&B from £145.
À la carte £30–£35.

SHIPSTON-ON-STOUR Warwickshire

## THE BOWER HOUSE

On the pretty square of a historic market town on the edge of the Cotswolds, this Grade II listed Georgian house has been restored with 'immense panache and impeccable taste'. A restaurant-with-rooms that attracts diners with its seasonal menus of local produce (caramelised shallot tart; Hereford beef fillet, rainbow chard, bone marrow), it is admired, too, for its 'first-class' accommodation. Through a separate entrance, the 'elegant' bedrooms are reached via a steep staircase. They're worth the climb: 'Every possible need had been thought of in our spacious room and well-lit bathroom, from home-made biscuits and the latest glossies to good-quality toiletries and large bath towels.' Breakfast is served till late.

MAP 3:D6
Market Place
Shipston-on-Stour CV36 4AG
T: 01608 663333
w: thebowerhouseshipston.com

BEDROOMS: 5.
OPEN: all year except 25/26 Dec, restaurant closed Sun eve, Mon.
FACILITIES: bar, interlinked dining rooms, in-room TV (Freeview), dining areas wheelchair accessible.
BACKGROUND MUSIC: 'gentle, happy' in restaurant.
LOCATION: town centre.
CHILDREN: all ages 'warmly welcomed'.
DOGS: allowed in bar area of restaurant.
CREDIT CARDS: Amex, MC, Visa.
PRICES: per room B&B £99–£185.
À la carte £35. 2-night min. stay bank holidays, summer weekends.

**NEW**

SHREWSBURY Shropshire

# DARWIN'S TOWNHOUSE

Ripe for discovery, this Grade II* listed building with 18th-century origins has evolved into a contemporary B&B that pays homage to the town's most revered son, Charles Darwin. The sitting room and snug have ample space for repose; there are board games, books and an honesty bar. Individually decorated bedrooms, some overlooking the sunken garden, have appropriate curiosities and 'a number of thoughtful touches': dressing gowns, a digital alarm radio, tea- and coffee-making facilities. A 'delicious' breakfast is served in the conservatory – 'and the options appeared endless'. Discount cards are offered to residents for two sister restaurants, both within a ten-minute walk of the B&B. The River Severn is steps away.

**25% DISCOUNT VOUCHERS**

MAP 3:B4
37 St Julian's Friars
Shrewsbury SY1 1XL
T: 01743 343829
W: darwinstownhouse.com

BEDROOMS: 19. 5 on ground floor, 8 in garden annexe, 1 suitable for disabled.
OPEN: all year, continental breakfast only on 25 Dec.
FACILITIES: lounge, snug (honesty bar), conservatory breakfast room, in-room TV, garden.
BACKGROUND MUSIC: in lounge, snug.
LOCATION: in town centre.
CHILDREN: all ages welcomed.
DOGS: allowed in garden bedrooms, not in breakfast room.
CREDIT CARDS: Amex, MC, Visa.
PRICES: per room B&B £100–£185.
À la carte (at sister restaurants) £25.

SHREWSBURY Shropshire

# LION AND PHEASANT

Modern style and characterful original features merge at this centrally located 16th-century coaching inn with 'easy access to all parts of the city'. The buzzy bar is a local gathering place, where 'friendly staff' dish out regional real ales; a fire burns in the inglenook fireplace in the cooler months. In the split-level restaurant, chef Callum Smith's well-regarded cooking focuses on Shropshire produce: artichoke and truffle velouté; rabbit Wellington. Contemporary bedrooms have a simple country air, 'a comfortable bed', 'a good shower'. Some have river views; one, in the eaves, has an array of exposed timbers. (Rooms at the front may have some street noise.) Close by: riverside walks and medieval streetscapes.

MAP 3:B4
49–50 Wyle Cop
Shrewsbury SY1 1XJ
T: 01743 770345
W: lionandpheasant.co.uk

BEDROOMS: 22.
OPEN: all year except 25/26 Dec.
FACILITIES: bar, wine bar, restaurant, function room, in-room TV (Freeview), garden terrace, parking (narrow entrance).
BACKGROUND MUSIC: in public areas, occasional live music in bar.
LOCATION: central, near English Bridge.
CHILDREN: all ages welcomed.
DOGS: allowed on garden terrace only.
CREDIT CARDS: MC, Visa.
PRICES: per room B&B £130–£270.
À la carte £38.

SISSINGHURST Kent

## THE MILK HOUSE

A village-hub feel spills out of Dane and Sarah Allchorne's 'enjoyable' pub-with-rooms, a 16th-century hall house updated with a jocund dairy theme. There's 'plenty of atmosphere' here: locals and visitors come for the bar bites, wood-fired pizzas, cask ales and local beers, served under timber beams or in the large, sunny garden; the rustic dining room has a seasonal menu of creative modern plates, their ingredients sourced from within a 20-mile radius. Upstairs, bedrooms with names such as Byre and Buttery are modishly understated, with a 'very comfortable' bed, and fresh flowers in milk pails. (Rear rooms are quieter.) Vita Sackville-West's Sissinghurst Castle and gardens are 20 minutes away on foot.

MAP 2:D5
The Street
Sissinghurst TN17 2JG
T: 01580 720200
W: themilkhouse.co.uk

BEDROOMS: 4.
OPEN: all year.
FACILITIES: bar, restaurant, private dining room, in-room TV (Freeview), terrace, large garden, duck pond, parking.
BACKGROUND MUSIC: in bar and restaurant.
LOCATION: in village.
CHILDREN: all ages welcomed.
DOGS: allowed in bar and garden, not in bedrooms.
CREDIT CARDS: Amex, MC, Visa.
PRICES: per room B&B £95–£145. 2-night min. stay at weekends.

SOMERTON Somerset

## THE WHITE HART

'There's a good atmosphere' at this bang-up-to-date pub-with-rooms, a foodie destination skirting the Somerset Levels. 'Superb staff' welcome tourists and locals, who come to the popular bar for cocktails, local ciders and organic wines. In the wood-floored restaurant and courtyard garden, 'delicious' West Country produce turns up in pizzas, pub classics and 'some interesting dishes'. Some of the 'well-presented' bedrooms are eclectically decorated, while others are simpler; all have a large bed, fluffy towels, natural toiletries. At breakfast: an Old Spot sausage ciabatta, avocado and harissa on toast, and more. Part of the Stay Original Company; see also Timbrell's Yard, Bradford-on-Avon, and The Swan, Wedmore (Shortlist entries).

MAP 1:C6
Market Place
Somerton TA11 7LX
T: 01458 272273
W: whitehartsomerton.com

BEDROOMS: 8.
OPEN: all year.
FACILITIES: bar, restaurant, in-room smart TV, large courtyard garden, bicycle storage.
BACKGROUND MUSIC: in bar.
LOCATION: in town centre.
CHILDREN: all ages welcomed.
DOGS: allowed in bedrooms, bar, terrace and garden.
CREDIT CARDS: MC, Visa.
PRICES: per room B&B £85–£160, D,B&B £120–£195. À la carte £27.

## SOUTH ALKHAM Kent
# ALKHAM COURT

Take in stunning sunsets over the 'beautiful' Alkham valley from Wendy and Neil Burrows's much-liked farmhouse – a 'haven', say Guide readers in 2020, 'run by wonderful, engaging hosts'. B&B guests are offered home-made cake on arrival; a picnic for walks on the Kent Downs; an evening bowl of soup, with warm, crusty rolls; the spa barn with a hot tub and sauna to unwind in. Country-style bedrooms each have a private entrance, and treats within: flowers, robes and slippers, a coffee machine, biscuits and sherry. The hosts 'have a love for the area', and can enthusiastically advise on diversions in countryside and along the coast. In the morning: 'The best breakfast I've had in England for a very long time!'

**25% DISCOUNT VOUCHERS**

MAP 2:D5
Meggett Lane
South Alkham  CT15 7DG
T: 01303 892056
W: alkhamcourt.co.uk

BEDROOMS: 4. 3 on ground floor, 1 suitable for disabled. Plus 2 shepherd's huts for self-catering.
OPEN: all year except 24/25 Dec.
FACILITIES: sitting/breakfast room, in-room TV (Freeview), spa barn, large garden, 60-acre farm.
BACKGROUND MUSIC: none.
LOCATION: in a rural location near Dover, 5 mins from M20, 10 mins from Eurotunnel.
CHILDREN: all ages welcomed.
DOGS: allowed (not unattended) in 1 bedroom, on lead at all times outside.
CREDIT CARDS: Amex, MC, Visa.
PRICES: per room B&B single £85–£100, double £140–£175. 2-night min. stay at bank holiday weekends and in high season.

**NEW**

## SOUTH HARTING Sussex
# THE WHITE HART

Traditional pub values attract locals, ramblers and overnighters to this dog- and family-friendly 16th-century inn, in a peaceful South Downs village close to the National Trust's Uppark House. There's character in the beams and log fires of the wood- and flagstone-floored bar, a setting that's just right for the range of restorative ales, wines and spirits; in the walled garden, picnic tables and parasols await clement weather. Wraps and baguette sandwiches make light lunches; heartier fare, on frequently changing menus, might include ham, egg and chips or more modern cep gnocchi, artichokes, wild mushrooms. Well-refurbished bedrooms have country charm in their exposed timbers, plaids and patterns.

MAP 2:E3
The Street
South Harting  GU31 5QB
T: 01730 825124
W: the-whitehart.co.uk

BEDROOMS: 7. 4 in annexe.
OPEN: all year except evening of 25/26 Dec, 1 Jan.
FACILITIES: bar, restaurant, snug, in-room TV, terrace, garden.
BACKGROUND MUSIC: in public spaces.
LOCATION: in village, 4½ miles SE of Petersfield.
CHILDREN: all ages welcomed.
DOGS: allowed in some bedrooms, bar, snug.
CREDIT CARDS: Amex, MC, Visa.
PRICES: per room B&B £84–£154. D,B&B £139–£204. À la carte £30.

SOUTHAMPTON Hampshire
# SOUTHAMPTON HARBOUR HOTEL

Taste life at sea at this contemporary, ocean liner-like hotel jutting out over a private marina. Ship-shape inside, it is bright and lively; porthole-shaped mirrors, vintage glass fish floats and a giant lobster add nautical fun. Bedrooms and suites, several with a Juliet balcony, are cheerily decorated with some retro touches, and supplied with bathrobes, slippers, a coffee machine, and decanters of gin and sherry. Order cocktails, light bites and wood-fired pizzas in the buzzy sixth-floor bar over wonderful (if also industrial) harbour views; the award-winning Jetty restaurant pairs locally caught seafood with seasonal produce, eaten on the terrace in good weather. The sleek spa and gym are a plus.

MAP 2:E2
5 Maritime Walk
Southampton SO14 3QT
T: 02381 103456
W: southampton-harbour-hotel.co.uk

BEDROOMS: 117. 8 suites, some suitable for disabled.
OPEN: all year.
FACILITIES: 2 bar/restaurants, café, in-room TV (Freeview), civil wedding licence, function facilities, spa (indoor swimming pool, hydrotherapy pool, sauna, steam room, treatment rooms, juice bar), gym, terrace, valet parking.
BACKGROUND MUSIC: in public areas, DJ in bar at weekend.
LOCATION: on the marina.
CHILDREN: all ages welcomed.
DOGS: only assistance dogs allowed.
CREDIT CARDS: Amex, MC, Visa.
PRICES: per room B&B £156–£1,026, D,B&B £206–£1,076. À la carte £35, tasting menu £65. 2-night min. stay during Southampton Boat Show and Cowes Week.

SOUTHWOLD Suffolk
# THE SWAN

A hip, jazzy refurbishment has brought stripped wooden floorboards, green velvet sofas and 'small but effective pink touches' to this Southwold stalwart, which has stood on the market square, minutes from the seafront, for centuries. It is owned by Adnams, the brewers. Some visitors find the makeover 'impressive', others call it 'incongruous'. Still: 'We recommend this very good hotel,' say regular Guide readers this year, after a return visit. 'Light, airy and well fitted-out', seasidey bedrooms are supplied with 'very nice touches', such as good biscuits and complimentary gin. Pub classics mix with imaginative options in the banquette-lined Tap Room and bar; in the restaurant, 'the food is particularly good'.

MAP 2:B6
Market Place
Southwold IP18 6EG
T: 01502 722186
W: theswansouthwold.co.uk

BEDROOMS: 35. 12 in garden extension, 1 suitable for disabled.
OPEN: all year.
FACILITIES: 2 restaurants, lounge, private dining rooms, in-room TV, civil wedding licence, large garden.
BACKGROUND MUSIC: in restaurant.
LOCATION: on market square.
CHILDREN: all ages welcomed.
DOGS: allowed in some garden rooms, not in main hotel building.
CREDIT CARDS: MC, Visa.
PRICES: per room B&B £189–£430, D,B&B £270–£490. À la carte £35. 1-night bookings generally refused in summer.

## STOKE BY NAYLAND Suffolk
# THE CROWN

With white-painted walls and a peg-tiled roof, this 'smartly renovated' inn, one of Suffolk's oldest pubs, stands in landscaped gardens that melt into Constable country. It is owned and run by the East Anglia-based Chestnut group. The popular bar and dining room open on to a terrace for alfresco drinks and meals; inside or out, diners pick from a menu that highlights locally sourced ingredients (particularly the freshest fish from the east coast). Bedrooms are in a 'beautifully presented' annexe behind the pub. They vary in size and decor; the best have French windows on to a private terrace overlooking lawns and fields. At breakfast, choose between omelettes, Scotch porridge, bubble and squeak, and more.

MAP 2:C5
Park Street
Stoke by Nayland CO6 4SE
T: 01206 262001
W: crowninn.net

BEDROOMS: 11. All in annexe, 8 on ground floor, 1 suitable for disabled.
OPEN: all year except 25/26 Dec.
FACILITIES: bar, restaurant, snug, reception area with seating, terrace, wine shop, in-room TV (BT, Freeview), garden, parking, public rooms wheelchair accessible, adapted toilet.
BACKGROUND MUSIC: none.
LOCATION: village centre.
CHILDREN: all ages welcomed.
DOGS: allowed in parts of restaurant, not in bedrooms.
CREDIT CARDS: Amex, MC, Visa.
PRICES: per room B&B single £110–£210, double £145–£295. À la carte £35.

## STOW-ON-THE-WOLD Gloucestershire
# THE OLD STOCKS INN

In a historic wool town, the classic Cotswold-stone exterior of this 'likeable' 17th-century inn gives way to a cool, contemporary decor that mixes wooden beams and ancient floorboards with Scandi-chic furnishings, a fine cocktail list and a family-friendly feel. Past the board games in the bar, colourful bedrooms have a large bed, a coffee machine and a free minibar stocked with soft drinks, fresh milk and local snacks. 'Quirky' features abound: exposed stone walls in one room; a private, slanted staircase in another; 'some creaks and footfalls from neighbouring rooms'. In the restaurant, modern dishes include interesting vegetarian options; in spring and summer, the pizza oven fires up in the walled garden.

MAP 3:D6
The Square
Stow-on-the-Wold GL54 1AF
T: 01451 830666
W: oldstocksinn.com

BEDROOMS: 16. 3 in garden annexe.
OPEN: all year except 24/25 Dec, restaurant closed for lunch Mon–Thurs.
FACILITIES: restaurant, bar, library, coffee shop, private dining room, in-room TV (Freeview), terrace.
BACKGROUND MUSIC: in all public areas.
LOCATION: in town centre.
CHILDREN: all ages welcomed.
DOGS: allowed in 3 bedrooms, bar, library, coffee shop.
CREDIT CARDS: Amex, MC, Visa.
PRICES: per room B&B £129–£289, D,B&B £210–£350. À la carte £35. 1-night bookings sometimes refused Sat night.

STRATFORD-UPON-AVON Warwickshire
# THE TOWNHOUSE
In a 400-year-old Grade II listed building across the road from the Guildhall, this style-savvy hotel and restaurant occupies a prime spot in the medieval market town. Colourful bedrooms vary in size, but all have a large bed and a flair for the theatrical, with an elaborately framed mirror here, a suede chaise longue there, perhaps a claw-footed bathtub in the bathroom. Interconnecting rooms suit a family. Locals, tourists and a thespian or two gather in the all-day bistro and atmospheric bar: hung with heavy drapes, and decorated with eye-catching photographs and ornaments, it's a quirky, inviting spot for breakfast, lunch or dinner. Pre-theatre diners are entertained by a local pianist. A Brakspear pub.

MAP 3:D6
16 Church Street
Stratford-upon-Avon CV37 6HB
T: 01789 262222
W: stratfordtownhouse.co.uk

BEDROOMS: 12. 1 on ground floor suitable for disabled.
OPEN: all year.
FACILITIES: bar, dining room, library, in-room TV, function facilities.
BACKGROUND MUSIC: in public areas, occasional live music.
LOCATION: town centre, 5 mins' walk from Royal Shakespeare Theatre.
CHILDREN: not under 16.
DOGS: not allowed.
CREDIT CARDS: MC, Visa.
PRICES: per room B&B £140–£190, D,B&B £190–£215. À la carte £28. 1-night bookings generally refused weekends.

STRATFORD-UPON-AVON Warwickshire
# WHITE SAILS
Tim and Denise Perkin run their well-regarded B&B in a suburban house, close to the farmhouse where Anne Hathaway lived as a child. The hosts maintain a home-away-from-home atmosphere, with help-yourself extras (sherry, espresso coffee, home-made treats) in the compact lounge, and a manicured garden to sit in on warm days. 'Clean and comfy' bedrooms, including one with a four-poster bed, are well supplied with bathrobes, a digital radio and home-baked cake; chilled water and fresh milk are in a silent fridge. Breakfast is a feast of home-made granola, bread and cakes; cooked-to-order dishes include eggs Benedict or smoked haddock with poached eggs. The RSC theatres are a 20-minute stroll away.

MAP 3:D6
85 Evesham Road
Stratford-upon-Avon CV37 9BE
T: 01789 550469
W: white-sails.co.uk

BEDROOMS: 4.
OPEN: all year except Christmas and New Year's Day.
FACILITIES: lounge, dining room, in-room TV (Freeview), garden, bicycle storage.
BACKGROUND MUSIC: in breakfast room.
LOCATION: 1 mile W of centre.
CHILDREN: not under 12.
DOGS: not allowed.
CREDIT CARDS: Amex, MC, Visa.
PRICES: per room B&B single £95–£120, double £110–£135. 2-night min. stay May–Sept.

## SUMMERHOUSE Co. Durham

### THE RABY HUNT RESTAURANT AND ROOMS

Way above par, James Close, a former golf professional and self-taught chef, has two Michelin stars for his seemingly simple, visually stunning cooking. His tiny restaurant-with-rooms, in a creeper-covered, Grade II listed 19th-century drover's inn, is in a rural hamlet. An open-view kitchen in the modern restaurant lets diners watch the drama as a busy team prepares the tasting menu of multiple courses. Up close, the Kitchen Table has front-row seats for six. A chocolate skull is a theatrical finale to the series of palate-thrilling plates – perhaps razor clam, almond and celeriac; mango, yuzu and coconut tart. Stay for breakfast: there are three contemporary bedrooms; more are planned.

25% DISCOUNT VOUCHERS

MAP 4:C4
Summerhouse DL2 3UD
T: 01325 374237
W: rabyhuntrestaurant.co.uk

BEDROOMS: 3.
OPEN: all year, except Christmas, New Year, restaurant closed Sun–Tues.
FACILITIES: restaurant, in-room TV.
BACKGROUND MUSIC: in restaurant.
LOCATION: 6 miles NW of Darlington.
CHILDREN: not under 12.
DOGS: not allowed.
CREDIT CARDS: Amex, MC, Visa.
PRICES: per room B&B £225. Tasting menu (14–18 courses) £170 per person, Kitchen Table menu £205 per person.

**NEW**

## TARPORLEY Cheshire

### 32 BY THE HOLLIES

Put to creditable use, a former bank in a handsome building on the High Street now serves as a 'buzzy', all-day restaurant, with bedrooms above. It is owned by the founders of the Hollies Farm Shop in a neighbouring village, which provides Cheshire produce for the 'tempting menus'. Cooked in an open kitchen, 'tasty' dishes such as pot-roast chicken are served in 'generous portions' by 'engaging, efficient staff'; the lounge and bar, with their cheerful velvet seating, make an 'alluring' space for drinking and dining. Stay over: 'plush' bedrooms in varying sizes have an underfloor-heated bathroom. In the morning, 'well-cooked' breakfasts, with 'coffee-shop-standard lattes', leave guests 'fully satisfied'.

MAP 3:A5
32 High Street
Tarporley CW6 0DY
T: 01829 738958
W: 32bythehollies.co.uk

BEDROOMS: 5.
OPEN: all year.
FACILITIES: bar, lounge, restaurant, in-room smart TV, terrace.
BACKGROUND MUSIC: in public spaces.
LOCATION: in village centre, 11 miles SE of Chester.
CHILDREN: all ages welcomed.
DOGS: not allowed.
CREDIT CARDS: Amex, MC, Visa.
PRICES: per room B&B from £159. À la carte £34.

TAUNTON Somerset

## THE CASTLE AT TAUNTON

'Beautifully furnished and very comfortable', this traditional hotel, in a wisteria-festooned medieval castle, has character and history to spare. Extended and rebuilt over centuries, it is today run by the third generation of the Chapman family, who have owned it since 1950. The buzzy brasserie serves 'delicious' food; its early-dining set menus, blackboard specials and sharing platters might include goat's cheese, hazelnut, peach; Somerset lamb chops, green beans. 'Cheerful' bedrooms, some newly refurbished, have a turn-down service at night. 'Excellent' breakfasts include a buffet with home-made bread and jams, plus 'piping hot' cooked dishes. 'The little gardens are a pleasant place to explore.'

**25% DISCOUNT VOUCHERS**

MAP 1:C5
Castle Green
Taunton TA1 1NF
T: 01823 272671
W: the-castle-hotel.com

BEDROOMS: 44. 2 suitable for disabled.
OPEN: all year.
FACILITIES: lift, lounge/bar, snug, restaurant, private dining/meeting rooms, in-room TV (Freeview), civil wedding licence, ¼-acre garden, public rooms wheelchair accessible, adapted toilet.
BACKGROUND MUSIC: 'easy listening' in bar, restaurant.
LOCATION: town centre.
CHILDREN: all ages welcomed.
DOGS: allowed in bedrooms, bar.
CREDIT CARDS: Amex, MC, Visa.
PRICES: per room B&B £165–£255, D,B&B £209–£299. À la carte £30, set menu £11.95 (2 courses, served 12 pm–3 pm, 6 pm–7 pm Mon–Fri).

TAVISTOCK Devon

## TAVISTOCK HOUSE HOTEL

Pristine throughout, Brad and Gill Walker's lawn-fronted town house hotel is a harmonious mix of crisp, modern design and well-maintained original features. The house, built by the Duke of Bedford in 1850, is five minutes' walk from the town square. Well-appointed bedrooms (some snug) are supplied with silk duvets, teas and a capsule coffee machine; bath- and shower rooms have under-floor heating. Up-to-date tech includes a Netflix-enabled smart TV and a tablet computer to access free online newspapers. Hearty breakfasts and light lunches, including vegan and vegetarian options, are served in a serene room decorated with contemporary artwork. An honesty bar supplies aperitifs and nightcaps.

MAP 1:D4
50 Plymouth Road
Tavistock PL19 8BU
T: 01822 481627
W: tavistockhousehotel.co.uk

BEDROOMS: 6. 1 on ground floor.
OPEN: all year except 25/26 Dec, 31 Dec, 1 Jan.
FACILITIES: lounge/breakfast room (honesty bar), in-room smart TV (Freeview, Netflix), front garden.
BACKGROUND MUSIC: in public areas.
LOCATION: in town centre.
CHILDREN: not under 9.
DOGS: not allowed.
CREDIT CARDS: MC, Visa.
PRICES: per room B&B £104–£144. 2-night min. stay most weekends.

THORNHAM Norfolk

# THE LIFEBOAT INN

A silent observer, this 16th-century beer house, in a 'spectacular' location on the north Norfolk coast, has taken in the changing landscape across salt marsh and sea for hundreds of years. Today a family-friendly, dog-welcoming inn (Agellus Hotels), it has an oak-beamed bar with settles and open fires; a relaxed restaurant serving seasonal dishes and daily specials; a conservatory crowned by a 200-year-old vine; and cosy, up-to-date bedrooms with views of countryside or coast. (A pitch-penny slot in a bar bench adds extra character.) Sit down to a hearty meal, or go solo along the Coast Path to Holme Dunes – the company of migrating birds, natterjack toads and dragonflies can be just as delicious.

MAP 2:A5
Ship Lane
Thornham  PE36 6LT
T: 01485 512236
W: lifeboatinnthornham.com

BEDROOMS: 13. 1 on ground floor, in cottage.
OPEN: all year.
FACILITIES: bar, 2 lounge areas, conservatory, restaurant, meeting room, private dining room, in-room smart TV (Freeview), terrace, garden, parking.
BACKGROUND MUSIC: all day in restaurant, bar.
LOCATION: in a small coastal village, 14 miles NE of Hunstanton.
CHILDREN: all ages welcomed.
DOGS: allowed in bedrooms, public rooms.
CREDIT CARDS: MC, Visa.
PRICES: per room B&B £145–£225. À la carte £28. 2-night min. stay preferred.

THORNTON HOUGH Merseyside

# MERE BROOK HOUSE

'A home away from home', this relaxed Edwardian country house is a 'peaceful haven' set within a dell of mature trees. Lorna Tyson and her husband, Donald, a farmer, run it with 'thoughtful hospitality' and a laid-back approach – 'no notices or rules anywhere!' Pretty bedrooms are in the main building and a converted coach house 20 yards away. Individually decorated, rooms overlook the garden or countryside. Both buildings have their own lounge and residents' kitchen stocked with help-yourself home-made cakes, cheese, juice and hot drinks. Breakfast in the conservatory has super-local ingredients, including honey from garden beehives, milk from the Tysons' dairy cows, apple juice from orchard fruit.

**25% DISCOUNT VOUCHERS**

MAP 4:E2
Thornton Common Road
Thornton Hough  CH63 0LU
T: 07713 189949
W: merebrookhouse.co.uk

BEDROOMS: 8. 4 in coach house, 3 on ground floor, 2 wheelchair accessible.
OPEN: all year, limited availability over Christmas, New Year.
FACILITIES: 3 lounges, conservatory, dining room, guest kitchens, in-room TV (Freeview), wedding/function facilities, 1-acre garden in 4-acre grounds.
BACKGROUND MUSIC: none.
LOCATION: centre of Wirral peninsula, 20 mins' drive from Chester and Liverpool.
CHILDREN: all ages welcomed.
DOGS: only assistance dogs allowed.
CREDIT CARDS: MC, Visa.
PRICES: per room B&B £79–£139.

THURNHAM Kent
## THURNHAM KEEP

A long drive through landscaped gardens reveals this 'simply wonderful' B&B, where visitors are rewarded with a sweet welcome: 'the best shortbread ever'. Built from the ruins of Thurnham Castle, Amanda Lane's 'magnificent place', her childhood home, stands in a 'perfect setting' on the crest of the North Downs. Up an oak staircase, each traditionally furnished bedroom has its own style. In two, a huge, original Edwardian bath in the bathroom; in all, soft pastels and period furniture. A spacious suite is in converted stables. A 'lavish and tasty' breakfast, served communally, brings home-made jams, garden honey, fresh-from-the-coop eggs. Supper might be arranged in advance; plenty of nearby pubs, too.

MAP 2:D4
Castle Hill
Thurnham  ME14 3LE
T: 01622 734149
W: thurnhamkeep.co.uk

BEDROOMS: 3. Plus self-catering suite in grounds.
OPEN: Mar–Oct.
FACILITIES: sitting room, dining room, conservatory, billiard room, in-room TV (Freeview), 7-acre terraced garden, terrace, heated outdoor swimming pool (May–Sept), tennis, parking.
BACKGROUND MUSIC: none.
LOCATION: 3 miles from Maidstone.
CHILDREN: not under 10.
DOGS: not allowed.
CREDIT CARDS: Amex, MC, Visa.
PRICES: per room B&B single £140–£150, double £150–£170. 2-night min. stay at weekends.

TISBURY Wiltshire
## THE COMPASSES INN

Reached down rural lanes bordered by hedgerows, Ben Maschler's contemporary country pub-with-rooms occupies a thatch-roofed 14th-century inn whose flagstone floors and ancient beams lend it much character. There are nooks and crannies, and candles lit on wooden tables; a fire burns in the inglenook fireplace when the mercury dips. Come hungry, as the locals do: Paddy Davy's 'exceptional' cooking, including sophisticated pub standbys, is ably accompanied by cocktails and local ales. Above the pub, 'simple but more than adequate' bedrooms are pleasingly pared back; modern bathrooms and shower rooms are supplied with British-made toiletries. The Nadder valley's footpaths and sheep trails start from the door.

MAP 2:D1
Lower Chicksgrove
Tisbury  SP3 6NB
T: 01722 714318
W: thecompassesinn.com

BEDROOMS: 4. Plus 3-bed self-catering cottage.
OPEN: all year except 25 Dec.
FACILITIES: bar, restaurant, in-room TV (Freeview), ¼-acre garden.
BACKGROUND MUSIC: none, occasional live music events.
LOCATION: 2 miles E of Tisbury.
CHILDREN: all ages welcomed.
DOGS: allowed in bedrooms, public areas.
CREDIT CARDS: MC, Visa.
PRICES: per room B&B single £110, double £120. À la carte £30. 2-night min. stay summer and bank holiday weekends.

TOPSHAM Devon

# THE SALUTATION INN

Behind its blue-and-cream facade, this Georgian
inn stands in the centre of an old ship-building
town at the head of the Exe estuary. Sleekly
updated with a nod to its maritime past, it is a
family-owned restaurant-with-rooms run by
chef/patron Tom Williams-Hawkes and his wife,
Amelia, with 'particularly helpful' staff. 'The
main attraction is clearly the food': 'adventurous,
imaginatively presented' tasting menus, including
ones for vegetarians, use an abundance of locally
sourced produce. Light meals and afternoon teas
may be taken in the GlassHouse atrium café.
Bedrooms (some snug, with a 'bijou' shower
room) are modern and restrained; hot drinks and
snacks are in a shared kitchen. 'Good' breakfasts
have 'some unusual dishes'.

MAP 1:C5
68 Fore Street
Topsham  EX3 0HL
T: 01392 873060
W: salutationtopsham.co.uk

BEDROOMS: 6.
OPEN: all year except 25 Dec evening,
26 Dec, 1 Jan, restaurant and café
closed Sun eve.
FACILITIES: 2 lounges, restaurant, café,
meeting/function room, in-room TV
(Freeview), walled yard with seating,
parking, restaurant wheelchair
accessible, adapted toilet.
BACKGROUND MUSIC: in public areas.
LOCATION: town centre.
CHILDREN: all ages welcomed.
DOGS: allowed in bedrooms, public
rooms.
CREDIT CARDS: MC, Visa.
PRICES: per room B&B single
£115–£205, double £135–£230. Set
menus £45–£85. 2-night min. stay on
weekends May–Sept.

TORQUAY Devon

# MEADFOOT BAY

'Kick off your shoes' at Phil Hartnett and Vicki
Osborne's relaxed B&B, in a Victorian villa
close to the beach and Coast Path. The graceful,
light-filled sitting room has deep sofas under
a chandelier; here, and throughout the house,
manager Jody Miller and his friendly team
encourage a 'home away from home' feel. Clean-
cut, individually decorated bedrooms in varying
sizes have all the amenities (tea and coffee, plus
fresh milk and chilled water in the mini-fridge);
three have a private terrace. There's modern
British cuisine in the brasserie; sandwiches and
sharing platters in the bar. Cooked-to-order dishes
accompany home-made muesli and granola, and
locally made jams and marmalades at breakfast.

MAP 1:D5
Meadfoot Sea Road
Torquay  TQ1 2LQ
T: 01803 294722
W: meadfoot.com

BEDROOMS: 15. 1 on ground floor.
OPEN: all year, restaurant closed Sun
eve and Mon eve Oct–Mar (bar menu
available).
FACILITIES: lounge, bar, dining room,
library, in-room TV (Freeview),
terrace, parking, all ground-floor
public areas wheelchair accessible.
BACKGROUND MUSIC: in public areas.
LOCATION: 3 mins' walk behind
Meadfoot beach, 15 mins' walk from
Torquay harbour.
CHILDREN: not under 15.
DOGS: allowed in 1 bedroom with own
entrance, not inside main hotel.
CREDIT CARDS: Amex, MC, Visa.
PRICES: per room B&B £85–£220,
D,B&B £125–£260. À la carte £28.
2-night min. stay in high season and
on bank holidays.

TRESCO Isles of Scilly
# THE NEW INN

Just off the beach, the only pub on Robert Dorrien-Smith's private, car-free island is a 'relaxed' gathering place for locals and holidaymakers alike. It has 'lovely accommodation', and unfussy menus showcasing Scillonian produce: Bryher crab mac and Cheddar, Cornish mackerel burgers, baked Salakee Farm duck egg. By the 'well-stocked bar', a wood-burning stove is fired up on chilly days; in good weather, move in to the 'pretty' canopied garden. Bedrooms newly updated in a breezy, beachy palette are supplied with specialist teas and ground coffee; many have views of the harbour. Guests may access the tennis and spa facilities at Tresco Island Spa (extra charge), a few minutes' stroll along the harbourfront.

MAP 1: inset C1
New Grimsby
Tresco TR24 0QQ
T: 01720 422849
W: tresco.co.uk/staying/the-new-inn

BEDROOMS: 16. Some on ground floor.
OPEN: all year, limited opening in winter months.
FACILITIES: bar, residents' lounge, restaurant, in-room TV (Freeview), patio, garden, pavilion, heated outdoor swimming pool (seasonal), use of Tresco Island Spa facilities (extra fee).
BACKGROUND MUSIC: in pub and restaurant, occasional live music events.
LOCATION: near New Grimsby harbour.
CHILDREN: all ages welcomed.
DOGS: allowed in public bar, beer garden, assistance dogs allowed in bedrooms.
CREDIT CARDS: MC, Visa.
PRICES: per room B&B £120–£205. À la carte £35.

TROUTBECK Cumbria
# BROADOAKS

The views stretch to Windermere and the Langdale Pikes from this 19th-century stone-and-slate country house, which stands in large, landscaped grounds, in a green valley that leads to the rushing river. A 'very welcoming' hotel, it is owned by Tracey Robinson and Joanna Harbottle. In the main house, coach house and other buildings in the grounds, modern bedrooms have their own style, plus, perhaps, a log fire, a roll-top bath or a private decked terrace. Evenings, canapés are served in the handsome Arts and Crafts music room before guests tuck in to 'excellent' French-accented Cumbrian fare in the restaurant. There's plenty of choice at breakfast, from Cartmel Valley kippers to omelettes and griddled pancakes.

MAP 4: inset C2
Bridge Lane
Troutbeck LA23 1LA
T: 01539 445566
W: broadoakscountryhouse.co.uk

BEDROOMS: 20. Some on ground floor, 5 in coach house, 4 detached suites in grounds.
OPEN: all year.
FACILITIES: sitting room, music room, bar, restaurant, orangery, in-room TV (Freeview), civil wedding licence, 8-acre grounds, complimentary access to nearby spa.
BACKGROUND MUSIC: 'on low volume' in public areas.
LOCATION: 2 miles N of Bowness-on-Windermere.
CHILDREN: all ages welcomed.
DOGS: allowed in some bedrooms, on lead in garden, bar and lounge.
CREDIT CARDS: MC, Visa.
PRICES: per room B&B £155–£355, D,B&B £185–£395. Set menu £47.50.

TRUSHAM Devon

# THE CRIDFORD INN

With cob walls, a thatched roof and wide stone fireplaces, this rural Teign valley pub looks the part of the county's – possibly England's – oldest inn. Reached via a single-track road, the traditional Devon longhouse was a nunnery, property of Buckfast Abbey, when it was listed in the Domesday Book. Today, it is an unassuming, dog-friendly inn owned by Paul and Ness Moir. The slate-floored pub and restaurant host Sunday roasts, pie-and-pint evenings and everyday lunches and dinners; a suntrap terrace invites alfresco meals and drinks. Simply decorated bedrooms have exposed beams, sloping ceilings and all the modern amenities. Exeter is 25 minutes away by car; all around are fields and country lanes.

25% DISCOUNT VOUCHERS

MAP 1:D4
Trusham TQ13 0NR
T: 01626 853694
W: thecridfordinn.co.uk

BEDROOMS: 4. Plus 2-bed cottage.
OPEN: all year.
FACILITIES: bar, restaurant, private dining room, in-room TV (Freeview), terrace, drying shed, pub and restaurant wheelchair accessible.
BACKGROUND MUSIC: 'very light' in bar.
LOCATION: in village, 12 miles SW of Exeter.
CHILDREN: all ages welcomed.
DOGS: allowed in 3 bedrooms, public rooms.
CREDIT CARDS: MC, Visa.
PRICES: per room B&B single £49–£109, double £59–£129. À la carte £25. 1-night bookings refused weekends in high season.

TUNBRIDGE WELLS Kent

# THE MOUNT EDGCUMBE

Overlooking the Common, Sally Hignett and Robert Hogben's contemporary inn is surrounded by trees and green space, a short walk from the town centre. Local families, dog owners and real-ale connoisseurs come for the seasonal menu of sharing platters and modern pub dishes served in the informal restaurant, set over two floors. In warm weather, parasols spring up over picnic tables on the large patio; cooler days signal a retreat to the snug bar, in a remarkable 6th-century sandstone cave. Stylish bedrooms in harmonious hues are on the upper floor of the Georgian building. Each is supplied with biscuits, a capsule coffee machine and all-natural toiletries; views are over leafy trees or the Edgcumbe Rocks.

MAP 2:D4
The Common
Tunbridge Wells TN4 8BX
T: 01892 618854
W: themountedgcumbe.com

BEDROOMS: 6.
OPEN: all year, restaurant closed 25 Dec.
FACILITIES: bar, restaurant, cave, in-room TV (Freeview), garden.
BACKGROUND MUSIC: in bar, restaurant.
LOCATION: ½ mile from Tunbridge Wells train station.
CHILDREN: all ages welcomed.
DOGS: in bar, restaurant, garden, not in bedrooms.
CREDIT CARDS: Amex, MC, Visa.
PRICES: per room B&B single £95–£185, double £110–£200. À la carte £30.

## ULVERSTON Cumbria
# THE BAY HORSE

'The view and the tranquillity are just wonderful.'
Overlooking the Levens estuary, Robert Lyons
and Lesley Wheeler's traditional pub-with-rooms
is a fine spot to watch the tide race in – a thrilling
sight. The inn was once a stop-over for coaches
and horses crossing the sands to Lancaster.
These days, its 'amiable' comforts draw back
birdwatchers, cyclists, walkers, dog owners and
fishermen year after year. A community hub, it
is popular with locals for casual bar meals, and
candlelit dinners served in the freshly decorated
conservatory restaurant by the water's edge.
Homely bedrooms are supplied with board
games, books and magazines; six rooms have an
estuary-view balcony. Breakfasts are 'exceptional'.

MAP 4: inset C2
Canal Foot
Ulverston LA12 9EL
T: 01229 583972
W: thebayhorsehotel.co.uk

BEDROOMS: 9.
OPEN: all year, restaurant closed Mon
lunchtime (light bites available).
FACILITIES: bar/lounge, conservatory
restaurant, in-room TV (Freeview),
picnic area, parking, bar and
restaurant wheelchair accessible.
BACKGROUND MUSIC: in bar, restaurant.
LOCATION: 1½ miles from town centre.
CHILDREN: not under 10.
DOGS: well-behaved dogs allowed in
bedrooms, not in restaurant.
CREDIT CARDS: Amex, MC, Visa.
PRICES: per room B&B £95–£117,
D,B&B (2-night min.) £160–£185.
À la carte £40. 2-night min. stay
preferred.

## UPTON MAGNA Shropshire
# THE HAUGHMOND

'Clearly very popular', Mel and Martin Board's
whitewashed 17th-century village inn draws
ramblers, cyclists, locals and their dogs.
Reservations are recommended for the well-
regarded restaurant, where the 'first-class' country
fare might include such modern dishes as duck
egg, mushrooms, pearl barley, truffle. Above the
bar, straightforward bedrooms, all solid oak and
crisp bedlinen, are named after British deer: Sika
has a Juliet balcony with countryside views; Red,
a sweeping vista towards the Wrekin. Two rooms
in a converted barn, with easy access to public
footpaths over the fields, are ideal for guests
travelling with their dog. Stop in at the on-site
farm shop for a packed lunch before striding out.

MAP 3:B5
Pelham Road
Upton Magna SY4 4TZ
T: 01743 709918
W: thehaughmond.co.uk

BEDROOMS: 7. 2, on ground floor, in
annexe.
OPEN: all year except Christmas Day,
New Year's Day, restaurant closed
Mon.
FACILITIES: bar/brasserie, breakfast
room, conservatory, in-room smart
TV, terrace, ½-acre garden, parking.
BACKGROUND MUSIC: 'on low volume'
in public areas.
LOCATION: 4 miles from Shrewsbury.
CHILDREN: all ages welcomed.
DOGS: allowed in bedrooms (own bed
required), on lead in public areas.
CREDIT CARDS: MC, Visa.
PRICES: per room B&B single £80–£100,
double £90–£120. À la carte £30.

WARTLING Sussex

# WARTLING PLACE

Rowena and Barry Gittoes 'cater for every need' at their Grade II listed former Georgian rectory, which stands in 'beautiful' gardens close to the Pevensey Levels nature reserve. Downstairs are prints, pictures, blue-and-white bibelots; comfortable seating in the drawing room. In the 'delightful' bedrooms: 'real coffee' and Fairtrade teas; perhaps an antique four-poster bed, and rural views towards the South Downs. Wake to a 'delicious' breakfast served in the large dining room, or opt to have it in your bedroom. Besides fruit, cereals and yogurt, there's smoked salmon from Hastings, locally produced sausages and eggs, herbs from the garden. 'Convenient for Glyndebourne and the coast.'

MAP 2:E4
Wartling BN27 1RY
T: 01323 832590
W: wartlingplace.co.uk

BEDROOMS: 4. Plus 2-bed self-catering cottage, suitable for disabled.
OPEN: all year.
FACILITIES: drawing room, dining room, in-room TV (Freeview), 3-acre garden, parking.
BACKGROUND MUSIC: none.
LOCATION: 5 miles E of Hailsham.
CHILDREN: not under 12.
DOGS: not allowed.
CREDIT CARDS: Amex, MC, Visa.
PRICES: per room B&B single £105–£120, double £140–£165. 1-night bookings refused peak-season weekends.

WARWICK Warwickshire

# PARK COTTAGE

Hanging baskets of colourful blooms, along with wonderfully wonky timbers, front Janet and Stuart Baldry's Grade II listed 15th-century house next to the entrance to Warwick Castle. Warm and welcoming, the owners exhibit 'one of the great advantages of the British B&B – truly attentive care and concern for their guests'. Across sloping floors and up a steep, narrow staircase, the 'comfortable' bedrooms are all different. One has an antique four-poster bed; another, a king-size spa bath; a third, access to the pretty patio garden, home to a 300-year-old listed tree. 'Splendid breakfasts, expertly cooked' by the host, are served at tables set on the original sandstone floor of the former castle dairy.

**25% DISCOUNT VOUCHERS**

MAP 3:C6
113 West Street
Warwick CV34 6AH
T: 01926 410319
W: parkcottagewarwick.co.uk

BEDROOMS: 7. 2 on ground floor, plus 2 adjoining self-catering cottages.
OPEN: all year except Christmas, New Year.
FACILITIES: reception/sitting area, breakfast room, in-room TV (Freeview), small garden, parking.
BACKGROUND MUSIC: none.
LOCATION: town centre.
CHILDREN: all ages welcomed.
DOGS: allowed by prior arrangement in bedrooms (not unattended, own bed required), on lead in public areas.
CREDIT CARDS: Amex, MC, Visa.
PRICES: per room B&B single £82, double from £92. 1-night bookings sometimes refused.

## WATCHET Somerset
# SWAIN HOUSE

Jason Robinson's chic B&B occupies a refurbished 18th-century house in the heart of the historic harbour town that inspired Samuel Taylor Coleridge. Steps from the statue of the Ancient Mariner on the quay, this stylish spot has large, thoughtfully equipped bedrooms: find teas and coffee, plus a flask of fresh milk; fluffy towels, waffle bathrobes and high-end toiletries; a roll-top slipper bath and walk-in shower in the bathroom. Home-cooked dishes at the 'beautifully laid out' breakfast include a full veggie option; in the evening, a light cheese or charcuterie supper is available. From here, ramble along the Coleridge Way – picnic lunches can be arranged – or easily access the heritage West Somerset Railway.

**25% DISCOUNT VOUCHERS**

MAP 1:B5
48 Swain Street
Watchet TA23 0AG
T: 01984 631038
W: swain-house.com

BEDROOMS: 4.
OPEN: all year except Christmas, New Year.
FACILITIES: lounge, dining room, in-room TV (Freeview).
BACKGROUND MUSIC: none.
LOCATION: 100 yds from harbour marina.
CHILDREN: not under 12.
DOGS: not allowed.
CREDIT CARDS: Amex, MC, Visa.
PRICES: per room B&B single from £125, double £140.

## WATERGATE BAY Cornwall
# WATERGATE BAY

'The whole family feels welcome' at this 'great' seaside hotel, which stands in a 'fabulous' location, on a two-mile stretch of sandy, dog-friendly beach. The modern building is breezy and bright inside, with a host of facilities that ensure there's a pursuit to suit everyone: surf lessons at the Extreme Academy; deep relaxation at the Swim Club; for young guests, dedicated play areas, and an activity club during the school holidays. At mealtimes, choose between American-style classics at Zacry's; salads and sharing platters in the Living Space; fresh seafood at the Beach Hut. At the end of the day, wind down in one of the 'extremely comfortable' bedrooms. Each has a coastal vibe; many have views to match.

MAP 1:D2
On the beach
Watergate Bay TR8 4AA
T: 01637 860543
W: watergatebay.co.uk

BEDROOMS: 73. 2 on ground floor, suitable for disabled, 4 apartments.
OPEN: all year.
FACILITIES: lounge/bar, 3 restaurants, in-room TV (Freeview), civil wedding licence, spa (indoor/outdoor swimming pool, sauna, hot tub, treatments), children's play areas, terrace, sun deck.
BACKGROUND MUSIC: all day in public spaces.
LOCATION: 5 miles N of Newquay.
CHILDREN: all ages welcomed.
DOGS: 'welcomed with open arms' in some bedrooms, 2 restaurants.
CREDIT CARDS: MC, Visa.
PRICES: per room B&B £190–£365, D,B&B £240–£420. À la carte (Zacry's restaurant) £40.

WEDMORE Somerset

## THE SWAN

The 'lovely, informal atmosphere' at this 'good-value' pub-with-rooms brings locals and tourists to the pleasingly updated 18th-century beer house, in a lively village in the Somerset Levels. The dog-friendly bar's the place for local real ales and ciders, and an all-day snack menu; at lunch and dinner, perhaps eaten alfresco on the garden terrace, local produce shines in unfussy gastropub dishes such as confit duck, sweet potato and root vegetable terrine. Upstairs, 'smart', rustic-chic bedrooms are well stocked with ground coffee and 'super' toiletries. 'Breakfast is a real treat.' Part of the Stay Original Company; see also Timbrell's Yard, Bradford-on-Avon, and The White Hart, Somerton (Shortlist entries).

MAP 1:B6
Cheddar Road
Wedmore BS28 4EQ
T: 01934 710337
W: theswanwedmore.com

BEDROOMS: 7.
OPEN: all year.
FACILITIES: bar, restaurant, in-room TV, civil wedding licence, function facilities, terrace, large garden, parking.
BACKGROUND MUSIC: in bar.
LOCATION: village centre.
CHILDREN: all ages welcomed.
DOGS: allowed in bedrooms, public rooms.
CREDIT CARDS: MC, Visa.
PRICES: per room B&B £85–£195, D,B&B £120–£230. À la carte £27.

WESTGATE Co. Durham

## WESTGATE MANOR

In the Durham Dales, a landscape of moors and hills, this large Victorian manor house is run as a guest house by 'welcoming, friendly and helpful' hosts Kathryn and Stuart Dobson. Huge windows in the wood burner-warmed lounge gaze across the rolling slopes (look out for grazing sheep, strolling pheasants and deer); elsewhere in the house, there are chandeliers, antique furnishings, and displays of fresh flowers. 'Beautiful', traditionally decorated bedrooms have exposed beams and countryside views; a bathroom with a walk-in shower, roll-top bath and under-floor heating. Two rooms interconnect to accommodate a family. Evening meals, taken, perhaps, in the orangery, may be ordered in advance.

**25% DISCOUNT VOUCHERS**

MAP 4:B3
Westgate DL13 1JT
T: 01388 517371
W: westgatemanor.co.uk

BEDROOMS: 5.
OPEN: all year except Christmas, New Year.
FACILITIES: lounge, dining room, orangery, garden room, in-room TV (Freeview), patio, secure bike storage, parking.
BACKGROUND MUSIC: in reception, dining room.
LOCATION: 40 mins' drive from Durham.
CHILDREN: all ages welcomed.
DOGS: not allowed.
CREDIT CARDS: Amex, MC, Visa.
PRICES: per room B&B £129–£145. À la carte £27.

WESTLETON Suffolk

# THE WESTLETON CROWN

Within a ten-minute drive – perhaps less as the crow flies – of the RSPB nature reserve at Minsmere, this updated 12th-century coaching inn makes a good base for birders, walkers, cyclists and seaside-seekers. Wood fires, deep armchairs, snug corners and a dog-friendly approach create an informal, inviting atmosphere in the bar and lounge; at mealtimes, diners sit in the traditional dining room, bright conservatory or terraced courtyard for the 'very good' food. Very good, too: the well-considered vegan and vegetarian options from breakfast to dinner. Modern bedrooms are unfussily decorated; two will suit a family. A circular walk calls for a pit stop at sister inn The Ship at Dunwich (see Shortlist entry).

MAP 2:B6
The Street
Westleton IP17 3AD
T: 01728 648777
W: westletoncrown.co.uk

BEDROOMS: 34. Most in cottages, converted stables and purpose-built blocks in grounds, 1 suitable for disabled.
OPEN: all year.
FACILITIES: bar, lounge, snug, 2 dining areas, in-room TV (Freeview), civil wedding licence, terraced garden.
BACKGROUND MUSIC: all day in dining areas.
LOCATION: in countryside, 3 miles from Dunwich beach.
CHILDREN: all ages welcomed.
DOGS: allowed in bar/lounge, bedrooms.
CREDIT CARDS: Amex, MC, Visa.
PRICES: per room B&B £110–£215, D,B&B £160–£300. À la carte £30. 2-night min. stay at weekends.

WHEATHILL Shropshire

# THE OLD RECTORY

A cheerful welcome awaits horses, hikers and hounds at Izzy Barnard's flower-filled Georgian house in prime Shropshire hacking and walking country. Piles of books and, in cool weather, a blazing fire in the drawing room help guests wind down; the soothing sauna completes the job. Country-style bedrooms have homely comforts, with a large bed, antique furnishings and biscuits. Horses and dogs have their own quarters. Ask for a four-course dinner, served communally and by candlelight, or sit down, simply, to soup and a sandwich. At breakfast, there's home-made bread and jams, and home-cured bacon; knitted cosies keep warm the eggs from resident ducks. Guides and route cards detail nearby bridleways.

MAP 3:C5
Wheathill WV16 6QT
T: 01746 787209
W: theoldrectorywheathill.com

BEDROOMS: 3.
OPEN: all year except Christmas, Jan.
FACILITIES: drawing room, dining room, in-room TV (Freeview), sauna, 7-acre gardens, boot room, tack room, loose boxes for horses.
BACKGROUND MUSIC: none.
LOCATION: 7 miles from Ludlow.
CHILDREN: all ages welcomed, by arrangement.
DOGS: allowed in boot room.
CREDIT CARDS: MC, Visa.
PRICES: per room B&B single £80–£125, double £95–£139. Set dinner £35, supper tray £10. 2-night min. stay preferred for Yellow Room.

WILLIAN Hertfordshire

## THE FOX AT WILLIAN

By the parish church in a quiet village mentioned in the Domesday Book, this white-painted pub has been spruced up to become a contemporary country inn with well-cooked food and fresh-as-a-daisy accommodation. Locals mix with townies on a getaway in the pared-back bar and neat dining room, where those in search of sustenance find all-day refreshments, pub classics and ambitious, inspired-by-the-seasons cooking. Staying guests check in to handsomely decorated bedrooms that combine rustic features with modern amenities (air conditioning, rainfall showers); dog-friendly garden rooms have their own terrace for an alfresco tipple. Part of Anglian Country Inns; see also The White Horse, Brancaster Staithe (main entry).

MAP 2:C4
Willian SG6 2AE
T: 01462 480233
W: foxatwillian.co.uk

BEDROOMS: 8. 4, in garden annexe, on ground floor.
OPEN: all year, restaurant closed Sun eve (bar food available).
FACILITIES: bar, restaurant, conservatory, in-room TV (Sky, Freeview), 2 terraces, public areas wheelchair accessible.
BACKGROUND MUSIC: in bar.
LOCATION: in village, 2 miles S of Letchworth Garden City.
CHILDREN: all ages welcomed.
DOGS: small dogs (and cats) allowed in garden bedrooms, bar.
CREDIT CARDS: Amex, MC, Visa.
PRICES: per room B&B single £85–£115, double £95–£130, D,B&B £150–£185. À la carte £35.

WOLTERTON Norfolk

## THE SARACEN'S HEAD

The north Norfolk countryside stretches away in all directions from Tim and Janie Elwes's 'enjoyable' Georgian inn, which stands in 'a beautifully rural setting' not far from the coast. The ivy-covered 19th-century building was designed to mimic a Tuscan farmhouse; it has bright public spaces, cosy-making wood burners, books and maps to browse. Bedrooms on the upper floors are simply decorated, though no less cheery for it. Each is supplied with hot chocolate, teas, ground coffee and a cafetière, plus natural Norfolk toiletries. In the earthy-toned restaurant, local produce studs the blackboard menu – think Brancaster-smoked salmon, Cromer crab, East Anglian cheeses. Aylsham, a 'delightful' town, is ten minutes' drive away.

MAP 2:A5
Wall Road
Wolterton NR11 7LZ
T: 01263 768909
W: saracenshead-norfolk.co.uk

BEDROOMS: 6.
OPEN: all year except 5 days over Christmas, bar and restaurant closed Sun eve–Mon lunch Nov–late Apr.
FACILITIES: lounge, bar, restaurant, in-room TV (Freeview), courtyard, 1-acre garden, restaurant and bar wheelchair accessible, no adapted toilet.
BACKGROUND MUSIC: in bar and dining rooms.
LOCATION: 5 miles N of Aylsham.
CHILDREN: all ages welcomed.
DOGS: allowed in bedrooms, back bar (booking required), not in restaurant.
CREDIT CARDS: MC, Visa.
PRICES: per room B&B single £75, double £110. À la carte £36.

WOODBRIDGE Suffolk
## THE CROWN

Coolly contemporary yet 'warm and welcoming',
this updated 16th-century coaching inn is in the
centre of an animated riverside town, within easy
reach of the Suffolk coast. New England-style
bedrooms (some snug) have local magazines
and a 'well-stocked' hospitality tray; British-
made toiletries are 'a definite plus'. (Some traffic
noise may be audible.) Downstairs, the wooden
sailing skiff in the glass-roofed bar is a nod to
the area's nautical heritage. Eat in: pub classics
and more modern dishes – grilled sea bass and
lime tagliatelle; a vegan pizza – are 'promptly
served' in the split-level restaurant and on the
wide terrace. Part of The Hotel Folk; see also The
Swan Hotel & Spa, Lavenham (Shortlist entry).

MAP 2:C5
Thoroughfare
Woodbridge IP12 1AD
T: 01394 384242
W: thecrownatwoodbridge.co.uk

BEDROOMS: 10.
OPEN: all year.
FACILITIES: restaurant, bar, private
dining room, in-room TV (Sky),
terrace, parking, restaurant and bar
wheelchair accessible.
BACKGROUND MUSIC: in public areas,
plus regular live music.
LOCATION: town centre.
CHILDREN: all ages welcomed.
DOGS: allowed in bar.
CREDIT CARDS: Amex, MC, Visa.
PRICES: per room B&B £95–£210,
D,B&B £145–£260. À la carte £34.
1-night bookings refused Sat.

WOODCHESTER Gloucestershire
## WOODCHESTER VALLEY VINEYARD

Amid the green fields of the Stroud valleys, Fiona
Shiner's family-owned vineyard and winery
shelter a modern B&B. Spacious duplex suites
in a sympathetically restored barn each have
a mini-kitchenette and a log burner-warmed
sitting area; private terraces and huge windows
take in long-reaching views across the valley
and vine-covered hills. Set off on the walking or
cycling routes that wind through this part of the
south Cotswolds; return for a vineyard tour and
a tasting of the award-winning wines. Breakfast
hampers (charged extra) include freshly baked
bread, croissants, preserves, yogurt, fresh fruit and
juice. Stop by the Cellar Door shop to stock up on
bottles from the vineyard before heading home.

MAP 3:E5
Convent Lane
Woodchester GL5 5HR
T: 07808 650883
W: woodchestervalleyvineyard.co.uk

BEDROOMS: 3. 1 suitable for disabled,
plus 2-bed farmhouse available for
self-catering.
OPEN: all year.
FACILITIES: tasting room, in-room TV
(Sky), vineyard, winery (tours, tutored
tastings).
BACKGROUND MUSIC: none.
LOCATION: in south Cotswolds, 3 miles
from Stroud.
CHILDREN: not under 12.
DOGS: allowed in farmhouse.
CREDIT CARDS: Amex, MC, Visa.
PRICES: per room £120–£160.
Continental breakfast hamper £20.
2-night min. stay at weekends.

## WOOLACOMBE Devon

# WATERSMEET

On the South West Coast Path, this former Edwardian gentleman's retreat has 'wonderful' cliff-top views over an expanse of sea and sand. Run with 'friendly, helpful staff', the 'comfortable, relaxed' hotel makes full use of its location. Its lounges, large, glass-fronted terrace and gardens have spectacular seascape panoramas and glorious sunsets; all but three bedrooms look out to Lundy Island and Baggy Point. In the informal bistro and candlelit restaurant (every table with a view over the sea), local produce features on British menus – John Dory, crab mayonnaise, samphire; Exmoor beef sirloin, roast shallots. Breakfast is 'good and plentiful'. Walks through National Trust land; a beach on the doorstep.

MAP 1:B4
Mortehoe
Woolacombe  EX34 7EB
T: 01271 870333
W: watersmeethotel.co.uk

BEDROOMS: 27. 3 on ground floor, 1 suitable for disabled.
OPEN: all year.
FACILITIES: lift, lounge, snug, bar, restaurant, bistro, in-room TV (Freeview), civil wedding licence, function facilities, terrace, ½-acre garden, indoor and heated outdoor swimming pools, treatment room, restaurant wheelchair accessible.
BACKGROUND MUSIC: in public areas.
LOCATION: behind beach, slightly N of village centre.
CHILDREN: all ages welcomed.
DOGS: not allowed.
CREDIT CARDS: MC, Visa.
PRICES: per room B&B £120–£300, D,B&B £210–£410. À la carte (bistro) £40, 2- and 3-course menus (restaurant) £42–£50.

## WORCESTER Worcestershire

# THE MANOR COACH HOUSE

Within easy reach of the city centre and Worcester cathedral, this 'spotless' B&B is in a 'peaceful' rural hamlet, just right for 'a good night's sleep'. An enthusiastic, hands-on hostess, Chrissie Mitchell greets arriving guests with tea, cake and local information. Recently refurbished, the 'comfortable, immaculate' bedrooms are in converted outbuildings set around a courtyard; each room has its own entrance. 'The facilities are excellent': there's fresh milk for tea and coffee, plus bathrobes and toiletries. A duplex family suite (suitable for children over four because of the stairs) also has a kitchenette. Special diets can be catered for, at breakfast; at dinner, local pubs are within walking distance.

MAP 3:C5
Hindlip Lane
Worcester  WR3 8SJ
T: 01905 456457
W: manorcoachhouse.co.uk

BEDROOMS: 5. All in converted outbuildings, 3 on ground floor, plus 2 self-catering units.
OPEN: all year except Christmas.
FACILITIES: breakfast room, in-room TV (Freeview), 1-acre garden.
BACKGROUND MUSIC: none.
LOCATION: in Hindlip, 2 miles from city centre.
CHILDREN: all ages welcomed.
DOGS: not allowed.
CREDIT CARDS: MC, Visa.
PRICES: per room B&B single £74–£80, double £74–£95.

YELVERTON Devon

# CIDER HOUSE

Birdsong fills the morning at this sophisticated B&B, in the sprawling grounds of the National Trust's Buckland Abbey. Once the medieval abbey's brew house, the refreshed, refreshing stone-built home is run with bonhomie by Bertie and Bryony Hancock. There are flowers in the drawing room, plus guidebooks and magazines; country-chic bedrooms with home-baked biscuits have restorative views through mullioned windows. Two cocooning, custom-built shepherd's huts in a wooded copse are just right for stargazing. Guests breakfast on orchard fruit, honey from garden bees, eggs from the hosts' rare-breed chickens. Residents receive passes for the abbey, and can explore its gardens outside public visiting times.

MAP 1:D4
Buckland Abbey
Yelverton PL20 6EZ
T: 01822 259062
W: cider-house.co.uk

BEDROOMS: 4. Plus 2 adult-only self-catering shepherd's huts.
OPEN: all year, shepherd's huts open Mar–Oct.
FACILITIES: drawing room, in-room TV (Freeview), terrace, garden, 700-acre grounds, parking.
BACKGROUND MUSIC: none.
LOCATION: 1 mile from village, 4 miles N of Plymouth.
CHILDREN: not under 16.
DOGS: not allowed.
CREDIT CARDS: MC, Visa.
PRICES: per room B&B single £125–£175, double £140–£190. 2-night min. stay preferred at weekends.

YORK Yorkshire

# BAR CONVENT

Next to the city's medieval walls, England's oldest active convent houses a community of sisters, who share their peaceful garden, domed chapel and antique religious texts with B&B guests. Immaculate bedrooms (some designed by Olga Polizzi) in the Grade I listed building vary in size; two accommodate a family of three. In a Victorian atrium, the café serves breakfast, morning coffee, light lunches and afternoon tea, plus a selection of daily specials. On a warm day, the suntrap garden is ideal for alfresco meals and snacks. There's a communal kitchen for DIY dinners; York's eateries are on the doorstep. Guests enjoy a discounted entrance to the on-site Living Heritage Centre and the 17th-century convent.

MAP 4:D4
17 Blossom Street
York YO24 1AQ
T: 01904 643238
W: bar-convent.org.uk

BEDROOMS: 20. 4 with shared bathrooms.
OPEN: all year except some days over Christmas, café closed Sun except for residents' breakfast.
FACILITIES: lift (to 1st and 2nd floors), sitting room, kitchen, licensed café, meeting rooms, in-room TV (Freeview), ¼-acre garden, Victorian atrium, 18th-century chapel, museum, shop.
BACKGROUND MUSIC: none.
LOCATION: 5 mins' walk from the railway station.
CHILDREN: all ages welcomed (guest kitchen, with use of washing machine for small additional charge).
DOGS: only assistance dogs allowed.
CREDIT CARDS: MC, Visa.
PRICES: per room B&B single £40–£86, double £80–£150.

YORK Yorkshire

## THE BLOOMSBURY

Steve and Tricia Townsley's 'beautiful' Victorian town house B&B is a scenic riverside walk away from the city centre. 'Superb hosts', the Townsleys welcome guests with a hot drink and 'a slice of something sweet'. Most of the 'extremely comfortable' bedrooms, each individually decorated and supplied with tea and coffee, are up the original staircase. (Fresh milk is available for the asking.) In the morning, breakfast is taken in a room overlooking the courtyard garden. There's plenty of locally sourced fare on offer: sausages and thick-cut bacon from the butcher 200 yards away; ground coffee from an independent merchant nearby; 'fabulous porridge with a tot of whisky'. Off-street parking is a plus.

**25% DISCOUNT VOUCHERS**

MAP 4:D4
127 Clifton
York YO30 6BL
T: 01904 634031
W: bloomsburyhotel.co.uk

BEDROOMS: 4. 1 on ground floor.
OPEN: Feb–22 Dec.
FACILITIES: sitting/dining room, in-room TV (Freeview), terrace, 'secret' courtyard garden, parking.
BACKGROUND MUSIC: 'relaxing hits from the 1950s to the present day' in dining room at breakfast.
LOCATION: within a mile of the city centre, 15 mins' walk from York Minster.
CHILDREN: not allowed.
DOGS: not allowed (resident dog).
CREDIT CARDS: MC, Visa.
PRICES: per person B&B single £50–£75, double £40–£60. 2-night min. stay.

**NEW**

YORK Yorkshire

## GRAYS COURT

Hidden down a narrow cobbled street, this 'fantastically located' hotel is set in leafy gardens within the city's medieval walls. With parts dating back to 1080, it has been sympathetically updated without losing its historic charm. Among the elegant, unstuffy sitting rooms, there is a peaceful library and a Jacobean oak-panelled gallery with original paintings, plush seating and recessed nooks. Afternoon tea is offered on arrival, but save room for the 'excellent', seasonally inspired tasting menu in the Bow Room restaurant. Up flights of stairs, handsomely furnished bedrooms have a modern bathroom, perhaps with a copper bath. Views take in the Minster, the cobbled courtyard and the 'beautiful' walled garden.

MAP 4:D4
Chapter House Street
York YO1 7JH
T: 01904 612613
W: grayscourtyork.com

BEDROOMS: 12.
OPEN: all year.
FACILITIES: bar, restaurant, 2 reception rooms, library, long gallery, in-room TV, civil wedding licence, function facilities, terrace, ½-acre garden, parking (booking required).
BACKGROUND MUSIC: none.
LOCATION: in the Minster quarter.
CHILDREN: all ages welcomed.
DOGS: small, well-behaved dogs allowed in 1 bedroom.
CREDIT CARDS: Amex, MC, Visa.
PRICES: per room B&B £200–£290. Tasting menu £70. 1-night bookings sometimes refused weekends.

ABERDEEN
# ATHOLL HOTEL

The soaring spires of this granite Victorian Gothic Revival building make this traditional hotel an easy-to-spot beacon. In a quiet location within reach of the city centre and convenient for the airport, it has plenty of parking space, and is popular with business travellers. Fuss-free bedrooms, including single rooms and family suites, have tartan bed covers and cushions; an array of amenities includes a tea and coffee tray, a hairdryer, an iron and ironing board. The restaurant, bar and lounge serve generously portioned, straightforward dishes such as sesame-baked salmon or braised ox cheeks. At breakfast, try tattie scones or smoked Finnan haddie. Castles, distilleries and golf courses are close by.

MAP 5:C3
54 King's Gate
Aberdeen AB15 4YN
T: 01224 323505
W: atholl-aberdeen.co.uk

BEDROOMS: 34. 2 suitable for disabled.
OPEN: all year, restaurant closed 1 Jan.
FACILITIES: lift (to 1st floor), lounge, bar, restaurant, in-room TV (Sky Sports), wedding/function facilities, patio, parking.
BACKGROUND MUSIC: in restaurant.
LOCATION: 1½ miles W of city centre.
CHILDREN: all ages welcomed.
DOGS: only assistance dogs allowed.
CREDIT CARDS: Amex, MC, Visa.
PRICES: per room B&B single £69–£99, double £89–£119. À la carte £32.

ABERFELDY Perth and Kinross
# FORTINGALL HOTEL

In a 'beautiful, tranquil' part of Highland Perthshire, Mags and Robbie Cairns's unpretentious country hotel occupies an old coaching inn at the entrance to Glen Lyon. Sheep-dotted fields stretch away in front of it; the village churchyard, in which stands the centuries-old Fortingall yew, is next door. A place to mingle, the bar has pictures and photographs, pickled eggs and crisps; here, and in the lounge and dining room, chef David Dunn's 'generally very good' cooking uses local meat and game, plus lobster 'from a friend's boat on the Forth'. Bedrooms are 'fresh and bright', and supplied with coffee, shortbread and a decanter of whisky. Walking, cycling, climbing, fishing and shooting on the doorstep.

MAP 5:D2
Old Street
Aberfeldy PH15 2NQ
T: 01887 830367
W: fortingall.com

BEDROOMS: 11.
OPEN: all year.
FACILITIES: bar, lounge, library, dining room, function room, in-room TV, wedding facilities, garden, secure bicycle storage.
BACKGROUND MUSIC: in restaurant, live folk music in bar on Fri nights.
LOCATION: 8 miles W of Aberfeldy.
CHILDREN: all ages welcomed.
DOGS: allowed.
CREDIT CARDS: MC, Visa.
PRICES: per room B&B single £100, double £190–£230, D,B&B single £150, double £260–£300.

**ALLANTON** Scottish Borders

## ALLANTON INN

A family-run affair for more than a decade, Katrina and William Reynolds's 18th-century coaching inn is a 'good-value' base for walkers, cyclists, fisherfolk and visitors in search of a tranquil rural break. The relaxed restaurant-with-rooms has 'a happy blend of modern furnishings and artwork, and the feel of a traditional country pub'; the bar has a 'spectacular' menu of 40 gins. In the recently refreshed bedrooms, pleasing treats include Scottish biscuits, Highland toiletries and helpful information on local walks. From morning to night, Borders produce is the taste of the day: expect home-baked breads, local meats and cheeses, Scottish seafood platters. The owners have a wealth of local knowledge.

MAP 5:E3
Main Street
Allanton TD11 3JZ
**T:** 01890 818260
**W:** allantoninn.co.uk

**BEDROOMS:** 6.
**OPEN:** all year except 25/26 Dec.
**FACILITIES:** bar, 2 restaurant areas, in-room TV (Freeview), wedding/function facilities, large garden, bicycle storage, drying room, parking.
**BACKGROUND MUSIC:** in bar, restaurant.
**LOCATION:** village centre.
**CHILDREN:** all ages welcomed.
**DOGS:** allowed in some areas, by prior arrangement.
**CREDIT CARDS:** Amex, MC, Visa.
**PRICES:** per room B&B £80–£105, D,B&B £135–£145.

**APPLECROSS** Highland

## APPLECROSS INN

The scenic, single-track Bealach na Ba winds and turns across the remote Applecross peninsula before it leads to Judith Fish's unpretentious hostelry, where low-key charm and cheer spill on to the shoreside terrace. Outside, the views stretch across the Inner Sound of Raasay; inside, malt whiskies, Scottish gins and Applecross ale are just right for sipping by the peat fire. In the small dining room or alfresco, order ultra-fresh seafood, perhaps prawns and king scallops straight from the bay; in spring and summer, a food truck sells fish and chips, coffees and sweet treats. Well-equipped bedrooms have no TV, but superlative water views (and perhaps some pub noise). Cyclists, walkers, kayakers welcomed.

MAP 5:C1
Shore Street
Applecross IV54 8LR
**T:** 01520 744262
**W:** applecrossinn.co.uk

**BEDROOMS:** 7. 1 on ground floor.
**OPEN:** all year, no accommodation for 2 weeks over Christmas, New Year, restaurant closed 25 Dec, 1/2 Jan.
**FACILITIES:** bar, dining room, beer garden, bicycle storage, bar, dining room wheelchair accessible, adapted toilet.
**BACKGROUND MUSIC:** in bar.
**LOCATION:** 85 miles W of Inverness, opposite the Isle of Skye, approx. 2 hours' drive.
**CHILDREN:** all ages welcomed, not in bar after 9 pm.
**DOGS:** allowed in 2 bedrooms (own bedding required), on lead in bar.
**CREDIT CARDS:** Amex, MC, Visa.
**PRICES:** per person B&B single £90–£170, double £70–£85. À la carte £35.

AUCHENCAIRN Dumfries and Galloway
# BALCARY BAY HOTEL

In 'suitably isolated splendour' on the shores of
the Solway Firth, Graeme Lamb's hotel gazes
across the water to Hestan Isle and the peaks of
the Lake District. Once a hideout for 17th-century
smugglers, the white-painted building today is
more likely to host 'mostly retirees like us, who
return year after year'. Many bedrooms have bay
views, while others overlook the mature gardens
(and Charlie, the resident pheasant). They are
contemporary and comfortable, though guests
this year thought a spruce-up would be welcome.
Lunch in the bright conservatory; at dinner, dress
up for 'very good, well-presented' meals in the
restaurant. Save room for sweets: 'the desserts
deserve particular mention'.

MAP 5:E2
Shore Road
Auchencairn  DG7 1QZ
T: 01556 640217
W: balcary-bay-hotel.co.uk

BEDROOMS: 20. 3 on ground floor,
1 suitable for disabled.
OPEN: 5 Feb–28 Nov.
FACILITIES: 2 lounges, cocktail bar,
conservatory, restaurant, free Wi-Fi
in reception area, in-room TV
(Freeview), 3-acre grounds, public
areas wheelchair accessible.
BACKGROUND MUSIC: none.
LOCATION: 2 miles SW of village.
CHILDREN: all ages welcomed.
DOGS: allowed in bedrooms, not in
public rooms (max. 2 small dogs or
1 large dog per room).
CREDIT CARDS: MC, Visa.
PRICES: per person B&B £80–£96,
D,B&B (min. 2 nights) £105–£133. Set
dinner (restaurant) £37–£49, à la carte
(conservatory and bar) £30. 1-night
bookings usually refused weekends.

BALLYGRANT Argyll and Bute
# KILMENY COUNTRY HOUSE

Surrounded by farmland on the southernmost
of the Inner Hebrides islands, this white-painted
19th-century house is owned by 'fabulous hosts'
Margaret and Blair Rozga. B&B guests are given a
sweet welcome, with home-baked treats and tea.
The Rozgas' home is handsomely furnished in
country house style; the traditional, individually
designed bedrooms have antiques and 'spectacular
views' across hills, glen and countryside. Some
rooms are capacious (a suite with its own kitchen
suits a family); others have access to a sheltered
garden; all have tea, coffee, home-made biscuits,
and fresh milk in the mini-fridge. Substantial
breakfasts with home-made bread, oatcakes and
preserves are 'worth getting up for'.

MAP 5:D1
Ballygrant
Isle of Islay  PA45 7QW
T: 01496 840668
W: kilmeny.co.uk

BEDROOMS: 5. 2 on ground floor.
OPEN: Mar–Oct.
FACILITIES: drawing room, dining
room, sun lounge, in-room TV
(Freeview), ½-acre garden.
BACKGROUND MUSIC: none.
LOCATION: ½ mile S of Ballygrant,
10 mins' drive to Port Askaig.
CHILDREN: not under 5.
DOGS: allowed in some bedrooms, not
in public rooms.
CREDIT CARDS: none accepted.
PRICES: per room B&B £155–£185.
1-night bookings sometimes refused.

## BARCALDINE Argyll and Bute
## ARDTORNA

'Thoroughly recommended', Sean and Karen O'Byrne's light, bright, super-modern, eco-friendly house is all Scandi style, with 'lovely views' of Loch Creran to boot. Fresh-from-the-oven scones are part of a generous greeting; home-made whisky cream liqueur is further temptation. Spruced-up, loch-view bedrooms have a king-size bed and under-floor heating, plus chocolates and good toiletries. Fruit smoothies accompany the 'good' breakfast in the glass-fronted dining room. Choose among sweet and savoury pancakes, griddled waffles and a Scottish platter with Stornoway black pudding and tattie scones. The 'very helpful' hosts assist with planning day-trips to castles, islands and the best spots for a dram.

MAP 5:D1
Mill Farm
Barcaldine PA37 1SE
T: 01631 720125
W: ardtorna.co.uk

**BEDROOMS:** 4.
**OPEN:** Apr–Nov.
**FACILITIES:** dining room, in-room TV (Freeview), 1-acre farmland, parking.
**BACKGROUND MUSIC:** traditional in restaurant.
**LOCATION:** 12 miles N of Oban.
**CHILDREN:** not under 12.
**DOGS:** not allowed.
**CREDIT CARDS:** MC, Visa.
**PRICES:** per person B&B £75–£100.

## BRIDGEND Argyll and Bute
## BRIDGEND HOTEL

There's whisky galore on the Inner Hebrides island of Islay; bonhomie in the bar of this friendly hotel. Simply, airily decorated bedrooms are supplied with local toiletries and Scottish tablet; a family suite has bunk beds for the children. The restaurant's daily-changing menu includes plenty of local produce: game from Islay estates, vegetables from the community garden, Loch Gruinart oysters. More casual dining is in the public bar; whiskies, gins and ales from the island may also be sipped in a tartan-carpeted lounge warmed by a blazing fire. After a breakfast kipper, set out to spot seal and sea eagle, visit distilleries, or 'follow a stream through woods and farms to a local craft centre'.

MAP 5:D1
Bridgend
Isle of Islay PA44 7PB
T: 01496 810212
W: bridgend-hotel.com

**BEDROOMS:** 11. 1 family room with bunk bed.
**OPEN:** all year except Christmas and New Year's Day.
**FACILITIES:** lounge bar, public bar, restaurant, in-room TV (Freeview), wedding facilities, drying room, terrace, garden, ½-acre grounds, parking, public areas wheelchair accessible, adapted toilet.
**BACKGROUND MUSIC:** in public areas.
**LOCATION:** centre of small village.
**CHILDREN:** all ages welcomed.
**DOGS:** well-behaved dogs allowed in bedrooms, bar.
**CREDIT CARDS:** Amex, MC, Visa.
**PRICES:** per room B&B £120–£195. À la carte £30. 1-night bookings sometimes refused during Islay Festival end May/early June.

**BROADFORD** Highland

# TIGH AN DOCHAIS

Huge windows bring 'glorious views' of Broadford Bay and the Cuillin hills into Neil Hope and Lesley Unwin's 'beautiful', architect-designed house on the Isle of Skye. Cross the footbridge to the front door: the modern B&B is 'equal to any first-class hotel'. Plump sofas sit by a log-burning stove in the book-lined, open-plan lounge/dining area; on the floor below, tartan-accented bedrooms have uninterrupted views of the seascape. Breakfast, served communally, has home-baked bread, locally smoked haddock, Skye sausages – 'delicious'. 'Perfect' evening meals can be arranged. Step on to the beach from the bottom of the garden; the 'friendly hosts' offer 'helpful information' for excursions further afield.

MAP 5:C1
13 Harrapool
Broadford
Isle of Skye IV49 9AQ
T: 01471 820022
W: skyebedbreakfast.co.uk

BEDROOMS: 3.
OPEN: Mar–end Nov.
FACILITIES: lounge/dining area, in-room TV (Freesat), ½-acre garden.
BACKGROUND MUSIC: traditional, occasionally, during breakfast.
LOCATION: 1 mile E of Broadford.
CHILDREN: all ages welcomed (no special facilities, must take own room).
DOGS: not allowed.
CREDIT CARDS: MC, Visa.
PRICES: per room B&B single £90, double £120, D,B&B £170. Set menu £25.

**BRUICHLADDICH** Argyll and Bute

# LOCH GORM HOUSE

On this southernmost island of the Inner Hebrides, 'friendly, helpful' hostess Fiona Doyle runs her 'clean, comfortable' B&B in a stone-built house, steps from the shores of Loch Indaal. Come up the garden path: past the large drawing room, cosily decorated, 'excellently appointed' bedrooms have 'stunning views' over the bay or across neighbouring fields. 'Our room had fresh flowers, an amazing selection of teas, a good shower. After the delicious scones upon arrival, we enjoyed a quiet night's sleep.' 'Good breakfasts, too.' Fiona has a wealth of local information to share, and can recommend restaurants, walks and distilleries; wellies, coats and beach towels may be borrowed for coastal wanderings.

**25% DISCOUNT VOUCHERS**

MAP 5:D1
Bruichladdich
Isle of Islay PA49 7UN
T: 01496 850139
W: lochgormhouse.com

BEDROOMS: 3.
OPEN: Mar–Dec.
FACILITIES: drawing room, dining room, in-room TV (Freeview), 1-acre garden, drying facilities.
BACKGROUND MUSIC: none.
LOCATION: on seafront, outside village.
CHILDREN: all ages welcomed.
DOGS: well-behaved dogs 'sometimes' allowed, not in bedrooms.
CREDIT CARDS: MC, Visa.
PRICES: per room B&B £135–£155.

**NEW**

COVE Argyll and Bute

# KNOCKDERRY HOUSE HOTEL

Romantic turrets and towers add to the Scottish country house experience at Murdo and Beth Macleod's listed baronial building by the shores of Loch Long. In manicured lawns, the dog-friendly hotel is near the Arrochar Alps, and surrounded by coastal walks and forest paths. Inside, homely lounges have notable stained glass, original fireplaces, wood panelling and tartan carpets; guidebooks, novels and traditional board games to entertain. Among well-equipped bedrooms furnished with character, the best have views over the water towards the Argyllshire hills. From varied breakfasts to modern dinners, Scottish provenance is featured in the restaurant, once a chapel and music room, overlooking the loch.

MAP 5:D1
Shore Road
Cove  G84 0NX
**T:** 01436 842283
**W:** www.knockderryhouse.co.uk

**BEDROOMS:** 15.
**OPEN:** all year except 16 Dec–3 Jan.
**FACILITIES:** drawing room, 2 dining rooms, billiard room/library, in-room TV, civil wedding licence, function facilities, ½-acre garden, dining areas wheelchair accessible.
**BACKGROUND MUSIC:** in restaurant.
**LOCATION:** on a peninsula in the Firth of Clyde, 17 miles from Helensburgh.
**CHILDREN:** all ages welcomed (though there are no special facilities).
**DOGS:** in 4 bedrooms, public rooms, specific dining room.
**CREDIT CARDS:** Amex, MC, Visa.
**PRICES:** per room B&B £95–£225, D,B&B £175–£310. À la carte £44.50.

DORNOCH Highland

# 2 QUAIL

'Friendly, thoughtful hosts', 'a comfortable bed' and 'delicious breakfasts' add up to 'a good stay' at Kerensa and Michael Carr's B&B, close to the cathedral and Royal Dornoch Golf Club. The late-Victorian sandstone town house has a wood-burning stove and a well-stocked library in the cosy, tartan-carpeted lounge; many family antiques are displayed throughout the home. Traditionally decorated bedrooms have tea- and coffee-making facilities, plus 'fluffy towels' and a 'good' power shower in the bathroom. Breakfast is served from 7 am ('for those with an early tee time'). The sands of Dornoch Firth are nearby; the Carrs have much helpful advice to offer on exploring this patch of the Highlands.

MAP 5:B2
Castle Street
Dornoch  IV25 3SN
**T:** 01862 811811
**W:** 2quail.com

**BEDROOMS:** 3.
**OPEN:** all year except Christmas.
**FACILITIES:** fully licensed lounge/library, dining room, in-room TV (Freeview).
**BACKGROUND MUSIC:** none.
**LOCATION:** town centre.
**CHILDREN:** 'babes in arms', over-10s welcomed.
**DOGS:** only assistance dogs allowed.
**CREDIT CARDS:** Amex, MC, Visa.
**PRICES:** per room B&B £95–£145.

**NEW**

DRUMNADROCHIT Highland
# THE LOCH NESS INN

In a village on the Great Glen Way, hikers
and cyclists stop for the simple comforts of this
160-year-old coaching inn. Visitors mingle with
locals in the bar, over Scottish whiskies and gins,
hand-pulled ciders and locally brewed real ales;
in the slate-floored restaurant, ingredients for
classic pub dishes are drawn from nearby waters,
farms and estates. Throughout, nature paintings
by a local artist add interest. Accommodation is
in fuss-free bedrooms made homely with wool
throws and tweedy cushions, tea and coffee,
Scottish toiletries; budget-friendly bunkhouse
rooms overlooking the River Coiltie suit groups
or a family. Hearty breakfast choices include
porridge, smoked haddock and a 'full Highland'.

MAP 5:C2
Drumnadrochit IV63 6UW
T: 01456 450991
W: staylochness.co.uk

BEDROOMS: 11. 4 in annexe, 1 on
ground floor suitable for disabled, plus
bunkhouse.
OPEN: all year except 25 Dec.
FACILITIES: bar, restaurant, in-room
TV, wedding facilities, beer garden,
'courtesy bus' for local pick-ups and
drop-offs.
BACKGROUND MUSIC: in bar, restaurant.
LOCATION: off the A82, in village
16 miles SW of Inverness.
CHILDREN: all ages welcomed.
DOGS: clean, well-behaved dogs
allowed in 1 bedroom, bar.
CREDIT CARDS: Amex, MC, Visa.
PRICES: per room B&B £60–£200.
À la carte £25.

DULNAIN BRIDGE Highland
# MUCKRACH COUNTRY HOUSE HOTEL

Surrounded by peaceful pastureland in the
Cairngorms national park – a happy setting for
the two resident long-horned bulls – the Cowap
family's restored Victorian shooting lodge is
within reach of a host of Highland activities.
Local artwork, modern furnishings and Scottish
flourishes brighten the panelled public areas; in
good weather, parasols come up over the twin-
tiered terrace. In the conservatory restaurant,
candlelit at night, 'home-style cooking with a
twist' might include Highland venison carpaccio
or whole Scottish langoustines. Handsome
bedrooms are kitted out with up-to-date tech,
bathrobes and Highland toiletries. Kick-start the
day with an extensive breakfast menu.

MAP 5:C2
Dulnain Bridge PH26 3LY
T: 01479 851227
W: muckrach.com

BEDROOMS: 16. 5 in garden annexe, plus
3-bed self-catering lodge with hot tub.
OPEN: all year.
FACILITIES: drawing room, library,
bar, conservatory restaurant/coffee
shop, private dining room, in-room
TV (Freeview), wedding facilities,
meeting facilities, drying room,
terraced patio, 1-acre grounds.
BACKGROUND MUSIC: in public areas.
LOCATION: outskirts of Dulnain
Bridge, 5 miles from Grantown-on-
Spey.
CHILDREN: all ages welcomed.
DOGS: well-behaved dogs allowed in
5 bedrooms in garden annexe, on lead
in library.
CREDIT CARDS: Amex, MC, Visa.
PRICES: per room B&B £110–£310.
À la carte £30.

**DUNDEE**

# TAYPARK HOUSE

In mature grounds just beyond the city centre, this sympathetically restored baronial mansion takes in reaching views over Dundee's Botanical Gardens. A hotel with romantic inclinations, it is popular with wedding parties. There are Scottish gins, local craft beers and ciders in the wood-floored, leather-armchaired bar; when the temperature drops, a fire is lit in the marble fireplace. A smart-rustic café serves lunch and dinner in the high season. Bedrooms are decorated in a muted modern palette; they may have a private terrace, or poetry on the walls. Four new rooms in converted stables are quirkier, with a shared living room. Breakfast has porridge oats, Arbroath smokies, vegan haggis.

MAP 5:D3
484 Perth Road
Dundee DD2 1LR
T: 01382 643777
W: tayparkhouse.co.uk

BEDROOMS: 18. 4 in garden annexe, 4 in converted stables, some on ground floor, 1 suitable for disabled.
OPEN: all year except 24–26 Dec, reduced meal service Jan–Mar.
FACILITIES: drawing room, cocktail bar/lounge, café, in-room TV (Freeview), billiard room, wedding/function facilities, mature gardens (garden bar, pizza oven open in summer).
BACKGROUND MUSIC: 'atmospheric' in public areas.
LOCATION: in Tayside area of city, 1½ miles from Dundee University.
CHILDREN: all ages welcomed.
DOGS: only assistance dogs allowed.
CREDIT CARDS: MC, Visa.
PRICES: per person B&B single £50–£150, double £60–£160.
À la carte £30.

**NEW**

**DUNNING Perth and Kinross**

# THE KIRKSTYLE INN & ROOMS

Genial Scottish hospitality and a traditional pub ethos are preserved in this welcoming village inn, a log-fire-warmed, fiddle-accompanied hark back to the past. Well-worn leather armchairs and eclectic bits and pieces dot the stone-walled bar, where the wide range of drinks includes the pub's own gin and 'Risky Kelt' beer. Hungry guests might find a beef-and-ale pie or Tamworth pork chop on the weekly menu; daily specials are marked on a blackboard. Ten paces from the door, simply furnished bedrooms in a separate building have a large orthopaedic bed and, perhaps, a slipper bath in the modern bathroom. In the morning, a continental breakfast (freshly baked croissants, muesli, yogurt, fruit) is delivered to the room.

MAP 5:D2
Kirkstyle Square
Dunning PH2 0RR
T: 01764 684248
W: thekirkstyleinn.co.uk

BEDROOMS: 4. All in adjacent building.
OPEN: all year except 25/26 Dec, 1 Jan.
FACILITIES: bar, lounge, snug, dining room, in-room smart TV (Freeview), wedding facilities, beer garden.
BACKGROUND MUSIC: in public areas, occasional live fiddle music.
LOCATION: in village, 10 miles SW of Perth.
CHILDREN: all ages welcomed.
DOGS: 'very welcome' in all areas, not on beds.
CREDIT CARDS: Amex, MC, Visa.
PRICES: per room B&B £105–£155, D,B&B £150–£185. À la carte £40.

EDINBURGH

# THE BALMORAL

'As well as being a "grand" hotel, the Balmoral is a very nice hotel – the two not necessarily being the same thing,' say regular readers about this Edinburgh icon. Fronted by a kilted doorman, the Victorian railway stop-over is today a thoroughly 21st-century hotel (Rocco Forte Hotels) with a Michelin-starred restaurant, a chic brasserie, an award-winning spa and a choice of inviting places to take tea – or a dram, from among some 500 varieties of whisky. Elegant bedrooms have an 'extremely comfortable' bed, a marble bathroom, robes and slippers; many look towards Edinburgh Castle and Arthur's Seat. Savour the place: the hotel clock has been set three minutes fast since 1902, so no one misses their train.

**25% DISCOUNT VOUCHERS**

MAP 5:D2
1 Princes Street
Edinburgh EH2 2EQ
**T:** 0131 556 2414
**W:** roccofortehotels.com/hotels-and-resorts/the-balmoral-hotel

**BEDROOMS:** 187. 3 suitable for disabled.
**OPEN:** all year.
**FACILITIES:** drawing room, tea lounge, 2 bars, restaurant, brasserie, in-room TV (Freeview), wedding facilities, conferences, 15-metre indoor swimming pool, spa, gym, valet parking.
**BACKGROUND MUSIC:** in restaurant, brasserie, bars and lobby.
**LOCATION:** city centre.
**CHILDREN:** all ages welcomed.
**DOGS:** allowed in bedrooms, public areas where food and drink are not served.
**CREDIT CARDS:** Amex, MC, Visa.
**PRICES:** per room B&B from £200. À la carte £80 (restaurant), £42.50 (brasserie).

EDINBURGH

# THE DUNSTANE HOUSES

Heathery tones and tweedy fabrics bring a breath of fresh Orkney air to this family-owned hotel, in a peaceful area just beyond the city centre. It occupies two recently refurbished Victorian villas – Dunstane House, and Hampton House, opposite. From 'cosy wee singles and doubles' to luxurious, high-ceilinged suites, bedrooms are kitted out in heritage style and supplied with pampering Scottish products and home-made shortbread. In Ba' Bar, find monochrome photographs and a wide selection of rare and vintage craft spirits; in the clubby lounge, velvet armchairs and sofas. A short menu of unfussy modern Scottish dishes is available all day. Buses to the centre and the airport stop right outside.

**25% DISCOUNT VOUCHERS**

MAP 5:D2
4 West Coates and 5 Hampton Terrace
Edinburgh EH12 5JQ
**T:** 0131 337 6169
**W:** thedunstane.com

**BEDROOMS:** 35. 18 in Hampton House, opposite.
**OPEN:** all year.
**FACILITIES:** lounge/bar, conservatory, residents' lounge and breakfast room in Hampton House, in-room TV (Freeview), wedding facilities, garden, parking.
**BACKGROUND MUSIC:** in bar, lounge.
**LOCATION:** in Murrayfield, just west of city centre.
**CHILDREN:** all ages welcomed.
**DOGS:** not allowed.
**CREDIT CARDS:** Amex, MC, Visa.
**PRICES:** per room B&B single £125–£295, double £154–£525. Prix fixe menu £28 (2 courses), £34 (3 courses). 2-night min. stay preferred Sat in peak season.

## EDINBURGH
# FINGAL

All is shipshape on this plushly revamped former Northern Lighthouse supply ship, floating moments away from the buzzy Leith neighbourhood. Once serving Scottish islands, this now-luxury liner today serves up cocktails and fine dining before rocking guests to sleep in decadent berths. All curving wood, thick carpets and glossy brass, the Art Deco interiors gleam glamour. Porthole-lined cabins have a huge bed draped in a custom-woven throw; a rain shower, under-floor heating and good toiletries in the bathroom. First-class cabins open on to the deck; those on the starboard have the best views. There are simple modern suppers in the evening; at breakfast, haggis and black pudding complete the full Scottish.

MAP 5:D2
Alexandra Dock
Edinburgh EH6 7DX
T: 0131 357 5000
W: fingal.co.uk

BEDROOMS: 23.
OPEN: all year except Christmas.
FACILITIES: bar, dining room, ballroom, in-room TV, deck.
BACKGROUND MUSIC: none.
LOCATION: berthed at the port of Leith.
CHILDREN: all ages welcomed.
DOGS: not allowed.
CREDIT CARDS: Amex, MC, Visa.
PRICES: per room B&B £220–£1,200. À la carte £25.

## EDINBURGH
# 21212

Paul Kitching and Katie O'Brien's well-regarded restaurant-with-rooms occupies a finely refurbished Georgian town house facing the Royal Terrace Gardens. Airy spaces have a laid-back glamour: a vast Caravaggio copy here; a sculpted Greek-style head there; still elsewhere, a dazzling chandelier. Sit with an aperitif in the first-floor drawing room before heading in to the elegant dining room for Paul Kitching's Michelin-rated weekly-changing menu. On the cards, perhaps: saffron risotto, chive oil; baked scallops, shellfish bisque. On the top two levels of the house, large, crisply styled bedrooms each have a sitting area and views over the garden or towards the firth – just the place to digest, and rest.

MAP 5:D2
3 Royal Terrace
Edinburgh EH7 5AB
T: 0131 523 1030
W: 21212restaurant.co.uk

BEDROOMS: 4.
OPEN: all year except 25/26 Dec, 1 Jan, 12 days Jan and Sept, restaurant closed Sun–Tues.
FACILITIES: drawing room, restaurant, private dining rooms, in-room TV (Freeview).
BACKGROUND MUSIC: in reception area.
LOCATION: 5 mins' walk from city centre.
CHILDREN: not under 5.
DOGS: not allowed.
CREDIT CARDS: Amex, MC, Visa.
PRICES: per room B&B £95–£295. À la carte £70. 1-night bookings refused weekends in Aug, New Year's Eve.

ELGOL Highland

# CORUISK HOUSE

Remote and romantic, Clare Winskill and Iain Roden's peaceful restaurant-with-rooms is reached down a single-track road through wild croft land, past grazing sheep. In an original Skye 'black house', it has quaintly low ceilings, a stone-walled snug and a conservatory dining room with views towards mountains and the islands of Rum and Eigg. Simply styled, modern-rustic bedrooms and suites are upstairs, and in the house next door. A four-course menu of Iain Roden's flavoursome, island ingredient-led cooking is served at 7 pm; dishes might include lobster bisque, black treacle bread; venison fillet, juniper tuile, pear and thyme crumble. Next day, set off on a scenic walk or take a dip in a loch or river nearby.

**25% DISCOUNT VOUCHERS**

MAP 5:C1
Elgol
Isle of Skye  IV49 9BL
T: 01471 866330
W: coruiskhouse.com

BEDROOMS: 5. 2 suites (1 with 2 bedrooms) in The Steading, next door.
OPEN: Mar–end Oct.
FACILITIES: sitting room/snug, 2 dining rooms (1 conservatory), in-room TV (Freeview) in 2 suites, humanist wedding facilities, front lawn, restaurant wheelchair accessible.
BACKGROUND MUSIC: none.
LOCATION: ½ mile NE of Elgol, 22 miles SW of Kyle of Lochalsh.
CHILDREN: not under 14.
DOGS: well-behaved dogs allowed in restaurant 'as long as other guests are comfortable with it' (resident dogs).
CREDIT CARDS: MC, Visa.
PRICES: per room B&B £160–£430. 4-course set menu £60.

**NEW**

FETTERCAIRN Aberdeenshire

# RAMSAY ARMS HOTEL & RESTAURANT

A grand archway, built to commemorate a visit by Queen Victoria and Prince Albert in 1861, graces this tiny village at the foot of the Cairn O' Mount. A recent visitor was 'absolutely charmed' by the hotel opposite, thanks to 'the warmth of the welcome; the excellent food, cooked using local fare; and the big-hearted way in which the place fits into the community'. The busy bar has malt whiskies and real ales; at mealtimes, perhaps in the oak-panelled restaurant, are pub favourites and more sophisticated dishes (loin of Scottish venison, cauliflower purée, wild mushrooms, say). Most of the straightforward, if old-fashioned, bedrooms have green views. The Fettercairn distillery is a snifter away.

MAP 5:C3
Burnside Road
Fettercairn  AB30 1XX
T: 01561 340334
W: ramsayarmshotel.com

BEDROOMS: 12.
OPEN: all year.
FACILITIES: lounge, bar, restaurant, in-room TV, function facilities, garden.
BACKGROUND MUSIC: in public areas.
LOCATION: in village, midway between Aberdeen and Dundee.
CHILDREN: all ages welcomed.
DOGS: not allowed.
CREDIT CARDS: MC, Visa.
PRICES: per room B&B single £69.95, double £98, family £115.

**FORT WILLIAM** Highland

# THE LIME TREE

Guests praise the 'true hospitality' at David Wilson's loch-facing hotel, restaurant and modern art gallery, in a converted former manse, a stroll from the old fort walls. Handsome bedrooms in the main building and an extension are 'comfortable and well-equipped'; rooms overlooking the water book quickly. 'Generous portions' of 'tasty, innovative' dishes are served at dinner in the 'cosy' dining room: Highland venison, haggis bonbon, perhaps, or crayfish tails, samphire and saffron dumplings. At breakfast: 'perfectly cooked hot dishes'. Loch Linnhe may be mesmerising, but turn your gaze inward: works by the host, a Highland artist, and others are displayed throughout the hotel and in the gallery.

MAP 5:C1
Achintore Road
Fort William  PH33 6RQ
**T:** 01397 701806
**w:** limetreefortwilliam.co.uk

**BEDROOMS:** 9. 4 in modern extension, plus 2-bed self-catering cottage.
**OPEN:** all year except Christmas, last 3 weeks Jan.
**FACILITIES:** 3 lounges, restaurant, art gallery, in-room TV (Freeview), garden, drying room, bicycle storage, parking.
**BACKGROUND MUSIC:** 'low' in restaurant in evening.
**LOCATION:** 5 mins' walk from town centre.
**CHILDREN:** all ages welcomed.
**DOGS:** allowed in bedrooms, separate dining area.
**CREDIT CARDS:** Amex, MC, Visa.
**PRICES:** per room B&B £70–£165. À la carte £40.

**GLASGOW**

# 15GLASGOW

Between George Square and the Kelvingrove museum, Lorraine Gibson's 'outstanding' B&B occupies a 19th-century terrace house opposite private gardens. Original fireplaces, sash windows and intricate cornicing in the former merchants' home are complemented by well-considered modern decor. Spacious, high-ceilinged bedrooms have a large bed and mood lighting; from two vast suites, huge windows overlook gardens front or rear. Ordered the night before, breakfast is eaten in the room, or communally in the lounge. Expect 'freshly squeezed orange juice, a fruit salad bursting with variety, a piping hot Scottish cooked, all first class'. The city's attractions are within walking distance; good eateries are close.

MAP 5:D2
15 Woodside Place
Glasgow  G3 7QL
**T:** 0141 332 1263
**w:** 15glasgow.com

**BEDROOMS:** 5.
**OPEN:** all year.
**FACILITIES:** lounge, in-room TV (Freeview), small garden, limited parking.
**BACKGROUND MUSIC:** none.
**LOCATION:** between town centre and West End.
**CHILDREN:** not under 6.
**DOGS:** allowed in bedrooms, not in public spaces.
**CREDIT CARDS:** MC, Visa.
**PRICES:** per room B&B £110–£180.

**GLENEGEDALE** Argyll and Bute
# GLENEGEDALE HOUSE

A slice of home baking greets arriving guests at Graeme and Emma Clark's much-praised island guest house, which stands in large gardens against a vista of the Mull of Oa and the Atlantic beyond. The consummate hosts enthusiastically dispense heaps of local knowledge, perhaps over a dram of Islay malt by the peat fire. Evenings, ask for a platter of charcuterie, cheese or local seafood – they come with home-baked bread and oatcakes – then retire to a handsome bedroom stocked with spoiling extras (Scottish-blended teas; Highland chocolates). The award-winning breakfast includes poached and fresh fruit; porridge laced with whisky. Close to the island's small airfield; ferry terminals a short drive away.

MAP 5:D1
Glenegedale
Isle of Islay PA42 7AS
**T:** 01496 300400
**W:** glenegedalehouse.co.uk

**BEDROOMS:** 4. 1 on ground floor, plus 4-bed self-catering house.
**OPEN:** all year except Christmas and New Year.
**FACILITIES:** bar, morning room, drawing room, dining room, music room, in-room TV (Freeview), wedding facilities, garden, parking, public rooms wheelchair accessible.
**BACKGROUND MUSIC:** none.
**LOCATION:** 4 miles from Port Ellen, 6 miles from Bowmore.
**CHILDREN:** not under 12.
**DOGS:** not allowed.
**CREDIT CARDS:** Amex, MC, Visa.
**PRICES:** per room B&B £115–£195.

**GLENFINNAN** Highland
# THE PRINCE'S HOUSE

At the head of Loch Shiel, 'friendly, attentive' hosts Ina and Kieron Kelly ably continue the tradition of this former coaching inn, where 17th-century travellers stopped in along the Road to the Isles. Traditionally decorated bedrooms are all on the first floor, under sloped ceilings; the best, with a Jacobean four-poster bed, is equipped with bathrobes, fresh flowers, a decanter of whisky mac. Book ahead to dine on Kieron's six-course fixed menu in the panelled restaurant; his dishes highlight locally sourced seasonal ingredients such as fish and shellfish from the boats at Mallaig, and beef from Highland butchers. Simpler fare is found in the Stage House Bistro, a 1980s extension overlooking a burn.

**25% DISCOUNT VOUCHERS**

MAP 5:C1
Glenfinnan PH37 4LT
**T:** 01397 722246
**W:** glenfinnan.co.uk

**BEDROOMS:** 9.
**OPEN:** mid-Mar–end Oct, end Dec–early Jan, restaurant open Easter–end Sept.
**FACILITIES:** restaurant, bistro/bar, in-room TV (Freeview), small front lawn.
**BACKGROUND MUSIC:** in bar, bistro, restaurant.
**LOCATION:** 17 miles NW of Fort William, 330 yards from Glenfinnan station.
**CHILDREN:** all ages welcomed.
**DOGS:** not allowed.
**CREDIT CARDS:** Amex, MC, Visa.
**PRICES:** per room B&B single £85–£120, double £160–£260. 6-course set menu (restaurant) £65, à la carte (bistro) £30.

GRANDTULLY Perth and Kinross

# THE GRANDTULLY HOTEL BY BALLINTAGGART

Surrounded by 'spectacular' scenery, this artfully
restored Victorian hotel is the sophisticated hub
of a small Perthshire village. It is run by chef/
patron Chris Rowley, his wife, Rachel, and his
brother, Andrew. Locals and tourists gather in
the convivial bar and informal dining room for
drinks and inventive daily-changing menus that
highlight locally sourced, foraged and home-
grown ingredients – parsnip and Strathtay honey
soup, say, or Loch Etive sea trout, sea kale. Boldly
coloured modern bedrooms have a wide bed
draped with locally woven tweeds; some rooms
overlook the River Tay. Breakfast is best walked
off in the surrounding glens. The family team also
run Ballintaggart Farm cookery school, nearby.

MAP 1:D2
Grandtully PH9 0PL
T: 01887 447000
W: ballintaggart.com

BEDROOMS: 8. Some interconnecting,
suitable for a family.
OPEN: all year except Christmas.
FACILITIES: bar, library, restaurant,
private dining room, in-room TV
(Freeview), civil wedding licence,
terrace, garden, shop, ground-floor
public areas wheelchair accessible.
BACKGROUND MUSIC: in public areas.
LOCATION: in village.
CHILDREN: all ages welcomed.
DOGS: not allowed.
CREDIT CARDS: MC, Visa.
PRICES: per room B&B £140–£200.
À la carte £27.

INNERLEITHEN Scottish Borders

# CADDON VIEW

'It's a delight to stay' at Lisa and Stephen Davies's
'great-value' guest house in the Tweed valley,
say visitors who laud the friendly welcome and
home-baked treats on offer. Bedrooms have a
simple country air, a 'spotless' modern bathroom
and all the amenities (tea- and coffee-making
facilities, fresh milk, a radio/alarm clock);
secondary glazing reduces traffic noise. Outdoorsy
adventures in the Borders, many from the door,
are plentiful; indoor pursuits, too, with books,
board games, and a blazing fire in the drawing
room. Light lunches and home-made cakes are
served in the conservatory café, along with 'very
good' seasonal Scottish dishes at dinner several
nights a week. 'Excellent' breakfasts, too.

## 25% DISCOUNT VOUCHERS

MAP 5:E2
14 Pirn Road
Innerleithen EH44 6HH
T: 01896 830208
W: caddonview.co.uk

BEDROOMS: 8.
OPEN: all year except Christmas, café
closed Sun and Mon evenings, dinner
Tues and Wed by reservation only.
FACILITIES: snug bar, drawing room,
breakfast room, café/bistro, in-room
TV (Freeview), ½-acre mature
garden, storage for bicycles and
fishing gear, parking.
BACKGROUND MUSIC: in breakfast room,
local radio in café during the day.
LOCATION: 400 yds from town centre.
CHILDREN: well-behaved children of all
ages welcomed.
DOGS: allowed in 1 bedroom, bar,
drawing room, café 'if no other guests
object'.
CREDIT CARDS: MC, Visa.
PRICES: per room B&B £55–£135. Set
menus £22–£28.

INVERNESS Highland
# BUNCHREW HOUSE

In a 'lovely position' by Beauly Firth, this
handsome 17th-century mansion stands in large
grounds that lead into woodland laced with
walking paths – look out for the brown hares
and roe deer who like to visit. Within the hotel
are traditionally styled bedrooms and suites
with period details, each looking over garden
or lake; one has its own conservatory. There are
two fireplaces in the drawing room, and a fine
collection of malt whiskies in the clubby bar; in
the wood-panelled restaurant, Scottish dishes
at dinner might include roast loin of Highland
lamb, spinach and mushroom stuffing. At
breakfast, fuel up on a Highland Scottish grill or
pancakes with maple-glazed bacon. 'We had a
very pleasant stay.'

MAP 5:C2
Inverness IV3 8TA
T: 01463 234917
W: bunchrewhousehotel.com

BEDROOMS: 16. 1 on ground floor.
OPEN: all year except 15–30 Jan.
FACILITIES: bar, drawing room,
restaurant, private dining room,
civil wedding licence, in-room
TV (Freeview), terrace, garden,
woodlands, electric car charging
points, public areas wheelchair
accessible.
BACKGROUND MUSIC: in public areas.
LOCATION: on the A862 Beauly/
Dingwall road, 3 miles from Inverness
city centre.
CHILDREN: all ages welcomed.
DOGS: allowed in bar, not in restaurant.
CREDIT CARDS: Amex, MC, Visa.
PRICES: per room B&B £95–£395.
Prix fixe dinner £45 (2 courses), £55
(3 courses), 7-course tasting menu £75.

INVERNESS Highland
# MOYNESS HOUSE

On a quiet residential street, John and Jane
Martin's good-value B&B is within a short walk,
over the River Ness, of the centre. The modest
Victorian villa, built in 1880, was once home to
Highland literary giant Neil M Gunn – browse
a collection of his books in the homely sitting
room. Upstairs, simply styled bedrooms are
supplied with tea- and coffee-making facilities,
bathrobes and locally made toiletries; two rooms
can accommodate a family. At breakfast, help
yourself to yogurt, stewed and fresh fruit, and
glasses of juice; 'tasty' cooked dishes use eggs from
the garden hens. Restaurants are a stroll away.
The Martins have plentiful tips about the city and
surrounding area, and can help arrange tours.

MAP 5:C2
6 Bruce Gardens
Inverness IV3 5EN
T: 01463 236624
W: moyness.co.uk

BEDROOMS: 7.
OPEN: Feb–Dec, except 25 Dec.
FACILITIES: sitting room, dining room,
in-room TV (Freeview), ¼-acre
garden, parking.
BACKGROUND MUSIC: at breakfast.
LOCATION: 10 mins' walk from city
centre.
CHILDREN: all ages welcomed.
DOGS: not allowed.
CREDIT CARDS: MC, Visa.
PRICES: per room B&B single from
£86, double from £98.

**KELSO** Scottish Borders

# THE OLD PRIORY BED AND BREAKFAST

There's a welcoming, home-away-from-home feel at the Girdwood family's B&B, in a Georgian town house near the old parish church in this cobbled market town. Spacious bedrooms are traditionally furnished with antiques and supplied with silk-filled duvets, large, fluffy towels and a hospitality tray; most rooms overlook the pretty garden. One suite, with a separate twin-bedded room, is ideal for a family. In the morning, light fills the breakfast room, where appreciative guests find 'plenty of cooked choices – even a vegetarian haggis!' The helpful hosts have plenty of local knowledge, and can advise on castles and cask ales, bookshops and sandy beaches. Kelso Abbey and many restaurants are a stroll away.

MAP 5:E3
33/35 Woodmarket
Kelso  TD5 7AT
**T:** 01573 223030
**W:** theoldpriorykelso.com

**BEDROOMS:** 5. 2 on ground floor, suitable for disabled, 1 family suite.
**OPEN:** Feb–Dec, open at Christmas, New Year.
**FACILITIES:** dining room, conservatory/ sitting room, in-room TV (Freeview), garden, parking.
**BACKGROUND MUSIC:** none.
**LOCATION:** in town centre.
**CHILDREN:** all ages welcomed (in family room).
**DOGS:** allowed in 1 bedroom (resident dogs).
**CREDIT CARDS:** not accepted.
**PRICES:** per room B&B single £80–£110, double £90–£120. 1-night bookings often refused weekends 'but we try to accommodate if we can'.

**NEW**

**KILCHRENAN** Argyll and Bute

# ARDANAISEIG

Swing round a winding road to this turreted, Jacobean-style baronial mansion – 'a palatial old joint' – in a 'beautiful' setting on the shores of Loch Awe. It has been owned since 1995 by antiques dealer Bennie Gray, who has filled it with a dazzling, in parts 'quirky', collection of artwork and statuary. From the marble-pillared drawing room, soak up 'superb romantic views' over gardens, loch and woodland across to the distant peak of Ben Lui. 'Well-furnished' bedrooms (some 'giant', with a four-poster bed, fireplace or roll-top bath) are supplied with biscuits, Scottish toiletries and fresh flowers. As evening draws in, sit in the informal dining room for a three-course menu of Inverawe salmon, local beef or venison.

MAP 5:D1
Kilchrenan  PA35 1HE
**T:** 01866 833333
**W:** ardanaiseig.com

**BEDROOMS:** 19. Some on ground floor, 1 in Boatshed. Plus self-catering cottage.
**OPEN:** all year.
**FACILITIES:** drawing room, library/bar, restaurant, in-room TV (Freeview), wedding facilities, 120-acre lochside grounds (walled garden, crannog, woodlands).
**BACKGROUND MUSIC:** in bar, restaurant.
**LOCATION:** 4 miles E of Kilchrenan.
**CHILDREN:** all ages welcomed.
**DOGS:** allowed in some bedrooms, public rooms.
**CREDIT CARDS:** Amex, MC, Visa.
**PRICES:** per room B&B £90–£260, D,B&B £140–£350. À la carte £42.

**KINCLAVEN** Perth and Kinross

# BALLATHIE HOUSE

A Victorian ghost, a Russian duke and a former Prince of Wales have all graced this 'lovely' Scottish country house in a 'delightful position' on the River Tay. Run by the Milligan family since 2005, the turreted and gabled pile has roaring fires, inviting sofas, a wood-panelled bar and 'numerous monster salmon in glass cases' – a nod to the days when it was famed for Scotland's best autumn fishing. Dog-friendly bedrooms in the main house, riverside annexe and lodge blend traditional grandeur with contemporary comforts. A farm-to-fork ethos underpins the modern Scottish menus in the elegant dining room. Breakfast on kippers or Stornoway black pudding, perhaps, before a garden stroll or woodland walk.

MAP 5:D2
Kinclaven PH1 4QN
**T:** 01250 883268
**w:** ballathiehousehotel.com

**BEDROOMS:** 53. 16 in riverside building, 12 in Sportsman's Lodge, some on ground floor, 1 suitable for disabled.
**OPEN:** all year.
**FACILITIES:** lounge, morning room, bar, restaurant, terrace room, private dining rooms, in-room TV (Freeview), wedding/function facilities, 290-acre estate (golf, fishing, clay pigeon shooting).
**BACKGROUND MUSIC:** in bar, main hall.
**LOCATION:** 1½ miles SW of Kinclaven.
**CHILDREN:** all ages welcomed.
**DOGS:** allowed in some bedrooms, public rooms, not in restaurant and lounge.
**CREDIT CARDS:** MC, Visa.
**PRICES:** per room B&B £79–£159, D,B&B £179–£259. Set dinner £55. 1-night bookings refused Christmas, New Year.

**NEW**

**KINLOCH RANNOCH** Perth and Kinross

# DUNALASTAIR HOTEL SUITES

Deeply rooted in a remote village on the edge of Loch Rannoch, this stone-built Victorian hotel with a contemporary, design-led interior stands in harmony with its Scottish heritage. From sleek lounge to modern brasserie and fine-dining table, natural materials and tawny tones reflect the glorious Highland scenery that surrounds. Each understated suite is equipped with tea, coffee, shortbread and fresh milk, plus robes, slippers and toiletries in a gleaming bathroom; some have a mini-kitchen with a microwave and a fridge. Many superior suites look toward Highland peaks. All-day menus in the brasserie revitalise hungry travellers back after a day's walking, cycling or general wilderness exploring.

MAP 5:D2
1 The Square
Kinloch Rannoch PH16 5PW
**T:** 01882 580444
**w:** dunalastairhotel.com

**BEDROOMS:** 32. 2 suitable for disabled.
**OPEN:** all year.
**FACILITIES:** lounge, brasserie, restaurant, in-room TV, room service, wedding/function facilities, boot room, courtyard, lounge and brasserie wheelchair accessible.
**BACKGROUND MUSIC:** in public rooms.
**LOCATION:** in village at the eastern end of Loch Rannoch.
**CHILDREN:** all ages welcomed.
**DOGS:** not allowed.
**CREDIT CARDS:** Amex, MC, Visa.
**PRICES:** per room B&B (continental) £99–£999. Cooked breakfast £9.95. À la carte (brasserie) £55, 7-course tasting menu (Library restaurant) £69.95.

KIPPEN Stirling
## THE CROSS KEYS

'Pub, food, rooms, log fires': the writing's, happily, on the white-painted wall of Debby McGregor and Brian Horsburgh's unassuming country inn. All friendly bustle, Sunday roasts and real ales, it has stood in this village, on the edge of Loch Lomond and the Trossachs national park, for centuries. Today, its award-winning pub grub includes such dishes as cured beetroot and pink gin salmon; venison or veggie haggis burgers. In clement weather, locals, walkers, families and their dogs head to the beer garden for views of the Gargunnock and Fintry hills; in winter, a fire warms the rustic, stone-walled bar. No-frills, good-value bedrooms have crisp linens on a comfortable bed; breakfast is worth waking for.

MAP 5:D2
Main Street
Kippen FK8 3DN
T: 01786 870293
W: kippencrosskeys.com

BEDROOMS: 3.
OPEN: all year except Christmas Day, New Year's Day.
FACILITIES: bar/dining areas, private dining room, in-room TV (Freeview), terrace, small beer garden.
BACKGROUND MUSIC: in bar.
LOCATION: 10 miles W of Stirling.
CHILDREN: all ages welcomed.
DOGS: allowed.
CREDIT CARDS: MC, Visa.
PRICES: per room B&B single £69, double £89–£109. À la carte £26.

LOCHEPORT Western Isles
## LANGASS LODGE

On an island of white-sand beaches, lochs and peat bogs, Amanda and Niall Leveson Gower run their 'handsome' sporting lodge as a family-friendly hotel. Lodge bedrooms are snug and traditional; there are larger ones in a 'slightly barn-like' annexe built into the hillside. Guests eat in the conservatory off the 'cosy' bar, or choose from a daily-changing menu in the restaurant, which has 'fabulous views over the pretty garden, across Loch Eport to Ben Eaval'; modern plates use locally fished, foraged, dived and hunted produce. North Uist is 'a paradise for wildlife', where you'll spot otter and seal, and hear the rasp of the corncrake. Hamersay House Hotel, Lochmaddy (see next entry), is under the same ownership.

MAP 5: inset A1
Locheport
Isle of North Uist HS6 5HA
T: 01876 580285
W: langasslodge.co.uk

BEDROOMS: 11. Some in extension, 1 suitable for disabled.
OPEN: Apr–end Oct.
FACILITIES: conservatory, bar, restaurant, in-room TV (Freeview), 11-acre garden in 200-acre grounds, bar and restaurant wheelchair accessible, adapted toilet.
BACKGROUND MUSIC: in public rooms.
LOCATION: 7½ miles SW of Lochmaddy.
CHILDREN: all ages welcomed.
DOGS: allowed in bedrooms and public rooms, not in restaurant.
CREDIT CARDS: MC, Visa.
PRICES: per room B&B single £95–£130, double £105–£165, family room £150–£240. À la carte (bar) £34, set menu (restaurant) £35–£40.

## LOCHMADDY Western Isles
## HAMERSAY HOUSE HOTEL

The cheery blue-and-white exterior of this laid-back island hotel is matched by the maritime feel in its neat bedrooms and modern brasserie, giving the place a spirit that's nautical but nice. It is owned and run by Amanda and Niall Leveson Gower (see also Langass Lodge, Locheport, previous entry). Bedrooms look over Lochmaddy harbour and towards the Lees; one room can accommodate a family. In the brasserie, a daily specials board lists the freshest local fare, perhaps just-landed seafood, or vegetables from the garden. The hotel is within an easy drive of white-sand beaches; friendly staff can advise on boat trips, fishing and walks. Well placed for the ferries; a village shop and pub are close by.

MAP 5: inset A1
Lochmaddy
Isle of North Uist  HS6 5AE
T: 01876 500700
W: hamersayhouse.co.uk

BEDROOMS: 9.
OPEN: all year except Christmas, New Year.
FACILITIES: bar, restaurant, in-room TV (Freeview), gym, garden, parking.
BACKGROUND MUSIC: in restaurant in evening.
LOCATION: on the edge of the village.
CHILDREN: all ages welcomed.
DOGS: allowed in bedrooms, public rooms.
CREDIT CARDS: MC, Visa.
PRICES: per room B&B £90–£145. À la carte £30.

**NEW**

## MEIKLEOUR Perth and Kinross
## THE MEIKLEOUR ARMS

In a Victorian fishing lodge on the Meikleour estate, owned by the same Franco-Scottish family since 1362, this friendly country inn benefits from a verdant woodland setting and a double-bank salmon beat on the River Tay. The dog-friendly pub and oak-beamed restaurant are airy spaces with modern rustic touches; a cheering wood-burner blazes between the two. Select a real ale, artisanal gin, one of more than 50 malts or the house Claret, before tucking in to classic dishes made with produce from the estate's fields, forest and kitchen garden. Spacious bedrooms (some in outlying cottages) have a rural French ambience and a decanter of sherry. The record-breaking Meikleour Beech Hedge is close by.

MAP 5:D2
Meikleour  PH2 6EB
T: 01250 883206
W: meikleourarms.co.uk

BEDROOMS: 20. 9 in cottages by walled garden of Meikleour House, a short distance away. Plus 5 serviced cottages in converted stables.
OPEN: all year.
FACILITIES: residents' lounge, pub, restaurant, private dining room, in-room TV, beer garden, large grounds and woodlands, 1.7-mile salmon fishing beat on river, restaurant wheelchair accessible.
BACKGROUND MUSIC: in pub.
LOCATION: 12 miles N of Perth.
CHILDREN: all ages welcomed.
DOGS: welcomed in ground-floor and cottage bedrooms, pub.
CREDIT CARDS: MC, Visa.
PRICES: per room B&B single £75–£135, double £85–£145. À la carte £29.

MELROSE Scottish Borders

## BURT'S

On the market square of a pretty Borders town, the Henderson family has owned and run this well-established hotel for nearly 50 years. Flower boxes fronting the listed 18th-century building extend a colourful welcome; inside, the popular restaurant (dark wood, light tartans, trophy fish) and bistro bar satisfy diners hungry for modern Scottish dishes, light lunchtime bites and hearty suppers. Bedrooms are tastefully decorated in soothing shades; each has tea- and coffee-making facilities and Scottish toiletries. A sustaining breakfast supports the next day's activities: golfing, walking, fishing on the River Tweed, or wandering the lively town. The Hendersons also own The Townhouse, across the street.

MAP 5:E3
Market Square
Melrose TD6 9PN
T: 01896 822285
W: burtshotel.co.uk

BEDROOMS: 20.
OPEN: all year, no accommodation 24–26 Dec.
FACILITIES: lobby lounge, residents' lounge, bistro bar, restaurant, private dining room, in-room TV (Freeview), wedding facilities, function facilities, ½-acre garden, parking.
BACKGROUND MUSIC: in public areas.
LOCATION: town centre.
CHILDREN: all ages welcomed, not under 8 in restaurant.
DOGS: allowed in some bedrooms, bistro bar, not in restaurant.
CREDIT CARDS: Amex, MC, Visa.
PRICES: per person B&B single from £79, double from £74, D,B&B (2-night min. stay) single from £112, double from £108. À la carte £42.

MOFFAT Dumfries and Galloway

## HARTFELL HOUSE & THE LIMETREE RESTAURANT

Take a short detour off the scenic Southern Upland Way to find 'exquisite views, fantastic cooking and good-value accommodation' at Robert and Mhairi Ash's 'lovely' Victorian house. It stands on a 'quiet drive' in a conservation town known for its outdoor activities. The highlight is the food, guests say: chef Matt Seddon's modern Scottish dishes, on a frequently changing, Michelin-rated menu, are 'thoroughly enjoyable'. A plus: vegetarian and other diets are well catered for, with advance notice. Traditionally furnished bedrooms have tea- and coffee-making facilities and Scottish toiletries; some rooms are snug, while others accommodate a family. Breakfast is 'excellent'. Easy access to the M74.

MAP 5:E2
Hartfell Crescent
Moffat DG10 9AL
T: 01683 220153
W: hartfellhouse.co.uk

BEDROOMS: 7. Plus self-catering cottage in the grounds.
OPEN: all year except Mon, Christmas, restaurant closed Sun, Mon.
FACILITIES: lounge, restaurant, in-room TV (Freeview), garden, cooking classes, bicycle storage, parking.
BACKGROUND MUSIC: in restaurant.
LOCATION: 5 mins' walk from town centre.
CHILDREN: all ages welcomed.
DOGS: not allowed.
CREDIT CARDS: MC, Visa.
PRICES: per room B&B single £55–£75, double £80–£95, D,B&B double £142–£157. Set menu £25 (2 courses), £31 (3 courses).

**NAIRN Highland**

# SUNNY BRAE

'The panorama of the sea' is an attraction at this 'good-value' B&B on the Moray coast; the welcome, by 'friendly, personable' hosts John Bochel and Rachel Philipsen, is another. There's 'a domestic feel' at this house across the road from the beach: books are available for borrowing; pretty suntrap gardens have plentiful seating. 'Airy, comfortable' bedrooms, some with views over the Moray Firth, are supplied with bottled water and bathrobes. In the evening, ask for recommendations, readily provided, of nearby places to eat, or simply stay in – a cheese board or charcuterie platter can be arranged. Next day, breakfast is 'very good indeed'. Dolphins, dunes and whisky distilleries are within easy reach.

MAP 5:C2
Marine Road
Nairn IV12 4EA
T: 01667 452309
W: sunnybraenairn.co.uk

**BEDROOMS:** 8. 1 suitable for disabled.
**OPEN:** Mar–end Oct.
**FACILITIES:** lounge, dining room, in-room TV (Freeview), terrace, front and rear gardens, parking.
**BACKGROUND MUSIC:** none.
**LOCATION:** 5 mins' walk from town centre, 2 mins from beach.
**CHILDREN:** all ages welcomed.
**DOGS:** only guide dogs allowed.
**CREDIT CARDS:** MC, Visa.
**PRICES:** per room B&B £85–£145. À la carte £35.

**PEEBLES Scottish Borders**

# CRINGLETIE HOUSE

In sweeping lawns within acres of woodland, this secluded baronial mansion is a 'little jewel'. Inside, log fires, a frescoed ceiling, custom-created tartan and an old service bell in public rooms add to the grand ambience, though 'friendly', mainly local, staff encourage an easy, home-away-from-home feel. Individually decorated bedrooms and suites vary in size and style: some are snug, some more modern; all have views over the green grounds. At lunch and dinner, seasonal Borders produce is served in the Sutherland restaurant, whose vista stretches down the valley to Peebles. The extensive grounds invite exploration, with sculptures, a listed walled garden, a one-mile nature trail and outdoor games.

MAP 5:E2
off Edinburgh Road
Peebles EH45 8PL
T: 01721 725750
W: cringletie.com

**BEDROOMS:** 14. 1 suitable for disabled, plus 2-bed cottage, with hot tub, in grounds.
**OPEN:** all year except 2–3 weeks Jan.
**FACILITIES:** lift to all floors, bar, lounge, conservatory, garden room, restaurant, in-room TV (Freeview), wedding facilities, 28-acre grounds (nature trail, walled garden, woodland), parking, electric car charging points, hotel fully wheelchair accessible.
**BACKGROUND MUSIC:** in public areas.
**LOCATION:** 2 miles N of Peebles.
**CHILDREN:** all ages welcomed.
**DOGS:** allowed in bedrooms, not in public rooms.
**CREDIT CARDS:** MC, Visa.
**PRICES:** per room B&B single £197.50–£210, double £210–£235, D,B&B £320–£360. Prix fixe menu £55.

**PEEBLES** Scottish Borders

# THE TONTINE

'The atmosphere and service are absolutely first class' at Kate and Gordon Innes's hotel, on the High Street of a busy, arty town on the River Tweed. Locals and tourists pop in for afternoon teas and cocktail evenings; at weekends, keen cyclists and golfers gather over real ales beside the open fire in the lounge. At lunch and dinner, seasonal menus in the high-ceilinged, chandelier-lit restaurant and informal bistro might include cullen skink; Border beef and Broughton ale pie. Bedrooms are spread between the main 19th-century building and a more modern annexe (connected by a glass-sided corridor); dogs in annexe rooms have a blanket, a bowl and a treat. Maps point the way to country walks.

MAP 5:E2
High Street
Peebles  EH45 8AJ
**T:** 01721 720892
**W:** tontinehotel.com

**BEDROOMS:** 36. 20 in Riverside Lodge annexe.
**OPEN:** all year.
**FACILITIES:** lift, bar, lounge, bistro, restaurant, private dining/meeting room, in-room TV (Freeview), wedding facilities, 2 garden areas, drying room, secure bicycle storage, parking, all public rooms wheelchair accessible.
**BACKGROUND MUSIC:** in public areas.
**LOCATION:** in town centre.
**CHILDREN:** all ages welcomed.
**DOGS:** allowed in 10 annexe bedrooms, bar, bistro, garden.
**CREDIT CARDS:** MC, Visa.
**PRICES:** per room B&B single £55–£135, double £100–£145, D,B&B single £85–£165, double £160–£205. À la carte from £25.

**PERTH** Perth and Kinross

# SUNBANK HOUSE

Within easy walking distance of the bustling centre, this 'lovely, comfortable' Victorian house is set back from the road amid mature, 'well-tended' gardens. It is owned and personably run as a small, 'good-value' hotel by 'friendly, informative' hosts Finlay and Agnes Gillies. Traditional by design, bedrooms have 'a pleasant ambience' and all the necessary amenities (tea- and coffee-making facilities, toiletries); two rooms suit a family. Pre-dinner drinks may be taken in the lounge before a 'tasty, satisfying' meal is served in the 'airy' dining room overlooking the garden. Vegetarians have a separate menu. At breakfast, 'a good selection' of cereals and fruit may be followed by a 'very good' full Scottish.

MAP 5:D2
50 Dundee Road
Perth  PH2 7BA
**T:** 01738 479888
**W:** sunbankhouse.com

**BEDROOMS:** 10. 3 on ground floor.
**OPEN:** all year except Christmas.
**FACILITIES:** lounge/bar, restaurant, in-room TV (Freeview), function facilities, terrace, ½-acre garden, parking, ground floor wheelchair accessible.
**BACKGROUND MUSIC:** in restaurant.
**LOCATION:** ½ mile from centre.
**CHILDREN:** all ages welcomed.
**DOGS:** allowed in some bedrooms.
**CREDIT CARDS:** Amex, MC, Visa.
**PRICES:** per room B&B single from £59, double from £80. À la carte £34.

## PITLOCHRY Perth and Kinross
# CRAIGATIN HOUSE AND COURTYARD

Amid two acres of gardens and woodland – look out for wandering pheasants – this Victorian house has been brought up to date with bright, modern rooms and a lofty, glass-fronted extension overlooking the neat lawn. It is owned and amiably run by Lynne Fordyce and John Watters. Smart, contemporary bedrooms are in the main house and converted stables. They vary in size and character – some have original Georgian wooden shutters, others a skylight – but all are thoughtfully equipped with hot drinks, bottles of water and locally made biscuits. A log-burning stove warms the spacious lounge. At breakfast, choose between omelettes, French toast, apple pancakes and a traditional Scottish.

**25% DISCOUNT VOUCHERS**

MAP 5:D2
165 Atholl Road
Pitlochry PH16 5QL
T: 01796 472478
W: craigatinhouse.co.uk

**BEDROOMS:** 14. 7 in courtyard, 2 on ground floor, 1 suitable for disabled.
**OPEN:** Feb–Nov, New Year.
**FACILITIES:** lounge, 2 breakfast rooms, in-room TV (Freeview), 2-acre garden, lounge/breakfast room wheelchair accessible.
**BACKGROUND MUSIC:** in lounge, breakfast rooms.
**LOCATION:** 10 mins' walk to town centre.
**CHILDREN:** not under 14.
**DOGS:** not allowed.
**CREDIT CARDS:** Amex, MC, Visa.
**PRICES:** per room B&B single £105–£135, double £115–£145. 1-night bookings sometimes refused Sat.

## PITLOCHRY Perth and Kinross
# DALSHIAN HOUSE

Martin and Heather Walls's 'blissfully remote', good-value B&B is in a white-painted Georgian house, in gardens and woodland on the outskirts of town. Wild birds and red squirrels are frequent visitors, and no wonder – this is a 'warm, friendly' place where everything, from the comfy lounge, with a wood-burning stove and magazines, to the individually styled bedrooms, has the feel of a private home. 'Outstanding' breakfasts feature home-baked breads, local honey, compotes and poached fruit; hot dishes are cooked to order. Start the day with a bowl of whisky-laced Scottish porridge, then set off to explore: the hosts can advise on forest rambles and hilly hikes, and will pack a picnic lunch on request.

**25% DISCOUNT VOUCHERS**

MAP 5:D2
Old Perth Road
Pitlochry PH16 5TD
T: 01796 472173
W: dalshian.co.uk

**BEDROOMS:** 7.
**OPEN:** all year except Christmas.
**FACILITIES:** lounge, dining room, in-room TV (Freeview), 1-acre garden.
**BACKGROUND MUSIC:** none.
**LOCATION:** 1 mile S of centre.
**CHILDREN:** not under 9.
**DOGS:** not allowed.
**CREDIT CARDS:** MC, Visa.
**PRICES:** per person B&B £37–£47. 1-night bookings refused New Year.

PITLOCHRY Perth and Kinross
## PINE TREES HOTEL

Roe deer sometimes wander the wooded grounds
of this white-painted Victorian mansion, in 'a
delightful setting' on the outskirts of Pitlochry.
Recently refurbished, the hotel has stately public
spaces filled with oriental carpets, deep armchairs,
single malt whiskies and a judicious use of tartan.
An impressive wood-and-wrought iron staircase
leads to individually decorated main-house
bedrooms. Ground-floor rooms are in a converted
coach house or annexe nearby, and have dedicated
parking. In the garden-facing restaurant, hearty
dishes use Scottish produce, perhaps Orkney
herring or cheeses from the Isle of Mull. The
town centre is a 10-minute walk away; fishing,
golf and hill walking are within reach.

MAP 5:D2
Strathview Terrace
Pitlochry PH16 5QR
T: 01796 472121
W: pinetreeshotel.co.uk

BEDROOMS: 31. 3 in annexe, 6 in coach
house, 7 on ground floor, plus 2-bed
apartment.
OPEN: all year, special packages at
Christmas, New Year.
FACILITIES: bar, 3 lounges, restaurant,
in-room TV (Freeview), 7-acre
grounds, parking.
BACKGROUND MUSIC: in bar, restaurant.
LOCATION: ¼ mile N of town centre.
CHILDREN: all ages welcomed.
DOGS: well-behaved dogs allowed in
bedrooms, one lounge; only guide
dogs allowed in restaurant, bar
lounge.
CREDIT CARDS: Amex, MC, Visa.
PRICES: per room B&B £105–£189,
D,B&B £155–£239. Prix fixe menu
£28.50 (2 courses), £35 (3 courses).

**NEW**

PITLOCHRY Perth and Kinross
## SAORSA 1875

From clear-eyed ethics to contemporary style,
nothing is compromised at the McLaren-Stewart
family's vegan hotel and restaurant, in woodlands
and gardens overlooking the town. Everything in
the Victorian gabled house has been sustainably
sourced: the plump pillows, fine linens and
Scottish toiletries in the colourful bedrooms; the
vegan liqueurs and biodynamic wines at the bar;
the right-on cleaning products used behind the
scenes. A supper-club atmosphere reigns each
evening, as guests, including the 'plant-curious',
mingle at a communal table for an inspired five-
course menu, with asparagus and chargrilled
artichoke hearts, say, or butternut squash risotto,
sage crisps. Breakfast is a lavish cold spread.

**25% DISCOUNT VOUCHERS**

MAP 5:D2
2 East Moulin Road
Pitlochry PH16 5DW
T: 01796 475217
W: saorsahotel.com

BEDROOMS: 11.
OPEN: all year.
FACILITIES: bar, snug, lounge,
restaurant, 2-acre grounds.
BACKGROUND MUSIC: in public areas.
LOCATION: in town.
CHILDREN: all ages welcomed.
DOGS: allowed (resident dogs).
CREDIT CARDS: MC, Visa.
PRICES: per room B&B (continental)
£130–£220, D,B&B £175–£310.
À la carte £45. 1-night bookings
refused Christmas/New Year, Etape
Caledonia weekend.

## PORTREE Highland
# MARMALADE HOTEL

In landscaped gardens, overlooking the island's
main harbour town, this refurbished Edwardian
country house has a coolly contemporary interior
and views that stretch to the bay. Bedrooms
vary in size, with one room ideal for a family of
three; all are packed with welcome extras such as
handmade Scottish soaps and a coffee machine.
Rooms in an extension completed in 2020 have
floor-to-ceiling windows to take in the best views.
Choose Skye mussels or an Aberdeen Angus
steak at dinner in the modern restaurant; a full
Scottish or porridge with a dash of whisky in the
morning. On a fine day, the garden terrace, its
vista reaching to the Cuillin hills, is the place to
be. Part of the Perle Hotels group.

MAP 5:C1
Home Farm Road
Portree
Isle of Skye IV51 9LX
T: 01478 611711
W: marmaladehotel.co.uk

**BEDROOMS:** 34. 23 in extension,
some on ground floor, 1 suitable for
disabled.
**OPEN:** all year except 24–26 Dec.
**FACILITIES:** bar/restaurant, lounge,
in-room TV (Freeview), wedding
facilities, 2-acre grounds.
**BACKGROUND MUSIC:** in lounge, bar/
restaurant.
**LOCATION:** town centre.
**CHILDREN:** not under 12.
**DOGS:** not allowed.
**CREDIT CARDS:** Amex, MC, Visa.
**PRICES:** per room B&B £150–£370.
À la carte £35.

## RATHO Midlothian
# THE BRIDGE INN AT RATHO

Beside a bridge over the Union Canal, Graham
and Rachel Bucknall's genial pub-with-rooms is
conveniently sited for Edinburgh airport. Fires
burn in a bar popular with locals; in the 'inviting'
dining room, local produce influences the menu
of pub classics (fish and chips; Mull Cheddar
macaroni) and more elaborate dishes (glazed duck
breast, confit duck leg pancakes, creamed kale).
'Snug', modestly furnished bedrooms are 'warm
and clean'; all four have a canal view. Breakfast
brings sausages from rare-breed pigs, and freshly
laid chicken and duck eggs from Ratho Hall, just
across the canal – fuel for the seven-mile walk
down the towpath to Edinburgh. Sister hotel
The Ship Inn is in Elie (see main entry).

MAP 5:D2
27 Baird Road
Ratho EH28 8RA
T: 0131 333 1320
W: bridgeinn.com

**BEDROOMS:** 4.
**OPEN:** all year except 25–26 Dec.
**FACILITIES:** 2 bars, restaurant, in-room
TV (Freeview), wedding facilities,
terrace (beer garden, boat shed), bar
and restaurant wheelchair accessible,
adapted toilet.
**BACKGROUND MUSIC:** 'relaxed' all day,
monthly live music nights.
**LOCATION:** in village, 7 miles W of
Edinburgh.
**CHILDREN:** all ages welcomed.
**DOGS:** allowed in main bar only.
**CREDIT CARDS:** MC, Visa.
**PRICES:** per room B&B £115–£185.
À la carte £35.

## ST ANDREWS Fife
## RUFFLETS

One of Scotland's first country house hotels, this turreted 1920s mansion in tranquil, 'elegant' gardens is owned by Mark and Christopher Forrester, grandsons of two of the original founders. Its traditional standards are upheld by long-serving manager Stephen Owen, who runs the hotel with 'extremely welcoming', 'helpful' staff. 'Superb' bedrooms are packed with thoughtful touches (home-made shortbread, a hot-water bottle for a chilly night, Rufus the teddy bear); some have a private balcony. Produce from the kitchen garden and local suppliers feature in light lunches and modern Scottish dishes in the bar and restaurant. The ever-popular afternoon tea may be taken on the terrace on clement days.

MAP 5:D3
Strathkinness Low Road
St Andrews KY16 9TX
T: 01334 472594
W: rufflets.co.uk

BEDROOMS: 23. Some in Gatehouse and Rufflets Lodge, 4 on ground floor, 1 suitable for disabled, plus 3 self-catering cottages in gardens.
OPEN: all year.
FACILITIES: bar, drawing room, library, restaurant, in-room TV (Freeview), wedding facilities, function facilities, 10-acre grounds (formal gardens, kitchen garden and woodland).
BACKGROUND MUSIC: in bar, restaurant.
LOCATION: 2 miles W of town.
CHILDREN: all ages welcomed.
DOGS: allowed in some bedrooms, bar.
CREDIT CARDS: Amex, MC, Visa.
PRICES: per room B&B £145–£315, D,B&B £180–£385. À la carte £40.

**NEW**

## ST FILLANS Perth and Kinross
## ACHRAY HOUSE HOTEL

Laura Muirhead's small hotel stands, in a picture-perfect setting, by the shores of Loch Earn, in a conservation village within Loch Lomond and the Trossachs national park. Newly refurbished bedrooms are supplied with teas and a coffee machine, biscuits and Scottish-made toiletries; most rooms overlook the loch and the hills beyond. Two garden rooms open on to a small courtyard – ideal for guests with dogs. The conservatory restaurant has regularly changing menus, perhaps with home-smoked salmon, venison fillet, haggis bonbons; in the lounge, deep sofas invite guests to settle in. Sunday lunch is served until 4 pm. Within easy reach: scenic walks, watersports, fishing, golf, a 'whisky journey' in the bar.

MAP 5:D2
On Loch Earn
St Fillans PH6 2NF
T: 01764 685320
W: achrayhouse.com

BEDROOMS: 9. Plus 1 self-catering cottage.
OPEN: all year.
FACILITIES: bar, lounge, conservatory, restaurant, in-room TV (Sky), civil wedding licence, terrace, large foreshore, bar and restaurant wheelchair accessible.
BACKGROUND MUSIC: in lobby, bar, restaurant.
LOCATION: at the eastern end of Loch Earn, 6 km W of Comrie.
CHILDREN: 'not ideal for small children, but call to discuss'.
DOGS: allowed in 3 bedrooms, conservatory, bar.
CREDIT CARDS: Amex, MC, Visa.
PRICES: per room B&B £79–£190. À la carte £28.

**NEW**

SCOURIE Highland
## SCOURIE HOTEL

The Campbell family's old coaching inn has long been a mecca for fisherfolk, who come hoping to catch wild brown trout and salmon from the lochs and lochans around. Other visitors rejoice in the spectacular mountain scenery, white sandy bays, and genuine Scottish hospitality extended by this remote hotel. Bonhomie begins with tea and scones by roaring fires in lounges full of fishing memorabilia; tall tales are exchanged over drinks in the bar. At 7.30 pm, a gong summons diners to an 'excellent' set dinner focused on seafood and shellfish, Highland game and meat, and garden vegetables. Drift off to peaceful sleep in a freshly redecorated, TV-less bedroom. A path at the back of the hotel leads to the harbour.

MAP 5:B2
Scourie IV27 4SX
T: 01971 502396
W: scouriehotel.com

BEDROOMS: 21. 2 in garden annexe.
OPEN: mid-Apr–early Oct.
FACILITIES: 2 bars, 2 lounges, restaurant, 7-acre grounds (gardens, paddock, orchard).
BACKGROUND MUSIC: none.
LOCATION: in a village on the North Coast 500 route.
CHILDREN: all ages welcomed.
DOGS: allowed, except in dining area.
CREDIT CARDS: MC, Visa.
PRICES: per room B&B £105–£170, D,B&B £140–£240. Set menu £35.

SOUTH GALSON Western Isles
## GALSON FARM GUEST HOUSE

On the north-west coast of the island, a 'peaceful area teeming with wildlife', this traditional Hebridean farmhouse displays rugged views across to the Butt of Lewis. It is run as a 'high-quality' guest house by Elaine Fothergill and Richard Inger, who are part of a small crofting community here. Rustic and homely, it has comfortable bedrooms decorated with paintings and locally crafted pottery; a mini-fridge contains fresh milk and water. Guests have use of a TV lounge (with a fire, in chilly weather) and a quiet reading room overlooking the surging Atlantic. Served communally, a simple Aga-fresh supper may be arranged in advance. 'Excellent' breakfasts fuel exploration of beaches, mountains and burns.

MAP 5:B1
South Galson
Isle of Lewis HS2 0SH
T: 01851 850492
W: galsonfarm.co.uk

BEDROOMS: 4. Plus 6-bunk hostel available for sole occupancy, self-catering.
OPEN: all year except Christmas, New Year.
FACILITIES: 2 lounges, dining room, ¼-acre garden, drying facilities, bicycle storage, parking.
BACKGROUND MUSIC: in dining room, lounge.
LOCATION: on the coast, 7½ miles SW of the port of Ness, 20 miles from Stornoway.
CHILDREN: not under 16.
DOGS: only assistance dogs allowed (animals on site).
CREDIT CARDS: Amex, MC, Visa.
PRICES: per room B&B single £76, double £95–£115. Dinner £25 (2 courses).

## STIRLING
# VICTORIA SQUARE

Within strolling distance of the city centre, Kari
and Phillip Couser's serene Victorian guest
house overlooks a tree-lined square. Bedrooms
decorated with William Morris-designed
wallpapers are each different from the other;
superior rooms might have bay-window seating
or a view towards Stirling Castle. Afternoon tea,
with finger sandwiches and Osborne pudding
loaf (a favourite of Queen Victoria's), is served
in the lounge or rebuilt Victorian conservatory;
Tuesdays to Saturdays, a succinct, interesting
menu is available at dinner. For guests who opt
for a quiet night in, a 'room picnic' of Scottish
pastrami and Morangie brie, with an optional
bottle of wine or champagne, may be arranged.

MAP 5:D2
12 Victoria Square
Stirling  FK8 2QZ
T: 01786 473920
W: victoriasquare.scot

BEDROOMS: 10. 1 on ground floor.
OPEN: all year except Christmas,
restaurant closed Sun, Mon.
FACILITIES: lounge, breakfast room,
orangery restaurant, in-room smart
TV (Freeview).
BACKGROUND MUSIC: quiet, in
restaurant.
LOCATION: ½ mile from town centre.
CHILDREN: not under 12.
DOGS: not allowed.
CREDIT CARDS: MC, Visa.
PRICES: per room B&B £75–£190. Prix
fixe menu £29.95 (2 courses), £38.95
(3 courses).

## THORNHILL Dumfries and Galloway
# TRIGONY HOUSE

Jan and Adam Moore's relaxed, pet-friendly
country hotel is in an 18th-century sporting lodge
surrounded by mature gardens and woodland.
There are fire-warmed sitting areas and an
oak-panelled staircase; a Finnish sauna cabin and
hot tub are in the grounds. Sit in the charming
restaurant overlooking the neat lawn: 'The great
strength at this hotel is the food – imaginative
without being pretentious'. The same menu may
be taken in the bar, where dogs are welcomed.
Simply decorated in country style, bedrooms
have home-made shortbread and fresh coffee;
a garden suite has a conservatory and private
garden. At breakfast, opt for 'creamy porridge,
just as it should be; plump kippers; sausages full
of flavour'.

**25% DISCOUNT VOUCHERS**

MAP 5:E2
Closeburn
Thornhill DG3 5EZ
T: 01848 331211
W: trigonyhotel.co.uk

BEDROOMS: 9. 1 on ground floor.
OPEN: all year except 25–27, 31 Dec.
FACILITIES: bar, lounge, dining room,
in-room TV (Freeview), spa treatment
room in private garden (outdoor
wood-fired hot tub, sauna cabin),
wedding facilities, 4-acre grounds.
BACKGROUND MUSIC: in bar in evening.
LOCATION: 1 mile S of Thornhill.
CHILDREN: all ages welcomed.
DOGS: well-behaved dogs 'not only
allowed but welcomed' in bedrooms,
bar, grounds, not in dining room.
CREDIT CARDS: Amex, MC, Visa.
PRICES: per room B&B £130–£175,
D,B&B £200–£245. À la carte £35.
1-night bookings sometimes
refused Sat.

**ABERGELE** Conwy

# THE KINMEL ARMS

Well placed for walks in countryside and along
the coast, this Elwy valley inn (Tir Prince group)
stands around the corner from the parish church,
in a small village surrounded by green fields.
Come in to find locals, and local real ales, in the
relaxed bar; brasserie-style dishes, including
interesting gluten-free picks, are served in the
conservatory restaurant. Large, oak-floored
bedrooms each have a decked balcony with rural
views – just right for the morning bird chorus.
A generous spread of fruit, juices, home-made
granola, pastries, hams and local cheeses is placed
in each room's mini-kitchenette for breakfast
in pyjamas; continental and cooked options are
served in the restaurant from 9 am.

MAP 3:A3
St George
Abergele LL22 9BP
T: 01745 832207
W: thekinmelarms.co.uk

BEDROOMS: 4. 2 on ground floor.
OPEN: all year.
FACILITIES: bar, restaurant, private
dining room, deli/shop, tea rooms,
in-room TV (Freeview), small garden,
parking.
BACKGROUND MUSIC: 'subtle' in bar
area.
LOCATION: 15 mins' drive from
Llandudno.
CHILDREN: all ages welcomed.
DOGS: small dogs allowed in bar area,
1 bedroom (restrictions apply).
CREDIT CARDS: MC, Visa.
PRICES: per room B&B £135–£175,
D,B&B from £195. À la carte £32.

**NEW**

**ABERYSTWYTH** Ceredigion

# NANTEOS MANSION

Sheep-spotted hills stretch away from this
Grade I listed manor house, which stands in
tranquil seclusion in its own wooded grounds.
Sympathetically restored, the Georgian property
retains vestiges of its past in its stained glass,
carved fireplaces and grand staircase. Bedrooms
and sumptuous suites are decorated in keeping
with the period of the house, but hold thoughtful
modern comforts, including activity packs for
young guests. In the chandelier-lit dining room,
the food is keenly contemporary: Welsh lamb
rump, miso leeks, buttered potatoes, say. Lighter
dishes are available in the bar. Served in the
mansion's former kitchen, where copper pans line
a vast wood dresser, breakfast has good choice.

**25% DISCOUNT VOUCHERS**

MAP 3:C3
Rhydyfelin
Aberystwyth SY23 4LU
T: 01970 600522
W: nanteos.com

BEDROOMS: 22. 3 on ground floor,
1 suitable for disabled. Plus 4-bed
mews house.
OPEN: all year.
FACILITIES: bar, lounge, restaurant, tea
room, in-room smart TV (Freeview),
civil wedding licence, 30-acre grounds
(gardens, woodland), ground-floor
public areas all wheelchair accessible.
BACKGROUND MUSIC: in reception, bar.
LOCATION: 4 miles SE of Aberystwyth.
CHILDREN: all ages welcomed.
DOGS: in 3 bedrooms, not in restaurant.
CREDIT CARDS: Amex, MC, Visa.
PRICES: per room B&B single £90–£130,
double £125–£300, D,B&B £128–£380.
À la carte £39.

AMROTH Pembrokeshire

# MELLIEHA GUEST HOUSE

'Excellent, informative hosts' Julia and Stuart
Adams run their tranquil B&B in a forested valley,
with easy access to the Pembrokeshire Coast Path
and the beach. 'The Adamses take a real interest
in their guests. We were warmly welcomed,
then served tea and the lightest of scones on the
sunny terrace, where we enjoyed the view of the
immaculate garden and the sea,' report Guide
readers this year. 'Spotless' bedrooms have views
over the garden and green valley, or towards
Carmarthen Bay. 'Our room wasn't large, but
there were comfortable beds and many thoughtful
touches, such as fresh milk for our morning tea.'
'Well-presented' breakfasts (perhaps of cockles
and laverbread) are ordered the night before.

**25% DISCOUNT VOUCHERS**

MAP 3:D2
Amroth SA67 8NA
T: 01834 811581
W: mellieha.co.uk

BEDROOMS: 5.
OPEN: all year except over Christmas,
New Year.
FACILITIES: lounge, breakfast room,
in-room TV, no mobile signal, 1-acre
garden, parking.
BACKGROUND MUSIC: none.
LOCATION: 150 yards from Amroth
seafront, 2 miles E of Saundersfoot.
CHILDREN: not under 12.
DOGS: only assistance dogs allowed.
CREDIT CARDS: MC, Visa.
PRICES: per room B&B £85–£110.
2-night min. stay preferred weekends
May–Sept.

BALA Gwynedd

# PALE HALL

In a woodland garden that stretches to the River
Dee, this historic Victorian manor is today a
sumptuous hotel rich in antiques and fine original
features. Smaller pleasures abound, too: board
games in the library, lawn games outside, a pond
whose every fish is named Alan. Individually
decorated bedrooms (some dog friendly) have
little luxuries, such as organic toiletries and
complimentary Madeira. A barn and stables in the
grounds were being converted into duplex suites
as the Guide went to print. At mealtimes in the
Henry Robertson fine dining room or informal
Huntsman bistro, sustainably sourced produce is
the focus of chef Gareth Stevenson's cooking. Just
beyond, Snowdonia national park appeals.

MAP 3:B3
Bala LL23 7PS
T: 01678 530285
W: palehall.co.uk

BEDROOMS: 18. 1 suitable for disabled.
OPEN: all year.
FACILITIES: Grand Hall, lounge,
library, restaurant, bar/bistro,
Venetian dining room, in-room TV
(Freeview), room service, meeting/
function facilities, civil wedding
licence, 50-acre grounds, electric car
charging points.
BACKGROUND MUSIC: in Grand Hall,
restaurants.
LOCATION: 2 miles from Bala.
CHILDREN: all ages welcomed.
DOGS: 'well-behaved dogs' allowed
in 7 bedrooms, Grand Hall, bistro,
on lead at all times in gardens and
public areas.
CREDIT CARDS: Amex, MC, Visa.
PRICES: per room B&B £275–£860,
D,B&B £385–£1,010. Tasting menu
£70 (5 courses), £90 (8 courses),
à la carte £45–£50.

BEAUMARIS Anglesey

# THE BULL – BEAUMARIS

In a lively seaside town known equally for its medieval castle and its ice cream parlour, this ancient coaching inn is today a 'friendly' hotel with updated bedrooms, a stylish restaurant, and a well-preserved pub whose wonky doors, open fireplace and old photographs create much atmosphere. Individually decorated bedrooms (some clean lined and contemporary, some more flamboyant, one with a mahogany four-poster bed) are in the main building and the 17th-century Townhouse down the street; each is supplied with Welsh biscuits and a capsule coffee machine. At lunch and dinner, the modern menu (Welsh beef fillet, herb gnocchi; Thai-spiced Menai mussels, fries) may be served alfresco in the paved courtyard.

MAP 3:A3
Castle Street
Beaumaris LL58 8AP
T: 01248 810329
W: bullsheadinn.co.uk

BEDROOMS: 25. 13 in Townhouse, 1 in courtyard, 2 on ground floor, 1 suitable for disabled.
OPEN: all year except 24/25 Dec, limited bar and restaurant opening over Christmas period.
FACILITIES: lift (in Townhouse), residents' lounge, bar, restaurant, in-room TV (Freeview), courtyard, restaurant wheelchair accessible.
BACKGROUND MUSIC: in restaurant at mealtimes.
LOCATION: town centre.
CHILDREN: all ages welcomed, no children in bar after 9 pm.
DOGS: allowed in 2 bedrooms, bar.
CREDIT CARDS: Amex, MC, Visa.
PRICES: per room B&B single £110–£175, double £115–£180, D,B&B single £130–£195, double £145–£240. À la carte £29.

CARDIFF

# NEW HOUSE COUNTRY HOTEL

Panoramic views sweep over the city and the Severn estuary from this dog-friendly hotel in the rolling hills just north of the city centre. A tiered fountain at the entrance adds country house appeal to the creeper-covered, Grade II listed manor house; stone steps lead to elegant rooms that look out on to lush greenery. Afternoon tea may be taken in the lounges; Welsh ingredient-focused dishes in the restaurant might include Brecon gin-cured gravlax, or lamb shank, roasted garlic and pea risotto. Individually decorated with lively patterns and a flair for colour, modern bedrooms are supplied with ethically produced toiletries. Part of the Town & Country Collective; see also The Bear, Cowbridge, and The West House, Llantwit Major (Shortlist entries).

MAP 3:E4
Thornhill Road
Cardiff CF14 9UA
T: 02920 520280
W: townandcountrycollective.co.uk/newhouse

BEDROOMS: 37. 29 in annexe, connected via lounges.
OPEN: all year except 26 Dec, 1 Jan.
FACILITIES: 3 lounges, library, restaurant, in-room TV (Freeview), civil wedding licence, gym, 9-acre grounds.
BACKGROUND MUSIC: in restaurant.
LOCATION: in Thornhill suburb, 7 miles from Cardiff city centre.
CHILDREN: all ages welcomed.
DOGS: allowed in 3 bedrooms, 2 lounges, parts of garden, not in restaurant.
CREDIT CARDS: Amex, MC, Visa.
PRICES: per room B&B £90–£120, D,B&B £149.50–£250. À la carte £35.

COWBRIDGE Vale of Glamorgan

# THE BEAR

Between Cardiff and the coast, this well-located hotel has for centuries been the hub of the fashionable market town. The panelled lounge and grill bar (look out for the remains of a medieval fireplace) are a local gathering spot; when the sun's out, find a table under the courtyard pergola. From light lunches to grill dinners, modern dishes in the bar and atmospheric Cellars restaurant feature Welsh produce. Stay over, like the Plas Llanmihangel gentry did while attending local balls and races: some of the up-to-date bedrooms accommodate a dog or a family. Residents have gym access at a leisure centre nearby. Part of the Town & Country Collective; see also The West House, Llantwit Major (Shortlist entry).

MAP 3:E3
63 High Street
Cowbridge CF71 7AF
T: 01446 774814
W: townandcountrycollective.co.uk/
    thebear

BEDROOMS: 33. Some on ground floor, some in annexe, plus self-catering apartments.
OPEN: all year.
FACILITIES: lounge/bar, grill/bar, restaurant, in-room TV, civil wedding licence, conference facilities, courtyard, secure bicycle storage, parking.
BACKGROUND MUSIC: in restaurant.
LOCATION: town centre.
CHILDREN: all ages welcomed.
DOGS: allowed in bedrooms, bar.
CREDIT CARDS: MC, Visa.
PRICES: per room B&B £105–£145. À la carte £30.

DOLGELLAU Gwynedd

# Y MEIRIONNYDD

In a town of granite and slate, Marc Russell and Nicholas Banda's handsome, contemporary restaurant-with-rooms makes a fine base for expeditions in Snowdonia national park. Days spent hiking and biking the mountain paths end in cosy, freshly decorated bedrooms. Each is equipped with a wide bed and luxurious linen, Welsh blankets and slippers; a selection of books completes nights in. Every room has its own character, with a rugged, exposed stone wall, say, or views of Cadair Idris over neighbouring rooftops. There are Welsh gins in the friendly bar; modern plates of local produce in the smart cellar restaurant (once the county jail). Packed lunches, with a map and a rug, are available.

MAP 3:B3
Smithfield Square
Dolgellau LL40 1ES
T: 01341 422554
W: themeirionnydd.com

BEDROOMS: 5. 1 on ground floor.
OPEN: all year except 4–18 Jan, 2–9 Nov, 22–27 Dec, restaurant closed Sun, Mon.
FACILITIES: bar, restaurant, in-room TV, terrace, bicycle storage.
BACKGROUND MUSIC: in bar, restaurant.
LOCATION: town centre.
CHILDREN: not under 6.
DOGS: only assistance dogs allowed.
CREDIT CARDS: Amex, MC, Visa.
PRICES: per room B&B £89–£135, D,B&B £141–£187. À la carte £28.50. 2-night min. stay at weekends.

MAP 3:D2
Llanarthne SA32 8HJ
T: 01558 668778
W: llwynhelygcountryhouse.co.uk

LLANARTHNE Carmarthenshire
# LLWYN HELYG

In 'magnificent countryside', Fiona and Caron Jones's modern house, all marble, polished granite and honey-coloured wood inside, has 'an unexpected "wow" factor'. Another source of 'wow': a state-of-the-art sound system in an acoustically designed, vaulted listening room. Guests are invited to bring their own music or choose from the hosts' large library. Past the 'massive' entrance hall, a double staircase leads to spacious, 'elegant' bedrooms, each with a 'top-quality' bed and a 'luxurious' bathroom with a spa bath. The sunny breakfast room overlooks a formal pond, with views of the Tywi valley beyond. Dining recommendations are readily supplied. The National Botanic Garden of Wales is nearby.

BEDROOMS: 3.
OPEN: all year except 10 days over Christmas.
FACILITIES: 4 lounges, listening room, breakfast room, in-room TV (Freeview), 3-acre garden.
BACKGROUND MUSIC: none.
LOCATION: 8 miles W of Llandeilo, 9 miles E of Carmarthen.
CHILDREN: not under 16.
DOGS: not allowed.
CREDIT CARDS: MC, Visa.
PRICES: per room B&B single £110, double £135–£155.

MAP 3:B3
Llwynaire
Llanbrynmair SY19 7DX
T: 01650 519228
W: theroystonwales.com

LLANBRYNMAIR Powys
# THE ROYSTON

Relish a Victorian gentleman's residence in ten acres of gardens and pasture. Off a single-track road, welcoming hosts Rob Perham and Clive Sweeting have given their double-fronted guest house new life with deep hues, contemporary artwork and vintage-inspired style. There's a wood-burning stove and an honesty bar in the lounge; fire pits outside. Moody-toned, well-equipped bedrooms are lifted by interesting ornaments picked up during the owners' travels; there's no TV – instead, gaze through the windows at the Cambrian mountains, the kitchen garden or surrounding fields and hills. From breakfast and dinner to packed lunches and picnics, much of the food is home-made, home-grown or locally sourced.

BEDROOMS: 7.
OPEN: all year except Christmas, New Year.
FACILITIES: lounge, dining room, 10-acre grounds.
BACKGROUND MUSIC: none.
LOCATION: in rural setting N of Llanbrynmair.
CHILDREN: not under 12.
DOGS: allowed in 2 bedrooms, not in lounge, on lead at all times.
CREDIT CARDS: MC, Visa.
PRICES: per room B&B £110–£159. À la carte £22 (2 courses), £26 (3 courses).

LLANDDEINIOLEN Gwynedd

# TY'N RHOS

On a secluded farmstead, the Murphy family's 'friendly' hotel is in 'lovely countryside' overlooking the Isle of Anglesey. Sheep and cattle graze in fields beyond the gardens; binoculars are provided for watching the varied bird life. Each named after a wildflower, 'comfortable, well-equipped' bedrooms are in the creeper-covered house or around the courtyard; some open on to the lush garden. Take pre-dinner drinks in the bar, lounge or conservatory – or on the patio in fine weather – before a hearty meal, perhaps of 'wonderfully flavoursome' local lamb. A 'decent' buffet at breakfast has cereals, yogurts, pastries and home-made granola; 'very good' cooked options include haddock with Welsh rarebit.

MAP 3:A3
Llanddeiniolen LL55 3AE
T: 01248 670489
W: tynrhos.co.uk

BEDROOMS: 19. 7 in converted outbuilding, 2 on ground floor.
OPEN: all year except Christmas, New Year.
FACILITIES: lounge, bar, restaurant, conservatory, in-room TV, 1-acre garden, patio, parking, most public areas wheelchair accessible.
BACKGROUND MUSIC: in public areas.
LOCATION: 12 mins' drive from the Llanberis train, 4 miles from Bangor and Caernarfon.
CHILDREN: all ages welcomed, no 'small children' in restaurant in evening.
DOGS: allowed in some bedrooms, garden.
CREDIT CARDS: MC, Visa.
PRICES: per room B&B single £80–£95, double £90–£190, D,B&B (2-night min. stay) single £115–£125, double £160–£260. Set menu £36.50 (2 courses), £42.50 (3 courses).

LLANDUDNO Conwy

# ESCAPE

There's a touch of fun at Sam Nayar and Gaenor Loftus's design-conscious B&B, in a white stucco Victorian villa just up the street from the Great Orme Tramway. Modern and vintage furnishings are set against a backdrop of period features such as stained-glass windows and oak panelling; bedrooms have plenty of personality. Choose a room with a copper bathtub, and a pair of restored cocktail chairs in the bay window, perhaps; one, in the loft, has a cosy lounge area, while another, smaller but no less stylish, has panoramic views of the town and distant hills. In every room: high-end toiletries and high-spec technology. Breakfast is served at the table. The beach and the pier are a short stroll away.

MAP 3:A3
48 Church Walks
Llandudno LL30 2HL
T: 01492 877776
W: escapebandb.co.uk

BEDROOMS: 9.
OPEN: all year except 18–26 Dec.
FACILITIES: lounge (honesty bar), breakfast room, in-room TV (Freeview), front garden, limited parking.
BACKGROUND MUSIC: at breakfast.
LOCATION: 1 mile from town and coast.
CHILDREN: not under 10.
DOGS: not allowed.
CREDIT CARDS: Amex, MC, Visa.
PRICES: per room B&B £105–£160. Min. 2-night stay at weekends, 3 nights on bank holidays.

MAP 3:A3
17 North Parade
Llandudno LL30 2LP
T: 01492 860330
W: osbornehouse.co.uk

## LLANDUDNO Conwy
# OSBORNE HOUSE

On the promenade, this small, family-owned hotel is furnished with 'impressive grandeur', from the 'splendid' public rooms, all oil paintings and gilded mirrors, to the sea-facing suites on its upper floors. Each well-supplied suite has a large sitting room, a marble bathroom, and a working gas fire in a marble fireplace. 'We were pleasantly surprised by the elegance of our characterful room,' report Guide readers this year, although a closer eye on housekeeping wouldn't be out of place. 'Tasty, generously portioned' dishes are served all day in the 'ornate' Victorian dining room; a 'good' continental breakfast is taken in the suite. Guests may use the spa and gym at sister hotel The Empire, around the corner.

BEDROOMS: 6 suites.
OPEN: all year except 15–27 Dec.
FACILITIES: sitting room, bar, café/bistro, in-room TV (Freeview), small patio, parking.
BACKGROUND MUSIC: in public rooms.
LOCATION: on the promenade.
CHILDREN: not under 14.
DOGS: only assistance dogs allowed.
CREDIT CARDS: Amex, MC, Visa.
PRICES: per room B&B £135–£205, D,B&B £160–£235. À la carte £25.
1-night bookings refused weekends.

MAP 3:A4
Ruthin Road
Llanferres CH7 5SN
T: 01352 810225
W: druid-inn.co.uk

## LLANFERRES Denbighshire
# THE DRUID INN

Close to Offa's Dyke Path, this unpretentious country pub, a 'friendly' gathering spot for locals, is a 'lovely' find. Within the white-painted building, the cosy bar has exposed stone walls and low beams; a log fire burns when the temperature dips. Classic pub dishes such as gammon steak and fish pie are served alongside more modern, veggie-friendly options (garden pea and spinach burger, sweet potato roulade, etc) in the traditional dining room. Neat, modest bedrooms have an en suite shower room; a separate guest bathroom has a tub for a soak. The surrounding area is ripe for gentle countryside rambles and wilder mountain-biking excursions into the Clwydian hills; luggage transfers can be arranged.

BEDROOMS: 5.
OPEN: all year, but no food served Christmas Day.
FACILITIES: bar, snug, restaurant, pool room, in-room TV (Freeview), garden, parking.
BACKGROUND MUSIC: in public spaces.
LOCATION: edge of village, close to Offa's Dyke Path.
CHILDREN: all ages welcomed.
DOGS: allowed in some bedrooms, bar, pool room.
CREDIT CARDS: MC, Visa.
PRICES: per room B&B single £60–£72, double £85. À la carte £24.

## LLANSTEFFAN Carmarthenshire

# MANSION HOUSE LLANSTEFFAN

Carmarthenshire native Wendy Beaney and her husband, David, run this 'stylishly minimalist' restaurant-with-rooms in their thoughtfully restored Georgian mansion, which stands in wooded gardens overlooking the Tywi estuary. The 'excellent' view from the period dining room is fine accompaniment for Paul Owen's seasonal menus of locally farmed vegetables, Welsh meats and Carmarthen Bay seafood. Bedrooms with garden or river views are supplied with a host of extras: home-made treats, bathrobes, Welsh toiletries. Norman castles at Llansteffan and Laugharne, and the botanic gardens' futuristic greenhouse, are equally within reach; Dylan Thomas's contemplative boathouse is a half-hour's drive away.

MAP 3:D2
Pantyrathro
Llansteffan SA33 5AJ
T: 01267 241515
W: mansionhousellansteffan.co.uk

BEDROOMS: 8. 2 interconnecting rooms on ground floor, 1 suitable for disabled.
OPEN: all year, restaurant closed Sun eve except for residents, also Mon, Nov–mid-Feb.
FACILITIES: large open-plan bar/reception area, lounge, restaurant, in-room TV (Freeview), civil wedding licence, conference facilities, 5-acre grounds, parking.
BACKGROUND MUSIC: in public spaces.
LOCATION: 2 miles to Llansteffan village, beach and castle.
CHILDREN: all ages welcomed.
DOGS: not allowed.
CREDIT CARDS: Amex, MC, Visa.
PRICES: per room B&B £145–£220. À la carte £30.

## LLANTWIT MAJOR Vale of Glamorgan

# THE WEST HOUSE

The dramatic cliffs and secluded coves of the Glamorgan Heritage Coast are within easy reach of this modern hotel, in a quiet town of medieval streets and old stone buildings, a few minutes' drive from the beach. Updated bedrooms vary in size and decor; guests travelling with their dog may request (at extra charge) one of the Fido-friendly rooms – they're supplied with a dog bed, towel and treats, and have access to the walled garden. Sandwiches, light bites and straightforward British classics are served in the restaurant, along with interesting vegetarian options, perhaps Glamorgan leek, carrot and Cheddar hash. Part of the Town & Country Collective; see also New House Country Hotel, Cardiff and The Bear, Cowbridge (Shortlist entries).

MAP 3:E3
West Street
Llantwit Major CF61 1SP
T: 01446 792406
W: townandcountrycollective.co.uk/west-house

BEDROOMS: 22. 1 on ground floor.
OPEN: all year, restaurant closed Sun evening.
FACILITIES: bar, restaurant, snug, conservatory, in-room TV, civil wedding licence, terrace, garden, parking.
BACKGROUND MUSIC: in public areas.
LOCATION: 10 mins' walk from town centre.
CHILDREN: all ages welcomed.
DOGS: allowed in some bedrooms, separate eating area.
CREDIT CARDS: MC, Visa.
PRICES: per room B&B £129–£149, D,B&B £169–£189. À la carte £20.

## LLANWRTYD WELLS Powys
# LASSWADE COUNTRY HOUSE

The sheep-dotted landscape stretches to the Epynt hills behind Roger and Emma Stevens's semi-rural restaurant-with-rooms, in a small mid-Wales town that's a gateway to the Cambrian mountains. The decor may be old fashioned ('boutique and high luxury we are not'), but the Stevenses – chatty, congenial hosts – have created a welcoming, home-away-from-home atmosphere. Guests take pre-dinner drinks on the garden patio or in the fire-warmed drawing room before sitting down to Roger's 'very good', Slow Food-inspired menus in the traditional dining room. On the upper floors, most of the homely bedrooms have 'superb' mountain views. Gardens and National Trust properties are within reach.

**25% DISCOUNT VOUCHERS**

MAP 3:D3
Station Road
Llanwrtyd Wells LD5 4RW
T: 01591 610515
W: lasswadehotel.co.uk

BEDROOMS: 8.
OPEN: 2 Mar–19 Dec, closed Sun eve, Mon eve.
FACILITIES: drawing room, restaurant, conservatory, in-room TV (Freeview), patio, small garden, parking, electric vehicle charging point.
BACKGROUND MUSIC: pianola in restaurant.
LOCATION: edge of town.
CHILDREN: all ages welcomed, not under 8 in restaurant.
DOGS: not allowed except by prior arrangement.
CREDIT CARDS: MC, Visa.
PRICES: per room B&B single £70–£90, double £95–£130, D,B&B £126–£160, except during Royal Welsh Show week. Set menu £36.

## MOYLEGROVE Pembrokeshire
# THE OLD VICARAGE B&B

Coastal walks, sunset dinners and fireside chess are all within reach at Meg and Jaap van Soest's modern B&B, in a hill-top Edwardian vicarage that has peered over the village for well over a century. High-ceilinged, large-windowed rooms let in the day's light – all the better to take in the house's appealing, pared-back style. Downstairs, there's a flutter of books, maps and guides; in the unfussy bedrooms are a large bed, fresh milk and coffee, quality teas, and a shower room with Welsh toiletries. Plans are afoot for a snug bar area. To accompany the valley views at breakfast: home-baked breads; Pembrokeshire honey; local bacon, sausages and eggs; good veggie options. Home-cooked dinners on request.

MAP 3:D2
Moylegrove SA43 3BN
T: 01239 881711
W: oldvicaragemoylegrove.co.uk

BEDROOMS: 5.
OPEN: all year.
FACILITIES: sitting room, dining room, in-room TV (Freeview), 1-acre garden.
BACKGROUND MUSIC: in dining room in evening.
LOCATION: 500 yards from village, 13 miles N of Fishguard.
CHILDREN: all ages welcomed.
DOGS: allowed, not in dining room.
CREDIT CARDS: MC, Visa.
PRICES: per room B&B £100–£110. Dinner £35.

NANT GWYNANT Gwynedd
## PEN-Y-GWRYD HOTEL

Built in 1810, this 'eccentric' hotel at the foot of
Snowdonia retains the spirit of a mountaineers'
hostel, along with a wealth of memorabilia
commemorating mountaineering's golden age.
It is owned by the Pullee family, who hosted
Sir Edmund Hillary and Tenzing Norgay as
they trained to climb Everest. In the former
farmhouse-turned-coaching inn, most of the
bedrooms (not all with an en suite bathroom) are
traditionally decorated; three newly refurbished
rooms in the annexe have French windows
leading to a balcony, and a roll-top bath in the
bathroom. In the grounds: a sauna, and a tree-
bordered lake for swimming or sunning by. A
gong heralds a hearty home-cooked set dinner of
locally sourced produce.

MAP 3:A3
Nant Gwynant LL55 4NT
T: 01286 870211
w: pyg.co.uk

BEDROOMS: 18. 1 on ground floor, some
in annexe.
OPEN: Mar–mid-Nov, weekends mid-
Nov–New Year.
FACILITIES: bar, 3 snugs, residents' bar/
lounge, dining room, in-room TV
(Freeview) in some rooms, chapel,
1-acre grounds (natural swimming
lake, sauna).
BACKGROUND MUSIC: none.
LOCATION: between Beddgelert and
Capel Curig.
CHILDREN: all ages welcomed.
DOGS: allowed in some bedrooms,
public rooms except dining room.
CREDIT CARDS: MC, Visa.
PRICES: per person B&B £47.50–£75,
D,B&B £73.50–£111. Set dinner
£29–£39. 1-night bookings often
refused weekends.

NARBERTH Pembrokeshire
## CANASTON OAKS

The friendly owners 'go the extra mile' at this
well-restored Pembrokeshire longhouse, a short
drive from a pleasant market town. Eleanor and
David Lewis run the 'very good' B&B with their
daughter, Emma Millership. Spotless bedrooms
in a lake-view lodge or in converted barns with
their own front door have thoughtful extras such
as dressing gowns and candles; 'the fresh milk is
a lovely touch'. A family might request a suite of
interconnecting rooms with a countryside-facing
terrace. In the morning, feast on thick Welsh
yogurt, heather honey and home-poached fruit;
perhaps also porridge with Penderyn whisky, or
smoked haddock fishcakes. An amble by the river
awaits. 'Five star at every level.'

MAP 3:D2
Canaston Bridge
Narberth SA67 8DE
T: 01437 541254
w: canastonoaks.co.uk

BEDROOMS: 10. 7 around courtyard, 2
suitable for disabled, plus 1-bed self-
catering apartment.
OPEN: all year except Christmas.
FACILITIES: lounge, dining room, in-
room TV (Freeview), 1-acre grounds,
parking.
BACKGROUND MUSIC: at breakfast in
dining room.
LOCATION: 2 miles W of Narberth.
CHILDREN: all ages welcomed.
DOGS: well-behaved dogs allowed in
3 barn suites, not in dining area, on
lead in all public areas.
CREDIT CARDS: MC, Visa.
PRICES: per room B&B £90–£175. Set
menu £21 (2 courses), £26 (3 courses).
1-night bookings sometimes refused
peak times.

NEWTOWN Powys

## THE FOREST COUNTRY GUEST HOUSE

In mid-Wales countryside, Paul and Michelle Martin's family-friendly B&B is ringed by large, flower-filled gardens. A peaceful, homely retreat, the Victorian house has books, maps and games in the drawing room, plus an antique Bechstein grand piano to play; children may run free in the timber fort and outdoor play area. Up the 19th-century oak staircase, traditional country-style bedrooms have period furniture and views of fields graced by a herd of rare-breed sheep; one large room has a four-poster bed. DIY snacks and meals are easy in a shared guest kitchenette, and guests are welcome to bring their own drinks. Eggs from the Martins' free-range hens and ducks supply the organic breakfasts.

MAP 3:C4
Gilfach Lane
Newtown SY16 4DW
T: 01686 621821
W: bedandbreakfastnewtown.co.uk

BEDROOMS: 5. 1 room adapted for limited mobility, accessed by stairs, plus 4 self-catering cottages.
OPEN: all year except Christmas, New Year, self-catering cottages open all year.
FACILITIES: sitting room, dining room, kitchenette, games room, in-room TV (Freeview), 4-acre garden, tennis, parking, secure bicycle storage.
BACKGROUND MUSIC: none.
LOCATION: 1 mile from Kerry village, 3 miles from Newtown.
CHILDREN: all ages welcomed.
DOGS: allowed in cottages and in kennels in the grounds.
CREDIT CARDS: MC, Visa.
PRICES: per room B&B single £70–£85, double £80–£115. 1-night bookings sometimes refused bank holidays and busy weekends.

PENARTH Vale of Glamorgan

## HOLM HOUSE

Overlooking the Bristol Channel, this contemporary hotel and spa rests on a leafy avenue, minutes from the seafront. The former Victorian private home has been sleekly updated: there are cocktails and mocktails at the curving bar; light fills the coastal-chic restaurant (candlelit at night). Sit by the open fire in the snug in cool weather – a mug of hot chocolate or mulled wine's optional; on a clear day, head for the new garden bar on the sea-facing lawn. Varying in size, neat, modern bedrooms are supplied with good-quality coffee and tea, plus bathrobes, slippers and high-end toiletries. Breakfast on freshly baked pastries, plus pancakes, omelettes or a full Welsh, then stroll to the town's Art Deco pier.

### 25% DISCOUNT VOUCHERS

MAP 3:E4
Marine Parade
Penarth CF64 3BG
T: 029 2070 6029
W: holmhousehotel.com

BEDROOMS: 13. 2 in coach house, 2 on ground floor, 1 suitable for disabled.
OPEN: all year.
FACILITIES: lounge, snug, bar/restaurant, private dining room, in-room TV (Sky), civil wedding licence, large garden (garden bar), spa, hydrotherapy swimming pool, gym.
BACKGROUND MUSIC: all day in public areas.
LOCATION: seafront location on the edge of town, 5 miles from Cardiff.
CHILDREN: all ages welcomed.
DOGS: allowed in 2 bedrooms, lounge, garden.
CREDIT CARDS: MC, Visa.
PRICES: per room B&B £115–£285, D,B&B £175–£345. À la carte from £35.

## PORTMEIRION Gwynedd
# HOTEL PORTMEIRION

Amid the architectural astonishment that is
Sir Bertram Clough Williams-Ellis's Italianate
village, on the edge of a tidal estuary, this early
Victorian villa is today a 'comfortably furnished'
hotel run with 'friendly, welcoming' staff. Its
traditional bedrooms have 'wonderful' estuary
and mountain views; more modern rooms in
Castell Deudraeth overlook the walled garden;
some others yet, in cottages in the grounds, have
a private patio or terrace. There are plenty of
options at mealtimes, including the Art Deco
dining room, where 'the service is slick and
professional', and the menu has 'good choice'.
Busy during the day, the village, come evening,
is 'a delightful haven in which to wander in
relative solitude'.

MAP 3:B3
Minffordd
Portmeirion  LL48 6ER
T: 01766 770000
W: portmeirion-village.com

BEDROOMS: 59. 11 in Castell
Deudraeth, 34 in village, some on
ground floor, 1 suitable for disabled.
OPEN: all year, hotel and village rooms
closed 22–27 Nov, Castell Deudraeth
rooms closed 3–8 Jan.
FACILITIES: lift, 4 lounges, bar,
restaurant, brasserie in Castell,
in-room TV, civil wedding licence,
130-acre grounds, outdoor heated
swimming pool (summer).
BACKGROUND MUSIC: in public areas,
occasional live music in lounges.
LOCATION: 2 miles SE of Porthmadog.
CHILDREN: all ages welcomed.
DOGS: only assistance dogs allowed.
CREDIT CARDS: Amex, MC, Visa.
PRICES: per room B&B £114–£344,
D,B&B £164–£430. 2-night min. stay
most Sat.

## RHOSNEIGR Anglesey
# SANDY MOUNT HOUSE

A beach-house vibe breezes through Louise
and Phil Goodwin's restaurant-with-rooms,
in a seaside village on the Anglesey Coast
Path. Wicker chairs, sand-bleached floors and
weathered wooden tables encourage a laid-back
atmosphere; families and dogs are welcomed in
equal measure. Real ales, craft beers and cocktails
accompany small plates in the 'lively' bar; the
open kitchen turns out robust dishes (marinated
courgettes, roasted beetroot meringue, say, or
brown-sugar-cured belly pork, Mon Las cheese,
candied walnut) for diners in the restaurant or
on the heated terrace. Bedrooms, upstairs, are
modern and very smart. Two have window seats
with sea views; all are supplied with home-made
biscuits and cosseting amenities.

MAP 3:A2
High Street
Rhosneigr  LL64 5UX
T: 01407 253102
W: sandymounthouse.co.uk

BEDROOMS: 7.
OPEN: all year, limited hours over
Christmas.
FACILITIES: bar, restaurant,
conservatory, private dining rooms,
in-room TV, terrace, garden, bar and
restaurant wheelchair accessible.
BACKGROUND MUSIC: in bar, restaurant,
on front terrace.
LOCATION: in village, close to beach.
CHILDREN: all ages welcomed.
DOGS: allowed in 2 bedrooms, bar, on
front terrace.
CREDIT CARDS: Amex, MC, Visa.
PRICES: per room B&B £140–£360.
À la carte £35.

ROCH Pembrokeshire

# ROCH CASTLE HOTEL

In a dramatic setting, on a rocky outcrop above the Pembrokeshire landscape, this 12th-century Norman castle reigns over a panorama that takes in St Brides Bay and the Preseli hills. Rugged stone gives way to clean-cut, contemporary B&B accommodation. A curving staircase leads to moody bedrooms, a couple in the tower and upper turrets; each is supplied with robes, slippers and aromatherapy toiletries, tea- and coffee-making facilities and a fridge. Still higher, the Sun Room, with floor-to-ceiling glass walls and an open-air viewing platform, merits the climb. Free transfers take residents to sister hotel Twr y Felin, St Davids (see main entry), for dinner; at breakfast, find laverbread and local honey.

**25% DISCOUNT VOUCHERS**

MAP 3:D1
Church Road
Roch  SA62 6AQ
T: 01437 725566
W: rochcastle.com

BEDROOMS: 6.
OPEN: all year.
FACILITIES: lounge, study, breakfast room, sunroom (honesty bar), in-room TV (Freeview), civil wedding licence, 19-acre grounds, electric car charging points.
BACKGROUND MUSIC: in lounges, breakfast room.
LOCATION: 7 miles NW of Haverfordwest.
CHILDREN: not under 12.
DOGS: not allowed.
CREDIT CARDS: Amex, MC, Visa.
PRICES: per room B&B £220–£260, D,B&B £290–£340. 2- or 3-night min. stay at weekends and peak times; also available for exclusive use.

ST DAVIDS Pembrokeshire

# CRUG-GLAS

'The friendliness and warmth of the people' stand out at the Evans family's relaxed restaurant-with-rooms, in a Georgian farmhouse on a working Pembrokeshire farm. The family home is filled with photographs and inherited pieces – a generations-old dresser houses the honesty bar. Bedrooms in the main building, a converted barn and a coach house each have their own style: one has a copper bath in the room; another, a window seat overlooking countryside. The main draw is Janet Evans's 'cleverly cooked, imaginatively presented' dinners, with beef from home-reared cows. In the morning, there's 'superb choice', including 'absolutely beautiful, thick-cut sweet bacon', at breakfast. The coast is close.

MAP 3:D1
St Davids  SA62 6XX
T: 01348 831302
W: crug-glas.co.uk

BEDROOMS: 7. 2 in converted outbuildings, 1 on ground floor.
OPEN: all year except 24–26 Dec.
FACILITIES: drawing room, dining room, in-room TV (Freeview), civil wedding licence, function facilities, 1-acre garden on 600-acre farm.
BACKGROUND MUSIC: classical.
LOCATION: 3½ miles NE of St David's.
CHILDREN: babes-in-arms and over-11s welcomed.
DOGS: allowed in cottage.
CREDIT CARDS: MC, Visa.
PRICES: per room B&B £150–£190. À la carte £35.

ST DAVIDS Pembrokeshire
## PENRHIW PRIORY

A peaceful retreat within easy walking distance of the town, this late Victorian mansion stands in acres of landscaped gardens, enveloped by woodland paths, a river and a wildflower meadow. It is modern inside, with soberly decorated rooms and dramatic abstract artwork. Accommodation is in well-proportioned bedrooms supplied with cosseting extras: bathrobes and slippers, aromatherapy toiletries. A suite in the coach house has a private terrace and views of Carn Llidi. Mingle with fellow guests over a drink and snacks from the honesty bar; at dinner, complimentary transfers to and from the well-regarded Blas restaurant at sister hotel Twr y Felin (see main entry), on the other side of town, can be arranged.

**25% DISCOUNT VOUCHERS**

MAP 3:D1
St Davids SA62 6PG
T: 01437 725588
W: penrhiwhotel.com

BEDROOMS: 8. 2 in coach house, 1 on ground floor.
OPEN: all year.
FACILITIES: lounge, drawing room, breakfast room, study, in-room TV, civil wedding licence, 12-acre grounds.
BACKGROUND MUSIC: soft jazz/classical in breakfast room.
LOCATION: 10 mins' walk from St Davids cathedral and town centre.
CHILDREN: not under 12, except for exclusive-use bookings.
DOGS: not allowed.
CREDIT CARDS: Amex, MC, Visa.
PRICES: per room B&B £180–£250, D,B&B £290–£360. 2-night min. stay in summer months.

SAUNDERSFOOT Pembrokeshire
## ST BRIDES SPA HOTEL

The panoramic views of Saundersfoot harbour and the coastline from this modern hotel above Carmarthen Bay are 'exceptional' – and the inward calm that washes over guests in the award-winning spa isn't bad, either. Seaside splendour comes to the fore here: light floods in through floor-to-ceiling windows, ocean air through glass doors. 'Very pleasant' bedrooms are styled in breezy nautical hues; some have a balcony. A bonus: residents get a 90-minute session in the spa's hydro pool. In the restaurant and bar, or on the terrace, Pembrokeshire produce and locally landed fish feature on regularly changing menus. In the village, a downhill stroll away, a modern chippy and beach barbecue are offshoots.

MAP 3:D2
St Brides Hill
Saundersfoot SA69 9NH
T: 01834 812304
W: stbridesspahotel.com

BEDROOMS: 34. 1 suitable for disabled. Plus six 2-bed apartments in grounds, 12 self-catering in village.
OPEN: all year.
FACILITIES: lift, lounge, bar, restaurant, Gallery dining area, meeting/function rooms, in-room TV, civil wedding licence, terraces, art gallery, spa (treatments, infinity pool), public areas wheelchair accessible, adapted toilet.
BACKGROUND MUSIC: all day in public areas.
LOCATION: 3 mins' walk to village.
CHILDREN: all ages welcomed.
DOGS: allowed in some ground-floor apartments.
CREDIT CARDS: Amex, MC, Visa.
PRICES: per room B&B single £145–£230, double £190–£350, D,B&B (at limited times of year) double £210–£430. À la carte £40.

ST ANNE Alderney
## THE BLONDE HEDGEHOG

Tranquil Alderney, the northernmost of the inhabited Channel Islands, is roused from hibernation by Julie-Anne Uggla's contemporary, eco-conscious hotel. The lively restaurant, marble-topped bar and chic bedrooms span a Victorian pub, a Georgian town house and an 18th-century cottage on a cobbled street; with plentiful use of natural materials, a modern rustic ambience connects them all. Driven by the seasons and supplies from the kitchen garden, flavourful, unfussy dishes are served in the stylish restaurant, which opens on to a terraced garden. Eat well, then retire to one of the well-equipped, handsome-hued bedrooms or suites. Next day, island activities, with a picnic, can be arranged.

MAP 1: inset D6
6 Le Huret
St Anne GY9 3TR
T: 01481 823230
w: blondehedgehog.com

BEDROOMS: 9. 5 in adjacent town house, 2 on ground floor, plus 3-bed cottage opposite.
OPEN: all year.
FACILITIES: bar, snug, restaurant, in-room TV, cinema/games room, ¼-acre garden, ground-floor public rooms wheelchair accessible.
BACKGROUND MUSIC: in bar, restaurant.
LOCATION: town centre.
CHILDREN: all ages welcomed.
DOGS: allowed in bar, garden, cottage, assistance dogs allowed throughout.
CREDIT CARDS: Amex, MC, Visa.
PRICES: per room B&B single £150–£300, double £180–£420, D,B&B £250–£500. À la carte £40.
1-night bookings refused during Alderney week.

ST BRELADE Jersey
## LA HAULE MANOR

A short waterfront stroll from the village, this well-positioned Georgian manor house stands in gardens overlooking St Aubin's Bay. Complimentary transfers are provided to and from the airport; a welcome glass of bubbly on arrival sets the tone. Past a high-ceilinged, chandeliered sitting room, many of the traditionally decorated bedrooms have Louis XV-style furnishings and broad sea views. On a fine day, stretch out on one of the parasol-shaded loungers around the swimming pool, perhaps with a sandwich from the bar. Free transport takes guests to sister hotel La Place for dinner; alternatively, local eateries are within walking distance. A plus: a bus for getting around the island stops right outside.

MAP 1: inset E6
La Neuve Route
St Brelade JE3 8BS
T: 01534 746013
w: lahaulemanor.com

BEDROOMS: 16. Some on ground floor, plus 2 self-catering apartments.
OPEN: all year.
FACILITIES: bar, sitting room, TV room, breakfast room, in-room TV, terrace, garden, outdoor heated swimming pool, hot tub, parking.
BACKGROUND MUSIC: in bar, breakfast room.
LOCATION: 10 mins' bayfront walk from St Aubin village.
CHILDREN: all ages welcomed.
DOGS: only assistance dogs allowed.
CREDIT CARDS: MC, Visa.
PRICES: per room B&B £107–£220.
1-night bookings sometimes refused weekends in high season.

ST MARTIN Guernsey

## BELLA LUCE HOTEL

Renoir was once drawn to this spot, above Moulin Huet Bay, to capture the ever-changing scene in his Guernsey paintings. Today, it's the Wheadon family's luxurious small hotel, in a tastefully restored Norman manor house, that attracts. Elegant bedrooms, some with a separate sitting area, are supplied with magazines, bathrobes and slippers. Comfortable, too, is the atmospheric cellar lounge, watched over by the traditional copper stills that turn out the owners' small-batch gins. Candles are lit in the evening in the garden-facing restaurant, where diners tuck in to 'outstanding' modern European dishes; in good weather, choose to eat alfresco, under fairy lights and the spread of the tulip tree.

MAP 1: inset E5
La Fosse
St Martin GY4 6EB
T: 01481 238764
w: bellalucehotel.com

BEDROOMS: 23. 2 on ground floor.
OPEN: Apr–Oct.
FACILITIES: bar, snug, 2 restaurants, cellar lounge, private dining room, in-room TV (Freeview), room service, civil wedding licence, function facilities, 2-acre garden, courtyard, outdoor swimming pool, spa, parking.
BACKGROUND MUSIC: in public spaces.
LOCATION: 2 miles from town centre and airport.
CHILDREN: all ages welcomed.
DOGS: not allowed.
CREDIT CARDS: Amex, MC, Visa.
PRICES: per room B&B £144–£235, D,B&B £189–£285. À la carte £38.

ST PETER PORT Guernsey

## LA COLLINETTE HOTEL

The seagulls call over St Peter Port and this unpretentious hotel, where a relaxed, family-friendly atmosphere reigns. Cheery window boxes out front, the Georgian building has been owned and run by the Chambers family since 1960. Cyril Fortier is the long-serving manager. Most of the bright bedrooms have views of the sea; all have tea, coffee and biscuits. Improvements continue: beds and armchairs were recently replaced. At mealtimes, uncomplicated dishes in the informal restaurant might feature Guernsey lobsters and scallops. Visit the German Naval Underground Museum, in former bunkers under today's self-catering accommodation, before heading to the port, a 15-minute stroll away through historic Candie Gardens.

MAP 1: inset E5
St Jacques
St Peter Port GY1 1SN
T: 01481 710331
w: lacollinette.com

BEDROOMS: 23. Plus 14 self-catering cottages and apartments.
OPEN: all year.
FACILITIES: lounge, bar, restaurant, in-room TV (Sky, Freeview), 2-acre garden, outdoor heated swimming pool, children's pool, play area, gym, spa treatments, restaurant and bar wheelchair accessible.
BACKGROUND MUSIC: in bar, restaurant.
LOCATION: less than 1 mile W of town centre.
CHILDREN: all ages welcomed.
DOGS: not allowed.
CREDIT CARDS: MC, Visa.
PRICES: per person B&B from £60.

**BELFAST**

# THE OLD RECTORY

In a leafy suburb, a short bus ride from the centre, Mary Callan makes visitors to her Victorian guest house feel 'very welcome'. The 'nicely furnished' drawing room has board games and books to borrow; a hot whiskey for cool days. Bedrooms are supplied with tea- and coffee-making facilities, biscuits and magazines; there's fresh milk in a mini-fridge on each landing. 'My comfortable upper-floor room had views of the hills west of Belfast; a compact but perfectly good bathroom.' A light supper (home-made soup, beef chilli, frittata, etc) may be requested in advance; in the morning, 'splendid' breakfasts by an open fire 'cater for vegetarians as generously as they do for meat-eaters'. The hostess has much local knowledge to share.

MAP 6:B6
148 Malone Road
Belfast BT9 5LH
T: 028 9066 7882
W: anoldrectory.co.uk

BEDROOMS: 6. 1, on ground floor, suitable for disabled.
OPEN: all year except Christmas, New Year, 2 weeks mid-July.
FACILITIES: drawing room, dining room, in-room TV (Freeview), garden, parking.
BACKGROUND MUSIC: none.
LOCATION: just under 2 miles from city centre.
CHILDREN: all ages welcomed.
DOGS: not allowed.
CREDIT CARDS: MC, Visa.
PRICES: per room B&B £58–£98. 2-night min. stay May–Sept.

**BELFAST**

# RAVENHILL HOUSE

A short bus ride from the city centre, this handsomely restored red-brick B&B is close to popular restaurants, shops and a leafy park. Olive and Roger Nicholson, the owners, provide a warm welcome for arriving guests, with tea and oven-fresh treats. Cosy bedrooms in the Victorian house are decorated with floral prints; in each, there's good seating, home-baked shortbread, a vintage Hacker radio. In a book-lined room with a wood-burning stove, a wide-ranging breakfast is served – until 10 am at weekends. The Nicholsons mill their own flour from organic Irish rye grain for the freshly baked sourdough bread; there are also home-made marmalades and jellies, spiced fruit compotes and good vegetarian options.

MAP 6:B6
690 Ravenhill Road
Belfast BT6 0BZ
T: 028 9028 2590
W: ravenhillhouse.com

BEDROOMS: 5.
OPEN: Feb–15 Dec.
FACILITIES: sitting room/breakfast room, in-room TV (Freeview), small garden, parking.
BACKGROUND MUSIC: Radio 3 at breakfast.
LOCATION: 2 miles S of city centre.
CHILDREN: not under 10.
DOGS: not allowed.
CREDIT CARDS: Amex, MC, Visa.
PRICES: per room B&B £85–£140. 2-night min. stay preferred at busy weekends.

## BUSHMILLS Co. Antrim
## BUSHMILLS INN

A short stroll from the world's oldest distillery, there are peat fires, cosy nooks, a 'secret' library and well-considered bedrooms at this amiable 17th-century coaching inn on the Causeway Coastal Route. Many of the clean-cut bedrooms, each with a sitting area, have a partial view of the River Bush; all are supplied with tea- and coffee-making facilities, bathrobes and slippers. 'Our room was excellent, and very quiet.' In the public rooms, choose an ambience to suit. Eat modern dishes in the garden-facing restaurant or alfresco on the patio; hunker down in the Gas bar, still lit by Victorian gas light, for a Guinness-and-oyster pairing and a Saturday-night live music session – in all, 'a real plus'.

MAP 6:A6
9 Dunluce Road
Bushmills BT57 8QG
T: 028 2073 3000
W: bushmillsinn.com

BEDROOMS: 41. Some, on ground floor, suitable for disabled.
OPEN: all year, no accommodation 24–25 Dec.
FACILITIES: lift, bar, lounge, restaurant, loft, cinema, in-room TV (Freeview), conference facilities, patio, 2-acre garden, parking.
BACKGROUND MUSIC: in public areas, live traditional Irish music sessions every Sat in bar.
LOCATION: in village centre, 2 miles from Giant's Causeway.
CHILDREN: all ages welcomed.
DOGS: allowed on outside patio area.
CREDIT CARDS: Amex, MC, Visa.
PRICES: per room B&B £130–£460.
À la carte £60.

## CARAGH LAKE Co. Kerry
## ARD NA SIDHE
## COUNTRY HOUSE HOTEL

On the wooded shores of Lough Caragh, silent glades in the extensive gardens of this Irish sandstone-built manor house are ripe for discovery; hidden pathways open on to the water, and the mountains beyond. The serene hotel, once a grand private home, has an elegant restaurant for candlelit dinners; afternoon tea is taken in the fire-warmed lounge, or on the terrace in fine weather. In the main house and around a rustic courtyard, handsome bedrooms have antique furnishings and a deep mattress; no TV, but, perhaps, the sound of the water coming to shore. A picnic hamper can be arranged for days out; there's also boating and fishing on the lake. Guests have access to leisure facilities at a sister hotel.

MAP 6:D4
Caragh Lake V93 HV57
T: 00 353 66 976 9105
W: ardnasidhe.com

BEDROOMS: 18. 1 on ground floor, suitable for disabled, 8 in Garden House.
OPEN: Apr–Oct.
FACILITIES: lounge, library, restaurant, terrace, 32-acre grounds.
BACKGROUND MUSIC: in lounge, library.
LOCATION: on the shores of Lough Caragh.
CHILDREN: all ages welcomed.
DOGS: not allowed.
CREDIT CARDS: Amex, MC, Visa.
PRICES: per room B&B double €230–€360, D,B&B €330–€460.
À la carte €60.

CARLINGFORD Co. Louth

# GHAN HOUSE

A tree's length from the medieval town, the Carroll family's listed Georgian house sits within castellated walled gardens, with views of the mountains that surround. It is run by Paul Carroll; his mother, Joyce, tends the garden and adorns the rooms with freshly cut flowers. The house is filled with family photographs and heirlooms, squashy sofas, antique French beds and claw-footed baths. Log-burners warm the drawing room and 'elegant' dining room, where modern Irish menus based on produce from lough and countryside might include scallops, salmon or braised shoulder of wild Wicklow venison. Traditionally decorated bedrooms have a modern bathroom; home-made biscuits to go with garden or mountain views.

MAP 6:B6
Old Quay Lane
Carlingford A91 DXY5
T: 00 353 42 937 3682
W: ghanhouse.com

BEDROOMS: 12. 8 in garden annexe, 4 on ground floor.
OPEN: all year except 24–26, 31 Dec, 1–2 Jan.
FACILITIES: bar, lounge, restaurant, 3 private dining rooms, in-room smart TV (Freeview), wedding facilities, 3-acre garden, parking, electric car charging point.
BACKGROUND MUSIC: in bar, restaurant.
LOCATION: 'a tree length' from town.
CHILDREN: all ages welcomed.
DOGS: allowed in kennels in converted stables, not in bedrooms or public rooms.
CREDIT CARDS: Amex, MC, Visa.
PRICES: per person B&B €85–€125, D,B&B €130–€180. 6-course tasting menu from €45, 4-course menu from €55, 3-course early menu €35.

CLIFDEN Co. Galway

# BLUE QUAY ROOMS

In a colourful coastal town between the mountains and the sea, Paddy and Julia Foyle's good-value B&B above the harbour is in a jauntily refurbished building, minutes from the town centre. Sister to The Quay House on the waterfront (see main entry), it is managed by the Foyles' son, Toby, and Pauline Petit. The 200-year-old building has been painted an emphatic blue; within, playful, modern decor (spot the gold lobster on the wood-burning stove) adds to the fresh, airy atmosphere. Past cosy sitting areas, all but one of the simply decorated bedrooms upstairs look across the harbour. Over an imaginative breakfast, the hosts have much local information to share. An ideal base for walkers and cyclists.

MAP 6:C4
Seaview
Clifden H71 WE02
T: 00 353 87 621 7616
W: bluequayrooms.com

BEDROOMS: 8. Plus 2-bed self-catering apartment.
OPEN: Apr–Oct.
FACILITIES: sitting area, breakfast room, garden.
BACKGROUND MUSIC: none.
LOCATION: close to town centre.
CHILDREN: not under 10.
DOGS: not allowed.
CREDIT CARDS: none accepted.
PRICES: per room B&B single €65–€75, double €70–€100.

COBH Co. Cork

# KNOCKEVEN HOUSE

A gracious hostess in an elegant Victorian house, Pam Mulhaire welcomes B&B guests with hot drinks and home-baked scones. High above Cork harbour, on the outskirts of the historic port town, hers is a peaceful place to be. Past the drawing room, where a fire blazes on cool days, spacious, high-ceilinged bedrooms are filled with period pieces and flower arrangements. They're well supplied, too, with thick towels, terry cloth robes and high-end toiletries. Communal breakfasts, served at a mahogany table in the garden-facing dining room, have plenty of organic produce, plus home-baked brown bread. (Gluten-free options are available for the asking.) Pam has plenty of advice on sightseeing spots nearby.

MAP 6:D5
Rushbrooke
Cobh P24 E392
T: 00 353 21 481 1778
W: knockevenhouse.com

BEDROOMS: 5.
OPEN: 1 Jan–20 Dec.
FACILITIES: drawing room, dining room, in-room TV, 2-acre grounds.
BACKGROUND MUSIC: at breakfast.
LOCATION: 1 mile W of centre.
CHILDREN: all ages welcomed.
DOGS: not allowed.
CREDIT CARDS: MC, Visa.
PRICES: per person B&B €60–€65.

COLLINSTOWN Co. Westmeath

# LOUGH BAWN HOUSE

Four generations of Verity Butterfield's family have lived in this 'impressive' Georgian house, with 'divine' views down rolling meadow to a spring-fed lough. The 'lovely hostess' welcomes guests with afternoon tea before an open fire in the 'cosy' drawing room packed with family heirlooms, books and an abundance of flowers. Home-cooked dinners (by pre-arrangement), served in an elegant dining room, are 'a real treat'. Pretty, country house-style bedrooms overlook the garden or lake; two share a 'wonderful' bathroom (wooden floors, a vast bathtub and 'glorious' walk-in shower). At breakfast, soda bread, granola and preserves are all home made. Lots of walks, and swimming in the lake.

MAP 6:C5
Lough Bane
Collinstown N91 EYX4
T: 00 353 44 966 6186
W: loughbawnhouse.com

BEDROOMS: 4. 2 share a bathroom.
OPEN: all year except Dec.
FACILITIES: 2 sitting rooms, dining room, 50-acre parkland, wild swimming lake.
BACKGROUND MUSIC: none.
LOCATION: beside lake, near village.
CHILDREN: all ages welcomed.
DOGS: allowed by prior arrangement in 2 bedrooms, public rooms (resident dogs).
CREDIT CARDS: MC, Visa.
PRICES: per room B&B single from €85, double €140–€170. Dinner €50. 2-night min. stay at weekends May, June.

**NEW**

## CORK

# MONTENOTTE HOTEL

In an elevated position, this large, modern hotel perches above tiered gardens, taking in an impressive panorama over the city and harbour. With chandeliers hanging from the trees, and a duo of colourful china dogs as greeters, the plushly furnished public spaces are injected with a sense of fun. Diners gather in curving booths in the bistro and on sofas on the spacious terrace for all-day menus of snacks, salads and uncomplicated dishes (grilled sea bass; chestnut gnocchi). Brightly decorated bedrooms, some for a family, are equipped with magazines, bottled waters and hot drinks. There are nightly cinema screenings, and treatments in the spa; the restored Victorian sunken garden is worth a wander.

MAP 6:D5
Middle Glanmire Road
Cork  T23 E9DX
T: 00 353 21 453 0050
W: themontenottehotel.com

BEDROOMS: 107. Some suitable for disabled, plus 26 self-catering apartments.
OPEN: all year except 24–26 Dec.
FACILITIES: lobby, bistro, in-room TV, wedding facilities, spa (20-metre indoor swimming pool, sauna, steam room, hot tub, treatments), cinema, terrace, Victorian gardens and woodland.
BACKGROUND MUSIC: in lobby, restaurant, live piano music at Sunday lunch.
LOCATION: St Luke's Cross district.
CHILDREN: all ages welcomed.
DOGS: only assistance dogs allowed.
CREDIT CARDS: Amex, MC, Visa.
PRICES: per room €139–€279. Breakfast €15, à la carte €55.

## DONEGAL TOWN Co. Donegal

# ARD NA BREATHA

Within their working farm, Theresa and Albert Morrow's rustic B&B yields a genuine welcome. 'Simple, cosy' bedrooms are in an adjoining building, reached via a covered walkway; there are king-size beds, wool rugs, pine furnishings. The Morrows start their day at dawn, rising to lamb sheep when needed, but encourage guests to take their French toast and scrambled eggs (cooked to order and served in the main house) at a more civilised hour. Books, an honesty bar and a turf fire create a homely atmosphere in the residents' lounge. Dinner can be arranged for groups of ten or more, but the hosts are helpful with advice and booking for local eating options. Donegal is a ten-minute walk along a quiet path.

MAP 6:B5
Drumrooske Middle
Donegal Town
T: 00 353 74 972 2288
W: ardnabreatha.com

BEDROOMS: 6. All in adjoining annexe.
OPEN: mid-Feb–end Oct.
FACILITIES: bar, lounge, restaurant, in-room TV (Freeview), 1-acre grounds.
BACKGROUND MUSIC: in bar, restaurant at breakfast.
LOCATION: 1¼ miles NE of town centre.
CHILDREN: all ages welcomed.
DOGS: allowed in bedrooms (not unattended), sitting room, garden.
CREDIT CARDS: MC, Visa.
PRICES: per person B&B €35–€63. À la carte (for groups of 10 or more) €39.

DUBLIN
## ARIEL HOUSE

Within easy reach of the centre, Jennie
McKeown's 'warmly welcoming' guest house
occupies three connected Victorian town houses
in the Ballsbridge neighbourhood. A series of
stone steps from the leafy street rises to the front
door; just beyond, sympathetically restored
interiors retain gracious original features:
Flemish brickwork, ornate stained glass, huge
sash windows. Elegant bedrooms are styled
with antiques and Victorian-inspired fabrics;
spacious family rooms in the modern wing can
accommodate a group of four. A thoughtful
touch: complimentary home-baked cakes and
biscuits appear in the afternoon. Breakfast – a
feast of locally sourced produce – is served in a
bright room with a garden-facing conservatory.

MAP 6:C6
50–54 Lansdowne Road
Dublin 4
T: 00 353 1 668 5512
W: ariel-house.net

BEDROOMS: 37. 8 in mews, attached to
main house.
OPEN: all year except end Dec–early
Jan.
FACILITIES: drawing room, dining
room, in-room TV, garden, limited
parking.
BACKGROUND MUSIC: at breakfast in
dining room.
LOCATION: in Ballsbridge area, about
1½ miles from city centre.
CHILDREN: all ages welcomed.
DOGS: not allowed.
CREDIT CARDS: Amex, MC, Visa.
PRICES: per room B&B €99–€260.

**NEW**

DUBLIN
## SCHOOLHOUSE HOTEL

In Ballsbridge, a tree-lined residential district
within walking distance of the centre, this 19th-
century schoolhouse by the Grand Canal is today
a hotel with a restaurant and a 'very jolly' bar.
The Victorian building flaunts distinctive turrets
and high chimneys; an original wooden staircase,
panelled walls and a stone fireplace within.
Period-style bedrooms (some in the basement)
are decorated with pastel shades and William
Morris patterns; the best rooms have canal or
garden views, or access to the lawn. Pub classics
and 'basic' bistro dishes (beetroot and goat's cheese
salad; chargrilled chicken burger) are served all
day under a vaulted ceiling in the restaurant and
lively bar, or alfresco on the terrace.

MAP 6:C6
2–8 Northumberland Road
Dublin 4
T: 00 353 1 667 5014
W: schoolhousehotel.com

BEDROOMS: 31. Some on ground floor.
OPEN: all year except 24–26 Dec.
FACILITIES: bar, restaurant, private
dining/meeting room, in-room TV,
wedding facilities, ½-acre garden,
limited parking.
BACKGROUND MUSIC: in bar, restaurant.
LOCATION: in Ballsbridge
neighbourhood, 15 mins' walk from
St Stephen's Green.
CHILDREN: all ages welcomed.
DOGS: only assistance dogs allowed.
CREDIT CARDS: Amex, MC, Visa.
PRICES: per person B&B €89–€399. Set
menus €25 (2 courses), €30 (3 courses).
À la carte €42.

INIS MEAIN Co. Galway

# INIS MEAIN RESTAURANT AND SUITES

At one with the elements, Ruairí and Marie-Thérèse de Blacam's sustainably run restaurant-with-suites was designed to blend in to the landscape of its remote Aran island setting. Wood, lime, stone and wool give form to the large, linear architectural suites; each has vast views from an outdoor seating area. Succinct menus use the best of prime island produce, the restaurant's greenhouse and the surrounding waters, with such dishes as beetroot carpaccio; lobster with aïoli. Breakfast is delivered to the door. The two- or four-night booking packages include a daily hotpot lunch and use of an exploration kit with the essentials: bicycles, fishing rods, swimming towels, binoculars, nature guides and maps.

MAP 6:C4
Inis Meáin
Aran Islands H91 NX86
T: 00 353 86 826 6026
W: inismeain.com

BEDROOMS: 5 suites.
OPEN: Wed–Sat, Apr–Aug; Mon–Thurs, Mar, Sept–Oct.
FACILITIES: restaurant, 3-acre grounds.
BACKGROUND MUSIC: none.
LOCATION: centre of a small island, 15 miles off the Galway coast; 40-min. ferry from Ros a' Mhíl; 7-min. flight from Connemara airport.
CHILDREN: not under 12.
DOGS: not allowed.
CREDIT CARDS: MC, Visa.
PRICES: per suite B&B €480–€700, includes daily hotpot lunch, exploration kit (bicycles, fishing rods, walking sticks, binoculars, etc), collections to and from ferry port or airport. Set 4-course dinner €75. 2-night min. stay Apr–Aug, 4-night min. stay Mar, Sept–Oct.

KANTURK Co. Cork

# GLENLOHANE

History is in the walls of this ivy-clad Georgian country house, which stands in lawns and parkland in the Blackwater valley, surrounded by the stately trees that have looked over it for centuries. Visitors come to stay 'as if with friends', welcomed by Desmond and Melanie Sharp Bolster, and their son, Gordon, the ninth and tenth generations of the family to live here since the house was built in 1741. From the book-lined study to the airy drawing room, the gracious interior brims with heirlooms and memorabilia; spacious country-style bedrooms are fittingly old-fashioned. The hosts can recommend nearby eateries; alternatively, give a day's notice and dine in. Irish breakfasts are cooked on the Aga.

MAP 6:D5
Kanturk P51 CK31
T: 00 353 29 50014
W: glenlohane.com

BEDROOMS: 3. Plus 3-bed self-catering wheelchair-accessible cottage nearby.
OPEN: all year.
FACILITIES: drawing room, library, dining room, walled garden (terraced lawns, croquet), 250-acre farmland.
BACKGROUND MUSIC: none.
LOCATION: 1½ miles E of town.
CHILDREN: not under 12.
DOGS: not allowed.
CREDIT CARDS: Amex, MC, Visa.
PRICES: per room B&B single €135–€150, double €235–€250, D,B&B double €285–€300. 2-night min. stay preferred.

## KENMARE Co. Kerry
# BROOK LANE HOTEL

'A genuine sense of hospitality' – and an interesting collection of local art – fill Una and Dermot Brennan's 'attractively priced' hotel, in a pretty town between the Ring of Beara and the Ring of Kerry. Modern bedrooms are supplied with bottled water and a yoga mat, plus bathrobes and slippers in the bathroom; freshly brewed tea and coffee are brought to the room, on request, with home-baked biscuits. At lunch and dinner, find a spot in Casey's bar/restaurant for comforting bistro-style dishes such as Kenmare Bay seafood chowder or rare-breed sausage cassoulet. Sister restaurant No. 35 is 15 minutes' walk away. Plenty of choice at breakfast, from potato cakes to porridge with a slug of Jameson.

MAP 6:D4
Sneem Road
Kenmare V93 T289
T: 00 353 64 664 2077
W: brooklanehotel.com

BEDROOMS: 22. 9 on ground floor, 1 suitable for disabled.
OPEN: all year except 24–26 Dec.
FACILITIES: lift, bar/restaurant, library, reception area (seating, open fire), in-room TV, wedding facilities, parking, public areas wheelchair accessible, adapted toilet.
BACKGROUND MUSIC: in public areas, live music events in Casey's bar.
LOCATION: 5 mins' walk from town centre.
CHILDREN: all ages welcomed.
DOGS: not allowed.
CREDIT CARDS: MC, Visa.
PRICES: per room B&B single €80–€155, double €115–€285. À la carte €35.

## KILKENNY Co. Kilkenny
# ROSQUIL HOUSE

Across the River Nore from the medieval town, Phil and Rhoda Nolan's friendly B&B is well located for visiting Kilkenny's castle and cathedral. Bedrooms of varied sizes are neatly and simply styled; families have a choice of rooms, including a separate self-catering apartment with its own entrance. The extensive breakfast, made with local produce, is a point of pride: there are fresh and poached fruit, local cheeses, home-made granola and home-baked bread; Phil's cooked-to-order dishes include a full Irish and a choice of omelettes. Experienced, enthusiastic hosts, the Nolans are well placed to advise on local heritage spots and trips further afield; woodland and riverbank walks are within easy reach.

MAP 6:D5
Castlecomer Road
Kilkenny R95 P962
T: 00 353 56 772 1419
W: rosquilhouse.com

BEDROOMS: 7. 1 on ground floor, plus a self-catering apartment.
OPEN: all year except over Christmas period.
FACILITIES: lounge, dining room, in-room TV, smoking patio, ¼-acre garden.
BACKGROUND MUSIC: Irish or classical music in reception and dining room.
LOCATION: 5 mins' drive from town centre.
CHILDREN: all ages welcomed.
DOGS: allowed, by prior arrangement.
CREDIT CARDS: MC, Visa.
PRICES: per room B&B €85–€110.

**NEW**

MAP 6:D5
45 Main Street
Kinsale P17 K651
T: 00 353 21 477 4373
W: gilesnormantownhouse.com

### KINSALE Co. Cork

# GILES NORMAN TOWNHOUSE

Ready for its close-up, this Georgian town house in the centre of the historic harbour town has been stylishly renovated to include urbane, understated guestrooms close to the quays. It is owned by landscape photographer Giles Norman and his wife, Catherine, who have hung fine black-and-white photographic prints throughout the house. Above the gallery and shop on the ground floor, chic, contemporary bedrooms up the stairs are equipped with teas and a coffee machine, plus organic Irish toiletries; most have waterfront views. A spacious suite with handsome beams is under the eaves. No meals are served, but the bars, cafés and notable restaurants of the foodie town are within a few minutes' walk.

BEDROOMS: 5.
OPEN: 10 Mar–12 Dec.
FACILITIES: in-room TV.
BACKGROUND MUSIC: none.
LOCATION: in town centre.
CHILDREN: not allowed.
DOGS: not allowed.
CREDIT CARDS: MC, Visa.
PRICES: per room €130–€230. 1-night bookings refused bank holiday weekends.

**NEW**

MAP 6:C4
Kincora Road
Lisdoonvarna V95 P234
T: 00 353 65 707 4300
W: wildhoneyinn.com

### LISDOONVARNA Co. Clare

# WILD HONEY INN

Discerning diners make a beeline for chef/patron Aidan McGrath's 19th-century pub-with-rooms (the first in Ireland to win a Michelin star), which he runs with his partner, Kate, in a spa town on the edge of the Burren. In the informal bar and dining room, the refined bistro cooking uses flavourful Irish produce – organic vegetables, freshly picked berries, seasonal game, wild fish straight off the day boat. Typical dishes on the fixed-price menus: Lough Neagh smoked eel, fennel, apple; Irish Hereford rib-eye, crisp-fried celeriac. Simply decorated bedrooms, some snug, have a traditional country charm; the best have countryside views or a terrace with garden access. Delicious breakfasts fuel nature walks nearby.

BEDROOMS: 13. Some on ground floor.
OPEN: Mar–end Oct, restaurant closed Sun–Wed in Mar, Apr, Oct; Sun, Mon in May–Sept.
FACILITIES: bar, lounge, restaurant, library, in-room TV, garden.
BACKGROUND MUSIC: 'easy listening' in bar in evening, classical radio at breakfast.
LOCATION: on the edge of town.
CHILDREN: not under 12 in restaurant, not under 14 overnight.
DOGS: not allowed.
CREDIT CARDS: MC, Visa.
PRICES: per room B&B €170–€220, D,B&B from €320. Prix fixe menu €75. 2-night min. stay at weekends.

MAGHERAFELT Co. Londonderry
## LAUREL VILLA TOWNHOUSE
B&B guests find a fascinating collection of
books and memorabilia behind the bright red
door of Eugene and Gerardine Kielt's elegant
villa, a literary haven for Seamus Heaney fans.
Bedrooms, each named after a great Ulster poet,
display framed works and portraits of the writers;
each room has a desk among its period pieces, and
a host of modern amenities (tea-/coffee-making
facilities; blackout curtains; a power shower in the
bathroom). Home-baked scones and a full Ulster
are served at breakfast in the wood-panelled
dining room, beneath Heaney poems on scrolls.
Eugene Kielt, a Blue Badge guide, gives award-
winning tours of the area, revealing the everyday
landscapes that inspired the poet and playwright.

MAP 6:B6
60 Church Street
Magherafelt BT45 6AW
T:  028 7930 1459
W: laurel-villa.com

BEDROOMS: 4.
OPEN: all year.
FACILITIES: 2 lounges, dining room,
in-room TV, patio, ¼-acre garden,
parking.
BACKGROUND MUSIC: none.
LOCATION: town centre.
CHILDREN: all ages welcomed.
DOGS: not allowed.
CREDIT CARDS: MC, Visa.
PRICES: per room B&B single £70,
double £95.

PORTMAGEE Co. Kerry
## THE MOORINGS
On the waterfront of the working fishing village,
this brightly painted Irish tavern and family-run
guest house is full of all the nooks, crannies and
maritime memorabilia a guest hopes to find. A
lively spot, it is well liked by locals for its buzzy
bar and straight-off-the-boat seafood. Upstairs,
simply decorated modern bedrooms have all the
basics: a drinks tray, toiletries, an iron and ironing
board. Some, with an extra bed, can accommodate
a family; others, with a separate sea-view sitting
area, have a spa bath in the bathroom. Home-
made brown breads and a full Irish, with local
sausages, bolster a day of wildlife-watching along
the coast. Boats to the Skellig islands leave from
the pier, steps away.

MAP 6:D4
Main Street
Portmagee V23 RX05
T:  00 353 66 947 7108
W: moorings.ie

BEDROOMS: 16. Some in annexe.
OPEN: all year except Christmas and
New Year, restaurant closed Mon/
Tues Mar–Oct.
FACILITIES: bar, restaurant, in-room
TV.
BACKGROUND MUSIC: in bar.
LOCATION: 10 miles from the Ring of
Kerry (N70).
CHILDREN: all ages welcomed.
DOGS: not allowed.
CREDIT CARDS: Amex, MC, Visa.
PRICES: per room B&B single €70–€160,
double €100–€170.

RAMELTON Co. Donegal

# FREWIN

From the stained-glass windows and airy, white-linened bedrooms to the bone china cups at tea, there's an old-world charm at this creeper-covered former rectory, on the outskirts of a Georgian port town on the Wild Atlantic Way. The B&B is owned and run by Regina Gibson and Thomas Coyle, who have restored the home with period flair. Antiques and potted plants share the sitting room; spacious, traditionally decorated bedrooms, each with a compact bathroom, might have a four-poster bed, a roll-top bath or a separate sitting area. Communal breakfasts have a view on the mature wooded grounds. The congenial hosts can help arrange golf, fishing, horse riding and guided hikes in the Bluestack mountains.

MAP 6:B5
Rectory Road
Ramelton
T: 00 353 74 915 1246
W: frewinhouse.com

BEDROOMS: 3. Plus cottage in grounds.
OPEN: Mar–end Oct, by special arrangement for small groups in Feb and Nov.
FACILITIES: sitting room, library, dining room, 2-acre garden.
BACKGROUND MUSIC: none.
LOCATION: outskirts of town.
CHILDREN: not under 12.
DOGS: not allowed.
CREDIT CARDS: MC, Visa.
PRICES: per person B&B single €90–€125, double €85–€95.

RATHNEW Co. Wicklow

# HUNTER'S

In 'lovely' grounds by the River Vartry, this rambling, 'extremely comfy' property enveloped in olde-worlde charm is a 'special' place, says a Guide reader this year. 'It's like walking back in time.' Said to be Ireland's oldest coaching inn, it has been owned by the same family for almost 200 years; the current stewards, the Gelletlie brothers, run it with 'acceptable eccentricity'. Antiques, old prints and floral fabrics decorate the rooms; most of the chintz-filled bedrooms overlook the 'inspiring' garden. In the dining room: crisp table linens and 'delicious' classic cuisine. Throughout, 'the staff really make an effort'. 'Well worth a stop-over from the Rosslare ferry.' Gardens and golf courses are close.

**25% DISCOUNT VOUCHERS**

MAP 6:C6
Newrath Bridge
Rathnew  A67 TN30
T: 00 353 404 40106
W: hunters.ie

BEDROOMS: 16. 1 on ground floor.
OPEN: all year except 24–26 Dec.
FACILITIES: drawing room, lounge, bar, dining room, private dining room, in-room TV (Freeview), 5-acre grounds, golf, tennis, fishing nearby.
BACKGROUND MUSIC: none.
LOCATION: 1 mile SE of Ashford.
CHILDREN: all ages welcomed.
DOGS: allowed in bedrooms only, by arrangement.
CREDIT CARDS: MC, Visa.
PRICES: per person B&B €70–€80, D,B&B €100–€145. Set dinner from €32.75, à la carte from €29.75.

RECESS Co. Galway

## LOUGH INAGH LODGE

In the embrace of mountains, this Victorian fishing lodge stands in 'a spectacular position' before a panorama of Lough Inagh. It has been owned by the O'Connor family for over 30 years. The library and well-appointed sitting room are decorated with antiques and artwork; when the weather calls for it, a fire burns in the open fireplaces. In the dining room, Irish food with French flair (perhaps Killary lobster with lemon butter) is served on white table linens; the panelled bar has simpler fare. Among the traditionally furnished bedrooms, those with a lough view are 'worth the extra'. Days out include walks by the lake, and fishing accompanied by a ghillie; Kylemore Abbey and its Victorian walled garden are a short, scenic drive away.

MAP 6:C4
Recess
T: 00 353 95 34706
W: loughinaghlodgehotel.ie

BEDROOMS: 13. 4 on ground floor, 1 suitable for disabled.
OPEN: Mar–Dec.
FACILITIES: sitting room, bar, library, dining room, in-room TV (Freeview), wedding facilities, 14-acre grounds.
BACKGROUND MUSIC: none.
LOCATION: 3 miles N of Recess, on the lough's eastern shore.
CHILDREN: all ages welcomed.
DOGS: allowed in bedrooms, public rooms.
CREDIT CARDS: Amex, MC, Visa.
PRICES: per room B&B single from €90, double €165–€255. À la carte €50.

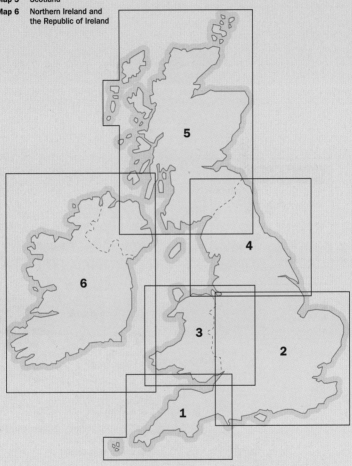

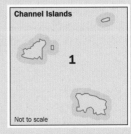

Channel Islands

1

Not to scale

# MAP 1 · SOUTH-WEST ENGLAND

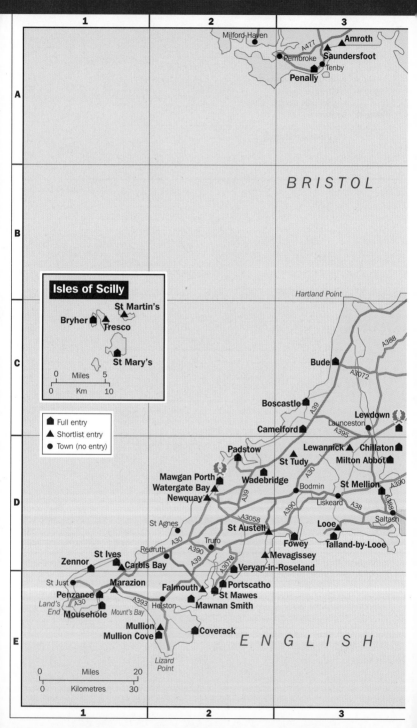

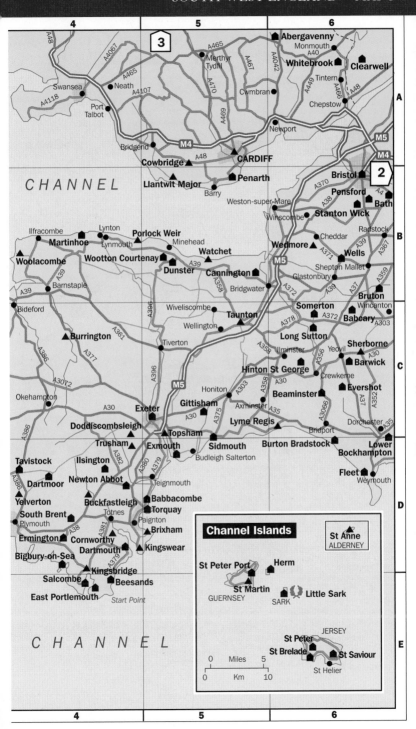

**3**

**2**

| | 4 | 5 | 6 | |
|---|---|---|---|---|

A48
A4067
A465
Swansea
Neath
A4107
Port Talbot
A4118
Bridgend
M4
A48
Cowbridge
CARDIFF
Merthyr Tydfil
A465
A467
A470
A42
Cwmbran
A469
Newport
Abergavenny
Monmouth
A40
Whitebrook
A449
Tintern
A466
Clearwell
A48
Chepstow
M5
M4

CHANNEL

Llantwit Major
Barry
Penarth
Weston-super-Mare
Bristol
A370
A38
Pensford
Bath
A4
Radstock
A39
A367
A359

Ilfracombe
Lynton
Porlock Weir
Minehead
Martinhoe
Lynmouth
Woolacombe
Wootton Courtenay
Dunster
A39
Watchet
Cannington
Bridgwater
A358
M5
Stanton Wick
Wedmore
A371
Cheddar
Winscombe
Wells
Shepton Mallet
Glastonbury
A37
Bruton
Wincanton

Barnstaple
A39
Bideford
Burrington
A361
Wiveliscombe
Taunton
Wellington
Tiverton
A396
A386
A371
A3072
Okehampton
A30
A386
M5

Somerton
A372
Babcary
A303
Long Sutton
A378
Ilminster
A356
Yeovil
Sherborne
A30
Barwick
Hinton St George
A358
Crewkerne
Evershot
A358
Honiton
A303
A35
Beaminster
A30
A37
A352
Exeter
Doddiscombsleigh
Gittisham
Axminster
A375
Lyme Regis
A3066
Bridport
Dorchester
A35
Lower Bockhampton

Trusham
Topsham
Exmouth
Sidmouth
Budleigh Salterton
Burton Bradstock
Tavistock
Ilsington
A382
A380
A379
Teignmouth
Fleet
Weymouth
Dartmoor
Newton Abbot
Yelverton
Buckfastleigh
Totnes
Babbacombe
Torquay
South Brent
Plymouth
A38
A381
Paignton
Brixham
Ermington
Cornworthy
Dartmouth
Kingswear
Bigbury-on-Sea
A379
Salcombe
Kingsbridge
Beesands
East Portlemouth
Start Point

CHANNEL

**Channel Islands**

St Anne
ALDERNEY

St Peter Port
Herm
St Martin
GUERNSEY
Little Sark
SARK

JERSEY
St Peter
St Brelade
St Saviour
St Helier

0 Miles 5
0 Km 10

MAP 2 • SOUTHERN ENGLAND

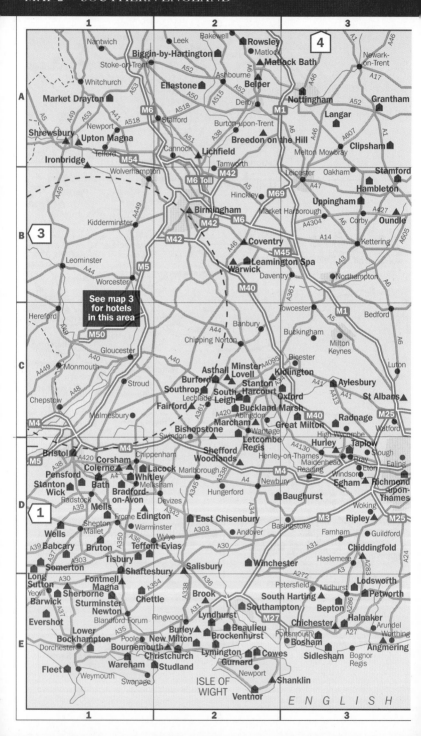

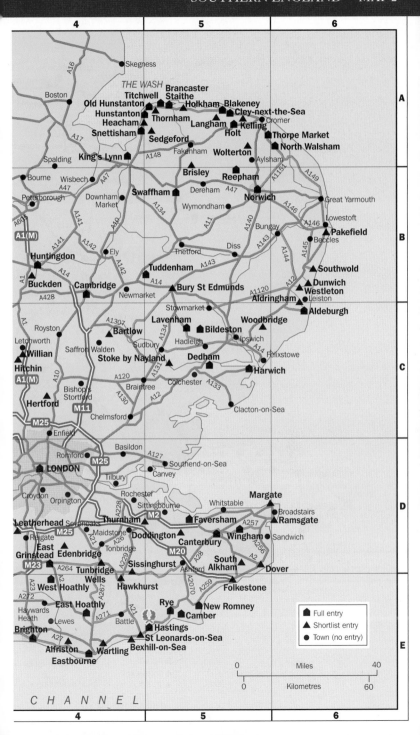

**4**　　**5**　　**6**

Skegness

Boston

A16

A17

*THE WASH*

Brancaster
Staithe
Titchwell　Holkham　Blakeney
Old Hunstanton　　　　Cley-next-the-Sea
Hunstanton　Thornham　　　Cromer
Heacham　Langham　Kelling
Snettisham　　Holt
Sedgeford　　Wolterton　Thorpe Market
Fakenham　　　　North Walsham

A148

King's Lynn

Spalding

Bourne　Wisbech
A47　A47
Peterborough　A141
Downham
Market
A605　A1(M)
A142　Ely
A141
Huntingdon
A1　A142
Buckden
A428　Cambridge
Newmarket

A17

Brisley　Reepham

Swaffham
Dereham
A134
Wymondham
Norwich
Great Yarmouth
A146
Lowestoft
A1151　A149
Aylsham
A140
Bungay　A146
A145　Pakefield
Beccles
A11　Diss
Thetford　A143
A143　Southwold
Tuddenham　A144　Dunwich
Bury St Edmunds　Westleton
A14　A1120　Aldringham
A1307　Stowmarket　Leiston
Bartlow　Lavenham　Aldeburgh
Royston　Bildeston　Woodbridge
Letchworth　Sudbury　Hadleigh
Willian　Saffron Walden　Stoke by Nayland
Hitchin　Dedham　Ipswich
A1(M)　A120　Felixstowe
A10　Braintree　Harwich
Hertford　Bishop's　Colchester　A133
M11　Stortford　A12　Clacton-on-Sea
M25　A130　Chelmsford
Enfield

Basildon
Romford　M25　A127　Southend-on-Sea
LONDON　Tilbury　Canvey
Croydon　Orpington　Rochester　Whitstable　Margate
Leatherhead　Sevenoaks　Sittingbourne　M2　Broadstairs
Reigate　M25　Thurnham　Faversham　Ramsgate
East　Maidstone　Doddington　A257　Sandwich
Grinstead　Edenbridge　Tonbridge　Canterbury　Wingham
M23　A264　Sissinghurst　M20　South　Dover
West Hoathly　Tunbridge　Ashford　Alkham
Wells　Hawkhurst　A2070　Folkestone
East Hoathly　A21　Rye　New Romney
Brighton　Battle　Camber
Alfriston　Hastings
Eastbourne　Wartling　St Leonards-on-Sea
Bexhill-on-Sea
Haywards
Heath　Lewes

A16
A47
A1
A14
A134
A11
A140
A143
A144
A145
A146
A149
A1151
A1120
A12
A133
A130
A127
A228
A21
A26
A229
A28
A2
A256
A257
A20
A259
A2070
A271
A27
A272
A23
A267
A264
A26

*Miles*
0　　　　40
0　　　　60
*Kilometres*

■ Full entry
▲ Shortlist entry
● Town (no entry)

C H A N N E L

**4**　　**5**　　**6**

# MAP 3 · WALES AND THE COTSWOLDS

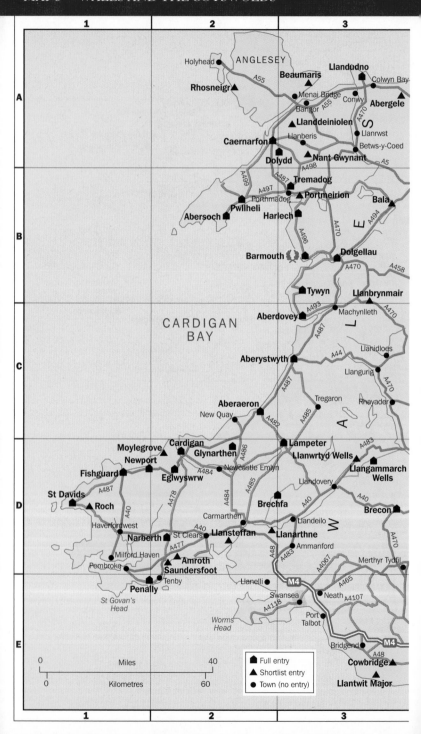

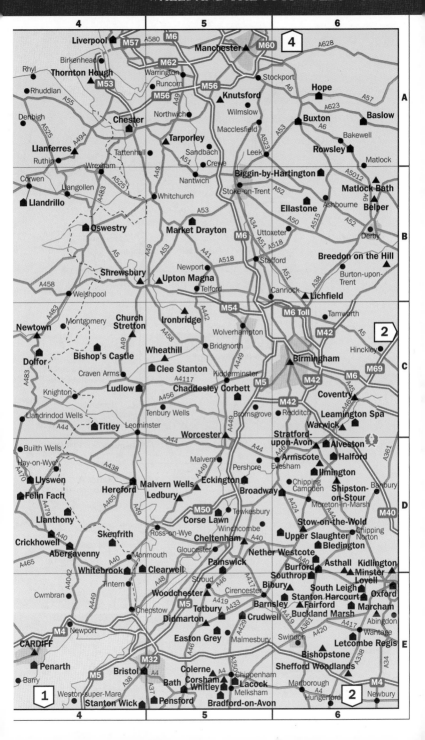

MAP 4 • THE NORTH OF ENGLAND AND THE LAKE DISTRICT

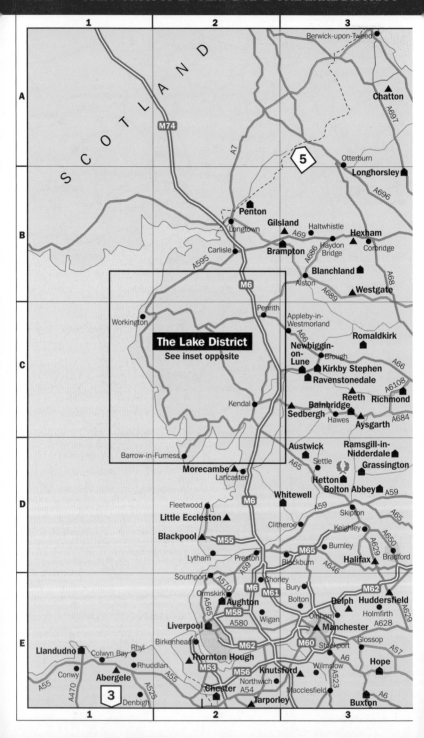

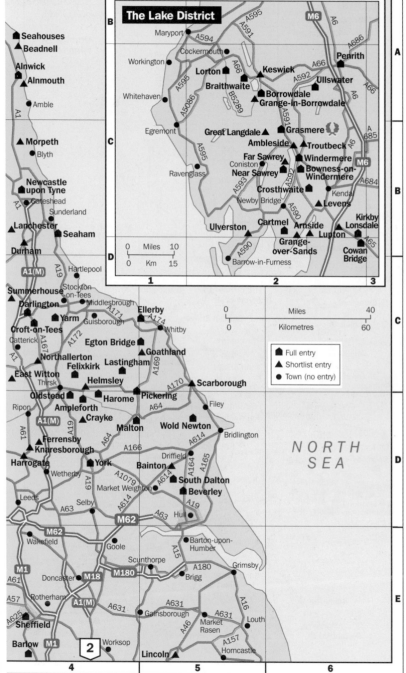

**4** **5** **6**

## The Lake District

B

Maryport
A594
M6 A6

A595 A591

A

Cockermouth
Workington A66 A686 Penrith
Lorton Keswick A592 Ullswater
Braithwaite A595 A66 A6
B5289
Whitehaven Borrowdale
A5086 Grange-in-Borrowdale A66

Egremont Great Langdale Grasmere A685 A
A591
Ambleside Troutbeck
C Far Sawrey Windermere A6 M6
Coniston
Ravenglass Near Sawrey Bowness-on-Windermere
A595 A593 Windermere A684
Crosthwaite
Newby Bridge A590 Kendal Levens

Ulverston Cartmel Arside Kirkby B
A590 Arnside Lonsdale
Grange- Lupton
over-Sands A65
0 Miles 10 Cowan
Barrow-in-Furness Bridge
D 0 Km 15

**1** **2** **3**

A19
Hartlepool
A1(M) Stockton-on-Tees
Summerhouse
Darlington Middlesbrough
Yarm A171 Ellerby C
A174
Croft-on-Tees Guisborough Whitby
Catterick A172
Egton Bridge
A1 Northallerton A169 Goathland
Felixkirk Lastingham
East Witton Helmsley A170 Scarborough
Thirsk
Oldstead Harome Pickering
Ampleforth Filey D
Ripon A1(M) Crayke A64
Malton Wold Newton
A61 Ferrensby A166 Bridlington
Knaresborough Driffield A614
Harrogate A19 A164 A165 NORTH
York Bainton SEA
Wetherby A1079 A614 South Dalton
Leeds A19 Market Weighton Beverley
Selby A614
A63 Hull
A62 A63 A19
M62
Wakefield Goole Barton-upon-Humber
M1 M62 A15
Scunthorpe Grimsby
M1 Doncaster M18 M180 Brigg
A61 Gainsborough A631 Louth E
A57 A1(M) A631 A16
A625 A46 Market Rasen
Sheffield A631
A157 Horncastle
Barlow M1 **2** Worksop Lincoln

**4** **5** **6**

Full entry
Shortlist entry
Town (no entry)

0 Miles 40
0 Kilometres 60

# MAP 5 · SCOTLAND

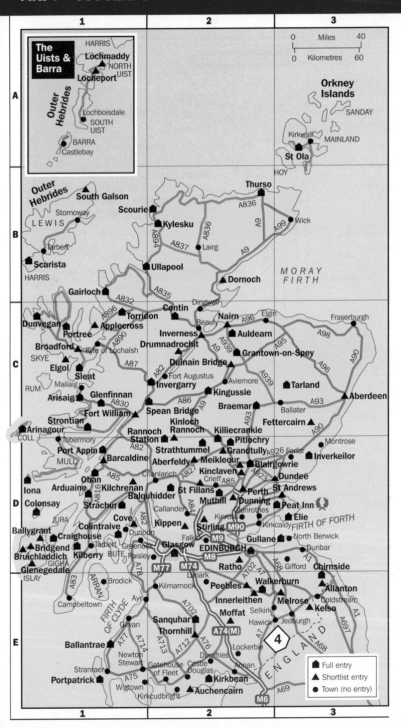

**The Uists & Barra**

Outer Hebrides

HARRIS
▲ Lochmaddy
NORTH UIST
▲ Locheport

● Lochboisdale
SOUTH UIST

● BARRA
Castlebay

**Orkney Islands**

SANDAY

MAINLAND

Kirkwall

■ **St Ola**

HOY

0 — Miles — 40
0 — Kilometres — 60

Outer Hebrides

▲ **South Galson**

● Stornoway

LEWIS

■ **Scarista**

● Tarbert

HARRIS

▲ **Thurso**

■ **Scourie**

▲ **Kylesku**

A836

A894
A837
● Lairg
A836
A9

● Wick
A99

*M O R A Y FIRTH*

▲ **Ullapool**

▲ **Dornoch**

A835

▲ **Gairloch**

A832

● Dingwall

■ **Contin**

▲ **Torridon**

▲ **Applecross**

A896
A890

Beauly

▲ **Nairn**
A96
● Elgin

■ **Auldearn**

■ **Fraserburgh**

A98

▲ **Dunvegan**

▲ **Portree**

▲ **Broadford**

SKYE

● Kyle of Lochalsh

■ **Inverness**

■ **Drumnadrochit**

A82
A9
A939

▲ **Grantown-on-Spey**

A95
A96
A90

▲ **Elgol**

▲ **Sleat**

RUM

A87

● Fort Augustus

■ **Dulnain Bridge**

● Aviemore

A939

▲ **Tarland**

▲ **Glenfinnan**

A830

● Mallaig

▲ **Invergarry**

A82

■ **Kingussie**

▲ **Aberdeen**

▲ **Arisaig**

A86

■ **Braemar**

● Ballater
A93

■ **Strontian**

▲ **Fort William**

▲ **Spean Bridge**

A9

A93

▲ **Fettercairn**
A90

● Montrose

▲ **Arinagour**

COLL

● Tobermory

■ **Rannoch Station**

■ **Kinloch Rannoch**

▲ **Killiecrankie**

A9

▲ **Port Appin**

A82

▲ **Strathtummel**

■ **Pitlochry**

● Forfar

▲ **Barcaldine**

■ **Aberfeldy**

▲ **Meikleour**

▲ **Grandtully**
A926

■ **Inverkeilor**

MULL

● Crianlarich

A827

■ **Blairgowrie**

▲ **Oban**

A85

■ **Kinclaven**

● Crieff
A85

■ **Dundee**

▲ **Iona**

▲ **Arduaine**

A819

▲ **Kilchrenan**

▲ **Balquhidder**

■ **St Fillans**

A822

■ **Perth**

A923

■ **St Andrews**

▲ **Colonsay**

▲ **Strachur**

■ **Muthill**

■ **Dunning**

■ **Peat Inn**

JURA

▲ **Cove**

● Callander

A84

● Kinross

● Glenrothes

■ **Elie**

*FIRTH OF FORTH*

▲ **Ballygrant**

▲ **Colintraive**

A83

■ **Kippen**

▲ **Stirling**

● Kirkcaldy

● North Berwick

▲ **Craighouse**

● Dunoon

A82

● Falkirk

M90

M9

▲ **Gullane**

▲ **Bridgend**

● Tarbert

● Greenock

▲ **Glasgow**

M8

● Dunbar

▲ **Bruichladdich**

▲ **Kilberry**

BUTE

● Paisley

■ **EDINBURGH**

A1

▲ **Glenegedale**

ISLAY

GIGHA

M77

M74

■ **Ratho**

A702
A7

● Gifford

■ **Chirnside**

ARRAN

● Brodick

A78

● Lanark

■ **Peebles**

■ **Walkerburn**

▲ **Allanton**

● Campbeltown

*FIRTH OF CLYDE*

● Kilmarnock

■ **Innerleithen**

■ **Melrose**

● Coldstream

■ **Kelso**

● Ayr

A702

■ **Moffat**

● Selkirk

■ **Ballantrae**

● Girvan

A77
A714

▲ **Sanquhar**

▲ **Thornhill**

A74(M)

● Hawick

● Jedburgh

A68
A697

**4**

A713
A712
A76

● Lockerbie

● Stranraer

▲ **Portpatrick**

● Newton Stewart

A75

● Gatehouse of Fleet

● Castle Douglas

● Dumfries

● Annan

A74

*E N G L A N D*

A69

● Wigtown

● Kirkcudbright

■ **Kirkbean**

▲ **Auchencairn**

M6

A68

■ Full entry
▲ Shortlist entry
● Town (no entry)

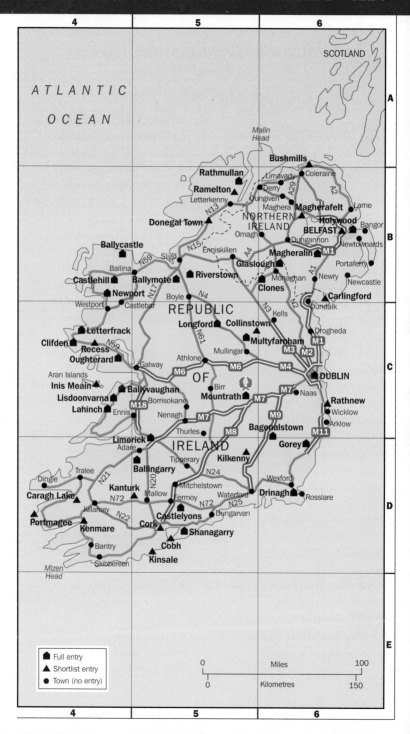

SCOTLAND

*ATLANTIC*

*OCEAN*

Malin
Head

Bushmills

Rathmullan
Limavady Coleraine
Ramelton Derry
Letterkenny Dungiven A29 R2 Larne
N13 Maghera Magherafelt
NORTHERN Holywood Bangor
Donegal Town IRELAND BELFAST
Omagh Dungannon Newtownards
N15 Enniskillen A4 Magheralin M1
Ballycastle N59 Sligo Glasclough A1 Portaferry
Ballina Riverstown Monaghan Newry Newcastle
Castlehill Ballymote N17 Clones A3
Newport Boyle N4 Dundalk Carlingford
Westport Castlebar
REPUBLIC N3 Kells Drogheda
Letterfrack Longford Collinstown M1
Clifden N61 Multyfaroham M3
Recess OF Mullingar M2
Oughterard Galway M6 Athlone M6 M4
Aran Islands Birr DUBLIN
Inis Meáin Ballyvaughan Mountrath M7 Naas
Lisdoonvarna M18 Borrisokane M7 Rathnew
Lahinch Nenagh M9 Wicklow
Ennis M7 Arklow
Limerick Thurles M8 Bagenalstown M11
Adare IRELAND Gorey
Ballingarry Tipperary Kilkenny
Tralee N21 Mitchelstown N24 Wexford
Dingle Kanturk Mallow Waterford Drinagh
Caragh Lake N72 Fermoy N72 Dungarvan Rosslare
Killarney N25
Portmagee N22 Castlelyons
Kenmare Cork Shanagarry
Bantry Cobh
Mizen Skibbereen Kinsale
Head

**Legend:**
- ■ Full entry
- ▲ Shortlist entry
- ● Town (no entry)

Miles
0 — 100
0 — 150
Kilometres

# ALPHABETICAL LIST OF HOTELS
(S) indicates a Shortlist entry

# INDEX OF HOTELS BY COUNTY
(S) indicates a Shortlist entry

# FREQUENTLY ASKED QUESTIONS

## HOW DO YOU CHOOSE A GOOD HOTEL?

The hotels we like are relaxed, unstuffy and personally run. We do not have a specific template: our choices vary greatly in style and size. Most of the hotels in the Guide are family owned and family run. These are places where the needs and comfort of the guest are put ahead of the convenience of the management.

## YOU ARE A HOTEL GUIDE – WHY DO YOU INCLUDE SO MANY PUBS AND B&BS?

Attitudes and expectations have changed considerably since the Guide was founded in the 1970s. Today's guests expect more informality, less deference. There has been a noticeable rise in the standards of food and accommodation in pubs and restaurants. This is demonstrated by the number of such places suggested to us by our readers. While pubs may have a more relaxed attitude than some traditional hotels, we ensure that only those that maintain high standards of service are included in our selections. The best B&Bs have always combined a high standard of accommodation with excellent value for money. Expect the bedrooms in a pub or B&B listed in the Guide to be well equipped, with thoughtful extras. B&B owners invariably know how to serve a good breakfast.

## WHAT ARE YOUR LIKES AND DISLIKES?

We like
* Flexible times for meals.
* Two decent armchairs in the bedroom.
* Good bedside lighting.
* Proper hangers in the wardrobe.
* Fresh milk with the tea tray in the room.

We dislike
* Intrusive background music.
* Stuffy dress codes.
* Bossy notices and house rules.
* Hidden service charges.
* Packaged fruit juices at breakfast.

## WHY DO YOU DROP HOTELS FROM ONE YEAR TO THE NEXT?

Readers are quick to tell us if they think standards have slipped at a hotel. If the evidence is overwhelming, we drop the hotel from the Guide or perhaps downgrade it to the Shortlist. Sometimes we send inspectors just to be sure. When a hotel is sold, we look for reports since the new owners took over, otherwise we inspect or omit it.

## WHY DO YOU ASK FOR 'MORE REPORTS, PLEASE'?

When we have not heard about a hotel for several years, we ask readers for more reports. Sometimes readers returning to a favourite hotel may not send a fresh report. Readers often respond to our request.

## WHAT SHOULD I TELL YOU IN A REPORT?

How you enjoyed your stay. We welcome reports of any length. We want to know what you think about the welcome, the service, the building and the facilities. Even a short report can tell us a great deal about the owners, the staff and the atmosphere.

## HOW SHOULD I SEND YOU A REPORT?

You can email us at editor@goodhotelguide.com. Or you can write to us at the address given on the report form at the end of the book, or send a report via the GHG's website: goodhotelguide.com.

Please send your reports to:
**The Good Hotel Guide**, 50 Addison Avenue, London W11 4QP, England.

Unless asked not to, we assume that we may publish your name. If you would like more report forms please tick ☐ Alternatively, you can either photostat this form or submit a review on our website: goodhotelguide.com

NAME OF HOTEL: _____
ADDRESS: _____
_____

Date of most recent visit: _____ Duration of stay: _____

☐ New recommendation                    ☐ Comment on existing entry

Report:

I am not connected directly or indirectly with the management or proprietors

Signed: _____

Name:    (CAPITALS PLEASE) _____

Address: _____

_____

Email address: _____